W9-CDL-717

The Life and Opinions of
TRISTRAM SHANDY,
Gentleman

LAURENCE STERNE was born in 1713 at Clonmel in Ireland, the
son of an army ensign, Roger Sterne, and his wife Agnes. In 1723 or
1724 he left Ireland for school in Halifax, proceeding in 1733 to
Jesus College, Cambridge. He graduated BA in 1737 and entered
the Church of England as a deacon, being appointed curate at St.
Ives and obtaining the living of Sutton-on-the-Forest in Yorkshire
the following year. In 1741 Sterne married Elizabeth Lumley and
for twenty years lived the uneventful life of a provincial clergyman.
In 1759 he published the first two volumes of *The Life and Opinions
of Tristram Shandy, Gentleman* in York, and found himself immediately famous. Extravagantly praised for its humour and roundly
condemned for its indecency, *Tristram Shandy* was an enormous
literary success and Sterne was lionized both in London and Paris.
Seven subsequent volumes of *Tristram Shandy* appeared between
1761 and 1767. In 1760 Sterne published two volumes of his sermons under the title *The Sermons of Mr. Yorick*, adding two further
volumes in 1766. In 1767 he met Mrs Elizabeth Draper, 23-year-old
wife of an East India Company official with whom he enjoyed a brief
but intense sentimental friendship which bore literary fruit in *The
Journal to Eliza*. In February 1768 he published the two volumes of
A Sentimental Journey through France and Italy. Sterne died in
London of consumption on 18 March 1768.

IAN CAMPBELL ROSS is Professor of Eighteenth-Century Studies
in the School of English, and Fellow of Trinity College Dublin. His
books include *Laurence Sterne: A Life* (Oxford University Press,
2001).

OXFORD WORLD'S CLASSICS

*For over 100 years Oxford World's Classics have brought
readers closer to the world's great literature. Now with over 700
titles—from the 4,000-year-old myths of Mesopotamia to the
twentieth century's greatest novels—the series makes available
lesser-known as well as celebrated writing.*

*The pocket-sized hardbacks of the early years contained
introductions by Virginia Woolf, T. S. Eliot, Graham Greene,
and other literary figures which enriched the experience of reading.
Today the series is recognized for its fine scholarship and
reliability in texts that span world literature, drama and poetry,
religion, philosophy and politics. Each edition includes perceptive
commentary and essential background information to meet the
changing needs of readers.*

OXFORD WORLD'S CLASSICS

LAURENCE STERNE

The Life and Opinions of *Tristram Shandy,* Gentleman

Edited with an Introduction and Notes by
IAN CAMPBELL ROSS

OXFORD
UNIVERSITY PRESS

OXFORD
UNIVERSITY PRESS

Great Clarendon Street, Oxford OX2 6DP

Oxford University Press is a department of the University of Oxford.
It furthers the University's objective of excellence in research, scholarship,
and education by publishing worldwide in

Oxford New York

Auckland Cape Town Dar es Salaam Hong Kong Karachi
Kuala Lumpur Madrid Melbourne Mexico City Nairobi
New Delhi Shanghai Taipei Toronto

With offices in

Argentina Austria Brazil Chile Czech Republic France Greece
Guatemala Hungary Italy Japan Poland Portugal Singapore
South Korea Switzerland Thailand Turkey Ukraine Vietnam

Oxford is a registered trade mark of Oxford University Press
in the UK and in certain other countries

Published in the United States
by Oxford University Press Inc., New York

Tristram Shandy first published 1759–67
This edition © Ian Campbell Ross 1983, 2009

British Library Cataloguing in Publication Data

Data available

Library of Congress Cataloging in Publication Data

Data available

Printed in Great Britain
on acid-free paper by
Clays Ltd., Elcograf S.p.A.

ISBN 978-0-19-953289-6

11

CONTENTS

INTRODUCTION

'Read, read, read, read, my unlearned reader! read,—or
... you had better throw down the book at once'

(*Tristram Shandy*, III. xxxvi)

FOR the reader who has reached the thirty-sixth chapter of
the third volume of *The Life and Opinions of Tristram
Shandy, Gentleman* (1759–67), Tristram's mock-exasperated
appeal must seem as much provocation as exhortation. To its
earliest readers it was still more so. For a start, Volume III
only appeared at the beginning of 1761, a full twelve months
after Volumes I and II had established Sterne's work as the
most talked-about book of the age, yet the narrator-hero of
this fictional autobiography had only just managed to get
himself born. Tristram's rebuke to the 'unlearned' reader was
startling in a less immediately obvious way too. Sterne's,
however, was the kind of book that, virtually by definition,
addressed the 'unlearned' rather than learned reader. So, at
least, Samuel Johnson had suggested, in a celebrated essay in
The Rambler, 4 (1750), when he bluntly affirmed that the
'new species of writing'—the novel—was written to the
'young, the ignorant, and the idle': that is to say to youthful
readers who had time on their hands but knew little either of
real life or of the world of polite letters. Although contemporary periodicals increasingly reviewed new works of
prose fiction, they did so under such headings as 'Entertainment'. Novels were not, it was implied, to be taken too seriously and even Sterne himself, when ambitiously dedicating
the first London edition of the first two volumes to William
Pitt, asked the then-prime minister merely to take the book
'into the country with you; where, if I am ever told, it has
made you smile, or can conceive it has beguiled you of one
moment's pain—I shall think myself as happy as a minister
of state' ('To the Right Honourable Mr. PITT', p. 3).

The New Species of Writing

Like other novelists of his age, Laurence Sterne in fact took
the 'new species of writing' very seriously indeed. In 1740,

Samuel Richardson (1689–1761) unexpectedly found his *Pamela; or, Virtue Rewarded* (1740)—the story, told by herself, of a 15-year-old servant girl under threat of rape by her master—one of the most widely read, and debated, books of its day. Not content with his initial success, he subsequently considered the art of the novelist both in multiple revisions of *Pamela* itself and in his elaboration of the epistolary form in his masterpiece *Clarissa* (1747–8). Here, and when writing his final novel, *Sir Charles Grandison* (1753–4), he engaged in extensive correspondence with numerous readers, whose advice he urgently solicited (but did not always take). Henry Fielding (1707–54) began his career as a novelist by lampooning the morally improving *Pamela* in his wittily pointed parody *Shamela* (1741). Yet though he remained conscious that he was frequently addressing the 'mere English reader'—i.e. the reader ignorant of the classical languages of Latin and Greek—he responded to the innovations of Richardson by outlining his own theory of contemporary prose fiction in *The History of the Adventures of Joseph Andrews* (1742), and his masterpiece, *Tom Jones* (1749), dignifying his work as a 'comic epic-poem in prose'. The precocious Tobias Smollett (1721–71), meanwhile, prefaced his first novel, *The Adventures of Roderick Random* (1748), with a brief history of European literature that culminated in the kind of prose fiction he was writing himself, and went on to outline an influential theory of novelistic discourse in the preface to *The Adventures of Ferdinand Count Fathom* (1753). Nor were female novelists behindhand, with Charlotte Lennox (1720–1804), in *The Female Quixote; or, the Adventures of Arabella* (1752), incisively addressing the nature of modern prose fiction, and its perceived dangers and imaginative benefits to contemporary women readers—themselves mostly 'unlearned', since excluded from the benefits of education accorded their male counterparts in the eighteenth century.

What most immediately distinguished Sterne from his fellow-writers of fiction, in terms of developing a theory of the new species of writing, was the problematic relationship between *The Life and Opinions of Tristram Shandy, Gentleman* and other works of contemporary fiction, prominently signalled by the title itself. Of fictional 'lives'—like 'histories' and 'adventures'—there was no shortage, but what had the hero's 'opinions' to offer prospective purchasers? The uncertainty led to considerable confusion among the book's first critics and great delight among its earliest readers. If *Tristram Shandy* presents itself as a 'life' of its supposed author, then it is an autobiography of no common kind, for not only is the book's chronology notably disrupted but Tristram, as already noted, has the greatest difficulty even in getting himself born. In Daniel Defoe's *The Life and Strange Surprizing Adventures of Robinson Crusoe* (1719), the hero's opening sentence is the simple 'I was born in the year 1632, in the city of York, of a good family ...' and in Smollett's *Roderick Random* the hero writes, just as straightforwardly, 'I was born in the northern part of this United Kingdom, in the house of my grandfather, a gentleman of considerable fortune and influence.' Tristram Shandy's life begins rather differently:

I WISH either my father or my mother, or indeed both of them, as they were in duty both equally bound to it, had minded what they were about when they begot me; had they duly consider'd how much depended upon what they were then doing;—that not only the production of a rational Being was concern'd in it, but that possibly the happy formation and temperature of his body, perhaps his genius and the very cast of his mind;—and, for aught they knew to the contrary, even the fortunes of his whole house might take their turn from the humours and dispositions which were then uppermost:—Had they duly weighed and considered all this, and proceeded accordingly,—I am verily persuaded I should have made a quite different figure in the world, from that, in which the reader is likely to see me. (I.i.5)

How the reader is likely—or invited—to see Tristram is, however, far from clear. '[I]n writing what I have set about', he declares, 'I shall confine myself ... to [no] man's rules that ever lived' (I.iv.8). Accordingly, *Tristram Shandy* invokes, seriously or satirically, a profusion of literary models and models of literary heroism, including the Bible (Old and New Testaments), classical epic (including Homer's *Odyssey* and Virgil's *Aeneid*), classical romance (Xenophon's *Cyropaedia*), Renaissance tragedy (above all *Hamlet*), Renaissance prose romance (*Don Quixote*), and contemporary auto-biography (most pertinently, the actor and Poet Laureate Colley Cibber's *An Apology for the Life of Mr. Colley Cibber, Comedian* [1740; 2nd edn. 1750]). The very profusion of literary categories powerfully suggests that Sterne himself took a real delight in teasing his readers. If so, he would doubtless have been amused by the long-standing debate that has resulted from such generic instability, leading modern critics to argue, sometimes heatedly, about whether Sterne understood himself to be adding to a tradition of 'learned wit', or writing satire, or a novel.[1]

What still provokes critical uncertainty today, however, hugely entertained, as much as it greatly puzzled, contemporary readers, making *Tristram Shandy* the most talked about prose fiction since *Pamela*. The author of this apparently facetious and decidedly irreverent work was, improbably, a 46-year-old clergyman of the Church of England, entirely unknown beyond the confines of his two rural parishes in Yorkshire, and the ecclesiastical circles centred on York Minster. More surprisingly still, the work that turned the author into the greatest literary celebrity of his day was first published, obscurely, and at his own expense, in York, after Sterne failed to find a London publisher willing to take the financial risk. It is the engaging combination of an often challengingly eccentric and chronologically disrupted narrative, shot through with bawdy humour, serious reflection, and frequently poignant sentiment, that best reveals why initially perplexed readers found, and still find, *Tristram Shandy* to be one of the world's great comic novels.

Laurence Sterne: A Brief Life

There was little in the youth or early middle age of *Tristram Shandy*'s author to suggest a man likely so to bemuse or entertain the world. Laurence Sterne was born on 24 November 1713 at Clonmel in Ireland. His father Roger was an army ensign, and the boy's first ten years were marked by continual removals from barrack to barrack, from Ireland to England and back again. Aged 9 or 10, Sterne was accompanied by his father to school in Yorkshire. The boy would

---

[1] See, for example, D. W. Jefferson, '*Tristram Shandy* and the Tradition of Learned Wit', *Essays in Criticism*, 1 (1951), 225–48; Melvyn New, *Laurence Sterne as Satirist: A Reading of 'Tristram Shandy'* (Gainesville: University of Florida Press, 1969); Shaun Regan, 'Novelizing Scriblerus: *Tristram Shandy* and (Post-) Scriblerian Satire', *The Shandean*, 17 (2006), 9–33; Thomas Keymer, *Sterne, the Moderns and the Novel* (Oxford: Oxford University Press, 2002).

never see either his father or Ireland again. Roger Sterne died in 1731 and it was only thanks to the generosity of a cousin that Sterne was able to attend Jesus College, Cambridge, where he received a traditional humanist education, leaving him a strong Latinist, proficient in Greek, and with a knowledge of classical literature, philosophy, and divinity. Graduating in 1737, he was immediately ordained into the Church of England as a deacon, taking priest's orders the following year, and being inducted into his first living, at Sutton-on-the-Forest, eight miles north of York, in August 1738.

That Sterne so quickly acquired a parish of his own—not all eighteenth-century clergymen were so fortunate—was due to the influence of his uncle Dr. Jaques Sterne, Archdeacon of Cleveland and Precentor of York Minster. Under the watchful eye of Dr. Sterne, a man of strong Whig loyalties, the young clergyman turned party political writer, and was rewarded by starting out on a moderately successful ecclesiastical career in the highly politicized Established Church. Even though he soon renounced politics—breaking with his unforgiving uncle as a result—Sterne managed to acquire a second living, the parish of Stillington, adjacent to his first. In 1741 he married Elizabeth Lumley, who gave birth, in 1747, to a daughter, Lydia, the only one of the Sternes' children to survive infancy. For almost twenty years, Sterne lived a life that gave little indication of substantial literary aspiration. The political journalism he wrote in the Whig interest during the Yorkshire by-election of 1741 gained him a prebendal stall in York Minster but is in no way exceptional. In 1743, the *Gentleman's Magazine* in London accepted 'The Unknown World: Verses occasion'd by hearing a Pass-Bell': a gloomy sixty-four-line poem that has retrospective interest in introducing into Sterne's work the theme of death so important to his later fiction: *Tristram Shandy* is possibly unique among comic novels in alerting the reader to the death of all its principal characters, the dying Tristram only excluded. Sterne was, however, a noted preacher, and two of his sermons, including the celebrated 'The Abuses of Conscience', later ingeniously introduced into *Tristram Shandy*, were printed in York in 1747 and 1750. Thereafter, Sterne published nothing until, in 1759, he contributed to a long-standing

York ecclesiastical wrangle a mischievously witty shilling pamphlet, *A Political Romance*, also known as 'The History of a Good Warm Watch-Coat'.

To Sterne's dismay, *A Political Romance* caused such offence that the Archbishop of York ordered the pamphlet to be burnt (a few copies only survived the flames). Despite his initial, and deeply felt, disappointment, Sterne nevertheless took from his experience both the inspiration for a much more ambitious work and confidence in his ability to achieve it. Within weeks he had completed a draft of one volume of a book entitled *Tristram Shandy*. Ambitious of a wider readership, Sterne approached the well-respected London bookseller Robert Dodsley, asking £50 for the copyright. Although he turned down the book, Dodsley offered Sterne both encouragement and good advice as to ways in which he might give his work wider public appeal. Sterne took the rejection—and advice—in good heart and in the autumn of 1759 indicated his intention to have his book printed at his own expense, asking Dodsley to sell it for him in London on commission. Dodsley agreed.

The two small volumes that made up *The Life and Opinions of Tristram Shandy, Gentleman* were published in York early in December 1759. Word of the book spread quickly and *Tristram Shandy* was soon the talk of York and the surrounding area. Welcome as it was, however, provincial success paled in comparison to what might be achieved in the political and cultural metropolis of London. As agreed, Sterne sent about half the York-printed edition—probably no more than 500 copies in all—to Dodsley in the English capital. Not that Sterne thought *Tristram Shandy* would sell itself. On the contrary, he made imaginative (if not wholly scrupulous) efforts to bring his book to the attention of one of the age's principal arbiters of literary taste—the actor, playwright, and theatre-manager David Garrick—writing a letter of apparently objective praise of his own book, which he persuaded the London singer Kitty Fourmantel, most probably his mistress, to copy out to send to Garrick as though it were her own.

At the beginning of March 1760, Sterne travelled to London himself. On his first morning in the capital, he went early to Dodsley's shop in Pall Mall, to enquire about his work. Understandably, he was 'highly delighted', when told 'there was not such a Book to be had in London either for Love or money'.[2]

Sterne's success took in all classes of readers. The earliest magazine reviews suggest the bewilderment even professional readers experienced when faced with so puzzling a book. 'This is a humorous performance, of which we are unable to convey any distinct ideas to our readers,' admitted the *Critical Review*.[3] As far as the narrative of *Tristram Shandy* is concerned, the reviewer's inability was comprehensible, for how was one to describe a 'rhapsodical' work whose apparent hero—and actual narrator—was unable even to get himself born in the first two volumes? a work whose narrator, anxious to tell his readers all about himself and his opinions, seemed dismally to fail while managing, instead, to interest us in his uncle Toby, his father, the man-midwife who will eventually (and disastrously) bring him into the world, and the likeable but laughable Parson Yorick, and to entertain us with a sermon delivered by a military manservant to a congregation of three, one of whom soon falls asleep; his parents' marriage settlement; and the progress of King William's wars in Flanders.

Bewilderment did not preclude enjoyment. The 'humour' of this 'humane' book was much praised and Sterne himself compared with Rabelais and Cervantes, testifying not only to two of the author's most obvious sources of influence but to the measure of his literary achievement. The very profusion of descriptions accorded the book—'ingenious', 'droll', 'poignant', 'sensible', 'pathetick'—bolstered the reputation of a work that others found both 'entertaining' and 'profitable' (i.e. morally improving). Among those who relished the book—if not always without reserve—were David Garrick, the poets Thomas Gray and Charles Churchill, and the young Edmund Burke. David Hume called *Tristram Shandy* 'the best book that has been writ by any Englishman these thirty Years'.[4] Not all readers were so enthusiastic, and those who disliked *Tristram Shandy* included such eminent and

[2] John Croft, 'Anecdotes of Sterne Vulgarly Tristram Shandy', *The Whitefoord Papers*, ed. W. A. S. Hewins (Oxford, 1898), 227.

[3] *Critical Review*, 9 (Jan. 1760), 73.

[4] *The Letters of David Hume*, ed. J. Y. T. Greig, 2 vols. (Oxford: Oxford University Press, 1922), ii. 269.

equally diverse writers as Samuel Richardson, Oliver Gold-smith, and Horace Walpole. But if these, and others, com-plained—variously damning the book as 'bawdy', 'mean *dirty Wit*', or 'obscenity'—then Sterne was equally pleased. Reversing the sentiments of Colley Cibber—'I wrote more to be Fed, than be Famous'[5]—Sterne declared: 'I wrote not [to] be *fed*, but to be *famous*.'[6] Recognizing the incalculable value of controversy itself in promoting literary success, Sterne remarked gaily of a 'shilling pamphlet' attacking *Tris-tram Shandy*: 'I wish they would write a hundred such' (*Letters*, 107). His wish was all but granted for a host of imitations, squibs, parodies, burlesques, celebratory verses, and moral rejoinders appeared on the market.

James Dodsley, who had taken over the running of his brother's business, now paid £250 for the copyright of the first two volumes (five times what Sterne had originally asked). The second edition, on sale in London at the begin-ning of April, was a large one and boasted the additional attraction of an engraving after a design by William Hogarth. Again, Sterne had not left the matter to chance: 'I would give both my Ears . . . for no more than ten Strokes of *Howgarth's* witty Chissel, to clap at the Front of my next Edition of *Shandy*' (*Letters*, 99), he had written to a mutual acquaint-ance, and the artist took the hint. By the end of May, two volumes of Sterne's sermons, under the title of *The Sermons of Mr. Yorick*—the Shakespearian jester's name being that under which Sterne portrayed himself as the local parson in the first volume of *Tristram Shandy*—were available to eager purchasers. Again published by R. and J. Dodsley, the *Sermons* bore further evidence of the author's social and commercial acumen. Embellished with a prestigious engrav-ing after the celebrated portrait of the author painted by Sir Joshua Reynolds, the volumes also boasted a remarkably large and distinguished list of subscribers (some 650 in all). Indeed, during his lifetime and for many years afterwards, Sterne's literary reputation rested as much on his sermons as on his fiction.

[5] Colley Cibber, *A Letter from Mr. Cibber to Mr. Pope* (London, 1742), 9.
[6] *The Letters of Laurence Sterne*, ed. Lewis Perry Curtis (Oxford: Claren-don Press, 1935), 90; all further references are to this edition and included parenthetically in the text.

Only after three months did Sterne tear himself away
from the social round and get back to his family and parishes in Yorkshire. There, he spent much of the next two
years, writing. Volumes III and IV of *Tristram Shandy*
(again containing an engraving from an illustration by
Hogarth) appeared in January 1761 and Volumes V and VI
(under the imprint of a new publisher, T. Becket and P. A.
Dehondt) in December that year. The critical reception was
as exhilaratingly mixed as for the first volumes. 'One half
of the town abuse my book as bitterly, as the other half
cry it up to the skies,' Sterne wrote in February 1761, adding, 'the best is, they abuse and buy it' (*Letters*, 129). Nor
was it only the bawdy humour or irreverent wit of *Tristram Shandy* to which readers responded with such marked
enjoyment or distaste. Sterne's talent for pathos was widely
admired, and sentimental set-pieces such as the moving
story of the dying soldier Le Fever, or uncle Toby's oath
on Le Fever's death, in Volume VI, provoked from critics
such epithets as 'sublime'. Literary esteem apart, however,
one fact about the fifth and sixth volumes of Sterne's
work was inescapable: *Tristram Shandy* was no longer a
novelty.

Sterne was worried at the diminishing popularity of his
book but, at the beginning of 1762, he had more serious
cause for anxiety. 'I am very ill,' he told a correspondent,
'having broke a vessel in my lungs—hard writing in the
summer, together with preaching, which I have not strength
for, is ever fatal to me' (*Letters*, 150). Since his student days
at Cambridge, Sterne had suffered from consumption: i.e.
pulmonary tuberculosis. Now he attempted the most usual
eighteenth-century cure for those who could afford it: a
trip to the warmer shores of the Mediterranean. By mid-
January 1762, Sterne was in Paris where, fêted as he had
been upon *Tristram Shandy*'s first appearance, he remained
until July. The winter of 1762–3 Sterne and his family
passed at Toulouse; that of 1763–4 at the more fashionable
Montpellier.

Only after an absence from England of two years did
Sterne decide to return home. Back in Coxwold—a third
Yorkshire living he had acquired as one of the first material
fruits of his literary success—he spent the summer of 1764
working hard on *Tristram Shandy*. Two more volumes, the

seventh and eighth, appeared in London at the end of January 1765; Beginning with Tristram's determined flight from Death—who knocks importunately at the door—Volume VII offers an exhilarating account of Tristram's tour through France, an imaginative re-creation of Sterne's less happy experience of continental travel in search of health. These volumes were again a popular success and by mid-March Sterne was assuring David Garrick that 'I have had a lucrative winter's campaign here—Shandy sells well' (*Letters*, 235). As a result, Sterne decided he could support his wife and daughter in France and project for himself a tour to Italy, beginning in the autumn. In his absence, two further volumes of sermons appeared in January 1766, again boasting a distinguished subscription list. After spending Easter in Rome, he abruptly terminated his tour, paused only briefly in France to visit his wife and daughter, who had taken up residence there, and by June 1766 was at home in Yorkshire.

This time Sterne found the continuation of *Tristram Shandy* more difficult. Personal troubles and the desire to bring his novel to a satisfactory conclusion were both stumbling blocks. The final instalment of *Tristram Shandy*, on sale at the end of January 1767, consisted of just one volume instead of the usual two. Only 3,500 copies were printed instead of the 4,000 of previous volumes, a sure indication of the anticipated decline in demand. Reviews were as mixed as ever, though charges of indecency were more numerous, but Sterne seemed content: 'Have you got the 9th V. of Shandy?' he asked a correspondent in Paris; ''tis liked the best of all here' (*Letters*, 300).

There were two main reasons for Sterne's equanimity. First, he had plans for another work—*A Sentimental Journey through France and Italy*—that he believed would be a literary and financial success. Secondly, he had recently met Eliza Draper, the 23-year-old wife of an official of the East India Company. In the three months before she returned to her husband in India, Sterne formed a strong emotional attachment to her, seeing her frequently and writing during their brief separations. While Eliza was evidently flattered to have attracted the attention of so eminent an admirer, Sterne was deeply infatuated. Throughout the summer of 1767, after Eliza had begun her voyage to India, he kept that record of his daily thoughts and feelings known as the 'Journal to Eliza'.[7]

On the surface the Journal seems more often mawkish than sentimental. Read more carefully it also suggests the extent to which Sterne was resolutely—even heroically—attempting to give literary shape to his own emotional responses to Eliza and to her imminent or actual departure, while he was in the final stages of the consumption of which he knew himself to be dying. And, despite the physical deterioration brought on by his illness—evident in his correspondence—Sterne also managed to compose his second great work, *A Sentimental Journey*. Here, the imperfectly controlled—and sometimes equivocal—sentiment of the 'Journal' is transmuted by the unmistakable hand of a writer able to combine true sensibility with ironic detachment, with the result that *A Sentimental Journey* is a masterpiece of calculated ambiguity. The first part of the new book—a second was promised but was never written—appeared in London in February 1768 but Sterne himself lived barely long enough to learn of his work's success. On 18 March 1768 he died in his lodgings in London, aged 54.

'Did you ever read Laurence Sterne?'

It was almost a century and a half later that James Joyce described *Work in Progress* (later *Finnegans Wake*) as being made up of 'exactly what every novelist might use: man and woman, birth, childhood, night, sleep, marriage, prayer, death . . . Only I am trying to bring many planes of narrative within a single aesthetic purpose', and concluded by asking his correspondent, 'Did you ever read Laurence Sterne?'[8] Joyce's query, though, begs another, less rhetorical question: what *is* it to read Laurence Sterne? As his description of *Work*

---

[7] Lost for some sixty years, the journal was first published in Wilbur L. Cross's 1904 edition of Sterne's works under the title, suggested by Swift's *Journal to Stella*, by which it is still generally known; the editors of the Florida edition of the work (2002) preferred the title 'Continuation of the Bramine's Journal', following Sterne's private usage.

[8] See Eugene Jolas, 'My Friend James Joyce', in Seon Givens (ed.), *James Joyce: Two Decades of Criticism* (New York: Vanguard, 1948), quoted in Richard Ellmann, *James Joyce* (1959; rev. edn. Oxford: Oxford University Press, 1982), 554.

in Progress—and *Finnegans Wake* itself—makes clear, Joyce read *Tristram Shandy* as an encyclopedic work. This was undoubtedly appropriate, since Sterne was a great reader of encyclopedias himself, and his novel makes considerable use, acknowledged and unacknowledged, both of Renaissance compilations such as Robert Burton's *Anatomy of Melancholy* (1621, and subsequently) and of Enlightenment works like Ephraim Chambers's *Cyclopaedia; or, Universal Dictionary of Arts and Sciences* (1728, and subsequently). The universal aspirations of Chambers or of Joyce are appropriate too, since such aspirations are also those of Sterne's fictional hero.

Tristram tells his readers as much in the opening chapters of his work: 'I have undertaken, you see, to write not only my life but my opinions also; hoping and expecting that your knowledge of my character, and of what kind of a mortal I am, by the one, would give you a better relish for the other ... then nothing which has touched me will be thought trifling in its nature, or tedious in its telling' (I.vi.10). What has touched Tristram, the reader will soon discover, includes not only his own life but that of his family and their servants—along with his (and often their) opinions.

There is his father, Walter Shandy, an inveterate pedant with theories about everything, including—to Tristram's misfortune—childbirth and the naming and education of children. There is also his good-natured uncle Toby, a retired army captain, grievously wounded in the groin at the 1695 siege of Namur, who plays elaborate war-games on his bowling-green with his servant, Corporal Trim, a soldier with an unusual capacity for oratory (and a brother in a Portuguese prison). And there is Widow Wadman, who sees in Toby a prospective husband but who is anxious first to clear up the question of exactly *where* uncle Toby was wounded in the groin (Toby's answer will surprise her—and the reader). And if Tristram's mother, Elizabeth Shandy, has little to say for herself and will go out of the world without knowing whether the sun goes round the earth or vice versa, then there are the Shandy household servants Obadiah and Susannah, and Widow Wadman's maid Bridget, who in a private moment coaxes the information her mistress wants from Corporal Trim. Tristram must tell us, too, about Parson Yorick and Dr. Slop, already mentioned. And he must not omit the story of the dying soldier Le Fever, or forget to rehearse Slawkenbergius' tale of the stranger who astounds all Strasbourg with the size of his nose. In time, too, Tristram must explain how he came to lose his own nose while being born, how he came to be christened Tristram, how he was accidentally circumcised by a falling sash window at the age of 5. Though he will be put into breeches—an eighteenth-century rite of passage for male children—he will not, in fact, get much past his fifth year, though he will recount his adult experiences of travelling in France. But before proceeding on the story he has barely begun, he declares that there is one point 'necessary to be clear'd up' to satisfy himself and 'the reader'. The particular point relates, in characteristically mystifying fashion, to his mother's marriage settlement—without knowledge of which we cannot understand the circumstances that lead to Tristram's calamitous entry into the world. The application, however, is general, for no writer, Tristram insists, can go 'as a muleteer drives on his mule,—straight forward', without many a deviation or digression, and besides there will be:

Accounts to reconcile:
Anecdotes to pick up:
Inscriptions to make out:
Stories to weave in:
Traditions to sift:
Personages to call upon:
Panygericks to paste up at this door:
Pasquinades at that:—All which both the man and his mule are quite exempt from. To sum up all; there are archives at every stage to be look'd into, and rolls, records, documents, and endless genealogies, which justice ever and anon calls him back to stay the reading of:----In short, there is no end of it;-----(I.xiv.32–3)

If there be no end of it, Tristram—avowedly telling the story of his life—is unlikely to make rapid progress: a reflection that prompts the virtuoso passage beginning: 'I am this month one whole year older than I was this time twelve-month; and having got as you perceive, almost into the middle of my fourth volume—and no farther than to my first day's life—'tis demonstrative that I have three hundred and sixty-four days more life to write just now, than when I first set out . . .' and ends 'It must follow, an' please your worships, that the more I write, the more I shall have to write—and consequently, the more your worships read, the more your worships will have to read. Will this be good for your worships eyes?' (IV.XIII.228). 'Read, read, read, read, my unlearned reader! read ...'. Reading may be the solution but it is also the problem.

Had Walter Shandy been able to get his breeches on in time, perhaps the problem would never have arisen. It is just this failure on the part of the hero's father, however, that prevents his son being appropriately christened according to Walter's theory of names. Unfortunate in his conception—left prey by his mother's most untimely question, asked of her husband while they are engaged in coition: '*Pray, my dear ... have you not forgot to wind up the clock?*'—Tristram must endure nine months of 'melancholy dreams and fancies' in the womb (I.I.5–6). At birth, he is more unfortunate still: his nose crushed flat as a pancake to his face (III.XXVII.170). Accordingly, Walter Shandy hopes to remedy his child's fortunes in life by calling him Trismegistus. As Walter explains to his brother, 'This *Trismegistus* ... was the greatest (*Toby*) of all earthly beings—he was the greatest king—the greatest lawgiver—the greatest philosopher—and the greatest priest ...' and bestowing this name on his child 'shall bring all things to rights' (IV.XI.226). (But Walter cannot get his breeches on in time and, to save his modesty, passes on his choice of name to the curate via the maid, Susannah, who misremembers it, causing the hero-narrator to be christened Tristram, which, in Walter's theory of names, is the most unfortunate of all.)

Walter's theory of names is both magical and mad. Hermes Trismegistus is nonetheless a significant presence in Sterne's novel. Once believed to have been an Egyptian god-king, also known as Thoth (or Theuth), Hermes Trismegistus (his name means 'Thrice-Greatest') was, by the eighteenth century, considered an apocryphal figure, though his supposed writings, the hermetic philosophy embodying the totality of human knowledge, had been widely known, at least until the late seventeenth century. The continuing awareness of Hermes Trismegistus owed much to Plato, who credited him with the invention of arithmetic, calculation, astronomy, and—most importantly—writing. In a famous passage of *Phaedrus*, Plato has Socrates reprove Thoth, declaring that writing will simply cause those who read it to forget, trusting in the written word, but not using their memory: 'for that through trusting to writing, they will remember outwardly by means of foreign marks, and not inwardly by means of their own faculties.'[9] Hermes Trismegistus, the father and protector of knowledge, is, in this formulation, responsible also for its destruction.

Tristram's encyclopedic life and opinions is a work full of seeming knowledge, apparently gleaned from an imposing range of texts, ancient and modern, and expressed through citation, allusion, paraphrase, and open (and concealed) borrowings. As author, Tristram presents this learning for readers both present and future: his work, he is certain, 'shall be read, perused, paraphrased, commented and discanted upon—or to say it all in a word, shall be thumb'd over by Posterity' (IX.VIII.497). But will his readers be able to read?

——How could you, Madam, be so inattentive in reading the last chapter? I told you in it, *That my mother was not a papist.*—— Papist! You told me no such thing, Sir. Madam, I beg leave to repeat it over again, That I told you as plain, at least, as words, by direct inference, could tell you such a thing.—Then, Sir, I must have miss'd a page.--No, Madam,—you have not miss'd a word.——Then I was asleep, Sir.—My pride, Madam, cannot allow you that refuge.—— Then, I declare, I know nothing at all about the matter.—That, Madam, is the very fault I lay to your charge; and as a punishment for it, I do insist upon it that you immediately turn back, that is, as soon as you get to the next full stop, and read the whole chapter over again. (I.xx.47–8)

While Madam is engaged in her rereading, Tristram points out to the reader the sentence she has missed: the mystifying 'it was . . . *necessary* I should be born before I was christen'd'. Tristram elaborately explains this by quoting a judgement, delivered at the Sorbonne in 1733, in response to a query by a French obstetrician as to the legitimacy of conditionally baptizing an infant still in the womb, by means of holy water delivered through a squirt. This (Roman Catholic) dilemma caused much amusement among Sterne's (mainly Protestant) readers, but most believed that the facetious author had

---

[9] Plato, *Phaedrus*, § 135, trans. Henry Cary, in *The Works of Plato*, trans. Cary et al., 5 vols. (London: George Bell & Sons, 1901–6), i. 355.

invented the judgement, quoted complete, in French, in his book. In order to show that this was not the case, Sterne added to the first London edition a footnote indicating his source in a work by the Dutch physician Hendrick van Deventer.[10] In a book full of references to often arcane learning the added footnote seemed to guarantee the authenticity of much information elsewhere and to establish the author—whether Tristram or Sterne—as a man of real learning. It is for having allegedly learned nothing from their reading that Tristram repeatedly reproaches his 'unlearned' readers. Like Tristram, however, Sterne is a facetious writer and his reproach of his readers might equally be understood as self-reproof.

One of Sterne's favourite authors—quoted or paraphrased in *Tristram Shandy* more frequently than is immediately apparent—was the French essayist Michel de Montaigne (1533–92), with whom Sterne shared an outwardly casual attitude to books and reading. Outward appearance, though, belies a shared concern as to whether the primary value of books lay in providing knowledge of the external world or in their role in forming the self. In 'On Books' Montaigne both boasted of his dependence on other authors—'I do not number my Borrowings, I weigh them'[11]—and explained how only the internalization of the words of others has real value: 'I turn over Books, I do not study them; what I retain I do not know to be another's, and is only what my Judgment has made its Advantage of; Discourses and Imaginations in which it has been instructed. The Author, Place, Words, and other Circumstances, I immediately forget.'[12] While the extent of Sterne's learning was doubted in his own day—Sir Horace Mann, British minister at the court of Florence, enjoyed Sterne's work but thought it 'humbugging'—Sterne's extensive quotation, allusion, and paraphrase throughout *Tristram Shandy* did not become an issue until the very end of the eighteenth century. Then, a Manchester physician, John Ferriar, published his *Illustrations of Sterne* (1798; 2nd expanded edn. 1812), in which he drew censorious attention to the author's *unacknowledged* borrowings

[10] Vide Deventer. Paris Edit. 4to, 1734. p. 366 [Sterne's note].

[11] Michel de Montaigne, 'Of Books', *Essays*, trans. Charles Cotton, 3 vols. (6th edn.; London, 1743), iii. 86.

[12] Montaigne, 'Of Presumption', *Essays*, iii. 375.

throughout *Tristram Shandy*, noting especially Sterne's frequent use of Robert Burton's *Anatomy of Melancholy* (1621), though neither the work nor the author is ever mentioned in the body of the text. In 'On Literary Thievery', in *The Four Ages*, also published in 1798, William Jackson drew more benign attention to the extent of Sterne's borrowings—again, not always acknowledged—from Montaigne. Although the number of authors whom Sterne names, quotes, paraphrases, or cites is substantial, the cases of Burton and Montaigne are exemplary. At the outset of the third instalment of Sterne's novel, Tristram gives vent to an apparently heartfelt cry:

Tell me, ye learned, shall we for ever be adding so much to the *bulk*—so little to the *stock*?
Shall we for ever make new books, as apothecaries make new mixtures, by pouring only out of one vessel into another?
Are we for ever to be twisting, and untwisting the same rope? for ever in the same track—for ever at the same pace? (V.1.275)

It was John Ferriar who indicated that Sterne is in fact borrowing here from the preface to *The Anatomy of Melancholy*, 'Democritus Junior to the Reader', in which Robert Burton inveighs against plagiarism, denouncing modern authors as 'all theeves; they pilfer out of old Writers to stuffe up their new Comments'[13]—while immediately acknowledging that he had 'laboriously collected' his own book 'out of divers Writers'. The complex relationships between reading and writing and between reading and learning likewise concerned Montaigne. In 'On Books', the essayist linked 'lives' and 'opinions' as matters of complementary interest to him, recommending haphazard, promiscuous reading as the necessary way to come to a true knowledge of things: 'I am ... curious to know the Lives and Fortunes of these great Instructors of the World [philosophers], as to know the Diversities of their Doctrines and Opinions. In this Kind of Study ... a Man must tumble over, without Distinction, all Sorts of Authors, both antique and modern, as well barbarous and obsolete, as those of current Language, there to know the Things of which they variously treat.'[14]

---

[13] Robert Burton, 'Democritus Junior to the Reader', *The Anatomy of Melancholy* (5th edn.; Oxford, 1638), 7.
[14] 'Of Books', iii. 96.

Montaigne's view would not go unchallenged. In *Reflections upon the conduct of human life, with reference to the study of knowledge and learning* (1691), John Norris of Bemerton (1657–1712)—a writer whose work Sterne also knew well[15]—offered a cautionary view of books and learning, contrary to Montaigne's. There, Norris signalled his alarm at the way in which true learning was being supplanted by opinion, arguing that in the modern age ''tis counted Learning to have tumbled over a multitude of Books ... Thus ... it goes for Learning, to be acquainted with Mens *Opinions*.'[16] In writing deprecatingly of confusing learning with having 'tumbled over' books, Norris does not directly reproach Montaigne—though he evidently had him in mind—but rather anticipates a problem increasingly foregrounded in the rapid contemporary expansion of print culture.[17]

In the eighteenth century, contemporaries commented frequently and critically on the sheer number of printed works available (with prose fiction coming in for particular criticism): 'Complaints are daily made, nor without reason, of the number of useless books, with which town and country are drenched and surfeited,' one lamented.[18] Following John Locke's *Essay Concerning Human Understanding* (1690; 4th edn. 1700)—a work he frequently cites and whose theory of the association of ideas underpins much of the structure of *Tristram Shandy*—Tristram nevertheless notes that the availability of books is not the same as reading them, nor reading the same as understanding them:

Pray, Sir, in all the reading which you have ever read, did you ever read such a book as *Locke*'s Essay upon the Human Understanding?——Don't answer me rashly,--because many, I know, quote the book, who have not read it,---and many have read it who understand it not:---(II.ii.70)

[15] It was Norris who provided Sterne with one of *Tristram Shandy*'s most celebrated phrases: 'we live among riddles and mysteries' (IV.xvii.233); see Melvyn New, 'The Odd Couple: Laurence Sterne and John Norris of Bemerton', *PQ* 75 (1996), 361–85.

[16] John Norris, *Reflections upon the conduct of human life, with reference to the study of knowledge and learning* (London, 1691), 54.

[17] The still more rapid spread of the internet, with its speedily expanding electronic resources and multiple search engines, has reconfigured the problem for our own age.

[18] John Cleland, review of Tobias Smollett's *Peregrine Pickle*, in *The Monthly Review* (Mar. 1751), 335.

(The target of this joke, it should be added, is far from clear, since Sterne's use of Locke throughout *Tristram Shandy* depends heavily on those parts of the *Essay* that were well known through popularizations, such as those of Joseph Addison in *The Spectator*, suggesting that Sterne might have numbered himself among those who 'quote the book' but 'have not read it'.) For his own readers' benefit, Tristram declares that Locke's *Essay* is a history of what 'passes in a man's own mind'—an excellent description of Locke, and an even better one of *Tristram Shandy*. Sterne's joke is pointed, however, for Locke—the founding figure of English empiricism—insisted that in seeking knowledge men should use their own understandings and experience rather than relying on the authority of others: 'So much as we our selves consider and comprehend of Truth and Reason, so much we possess of real and true Knowledge. The floating of other mens Opinions in our brains, makes us not one jot the more knowing, though they happen to be true. What in them was Science, is in us but Opiniatry.'[19] What in learned readers is knowledge, Locke insists, is in the unlearned mere opinion. And, as the *Oxford English Dictionary* reminds us, using a quotation from John Norris, 'what we call *Opinion* ... is an imperfect Assent, or Judgment'.[20]

An 'imperfect Assent, or Judgment' is very much what Tristram constantly offers his readers in relating his 'Life and Opinions' and perhaps one of the most remarkable achievements of Sterne, the most singular practitioner of the 'new species of writing', was—as the title of his book brazenly suggests—to turn Locke and Norris on their heads and instead of searching after truth or knowledge, to offer opinion in their stead.[21] Yet though he vaunted his own singularity, Sterne was not here being either (wholly) facetious or giving rein to a merely personal preoccupation. In raising questions about reading and learning—above all in a form addressed to 'unlearned' readers—Sterne was rehearsing one

---

[19] John Locke, *Essay Concerning Human Understanding*, book I, ch. 4. § 22.

[20] John Norris, *An Essay toward the Theory of the Intelligible World*, 2 vols. (London, 1701–4 [1704]), ii. 130. See also *OED*: opinion, n. 3b.

[21] The first volumes of *Tristram Shandy* employ as motto the following sentiment from the *Manual* of the Stoic philosopher Epictetus: 'Not things, but opinions about things, trouble men.'

of the central cultural as well as philosophical anxieties of his age. More than any of his contemporaries, he was also capable of expressing this modern anxiety in a manner at once serious and captivating: 'Knowledge in most of its branches, and in most affairs', he would write in *A Sentimental Journey*, 'is like music in an Italian street, whereof those may partake, who pay nothing.'[22]

Sterne's amiable metaphor does not entirely conceal the problems his work addresses so light-heartedly. *The Life and Opinions of Tristram Shandy, Gentleman* is full of echoes of books glanced at, heard of, forgotten, or unknown, or references culled from such encyclopedic works as the *Anatomy of Melancholy* or the *Cyclopaedia*. (Sterne would surely have loved, and understood, Pierre Bayard's *How to Talk about Books you haven't Read* (2007), with the author's wittily thoughtful categories of 'Books You Don't Know', 'Books You Have Skimmed', 'Books You Have Heard of', 'Books You Have Forgotten'.[23]) In *Tristram Shandy*, Xenophon, Pufendorf, Saxo-Grammaticus, Montaigne, Tom Thumb, Daniel Waterland, Shakespeare, Virgil, Rabelais, Piereskius, Deventer, Ludovicus Sorbonensis, Giovanni della Casa, Virgil, Cervantes, Democritus, Prignitz, Cid Hamet, Aristotle, Norris, Locke, Plato, Hermes Trismegistus, and dozens of others crowd together, jostling each other—and the reader. What was true? what false? Which authors were real? which invented? If neither professional reviewers nor even learned readers could be sure, then might not any man or woman's opinions on this, or any other, work be as valid as theirs? Playful as it is, the laughter *Tristram Shandy* so abundantly provoked was often nervous enough, for no amount of humour could conceal the fact that virtually every contested area of eighteenth-century life—philosophy, theology, law, politics, gender, education, and medicine among them—has its part to play in the novel. No wonder then that the contemporary reaction to *Tristram Shandy* was so mixed, and the social influence of his writing a source of anxiety to many. If

[22] Laurence Sterne, *A Sentimental Journey through France and Italy*, ed. Ian Jack, in Ian Jack and Tim Parnell (eds.), Laurence Sterne, *A Sentimental Journey and other writings* (Oxford: Oxford University Press, 2003), 11.

[23] Pierre Bayard, *How to Talk about Books you haven't Read* (2007), trans. Jeffrey Mehlman (London: Granta, 2008).

Thomas Jefferson thought Sterne's writing formed 'the best course of morality that ever was written',[24] others feared the demotic confusion of virtue and vice they found there, so that William Warburton dismissed Sterne, shortly after his death, as 'the idol of the higher mob' and 'common jester to the many'.[25]

The Afterlife of Tristram Shandy

The controversy that surrounded *Tristram Shandy* had brought Sterne the fame he sought to a degree that could only have exceeded his wildest hopes. Yet the literary celebrity he enjoyed lasted a mere eight years before his premature death. The publication of *A Sentimental Journey* so shortly preceding that demise, early reviews understandably tended towards the respectful. Yet the admiration for Sterne's last work was none the less genuine and owed much to the increasing tendency—already discernible in the reception accorded the later volumes of *Tristram Shandy*—to read the author more as sentimentalist than satirist. In the *Monthly Review*, Ralph Griffiths wrote as much: 'Now, Reader, did we not tell thee . . . that the highest excellence of this genuine, this legitimate son of humour, lies not in his humorous but in his pathetic vein?'[26] By and large, the Reader was willing to concur. By adding 'the moral and the pathetic' to 'an original vein of humour', averred the *Political Register*, Sterne had produced his best work.[27] Readers were still ready for more, and Sterne's daughter obliged with three further volumes of sermons, culled from those her father had left, published under the more decorous title of *Sermons by the Late Rev. Mr. Sterne* (1769), a further edition of which was required before the year was out. Eliza Draper published Sterne's side of their mutual correspondence *Letters from Yorick to Eliza* in 1773 and a young acquaintance of Sterne's, William Combe, added *Sterne's Letters to his Friends on Various Occasions* two years later (though, in the absence of genuine

---

[24] Thomas Jefferson to Peter Carr, 10 Aug. 1787: *Writings* (New York: Literary Classics of the United States, 1984), 902.

[25] William Warburton to Charles Yorke, 4 Apr. 1768, *Letters from . . . Dr. Warburton . . . to the Hon. Charles Yorke* (1812), quoted in Alan B. Howes (ed.), *Sterne: The Critical Heritage* (London: Routledge & Kegan Paul), 205.

[26] *Monthly Review*, 38 (Mar. 1768), 185.

[27] *Political Register*, 2 (May 1768), 383.

correspondence, he seems to have forged most of the letters himself). It was in the same year that a more reliable edition of Sterne's correspondence appeared from the indefatigable Lydia, under the title *Letters of the Late Rev. Mr. Sterne* (1775). Two 'complete' editions of Sterne's works were soon available: one published in Dublin in 1775, the other appearing in London five years later. Despite this indication that there was an audience for the 'complete' Sterne, the volume entitled *Beauties of Sterne: Including all his Pathetic Tales, and most distinguished Observations on Life, Selected for the Heart of Sensibility* (1782) gives a more revealing insight into the way in which the writer's work became known to a wider public in the last decades of the eighteenth century. A patchwork of the most admired passages of sensibility from *Tristram Shandy*, *A Sentimental Journey*, and the sermons, arranged so as not to overwhelm the sentimental reader, *Beauties of Sterne* went through thirteen editions by 1799.

Even during his lifetime, however, Sterne's influence had been felt in ways that went far beyond mere simplification or popularization. So, the Irish writer Henry Brooke's *The Fool of Quality* (1765–70) reveals the influence both of Sterne's quirky narrative technique and of his sentimentalism. Shortly after the author's death, the hugely admired *The Man of Feeling* (1771) by the Scottish author Henry Mackenzie further intensified the sentimentalism of Sterne (and Richardson), while in France the *encyclopédiste* Denis Diderot found particular inspiration in *Tristram Shandy*'s structure, apparent in the ostentatiously disruptive narrative of *Jacques the Fatalist and his Master* (written c.1767–c.1778; pub. 1796). Among works by the English Romantics, Wordsworth's autobiographical poem *The Prelude* (1798; 1805; pub. 1850) and Coleridge's *Biographia Literaria* (1817) are unimaginable without the example of Sterne, and when attempting to describe his comic epic *Don Juan* (1819–24), Byron confided that 'I mean it for a poetic T. Shandy'. Among a host of nineteenth-century writers—including Jean Paul and E. T. A. Hoffmann in Germany, Ugo Foscolo in Italy, and Pushkin and Gogol in Russia[28]—whose admiration for Sterne found

---

[28] For a full and fascinating account of Sterne's European fortunes, see Peter de Voogd and John Neubauer (eds.), *The Reception of Laurence Sterne in Europe* (London: Thoemmes Continuum, 2004).

expression in their own works, there were some less predictable names. *Tristram Shandy* was Karl Marx's favourite book, as it was Friedrich Nietzsche's. In such cases, the importance of Sterne went beyond either sentiment or narrative technique. Goethe having earlier described Sterne as the most liberated spirit of his century, Nietzsche went a step further, proclaiming Sterne 'the most liberated spirit of all time'.[29]

All of these writers, of course, read Sterne through the prism of their own and their ages' literary, moral, and philosophical preoccupations. Unsurprisingly, the early twentieth century enrolled Sterne as a precursor of Modernism, admired and imitated by writers from Joyce to Luigi Pirandello. Another admirer, Virginia Woolf, had Sterne's jerkily unpredictable prose style in mind when she wrote that '[t]he order of the ideas, their suddenness and irrelevancy, is more true to life than to literature'.[30] The Russian Formalist Viktor Shklovsky offered a complementary view, famously calling *Tristram Shandy* the 'most typical novel in world literature'.[31] The roll-call of twentieth-century writers whose own engagements with life and literature were indebted to Sterne is long and varied, and includes Beckett, Borges, Calvino, B. S. Johnson, Nabokov, Perec, Queneau, Roth, Salman Rushdie, and Orhan Pamuk—while Milan Kundera coupled Sterne with Diderot as the two writers who taught the world to see the form of the novel as a 'great game'.[32] Since, in ludic fashion, Sterne also taught writers to value the visual aspects of the text—*Tristram Shandy* contains, among much else, a black leaf, a marbled leaf, a blank page for painting a picture of the Widow Wadman ('as like your mistress as you can—as unlike your wife as your conscience will let you—'tis all one to me' [VI.xxxviii.376]), the lines

---

[29] Friedrich Nietzsche, *Human, All Too Human*, trans. R. J. Hollingdale (1986; new edn. Cambridge: Cambridge University Press, 1996), 238–9.

[30] Virginia Woolf, 'The "Sentimental Journey"', *The Common Reader*, Second Series, in *Collected Essays*, 4 vols. (London: Hogarth Press, 1966), i. 96.

[31] Viktor Shklovsky [Viktor Shklvoskil], *Theory of Prose*, trans. Benjamin Sher, 2nd edn. (1929; Normal, Ill.: Dalkey Archive Press, 1990), 'The Novel as Parody', 170.

[32] 'Afterword: A Talk with the Author by Philip Roth', in Milan Kundera, *The Book of Laughter and Forgetting*, trans. Michael Henry Hein (1978; repr. Harmondsworth: Penguin, 1983), 231.

purporting to show Tristram's less than perfect attempts to construct a straight narrative line in Volumes I–V of his 'Life and Opinions', and the impressive flourish of Corporal Trim's stick—it is appropriate that Sterne's novel has more recently been re-imagined visually both by Martin Rowson in his sharply intelligent comic book *Tristram Shandy* (1997) and by the director Michael Winterbottom in his imaginative and very funny film adaptation, *A Cock and Bull Story* (2006).

The title of Winterbottom's film appropriately enough picks up on the celebrated ending to Sterne's nine-volume novel:

L -- d! said my mother, what is all this story about?—
A COCK and a BULL, said Yorick—And one of the best of its kind, I ever heard. (IX.xxxiii.539)

That *Tristram Shandy* should conclude with a bemused question and a highly ambiguous answer is certainly characteristic of its facetious author. Yet the question of whether readers have been wasting their time pertinently echoes those contemptuous fears the 'new species of writing' so often prompted. In *Tristram Shandy*, Sterne hits back. Nor was he alone. It was another clergyman-novelist, Francis Coventry, who had attacked the 'pride and pedantry of learned men, who are willing to monopolize reading to themselves, and therefore fastidiously decry all books that are on a level with common understandings, as empty, trifling and impertinent'.[33] Sterne takes this argument a stage further, writing a work that appealed to common and uncommon understandings alike, while often remaining as puzzling to the latter as to the former. And so the black leaf or the blank page or the marbled leaf is as open (or closed) to interpretation by the common as by the learned reader:

Read, read, read, read, my unlearned reader! read,—or by the knowledge of the great saint *Paraleipomenon*—I tell you beforehand, you had better throw down the book at once; for without *much reading*, by which your reverence knows, I mean *much knowledge*, you will be no more able to penetrate the moral of the next marbled page (motly emblem of my work!) than the world with all

---

[33] Francis Coventry, 'To Henry Fielding, Esq.', *The History of Pompey the Little; or the Life and Adventures of a Lap-Dog*, ed. Robert Adams Day (London: Oxford University Press, 1974), pp. xli–xlii.

its sagacity has been able to unravel the many opinions, transactions and truths which still lie mystically hid under the veil of the black one (III.XXXVI.180).

Let the modern reader of novels who doubts the democratic impulse and subversive power of the eighteenth century's 'new species of writing' turn to page 181 of the present edition of *The Life and Opinions of Tristram Shandy, Gentleman*, and penetrate, learnedly, the moral of Sterne's work.

NOTE ON THE TEXT

THE present text follows the first editions of the several volumes of *Tristram Shandy*:

> Vols. I and II: [York]: [A. Ward], 1760
> Vols. III and IV: London: R. and J. Dodsley, 1761
> Vols. V and VI: London: T. Becket and P. A. Dehondt, 1762
> Vols. VII and VIII: London: T. Becket and P. A. Dehon[d]t, 1765
> Vol. IX: London: T. Becket and P. A. Dehondt, 1767.

(Despite the dates given on the title pages, Volumes I and II were printed and published in York in December 1759; Volumes V and VI were advertised in London on 22 December 1761.)

For Volumes I and II, the British Library set of the first edition, catalogued as Ashley 1770, was used as copy-text; for the remaining volumes, the Bodleian set Godw. Subt. 111–16, 118. The marbled leaf on pp. 181–2 is reproduced from this Bodleian edition, Godw. Subt 111–12, [III] pp. 169–70, by courtesy of the Bodleian Library, University of Oxford. Obvious errors have been corrected and the long 's' has been eliminated throughout. The style CHAP. I. has been expanded to CHAPTER I etc., and running heads have been added. The running quotation marks in the left margin have been omitted and normal modern practice concerning quotations has been followed. Otherwise, the copy-text has been followed for accidentals, though substantive emendations from later editions in which Sterne took an interest have been incorporated. There has been no normalization of inconsistencies of spelling or italicization.

No attempt has been made to 'correct' errors arising from Sterne's over-hasty copying from sources such as Chambers's *Cyclopaedia* or Burton's *Anatomy of Melancholy*, as the retention of such minor deviations from his sources best indicates Sterne's ludic (and certainly non-scholarly) relationship to the great variety of materials on which he drew, with or without acknowledgement, and which he variously copied, paraphrased, alluded to, misremembered, or mistranscribed. Attention is drawn to some of Sterne's copying 'errors'—and the impossibility of 'correcting' these consistently—in the Notes (see n. 2 to III.xi or n. 4 to VII-I.xxxiii, for example). No authorial manuscript of *Tristram Shandy* survives but a fair copy by Sterne of the Le Fever episode in Volume VI was brought to light in 1991; the single substantive change from the published text is discussed in n. 1 to VI.x.

A list of textual emendations is given on pp. 602–4.

SELECT BIBLIOGRAPHY

Editions of Tristram Shandy

The Life and Opinions of Tristram Shandy, Gentleman. [York] and London, 1760–7.

The Life and Opinions of Tristram Shandy, Gentleman, ed. James Aiken Work. New York: Odyssey Press, 1940.

The Life and Opinions of Tristram Shandy, Gentleman, 3 vols., ed. Melvyn New and Joan New with Richard A. Davies and W. G. Day. Gainesville: University Press of Florida, 1978–84 (The Florida Edition of the Works of Laurence Sterne).

The Life and Opinions of Tristram Shandy, Gentleman, ed. Ian Campbell Ross. Oxford: Clarendon Press, 1983.

The Life and Opinions of Tristram Shandy, Gentleman, ed. Robert Folkenflik. New York: The Modern Library, 2004.

Editions of Other Works by Laurence Sterne

Sterne's Memoirs: A Hitherto Unrecorded Holograph Now Brought to Light in Facsimile, ed. Kenneth Monkman. Coxwold: The Laurence Sterne Trust, 1985.

Letters of Laurence Sterne, ed. Lewis Perry Curtis. Oxford: Clarendon Press, 1935.

The Letters, 2 vols., ed. Melvyn New and Peter de Voogd. Gainesville: University Press of Florida, 2009 (The Florida Edition of the Works of Laurence Sterne).

'Sterne's Rabelaisian Fragment', ed. Melvyn New, *PMLA* 88 (1972), 1083–92.

The Sermons of Laurence Sterne, 2 vols., ed. Melvyn New. Gainesville: University Press of Florida, 1996 (The Florida Edition of the Works of Laurence Sterne).

A Sentimental Journey through France and Italy. By Mr. Yorick, ed. Gardner D. Stout Jr. Berkeley and Los Angeles: University of California Press, 1967.

A Sentimental Journey through France and Italy and *Continuation of the Bramine's Journal*, ed. Melvyn New and W. G. Day. Gainesville: University Press of Florida, 2002 (The Florida Edition of the Works of Laurence Sterne).

A Sentimental Journey through France and Italy and Other Writings, ed. Ian Jack and Tim Parnell. Oxford: Oxford University Press, 2003.

Biographical Works

Cash, Arthur H. *Laurence Sterne: The Early and Middle Years*. London: Methuen, 1975.

— *Laurence Sterne: The Later Years*. London: Methuen, 1986.

Cross, Wilbur L. *The Life and Times of Laurence Sterne*. 3rd edn. New Haven: Yale University Press, 1929.

Fitzgerald, Percy. *Life of Laurence Sterne*. 3rd edn. London: Chatto & Windus, 1906.

Hartley, Lodwick. *Laurence Sterne: A Biographical Essay*. 1943; repr. Chapel Hill: University of North Carolina Press, 1968.

Ross, Ian Campbell. *Laurence Sterne: A Life*. Oxford: Oxford University Press, 2001.

Thompson, David. *Wild Excursions: The Life and Fiction of Laurence Sterne*. London: Weidenfeld & Nicolson, 1972.

Critical and Textual Studies

Monographs and edited collections

Byrd, Max. *Tristram Shandy*. London: George Allen & Unwin, 1985.

Cash, Arthur H., and Stedmond, John M. (eds.). *The Winged Skull: Papers from the Laurence Sterne Bicentenary Conference*. London: Methuen, 1971.

Fluchère, Henri. *Laurence Sterne: From Tristram to Yorick: An interpretation of 'Tristram Shandy'*, trans. and abridged Barbara Bray. 1961; Oxford: Oxford University Press, 1965.

Freedman, William. *Laurence Sterne and the Origins of the Musical Novel*. Athens, Ga.: University of Georgia Press, 1978.

Gerrard, William Blake. *Laurence Sterne and the Visual Imagination*. Aldershot: Ashgate, 2006.

Holtz, William V. *Image and Immortality: A Study of 'Tristram Shandy'*. Providence, RI: Brown University Press, 1970.

Howes, Alan B. *Yorick and the Critics: Sterne's Reputation in England, 1760–1868*, Yale Studies in English, 139. New Haven: Yale University Press, 1958.

— *Sterne: The Critical Heritage*. London: Routledge & Kegan Paul, 1974.

Iser, Wolfgang. *Laurence Sterne: 'Tristram Shandy'*, trans. David Henry Wilson. Cambridge: Cambridge University Press, 1988.

Keymer, Thomas (ed.), *Sterne, the Moderns, and the Novel*. Oxford: Oxford University Press, 2002.

— *Laurence Sterne's 'Tristram Shandy': A Casebook*. Oxford: Oxford University Press, 2006.

— *The Cambridge Companion to Laurence Sterne*. Cambridge: Cambridge University Press, 2009.

Kraft, Elizabeth. *Laurence Sterne Revisited*. New York: Twayne, 1996.

Lamb, Jonathan. *Sterne's Fiction and the Double Principle*. Cambridge: Cambridge University Press, 1989.

Lanham, Richard A. *'Tristram Shandy': The Games of Pleasure*. Berkeley and Los Angeles: University of California Press, 1973.

Loveridge, Mark. *Laurence Sterne and the Argument about Design*. London: Macmillan, 1982.

Moglen, Helene. *The Philosophical Irony of Laurence Sterne*. Gainesville: University Press of Florida, 1975.

Myer, Valerie Grosvenor (ed.). *Laurence Sterne: Riddles and Mysteries*. London: Vision and Barnes & Noble, 1984.

New, Melvyn. *Laurence Sterne as Satirist: A Reading of 'Tristram Shandy'*. Gainesville: University Press of Florida, 1969.

—— (ed.). *'The Life and Opinions of Tristram Shandy, Gentleman': Laurence Sterne*. London: Macmillan, 1992.

—— *'Tristram Shandy': A Book for Free Spirits*. New York: Twayne, 1994.

—— (ed.). *Critical Essays on Laurence Sterne*. New York: G. K. Hall, 1998.

Pierce, David, and Voogd, Peter de (eds.). *Laurence Sterne in Modernism and Postmodernism*. Amsterdam: Rodopi, 1996.

Rowson, Martin, *Laurence Sterne: The Life and Opinions of Tristram Shandy, Gentleman*. London: Picador, 1996, and Woodstock, NY: The Overlook Press, 1997.

Stedmond, John M. *The Comic Art of Laurence Sterne: Convention and Innovation in 'Tristram Shandy' and 'A Sentimental Journey'*. Toronto: University of Toronto Press, 1967.

Swearingen, James E. *Reflexivity in 'Tristram Shandy': An Essay in Phenomenological Criticism*. New Haven: Yale University Press, 1977.

Traugott, John. *Tristram Shandy's World: Sterne's Philosophical Rhetoric*. Berkeley and Los Angeles: University of California Press, 1954.

—— (ed.). *Laurence Sterne: A Collection of Critical Essays*. Englewood Cliffs, NJ: Prentice-Hall, 1968.

Voogd, Peter de, and Neubauer, John (eds.). *The Reception of Laurence Sterne in Europe*. London: Thoemmes Continuum, 2004.

Walsh, Marcus (ed.). *Laurence Sterne*. Harlow: Longman, 2002.

Watts, Carol. *The Cultural Work of Empire: The Seven Years' War and the Imagining of the Shandean State*. Edinburgh: Edinburgh University Press, 2007.

Book chapters and journal articles

Alter, Robert. 'Sterne and the Nostalgia for Reality', in *Partial Magic: The Novel as a Self-Conscious Genre*. Berkeley and Los Angeles: University of California Press, 1975, 30–56.

Booth, Wayne C. 'The Self-Conscious Narrator in Comic Fiction before *Tristram Shandy*', *PMLA* 67/2 (1952), 163–85; repr. in New (ed.), *Critical Essays*, 36–59.

—— 'Did Sterne Complete *Tristram Shandy*?', *Modern Philology*, 48/1 (1951), 172–83.

Brady, Frank. '*Tristram Shandy*: Sexuality, Morality, and Sensibility', *Eighteenth-Century Studies*, 4/1 (1970), 41–56.

Briggs, Peter M. 'Laurence Sterne and Literary Celebrity in 1760', *Age of Johnson*, 4 (1991), 251–80; repr. in Keymer, *Laurence Sterne's 'Tristram Shandy'*, 79–107.

Brissenden, R. F. 'The Sentimental Comedy: *Tristram Shandy*', in *Virtue in Distress: Studies in the Novel of Sentiment from Richardson to Sterne*. London: Macmillan, 1974, 187–217.

—— 'Sterne and Painting', in John Butt (ed.), *Of Books and Humankind: Essays and Poems Presented to Bonamy Dobrée*. London: Routledge & Kegan Paul, 1964, 93–108.

Brown, Marshall. 'Sterne's Stories', in *Preromanticism*. Stanford, Calif.: Stanford University Press, 1991, 261–300.

Campbell, Anne. '*Tristram Shandy* and the Seven Years' War: Beyond the Borders of the Bowling Green', *The Shandean*, 17 (2006), 106–20.

Carnochan, W. B. '"Which Way I Fly"', in *Confinement and Flight: An Essay on English Literature of the Eighteenth Century*. Berkeley and Los Angeles: University of California Press, 1977, 102–46.

Cash, Arthur H. 'The Birth of Tristram Shandy: Sterne and Dr. Burton', in R. F. Brissenden (ed.), *Studies in the Eighteenth Century*. Canberra: Australian National University Press, 1968, 133–54.

DePorte, Michael V. *Nightmares and Hobbyhorses: Swift, Sterne and Augustan Ideas of Madness*. San Marino, Calif.: The Huntington Library, 1974.

Donoghue, Frank. '"I wrote not to be fed but to be famous": Laurence Sterne', in *The Fame Machine: Book Reviewing and Eighteenth-Century Literary Careers*. Stanford, Calif.: Stanford University Press, 1996, 56–85.

Douglas, Mary. '*Tristram Shandy*: Testing for Ring Shape', in *Thinking in Circles: An Essay on Ring Composition*. New Haven: Yale University Press, 2007, 85–100.

Fanning, Christopher. 'On Sterne's Page: Spatial Layout, Spatial Form, and Social Spaces in *Tristram Shandy*', *Eighteenth-Century Fiction*, 10/4 (1998), 429–50.

Ginzburg, Carlo. 'A Search for Origins: Re-reading *Tristram Shandy*', in *No Island is an Island: Four Glances at English Literature in a World Perspective*. New York: Columbia University Press, 2000, 43–67.

Hammond, Brean, and Regan, Shaun. 'The Sympathetic Strain: Sterne and Sentimental Fiction', in *Making the Novel: Fiction and Society in Britain, 1660–1789*. Basingstoke: Palgrave Macmillan, 2006, 164–200.

Hawley, Judith. '"Hints and Documents" 1: A Bibliography for Tristram Shandy', *The Shandean*, 3 (1991), 9–36.

—— '"Hints and Documents" 2: A Bibliography for Tristram Shandy', *The Shandean*, 4 (1992), 49–65.

—— 'The Anatomy of *Tristram Shandy*', in Marie Mulvey Roberts and Roy Porter (eds.), *Literature and Medicine during the Eighteenth Century*. London: Routledge, 1993, 84–100.

—— 'Sterne and the *Cyclopaedia* Revisited', *The Shandean*, 15 (2004), 57–77.

Hunter, J. Paul. 'Clocks, Calendars, and Names: The Troubles of Tristram and the Aesthetics of Uncertainty', in J. Douglas Canfield and J. Paul Hunter (eds.), *Rhetorics of Order/Ordering Rhetorics in English Neoclassical Literature*. Newark: University of Delaware Press, 1989, 173–98.

Jefferson, D. W. '*Tristram Shandy* and the Tradition of Learned Wit', *Essays in Criticism*, 1/3 (1951), 225–48; repr. in Traugott (ed.), *Laurence Sterne* 148–67, and New (ed.), '*The Life and Opinions*', 17–35.

Josipovici, Gabriel. 'The Body in the Library', in *Writing and the Body: The Northcliffe Lectures 1981*. Brighton: Harvester Press, 1982, 1–33.

Keymer, Thomas. 'Sterne and Romantic Autobiography', in Thomas Keymer and Jon Mee (eds.), *The Cambridge Companion to English Literature from 1740 to 1830*. Cambridge: Cambridge University Press, 2004, 173–93.

Lamb, Jonathan. 'Sterne's Use of Montaigne', *Comparative Literature*, 32/1 (1980), 1–41.

Loveridge, Mark. 'Stories of Cocks and Bulls: The Ending of Tristram Shandy', *Eighteenth-Century Fiction*, 5/1 (1992), 35–54.

Lupton, Christina. '*Tristram Shandy*, David Hume and Epistemological Fiction', *Philosophy and Literature*, 27/1 (2003), 98–115.

Lynch, Jack. 'The Relicks of Learning: Sterne among the Renaissance Encyclopedists', *Eighteenth-Century Fiction*, 13/1 (2000), 1–17.

Moglen, Helen. '(W)holes and Noses: The Indeterminacies of Tristram Shandy', in *The Trauma of Gender: A Feminist Theory of the English Novel*. Berkeley and Los Angeles: University of California Press, 2001, 87–108.

Monkman, Kenneth. 'Bibliography of the Early Editions of Tristram Shandy', *The Library*, 5th ser. 25 (1970), 11–39.

—— 'Tristram in Dublin', *Transactions of the Cambridge Bibliographical Society*, 7 (1979), 343–68.

Mullan, John. 'Laurence Sterne and the "Sociality" of the Novel', in *Sentiment and Sociability: The Language of Feeling in the Eighteenth Century*. Oxford: Clarendon Press, 1988, 147–200.

New, Melvyn. 'Sterne, Warburton, and the Burden of Exuberant Wit', *Eighteenth-Century Studies*, 15/3 (1982), 245–74.

—— 'A Manuscript of the Le Fever Episode in *Tristram Shandy*', *The Scriblerian*, 23/2 (1991), 165–74.

—— et al. 'Scholia to the Florida Edition of the Works of Sterne from *The Scriblerian*, 1986–2005', *The Shandean*, 15 (2004), 135–64.

Nuttall, A. D. '*Tristram Shandy*', in *A Common Sky: Philosophy and the Literary Imagination*. London: Chatto & Windus for Sussex University Press, 1974, 45–91.

Ostovich, Helen. 'Reader as Hobby-Horse in *Tristram Shandy*', *Philological Quarterly*, 68 (1989), 325–42; repr. in Keymer, *Laurence Sterne's 'Tristram Shandy'*, 171–90.

Parnell, J. T. 'Swift, Sterne, and the Skeptical Tradition', *Studies in Eighteenth-Century Culture*, 23 (1994), 221–42; repr. in Keymer, *Laurence Sterne's 'Tristram Shandy'*, 23–49.

—— '"Que sçais-je?" Montaigne's *Apology*, *Hamlet* and *Tristram Shandy*: Enquiry and Sceptical Response', *Eighteenth-Century Ireland/Iris an dá chultúr*, 10 (1995), 148–55.

—— 'A Story Painted to the Heart? *Tristram Shandy* and Sentimentalism Reconsidered', *The Shandean*, 9 (1997), 122–35.

Porter, Roy. '"The whole secret of health": Mind, Body, and Medicine in *Tristram Shandy*', in John Christie and Sally Shuttleworth (eds.), *Nature Transfigured: Science and Literature 1700–1900*. Manchester: Manchester University Press, 1989, 61–84.

Preston, John. '*Tristram Shandy* (i): The Reader as Author' and '*Tristram Shandy* (ii): The Author as Reader', in *The Created Self: The Reader's Role in Eighteenth-Century Fiction*. London: Heinemann, 1970, 133–64, 165–95.

Price, Martin. 'Sterne: Art and Nature', in *To the Palace of Wisdom: Studies in Order and Energy from Dryden to Blake*. Garden City, NY: Doubleday, 1964, 313–42.

Regan, Shaun. 'Translating Rabelais: Sterne, Motteux, and the Culture of Politeness', *Translation and Literature*, 10/2 (2001), 174–99.

—— 'Print Culture in Transition: *Tristram Shandy*, the Reviewers, and the Consumable Text', *Eighteenth-Century Fiction*, Special Issue on *Fiction and Print Culture*, 14/3–4 (2002), 289–309.

—— 'Novelizing Scriblerus: *Tristram Shandy* and (Post-) Scriblerian Satire', *The Shandean*, 17 (2006), 9–33.

Rosenblum, Michael. 'The Sermon, the King of Bohemia, and the Art of Interpolation in *Tristram Shandy*', *Studies in Philology*, 75/4 (1978), 472–98.

Ross, Ian Campbell, and Nassar, Noha Saad. 'Trim (-tram), Like Master, Like Man: Servant and Sexton in Sterne's *Tristram Shandy* and *A Political Romance*', *Notes & Queries*, 36/1 (1989), 62–5.

Rothstein, Eric. '*Tristram Shandy*', in *Systems of Order and Inquiry in Later Eighteenth-Century Fiction*. Berkeley and Los Angeles: University of California Press, 1975, 62–108.

Seidel, Michael. 'Gravity's Inheritable Line: Sterne's *Tristram Shandy*', in *Satiric Inheritance: Rabelais to Sterne*. Princeton, NJ: Princeton University Press, 1979, 250–62.

Shklovskii, Viktor [Shklovsky, Viktor]. *Theory of Prose*, trans. Benjamin Sher, 2nd edn. Normal, Ill.: Dalkey Archive Press, 1990, 'A Parodying Novel: Sterne's *Tristram Shandy*', 147–70; also, trans. W. George Isaak, in John Traugott (1969), 66–89; trans. Richard Sheldon. *The Review of Contemporary Fiction*, 1 (1981), 190–211.

Spacks, Patricia Meyer. 'The Beautiful Oblique: *Tristram Shandy*', in *Imagining a Self: Autobiography and the Novel in Eighteenth-Century England*. Cambridge, Mass.: Harvard University Press, 1976, 127–57.

— '*Tristram Shandy* and the Development of the Novel', in *Novel Beginnings: Experiments in Eighteenth-Century English Fiction*. New Haven and London: Yale University Press, 2006, 254–76.

Stewart, Carol. 'The Anglicanism of *Tristram Shandy*: Latitudinarianism at the Limits', *British Journal for Eighteenth-Century Studies*, 28/2 (2005), 239–50.

Van Sant, Anne Jessie. 'Locating Experience in the Body: The Man of Feeling', in *Eighteenth-Century Sensibility and the Novel: The Sense in Social Context*. Cambridge: Cambridge University Press, 1993, 98–115.

Watt, Ian. 'The Comic Syntax of *Tristram Shandy*', in Bruce Thompson (ed.), *The Literal Imagination: Selected Essays*. Seattle: University of Washington Press, 2002, 126–42.

Wehrs, Donald R. 'Sterne, Cervantes, Montaigne: Fideistic Skepticism and the Rhetoric of Desire', *Comparative Literature Studies*, 25/2 (1988), 127–51.

Zimmermann, Everett. '*Tristram Shandy* and Narrative Representation', *Eighteenth Century: Theory and Interpretation*, 28/2 (1987), 127–47.

Journal

The Shandean (1986–present) is edited annually by Peter de Voogd and wholly given over to Sterne and his writings. The journal is an invaluable source of critical and textual studies of *Tristram Shandy*, only a small selection of which are mentioned above.

Film

A Cock and Bull Story (2006). Director: Michael Winterbottom. Cast: Steve Coogan, Rob Brydon, Gillian Anderson, Keeley Hawes, Shirley Henderson, Dylan Moran, Jeremy Northam, Naomie Harris, Kelly Macdonald, James Fleet, Ian Hart.

Further Reading in Oxford World's Classics

Sterne, Laurence. *A Sentimental Journey and Other Writings*, ed. Ian Jack and Tim Parnell.

A CHRONOLOGY OF LAURENCE STERNE

1713 (24 November) Born in Clonmel, Ireland, first son and second child of Roger Sterne, an army ensign, and Agnes Sterne.

1723 (or 1724) Goes to school in Halifax, leaving Ireland and his family for good.

1731 (31 July) Death of Roger Sterne at Port Antonio, Jamaica.

1733 Enters Jesus College, Cambridge, of which an ancestor, Richard Sterne, had been Master 1634–44, as a sizar.

1737 (January) BA; (6 March) admitted as a deacon in the Church of England and licensed assistant curate of St. Ives, Huntingdonshire.

1738 (18 February) Licensed assistant curate at Catton, Yorkshire; (20 August) ordained priest and collated to vicarage of Sutton-on-the-Forest, Yorkshire.

1740 (July) Awarded MA.

1741 (19 January) Admitted to the prebend of Givendale in York Minster; (30 March) marries Elizabeth Lumley; writes political propaganda for Whigs and is rewarded by the prebend of North Newbald.

1742 (8 January) Admitted as prebendary of North Newbald.

1743 (July) *Gentleman's Magazine* publishes 'The Unknown World: Verses occasion'd by hearing a Pass-Bell'.

1744 (14 March) Induced into a second living at Stillington, near Sutton; (1 November) the Sternes purchase the Tindal Farm which they work with little success until 1758.

1745 (1 October) Elizabeth Sterne gives birth to daughter, Lydia, who dies next day.

1747 (April) Preaches a charity sermon, *'The Case of Elijah and the Widow of Zerephath, consider'd'*, subsequently published in York; (1 December) birth of daughter, Lydia.

1750 (29 July) Preaches the sermon 'The Abuses of Conscience' in York Minster; (August) sermon published in York.

1759 (January) *A Political Romance* published in York; (December) *Tristram Shandy*, I–II, published in York.

1760 (January) *Tristram Shandy*, I–II, on sale in London where all subsequent volumes are first published; (29 March) licensed to the living of Coxwold, in Yorkshire, where he settles; (May) *The Sermons of Mr. Yorick*, I–II.

1761 (January) *Tristram Shandy*, III–IV; (December) *Tristram Shandy*, V–VI.

1762 (January) Leaves for France for reasons of health.

1764 (May) Returns to England.

1765 (January) *Tristram Shandy*, VII–VIII; (October) leaves England for France and Italy.

1766 (January) *The Sermons of Mr. Yorick*, III–IV; (June) returns to England.

1767 (January) *Tristram Shandy*, IX; meets Elizabeth Draper who leaves England to rejoin her husband in India in April; (April to November) writes *The Journal to Eliza*.

1768 (February) *A Sentimental Journal through France and Italy*, I–II; (18 March) Sterne dies at his Bond Street lodgings; (22 March) interred in the burial-ground of St. George's, Hanover Square, London.

1769 (June) *Sermons by the late Rev. Mr. Sterne*, V–VII, published by Lydia Sterne.

1904 *The Journal to Eliza* first published by Wilbur L. Cross in *The Works and Life of Laurence Sterne*, 12 vols.

1969 (8 June) Sterne's bones reburied in Coxwold churchyard.

W. Hogarth inv.ᵗ   Vol. 2. page 128.   S. Ravenet Sculp.ᵗ

THE

L I F E

A N D

O P I N I O N S

O F

TRISTRAM SHANDY,

Gentleman.

Ταρασσει τοὺς Ἀνθρώπους οὐ τὰ Πράγματα,
αλλα τὰ περι τῶν Πραγμάτων, Δογματα.

VOL. I.

1 7 6 0.

THE

L I F E

AND

O P I N I O N S

OF

TRISTRAM SHANDY,

GENTLEMAN.

Ταρασσει τοὺς 'Ανθρώπους οὐ τὰ Πράγματα,
αλλα τὰ περι τῶν Πραγμάτων, Δογματα.

VOL. I.

The SECOND EDITION.

L O N D O N :
Printed for R. and J. DODSLEY in *Pall-Mall*.
M.DCC.LX.

To the Right Honourable

Mr. P I T T.[1]

SIR,

NEVER poor Wight of a Dedicator had less hopes from his Dedication, than I have from this of mine; for it is written in a bye corner of the kingdom,[2] and in a retired thatch'd house, where I live in a constant endeavour to fence against the infirmities of ill health, and other evils of life, by mirth; being firmly persuaded that every time a man smiles,—but much more so, when he laughs, that it adds something to this Fragment of Life.

I humbly beg, Sir, that you will honour this book by taking it——(not under your Protection,——it must protect itself, but)—into the country with you; where, if I am ever told, it has made you smile, or can conceive it has beguiled you of one moment's pain——I shall think myself as happy as a minister of state;—— perhaps much happier than any one (one only excepted) that I have ever read or heard of.

I am, great Sir,
(and what is more to your Honour,)
I am, good Sir,
Your well wisher,
and most humble Fellow-Subject

THE AUTHOR.

CHAPTER I

I wish either my father or my mother, or indeed both of them, as they were in duty both equally bound to it, had minded what they were about when they begot me; had they duly consider'd how much depended upon what they were then doing;—that not only the production of a rational Being was concern'd in it, but that possibly the happy formation and temperature of his body, perhaps his genius and the very cast of his mind;—and, for aught they knew to the contrary, even the fortunes of his whole house might take their turn from the humours[1] and dispositions which were then uppermost:——Had they duly weighed and considered all this, and proceeded accordingly, ——I am verily persuaded I should have made a quite different figure in the world, from that, in which the reader is likely to see me.—Believe me, good folks, this is not so inconsiderable a thing as many of you may think it;—you have all, I dare say, heard of the animal spirits,[2] as how they are transfused from father to son, &c. &c.—and a great deal to that purpose:—Well, you may take my word, that nine parts in ten of a man's sense or his nonsense, his successes and miscarriages in this world depend upon their motions and activity, and the different tracks and trains you put them into; so that when they are once set a-going, whether right or wrong, 'tis not a halfpenny matter,--away they go cluttering like hey-go-mad; and by treading the same steps over and over again, they presently make a road of it, as plain and as smooth as a garden-walk, which, when they are once used to, the Devil himself sometimes shall not be able to drive them off it.

Pray, my dear, quoth my mother, *have you not forgot to wind up the clock?*——*Good G—!* cried my father, making an exclamation, but taking care to moderate his voice at the same time,——*Did ever woman, since the creation of the world, interrupt a man with such a silly question?* Pray, what was your father saying?——Nothing.

CHAPTER II

——Then positively, there is nothing in the question, that I can see, either good or bad.——Then let me tell you, Sir, it was a very unseasonable question at least,—because it scattered and dispersed the animal spirits, whose business it was to have escorted and gone hand-in-hand with the *HOMUNCULUS*,[1] and conducted him safe to the place destined for his reception.

The HOMUNCULUS, Sir, in how-ever low and ludicrous a light he may appear, in this age of levity, to the eye of folly or prejudice;—to the eye of reason in scientifick research, he stands confess'd— a BEING guarded and circumscribed with rights:——The minutest philosophers, who, by the bye, have the most enlarged understandings, (their souls being inversely as their enquiries) shew us incontestably, That the HOMUNCULUS is created by the same hand,—engender'd in the same course of nature,—endowed with the same loco-motive powers and faculties with us:——That he consists, as we do, of skin, hair, fat, flesh, veins, arteries, ligaments, nerves, cartileges, bones, marrow, brains, glands, genitals, humours, and articulations;——is a Being of as much activity,——and, in all senses of the word, as much and as truly our fellow-creature as my Lord Chancellor of England.—He may be benefited, he may be injured,—he may obtain redress;—in a word, he has all the claims and rights of humanity, which *Tully*,[2] *Puffendorff*, or the best ethick writers allow to arise out of that state and relation.

Now, dear Sir, what if any accident had befallen him in his way alone?——or that, thro' terror of it, natural to so young a traveller, my little gentleman had got to his journey's end miserably spent;——his muscular strength and virility worn down to a thread;—his own animal spirits ruffled beyond description,—and that in this sad disorder'd state of nerves, he had laid down a prey to sudden starts, or a series of melancholy dreams and fancies for nine long, long months together.——I tremble to think what a foundation had been laid for a thousand weaknesses both of body and mind, which no skill of the physician or the philosopher could ever afterwards have set thoroughly to rights.

CHAPTER III

To my uncle Mr. *Toby Shandy* do I stand indebted for the preceding anecdote, to whom my father, who was an excellent natural philosopher,[1] and much given to close reasoning upon the smallest matters, had oft, and heavily, complain'd of the injury; but once more particularly, as my uncle *Toby* well remember'd, upon his observing a most unaccountable obliquity, (as he call'd it) in my manner of setting up my top, and justifying the principles upon which I had done it,—the old gentleman shook his head, and in a tone more expressive by half of sorrow than reproach,—he said his heart all along foreboded, and he saw it verified in this, and from a thousand other observations he had made upon me, That I should neither think nor act like any other man's child:——*But alas!* continued he, shaking his head a second time, and wiping away a tear which was trickling down his cheeks, *My Tristram's misfortunes began nine months before ever he came into the world.*

——My mother, who was sitting by, look'd up,—but she knew no more than her backside what my father meant,--but my uncle, Mr. *Toby Shandy*, who had been often informed of the affair,—understood him very well.

CHAPTER IV

I know there are readers in the world, as well as many other good people in it, who are no readers at all,—who find themselves ill at ease, unless they are let into the whole secret from first to last, of every thing which concerns you.

It is in pure compliance with this humour of theirs, and from a backwardness in my nature to disappoint any one soul living, that I have been so very particular already. As my life and opinions are likely to make some noise in the world, and, if I conjecture right, will take in all ranks, professions, and denominations of men whatever,—be no less read than the *Pilgrim's Progress*[1] itself---and, in the end, prove the very thing which *Montaigne*[2] dreaded his essays should turn out, that is, a book for a parlour-window;—I find it necessary to consult every one a little in his turn; and therefore must beg pardon for going on a little further in the same way: For which cause, right glad I am, that I have begun the history of myself in the way I have done; and that I am able to go on tracing every thing in it, as *Horace*[3] says, *ab Ovo*.

Horace, I know, does not recommend this fashion altogether: But that gentleman is speaking only of an epic poem or a tragedy;—(I forget which)—besides, if it was not so, I should beg Mr. *Horace*'s pardon;—for in writing what I have set about, I shall confine myself neither to his rules, nor to any man's rules that ever lived.

To such, however, as do not choose to go so far back into these things, I can give no better advice, than that they skip over the remaining part of this Chapter; for I declare before hand, 'tis wrote only for the curious and inquisitive.

———————————— Shut the door. ————————————

I was begot in the night, betwixt the first *Sunday* and the first *Monday* in the month of *March*, in the year of our Lord one thousand seven hundred and eighteen. I am positive I was.— But how I came to be so very particular in my account of a thing which happened before I was born, is owing to another small anecdote known only in our own family, but now made public for the better clearing up this point.

My father, you must know, who was originally a *Turky* merchant,[4] but had left off business for some years, in order to retire to, and die upon, his paternal estate in the county of ———, was, I believe, one of the most regular men in every thing he did, whether 'twas matter of business, or matter of amusement, that ever lived. As a small specimen of this extreme exactness of his, to which he was in truth a slave,—he had made it a rule for many years of his life,—on the first *Sunday night* of every month throughout the whole year,—as certain as ever the *Sunday night* came,——to wind up a large house-clock which we had standing upon the back-stairs head, with his own hands:—And being somewhere between fifty and sixty years of age, at the time I have been speaking of,—he had likewise gradually brought some other little family concernments to the same period, in order, as he would often say to my uncle *Toby*, to get them all out of the way at one time, and be no more plagued and pester'd with them the rest of the month.

It was attended but with one misfortune, which, in a great

measure, fell upon myself, and the effects of which I fear I shall
carry with me to my grave; namely, that, from an unhappy
association of ideas which have no connection in nature, it so
fell out at length, that my poor mother could never hear the said
clock wound up,—but the thoughts of some other things unavoidably popp'd into her head,—& *vice versâ:*—which strange
combination of ideas, the sagacious *Locke*,[5] who certainly
understood the nature of these things better than most men,
affirms to have produced more wry actions than all other
sources of prejudice whatsoever.

But this by the bye.

Now it appears, by a memorandum in my father's pocket-
book, which now lies upon the table, "That on *Lady-Day*,
which was on the 25th of the same month in which I date my
geniture,—my father set out upon his journey to *London* with
my eldest brother *Bobby*, to fix him at *Westminster* school;"
and, as it appears from the same authority, "That he did not get
down to his wife and family till the *second week* in *May* following,"—it brings the thing almost to a certainty. However, what
follows in the beginning of the next chapter puts it beyond all
possibility of doubt.

————But pray, Sir, What was your father doing all *December,—January*, and *February?*——Why, Madam,—he was all
that time afflicted with a Sciatica.

CHAPTER V

ON the fifth day of *November*,[1] 1718, which to the æra fixed
on, was as near nine kalendar months as any husband could in
reason have expected,—was I *Tristram Shandy*, Gentleman,
brought forth into this scurvy and disasterous world of ours.—I
wish I had been born in the Moon, or in any of the planets,
(except *Jupiter* or *Saturn*,[2] because I never could bear cold
weather) for it could not well have fared worse with me in any of
them (tho' I will not answer for *Venus*) than it has in this vile,
dirty planet of ours,—which o' my conscience, with reverence
be it spoken, I take to be made up of the shreds and clippings of
the rest;——not but the planet is well enough, provided a man
could be born in it to a great title or to a great estate; or could
any how contrive to be called up to publick charges, and

employments of dignity or power;—but that is not my case;----
and therefore every man will speak of the fair as his own market
has gone in it;—for which cause I affirm it over again to be one
of the vilest worlds that ever was made;---for I can truly say,
that from the first hour I drew my breath in it, to this, that I can
now scarce draw it at all, for an asthma I got in scating against
the wind in *Flanders*;--I have been the continual sport of what
the world calls Fortune;³ and though I will not wrong her by
saying, She has ever made me feel the weight of any great or
signal evil;---yet with all the good temper in the world, I affirm
it of her, That in every stage of my life, and at every turn and
corner where she could get fairly at me, the ungracious Duchess
has pelted me with a set of as pitiful misadventures and cross
accidents as ever small HERO sustained.

CHAPTER VI

IN the beginning of the last chapter, I inform'd you exactly
when I was born;—but I did not inform you, *how*. *No*; that
particular was reserved entirely for a chapter by itself;—
besides, Sir, as you and I are in a manner perfect strangers to
each other, it would not have been proper to have let you into
too many circumstances relating to myself all at once.—You
must have a little patience. I have undertaken, you see, to write
not only my life, but my opinions also; hoping and expecting
that your knowledge of my character, and of what kind of a
mortal I am, by the one, would give you a better relish for the
other: As you proceed further with me, the slight acquaintance
which is now beginning betwixt us, will grow into familiarity;
and that, unless one of us is in fault, will terminate in friendship.——*O diem praeclarum!*¹——then nothing which has
touched me will be thought trifling in its nature, or tedious in its
telling. Therefore, my dear friend and companion, if you should
think me somewhat sparing of my narrative on my first setting
out,—bear with me,—and let me go on, and tell my story my
own way:——or if I should seem now and then to trifle upon
the road,——or should sometimes put on a fool's cap with a bell
to it, for a moment or two as we pass along,--don't fly off,—but
rather courteously give me credit for a little more wisdom than
appears upon my outside;—and as we jogg on, either laugh with

me, or at me, or in short, do any thing,——only keep your temper.

CHAPTER VII

In the same village where my father and my mother dwelt, dwelt also a thin, upright, motherly, notable, good old body of a midwife, who, with the help of a little plain good sense, and some years full employment in her business, in which she had all along trusted little to her own efforts, and a great deal to those of dame nature,—had acquired, in her way, no small degree of reputation in the world;—by which word *world*, need I in this place inform your worship, that I would be understood to mean no more of it, than a small circle described upon the circle of the great world, of four *English* miles diameter, or thereabouts, of which the cottage where the good old woman lived, is supposed to be the centre.——She had been left, it seems, a widow in great distress, with three or four small children, in her forty-seventh year; and as she was at that time a person of decent carriage,— grave deportment,——a woman moreover of few words, and withall an object of compassion, whose distress and silence under it call'd out the louder for a friendly lift: the wife of the parson of the parish was touch'd with pity; and having often lamented an inconvenience, to which her husband's flock had for many years been exposed, inasmuch, as there was no such thing as a midwife, of any kind or degree to be got at, let the case have been never so urgent, within less than six or seven long miles riding; which said seven long miles in dark nights and dismal roads, the country thereabouts being nothing but a deep clay, was almost equal to fourteen; and that in effect was sometimes next to having no midwife at all; it came into her head, that it would be doing as seasonable a kindness to the whole parish, as to the poor creature herself, to get her a little instructed in some of the plain principles of the business, in order to set her up in it. As no woman thereabouts was better qualified to execute the plan she had formed than herself, the Gentlewoman very charitably undertook it; and having great influence over the female part of the parish, she found no difficulty in effecting it to the utmost of her wishes. In truth, the parson join'd his interest with his wife's in the whole affair; and in order to do things as they should be, and give the poor soul as good a title by law to practise, as his wife had given by institution,——he chearfully paid the fees for the ordinaries[1] licence himself, amounting, in the whole, to the sum of eighteen shillings and fourpence; so that, betwixt them both, the good woman was fully invested in the real and corporal possession of her office, together with all its *rights, members, and appurtenances whatsoever*.

These last words, you must know, were not according to the old form in which such licences, faculties, and powers usually ran, which in like cases had heretofore been granted to the sisterhood. But it was according to a neat *Formula* of *Didius*[2] his own devising, who having a particular turn for taking to pieces, and new framing over again, all kind of instruments in that way, not only hit upon this dainty amendment, but coax'd many of the old licensed matrons in the neighbourhood, to open their faculties afresh, in order to have this whim-wham[3] of his inserted.

I own I never could envy *Didius* in these kinds of fancies of his:—But every man to his own taste.—Did not Dr. *Kunastrokius*,[4] that great man, at his leisure hours, take the greatest delight imaginable in combing of asses tails, and plucking the dead hairs out with his teeth, though he had tweezers always in his pocket? Nay, if you come to that, Sir, have not the wisest of men in all ages, not excepting *Solomon* himself,—have they not had their HOBBY-HORSES;[5]—their running horses,—their coins and their cockle-shells, their drums and their trumpets, their fiddles, their pallets,——their maggots and their butterflies?—and so long as a man rides his HOBBY-HORSE peaceably and quietly along the King's highway, and neither compels you or me to get up behind him,——pray, Sir, what have either you or I to do with it?

CHAPTER VIII

—*De gustibus non est disputandum*;[1]—that is, there is no disputing against HOBBY-HORSES; and, for my part, I seldom do; nor could I with any sort of grace, had I been an enemy to them at the bottom; for happening, at certain intervals and changes of the Moon, to be both fiddler and painter, according as the fly stings:---Be it known to you, that I keep a couple of pads myself, upon which, in their turns, (nor do I care who knows it) I frequently ride out and take the air;---tho' sometimes, to my shame be it spoken, I take somewhat longer journies than what a wise man would think altogether right.----But the truth is,---I am not a wise man;-----and besides am a mortal of so little consequence in the world, it is not much matter what I do; so I seldom fret or fume at all about it: Nor does it much disturb my rest when I see such great Lords and tall Personages as hereafter follow;---such, for instance, as my Lord A, B, C, D, E, F, G, H, I, K, L, M, N, O, P, Q, and so on, all of a row, mounted upon their several horses;--some with large stirrups, getting on in a more grave and sober pace;----others on the contrary, tuck'd up to their very chins, with whips across their mouths, scouring and scampering it away like so many little party-colour'd devils astride a mortgage,-----and as if some of them were resolved to break their necks.—So much the better—say I to myself;---for in case the worst should happen, the world will make a shift to do excellently well without them;—and for the rest,----why,----God speed them,----e'en let them ride on without any opposition from me; for were their lordships unhorsed this very night,------'tis ten to one but that many of them would be worse mounted by one half before tomorrow morning.

Not one of these instances therefore can be said to break in upon my rest.—But there is an instance, which I own puts me off my guard, and that is, when I see one born for great actions, and, what is still more for his honour, whose nature ever inclines him to good ones;----when I behold such a one, my Lord, like yourself, whose principles and conduct are as generous and noble as his blood, and whom, for that reason, a corrupt world cannot spare one moment;—when I see such a one, my Lord, mounted, though it is but for a minute beyond the time which my love to my country has prescribed to him, and my zeal for his glory wishes,—then, my Lord, I cease to be a philosopher, and in the first transport of an honest impatience, I wish the HOBBY-HORSE, with all his fraternity, at the Devil.

My Lord,
"I MAINTAIN this to be a dedication, notwithstanding its singularity in the three great essentials of matter, form, and place: I

beg, therefore, you will accept it as such, and that you will permit me to lay it, with the most respectful humility, at your Lordship's feet,--when you are upon them,--which you can be when you please;----and that is, my Lord, when ever there is occasion for it, and I will add, to the best purposes too. I have the honour to be,

> *My Lord,*
> *Your Lordship's most obedient,*
> *and most devoted,*
> *and most humble servant,*
> TRISTRAM SHANDY.

CHAPTER IX

I SOLEMNLY declare to all mankind, that the above dedication was made for no one Prince, Prelate, Pope, or Potentate,— Duke, Marquis, Earl, Viscount, or Baron of this, or any other Realm in Chistendom;-----nor has it yet been hawk'd about, or offered publickly or privately, directly or indirectly, to any one person or personage, great or small; but is honestly a true Virgin-Dedication untried on, upon any soul living.

I labour this point so particularly, merely to remove any offence or objection which might arise against it, from the manner in which I propose to make the most of it;---which is the putting it up fairly to publick sale; which I now do.

------Every author has a way of his own, in bringing his points to bear;--for my own part, as I hate chaffering and higgling for a few guineas in a dark entry;---I resolved within myself, from the very beginning, to deal squarely and openly with your Great Folks in this affair, and try whether I should not come off the better by it.

If therefore there is any one Duke, Marquis, Earl, Viscount, or Baron, in these his Majesty's dominions, who stands in need of a tight, genteel dedication, and whom the above will suit, (for by the bye, unless it suits in some degree, I will not part with it)------it is much at his service for fifty guineas;------which I am positive is twenty guineas less than it ought to be afforded for, by any man of genius.

My Lord, if you examine it over again, it is far from being a gross piece of daubing, as some dedications are. The design, your Lordship sees, is good, the colouring transparent,—the drawing not amiss;—or to speak more like a man of science,—and measure my piece in the painter's scale, divided into 20,—I believe, my Lord, the out-lines will turn out as 12,—the composition as 9,—the colouring as 6,—the expression 13 and a half,—and the design,—if I may be allowed, my Lord, to understand my own *design*, and supposing absolute perfection in designing, to be as 20,—I think it cannot well fall short of 19. Besides all this,—there is keeping in it, and the dark strokes in the HOBBY-HORSE, (which is a secondary figure, and a kind of back-ground to the whole) give great force to the principal lights in your own figure, and make it come off wonderfully; ——and besides, there is an air of originality in the *tout ensemble.*[1]

Be pleased, my good Lord, to order the sum to be paid into the hands of Mr. *Dodsley*,[2] for the benefit of the author; and in the next edition care shall be taken that this chapter be expunged, and your Lordship's titles, distinctions, arms and good actions, be placed at the front of the preceding chapter: All which, from the words, *De gustibus non est disputandum*, and whatever else in this book relates to HOBBY-HORSES, but no more, shall stand dedicated to your Lordship.---The rest I dedicate to the MOON, who, by the bye, of all the PATRONS or MATRONS I can think of, has most power to set my book a-going, and make the world run mad after it.

Bright Goddess,

If thou are not too busy with CANDID and Miss CUNE-GUND'S affairs,[3]--take *Tristram Shandy*'s under thy protection also.

CHAPTER X

WHATEVER degree of small merit, the act of benignity in favour of the midwife, might justly claim, or in whom that claim truly rested,—at first sight seems not very material to this history; ——certain however it was, that the gentlewoman, the parson's wife, did run away at that time with the whole of it: And yet, for my life, I cannot help thinking but that the parson himself, tho' he had not the good fortune to hit upon the design first,—yet, as he heartily concurred in it the moment it was laid before him, and as heartily parted with his money to carry it into execution, had a claim to some share of it,—if not to a full half of whatever honour was due to it.

The world at that time was pleased to determine the matter otherwise.

Lay down the book, and I will allow you half a day to give a probable guess at the grounds of this procedure.

Be it known then, that, for about five years before the date of the midwife's licence, of which you have had so circumstantial an account,—the parson we have to do with, had made himself a country-talk by a breach of all decorum, which he had committed against himself, his station, and his office;——and that was, in never appearing better, or otherwise mounted, than upon a lean, sorry, jack-ass of a horse, value about one pound fifteen shillings; who, to shorten all description of him, was full brother to *Rosinante*,[1] as far as similitude congenial could make him; for he answered his description to a hair-breadth in every thing,—except that I do not remember 'tis any where said, that *Rosinante* was broken winded; and that, moreover, *Rosinante*, as is the happiness of most *Spanish* horses, fat or lean,—was undoubtedly a horse at all points.

I know very well that the HERO's horse was a horse of chaste deportment, which may have given grounds for a contrary opinion: But it is certain at the same time, that *Rosinante*'s continency (as may be demonstrated from the adventure of the *Yanguesian* carriers[2]) proceeded from no bodily defect or cause whatsoever, but from the temperance and orderly current of his blood.—And let me tell you, Madam, there is a great deal of very good chastity in the world, in behalf of which you could not say more for your life.

Let that be as it may, as my purpose is to do exact justice to every creature brought upon the stage of this dramatic work,—I could not stifle this distinction in favour of Don *Quixote*'s horse;——in all other points the parson's horse, I say, was just such another,——for he was as lean, and as lank, and as sorry a jade, as HUMILITY herself could have bestrided.

In the estimation of here and there a man of weak judgment, it was greatly in the parson's power to have helped the figure of this horse of his,—for he was master of a very handsome demi-peak'd saddle, quilted on the seat with green plush, garnished with a double row of silver-headed studs, and a noble pair of shining brass stirrups, with a housing altogether suitable, of grey superfine cloth, with an edging of black lace, terminating in a deep, black, silk fringe, *poudrè d'or*,[3]—all which he had purchased in the pride and prime of his life, together with a grand embossed bridle, ornamented at all points as it should be.——But not caring to banter his beast, he had hung all these up behind his study door;—and, in lieu of them, had seriously befitted him with just such a bridle and such a saddle, as the figure and value of such a steed might well and truly deserve.

In the several sallies about his parish, and in the neighbouring visits to the gentry who lived around him,——you will easily comprehend, that the parson, so appointed, would both hear and see enough to keep his philosophy from rusting. To speak the truth, he never could enter a village, but he caught the attention of both old and young.----Labour stood still as he pass'd,---the bucket hung suspended in the middle of the well,——the spinning-wheel forgot its round,——even chuck-farthing and shuffle-cap[4] themselves stood gaping till he had got out of sight; and as his movement was not of the quickest, he had generally time enough upon his hands to make his observations,--to hear the groans of the serious,——and the laughter of the light-hearted;—all which he bore with excellent tranquility.—His character was,——he loved a jest in his heart—and as he saw himself in the true point of ridicule, he would say, he could not be angry with others for seeing him in a light, in which he so strongly saw himself: So that to his friends, who knew his foible was not the love of money, and who therefore made the less scruple in bantering the extravagance of his humour,—instead of giving the true cause,——he chose rather to join in the laugh against himself; and as he never carried one single ounce of flesh upon his own bones,[5] being altogether as spare a figure as his beast,—he would sometimes insist upon it, that the horse was as good as the rider deserved;—that they were, centaur-like,---both of a piece. At other times, and in other moods, when his spirits were above the temptation of false wit,—he would say, he found himself going off fast in a consumption; and, with great gravity, would pretend, he could not bear the sight of a fat horse without a dejection of heart, and a sensible alteration in his pulse; and that he had made choice of the lean one he rode upon, not only to keep himself in countenance, but in spirits.

At different times he would give fifty humourous and opposite reasons for riding a meek-spirited jade of a broken-winded
horse, preferably to one of mettle;—for on such a one he could
sit mechanically, and meditate as delightfully *de vanitate mundi
et fugâ sæculi*,[6] as with the advantage of a death's head before
him;—that, in all other exercitations, he could spend his time, as
he rode slowly along,——to as much account as in his study;—
that he could draw up an argument in his sermon,—or a hole in
his breeches, as steadily on the one as in the other;—that brisk
trotting and slow argumentation, like wit and judgment, were
two incompatible movements.--But that, upon his steed—he
could unite and reconcile every thing,—he could compose his
sermon,—he could compose his cough,——and, in case nature
gave a call that way, he could likewise compose himself to
sleep.—In short, the parson upon such encounters would assign
any cause, but the true cause,—and he with-held the true one,
only out of a nicety of temper, because he thought it did honour
to him.

But the truth of the story was as follows: In the first years of
this gentleman's life, and about the time when the superb saddle
and bridle were purchased by him, it had been his manner, or
vanity, or call it what you will,——to run into the opposite
extream.—In the language of the county where he dwelt, he was
said to have loved a good horse, and generally had one of the
best in the whole parish standing in his stable always ready for
saddling; and as the nearest midwife, as I told you, did not live
nearer to the village than seven miles, and in a vile country,
——it so fell out that the poor gentleman was scarce a whole
week together without some piteous application for his beast;
and as he was not an unkind-hearted man, and every case was
more pressing and more distressful than the last,—as much as he
loved his beast, he had never a heart to refuse him; the upshot of
which was generally this, that his horse was either clapp'd, or
spavin'd, or greaz'd;—or he was twitter-bon'd, or broken-
winded,[7] or something, in short, or other had befallen him
which would let him carry no flesh;—so that he had every nine
or ten months a bad horse to get rid of,—and a good horse to
purchase in his stead.

What the loss in such a balance might amount to, *communibus annis*,[8] I would leave to a special jury of sufferers in the same
traffic, to determine;—but let it be what it would, the honest
gentleman bore it for many years without a murmur, till at

length, by repeated ill accidents of the kind, he found it necessary to take the thing under consideration; and upon weighing
the whole, and summing it up in his mind, he found it not only
disproportion'd to his other expences, but withall so heavy an
article in itself, as to disable him from any other act of generosity in his parish: Besides this he considered, that, with half the
sum thus galloped away, he could do ten times as much good;
——and what still weighed more with him than all other considerations put together, was this, that it confined all his charity
into one particular channel, and where, as he fancied, it was the
least wanted, namely, to the child-bearing and child-getting part
of his parish; reserving nothing for the impotent,---nothing for
the aged,---nothing for the many comfortless scenes he was
hourly called forth to visit, where poverty, and sickness, and
affliction dwelt together.

For these reasons he resolved to discontinue the expence; and
there appeared but two possible ways to extricate him clearly
out of it;—and these were, either to make it an irrevocable law
never more to lend his steed upon any application whatever,—
or else be content to ride the last poor devil, such as they had
made him, with all his aches and infirmities, to the very end of
the chapter.

As he dreaded his own constancy in the first,——he very
chearfully betook himself to the second; and tho' he could very
well have explain'd it, as I said, to his honour,—yet, for that
very reason, he had a spirit above it; choosing rather to bear the
contempt of his enemies, and the laughter of his friends, than
undergo the pain of telling a story, which might seem a
panygeric upon himself.

I have the highest idea of the spiritual and refined sentiments
of this reverend gentleman, from this single stroke in his
character, which I think comes up to any of the honest refine-
ments of the peerless knight of *La Mancha*,[9] whom, by the
bye, with all his follies, I love more, and would actually have
gone further to have paid a visit to, than the greatest hero of
antiquity.

But this is not the moral of my story: The thing I had in view
was to shew the temper of the world in the whole of this
affair.—For you must know, that so long as this explanation
would have done the parson credit,—the devil a soul could find
it out,—I suppose his enemies would not, and that his friends
could not.—But no sooner did he bestir himself in behalf of the

midwife, and pay the expences of the ordinary's licence to set her up,—but the whole secret came out; every horse he had lost, and two horses more than ever he had lost, with all the circumstances of their destruction, were known and distinctly remembered.—The story ran like wild-fire.—"The parson had a returning fit of pride which had just seized him; and he was going to be well mounted once again in his life; and if it was so, 'twas plain as the sun at noon-day, he would pocket the expence of the licence, ten times told the very first year:——so that every body was left to judge what were his views in this act of charity."

What were his views in this, and in every other action of his life,—or rather what were the opinions which floated in the brains of other people concerning it, was a thought which too much floated in his own, and too often broke in upon his rest, when he should have been sound asleep.

About ten years ago this gentleman had the good fortune to be made entirely easy upon that score,——it being just so long since he left his parish,——and the whole world at the same time behind him,--and stands accountable to a judge of whom he will have no cause to complain.

But there is a fatality attends the actions of some men: Order them as they will, they pass thro' a certain medium which so twists and refracts them from their true directions——that, with all the titles to praise which a rectitude of heart can give, the doers of them are nevertheless forced to live and die without it.

Of the truth of which this gentleman was a painful example.——But to know by what means this came to pass,---- and to make that knowledge of use to you, I insist upon it that you read the two following chapters, which contain such a sketch of his life and conversation, as will carry its moral along with it.--When this is done, if nothing stops us in our way, we will go on with the midwife.

CHAPTER XI

YORICK was this parson's name, and, what is very remarkable in it, (as appears from a most antient account of the family, wrote upon strong vellum, and now in perfect preservation) it

had been exactly so spelt for near,——I was within an ace of
saying nine hundred years;——but I would not shake my credit
in telling an improbable truth, however indisputable in itself;
——and therefore I shall content myself with only saying,---It
had been exactly so spelt, without the least variation or transposition of a single letter, for I do not know how long; which is
more than I would venture to say of one half of the best
surnames in the kingdom; which, in a course of years, have
generally undergone as many chops and changes as their owners.—Has this been owing to the pride, or to the shame of the
respective proprietors?—In honest truth, I think, sometimes to
the one, and sometimes to the other, just as the temptation has
wrought. But a villainous affair it is, and will one day so blend
and confound us all together, that no one shall be able to stand
up and swear, "That his own great grand father was the man
who did either this or that."

This evil had been sufficiently fenced against by the prudent
care of the *Yorick*'s family, and their religious preservation of
these records I quote, which do further inform us, That the
family was originally of *Danish* extraction, and had been trans-
planted into *England* as early as in the reign of *Horwendillus*,[1]
king of *Denmark*, in whose court it seems, an ancestor of this
Mr. *Yorick*'s, and from whom he was lineally descended, held a
considerable post to the day of his death. Of what nature this
considerable post was, this record saith not;—it only adds,
That, for near two centuries, it had been totally abolished as
altogether unnecessary, not only in that court, but in every
other court of the Christian world.

It has often come into my head, that this post could be no
other than that of the king's chief Jester;---and that *Hamlet*'s
Yorick, in our *Shakespear*, many of whose plays, you know,
are founded upon authenticated facts,--was certainly the very
man.

I have not the time to look into *Saxo-Grammaticus*'s *Danish*
history,[2] to know the certainty of this;—but if you have leisure,
and can easily get at the book, you may do it full as well
yourself.

I had just time, in my travels through *Denmark* with Mr.
Noddy's eldest son, whom, in the year 1741, I accompanied as
governor, riding along with him at a prodigious rate thro' most
parts of *Europe*, and of which original journey perform'd by us
two, a most delectable narrative will be given in the progress of

this work. I had just time, I say, and that was all, to prove the truth of an observation made by a long sojourner in that country;----namely, "That nature was neither very lavish, nor was she very stingy in her gifts of genius and capacity to its inhabitants;--but, like a discreet parent, was moderately kind to them all; observing such an equal tenor in the distribution of her favours, as to bring them, in those points, pretty near to a level with each other; so that you will meet with few instances in that kingdom of refin'd parts; but a great deal of good plain houshold understanding amongst all ranks of people, of which every body has a share;" which is, I think, very right.

With us, you see, the case is quite different;—we are all ups and downs in this matter;—you are a great genius;--or 'tis fifty to one, Sir, you are a great dunce and a blockhead;---not that there is a total want of intermediate steps,—no,—we are not so irregular as that comes to;—but the two extremes are more common, and in a greater degree in this unsettled island, where nature, in her gifts and dispositions of this kind, is most whimsical and capricious; fortune herself not being more so in the bequest of her goods and chattels than she.

This is all that ever stagger'd my faith in regard to *Yorick*'s extraction, who, by what I can remember of him, and by all the accounts I could ever get of him, seem'd not to have had one single drop of *Danish* blood in his whole crasis;[3] in nine hundred years, it might possibly have all run out:----I will not philosophize one moment with you about it; for happen how it would, the fact was this:—That instead of that cold phlegm and exact regularity of sense and humours, you would have look'd for, in one so extracted;---he was, on the contrary, as mercurial and sublimated a composition,----as heteroclite a creature in all his declensions;-----with as much life and whim, and *gaité de cœur*[4] about him, as the kindliest climate could have engendered and put together. With all this sail, poor *Yorick* carried not one ounce of ballast; he was utterly unpractised in the world; and, at the age of twenty-six, knew just about as well how to steer his course in it, as a romping, unsuspicious girl of thirteen: So that upon his first setting out, the brisk gale of his spirits, as you will imagine, ran him foul ten times in a day of some body's tackling; and as the grave and more slow-paced were oftenest in his way,-----you may likewise imagine, 'twas with such he had generally the ill luck to get the most entangled. For aught I know there might be some mixture of unlucky wit at the bottom of such *Fracas*:---For, to speak the truth, *Yorick* had an invincible dislike and opposition in his nature to gravity;----not to gravity as such;----for where gravity was wanted, he would be the most grave or serious of mortal men for days and weeks together;---but he was an enemy to the affectation of it, and declared open war against it, only as it appeared a cloak for ignorance, or for folly; and then, whenever it fell in his way, however sheltered and protected, he seldom gave it much quarter.

Sometimes, in his wild way of talking, he would say, That gravity was an errant scoundrel; and he would add,—of the most dangerous kind too,----because a sly one; and that, he verily believed, more honest, well-meaning people were bubbled out of their goods and money by it in one twelve-month, than by pocket-picking and shop-lifting in seven. In the naked temper which a merry heart discovered, he would say, There was no danger,--but to itself:—whereas the very essence of gravity was design, and consequently deceit;---'twas a taught trick to gain credit of the world for more sense and knowledge than a man was worth; and that, with all its pretensions,---it was no better, but often worse, than what a *French* wit[5] had long ago defined it,---*viz. A mysterious carriage of the body to cover the defects of the mind*;—which definition of gravity, *Yorick*, with great imprudence, would say, deserved to be wrote in letters of gold.

But, in plain truth, he was a man unhackneyed and unpractised in the world, and was altogether as indiscreet and foolish on every other subject of discourse where policy is wont to impress restraint. *Yorick* had no impression but one, and that was what arose from the nature of the deed spoken of; which impression he would usually translate into plain *English* without any periphrasis,——and too oft without much distinction of either personage, time, or place;---so that when mention was made of a pitiful or an ungenerous proceeding,---he never gave himself a moment's time to reflect who was the Hero of the piece,----what his station,----or how far he had power to hurt him hereafter;---but if it was a dirty action,-----without more ado,-----The man was a dirty fellow,---and so on:---And as his comments had usually the ill fate to be terminated either in a *bon mot*, or to be enliven'd throughout with some drollery or humour of expression, it gave wings to *Yorick*'s indiscretion. In a word, tho' he never sought, yet, at the same time, as he seldom shun'd occasions of saying what came uppermost, and without much ceremony;----he had but too many temptations in life, of scattering his wit and his humour,—his gibes and his jests about him.----They were not lost for want of gathering.

What were the consequences, and what was *Yorick*'s catastrophe thereupon, you will read in the next chapter.

CHAPTER XII

THE *Mortgager* and *Mortgageé* differ the one from the other, not more in length of purse, than the *Jester* and *Jesteé* do, in that of memory. But in this the comparison between them runs, as the scholiasts call it, upon all-four; which, by the bye, is upon one or two legs more, than some of the best of *Homer*'s can pretend to;—namely, That the one raises a sum and the other a laugh at your expence, and think no more about it. Interest, however, still runs on in both cases;----the periodical or accidental payments of it, just serving to keep the memory of the affair alive; till, at length, in some evil hour,----pop comes the creditor upon each, and by demanding principal upon the spot, together with full interest to the very day, makes them both feel the full extent of their obligations.

As the reader (for I hate your *ifs*) has a thorough knowledge of human nature, I need not say more to satisfy him, that my Hero could not go on at this rate without some slight experience of these incidental mementos. To speak the truth, he had wantonly involved himself in a multitude of small book-debts of this stamp, which, notwithstanding *Eugenius*'s[1] frequent advice, he too much disregarded; thinking, that as not one of them was contracted thro' any malignancy;---but, on the contrary, from an honesty of mind, and a mere jocundity of humour, they would all of them be cross'd out in course.

Eugenius would never admit this; and would often tell him, that one day or other he would certainly be reckoned with; and he would often add, in an accent of sorrowful apprehension,--- to the uttermost mite. To which *Yorick*, with his usual carelessness of heart, would as often answer with a pshaw!---and if the subject was started in the fields,---with a hop, skip, and a jump, at the end of it; but if close pent up in the social chimney corner, where the culprit was barricado'd in, with a table and a couple of arm chairs, and could not so readily fly off in a tangent,---- *Eugenius* would then go on with his lecture upon discretion, in words to this purpose, though somewhat better put together.

Trust me, dear *Yorick*, this unwary pleasantry of thine will sooner or later bring thee into scrapes and difficulties, which no after-wit can extricate thee out of.——In these sallies, too oft, I see, it happens, that a person laugh'd at, considers himself in the light of a person injured, with all the rights of such a situation belonging to him; and when thou viewest him in that light too, and reckons up his friends, his family, his kindred, and allies,---- and musters up with them the many recruits which will list under him from a sense of common danger;---'tis no extravagant arithmetic to say, that for every ten jokes,---thou hast got a hundred enemies; and till thou hast gone on, and raised a swarm of wasps about thy ears, and art half stung to death by them, thou will never be convinced it is so.

I cannot suspect it in the man whom I esteem, that there is the least spur from spleen or malevolence of intent in these sallies. ——I believe and know them to be truly honest and sportive:--- But consider, my dear lad, that fools cannot distinguish this,-- and that knaves will not; and thou knowest not what it is, either to provoke the one, or to make merry with the other,-- whenever they associate for mutual defence, depend upon it, they will carry on the war in such a manner against thee, my dear friend, as to make thee heartily sick of it, and of thy life too.

REVENGE from some baneful corner shall level a tale of dishonour at thee, which no innocence of heart or integrity of conduct shall set right.——The fortunes of thy house shall totter,---thy character, which led the way to them, shall bleed on every side of it,--thy faith questioned,--thy works belied, --thy wit forgotten,--thy learning trampled on. To wind up the last scene of thy tragedy, CRUELTY and COWARDICE, twin ruffians, hired and set on by MALICE in the dark, shall strike together at all thy infirmities and mistakes:---the best of us, my dear lad, lye open there,---and trust me,----trust me, *Yorick*, *When to gratify a private appetite, it is once resolved upon, that an innocent and an helpless creature shall be sacrificed,'tis an easy matter to pick up sticks enew from any thicket where it has strayed, to make a fire to offer it up with.*

Yorick scarce ever heard this sad vaticination of his destiny read over to him, but with a tear stealing from his eye, and a promissory look attending it, that he was resolved, for the time to come, to ride his tit with more sobriety.—But, alas, too late!---a grand confederacy, with ***** and ***** at the head of it, was form'd before the first prediction of it.----The whole plan of the attack, just as *Eugenius* had foreboded, was put in execution all at once,-----with so little mercy on the side of the allies,---and so little suspicion in *Yorick*, of what was carrying on against him,---that when he thought, good easy man! full surely preferment was o' ripening,--they had smote his root, and then he fell, as many a worthy man had fallen before him.

Yorick, however, fought it out with all imaginable gallantry for some time; till, over-power'd by numbers, and worn out at length by the calamities of the war,----but more so, by the ungenerous manner in which it was carried on,---he threw down the sword; and though he kept up his spirits in appearance to the last,----he died, nevertheless, as was generally thought, quite broken hearted.

What inclined *Eugenius* to the same opinion, was as follows:

A few hours before *Yorick* breath'd his last, *Eugenius* stept in with an intent to take his last sight and last farewell of him: Upon his drawing *Yorick*'s curtain, and asking how he felt himself, *Yorick*, looking up in his face, took hold of his hand, ----and, after thanking him for the many tokens of his friendship to him, for which, he said, if it was their fate to meet hereafter,---he would thank him again and again.—He told him, he was within a few hours of giving his enemies the slip for ever.-----I hope not, answered *Eugenius*, with tears trickling down his cheeks, and with the tenderest tone that ever man spoke,---I hope not, *Yorick*, said he.--*Yorick* replied, with a look up, and a gentle squeeze of *Eugenius*'s hand, and that was all,--but it cut *Eugenius* to his heart.--Come,--come, *Yorick*, quoth *Eugenius*, wiping his eyes, and summoning up the man within him,-----my dear lad, be comforted,---let not all thy spirits and fortitude forsake thee at this crisis when thou most wants them;——who knows what resourses are in store, and what the power of God may yet do for thee?——*Yorick* laid his hand upon his heart, and gently shook his head;---for my part, continued *Eugenius*, crying bitterly as he uttered the words,—I declare I know not, *Yorick*, how to part with thee,——and would gladly flatter my hopes, added *Eugenius*, chearing up his voice, that there is still enough left of thee to make a bishop,--- and that I may live to see it.——I beseech thee, *Eugenius*, quoth *Yorick*, taking off his night-cap as well as he could with his left hand,——his right being still grasped close in that of *Eugenius*,——I beseech thee to take a view of my head.----I see nothing that ails it, replied *Eugenius*. Then, alas! my friend, said *Yorick*, let me tell you, that 'tis so bruised and misshapen'd with the blows which ***** and *****, and some others have so unhandsomely given me in the dark, that I might say with *Sancho Pança*,[2] that should I recover, and "Mitres thereupon be suffer'd to rain down from heaven as thick as hail, not one of 'em would fit it."——*Yorick*'s last breath was hanging upon his trembling lips ready to depart as he uttered this;---yet still it was utter'd with something of a *cervantick* tone;--and as he spoke it, *Eugenius* could perceive a stream of lambent fire lighted up for a moment in his eyes;----faint picture of those flashes of his spirit, which (as *Shakespear* said of his ancestor) were wont to set the table in a roar![3]

Eugenius was convinced from this, that the heart of his friend was broke; he squeez'd his hand,——and then walk'd softly out of the room, weeping as he walk'd. *Yorick* followed *Eugenius* with his eyes to the door,----he then closed them,—and never opened them more.

He lies buried in a corner of his church-yard, in the parish of————, under a plain marble slabb, which his friend *Eugenius*, by leave of his executors, laid upon his grave, with no more than these three words of inscription serving both for his epitaph and elegy.[4]

Alas, poor YORICK!

Ten times in a day has *Yorick*'s ghost the consolation to hear his monumental inscription read over with such a variety of plaintive tones, as denote a general pity and esteem for him; ——a foot-way crossing the church-yard close by the side of his grave,—not a passenger goes by without stopping to cast a look upon it,——and sighing as he walks on,

Alas, poor YORICK!

CHAPTER XIII

It is so long since the reader of this rhapsodical work has been parted from the midwife, that it is high time to mention her again to him, merely to put him in mind that there is such a body still in the world, and whom, upon the best judgment I can form upon my own plan at present,---I am going to introduce to him for good and all: But as fresh matter may be started, and much unexpected business fall out betwixt the reader and myself, which may require immediate dispatch;-----'twas right to take care that the poor woman should not be lost in the mean time;---because when she is wanted we can no way do without her.

I think I told you that this good woman was a person of no small note and consequence throughout our whole village and township;---that her fame had spread itself to the very out-edge and circumference of that circle of importance, of which kind every soul living, whether he has a shirt to his back or no,----has one surrounding him;--which said circle, by the way, whenever 'tis said that such a one is of great weight and importance in the *world*,-----I desire may be enlarged or contracted in your worship's fancy, in a compound-ratio of the station, profession, knowledge, abilities, height and depth (measuring both ways) of the personage brought before you.

In the present case, if I remember, I fixed it at about four or five miles, which not only comprehended the whole parish, but extended itself to two or three of the adjacent hamlets in the skirts of the next parish; which made a considerable thing of it. I must add, That she was, moreover, very well looked on at one large grange-house and some other odd houses and farms within two or three miles, as I said, from the smoke of her own chimney:----But I must here, once for all, inform you, that all this will be more exactly delineated and explain'd in a map, now in the hands of the engraver, which, with many other pieces and developments to this work, will be added to the end of the twentieth volume,---not to swell the work,—I detest the thought of such a thing;-----but by way of commentary, scholium, illustration, and key to such passages, incidents, or inuendos as shall be thought to be either of private interpretation, or of dark or doubtful meaning after my life and my opinions shall have been read over, (now don't forget the meaning of the

word) by all the *world*;--which, betwixt you and me, and in
spight of all the gentlemen reviewers in *Great-Britain*,[1] and of all
that their worships shall undertake to write or say to the contrary,----I am determined shall be the case.----I need not tell
your worship, that all this is spoke in confidence.

CHAPTER XIV

Upon looking into my mother's marriage settlement, in order
to satisfy myself and reader in a point necessary to be clear'd up,
before we could proceed any further in this history;---I had the
good fortune to pop upon the very thing I wanted before I had
read a day and a half straightforwards,--it might have taken me
up a month;--which shews plainly, that when a man sits down
to write a history,---tho' it be but the history of *Jack
Hickathrift*[1] or *Tom Thumb*, he knows no more than his heels
what lets and confounded hinderances he is to meet with in his
way,---or what a dance he may be led, by one excursion or
another, before all is over. Could a historiographer drive on his
history, as a muleteer drives on his mule,—straight forward;----
for instance, from *Rome* all the way to *Loretto*, without ever
once turning his head aside either to the right hand or to the
left,—he might venture to foretell you to an hour when he
should get to his journey's end;-----but the thing is, morally
speaking, impossible: For, if he is a man of the least spirit, he
will have fifty deviations from a straight line to make with this
or that party as he goes along, which he can no ways avoid. He
will have views and prospects to himself perpetually solliciting
his eye, which he can no more help standing still to look at than
he can fly; he will moreover have various

    Accounts to reconcile:
    Anecdotes to pick up:
    Inscriptions to make out:
    Stories to weave in:
    Traditions to sift:
    Personages to call upon:
    Panygericks to paste up at this door:
    Pasquinades at that:------All which both the man and his mule
are quite exempt from. To sum up all; there are archives at every
stage to be look'd into, and rolls, records, documents, and
endless genealogies, which justice ever and anon calls him back

to stay the reading of:----In short, there is no end of it;-----for my own part, I declare I have been at it these six weeks, making all the speed I possibly could,—and am not yet born:--I have just been able, and that's all, to tell you *when* it happen'd, but not *how*;---so that you see the thing is yet far from being accomplished.

These unforeseen stoppages, which I own I had no conception of when I first set out;---but which, I am convinced now, will rather increase than diminish as I advance,---have struck out a hint which I am resolved to follow;---and that is,---not to be in a hurry;---but to go on leisurely, writing and publishing two volumes of my life every year;[2]----which, if I am suffered to go on quietly, and can make a tolerable bargain with my bookseller, I shall continue to do as long as I live.

CHAPTER XV

THE article in my mother's marriage settlement, which I told the reader I was at pains to search for, and which, now that I have found it, I think proper to lay before him,—is so much more fully express'd in the deed itself, than ever I can pretend to do it, that it would be barbarity to take it out of the lawyer's hand:—It is as follows.

"And this Indenture further witnesseth, That the said *Walter Shandy*, merchant, in consideration of the said intended marriage to be had, and, by God's blessing, to be well and truly solemnized and consummated between the said *Walter Shandy* and *Elizabeth Mollineux* aforesaid, and divers other good and valuable causes and considerations him thereunto specially moving,—doth grant, covenant, condescend, consent, conclude, bargain, and fully agree to and with *John Dixon* and *James Turner*, Esqrs. the above-named trustees, &c. &c.— to wit,—That in case it should hereafter so fall out, chance, happen, or otherwise come to pass,—That the said *Walter Shandy*, merchant, shall have left off business before the time or times, that the said *Elizabeth Mollineux* shall, according to the course of nature, or otherwise, have left off bearing and bringing forth children;—and that, in consequence of the said *Walter Shandy* having so left off business, shall, in despight, and against the free will, consent, and good-liking of the said *Elizabeth Mollineux*,—make a departure from the city of *London*, in order to retire to, and dwell upon his estate at *Shandy-Hall*, in the county of——, or at any other country seat, castle, hall, mansion-house, messuage, or grainge-house, now purchased, or hereafter to be purchased, or upon any part or parcel thereof:—That then, and as often as the said *Elizabeth Mollineux* shall happen to be enceint with child or children severally and lawfully begot, or to be begotten, upon the body of the said *Elizabeth Mollineux* during her said coverture,——he the said *Walter Shandy* shall, at his own proper cost and charges, and out of his own proper monies, upon good and reasonable notice, which is hereby agreed to be within six weeks of her the said *Elizabeth Mollineux*'s full reckoning, or time of supposed and computed delivery,—pay, or cause to be paid, the sum of one hundred and twenty pounds of good and lawful money, to *John Dixon* and *James Turner*, Esqrs. or assigns,—upon Trust and confidence, and for and unto the use and uses, intent, end, and purpose following:—That is to say,—That the said sum of one hundred and twenty pounds shall be paid into the hands of the said *Elizabeth Mollineux*, or to be otherwise applied by them the said trustees, for the well and truly hiring of one coach, with able and sufficient horses, to carry and convey the body of the said *Elizabeth Mollineux* and the child or children which she shall be then and there enceint and pregnant with,—unto the city of *London*; and for the further paying and defraying of all other incidental costs, charges, and expences whatsoever,—in and about, and for, and relating to her said intended delivery and lying-in, in the said city or suburbs thereof. And that the said *Elizabeth Mollineux* shall and may, from time to time, and at all such time and times as are here covenanted and agreed upon,—peaceably and quietly hire the said coach and horses, and have free ingress, egress, and regress throughout her journey, in and from the said coach, according to the tenor, true intent, and meaning of these presents, without any let, suit, trouble, disturbance, molestation, discharge, hinderance, forfeiture, eviction, vexation, interruption, or incumberance whatsoever.—And that it shall moreover be lawful to and for the said *Elizabeth Mollineux*, from time to time, and as oft or often as she shall well and truly be advanced in her said pregnancy, to the time heretofore stipulated and agreed upon,—to live and reside in such place or places, and in such family or families, and with such relations, friends, and other persons within the said city of *London*, as she, at her own will and pleasure, notwithstanding her present coverture, and as if she was a *femme sole*[1] and unmarried,—shall think fit.— 𝔄𝔫𝔡 𝔱𝔥𝔦𝔰 𝔍𝔫𝔡𝔢𝔫𝔱𝔲𝔯𝔢 𝔣𝔲𝔯𝔱𝔥𝔢𝔯 𝔴𝔦𝔱𝔫𝔢𝔰𝔰𝔢𝔱𝔥, That for the more effectually carrying of the said covenant into execution, the said *Walter Shandy*, merchant, doth hereby grant, bargain, sell, release, and confirm unto the said *John Dixon* and *James Turner*, Esqrs. their heirs, executors, and assigns, in their actual possession, now being by virtue of an indenture of bargain and sale for a year to them the said *John Dixon* and *James Turner*, Esqrs. by him the said *Walter Shandy*, merchant, thereof made; which said bargain and sale for a year, bears date the day next before the date of these presents, and by force and virtue of the statute for transferring of uses into possessions,———— 𝔄𝔩𝔩 that the manor and lordship of *Shandy* in the county of————, with all the rights, members, and appurtenances thereof; and all and every the messuages, houses, buildings, barns, stables, orchards, gardens, backsides, tofts, crofts, garths, cottages, lands, meadows, feedings, pastures, marshes, commons, woods, underwoods, drains, fisheries, waters, and water-courses;—together with all rents, reversions, services, annuities, fee-farms, knights fees, views of frank-pledge, escheats, reliefs, mines, quarries, goods and chattels of felons and fugitives, felons of themselves, and put in exigent, deodands, free warrens,[2] and all other royalties and seignories, rights and jurisdictions, privileges and hereditaments whatsoever.———— 𝔄𝔫𝔡 𝔞𝔩𝔰𝔬 the advowson, donation, presentation and free disposition of the rectory or parsonage of *Shandy* aforesaid, and all and every the tenths, tythes, glebe-lands"————In three words,——"My mother was to lay in, (if she chose it) in *London*."

But in order to put a stop to the practice of any unfair play on the part of my mother, which a marriage article of this nature too manifestly opened a door to, and which indeed had never been thought of at all, but for my uncle *Toby Shandy*;--a clause was added in security of my father, which was this:—"That in case my mother hereafter should, at any time, put my father to the trouble and expence of a *London* journey upon false cries and tokens;————that for every such instance she should forfeit all the right and title which the covenant gave her to the next turn;————but to no more,--and so on, *toties quoties*,[3] in as effectual a manner, as if such a covenant betwixt them had not been made."—This, by the way, was no more than what was reasonable;—and yet, as reasonable as it was, I have ever thought it hard that the whole weight of the article should have fallen entirely, as it did, upon myself.

But I was begot and born to misfortunes;—for my poor mother, whether it was wind or water,—or a compound of both,—or neither;----or whether it was simply the mere swell of imagination and fancy in her;—or how far a strong wish and desire to have it so, might mislead her judgment;—in short, whether she was deceived or deceiving in this matter, it no way becomes me to decide.⁴ The fact was this, That, in the latter end of *September*, 1717, which was the year before I was born, my mother having carried my father up to town much against the grain,—he peremptorily insisted upon the clause;----so that I was doom'd, by marriage articles, to have my nose squeez'd as flat to my face, as if the destinies had actually spun me without one.

How this event came about,---and what a train of vexatious disappointments, in one stage or other of my life, have pursued me from the mere loss, or rather compression, of this one single member,---shall be laid before the reader all in due time.

CHAPTER XVI

My father, as any body may naturally imagine, came down with my mother into the country, in but a pettish kind of a humour. The first twenty or five-and-twenty miles he did nothing in the world but fret and teaze himself, and indeed my mother too, about the cursed expence, which he said might every shilling of it have been saved;—then what vexed him more than every thing else was the provoking time of the year,——which, as I told you, was towards the end of *September*, when his wall-fruit, and green gages especially, in which he was very curious, were just ready for pulling:—"Had he been whistled up to *London*, upon a *Tom Fool*'s errand in any other month of the whole year, he should not have said three words about it."

For the next two whole stages, no subject would go down, but the heavy blow he had sustain'd from the loss of a son, whom it seems he had fully reckon'd upon in his mind, and register'd down in his pocket-book, as a second staff for his old age, in case *Bobby* should fail him. "The disappointment of this, he said, was ten times more to a wise man than all the money which the journey, &c. had cost him, put together,---rot the hundred and twenty pounds,——he did not mind it a rush."

From *Stilton*, all the way to *Grantham*,[1] nothing in the whole affair provoked him so much as the condolences of his friends, and the foolish figure they should both make at church the first *Sunday*;——of which, in the satirical vehemence of his wit, now sharpen'd a little by vexation, he would give so many humorous and provoking descriptions,---and place his rib and self in so many tormenting lights and attitudes in the face of the whole congregation;---that my mother declared, these two stages were so truly tragicomical, that she did nothing but laugh and cry in a breath, from one end to the other of them all the way.

From *Grantham*, till they had cross'd the *Trent*, my father was out of all kind of patience at the vile trick and imposition which he fancied my mother had put upon him in this affair.--- "Certainly", he would say to himself, over and over again, "the woman could not be deceived herself;——if she could,—— what weakness!"——tormenting word! which led his imagination a thorny dance, and, before all was over, play'd the duce and all with him;——for sure as ever the word *weakness* was uttered, and struck full upon his brain,—so sure it set him upon running divisions upon how many kinds of weaknesses there were;——that there was such a thing as weakness of the body,——as well as weakness of the mind,----and then he would do nothing but syllogize within himself for a stage or two together, How far the cause of all these vexations might, or might not, have arisen out of himself.

In short, he had so many little subjects of disquietude springing out of this one affair, all fretting successively in his mind as they rose up in it, that my mother, whatever was her journey up, had but an uneasy journey of it down.——In a word, as she complained to my uncle *Toby*, he would have tired out the patience of any flesh alive.

CHAPTER XVII

THOUGH my father travelled homewards, as I told you, in none of the best of moods,---pshaw-ing and pish-ing all the way down,----yet he had the complaisance to keep the worst part of the story still to himself;—which was the resolution he had taken of doing himself the justice, which my uncle *Toby*'s clause

in the marriage settlement empowered him; nor was it till the
very night in which I was begot, which was thirteen months
after, that she had the least intimation of his design;---when my
father, happening, as you remember, to be a little chagrin'd and
out of temper,——took occasion as they lay chatting gravely in
bed afterwards, talking over what was to come,——to let her
know that she must accommodate herself as well as she could to
the bargain made between them in their marriage deeds; which
was to lye-in of her next child in the country to balance the last
year's journey.

My father was a gentleman of many virtues,—but he had a
strong spice of that in his temper which might, or might not, add
to the number.----'Tis known by the name of perseverance in a
good cause,—and of obstinacy in a bad one: Of this my mother
had so much knowledge, that she knew 'twas to no purpose to
make any remonstrance,—so she e'en resolved to sit down
quietly, and make the most of it.

CHAPTER XVIII

As the point was that night agreed, or rather determin'd, that
my mother should lye-in of me in the country, she took her
measures accordingly; for which purpose, when she was three
days, or thereabouts, gone with child, she began to cast her eyes
upon the midwife, whom you have so often heard me mention;
and before the week was well got round, as the famous Dr.
Maningham[1] was not to be had, she had come to a final determination in her mind,——notwithstanding there was a scientifick operator within so near a call as eight miles of us, and who,
moreover, had expressly wrote a five shillings book upon the
subject of midwifery, in which he had exposed, not only the
blunders of the sisterhood itself,——but had likewise superadded many curious improvements for the quicker extraction of
the fœtus in cross births, and some other cases of danger which
belay us in getting into the world; notwithstanding all this, my
mother, I say, was absolutely determined to trust her life and
mine with it, into no soul's hand but this old woman's only.—
Now this I like;—when we cannot get at the very thing we
wish,-----never to take up with the next best in degree to
it;---no; that's pitiful beyond description;—it is no more than a
week from this very day, in which I am now writing this book

for the edification of the world,---which is *March* 9, 1759,
------that my dear, dear *Jenny*[2] observing I look'd a little grave,
as she stood cheapening a silk of five-and-twenty shillings a
yard,---told the mercer, she was sorry she had given him so
much trouble;---and immediately went and bought herself a
yard-wide stuff of ten-pence a yard.---'Tis the duplication of
one and the same greatness of soul; only what lessen'd the
honour of it somewhat, in my mother's case, was, that she could
not heroine it into so violent and hazardous an extream, as one
in her situation might have wish'd, because the old midwife had
really some little claim to be depended upon,---as much, at least,
as success could give her; having, in the course of her practice of
near twenty years in the parish, brought every mother's son of
them into the world without any one slip or accident which
could fairly be laid to her account.

These facts, tho' they had their weight, yet did not altogether
satisfy some few scruples and uneasinesses which hung upon
my father's spirits in relation to this choice.---To say nothing of
the natural workings of humanity and justice,---or of the yearnings of parental and connubial love, all which prompted him to
leave as little to hazard as possible in a case of this kind;------he
felt himself concern'd in a particular manner, that all should go
right in the present case;---from the accumulated sorrow he lay
open to, should any evil betide his wife and child in lying-in at
Shandy-Hall.------He knew the world judged by events, and
would add to his afflictions in such a misfortune, by loading him
with the whole blame of it.------"Alas o'day!---had Mrs. *Shandy*, poor gentlewoman! had but her wish in going up to town
just to lye-in and come down again;---which, they say, she
begg'd and pray'd for upon her bare knees,------and which, in
my opinion, considering the fortune which Mr. *Shandy* got
with her,---was no such mighty matter to have complied with,
the lady and her babe might both of 'em have been alive at this
hour."

This exclamation, my father knew was unanswerable;----and
yet, it was not merely to shelter himself,---nor was it altogether
for the care of his offspring and wife that he seem'd so extremely
anxious about this point;---my father had extensive views of
things,------and stood, moreover, as he thought, deeply concern'd in it for the publick good, from the dread he entertained
of the bad uses an ill-fated instance might be put to.

He was very sensible that all political writers upon the subject had unanimously agreed and lamented, from the beginning of Queen *Elizabeth*'s reign down to his own time, that the current of men and money towards the metropolis, upon one frivolous errand or another,—set in so strong,—as to become dangerous to our civil rights;—tho', by the bye,——a *current* was not the image he took most delight in,-- a *distemper* was here his favourite metaphor, and he would run it down into a perfect allegory, by maintaining it was identically the same in the body national as in the body natural, where blood and spirits were driven up into the head faster than they could find their ways down;——a stoppage of circulation must ensue, which was death in both cases.

There was little danger, he would say, of losing our liberties by *French* politicks or *French* invasions;——nor was he so much in pain of a consumption from the mass of corrupted matter and ulcerated humours in our constitution,—which he hoped was not so bad as it was imagined;—but he verily feared, that in some violent push, we should go off, all at once, in a state-apoplexy;—and then he would say, *The Lord have mercy upon us all*.

My father was never able to give the history of this distemper,---without the remedy along with it.

"Was I an absolute prince, he would say, pulling up his breeches with both his hands, as he rose from his arm-chair, "I would appoint able judges, at every avenue of my metropolis, who should take cognizance of every fool's business who came there;---and if, upon a fair and candid hearing, it appeared not of weight sufficient to leave his own home, and come up, bag and baggage, with his wife and children, farmers sons, &c. &c. at his backside, they should be all sent back, from constable to constable, like vagrants as they were, to the place of their legal settlements. By this means, I shall take care, that my metropolis totter'd not thro' its own weight;—that the head be no longer too big for the body;---that the extreams, now wasted and pin'd in, be restored to their due share of nourishment, and regain, with it, their natural strength and beauty:--I would effectually provide, That the meadows and corn-fields, of my dominions, should laugh and sing;—that good chear and hospitality flourish once more;—and that such weight and influence be put thereby into the hands of the Squirality of my kingdom, as should counterpoise what I perceive my Nobility are now taking from them.

"Why are there so few palaces and gentlemen's seats, he would ask, with some emotion, as he walked a-cross the room, "throughout so many delicious provinces in *France?* Whence is it that the few remaining *Chateaus* amongst them are so dismantled,—so unfurnished, and in so ruinous and desolate a condition?—Because, Sir, (he would say) "in that kingdom no man has any country-interest to support;—the little interest of any kind, which any man has any where in it, is concentrated in the court, and the looks of the Grand Monarch;' by the sun-shine of whose countenance, or the clouds which pass a-cross it, every *French* man lives or dies."

Another political reason which prompted my father so strongly to guard against the least evil accident in my mother's lying-in the country,——was, That any such instance would infallibly throw a balance of power, too great already, into the weaker vessels of the gentry, in his own, or higher stations;—— which, with the many other usurped rights which that part of the constitution was hourly establishing,—would, in the end, prove fatal to the monarchical system of domestick government established in the first creation of things by God.

In this point he was entirely of Sir *Robert Filmer's* opinion, That the plans and institutions of the greatest monarchies in the eastern parts of the world, were, originally, all stolen from that admirable pattern and prototype of this houshold and paternal power;---which, for a century, he said, and more, had gradually been degenerating away into a mix'd government;——the form of which, however desirable in great combinations of the species,——was very troublesome in small ones,—and seldom produced any thing, that he saw, but sorrow and confusion.

For all these reasons, private and publick, put together,—my father was for having the man-midwife by all means,---my mother by no means. My father begg'd and intreated, she would for once recede from her prerogative in this matter, and suffer him to choose for her;—my mother, on the contrary, insisted upon her privilege in this matter, to choose for herself,—and have no mortal's help but the old woman's.—What could my father do? He was almost at his wit's end;——talked it over with her in all moods;—placed his arguments in all lights;— argued the matter with her like a christian,—like a heathen,— like a husband,—like a father,—like a patriot,—like a man:— My mother answered every thing only like a woman; which was a little hard upon her;—for as she could not assume and fight it

out behind such a variety of characters,—'twas no fair match;—
'twas seven to one.—What could my mother do?——She had
the advantage (otherwise she had been certainly overpowered)
of a small reinforcement of chagrin personal at the bottom
which bore her up, and enabled her to dispute the affair with my
father with so equal an advantage,——that both sides sung *Te
Deum*. In a word, my mother was to have the old woman,—and
the operator was to have licence to drink a bottle of wine with
my father and my uncle *Toby Shandy* in the back parlour,—for
which he was to be paid five guineas.

I must beg leave, before I finish this chapter, to enter a caveat
in the breast of my fair reader;—and it is this:——Not to take it
absolutely for granted from an unguarded word or two which I
have dropp'd in it,——"That I am a married man."---I own the
tender appellation of my dear, dear *Jenny*,----with some other
strokes of conjugal knowledge, interspersed here and there,
might, naturally enough, have misled the most candid judge in
the world into such a determination against me.---All I plead
for, in this case, Madam, is strict justice, and that you do so
much of it, to me as well as to yourself,—as not to prejudge or
receive such an impression of me, till you have better evidence,
than I am positive, at present, can be produced against me:---
Not that I can be so vain or unreasonable, Madam, as to desire
you should therefore think, that my dear, dear *Jenny* is my kept
mistress;—no,— that would be flattering my character in the
other extream, and giving it an air of freedom, which, perhaps, it
has no kind of right to. All I contend for, is the utter impossibility for some volumes, that you, or the most penetrating spirit
upon earth, should know how this matter really stands.----It is
not impossible, but that my dear, dear *Jenny!* tender as the
appellation is, may be my child.——Consider,—I was born in
the year eighteen.—Nor is there any thing unnatural or extravagant in the supposition, that my dear *Jenny* may be my friend.—
—Friend!—My friend.—Surely, Madam, a friendship between
the two sexes may subsist, and be supported without——Fy!
Mr. *Shandy*:—Without any thing, Madam, but that tender and
delicious sentiment,[5] which ever mixes in friendship, where
there is a difference of sex. Let me intreat you to study the pure
and sentimental parts of the best *French* Romances;——it will
really, Madam, astonish you to see with what a variety of chaste
expression this delicious sentiment, which I have the honour to
speak of, is dress'd out.

CHAPTER XIX

I WOULD sooner undertake to explain the hardest problem in Geometry, than pretend to account for it, that a gentleman of my father's great good sense,——knowing, as the reader must have observed him, and curious too, in philosophy,--wise also in political reasoning,—and in polemical (as he will find) no way ignorant,---could be capable of entertaining a notion in his head, so out of the common track,---that I fear the reader, when I come to mention it to him, if he is the least of a cholerick temper, will immediately throw the book by; if mercurial, he will laugh most heartily at it;—and if he is of a grave and saturnine cast, he will, at first sight, absolutely condemn as fanciful and extravagant; and that was in respect to the choice and imposition of Christian names, on which he thought a great deal more depended than what superficial minds were capable of conceiving.

His opinion, in this matter, was, That there was a strange kind of magick bias, which good or bad names, as he called them, irresistibly impress'd upon our characters and conduct.

The Hero of *Cervantes* argued not the point with more seriousness,----nor had he more faith,----or more to say on the powers of Necromancy in dishonouring his deeds,—or on DULCINEA'S[1] name, in shedding lustre upon them, than my father had on those of TRISMEGISTUS[2] or ARCHIMEDES,[3] on the one hand,—or of NYKY and SIMKIN[4] on the other. How many CÆSARS and POMPEYS, he would say, by mere inspiration of the names, have been render'd worthy of them? And how many, he would add, are there who might have done exceeding well in the world, had not their characters and spirits been totally depress'd and NICODEMUS'D[5] into nothing.

I see plainly, Sir, by your looks, (or as the case happen'd) my father would say,—that you do not heartily subscribe to this opinion of mine,—which, to those, he would add, who have not carefully sifted it to the bottom,—I own has an air more of fancy than of solid reasoning in it;----and yet, my dear Sir, if I may presume to know your character, I am morally assured, I should hazard little in stating a case to you,---not as a party in the dispute,—but as a judge, and trusting my appeal upon it to your own good sense and candid disquisition in this matter;——you are a person free from as many narrow prejudices of education as most men;—and, if I may presume to penetrate further into you,—of a liberality of genius above bearing down an opinion, merely because it wants friends. Your son!---your dear son,---from whose sweet and open temper you have so much to expect.—Your BILLY, Sir!—would you, for the world, have called him JUDAS?—Would you, my dear Sir, he would say, laying his hand upon your breast, with the genteelest address,---and in that soft and irresistible *piano* of voice, which the nature of the *argumentum ad hominem*[6] absolutely requires,—Would you, Sir, if a *Jew* of a godfather had proposed the name for your child, and offered you his purse along with it, would you have consented to such a desecration of him?——O my God! he would say, looking up, if I know your temper right, Sir,---you are incapable of it;——you would have trampled upon the offer;---you would have thrown the temptation at the tempter's head with abhorrence.

Your greatness of mind in this action, which I admire, with that generous contempt of money which you shew me in the whole transaction, is really noble;---and what renders it more so, is the principle of it;---the workings of a parent's love upon the truth and conviction of this very hypothesis, namely, That was your son called JUDAS,---the sordid and treacherous idea, so inseparable from the name, would have accompanied him thro' life like his shadow, and, in the end, made a miser and a rascal of him, in spight, Sir, of your example.

I never knew a man able to answer this argument.——But, indeed, to speak of my father as he was;—he was certainly irresistible, both in his orations and disputations;—he was born an orator;—Θεοδιδακτος.[7]—Persuasion hung upon his lips, and the elements of Logick and Rhetorick were so blended up in him,—and, withall, he had so shrewd guess at the weaknesses and passions of his respondent,——that NATURE might have stood up and said,—"This man is eloquent." In short, whether he was on the weak or the strong side of the question, 'twas hazardous in either case to attack him:—And yet, 'tis strange, he had never read *Cicero* nor *Quintilian de Oratore*,[8] nor *Isocrates*,[9] nor *Aristotle*,[10] nor *Longinus*[11] amongst the antients;——nor *Vossius*,[12] nor *Skioppius*,[13] nor *Ramus*,[14] nor *Farnaby*[15] amongst the moderns;—and what is more astonishing, he had never in his whole life the least light or spark of subtilty struck into his mind, by one single lecture upon *Crackenthorp*[16] or *Burgersdicius*,[17] or any *Dutch* logician or commentator;—he knew not so much as in what the difference of an argument *ad ignorantiam*,[18] and an argument *ad hominem* consisted; so that I well remember, when he went up along with me to enter my name at *Jesus College*[19] in ****,—it was a matter of just wonder with my worthy tutor, and two or three fellows of that learned society,---that a man who knew not so much as the names of his tools, should be able to work after that fashion with 'em.

To work with them in the best manner he could, was what my father was, however, perpetually forced upon;——for he had a thousand little sceptical notions of the comick kind to defend, ——most of which notions, I verily believe, at first enter'd upon the footing of mere whims, and of a *vive la Bagatelle*;[20] and as such he would make merry with them for half an hour or so, and having sharpen'd his wit upon 'em, dismiss them till another day.

I mention this, not only as matter of hypothesis or conjecture upon the progress and establishment of my father's many odd opinions,--but as a warning to the learned reader against the indiscreet reception of such guests, who, after a free and undisturbed enterance, for some years, into our brains,—at length claim a kind of settlement there,——working sometimes like yeast;—but more generally after the manner of the gentle passion, beginning in jest,—but ending in downright earnest.

Whether this was the case of the singularity of my father's notions,—or that his judgment, at length, became the dupe of his wit;—or how far, in many of his notions, he might, tho' odd, be absolutely right;——the reader, as he comes at them, shall decide. All that I maintain here, is, that in this one, of the influence of Christian names, however it gain'd footing, he was serious;—he was all uniformity;—he was systematical, and, like all systematick reasoners, he would move both heaven and earth, and twist and torture every thing in nature to support his hypothesis. In a word, I repeat it over again;—he was serious;—and, in consequence of it, he would lose all kind of patience whenever he saw people, especially of condition, who should have known better,——as careless and as indifferent about the name they imposed upon their child,—or more so, than in the choice of *Ponto* or *Cupid* for their puppy dog.

This, he would say, look'd ill;—and had, moreover, this particular aggravation in it, *viz.* That when once a vile name was wrongfully or injudiciously given, 'twas not like the case of a man's character, which, when wrong'd, might hereafter be clear'd;——and, possibly, sometime or other, if not in the man's life, at least after his death,—be, somehow or other, set to rights with the world: But the injury of this, he would say, could never be undone;---nay, he doubted even whether an act of parliament could reach it:——He knew as well as you, that the legislature assum'd a power over surnames;—but for very strong reasons, which he could give, it had never yet adventured, he would say, to go a step further.

It was observable, that tho' my father, in consequence of this opinion, had, as I have told you, the strongest likings and dislikings towards certain names;—that there were still numbers of names which hung so equally in the balance before him, that they were absolutely indifferent to him. *Jack, Dick,* and *Tom* were of this class: These my father call'd neutral names;—affirming of them, without a satyr, That there had been as many knaves and fools, at least, as wise and good men, since the world began, who had indifferently borne them;---so that, like equal forces acting against each other in contrary directions, he thought they mutually destroyed each others effects; for which reason, he would often declare, He would not give a cherry-stone to choose amongst them. *Bob,* which was my brother's name, was another of these neutral kinds of Christian names, which operated very little either way; and as my father happen'd to be at *Epsom,*[21] when it was given him,—he would oft times thank heaven it was no worse. *Andrew* was something like a negative quantity in Algebra with him;---'twas worse, he said, than nothing.---*William* stood pretty high:-----*Numps*[22] again was low with him;--and *Nick,* he said, was the DEVIL.

But, of all the names in the universe, he had the most unconquerable aversion for TRISTRAM;[23]---he had the lowest and most contemptible opinion of it of any thing in the world,---thinking it could possibly produce nothing in *rerum naturâ,*[24] but what was extreamly mean and pitiful: So that in the midst of a dispute on the subject, in which, by the bye, he was frequently involved,-----he would sometimes break off in a sudden and spirited EPIPHONEMA,[25] or rather EROTESIS,[26] raised a third, and sometimes a full fifth, above the key of the discourse,——and demand it categorically of his antagonist, Whether he would take upon him to say, he had ever remember'd,-----whether he had ever read,---or even whether he had ever heard tell of a man, call'd *Tristram,* performing any thing great or worth recording?—No---, he would say,---TRISTRAM!---The thing is impossible.

What could be wanting in my father but to have wrote a book to publish this notion of his to the world? Little boots it to the subtle speculatist to stand single in his opinions,----unless he gives them proper vent:---It was the identical thing which my father did;—for in the year sixteen, which was two years before I was born, he was at the pains of writing an express DISSERTATION simply upon the word *Tristram*,—shewing the world, with great candour and modesty, the grounds of his great abhorrence to the name.

When this story is compared with the title-page,---Will not the gentle reader pity my father from his soul?----to see an orderly and well-disposed gentleman, who tho' singular,—yet inoffensive in his notions,—so played upon in them by cross purposes;——to look down upon the stage, and see him baffled and overthrown in all his little systems and wishes; to behold a train of events perpetually falling out against him, and in so critical and cruel a way, as if they had purposedly been plann'd and pointed against him, merely to insult his speculations. ——In a word, to behold such a one, in his old age, ill-fitted for troubles, ten times in a day suffering sorrow;—ten times in a day calling the child of his prayers TRISTRAM!——Melancholy dissyllable of sound! which, to his ears, was unison to *Nicompoop*, and every name vituperative under heaven.——By his ashes! I swear it,—if ever malignant spirit took pleasure, or busied itself in traversing the purposes of mortal man,---it must have been here;---and if it was not necessary I should be born before I was christened, I would this moment give the reader an account of it.

CHAPTER XX

——How could you, Madam, be so inattentive in reading the last chapter? I told you in it, *That my mother was not a papist.*——Papist! You told me no such thing, Sir. Madam, I beg leave to repeat it over again, That I told you as plain, at least, as words, by direct inference, could tell you such a thing.—Then, Sir, I must have miss'd a page.--No, Madam,—you have not miss'd a word.——Then I was asleep, Sir.—My pride, Madam, cannot allow you that refuge.——Then, I declare, I know nothing at all about the matter.—That, Madam, is the very fault I lay to your charge; and as a punishment for it, I do insist upon it, that you immediately turn back, that is, as soon as you get to the next full stop, and read the whole chapter over again.

I have imposed this penance upon the lady, neither out of wantonness or cruelty, but from the best of motives; and therefore shall make her no apology for it when she returns back:— 'Tis to rebuke a vicious taste which has crept into thousands besides herself,—of reading straight forwards, more in quest of the adventures, than of the deep erudition and knowledge which a book of this cast, if read over as it should be, would infallibly impart with them.——The mind should be accustomed to make wise reflections, and draw curious conclusions as it goes along; the habitude of which made *Pliny* the younger[1] affirm, "That he never read a book so bad, but he drew some profit from it." The stories of *Greece* and *Rome*, run over without this turn and application,—do less service, I affirm it, than the history of *Parismus* and *Parismenus*,[2] or of the Seven Champions of *England*,[3] read with it.

——But here comes my fair Lady. Have you read over again the chapter, Madam, as I desired you?—You have: And did you not observe the passage, upon the second reading, which admits the inference?——Not a word like it! Then, Madam, be pleased to ponder well the last line but one of the chapter, where I take upon me to say, "It was *necessary* I should be born before I was christen'd." Had my mother, Madam, been a Papist, that consequence did not follow.*

It is a terrible misfortune for this same book of mine, but more so to the Republick of Letters;—so that my own is quite

---

* The *Romish* Rituals direct the baptizing of the child, in cases of danger, *before* it is born;—but upon this proviso, That some part or other of the child's body be seen by the baptizer:——But the Doctors of the *Sorbonne*, by a deliberation held amongst them, *April* 10, 1733,—have enlarged the powers of the midwives, by determining, That tho' no part of the child's body should appear,——that baptism shall, nevertheless, be administered to it by injection,— *par le moyen d'une petite Canulle.*—Anglicé, *a squirt.*—'Tis very strange that St. *Thomas Aquinas*, who had so good a mechanical head, both for tying and untying the knots of school-divinity,—should, after so much pains bestowed upon this,—give up the point at last, as a second *La chose impossible;*—"Infantes in maternis uteris existentes (quoth St. *Thomas*) baptizari possunt *nullo modo.*"—O *Thomas! Thomas!*

If the reader has the curiosity to see the question upon baptism, *by injection*, as presented to the Doctors of the *Sorbonne,*—with their consultation thereupon, it is as follows.[4]

swallowed up in the consideration of it,--that this self-same vile pruriency for fresh adventures in all things, has got so strongly into our habit and humours,—and so wholly intent are we upon satisfying the impatience of our concupiscence that way,—that nothing but the gross and more carnal parts of a composition will go down:—The subtle hints and sly communications of science fly off, like spirits, upwards;——the heavy moral escapes downwards; and both the one and the other are as much lost to the world, as if they were still left in the bottom of the ink-horn.

I wish the male-reader has not pass'd by many a one, as quaint and curious as this one, in which the female-reader has been detected. I wish it may have its effects;—and that all good people, both male and female, from her example, may be taught to think as well as read.

MEMOIRE presenté a Messieurs les Docteurs de SORBONNE.*[5]

Un Chirurgien Accoucheur, represente á Messieurs les Docteurs de Sorbonne, qu' il y a de cas, quoique trés rares, oú une mere ne sçauroit accoucher, & même oú l'enfant est tellement renfermé dans le sein de sa mere, qu' il ne fait parôitre aucune partie de son corps, ce qui seroit un cas, suivant les Rituels, de lui conférer, du moins sous condition, le baptême. Le Chirurgien, qui consulte, prétend, par le moyen d'une petite canulle, de pouvoir baptiser immediatement l'enfant, sans faire aucun tort á la mere.——Il demand si ce moyen, qu' il vient de proposer, est permis & légitime, et s'il peut s'en servir dans le cas qu' il vient d'exposer.

REPONSE.

LE Conseil estime, que la question proposée souffre de grandes difficultes. Les Théologiens posent d'un coté pour principe, que le baptême, qui est une naissance spirituelle, suppose une premiere naissance; il faut être né dans le monde, pour renâitre en Jesus Christ, *comme ils l'enseignent.* S. Thomas, 3 part. quæst. 88. artic. 11. *suit cette doctrine comme une verité constante; l'on ne peut, dit ce* S. Docteur, *baptiser les enfans qui sont renfermés dans le sein de leurs Meres, et* S. Thomas *est fondé sur ce, que les enfans ne sont point nés, & ne peuvent être comptés parmi les autres hommes; d'ou il conclud, qu'ils ne peuvent être l'object d'une action extérieure, pour recevoir par leur ministére les*

* Vide Deventer. Paris Edit. 4to, 1734. p. 366.[6]

sacremens nécessaires au salut: Pueri in maternis uteris existentes nondum prodierunt in lucem ut cum aliis hominibus vitam ducant; unde non possunt subjici actioni humanæ, ut per eorum ministerium sacramenta recipiant ad salutem. *Les rituels ordonnent dans la pratique ce que les theologiens ont établi sur les mêmes matiéres, & ils deffendent tous d'une maniére uniforme de baptiser les enfans qui sont renfermés dans le sein de leurs meres, s' ils ne font paroitre quelque partie de leurs corps. Le concours des théologiens, & des rituels, qui sont les régles des diocéses, parôit former une autorité qui termine la question presente; cependant le conseil de conscience considerant d'un coté, que le raisonnement des théologiens est uniquement fondé sur une raison de convenance, & que la deffense des rituels, suppose que l'on ne peut baptiser immediatement les enfans ainsi renfermés dans le sein de leurs meres, ce qui est contre la supposition presente; & d'un autre côté, considerant que les mêmes théologiens enseignent, que l'on peut risquer les sacremens qu'* Jesus Christ *á établis comme des moyens faciles, mais neéssaires pour sanctifier les hommes; & d'ailleurs estimant, que les enfans renfermés dans le sein de leurs meres, pourroient être cæpables de salut, parce qu'ils sont capables de damnation;—pour ces considerations, & eu égard a l'exposé, suivant lequel on assure avoir trouvé un moyen certain de baptiser ces enfans ainsi renfermés, sans faire aucun tort a la mere, le Conseil estime que l'on pourroit se servir du moyen proposé, dans la confiance qu'il a, que Dieu n' a point laissé ces sortes d'enfans sans aucuns secours, & supposant, comme il est exposé, que le moyen dont il s'agit est propre a leur procurer le baptême; cependant comme il s'agiroit, en autorisant la pratique proposée, de changer une régle universellement établie, le Conseil croit que celui qui consulte doit s'adresser a son évêque, & a qui il appartient de juger de l'utilité, & du danger du moyen proposé, & comme, sous le bon plaisir de l'evêque, le conseil estime qu'il faudroit recourir au Pape, qui a le droit d'expliquer les régles de l'eglise, et d'y déroger dans les cas, ou la loi ne sçauroit obliger, quelque sage & quelque utile que paroisse la maniére de baptiser dont il s'agit, le conseil ne pourroit l'approuver sans le concours de ces deux autorités. On conseile au moins à celui qui consulte, de s'adresser á son evêque, & de lui faire part de la presente décision, afin que, si le prélat entre dans les raisons sur lesquelles les docteurs soussignés s'appuyent, il puisse être autorisé dans le cas de nécessité, ou il risqueroit trop d'attendre que la permission fût demandée &*

*accordée d'employer le moyen qu'il propose si avantageux au
salut de l'enfant. Au reste le conseile, en estimant que l'on
pourroit s'en servir croit cependant, que si les enfans dont il
s'agit, venoient au monde, contre l'esperance de ceux qui se
séroient servis du même moyen, il séroit nécessaire de les baptiser
sous condition, & en cela le conseil se conforme a tous les rituels,
qui en autorisant le baptême d'un enfant qui fait paroître quelque partie de son corps, enjoignent néantmoins, & ordonnent de
le baptiser sous condition, s'il vient heureusement au monde.*

Déliberé en *Sorbonne*, le 10 *Avril*, 1733.

A. Le Moyne,

L. De Romigny,

De Marcilly.

Mr. *Tristram Shandy*'s compliments to Messrs. *Le Moyne,
De Romigny*, and *De Marcilly*, hopes they all rested well the
night after so tiresome a consultation.—He begs to know,
whether, after the ceremony of marriage, and before that of
consummation, the baptizing all the Homunculi at once,
slap-dash, by *injection*, would not be a shorter and safer cut still;
on condition, as above, That if the Homunculi do well and
come safe into the world after this, That each and every of them
shall be baptized again (*sous condition*.)——And provided, in
the second place, That the thing can be done, which Mr. *Shandy*
apprehends it may, *par le moyen d'une* petite canulle, and, *sans
faire aucun tort a le pere.*'

CHAPTER XXI

——I wonder what's all that noise, and running backwards and forwards for, above stairs, quoth my father, addressing himself, after an hour and a half's silence, to my uncle
Toby,——who you must know, was sitting on the opposite side
of the fire, smoking his social pipe all the time, in mute contemplation of a new pair of black-plush-breeches which he had
got on;—What can they be doing brother? quoth my father,—
we can scarce hear ourselves talk.

I think, replied my uncle *Toby*, taking his pipe from his
mouth, and striking the head of it two or three times upon the
nail of his left thumb, as he began his sentence,——I think, says
he:——But to enter rightly into my uncle *Toby*'s sentiments
upon this matter, you must be made to enter first a little into his

character, the out-lines of which I shall just give you, and then the dialogue between him and my father will go on as well again.

—Pray what was that man's name,---for I write in such a hurry, I have no time to recollect or look for it,——who first made the observation, "That there was great inconstancy in our air and climate?" Whoever he was, 'twas a just and good observation in him.----But the corollary drawn from it, namely, "That it is this which has furnished us with such a variety of odd and whimsical characters;"—that was not his;----it was found out by another man, at least a century and a half after him:— Then again,—that this copious store-house of original materials, is the true and natural cause that our Comedies are so much better than those of *France*, or any others that either have, or can be wrote upon the Continent;——that discovery was not fully made till about the middle of king *William*'s reign,---when the great *Dryden*,[1] in writing one of his long prefaces, (if I mistake not) most fortunately hit upon it. Indeed towards the latter end of queen *Anne*, the great *Addison*[2] began to patronize the notion, and more fully explained it to the world in one or two of his Spectators;—but the discovery was not his.—Then, fourthly and lastly, that this strange irregularity in our climate, producing so strange an irregularity in our characters,——doth thereby, in some sort, make us amends, by giving us somewhat to make us merry with when the weather will not suffer us to go out of doors,--that observation is my own;--and was struck out by me this very rainy day, *March* 26, 1759, and betwixt the hours of nine and ten in the morning.

Thus,---thus my fellow labourers and associates in this great harvest of our learning, now ripening before our eyes; thus it is, by slow steps of casual increase, that our knowledge physical, metaphysical, physiological, polemical, nautical, mathematical, ænigmatical, technical, biographical, romantical, chemical, and obstetrical, with fifty other branches of it, (most of 'em ending, as these do, in *ical*) have, for these two last centuries and more, gradually been creeping upwards towards that $Aκμὴ$[3] of their perfections, from which, if we may form a conjecture from the advances of these last seven years, we cannot possibly be far off.

When that happens, it is to be hoped, it will put an end to all kind of writings whatsoever;—the want of all kind of writing will put an end to all kind of reading;---and that in time, *As war begets poverty, poverty peace*,——must, in course, put an end to all kind of knowledge,---and then——we shall have all to begin over again; or, in other words, be exactly where we started.

———Happy! thrice happy Times! I only wish that the æra of my begetting, as well as the mode and manner of it, had been a little alter'd,--or that it could have been put off with any convenience to my father or mother, for some twenty or five-and-twenty years longer, when a man in the literary world might have stood some chance.———

But I forget my uncle *Toby*, whom all this while we have left knocking the ashes out of his tobacco pipe.

His humour was of that particular species, which does honour to our atmosphere; and I should have made no scruple of ranking him amongst one of the first-rate productions of it, had not there appear'd too many strong lines in it of a family-likeness, which shewed that he derived the singularity of his temper more from blood, than either wind or water, or any modifications or combinations of them whatever: And I have, therefore, oft times wondered, that my father, tho' I believe he had his reasons for it, upon his observing some tokens of excentricity in my course when I was a boy,—should never once endeavour to account for them in this way; for all the SHANDY FAMILY were of an original character throughout;———I mean the males,—the females had no character at all,—except, indeed, my great aunt DINAH,⁴ who, about sixty years ago, was married and got with child by the coachman, for which my father, according to his hypothesis of Christian names, would often say, She might thank her godfathers and godmothers.

It will seem very strange,———and I would as soon think of dropping a riddle in the reader's way, which is not my interest to do, as set him upon guessing how it could come to pass, that an event of this kind, so many years after it had happened, should be reserved for the interruption of the peace and unity, which otherwise so cordially subsisted, between my father and my uncle *Toby*. One would have thought, that the whole force of the misfortune should have spent and wasted itself in the family at first,—as is generally the case:—But nothing ever wrought with our family after the ordinary way. Possibly at the very time this happened, it might have something else to afflict it; and as afflictions are sent down for our good, and that as this had never done the SHANDY FAMILY any good at all, it might lye waiting till apt times and circumstances should give it an opportunity to discharge its office.———Observe, I determine nothing upon this.————My way is ever to point out to the curious, different tracts of investigation, to come at the first springs of the events I tell;—not with a pedantic *Fescue*,—or in the decisive Manner of *Tacitus*,[5] who outwits himself and his reader;—but with the officious humility of a heart devoted to the assistance merely of the inquisitive,--to them I write, ——and by them I shall be read,——if any such reading as this could be supposed to hold out so long, to the very end of the world.

Why this cause of sorrow, therefore, was thus reserved for my father and uncle, is undetermined by me. But how and in what direction it exerted itself, so as to become the cause of dissatisfaction between them, after it began to operate, is what I am able to explain with great exactness, and is as follows:

My uncle TOBY SHANDY, Madam, was a gentleman, who, with the virtues which usually constitute the character of a man of honour and rectitude,—possessed one in a very eminent degree, which is seldom or never put into the catalogue; and that was a most extream and unparallel'd modesty of nature;——tho' I correct the word nature, for this reason, that I may not prejudge a point which must shortly come to a hearing; and that is, Whether this modesty of his was natural or acquir'd.——Which ever way my uncle *Toby* came by it, 'twas nevertheless modesty in the truest sense of it; and that is, Madam, not in regard to words, for he was so unhappy as to have very little choice in them,—but to things;——and this kind of modesty so possess'd him, and it arose to such a height in him, as almost to equal, if such a thing could be, even the modesty of a woman: That female nicety, Madam, and inward cleanliness of mind and fancy, in your sex, which makes you so much the awe of ours.

You will imagine, Madam, that my uncle *Toby* had contracted all this from this very source;----that he had spent a great part of his time in converse with your sex; and that, from a thorough knowledge of you, and the force of imitation which such fair examples render irresistable,---he had acquired this amiable turn of mind.

I wish I could say so,----for unless it was with his sister-in-law, my father's wife and my mother,——my uncle *Toby* scarce exchanged three words with the sex in as many years;——no, he got it, Madam, by a blow.——A blow!---Yes, Madam, it was owing to a blow from a stone, broke off by a ball from the parapet of a horn-work[6] at the siege of *Namur*,[7] which struck full upon my uncle *Toby*'s groin.----Which way could that effect it? The story of that, Madam, is long and interesting;----but it would be running my history all upon heaps to give it you here.------'Tis for an episode hereafter; and every circumstance relating to it in its proper place, shall be faithfully laid before you:----'Till then, it is not in my power to give further light into this matter, or say more than what I have said already,-----That my uncle *Toby* was a gentleman of unparallel'd modesty, which happening to be somewhat subtilized and rarified by the constant heat of a little family-pride,-----they both so wrought together within him, that he could never bear to hear the affair of my aunt DINAH touch'd upon, but with the greatest emotion.------The least hint of it was enough to make the blood fly into his face;---but when my father enlarged upon the story in mixed companies, which the illustration of his hypothesis frequently obliged him to do,----the unfortunate blight of one of the fairest branches of the family, would set my uncle *Toby*'s honour and modesty o'bleeding; and he would often take my father aside, in the greatest concern imaginable, to expostulate and tell him, he would give him any thing in the world, only to let the story rest.

My father, I believe, had the truest love and tenderness for my uncle *Toby*, that ever one brother bore towards another, and would have done any thing in nature, which one brother in reason could have desir'd of another, to have made my uncle *Toby*'s heart easy in this, or any other point. But this lay out of his power.

------My father, as I told you, was a philosopher in grain,—speculative,—systematical;—and my aunt *Dinah*'s affair was a matter of as much consequence to him, as the retrogradation of the planets to *Copernicus*:[8]—The backslidings of *Venus* in her orbit fortified the *Copernican* system, call'd so after his name; and the backslidings of my aunt *Dinah* in her orbit, did the same service in establishing my father's system, which, I trust, will for ever hereafter be call'd the *Shandean System*, after his.

In any other family dishonour, my father, I believe, had as nice a sense of shame as any man whatever;------and neither he, nor, I dare say, *Copernicus*, would have divulged the affair in either case, or have taken the least notice of it to the world, but for the obligations they owed, as they thought, to truth.—*Amicus Plato*, my father would say, construing the words to my uncle *Toby*, as he went along, *Amicus Plato*; that is, DINAH was my aunt;—*sed magis amica veritas*[9]——but TRUTH is my sister.

This contrariety of humours betwixt my father and my uncle, was the source of many a fraternal squabble. The one could not bear to hear the tale of family disgrace recorded,——and the other would scarce ever let a day pass to an end without some hint at it.

For God's sake, my uncle *Toby* would cry,——and for my sake, and for all our sakes, my dear brother *Shandy*,——do let this story of our aunt's and her ashes sleep in peace;——how can you,——how can you have so little feeling and compassion for the character of our family:——What is the character of a family to an hypothesis? my father would reply.——Nay, if you come to that—what is the life of a family:——The life of a family!—my uncle *Toby* would say, throwing himself back in his arm-chair, and lifting up his hands, his eyes, and one leg. ——Yes the life,——my father would say, maintaining his point. How many thousands of 'em are there every year that comes cast away, (in all civilized countries at least)——and consider'd as nothing but common air, in competition of an hypothesis. In my plain sense of things, my uncle *Toby*, would answer,——every such instance is downright MURDER, let who will commit it.——There lies your mistake, my father would reply;——for, in *Foro Scientiæ*[10] there is no such thing as MURDER,——'tis only DEATH, brother.

My uncle *Toby* would never offer to answer this by any other kind of argument, than that of whistling half a dozen bars of *Lillabullero*.[11]——You must know it was the usual channel thro' which his passions got vent, when any thing shocked or surprised him;——but especially when any thing, which he deem'd very absurd, was offer'd.

As not one of our logical writers, nor any of the commentators upon them, that I remember, have thought proper to give a name to this particular species of argument,—I here take the liberty to do it myself, for two reasons. First, That, in order to prevent all confusion in disputes, it may stand as much distinguished for ever, from every other species of argument,——as the *Argumentum ad Verecundiam*,[12] *ex Absurdo*,[13] *ex Fortiori*,[14] or any other argument whatsoever:——And, secondly, That it may be said by my children's children, when my head is laid to rest,----that their learned grand-father's head had been busied to as much purpose once, as other people's:—That he had invented a name,---and generously thrown it into the TREAS-URY of the *Ars Logica*,[15] for one of the most unanswerable arguments in the whole science. And if the end of disputation is more to silence than convince,--they may add, if they please, to one of the best arguments too.

I do therefore, by these presents, strictly order and command, That it be known and distinguished by the name and title of the *Argumentum Fistulatorium*,[16] and no other;---and that it rank hereafter with the *Argumentum Baculinum*,[17] and the *Argumentum ad Crumenam*,[18] and for ever hereafter be treated of in the same chapter.

As for the *Argumentum Tripodium*,[19] which is never used but by the woman against the man;---and the *Argumentum ad Rem*,[20] which, contrarywise, is made use of by the man only against the woman:—As these two are enough in conscience for one lecture;——and, moreover, as the one is the best answer to the other,---let them likewise be kept apart, and be treated of in a place by themselves.

CHAPTER XXII

THE learned Bishop *Hall*,[1] I mean the famous Dr. *Joseph Hall*, who was Bishop of *Exeter* in King *James* the first's reign, tells us in one of his *Decads*, at the end of his divine art of meditation, imprinted at *London*, in the year 1610, by *John Beal*, dwelling in *Aldergate-street*, "That it is an abominable thing for a man to commend himself;"---and I really think it is so.

And yet, on the other hand, when a thing is executed in a masterly kind of a fashion, which thing is not likely to be found out;---I think it is full as abominable, that a man should lose the honour of it, and go out of the world with the conceit of it rotting in his head.

This is precisely my situation.

For in this long digression which I was accidentally led into, as in all my digressions (one only excepted) there is a master-stroke of digressive skill, the merit of which has all along, I fear, been overlooked by my reader,--not for want of penetration in him,—but because 'tis an excellence seldom looked for, or expected indeed, in a digression;---and it is this: That tho' my digressions are all fair, as you observe,—and that I fly off from what I am about, as far and as often too as any writer in

Great-Britain; yet I constantly take care to order affairs so, that my main business does not stand still in my absence.

I was just going, for example, to have given you the great out-lines of my uncle *Toby*'s most whimsical character;—when my aunt *Dinah* and the coachman came a-cross us, and led us a vagary some millions of miles into the very heart of the planetary system: Notwithstanding all this, you perceive that the drawing of my uncle *Toby*'s character went on gently all the time;---not the great contours of it,—that was impossible,---but some familiar strokes and faint designations of it, were here and there touch'd in, as we went along, so that you are much better acquainted with my uncle *Toby* now than you was before.

By this contrivance the machinery of my work is of a species by itself; two contrary motions are introduced into it, and reconciled, which were thought to be at variance with each other. In a word, my work is digressive, and it is progressive too,—and at the same time.

This, Sir, is a very different story from that of the earth's moving round her axis, in her diurnal rotation, with her progress in her elliptick orbit which brings about the year, and constitutes that variety and vicissitude of seasons we enjoy;---though I own it suggested the thought,—as I believe the greatest of our boasted improvements and discoveries have come from some such trifling hints.

Digressions, incontestably, are the sunshine;——they are the life, the soul of reading;---take them out of this book for instance,--you might as well take the book along with them;—one cold eternal winter would reign in every page of it; restore them to the writer;----he steps forth like a bridegroom,[2]—bids All hail; brings in variety, and forbids the appetite to fail.

All the dexterity is in the good cookery and management of them, so as to be not only for the advantage of the reader, but also of the author, whose distress, in this matter, is truely pitiable: For, if he begins a digression,---from that moment, I observe, his whole work stands stock-still;—and if he goes on with his main work,----then there is an end of his digression.

——This is vile work.—For which reason, from the beginning of this, you see, I have constructed the main work and the adventitious parts of it with such intersections, and have so complicated and involved the digressive and progressive movements, one wheel within another, that the whole machine, in general, has been kept a-going;---and, what's more, it shall be kept a-going these forty years, if it pleases the fountain of health to bless me so long with life and good spirits.

CHAPTER XXIII

I HAVE a strong propensity in me to begin this chapter very nonsensically, and I will not balk my fancy.—Accordingly I set off thus.

If the fixure of *Momus*'s glass,[1] in the human breast, according to the proposed emendation of that arch-critick, had taken place,——first, This foolish consequence would certainly have followed,--That the very wisest and the very gravest of us all, in one coin or other, must have paid window-money[2] every day of our lives.

And, secondly, That had the said glass been there set up, nothing more would have been wanting, in order to have taken a man's character, but to have taken a chair and gone softly, as you would to a dioptrical bee-hive,[3] and look'd in,-- view'd the soul stark naked;---observ'd all her motions,—her machinations;—traced all her maggots from their first engendering to their crawling forth;---watched her loose in her frisks, her gambols, her capricios; and after some notice of her more solemn deportment, consequent upon such frisks, &c.——then taken your pen and ink and set down nothing but what you had seen, and could have sworn to:---But this is an advantage not to be had by the biographer in this planet,—in the planet *Mercury* (belike) it may be so, if not better still for him;----for there the intense heat of the country, which is proved by computators, from its vicinity to the sun, to be more than equal to that of red hot iron,—must, I think, long ago have vitrified the bodies of the inhabitants, (as the efficient cause) to suit them for the climate (which is the final cause); so that, betwixt them both, all the tenements of their souls, from top to bottom, may be nothing else, for aught the soundest philosophy can shew to the contrary, but one fine transparent body of clear glass (bating the umbilical knot);---so, that till the inhabitants grow old and tolerably wrinkled, whereby the rays of light, in passing through them, become so monstrously refracted,-----or return reflected from their surfaces in such transverse lines to the eye, that a man cannot be seen thro';---his soul might as well, unless, for more ceremony,---or the trifling advantage which the umbilical point gave her,----might, upon all other accounts, I say, as well play the fool out o'doors as in her own house.

But this, as I said above, is not the case of the inhabitants of this earth;—our minds shine not through the body, but are wrapt up here in a dark covering of uncrystalized flesh and blood; so that if we would come to the specifick characters of them, we must go some other way to work.

Many, in good truth, are the ways which human wit has been forced to take to do this thing with exactness.

Some, for instance, draw all their characters with wind instruments.—*Virgil*[4] takes notice of that way in the affair of *Dido* and *Æneas*;—but it is as fallacious as the breath of fame;—and, moreover, bespeaks a narrow genius. I am not ignorant that the *Italians*[5] pretend to a mathematical exactness in their designations of one particular sort of character among them, from the *forte* or *piano* of a certain wind instrument they use,—which they say is infallible.—I dare not mention the name of the instrument in this place;--'tis sufficient we have it amongst us,—but never think of making a drawing by it;---this is ænigmatical, and intended to be so, at least, *ad populum*:[6]---And therefore I beg, Madam, when you come here, that you read on as fast as you can, and never stop to make any inquiry about it.

There are others again, who will draw a man's character from no other helps in the world, but merely from his evacuations;—but this often gives a very incorrect out-line,---unless, indeed, you take a sketch of his repletions too; and by correcting one drawing from the other, compound one good figure out of them both.

I should have no objection to this method, but that I think it must smell too strong of the lamp,—and be render'd still more operose, by forcing you to have an eye to the rest of his *Non-Naturals*.[7]——Why the most natural actions of a man's life should be call'd his Non-Naturals,---is another question.

There are others, fourthly, who disdain every one of these expedients;—not from any fertility of his own, but from the various ways of doing it, which they have borrowed from the honourable devices which the Pentagraphic Brethren* of the brush have shewn in taking copies.—These, you must know, are your great historians.

---

* Pentagraph, an instrument to copy prints and pictures mechanically, and in any proportion.

One of these you will see drawing a full-length character *against the light*;—that's illiberal,----dishonest,----and hard upon the character of the man who sits.

Others, to mend the matter, will make a drawing of you in the *Camera*;⁸---that is most unfair of all,---because, *there* you are sure to be represented in some of your most ridiculous attitudes.

To avoid all and every one of these errors, in giving you my uncle *Toby*'s character, I am determin'd to draw it by no mechanical help whatever;——nor shall my pencil be guided by any one wind instrument which ever was blown upon, either on this, or on the other side of the *Alps*;—nor will I consider either his repletions or his discharges,—or touch upon his Non-Naturals;---but, in a word, I will draw my uncle *Toby*'s character from his HOBBY-HORSE.

CHAPTER XXIV

IF I was not morally sure that the reader must be out of all patience for my uncle *Toby*'s character,——I would here previously have convinced him, that there is no instrument so fit to draw such a thing with, as that which I have pitch'd upon.

A man and his HOBBY-HORSE, tho' I cannot say that they act and re-act exactly after the same manner in which the soul and body do upon each other: Yet doubtless there is a communication between them of some kind, and my opinion rather is, that there is something in it more of the manner of electrified bodies,--and that by means of the heated parts of the rider, which come immediately into contact with the back of the HOBBY-HORSE.—By long journies and much friction, it so happens that the body of the rider is at length fill'd as full of HOBBY-HORSICAL matter as it can hold;----so that if you are able to give but a clear description of the nature of the one, you may form a pretty exact notion of the genius and character of the other.

Now the HOBBY-HORSE which my uncle *Toby* always rode upon, was, in my opinion, an HOBBY-HORSE well worth giving a description of, if it was only upon the score of his great singularity; for you might have travelled from *York* to *Dover*, —from *Dover* to *Penzance* in *Cornwall*, and from *Penzance* to *York* back again, and not have seen such another upon the road;

or if you had seen such a one, whatever haste you had been in, you must infallibly have stopp'd to have taken a view of him. Indeed, the gait and figure of him was so strange, and so utterly unlike was he, from his head to his tail, to any one of the whole species, that it was now and then made a matter of dispute, ——whether he was really a HOBBY-HORSE or no: But as the Philosopher[1] would use no other argument to the sceptic, who disputed with him against the reality of motion, save that of rising up upon his legs, and walking a-cross the room;—so would my uncle *Toby* use no other argument to prove his HOBBY-HORSE was a HOBBY-HORSE indeed, but by getting upon his back and riding him about;—leaving the world after that to determine the point as it thought fit.

In good truth, my uncle *Toby* mounted him with so much pleasure, and he carried my uncle *Toby* so well,——that he troubled his head very little with what the world either said or thought about it.

It is now high time, however, that I give you a description of him:—But to go on regularly, I only beg you will give me leave to acquaint you first, how my uncle *Toby* came by him.

CHAPTER XXV

THE wound in my uncle *Toby*'s groin, which he received at the siege of *Namur*, rendering him unfit for the service, it was thought expedient he should return to *England*, in order, if possible, to be set to rights.

He was four years totally confined,—part of it to his bed, and all of it to his room; and in the course of his cure, which was all that time in hand, suffer'd unspeakable miseries,—owing to a succession of exfoliations from the *oss pubis*,[1] and the outward edge of that part of the *coendix*[2] called the *oss illeum*,[3]——both which bones were dismally crush'd, as much by the irregularity of the stone, which I told you was broke off the parapet,—as by its size,—(though it was pretty large) which inclined the surgeon all along to think, that the great injury which it had done my uncle *Toby*'s groin, was more owing to the gravity of the stone itself, than to the projectile force of it,—which he would often tell him was a great happiness.

My father at that time was just beginning business in *London*, and had taken a house;—and as the truest friendship and cordiality subsisted between the two brothers,—and that my father thought my uncle *Toby* could no where be so well nursed and taken care of as in his own house,——he assign'd him the very best apartment in it.—And what was a much more sincere mark of his affection still, he would never suffer a friend or an acquaintance to step into the house on any occasion, but he would take him by the hand, and lead him up stairs to see his brother *Toby*, and chat an hour by his bed side.

The history of a soldier's wound beguiles the pain of it;—my uncle's visiters at least thought so, and in their daily calls upon him, from the courtesy arising out of that belief, they would frequently turn the discourse to that subject,—and from that subject the discourse would generally roll on to the siege itself.

These conversations were infinitely kind; and my uncle *Toby* received great relief from them, and would have received much more, but that they brought him into some unforeseen perplexities, which, for three months together, retarded his cure greatly; and if he had not hit upon an expedient to extricate himself out of them, I verily believe they would have laid him in his grave.

What these perplexities of my uncle *Toby* were,——'tis impossible for you to guess;—if you could,—I should blush; not as a relation,—not as a man,—nor even as a woman,—but I should blush as an author; inasmuch as I set no small store by myself upon this very account, that my reader has never yet been able to guess at any thing. And in this, Sir, I am of so nice and singular a humour, that if I thought you was able to form the least judgment or probable conjecture to yourself, of what was to come in the next page,—I would tear it out of my book.

END of the First Volume.

THE
L I F E
AND
O P I N I O N S
OF
TRISTRAM SHANDY,
GENTLEMAN.

*Ταρασσει τοὺς Ἀνθρώπους οὐ τὰ Πράγματα,
αλλα τὰ περι τῶν Πραγμάτων, Δογματα.*

VOL. II.

1760.

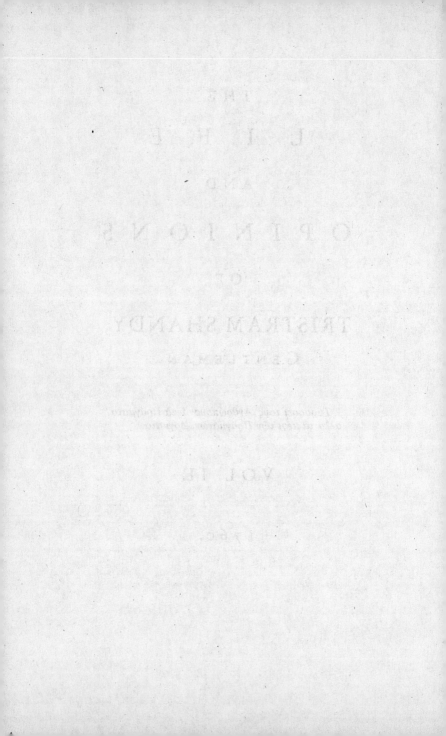

CHAPTER I

I HAVE begun a new book, on purpose that I might have room enough to explain the nature of the perplexities in which my uncle *Toby* was involved, from the many discourses and interrogations about the siege of *Namur*, where he received his wound.

I must remind the reader, in case he has read the history of King *William*'s wars,[1]—but if he has not,--I then inform him, that one of the most memorable attacks in that siege, was that which was made by the *English* and *Dutch* upon the point of the advanced counterscarp, before the gate of *St. Nicolas*, which inclosed the great sluice or water-stop, where the *English* were terribly exposed to the shot of the counter-guard[2] and demi-bastion of *St. Roch:* The issue of which hot dispute, in three words, was this; That the *Dutch* lodged themselves upon the counter-guard,---and that the *English* made themselves masters of the covered way[3] before *St. Nicolas*'s gate, notwithstanding the gallantry of the *French* officers, who exposed themselves upon the glacis sword in hand.

As this was the principal attack of which my uncle *Toby* was an eye-witness at *Namur*,——the army of the besiegers being cut off, by the confluence of the *Maes* and *Sambre*, from seeing much of each other's operations,—my uncle *Toby* was generally more eloquent and particular in his account of it; and the many perplexities he was in, arose out of the almost insurmountable difficulties he found in telling his story intelligibly, and giving such clear ideas of the differences and distinctions between the scarp and counterscarp,——the glacis and covered way,——the half-moon[4] and ravelin,——as to make his company fully comprehend where and what he was about.

Writers themselves are too apt to confound these terms; ——so that you will the less wonder, if in his endeavours to explain them, and in opposition to many misconceptions, that my uncle *Toby* did oft times puzzle his visiters; and sometimes himself too.

To speak the truth, unless the company my father led up stairs were tolerably clear-headed, or my uncle *Toby* was in one of his best explanatory moods, 'twas a difficult thing, do what he could, to keep the discourse free from obscurity.

What rendered the account of this affair the more intricate to my uncle *Toby*, was this,—that in the attack of the counterscarp before the gate of *St. Nicolas*, extending itself from the bank of the *Maes*, quite up to the great water-stop;—the ground was cut and cross-cut with such a multitude of dykes, drains, rivulets, and sluices, on all sides,—and he would get so sadly bewilder'd and set fast amongst them, that frequently he could neither get backwards or forwards to save his life; and was oft times obliged to give up the attack upon that very account only.

These perplexing rebuffs gave my uncle *Toby Shandy* more perturbations than you would imagine; and as my father's kindness to him was continually dragging up fresh friends and fresh inquirers,—he had but a very uneasy task of it.

No doubt my uncle *Toby* had great command of himself,—and could guard appearances, I believe, as well as most men;—yet any one may imagine, that when he could not retreat out of the ravelin without getting into the half-moon, or get out of the covered way without falling down the counterscarp, nor cross the dyke without danger of slipping into the ditch, but that he must have fretted and fumed inwardly:—He did so;—and these little and hourly vexations, which may seem trifling and of no account to the man who has not read *Hippocrates*,[5] yet, whoever has read *Hippocrates*, or Dr. *James Mackenzie*,[6] and has considered well the effects which the passions and affections of the mind have upon the digestion,—(Why not of a wound as well as of a dinner?)——may easily conceive what sharp paroxisms and exacerbations of his wound my uncle *Toby* must have undergone upon that score only.

—My uncle *Toby* could not philosophize upon it;—'twas enough he felt it was so,—and having sustained the pain and sorrows of it for three months together, he was resolved some way or other to extricate himself.

He was one morning lying upon his back in his bed, the anguish and nature of the wound upon his groin suffering him to lye in no other position, when a thought came into his head, that if he could purchase such a thing, and have it pasted down upon a board, as a large map of the fortifications of the town and citadel of *Namur*, with its environs, it might be a means of giving him ease.—I take notice of his desire to have the environs along with the town and citadel, for this reason,—because my uncle *Toby*'s wound was got in one of the traverses, about thirty toises[7] from the returning angle[8] of the trench, opposite to the salient angle⁹ of the demi-bastion¹⁰ of *St. Roch*;——so that he was pretty confident he could stick a pin upon the identical spot of ground where he was standing in when the stone struck him.

All this succeeded to his wishes, and not only freed him from a world of sad explanations, but, in the end, it prov'd the happy means, as you will read, of procuring my uncle *Toby* his HOBBY-HORSE.

CHAPTER II

THERE is nothing so foolish, when you are at the expence of making an entertainment of this kind, as to order things so badly, as to let your criticks and gentry of refined taste run it down: Nor is there any thing so likely to make them do it, as that of leaving them out of the party, or, what is full as offensive, of bestowing your attention upon the rest of your guests in so particular a way, as if there was no such thing as a critick (by occupation) at table.

——I guard against both; for, in the first place, I have left half a dozen places purposely open for them;—and, in the next place, I pay them all court,—Gentlemen, I kiss your hands,—I protest no company could give me half the pleasure,—by my soul I am glad to see you,——I beg only you will make no strangers of yourselves, but sit down without any ceremony, and fall on heartily.

I said I had left six places, and I was upon the point of carrying my complaisance so far, as to have left a seventh open for them,—and in this very spot I stand on;—but being told by a critick, (tho' not by occupation,---but by nature) that I had acquitted myself well enough, I shall fill it up directly, hoping, in the mean time, that I shall be able to make a great deal of more room next year.

——How, in the name of wonder! could your uncle *Toby*, who, it seems, was a military man, and whom you have represented as no fool,----be at the same time such a confused, pudding-headed, muddle-headed fellow, as---Go look.

So, Sir Critick, I could have replied; but I scorn it.——'Tis language unurbane,----and only befitting the man who cannot give clear and satisfactory accounts of things, or dive deep enough into the first causes of human ignorance and confusion. It is moreover the reply valiant,----and therefore I reject it; for

tho' it might have suited my uncle *Toby*'s character as a soldier
excellently well,---and had he not accustomed himself, in such
attacks, to whistle the *Lillabullero*,----as he wanted no courage,
'tis the very answer he would have given; yet it would by no
means have done for me. You see as plain as can be, that I write
as a man of erudition;---that even my similies, my allusions, my
illustrations, my metaphors, are erudite,----and that I must
sustain my character properly, and contrast it properly too,---
else what would become of me? Why, Sir, I should be undone;
----at this very moment that I am going here to fill up one place
against a critick,-----I should have made an opening for a
couple.

——Therefore I answer thus:

Pray, Sir, in all the reading which you have ever read, did you
ever read such a book as *Locke*'s Essay upon the Human
Understanding?——Don't answer me rashly,--because many, I
know, quote the book, who have not read it,---and many have
read it who understand it not:---If either of these is your case, as
I write to instruct, I will tell you in three words what the book
is.—It is a history.—A history! of who? what? where? when?
Don't hurry yourself.——It is a history-book, Sir, (which may
possibly recommend it to the world) of what passes in a man's
own mind; and if you will say so much of the book, and no
more, believe me, you will cut no contemptible figure in a
metaphysic circle.

But this by the way.

Now if you will venture to go along with me, and look
down into the bottom of this matter, it will be found that the
cause of obscurity and confusion, in the mind of man, is
threefold.

Dull organs, dear Sir, in the first place. Secondly, slight and
transient impressions made by objects when the said organs are
not dull. And, thirdly, a memory like unto a sieve, not able to
retain what it has received.----Call down *Dolly* your chamber-
maid, and I will give you my cap and bell[1] along with it, if I make
not this matter so plain that *Dolly* herself shall understand it as
well as *Malbranch*.[2]——When *Dolly* has indited her epistle to
Robin, and has thrust her arm into the bottom of her pocket
hanging by her right side;—take that opportunity to recollect
that the organs and faculties of perception, can, by nothing in
this world, be so aptly typified and explained as by that one
thing which *Dolly*'s hand is in search of.—Your organs are not

so dull that I should inform you---'tis an inch, Sir, of red seal-wax.

When this is melted and dropp'd upon the letter,—if *Dolly* fumbles too long for her thimble, till the wax is over harden'd, it will not receive the mark of her thimble from the usual impulse which was wont to imprint it. Very well: If *Dolly*'s wax, for want of better, is bees-wax, or of a temper too soft,—tho' it may receive,---it will not hold the impression, how hard soever *Dolly* thrusts against it; and last of all, supposing the wax good, and eke the thimble, but applied thereto in careless haste, as her Mistress rings the bell;——in any one of these three cases, the print, left by the thimble, will be as unlike the prototype as a brass-jack.

Now you must understand that not one of these was the true cause of the confusion in my uncle *Toby*'s discourse; and it is for that very reason I enlarge upon them so long, after the manner of great physiologists,—to shew the world what it did *not* arise from.

What it did arise from, I have hinted above, and a fertile source of obscurity it is,---and ever will be,---and that is the unsteady uses of words which have perplexed the clearest and most exalted understandings.

It is ten to one, (at *Arthur*'s)³ whether you have ever read the literary histories of past ages;—if you have,—what terrible battles, 'yclept logomachies, have they occasioned and perpetuated with so much gall and ink-shed,⁴---that a good natured man cannot read the accounts of them without tears in his eyes.

Gentle critick! when thou hast weigh'd all this, and consider'd within thyself how much of thy own knowledge, discourse, and conversation has been pestered and disordered, at one time or other, by this, and this only:——What a pudder⁵ and racket in Councils about οὐσὶα and ὑπόστασις;⁶ and in the Schools of the learned about power and about spirit;—about essences, and about quintessences;——about substances, and about space.——What confusion in greater Theatres from words of little meaning, and as indeterminate a sense;---when thou considers this, thou wilt not wonder at my uncle *Toby*'s perplexities,—thou wilt drop a tear of pity upon his scarp and his counterscarp;—his glacis and his covered-way;—his ravelin and his half-moon: 'Twas not by ideas,——by heaven! his life was put in jeopardy by words.

CHAPTER III

WHEN my uncle *Toby* got his map of *Namur* to his mind, he began immediately to apply himself, and with the utmost diligence, to the study of it; for nothing being of more importance to him than his recovery, and his recovery depending, as you have read, upon the passions and affections of his mind, it behoved him to take the nicest care to make himself so far master of his subject, as to be able to talk upon it without emotion.

In a fortnight's close and painful application, which, by the bye, did my uncle *Toby*'s wound, upon his groin, no good,—he was enabled, by the help of some marginal documents at the feet of the elephant, together with *Gobesius*'s[1] military architecture and pyroballogy, translated from the *Flemish*, to form his discourse with passable perspicuity; and, before he was two full months gone,—he was right eloquent upon it, and could make not only the attack of the advanced counterscarp with great order;——but having, by that time, gone much deeper into the art, than what his first motive made necessary,—my uncle *Toby* was able to cross the *Maes* and *Sambre*; make diversions as far as *Vauban*'s line,[2] the abbey of *Salsines*, &c. and give his visiters as distinct a history of each of their attacks, as of that of the gate of *St. Nicolas*, where he had the honour to receive his wound.

But the desire of knowledge, like the thirst of riches, increases ever with the acquisition of it. The more my uncle *Toby* pored over his map, the more he took a liking to it;—by the same process and electrical assimulation, as I told you, thro' which I ween the souls of connoisseurs themselves, by long friction and incumbition, have the happiness, at length, to get all be-virtu'd,—be-pictur'd,—be-butterflied, and be-fiddled.

The more my uncle *Toby* drank of this sweet fountain of science, the greater was the heat and impatience of his thirst, so that, before the first year of his confinement had well gone round, there was scarce a fortified town in *Italy* or *Flanders*, of which, by one means or other, he had not procured a plan, reading over as he got them, and carefully collating therewith the histories of their sieges, their demolitions, their improvements and new works, all which he would read with that intense application and delight, that he would forget himself, his wound, his confinement, his dinner.

In the second year my uncle *Toby* purchased *Ramelli*[3] and *Cataneo*, translated from the *Italian*;——likewise *Stevinus, Marolis*, the Chevalier *de Ville, Lorini, Cochorn, Sheeter*, the Count de *Pagan*, the Marshal *Vauban*, Mons. *Blondel*, with almost as many more books of military architecture, as Don Quixote was found to have of chivalry, when the curate and barber invaded his library.[4]

Towards the beginning of the third year, which was in *August*, ninety-nine, my uncle *Toby* found it necessary to understand a little of projectiles:——And having judged it best to draw his knowledge from the fountain-head, he began with *N. Tartaglia*,[5] who it seems was the first man who detected the imposition of a cannon-ball's doing all that mischief under the notion of a right line.——This *N. Tartaglia* proved to my uncle *Toby* to be an impossible thing.

————Endless is the Search of Truth!

No sooner was my uncle *Toby* satisfied which road the cannon-ball did not go, but he was insensibly led on, and resolved in his mind to enquire and find out which road the ball did go: For which purpose he was obliged to set off afresh with old *Maltus*,[6] and studied him devoutly.——He proceeded next to *Gallileo*[7] and *Torricellius*,[8] wherein, by certain geometrical rules, infallibly laid down, he found the precise path to be a PARABOLA,——or else an HYPERBOLA,——and that the parameter, or *latus rectum*[9], of the conic section of the said path, was to the quantity and amplitude in a direct *ratio*, as the whole line to the sine of double the angle of incidence, form'd by the breech upon an horizontal plane;——and that the semi-parameter,————stop! my dear uncle *Toby*,——stop!——go not one foot further into this thorny and bewilder'd track,——intricate are the steps! intricate are the mases of this labyrinth! intricate are the troubles which the pursuit of this bewitching phantom, KNOWLEDGE, will bring upon thee.——O my uncle! fly--fly--fly from it as from a serpent.——Is it fit, good-natur'd man! thou should'st sit up, with the wound upon thy groin, whole nights baking thy blood with hectic watchings?——Alas! 'twill exasperate thy symptoms,—— check thy perspirations,——evaporate thy spirits,——waste thy animal strength,——dry up thy radical moister,[10]——bring thee into a costive habit of body, impair thy health,——and hasten all the infirmities of thy old age.——O my uncle! my uncle *Toby*.

CHAPTER IV

I WOULD not give a groat for that man's knowledge in pen-craft, who does not understand this,——That the best plain narrative in the world, tack'd very close to the last spirited apostrophe to my uncle *Toby*,—would have felt both cold and vapid upon the reader's palate;—therefore I forthwith put an end to the chapter,—though I was in the middle of my story.

——Writers of my stamp have one principle in common with painters.—Where an exact copying makes our pictures less striking, we choose the less evil; deeming it even more pardonable to trespass against truth, than beauty.—This is to be understood *cum grano salis*;[1] but be it as it will,——as the parallel is made more for the sake of letting the apostrophe cool, than any thing else,—'tis not very material whether upon any other score the reader approves of it or not.

In the latter end of the third year, my uncle *Toby* perceiving that the parameter and semi-parameter of the conic section, angered his wound, he left off the study of projectiles in a kind of a huff, and betook himself to the practical part of fortification only; the pleasure of which, like a spring held back, returned upon him with redoubled force.

It was in this year that my uncle began to break in upon the daily regularity of a clean shirt,——to dismiss his barber unshaven,——and to allow his surgeon scarce time sufficient to dress his wound, concerning himself so little about it, as not to ask him once in seven times dressing how it went on: When, lo!—all of a sudden, for the change was as quick as lightening, he began to sigh heavily for his recovery,—complain'd to my father, grew impatient with the surgeon;—and one morning as he heard his foot coming up stairs, he shut up his books, and thrust aside his instruments, in order to expostulate with him upon the protraction of his cure, which, he told him, might surely have been accomplished at least by that time:—He dwelt long upon the miseries he had undergone, and the sorrows of his four years melancholy imprisonment;—adding, that had it not been for the kind looks, and fraternal chearings of the best of brothers,—he had long since sunk under his misfortunes.—My father was by: My uncle *Toby*'s eloquence brought tears into his eyes;—'twas unexpected.—My uncle *Toby*, by nature, was not eloquent;——it had the greater effect.—The Surgeon was confounded;—not that there wanted grounds for such, or greater, marks of impatience,—but 'twas unexpected too; in the four years he had attended him, he had never seen any thing like it in my uncle *Toby*'s carriage;—he had never once dropp'd one fretful or discontented word;—he had been all patience,—all submission.

—We lose the right of complaining sometimes by forbearing it;——but we oftener treble the force:—The Surgeon was astonished;—but much more so, when he heard my uncle *Toby* go on, and peremptorily insist upon his healing up the wound directly,——or sending for Monsieur *Ronjat*,[2] the King's Serjeant-Surgeon, to do it for him.

The desire of life and health is implanted in man's nature;—the love of liberty and enlargement is a sister passion to it: These my uncle *Toby* had in common with his species;——and either of them had been sufficient to account for his earnest desire to get well and out of doors;—but I have told you before that nothing wrought with our family after the common way;—and from the time and manner in which this eager desire shew'd itself in the present case, the penetrating reader will suspect there was some other cause or crotchet for it in my uncle *Toby*'s head:—There was so, and 'tis the subject of the next chapter to set forth what that cause and crotchet was. I own, when that's done, 'twill be time to return back to the parlour fire-side, where we left my uncle *Toby* in the middle of his sentence.

CHAPTER V

WHEN a man gives himself up to the government of a ruling passion,——or, in other words, when his HOBBY-HORSE grows head-strong,——farewell cool reason and fair discretion!

My uncle *Toby*'s wound was near well, and as soon as the surgeon recovered his surprize, and could get leave to say as much—he told him, 'twas just beginning to incarnate;[1] and that if no fresh exfoliation happen'd, which there was no signs of,—it would be dried up in five or six weeks. The sound of as many olympiads twelve hours before, would have convey'd an idea of shorter duration to my uncle *Toby*'s mind.—The succession of his ideas was now rapid,—he broil'd with impatience to put his design in execution;—and so, without consulting further with any soul living,—which, by the bye, I think is right, when you are predetermined to take no one soul's advice,—he privately ordered *Trim*, his man, to pack up a bundle of lint and dressings, and hire a chariot and four to be at the door exactly by twelve o'clock that day, when he knew my father would be upon 'Change.[2]——So leaving a bank-note upon the table for the surgeon's care of him, and a letter of tender thanks for his brother's,——he pack'd up his maps, his books of fortification, his instruments, &c.—and, by the help of a crutch on one side, and *Trim* on the other,——my uncle *Toby* embark'd for *Shandy-Hall*.

The reason, or rather the rise, of this sudden demigration,[3] was as follows:

The table in my uncle *Toby*'s room, and at which, the night before this change happened, he was sitting with his maps, &c. about him,—being somewhat of the smallest, for that infinity of great and small instruments of knowledge which usually lay crouded upon it;—he had the accident, in reaching over for his tobacco-box, to throw down his compasses, and in stooping to take the compasses up, with his sleeve he threw down his case of instruments and snuffers;—and as the dice took a run against him, in his endeavouring to catch the snuffers in falling,—he thrust Monsieur *Blondel* off the table and Count de *Pagan* o' top of him.

'Twas to no purpose for a man, lame as my uncle *Toby* was, to think of redressing all these evils by himself,—he rung his bell for his man *Trim*;—*Trim!* quoth my uncle *Toby*, pri'thee see what confusion I have here been making.—I must have some better contrivance, *Trim*.—Can'st not thou take my rule and measure the length and breadth of this table, and then go and bespeak me one as big again?—Yes, an' please your Honour, replied *Trim*, making a bow;——but I hope your Honour will be soon well enough to get down to your country seat, where,—as your Honour takes so much pleasure in fortification, we could manage this matter to a T.

I must here inform you, that this servant of my uncle *Toby*'s, who went by the name of *Trim*, had been a Corporal in my uncle's own company,——his real name was *James Butler*, ——but having got the nick-name of *Trim* in the regiment, my uncle *Toby*, unless when he happened to be very angry with him, would never call him by any other name.

The poor fellow had been disabled for the service, by a wound on his left knee by a musket-bullet, at the battle of *Landen*,[4] which was two years before the affair of *Namur*;— and as the fellow was well beloved in the regiment, and a handy fellow into the bargain, my uncle *Toby* took him for his servant, and of excellent use was he, attending my uncle *Toby* in the camp and in his quarters as valet, groom, barber, cook, semp-ster, and nurse; and indeed, from first to last, waited upon him and served him with great fidelity and affection.

My uncle *Toby* loved the man in return, and what attached him more to him still, was the similitude of their knowledge:— For Corporal *Trim*, (for so, for the future, I shall call him) by four years occasional attention to his Master's discourse upon fortified towns, and the advantage of prying and peeping conti-nually into his Master's plans, &c. exclusive and besides what he gained HOBBY-HORSICALLY, as a body-servant, *Non Hobby-Horsical per se*;——had become no mean proficient in the science; and was thought, by the cook and chamber-maid, to know as much of the nature of strong-holds as my uncle *Toby* himself.

I have but one more stroke to give to finish Corporal *Trim*'s character,--and it is the only dark line in it.—The fellow lov'd to advise,—or rather to hear himself talk; his carriage, however, was so perfectly respectful, 'twas easy to keep him silent when you had him so; but set his tongue a-going,—you had no hold of him;—he was voluble;--the eternal interlardings of *your Hon-our*, with the respectfulness of Corporal *Trim*'s manner, inter-ceeding so strong in behalf of his elocution,—that tho' you might have been incommoded,—you could not well be angry. My uncle *Toby* was seldom either the one or the other with him,—or, at least, this fault, in *Trim*, broke no squares with 'em.[5] My uncle *Toby*, as I said, loved the man;—and besides, as he ever looked upon a faithful servant,——but as a humble friend,—he could not bear to stop his mouth.——Such was Corporal *Trim*.[6]

If I durst presume, continued *Trim*, to give your Honour my advice, and speak my opinion in this matter.—Thou art wel-come, *Trim*, quoth my uncle *Toby*,—speak,—speak what thou thinkest upon the subject, man, without fear. Why then, replied *Trim*, (not hanging his ears and scratching his head like a country lout, but) stroking his hair back from his forehead, and standing erect as before his division.——I think, quoth *Trim*,

advancing his left, which was his lame leg, a little forwards,—
and pointing with his right hand open towards a map of *Dun-kirk*, which was pinn'd against the hangings,—I think, quoth
Corporal *Trim*, with humble submission to your Honour's
better judgement,—that these ravelins, bastions, curtins, and
hornworks make but a poor, contemptible, fiddle faddle piece
of work of it here upon paper, compared to what your Honour
and I could make of it, were we in the country by ourselves, and
had but a rood, or a rood and a half of ground to do what we
pleased with: As summer is coming on, continued *Trim*, your
Honour might sit out of doors, and give me the nography
——(call it ichnography, quoth my uncle)—of the town or
citadel, your Honour was pleased to sit down before,—and I
will be shot by your Honour upon the glacis of it, if I did not
fortify it to your Honour's mind.—I dare say thou would'st
Trim, quoth my uncle.—For if your Honour, continued the
Corporal, could but mark me the polygon, with its exact lines
and angles,——that I could do very well, quoth my uncle.—I
would begin with the fossé,[7] and if your Honour could tell me
the proper depth and breadth,—I can to a hair's breadth, *Trim*,
replied my uncle,—I would throw out the earth upon this hand
towards the town for the scarp,—and on that hand towards the
campaign[8] for the counterscarp,—very right, *Trim*, quoth my
uncle *Toby*,—and when I had sloped them to your mind,—an'
please your Honour, I would face the glacis, as the finest
fortifications are done in *Flanders*, with sods,—and as your
Honour knows they should be,——and I would make the walls
and parapets with sods too;—the best engineers call them
gazons, *Trim*, said my uncle *Toby*;—whether they are gazons or
sods, is not much matter, replied *Trim*, your Honour knows
they are ten times beyond a facing either of brick or stone;——I
know they are, *Trim*, in some respects,—quoth my uncle *Toby*,
nodding his head;—for a cannon-ball enters into the gazon right
onwards, without bringing any rubbish down with it, which
might fill the fossé, (as was the case at *St. Nicolas*'s *Gate*) and
facilitate the passage over it.

Your Honour understands these matters, replied Corporal
Trim, better than any officer in his Majesty's service;——but
would your Honour please to let the bespeaking of the table
alone, and let us but go into the country, I would work under
your Honour's directions like a horse, and make fortifications
for you something like a tansy,[9] with all their batteries, saps,

ditches, and pallisadoes, that it should be worth all the world's riding twenty miles to go and see it.

My uncle *Toby* blushed as red as scarlet as *Trim* went on;— but it was not a blush of guilt,—of modesty,—or of anger;— it was a blush of joy;—he was fired with Corporal *Trim's* project and description.—*Trim!* said my uncle *Toby*, thou hast said enough.—We might begin the campaign, continued *Trim*, on the very day that his Majesty and the Allies take the field, and demolish 'em town by town as fast as——*Trim*, quoth my uncle *Toby*, say no more.—Your Honour, continued *Trim*, might sit in your arm-chair, (pointing to it) this fine weather, giving me your orders, and I would——Say no more, *Trim*, quoth my uncle *Toby*.——Besides, your Honour would get not only pleasure and good pastime,—but good air, and good exercise, and good health,—and your Honour's wound would be well in a month. Thou hast said enough, *Trim*,—quoth my uncle *Toby*, (putting his hand into his breeches-pocket)—I like thy project mightily;—and if your Honour pleases, I'll, this moment, go and buy a pioneer's spade to take down with us, and I'll bespeak a shovel and a pick-ax, and a couple of——Say no more, *Trim*, quoth my uncle *Toby*, leaping up upon one leg, quite overcome with rapture,——and thrusting a guinea into *Trim's* hand.—— *Trim*, said my uncle *Toby*, say no more;--but go down, *Trim*, this moment, my lad, and bring up my supper this instant.

Trim ran down and brought up his Master's supper,—to no purpose:——*Trim's* plan of operation ran so in my uncle *Toby's* head, he could not taste it.—*Trim*, quoth my uncle *Toby*, get me to bed;—'twas all one.—Corporal *Trim's* description had fired his imagination,—my uncle *Toby* could not shut his eyes.--The more he consider'd it, the more bewitching the scene appeared to him;—so that, two full hours before day-light, he had come to a final determination, and had concerted the whole plan of his and Corporal *Trim's* decampment.

My uncle *Toby* had a little neat country-house of his own, in the village where my father's estate lay at *Shandy*, which had been left him by an old uncle, with a small estate of about one hundred pounds a-year. Behind this house, and contiguous to it, was a kitchen-garden of about half an acre;—and at the bottom of the garden, and cut off from it by a tall yew hedge, was a bowling-green, containing just about as much ground as Corporal *Trim* wished for;—so that as *Trim* uttered the words,

"A rood and a half of ground to do what they would with:"
——This identical bowling-green instantly presented itself, and
became curiously painted, all at once, upon the retina of my
uncle *Toby*'s fancy;——which was the physical cause of making
him change colour, or at least, of heightening his blush to that
immoderate degree I spoke of.

Never did lover post down to a belov'd mistress with more
heat and expectation, than my uncle *Toby* did, to enjoy this
self-same thing in private;—I say in private;—for it was sheltered from the house, as I told you, by a tall yew hedge, and was
covered on the other three sides, from mortal sight, by rough
holly and thickset flowering shrubs;—so that the idea of not
being seen, did not a little contribute to the idea of pleasure
preconceived in my uncle *Toby*'s mind.—Vain thought!
however thick it was planted about,——or private soever it
might seem,—to think, dear uncle *Toby*, of enjoying a thing
which took up a whole rood and a half of ground,—and not
have it known!

How my uncle *Toby* and Corporal *Trim* managed this matter,—with the history of their campaigns, which were no way
barren of events,—may make no uninteresting under-plot in the
epitasis[10] and working up of this drama.—At present the scene
must drop,—and change for the parlour fire-side.

CHAPTER VI

——What can they be doing, brother? said my father.—I
think, replied my uncle *Toby*,—taking, as I told you, his pipe
from his mouth, and striking the ashes out of it as he began his
sentence;----I think, replied he,—it would not be amiss,
brother, if we rung the bell.

Pray, what's all that racket over our heads, *Obadiah?*—quoth
my father;—my brother and I can scarce hear ourselves
speak.

Sir, answer'd *Obadiah*, making a bow towards his left shoulder,—my Mistress is taken very badly;—and where's *Susannah*
running down the garden there, as if they were going to ravish
her.——Sir, she is running the shortest cut into the town,
replied *Obadiah*, to fetch the old midwife.——Then saddle a
horse, quoth my father, and do you go directly for Dr. *Slop*, the
man-midwife, with all our services,—and let him know your

Mistress is fallen into labour,—and that I desire he will return with you with all speed.

It is very strange, says my father, addressing himself to my uncle *Toby*, as *Obadiah* shut the door,—as there is so expert an operator as Dr. *Slop* so near---that my wife should persist to the very last in this obstinate humour of hers, in trusting the life of my child, who has had one misfortune already, to the ignorance of an old woman;——and not only the life of my child, brother,—but her own life, and with it the lives of all the children I might, peradventure, have begot out of her hereafter.

Mayhap, brother, replied my uncle *Toby*, my sister does it to save the expence:—A pudding's end,—replied my father,—the Doctor must be paid the same for inaction as action,—if not better,—to keep him in temper.

—Then it can be out of nothing in the whole world, quoth my uncle *Toby*, in the simplicity of his heart,—but MODESTY: —My sister, I dare say, added he, does not care to let a man come so near her * * * *. I will not say whether my uncle *Toby* had compleated the sentence or not;—'tis for his advantage to suppose he had,—as, I think, he could have added no ONE WORD which would have improved it.

If, on the contrary, my uncle *Toby* had not fully arrived at his period's end,—then the world stands indebted to the sudden snapping of my father's tobacco-pipe, for one of the neatest examples of that ornamental figure in oratory, which Rhetoricians stile the *Aposiopesis*.[1]—Just heaven! how does the *Poco piu* and the *Poco meno*[2] of the *Italian* artists;—the insensible, more or less, determine the precise line of beauty in the sentence,[3] as well as in the statue! How do the slight touches of the chisel, the pencil, the pen, the fiddle-stick, *et cætera*,—give the true swell, which gives the true pleasure!—O my countrymen!—be nice;—be cautious of your language;——and never, O! never let it be forgotten upon what small particles your eloquence and your fame depend.

——"My sister, mayhap, quoth my uncle *Toby*, does not choose to let a man come so near her ****" Make this dash, ——'tis an Aposiopesis.—Take the dash away, and write Backside,—'tis Bawdy.—Scratch Backside out, and put *Cover'd-way* in,—'tis a Metaphor;—and, I dare say, as fortification ran so much in my uncle *Toby*'s head, that if he had been left to have added one word to the sentence,—that word was it.

But whether that was the case or not the case;—or whether the snapping of my father's tobacco-pipe so critically, happened thro' accident or anger,—will be seen in due time.

CHAPTER VII

Tho' my father was a good natural philosopher,——yet he was something of a moral philosopher too; for which reason, when his tobacco-pipe snapp'd short in the middle,——he had nothing to do,—as such,—but to have taken hold of the two pieces, and thrown them gently upon the back of the fire.—He did no such thing;—he threw them with all the violence in the world;—and, to give the action still more emphasis,--he started up upon both his legs to do it.

This look'd something like heat;—and the manner of his reply to what my uncle *Toby* was saying prov'd it was so.

—"Not choose, quoth my father, (repeating my uncle *Toby*'s words) to let a man come so near her——" By heaven, brother *Toby*! you would try the patience of a *Job*;—and I think I have the plagues of one already, without it.—— Why?—— Where?——Wherein?——Wherefore?—Upon what account, replied my uncle *Toby*, in the utmost astonishment.——To think, said my father, of a man living to your age, brother, and knowing so little about women!—I know nothing at all about them,—replied my uncle *Toby*; and I think, continued he, that the shock I received the year after the demolition of *Dunkirk*,[1] in my affair with widow *Wadman*;—which shock you know I should not have received, but from my total ignorance of the sex,---has given me just cause to say, That I neither know, nor do pretend to know, any thing about 'em, or their concerns either.——Methinks, brother, replied my father, you might, at least, know so much as the right end of a woman from the wrong.

It is said in *Aristotle's Master-Piece*,[2] "That when a man doth think of any thing which is past,---he looketh down upon the ground;---but that when he thinketh of something which is to come, he looketh up towards the heavens."

My uncle *Toby*, I suppose, thought of neither,---for he look'd horizontally.----Right end,---quoth my uncle *Toby*, muttering the two words low to himself, and fixing his two eyes insensibly as he muttered them, upon a small crevice, form'd by a bad joint in the chimney-piece.—Right end of a woman!——I declare, quoth my uncle, I know no more which it is, than the man in the moon;--and if I was to think, continued my uncle *Toby*, (keeping his eye still fix'd upon the bad joint) this month together, I am sure I should not be able to find it out.

Then brother *Toby*, replied my father, I will tell you.

Every thing in this world, continued my father, (filling a fresh pipe)----every thing in this earthly world, my dear brother *Toby*, has two handles;--not always, quoth my uncle *Toby*;---at least, replied my father, every one has two hands,----which comes to the same thing.----Now, if a man was to sit down coolly, and consider within himself the make, the shape, the construction, com-at-ability, and convenience of all the parts which constitute the whole of that animal, call'd Woman, and compare them analogically—I never understood rightly the meaning of that word,---quoth my uncle *Toby*.——ANALOGY, replied my father, is the certain relation and agreement, which different—Here a Devil of a rap at the door snapp'd my father's definition (like his tobacco-pipe) in two,---and, at the same time, crushed the head of as notable and curious a dissertation as ever was engendered in the womb of speculation;—it was some months before my father could get an opportunity to be safely deliver'd of it:—And, at this hour, it is a thing full as problematical as the subject of the dissertation itself,--(considering the confusion and distresses of our domestick misadventures, which are now coming thick one upon the back of another) whether I shall be able to find a place for it in the third volume or not.

CHAPTER VIII

IT is about an hour and a half's tolerable good reading since my uncle *Toby* rung the bell,[1] when *Obadiah* was order'd to saddle a horse, and go for Dr. *Slop*, the man-midwife;---so that no one can say, with reason, that I have not allowed *Obadiah* time enough, poetically speaking, and considering the emergency too, both to go and come;----tho', morally and truly speaking, the man, perhaps, has scarce had time to get on his boots.

If the hypercritick will go upon this; and is resolved after all to take a pendulum, and measure the true distance betwixt the ringing of the bell and the rap at the door;—and, after finding it to be no more than two minutes, thirteen seconds, and three fifths,----should take upon him to insult over me for such a breach in the unity, or rather probability, of time;—I would remind him, that the idea of duration and of its simple modes,[2] is got merely from the train and succession of our ideas,---and is the true scholastick pendulum,----and by which, as a scholar, I will be tried in this matter,----abjuring and detesting the jurisdiction of all other pendulums whatever.

I would, therefore, desire him to consider that it is but poor eight miles from *Shandy-Hall* to Dr. *Slop*, the man-midwife's house;—and that whilst *Obadiah* has been going those said miles and back, I have brought my uncle *Toby* from *Namur*, quite across all *Flanders*, into *England:*---That I have had him ill upon my hands near four years;---and have since travelled him and Corporal *Trim*, in a chariot and four, a journey of near two hundred miles down into *Yorkshire*;—all which put together, must have prepared the reader's imagination for the enterance of Dr. *Slop* upon the stage,——as much, at least, (I hope) as a dance, a song, or a concerto between the acts.

If my hypercritick is intractable,—alledging, that two minutes and thirteen seconds are no more than two minutes and thirteen seconds,---when I have said all I can about them;——and that this plea, tho' it might save me dramatically, will damn me biographically, rendering my book, from this very moment, a profess'd ROMANCE, which, before, was a book apocryphal:——If I am thus pressed—I then put an end to the whole objection and controversy about it all at once,---by acquainting him, that *Obadiah* had not got above threescore yards from the stable-yard before he met with Dr. *Slop*;—and indeed he gave a dirty proof that he had met with him,-----and was within an ace of giving a tragical one too.

Imagine to yourself;——but this had better begin a new chapter.

CHAPTER IX

IMAGINE to yourself a little, squat, uncourtly figure of a Doctor *Slop*,[1] of about four feet and a half perpendicular height, with a breadth of back, and a sesquipedality[2] of belly, which might have done honour to a Serjeant in the Horse-Guards.

Such were the out-lines of Dr. *Slop*'s figure, which,—if you have read *Hogarth*'s analysis of beauty,[3] and if you have not, I wish you would;—you must know, may as certainly be caracatur'd, and convey'd to the mind by three strokes as three hundred.

Imagine such a one,—for such, I say, were the out-lines of Dr. *Slop*'s figure, coming slowly along, foot by foot, waddling thro' the dirt upon the vertebræ of a little diminutive pony,—of a pretty colour;---but of strength,---alack!——scarce able to have made an amble of it, under such a fardel, had the roads been in an ambling condition.----They were not.——Imagine to yourself, *Obadiah* mounted upon a strong monster of a coach-horse, prick'd into a full gallop, and making all practicable speed the adverse way.

Pray, Sir, let me interest you a moment in this description.

Had Dr. *Slop* beheld *Obadiah* a mile off, posting in a narrow lane directly towards him, at that monstrous rate,—splashing and plunging like a devil thro' thick and thin, as he approach'd, would not such a phænomenon, with such a vortex of mud and water moving along with it, round its axis,—have been a subject of juster apprehension to Dr. *Slop* in his situation, than the *worst* of *Whiston*'s comets?[4]—To say nothing of the NUCLEUS; that is, of *Obadiah* and the coach-horse.—In my idea, the vortex alone of 'em was enough to have involved and carried, if not the Doctor, at least the Doctor's pony quite away with it. What then do you think must the terror and hydrophobia of Dr. *Slop* have been, when you read, (which you are just going to do) that he was advancing thus warily along towards *Shandy-Hall*, and had approach'd to within sixty yards of it, and within five yards of a sudden turn, made by an acute angle of the garden wall,—and in the dirtiest part of a dirty lane,—when *Obadiah* and his coach-horse turn'd the corner, rapid, furious,---pop,--- full upon him!-----Nothing, I think, in nature, can be supposed more terrible, than such a Rencounter,--so imprompt! so ill prepared to stand the shock of it as Dr. *Slop* was!

What could Dr. *Slop* do?---He cross'd himself †——Pugh! ----but the Doctor, Sir, was a Papist.——No matter; he had better have kept hold of the pummel.—He had so;—nay, as it happen'd, he had better have done nothing at all;---for in crossing himself he let go his whip,——and in attempting to save his whip betwixt his knee and his saddle's skirt, as it slipp'd, he lost his stirrup,—in losing which, he lost his seat;——and in the multitude of all these losses, (which, by the bye, shews what little advantage there is in crossing) the unfortunate Doctor lost his presence of mind. So that, without waiting for *Obadiah*'s onset, he left his pony to its destiny, tumbling off it diagonally, something in the stile and manner of a pack of wool, and without any other consequence from the fall, save that of being left, (as it would have been) with the broadest part of him sunk about twelve inches deep in the mire.

Obadiah pull'd off his cap twice to Dr. *Slop*;——once as he was falling,----and then again when he saw him seated.---Ill timed complaisance!——had not the fellow better have stopp'd his horse, and got off and help'd him?——Sir, he did all that his situation would allow;---but the MOMENTUM of the coach-horse was so great, that *Obadiah* could not do it all at once;——he rode in a circle three times round Dr. *Slop*, before he could fully accomplish it any how;---and at the last, when he did stop his beast, 'twas done with such an explosion of mud, that *Obadiah* had better have been a league off. In short, never was a Dr. *Slop* so beluted,[5] and so transubtantiated, since that affair came into fashion.

CHAPTER X

WHEN Dr. *Slop* entered the back parlour, where my father and my uncle *Toby* were discoursing upon the nature of women,——it was hard to determine whether Dr. *Slop*'s figure, or Dr. *Slop*'s presence, occasioned more surprize to them; for as the accident happened so near the house, as not to make it worth while for *Obadiah* to remount him,----*Obadiah* had led him in as he was, *unwiped, unappointed, unanealed,*[1] with all his stains and blotches on him.——He stood like *Hamlet*'s ghost, motionless and speechless, for a full minute and a half, at the parlour door, (*Obadiah* still holding his hand) with all the majesty of mud.[2] His hinder parts, upon which he had received his fall, totally besmear'd,----and in every other part of him, blotched over in such a manner with *Obadiah*'s explosion, that you would have sworn, (without mental reservation)[3] that every grain of it had taken effect.

Here was a fair opportunity for my uncle *Toby* to have triumph'd over my father in his turn;---for no mortal, who had beheld Dr. *Slop* in that pickle, could have dissented from so much, at least, of my uncle *Toby*'s opinion, "That mayhap his sister might not care to let such a Dr. *Slop* come so near her ****" But it was the *Argumentum ad hominem*; and if my uncle *Toby* was not very expert at it, you may think, he might not care to use it.—No; the reason was,—'twas not his nature to insult.

Dr. *Slop*'s presence, at that time, was no less problematical than the mode of it; tho', it is certain, one moment's reflection in my father might have solved it; for he had apprized Dr. *Slop* but the week before, that my mother was at her full reckoning; and as the Doctor had heard nothing since, 'twas natural and very political too in him, to have taken a ride to *Shandy-Hall*, as he did, merely to see how matters went on.

But my father's mind took unfortunately a wrong turn in the investigation; running, like the hypercritick's, altogether upon the ringing of the bell and the rap upon the door,--measuring their distance,—and keeping his mind so intent upon the operation, as to have power to think of nothing else,---commonplace infirmity of the greatest mathematicians! working with might and main at the demonstration, and so wasting all their strength upon it, that they have none left in them to draw the corollary, to do good with.

The ringing of the bell and the rap upon the door, struck likewise strong upon the sensorium of my uncle *Toby*,—but it excited a very different train of thoughts;—the two irreconcileable pulsations instantly brought *Stevinus*, the great engineer, along with them, into my uncle *Toby*'s mind:——What business *Stevinus* had in this affair,—is the greatest problem of all;—it shall be solved,—but not in the next chapter.

CHAPTER XI

WRITING, when properly managed, (as you may be sure I think mine is) is but a different name for conversation: As no one, who knows what he is about in good company, would venture to talk all;—so no author, who understands the just boundaries of decorum and good breeding, would presume to think all: The truest respect which you can pay to the reader's understanding, is to halve this matter amicably, and leave him something to imagine, in his turn, as well as yourself.

For my own part, I am eternally paying him compliments of

this kind, and do all that lies in my power to keep his imagination as busy as my own.

'Tis his turn now;—I have given an ample description of Dr. *Slop*'s sad overthrow, and of his sad appearance in the back parlour;—his imagination must now go on with it for a while.

Let the reader imagine then, that Dr. *Slop* has told his tale;——and in what words, and with what aggravations his fancy chooses:——Let him suppose that *Obadiah* has told his tale also, and with such rueful looks of affected concern, as he thinks will best contrast the two figures as they stand by each other: Let him imagine that my father has stepp'd up stairs to see my mother:—And, to conclude this work of imagination,—let him imagine the Doctor wash'd,——rubb'd down,—condoled with,—felicitated,—got into a pair of *Obadiah*'s pumps, stepping forwards towards the door, upon the very point of entering upon action.

Truce!—truce, good Dr. *Slop*!—stay thy obstetrick hand;—return it safe into thy bosom to keep it warm;—little do'st thou know what obstacles;—little do'st thou think what hidden causes retard its operation!—Hast thou, Dr. *Slop*,—hast thou been intrusted with the secret articles of this solemn treaty which has brought thee into this place?—Art thou aware that, at this instant, a daughter of *Lucina*[1] is put obstetrically over thy head? Alas! 'tis too true.—Besides, great son of *Pilumnus!*[2] what can'st thou do?—Thou has come forth unarm'd;—thou hast left thy *tire-tête*,[3]—thy new-invented *forceps*,—thy *crotchet*,—thy *squirt*, and all thy instruments of salvation and deliverance behind thee.——By heaven! at this moment they are hanging up in a green bays bag, betwixt thy two pistols, at thy bed's head!—Ring;—call;—send *Obadiah* back upon the coach-horse to bring them with all speed.

—Make great haste, *Obadiah*, quoth my father, and I'll give thee a crown;—and, quoth my uncle *Toby*, I'll give him another.

CHAPTER XII

YOUR sudden and unexpected arrival, quoth my uncle *Toby*, addressing himself to Dr. *Slop*, (all three of them sitting down to the fire together, as my uncle *Toby* began to speak)----instantly brought the great *Stevinus* into my head, who, you must know, is a favourite author with me.————Then, added my father, making use of the argument *Ad Crumenam*,---I will lay twenty guineas to a single crown piece, (which will serve to give away to *Obadiah* when he gets back) that this same *Stevinus* was some engineer or other,----or has wrote something or other, either directly or indirectly, upon the science of fortification.

He has so,—replied my uncle *Toby*.—I knew it, said my father;—tho', for the soul of me, I cannot see what kind of connection there can be betwixt Dr. *Slop*'s sudden coming, and a discourse upon fortification;—yet I fear'd it.—Talk of what we will, brother,—or let the occasion be never so foreign or unfit for the subject,---you are sure to bring it in: I would not, brother *Toby*, continued my father,---I declare I would not have my head so full of curtins and horn-works.—That, I dare say, you would not, quoth Dr. *Slop*, interrupting him, and laughing most immoderately at his pun.

Dennis[1] the critick could not detest and abhor a pun, or the insinuation of a pun, more cordially than my father;———he would grow testy upon it at any time;--but to be broke in upon by one, in a serious discourse, was as bad, he would say, as a fillip upon the nose;—he saw no difference.

Sir, quoth my uncle *Toby*, addressing himself to Dr. *Slop*, ———the curtins my brother *Shandy* mentions here, have nothing to do with bed-steads;—tho', I know, *Du Cange*[2] says, "That bed-curtains, in all probability, have taken their name from them;"---nor have the horn-works, he speaks of, any thing in the world to do with the horn-works of cuckoldom:— But the *curtin*, Sir, is the word we use in fortification, for that part of the wall or rampart which lies between the two bastions and joins them.----Besiegers seldom offer to carry on their attacks directly against the curtin, for this reason, because they are so well *flanked*; ('tis the case of other curtins, quoth Dr. *Slop*, laughing) however, continued my uncle *Toby*, to make them sure, we generally choose to place ravelins before them, taking care only to extend them beyond the fossé or ditch:— The common men, who know very little of fortification, confound the ravelin and the half-moon together,---tho' they are very different things;---not in their figure or construction, for we make them exactly alike in all points;---for they always consist of two faces, making a salient angle, with the gorges, not straight, but in form of a crescent.—Where then lies the difference? (quoth my father, a little testily)--In their situations, answered my uncle *Toby*:--For when a ravelin, brother, stands before the curtin, it is a ravelin; and when a ravelin stands before a bastion, then the ravelin is not a ravelin;--it is a half-moon;—a half-moon likewise is a half-moon, and no more, so long as it stands before its bastion;—but was it to change place, and get before the curtin,—'twould be no longer a half-moon; a half-moon, in that case, is not a half-moon;—'tis no more than a ravelin.—I think, quoth my father, that the noble science of defence has its weak sides,----as well as others.

—As for the horn-works (high! ho! sigh'd my father) which, continued my uncle *Toby*, my brother was speaking of, they are a very considerable part of an outwork;---they are called by the *French* engineers, *Ouvrage á corne*, and we generally make them to cover such places as we suspect to be weaker than the rest;--'tis form'd by two epaulments[3] or demi-bastions,—they are very pretty, and if you will take a walk, I'll engage to shew you one well worth your trouble.——I own, continued my uncle *Toby*, when we crown them,—they are much stronger, but then they are very expensive, and take up a great deal of ground; so that, in my opinion, they are most of use to cover or defend the head of a camp; otherwise the double tenaille[4] ——By the mother who bore us!——brother *Toby*, quoth my father, not able to hold out any longer,—you would provoke a saint;—here have you got us, I know not how, not only souse into the middle of the old subject again:—But so full is your head of these confounded works, that tho' my wife is this moment in the pains of labour,—and you hear her cry out,—yet nothing will serve you but to carry off the man-midwife.—— *Accoucheur*,[5]—if you please, quoth Dr. *Slop*.---With all my heart, replied my father, I don't care what they call you,——but I wish the whole science of fortification, with all its inventors, at the Devil;—it has been the death of thousands,——and it will be mine, in the end.--I would not, I would not, brother *Toby*, have my brains so full of saps, mines, blinds,[6] gabions,[7] palisadoes, ravelins, half-moons, and such trumpery, to be proprietor of *Namur*, and of all the towns in *Flanders* with it.

My uncle *Toby* was a man patient of injuries;—not from want of courage,—I have told you in the fifth chapter of this second book, "That he was a man of courage:"——And will add here, that where just occasions presented, or called it forth,---I know no man under whose arm I would sooner have taken shelter; nor did this arise from any insensibility or obtuseness of his intellectual parts;--for he felt this insult of my father's as feelingly as a man could do;----but he was of a peaceful, placid nature,—no jarring element in it,—all was mix'd up so kindly within him; my uncle *Toby* had scarce a heart to retalliate upon a fly.

—Go,---says he, one day at dinner, to an over-grown one which had buzz'd about his nose, and tormented him cruelly all dinner-time,—and which, after infinite attempts, he had caught at last, as it flew by him;---I'll not hurt thee, says my uncle *Toby*, rising from his chair, and going a-cross the room, with the fly in his hand,---I'll not hurt a hair of thy head:---Go, says he, lifting up the sash, and opening his hand as he spoke, to let it escape;—go poor Devil, get thee gone, why should I hurt thee?----This world surely is wide enough to hold both thee and me.

I was but ten years old when this happened;—but whether it was, that the action itself was more in unison to my nerves at that age of pity, which instantly set my whole frame into one vibration of most pleasurable sensation;—or how far the manner and expression of it might go towards it;—or in what degree, or by what secret magick,—a tone of voice and harmony of movement, attuned by mercy, might find a passage to my heart, I know not;—this I know, that the lesson of universal good-will then taught and imprinted by my uncle *Toby*, has never since been worn out of my mind: And tho' I would not depreciate what the study of the *Literæ humaniores*, at the university, have done for me in that respect, or discredit the other helps of an expensive education bestowed upon me, both at home and abroad since;—yet I often think that I owe one half of my philanthropy to that one accidental impression.

☞ This is to serve for parents and governors instead of a whole volume upon the subject.

I could not give the reader this stroke in my uncle *Toby*'s picture, by the instrument with which I drew the other parts of it,—that taking in no more than the mere HOBBY-HORSICAL likeness;—this is a part of his moral character. My father, in this patient endurance of wrongs, which I mention, was very different, as the reader must long ago have noted; he had a much more acute and quick sensibility of nature, attended with a little soreness of temper; tho' this never transported him to any thing which looked like malignancy;—yet, in the little rubs and vexations of life, 'twas apt to shew itself in a drollish and witty kind of peevishness:—He was, however, frank and generous in his nature,——at all times open to conviction; and in the little ebullitions of this subacid humour towards others, but particularly towards my uncle *Toby*, whom he truly loved;—he would feel more pain, ten times told, (except in the affair of my aunt *Dinah*, or where an hypothesis was concerned) than what he ever gave.

The characters of the two brothers, in this view of them, reflected light upon each other, and appear'd with great advantage in this affair which arose about *Stevinus*.

I need not tell the reader, if he keeps a HOBBY-HORSE,--that a man's HOBBY-HORSE is as tender a part as he has about him; and that these unprovoked strokes, at my uncle *Toby*'s could not be unfelt by him.—No;—as I said above, my uncle *Toby* did feel them, and very sensibly too.

Pray, Sir, what said he?—How did he behave?—Oh, Sir!—it was great: For as soon as my father had done insulting his HOBBY-HORSE,—he turned his head, without the least emotion, from Dr. *Slop*, to whom he was addressing his discourse, and look'd up into my father's face, with a countenance spread over with so much good nature;—so placid;—so fraternal;—so inexpressibly tender towards him;—it penetrated my father to his heart: He rose up hastily from his chair, and seizing hold of both my uncle *Toby*'s hands as he spoke:—Brother *Toby*, said he,—I beg thy pardon;—forgive, I pray thee, this rash humour which my mother gave me.⁸—My dear, dear brother, answer'd my uncle *Toby*, rising up by my father's help, say no more about it;—you are heartily welcome, had it been ten times as much, brother. But 'tis ungenerous, replied my father, to hurt any man;—a brother worse;—but to hurt a brother of such gentle manners,—so unprovoking,—and so unresenting;—'tis base:—By heaven, 'tis cowardly.——You are heartily welcome, brother, quoth my uncle *Toby*,—had it been fifty times as much.——Besides, what have I to do, my dear *Toby*, cried my father, either with your amusements or your pleasures, unless it was in my power (which it is not) to increase their measure?

—Brother *Shandy*, answer'd my uncle *Toby*, looking wistfully in his face,—you are much mistaken in this point;—for you do increase my pleasure very much, in begetting children for the *Shandy* Family at your time of life.——But, by that, Sir, quoth Dr. *Slop*, Mr. *Shandy* increases his own.——Not a jot, quoth my father.

CHAPTER XIII

My brother does it, quoth my uncle *Toby*, out of *principle*.—
In a family-way, I suppose, quoth Dr. *Slop*.—Pshaw!—said my
father,—'tis not worth talking of.

CHAPTER XIV

At the end of the last chapter, my father and my uncle *Toby*
were left both standing, like *Brutus* and *Cassius* at the close of
the scene [1] making up their accounts.

As my father spoke the three last words,—he sat down;—my
uncle *Toby* exactly followed his example, only, that before he
took his chair, he rung the bell, to order Corporal *Trim*, who
was in waiting, to step home for *Stevinus*;---my uncle *Toby*'s
house being no further off than the opposite side of the way.

Some men would have dropp'd the subject of *Stevinus*;—but
my uncle *Toby* had no resentment in his heart, and he went on
with the subject, to shew my father that he had none.

Your sudden appearance, Dr. *Slop*, quoth my uncle, resuming the discourse, instantly brought *Stevinus* into my head. (My
father, you may be sure, did not offer to lay any more wagers
upon *Stevinus*'s head)——Because, continued my uncle *Toby*,
the celebrated sailing chariot,[2] which belonged to Prince
Maurice,[3] and was of such wonderful contrivance and velocity,
as to carry half a dozen people thirty *German* miles, in I don't
know how few minutes,—was invented by *Stevinus*, that great
mathematician and engineer.

You might have spared your servant the trouble, quoth Dr.
Slop, (as the fellow is lame) of going for *Stevinus*'s account of it,
because, in my return from *Leyden* thro' the *Hague*, I walked as
far as *Schevling*, which is two long miles, on purpose to take a
view of it.

—That's nothing, replied my uncle *Toby*, to what the learned
Peireskius[4] did, who walked a matter of five hundred miles,
reckoning from *Paris* to *Schevling*, and from *Schevling* to *Paris*
back again, in order to see it,—and nothing else.

Some men cannot bear to be out-gone.

The more fool *Peireskius*, replied Dr. *Slop*. But mark,--'twas
out of no contempt of *Peireskius* at all;—but that *Peireskius*'s

indefatigable labour in trudging so far on foot out of love for the sciences, reduced the exploit of Dr. *Slop*, in that affair, to nothing;—the more fool *Peireskius*, said he again:—Why so?— replied my father, taking his brother's part, not only to make reparation as fast as he could for the insult he had given him, which sat still upon my father's mind;—but partly, that my father began really to interest himself in the discourse;——Why so?—said he. Why is *Peireskius*, or any man else, to be abused for an appetite for that, or any other morsel of sound knowledge? For, notwithstanding I know nothing of the chariot in question, continued he, the inventor of it must have had a very mechanical head; and tho' I cannot guess upon what principles of philosophy he has atchiev'd it;—yet certainly his machine has been constructed upon solid ones, be they what they will, or it could not have answer'd at the rate my brother mentions.

It answered, replied my uncle *Toby*, as well, if not better; for, as *Peireskius* elegantly expresses it, speaking of the velocity of its motion, *Tam citus erat, quam erat ventus*; which, unless I have forgot my Latin, is, that it was as swift as the wind itself.

But pray, Dr. *Slop*, quoth my father, interrupting my uncle, (tho' not without begging pardon for it, at the same time) upon what principles was this self-same chariot set a-going?----Upon very pretty principles to be sure, replied Dr. *Slop*;—and I have often wondered, continued he, evading the question, why none of our Gentry, who live upon large plains like this of ours,--- (especially they whose wives are not past child-bearing) attempt nothing of this kind; for it would not only be infinitely expeditious upon sudden calls, to which the sex is subject,—if the wind only served,—but would be excellent good husbandry to make use of the winds, which cost nothing, and which eat nothing, rather than horses, which (the Devil take 'em) both cost and eat a great deal.

For that very reason, replied my father, "Because they cost nothing, and because they eat nothing,"—the scheme is bad;— it is the consumption of our products, as well as the manufactures of them, which gives bread to the hungry, circulates trade,—brings in money, and supports the value of our lands;— and tho', I own, if I was a Prince, I would generously recompence the scientifick head which brought forth such contrivances;—yet I would as peremptorily suppress the use of them.

My father here had got into his element,—and was going on as prosperously with his dissertation upon trade, as my uncle

Toby had before, upon his of fortification;—but, to the loss of much sound knowledge, the destinies in the morning had decreed that no dissertation of any kind should be spun by my father that day;——for as he opened his mouth to begin the next sentence,

CHAPTER XV

IN popp'd Corporal *Trim* with *Stevinus*:—But 'twas too late, —all the discourse had been exhausted without him, and was running into a new channel.

—You may take the book home again, *Trim*, said my uncle *Toby*, nodding to him.

But pri'thee, Corporal, quoth my father, drolling,—look first into it, and see if thou can'st spy aught of a sailing chariot in it.

Corporal *Trim*, by being in the service, had learned to obey,—and not to remonstrate;——so taking the book to a side-table, and running over the leaves; an' please your Honour, said *Trim*, I can see no such thing;—however, continued the Corporal, drolling a little in his turn, I'll make sure work of it, an' please your Honour;—so taking hold of the two covers of the book, one in each hand, and letting the leaves fall down, as he bent the covers back, he gave the book a good sound shake.

There is something fallen out, however, said *Trim*, an' please your Honour; but it is not a chariot, or any thing like one:— Pri'thee Corporal, said my father, smiling, what is it then?—I think, answered *Trim*, stooping to take it up,—'tis more like a sermon,—for it begins, with a text of scripture, and the chapter and verse;—and then goes on, not as a chariot,—but like a sermon directly.

The company smiled.

I cannot conceive how it is possible, quoth my uncle *Toby*, for such a thing as a sermon to have got into my *Stevinus*.

I think 'tis a sermon, replied *Trim*,—but if it please your Honours, as it is a fair hand, I will read you a page;—for *Trim*, you must know, loved to hear himself read almost as well as talk.

I have ever a strong propensity, said my father, to look into things which cross my way, by such strange fatalities as these;— and as we have nothing better to do, at least till *Obadiah* gets back, I should be obliged to you, brother, if Dr. *Slop* has no objection to it, to order the Corporal to give us a page or two of it,—if he is as able to do it, as he seems willing. An' please your Honour, quoth *Trim*, I officiated two whole campaigns in *Flanders*, as Clerk to the Chaplain of the Regiment.—He can read it, quoth my uncle *Toby*, as well as I can.—*Trim*, I assure you, was the best scholar in my company, and should have had the next Halberd,[1] but for the poor fellow's misfortune. Corporal *Trim* laid his hand upon his heart, and made a humble bow to his Master;--then laying down his hat upon the floor, and taking up the sermon in his left hand, in order to have his right at liberty,—he advanced, nothing doubting,[2] into the middle of the room, where he could best see, and be best seen by, his audience.

CHAPTER XVI

——If you have any objection,—said my father, addressing himself to Dr. *Slop:* Not in the least, replied Dr. *Slop*;—for it does not appear on which side of the question it is wrote;——it may be a composition of a divine of our church, as well as yours,—so that we run equal risks.——'Tis wrote upon neither side, quoth *Trim*, for 'tis only upon *Conscience*, an' please your Honours.

Trim's reason put his audience into good humour,—all but Dr. *Slop*, who, turning his head about towards *Trim*, look'd a little angry.

Begin, *Trim*,——and read distinctly, quoth my father;—I will, an' please your Honour, replied the Corporal, making a bow, and bespeaking attention with a slight movement of his right hand.

CHAPTER XVII

——But before the Corporal begins, I must first give you a description of his attitude;——otherwise he will naturally stand represented, by your imagination, in an uneasy posture,—stiff,—perpendicular,—dividing the weight of his body equally upon both legs;—his eye fix'd, as if on duty;—his look determined,—clinching the sermon in his left hand, like his firelock:—In a word, you would be apt to paint *Trim*, as if he was standing in his platoon ready for action:——His attitude was as unlike all this as you can conceive.

He stood before them with his body swayed, and bent forwards just so far, as to make an angle of 85 degrees and a half upon the plain of the horizon;——which sound orators, to whom I address this, know very well, to be the true persuasive angle of incidence;—in any other angle you may talk and preach;—'tis certain,—and it is done every day;—but with what effect,—I leave the world to judge!

The necessity of this precise angle of 85 degrees and a half to a mathematical exactness,—does it not shew us, by the way,—how the arts and sciences mutually befriend each other?

How the duce Corporal *Trim*, who knew not so much as an acute angle from an obtuse one, came to hit it so exactly;—or whether it was chance or nature, or good sense or imitation, &c. shall be commented upon in that part of this cyclopædia of arts and sciences, where the instrumental parts of the eloquence of the senate, the pulpit, the bar, the coffee-house, the bed-chamber, and fire-side, fall under consideration.

He stood,—for I repeat it, to take the picture of him in at one view, with his body sway'd, and somewhat bent forwards,—his right leg firm under him, sustaining seven-eighths of his whole weight,—the foot of his left leg, the defect of which was no disadvantage to his attitude, advanced a little,—not laterally, nor forwards, but in a line betwixt them;—his knee bent, but that not violently,—but so as to fall within the limits of the line of beauty;[1]—and I add, of the line of science too;—for consider, it had one eighth part of his body to bear up;—so that in this case the position of the leg is determined,—because the foot could be no further advanced, or the knee more bent, than what would allow him, mechanically, to receive an eighth part of his whole weight under it,—and to carry it too.

☞ This I recommend to painters;—need I add,—to orators?—I think not; for, unless they practise it,—they must fall upon their noses.

So much for corporal *Trim*'s body and legs.—He held the sermon loosely,—not carelessly, in his left hand, raised something above his stomach, and detach'd a little from his breast;—his right arm falling negligently by his side, as nature and the laws of gravity order'd it,—but with the palm of it open and turned towards his audience, ready to aid the sentiment, in case it stood in need.

Corporal *Trim*'s eyes and the muscles of his face were in full harmony with the other parts of him;—he look'd frank,—unconstrained,—something assured,—but not bordering upon assurance.

Let not the critick ask how Corporal *Trim* could come by all this; I've told him it shall be explained;—but so he stood before my father, my uncle *Toby*, and Dr. *Slop*,—so swayed his body, so contrasted his limbs, and with such an oratorical sweep throughout the whole figure,—a statuary might have modell'd from it;——nay, I doubt whether the oldest Fellow of a College,—or the *Hebrew* Professor himself, could have much mended it.

Trim made a bow, and read as follows:

The SERMON.[2]

HEBREWS xiii. 18.

——*For we* trust *we have a good Conscience.*——

"TRUST!—Trust we have a good conscience!"

[Certainly, *Trim*, quoth my father, interrupting him, you give that sentence a very improper accent; for you curl up your nose, man, and read it with such a sneering tone, as if the Parson was going to abuse the Apostle.

He is, an' please your Honour, replied *Trim*. Pugh! said my father, smiling.

Sir, quoth Dr. *Slop*, *Trim* is certainly in the right; for the writer, (who I perceive is a Protestant) by the snappish manner in which he takes up the Apostle, is certainly going to abuse him,—if this treatment of him has not done it already. But from whence, replied my father, have you concluded so soon Dr. *Slop*, that the writer is of our Church?—for aught I can see yet,—he may be of any Church:—Because, answered Dr. *Slop*, if he was of ours,—he durst no more take such a licence,—than a bear by his beard:——If, in our communion, Sir, a man was to insult an Apostle,——a saint,—or even the paring of a saint's nail,—he would have his eyes scratched out.——What, by the saint? quoth my uncle *Toby*. No; replied Dr. *Slop*,—he would have an old house over his head.[3] Pray is the Inquisition an antient building, answered my uncle *Toby*, or is it a modern one?—I know nothing of architecture replied Dr. *Slop*.——An' please your Honours, quoth *Trim*, the Inquisition is the vilest——Pri'thee spare thy description, *Trim*, I hate the very name of

it, said my father.—No matter for that, answered Dr. *Slop*,—it
has its uses; for tho' I'm no great advocate for it, yet in such a
case as this, he would soon be taught better manners; and I can
tell him, if he went on at that rate, would be flung into the
Inquisition for his pains. God help him then, quoth my uncle
Toby. Amen, added *Trim*; for, heaven above knows, I have a
poor brother who has been fourteen years a captive in it.--I
never heard one word of it before, said my uncle *Toby*, hastily:—How came he there, *Trim*?——O, Sir! the story will
make your heart bleed,—as it has made mine a thousand
times;—but it is too long to be told now;—your Honour shall
hear it from first to last some day when I am working besides
you in our fortifications;——but the short of the story is this:
——That my brother *Tom* went over a servant to *Lisbon*,—and
then married a *Jew*'s widow, who kept a small shop, and sold
sausages, which, some how or other, was the cause of his being
taken in the middle of the night out of his bed, where he was
lying with his wife and two small children, and carried directly
to the Inquisition, where, God help him, continued *Trim*,
fetching a sigh from the bottom of his heart,—the poor honest
lad lies confined at this hour;—he was as honest a soul, added
Trim, (pulling out his handkerchief) as ever blood warm'd.——

——The tears trickled down *Trim*'s cheeks faster than he
could well wipe them away:—A dead silence in the room
ensued for some minutes.——Certain proof of pity!

Come, *Trim*, quoth my father, after he saw the poor fellow's
grief had got a little vent,—read on,—and put this melancholy
story out of thy head:—I grieve that I interrupted thee;—but
pri'thee begin the sermon again;—for if the first sentence in it is
matter of abuse, as thou sayest, I have a great desire to know
what kind of provocation the Apostle has given.

Corporal *Trim* wiped his face, and returning his handkerchief
into his pocket, and, making a bow as he did it,—he began
again.]

The SERMON.

HEBREWS xiii. 18.

——*For we* trust *we have a good conscience.*——

"TRUST! trust we have a good conscience! Surely if there is any
thing in this life which a man may depend upon, and to the
knowledge of which he is capable of arriving upon the most

indisputable evidence, it must be this very thing,—whether he has a good conscience or no."

[I am positive I am right quoth Dr. *Slop*.]

"If a man thinks at all, he cannot well be a stranger to the true state of this account;—he must be privy to his own thoughts and desires;—he must remember his past pursuits, and know certainly the true springs and motives which, in general, have governed the actions of his life."

[I defy him, without an assistant, quoth Dr. *Slop*.]

"In other matters we may be deceived by false appearances; and, as the Wise Man complains, *hardly do we guess aright at the things that are upon the earth, and with labour do we find the things that are before us*.⁴ But here the mind has all the evidence and facts within herself;--is conscious of the web she has wove;—knows its texture and fineness, and the exact share which every passion has had in working upon the several designs which virtue or vice has plann'd before her."

[The language is good, and I declare *Trim* reads very well, quoth my father.]

"Now,—as conscience is nothing else but the knowledge which the mind has within herself of this; and the judgment, either of approbation or censure, which it unavoidably makes upon the successive actions of our lives; 'tis plain you will say, from the very terms of the proposition,—whenever this inward testimony goes against a man, and he stands self-accused,—that he must necessarily be a guilty man.—And, on the contrary, when the report is favourable on his side, and his heart condemns him not;—that it is not a matter of *trust*, as the Apostle intimates,—but a matter of *certainty* and fact, that the conscience is good, and that the man must be good also."

[Then the Apostle is altogether in the wrong, I suppose, quoth Dr. *Slop*, and the Protestant divine is in the right. Sir, have patience, replied my father, for I think it will presently appear that St. *Paul* and the Protestant divine are both of an opinion.— As nearly so, quoth Dr. *Slop*, as East is to West;—but this, continued he, lifting both hands, comes from the liberty of the press.

It is no more, at the worst, replied my uncle *Toby*, than the liberty of the pulpit; for it does not appear that the sermon is printed, or ever likely to be.

Go on, *Trim*, quoth my father.]

"At first sight this may seem to be a true state of the case; and

I make no doubt but the knowledge of right and wrong is so truly impressed upon the mind of man,—that did no such thing ever happen, as that the conscience of a man, by long habits of sin, might (as the scripture assures it may) insensibly become hard;—and, like some tender parts of his body, by much stress and continual hard usage, lose, by degrees, that nice sense and perception with which God and nature endow'd it.—Did this never happen;—or was it certain that self-love could never hang the least bias upon the judgment;—or that the little interests below, could rise up and perplex the faculties of our upper regions, and encompass them about with clouds and thick darkness:—Could no such thing as favour and affection enter this sacred COURT:—Did WIT disdain to take a bribe in it;—or was asham'd to shew its face as an advocate for an unwarrantable enjoyment.——Or, lastly, were we assured, that INTEREST stood always unconcern'd whilst the cause was hearing,—and that passion never got into the judgment-seat, and pronounc'd sentence in the stead of reason, which is supposed always to preside and determine upon the case.—Was this truly so, as the objection must suppose;—no doubt then, the religious and moral state of a man would be exactly what he himself esteem'd it;—and the guilt or innocence of every man's life could be known, in general, by no better measure, than the degrees of his own approbation and censure.

"I own, in one case, whenever a man's conscience does accuse him, (as it seldom errs on that side) that he is guilty; and, unless in melancholy and hypochondriack cases, we may safely pronounce upon it, that there is always sufficient grounds for the accusation.

"But the converse of the proposition will not hold true;—— namely, that whenever there is guilt the conscience must accuse; and if it does not, that a man is therefore innocent.— This is not fact:—So that the common consolation which some good christian or other, is hourly administering to himself,— that he thanks God his mind does not misgive him; and that, consequently, he has a good conscience, because he has a quiet one,—is fallacious;—and as current as the inference is, and as infallible as the rule appears at first sight, yet, when you look nearer to it, and try the truth of this rule upon plain facts,—you see it liable to so much error from a false application;——the principle upon which it goes so often perverted;—the whole force of it lost, and sometimes so vilely cast away, that it is painful to produce the common examples from human life which confirm the account.

"A man shall be vicious and utterly debauched in his principles;—exceptionable in his conduct to the world; shall live shameless, in the open commission of a sin which no reason or pretence can justify;—a sin, by which, contrary to all the workings of humanity, he shall ruin for ever the deluded partner of his guilt;—rob her of her best dowry; and not only cover her own head with dishonour,—but involve a whole virtuous family in shame and sorrow for her sake.—Surely, you will think conscience must lead such a man a troublesome Life;—he can have no rest night or day from its reproaches.

"Alas! CONSCIENCE had something else to do, all this time, than break in upon him; as *Elijah* reproached the God *Baal,*[5]—this domestick God *was either talking, or pursuing, or was in a journey, or peradventure he slept and could not be awoke.*

"Perhaps HE was gone out in company with HONOUR to fight a duel;—to pay off some debt at play;——or dirty annuity, the bargain of his lust: Perhaps CONSCIENCE all this time was engaged at home, talking loud against petty larceny, and executing vengeance upon some such puny crimes as his fortune and rank in life secured him against all temptation of committing; so that he lives as merrily, [if he was of our church tho', quoth Dr. *Slop*, he could not]—"sleeps as soundly in his bed;—and at last meets death as unconcernedly;—perhaps much more so than a much better man."

[All this is impossible with us, quoth Dr. *Slop*, turning to my father,—the case could not happen in our Church.——It happens in ours, however, replied my father, but too often.—I own, quoth Dr. *Slop*, (struck a little with my father's frank acknowledgment)—that a man in the *Romish* Church may live as badly;—but then he cannot easily die so.—'Tis little matter, replied my father, with an air of indifference,—how a rascal dies.—I mean, answer'd Dr. *Slop*, he would be denied the benefits of the last sacraments.---Pray how many have you in all, said my uncle *Toby*,—for I always forget?——Seven, answered Dr. *Slop*.—Humph!—said my uncle *Toby*;--tho' not accented as a note of acquiescence,—but as an interjection of that particular species of surprize, when a man, in looking into a drawer, finds more of a thing than he expected.--Humph! replied my uncle *Toby*. Dr. *Slop*, who had an ear, understood my uncle *Toby* as well as if he had wrote a whole volume against the seven sacraments.[6]——Humph! replied Dr. *Slop*, (stating my uncle *Toby*'s argument over again to him)—Why, Sir, are there not seven cardinal virtues?—Seven mortal sins?—Seven golden candle-sticks?—Seven heavens?—'Tis more than I know, replied my uncle *Toby*.—Are there not seven wonders of the world?——Seven days of the creation?—Seven planets?—Seven plagues?—That there are, quoth my father, with a most affected gravity. But pri'thee, continued he, go on with the rest of thy characters, *Trim*.]

"Another is sordid, unmerciful, (here *Trim* waved his right hand) a strait-hearted, selfish wretch, incapable either of private friendship or publick spirit. Take notice how he passes by the widow and orphan in their distress, and sees all the miseries incident to human life without a sigh or a prayer." [And please your Honours, cried *Trim*, I think this is a viler man than the other.]

"Shall not conscience rise up and sting him on such occasions?——No; thank God there is no occasion; *I pay every man his own;—I have no fornication to answer to my conscience;—no faithless vows or promises to make up;—I have debauched no man's wife or child; thank God, I am not as other men, adulterers, unjust, or even as this libertine, who stands before me.*[7]

"A third is crafty and designing in his nature. View his whole life;——'tis nothing but a cunning contexture of dark arts and unequitable subterfuges, basely to defeat the true intent of all laws,—plain dealing and the safe enjoyment of our several properties.——You will see such a one working out a frame of little designs upon the ignorance and perplexities of the poor and needy man;—shall raise a fortune upon the inexperience of a youth, or the unsuspecting temper of his friend who would have trusted him with his life.

"When old age comes on, and repentance calls him to look back upon this black account, and state it over again with his conscience,——CONSCIENCE looks into the STATUTES at LARGE;—finds no express law broken by what he has done;—perceives no penalty of forfeiture of goods and chattels incurred;--sees no scourge waving over his head, or prison opening his gates upon him:—What is there to affright his conscience?—Conscience has got safely entrenched behind the Letter of the Law; sits there invulnerable, fortified with Cases and Reports so strongly on all sides,—that it is not preaching can dispossess it of its hold."

[Here Corporal *Trim* and my uncle *Toby* exchanged looks with each other,--Aye,---aye, *Trim!* quoth my uncle *Toby*, shaking his head,---these are but sorry fortifications, *Trim*.------O! very poor work, answered *Trim*, to what your Honour and I make of it.------The character of this last man, said Dr. *Slop*, interrupting *Trim*, is more detestable than all the rest;---and seems to have been taken from some pettifogging Lawyer amongst you:---Amongst us a man's conscience could not possibly continue so long *blinded*;---three times in a year, at least, he must go to confession. Will that restore it to sight, quoth my uncle *Toby?*--- Go on, *Trim*, quoth my father, or *Obadiah* will have got back before thou hast got to the end of thy sermon;---'tis a very short one, replied *Trim*.---I wish it was longer, quoth my uncle *Toby*, for I like it hugely.---*Trim* went on.]

"A fourth man shall want even this refuge;---shall break through all this ceremony of slow chicane;------scorns the doubtful workings of secret plots and cautious trains to bring about his purpose:---See the bare-faced villain, how he cheats, lies, perjures, robs, murders.------Horrid!------But indeed much better was not to be expected, in the present case,---the poor man was in the dark!---his priest had got the keeping of his conscience;---and all he would let him know of it, was, That he must believe in the Pope;---go to Mass;---cross himself;---tell his beads;---be a good Catholick, and that this, in all conscience, was enough to carry him to heaven. What;---if he perjures!---Why;---he had a mental reservation in it.---But if he is so wicked and abandoned a wretch as you represent him;---if he robs,---if he stabs,------will not conscience, on every such act, receive a wound itself? Aye,---but the man has carried it to confession;---the wound digests there, and will do well enough, and in a short time be quite healed up by absolution. O Popery! what hast thou to answer for?---when, not content with the too many natural and fatal ways, thro' which the heart of man is every day thus treacherous to itself above all things;---thou hast wilfully set open this wide gate of deceit before the face of this unwary traveller, too apt, God knows, to go astray of himself; and confidently speak peace to himself, when there is no peace.

"Of this the common instances which I have drawn out of life, are too notorious to require much evidence. If any man doubts the reality of them, or thinks it impossible for a man to be such a bubble[8] to himself,---I must refer him a moment to his own reflections, and will then venture to trust my appeal with his own heart.

"Let him consider in how different a degree of detestation, numbers of wicked actions stand *there*, tho' equally bad and vicious in their own natures;—he will soon find that such of them, as strong inclination and custom have prompted him to commit, are generally dress'd out and painted with all the false beauties, which a soft and a flattering hand can give them;—and that the others, to which he feels no propensity, appear, at once, naked and deformed, surrounded with all the true circumstances of folly and dishonour.

"When *David* surprized *Saul* sleeping in the Cave, and cut off the skirt of his robe,—we read his heart smote him for what he had done:—But in the matter of *Uriah*,[10] where a faithful and gallant servant, whom he ought to have loved and honoured, fell to make way for his lust,—where conscience had so much greater reason to take the alarm, his heart smote him not. A whole year had almost passed from the first commission of that crime, to the time *Nathan* was sent to reprove him; and we read not once of the least sorrow or compunction of heart which he testified, during all that time, for what he had done.

"Thus conscience, this once able monitor,—placed on high as a judge within us, and intended by our maker as a just and equitable one too,—by an unhappy train of causes and impediments, takes often such imperfect cognizance of what passes,—does its office so negligently,—sometimes so corruptly,—that it is not to be trusted alone; and therefore we find there is a necessity, an absolute necessity of joining another principle with it to aid, if not govern, its determinations.

"So that if you would form a just judgment of what is of infinite importance to you not to be misled in,——namely, in what degree of real merit you stand either as an honest man, an useful citizen, a faithful subject to your King, or a good servant to your God,--call in religion and morality.—Look,--What is written in the law of God?—How readest thou?——Consult calm reason and the unchangeable obligations of justice and truth;—what say they?

"Let CONSCIENCE determine the matter upon these reports;—and then if thy heart condemns thee not, which is the case the Apostle supposes,—the rule will be infallible, (here Dr. *Slop* fell asleep) *thou wilt have confidence towards God*;[11]—that is, have just grounds to believe the judgment thou hast past upon thyself, is the judgment of God; and nothing else but an anticipation of that righteous sentence which will be pronounced upon thee hereafter by that Being, to whom thou art finally to give an account of thy actions.

"*Blessed is the man*,[12] indeed then, as the author of the book of *Ecclesiasticus* expresses it, *who is not prick'd with the multitude of his sins: Blessed is the man whose heart hath not condemn'd him; whether he be rich, or whether he be poor, if he have a good heart*, (a heart thus guided and informed) *he shall at all times rejoice in a chearful countenance; his mind shall tell him more than seven watch-men that sit above upon a tower on high.*——[A tower has no strength, quoth my uncle *Toby*, unless 'tis flank'd.] In the darkest doubts it shall conduct him safer than a thousand casuists, and give the state he lives in a better security for his behaviour than all the clauses and restrictions put together, which law-makers are forced to multiply:—*Forced*, I say, as things stand; human laws not being a matter of original choice, but of pure necessity, brought in to fence against the mischievous effects of those consciences which are no law unto themselves; well intending, by the many provisions made,—that in all such corrupt and misguided cases, where principles and the checks of conscience will not make us upright,—to supply their force, and, by the terrors of goals and halters, oblige us to it."

[I see plainly, said my father, that this sermon has been composed to be preach'd at the Temple,—or at some Assize.—I like the reasoning,—and am sorry that Dr. *Slop* has fallen asleep before the time of his conviction;—for it is now clear, that the Parson, as I thought at first, never insulted St. *Paul* in the least;—nor has there been, brother, the least difference between them.—A great matter, if they had differed, replied my uncle *Toby*,—the best friends in the world may differ sometimes.—True,—brother *Toby*, quoth my father, shaking hands with him,—we'll fill our pipes, brother, and then *Trim* shall go on.

Well,—what do'st thou think of it? said my father, speaking to Corporal *Trim*, as he reach'd his tobacco-box.

I think, answered the Corporal, that the seven watch-men upon the tower, who, I suppose, are all centinels there,—are more, an' please your Honour, than were necessary;—and, to go on at that rate, would harrass a regiment all to pieces, which a commanding officer, who loves his men, will never do, if he can help it; because two centinels, added the Corporal, are as good as twenty.—I have been a commanding officer myself in the *Corps de Garde*[13] a hundred times, continued *Trim*, rising an inch higher in his figure, as he spoke,——and all the time I had the honour to serve his Majesty King *William*, in relieving the most considerable posts, I never left more than two in my life.——Very right, *Trim*, quoth my uncle *Toby*;—but you do not consider *Trim*, that the towers, in *Solomon*'s days, were not such things as our bastions, flank'd and defended by other works;—this, *Trim*, was an invention since *Solomon*'s death; nor had they horn-works, or ravelins before the curtin, in his time;—or such a fossé as we make with a cuvette[14] in the middle of it, and with cover'd-ways and counterscarps pallisadoed along it, to guard against a *Coup de main:*—So that the seven men upon the tower were a party, I dare say, from the *Corps de Garde*, set there, not only to look out, but to defend it.—They could be no more, an' please your Honour, than a Corporal's Guard.—My father smiled inwardly,—but not outwardly;—the subject between my uncle *Toby* and Corporal *Trim* being rather too serious, considering what had happened, to make a jest of:—So, putting his pipe into his mouth, which he had just lighted,—he contented himself with ordering *Trim* to read on. He read on as follows:]

"To have the fear of God before our eyes, and, in our mutual dealings with each other, to govern our actions by the eternal measures of right and wrong:—The first of these will comprehend the duties of religion;——the second, those of morality, which are so inseparably connected together, that you cannot divide these two *tables*,[15] even in imagination, (tho' the attempt is often made in practice) without breaking and mutually destroying them both.

"I said the attempt is often made, and so it is;—there being nothing more common than to see a man who has no sense at all of religion,——and indeed has so much honesty as to pretend to none, who would take it as the bitterest affront, should you but hint at a suspicion of his moral character,--or imagine he was not conscientiously just and scrupulous to the uttermost mite.

"When there is some appearance that it is so,—tho' one is unwilling even to suspect the appearance of so amiable a virtue as moral honesty, yet were we to look into the grounds of it, in the present case, I am persuaded we should find little reason to envy such a one the honour of his motive.

"Let him declaim as pompously as he chooses upon the

subject, it will be found to rest upon no better foundation than either his interest, his pride, his ease, or some such little and changeable passion as will give us but small dependence upon his actions in matters of great stress.

"I will illustrate this by an example.

"I know the banker I deal with, or the physician I usually call in [there is no need, cried Dr. *Slop*, (waking) to call in any physician in this case] to be neither of them men of much religion: I hear them make a jest of it every day, and treat all its sanctions with so much scorn, as to put the matter past doubt. Well;—notwithstanding this, I put my fortune into the hands of the one;—and, what is dearer still to me, I trust my life to the honest skill of the other.

"Now, let me examine what is my reason for this great confidence.——Why, in the first place, I believe there is no probability that either of them will employ the power I put into their hands to my disadvantage;—I consider that honesty serves the purposes of this life:—I know their success in the world depends upon the fairness of their characters.—In a word,—I'm persuaded that they cannot hurt me, without hurting themselves more.

"But put it otherwise, namely, that interest lay, for once, on the other side; that a case should happen, wherein the one, without stain to his reputation, could secrete my fortune, and leave me naked in the world;—or that the other could send me out of it, and enjoy an estate by my death, without dishonour to himself or his art:—In this case, what hold have I of either of them?—Religion, the strongest of all motives, is out of the question:—Interest, the next most powerful motive in the world, is strongly against me:—What have I left to cast into the opposite scale to balance this temptation?--Alas! I have nothing,—nothing but what is lighter than a bubble.—I must lay at the mercy of HONOUR, or some such capricious principle. ——Strait security for two of my most valuable blessings!—my property and my life.

"As, therefore, we can have no dependence upon morality without religion;—so, on the other hand, there is nothing better to be expected from religion without morality;—nevertheless, 'tis no prodigy to see a man whose real moral character stands very low, who yet entertains the highest notion of himself, in the light of a religious man.

"He shall not only be covetous, revengeful, implacable,

——but even a wanting in points in common honesty; yet, inasmuch as he talks aloud against the infidelity of the age,—is zealous for some points of religion,——goes twice a day to church,—attends the sacraments,—and amuses himself with a few instrumental parts of religion,—shall cheat his conscience into a judgment that, for this, he is a religious man, and has discharged truly his duty to God: And you will find that such a man, thro' force of this delusion, generally looks down with spiritual pride upon every other man who has less affectation of piety,--tho', perhaps, ten times more moral honesty than himself.

"*This likewise is a sore evil under the sun*; and I believe there is no one mistaken principle which, for its time, has wrought more serious mischiefs.—For a general proof of this,—examine the history of the *Romish* Church;—[Well, what can you make of that, cried Dr. *Slop?*]—see what scenes of cruelty, murders, rapines, blood-shed, [They may thank their own obstinacy, cried Dr. *Slop*] have all been sanctified by a religion not strictly governed by morality.

"In how many kingdoms of the world, [Here *Trim* kept waving his right hand from the sermon to the extent of his arm, returning it backwards and forwards to the conclusion of the Paragraph.]

"In how many kingdoms of the world has the crusading sword of this misguided saint-errant spared neither age, or merit, or sex, or condition?—and, as he fought under the banners of a religion which set him loose from justice and humanity, he shew'd none; mercilessly trampled upon both,——heard neither the cries of the unfortunate, nor pitied their distresses.

[I have been in many a battle, an' please your honour, quoth *Trim*, sighing, but never in so melancholy a one as this.—I would not have drawn a tricker[16] in it, against these poor souls,——to have been made a general officer.—Why, what do you understand of the affair? said Doctor *Slop*, looking towards *Trim* with something more contempt than the Corporal's honest heart deserved.—What do you know, friend, about this battle you talk of?——I know, replied *Trim*, that I never refused quarter in my life to any man who cried out for it;—but to a woman or a child, continued *Trim*, before I would level my musket at them, I would lose my life a thousand times.—Here's a crown for thee, *Trim*, to drink with *Obadiah* to-night, quoth my uncle *Toby*, and I'll give *Obadiah* another too.--God bless your honour, replied *Trim*,—I had rather these poor women and children had it.—Thou art an honest fellow, quoth my uncle *Toby*.----My father nodded his head,—as much as to say,—and so he is.————

But pri'thee, *Trim*, said my father, make an end,—for I see thou hast but a leaf or two left.]

Corporal Trim read on.

"If the testimony of past centuries in this matter is not sufficient,————consider, at this instant, how the votaries of that religion are every day thinking to do service and honour to God, by actions which are a dishonour and scandal to themselves.

"To be convinced of this, go with me for a moment into the Prisons of the inquisition. [God help, my poor brother *Tom*.] ————Behold *Religion*, with *Mercy* and *Justice* chained down under her feet,————there sitting ghastly upon a black tribunal, propp'd up with racks and instruments of torment. Hark!—hark! what a piteous groan! [Here *Trim*'s face turned as pale as ashes.] See the melancholy wretch who utter'd it—[Here the tears began to trickle down] just brought forth to undergo the anguish of a mock trial, and endure the utmost pains that a studied system of cruelty has been able to invent.—[D—n them all, quoth *Trim*, his colour returning into his face as red as blood.]—Behold this helpless victim delivered up to his tormentors,————his body so wasted with sorrow and confinement.—[Oh! 'tis my brother, cried poor *Trim* in a most passionate exclamation, dropping the sermon upon the Ground, and clapping his hands together————I fear 'tis poor *Tom*. My father's and my uncle *Toby*'s hearts yearn'd with sympathy for the poor fellow's distress,————even *Slop* himself acknowledged pity for him.—Why, *Trim*, said my father, this is not a history,—'tis a sermon thou art reading;—pri'thee begin the sentence again.]—Behold this helpless victim deliver'd up to his tormentors,—his body so wasted with sorrow and confinement, you will see every nerve and muscle as it suffers.

"Observe the last movement of that horrid engine! [I would rather face a cannon, quoth *Trim*, stamping.]————See what convulsions it has thrown him into!————Consider the nature of the posture in which he now lies stretched,—what exquisite tortures he endures by it!————[I hope tis not in *Portugal*.]—'Tis all nature can bear! Good God! see how it keeps his weary soul hanging upon his trembling lips! [I would not read another line of it, quoth *Trim*, for all this world;—I fear, an' please your Honours, all this is in *Portugal*, where my poor brother *Tom* is. I tell thee, *Trim*, again, quoth my father, 'tis not an historical account,—'tis a description.—'Tis only a description, honest man, quoth *Slop*, there's not a word of truth in it.—That's another story, replied my father.—However, as *Trim* reads it with so much concern,—'tis cruelty to force him to go on with it.--Give me hold of the sermon, *Trim*,--I'll finish it for thee, and thou may'st go. I must stay and hear it too, replied *Trim*, if your Honour will allow me;—tho' I would not read it myself for a Colonel's pay.——Poor *Trim*! quoth my uncle *Toby*. My father went on.]

—"Consider the nature of the posture in which he now lies stretch'd,—what exquisite torture he endures by it!—'Tis all nature can bear!—Good God! See how it keeps his weary soul hanging upon his trembling lips,—willing to take its leave, ——but not suffered to depart!——Behold the unhappy wretch led back to his cell! [Then, thank God, however, quoth *Trim*, they have not killed him]—See him dragg'd out of it again to meet the flames, and the insults in his last agonies, which this principle,—this principle, that there can be religion without mercy, has prepared for him. [Then, thank God,—he is dead, quoth *Trim*,—he is out of his pain,—and they have done their worst at him.—O Sirs!—Hold your peace, *Trim*, said my father, going on with the sermon, lest *Trim* should incense Dr. *Slop*,—we shall never have done at this rate.]

"The surest way to try the merit of any disputed notion is, to trace down the consequences such a notion has produced, and compare them with the spirit of Christianity;—'tis the short and decisive rule which our Saviour hath left us, for these and such-like cases, and it is worth a thousand arguments,——*By their fruits ye shall know them.*[17]

"I will add no further to the length of this sermon, than, by two or three short and independent rules deducible from it.

"*First*, Whenever a man talks loudly against religion,— always suspect that it is not his reason, but his passions which have got the better of his CREED. A bad life and a good belief are disagreeable and troublesome neighbours, and where they separate, depend upon it, 'tis for no other cause but quietness sake.

"*Secondly*, When a man, thus represented, tells you in any particular instance,——That such a thing goes *against* his conscience,—always believe he means exactly the same thing, as when he tells you such a thing goes *against* his stomach;—a present want of appetite being generally the true cause of both.

"In a word,—trust that man in nothing, who has not a CONSCIENCE in every thing.

"And, in your own case, remember this plain distinction, a mistake in which has ruined thousands,—that your conscience is not a law:--No, God and reason made the law, and have placed conscience within you to determine;—not like an *Asiatick* Cadi, according to the ebbs and flows of his own passions,—but like a *British* judge in this land of liberty and good sense, who makes no new law, but faithfully declares that law which he knows already written."

FINIS.

Thou hast read the sermon extremely well, *Trim*, quoth my father.—If he had spared his comments, replied Dr. *Slop*, he would have read it much better. I should have read it ten times better, Sir, answered *Trim*, but that my heart was so full.—That was the very reason, *Trim*, replied my father, which has made thee read the sermon as well as thou hast done; and if the clergy of our church, continued my father, addressing himself to Dr. *Slop*, would take part in what they deliver, as deeply as this poor fellow has done,—as their compositions are fine, (I deny it, quoth Dr. *Slop*) I maintain it, that the eloquence of our pulpits, with such subjects to inflame it,—would be a model for the whole world:—But, alas! continued my father, and I own it, Sir, with sorrow, that, like *French* politicians in this respect, what they gain in the cabinet they lose in the field.——'Twere a pity, quoth my uncle, that this should be lost. I like the sermon well, replied my father,—'tis dramatic,——and there is something in that way of writing, when skilfully managed, which catches the attention.———We preach much in that way with us, said Dr. *Slop*.—I know that very well, said my father,—but in a tone and manner which disgusted Dr. *Slop*, full as much as his assent, simply, could have pleased him.-----But in this, added Dr. *Slop*, a little piqued,——our sermons have greatly the advantage, that we never introduce any character into them below a patriarch or a patriarch's wife, or a martyr or a saint.—There are some very bad characters in this, however, said my father, and I do not think the sermon a jot the worse for 'em.—But pray, quoth my uncle *Toby*,——who's can this be?—How could it get into my *Stevinus*? A man must be as great a conjurer as *Stevinus*, said my father, to resolve the second question:—The first, I think, is not so difficult;—for unless my judgment greatly deceives me, ——I know the author, for 'tis wrote, certainly, by the parson of the parish.

The similitude of the stile and manner of it, with those my father constantly had heard preach'd in his parish-church, was the ground of his conjecture,—proving it as strongly, as an argument *a priori*, could prove such a thing to a philosophic mind, That it was *Yorick*'s and no one's else:——It was proved to be so *a posteriori*, the day after, when *Yorick* sent a servant to my uncle *Toby*'s house to enquire after it.

It seems that *Yorick*, who was inquisitive after all kinds of knowledge, had borrowed *Stevinus* of my uncle *Toby*, and had carelessly popp'd his sermon, as soon as he had made it, into the middle of *Stevinus*; and, by an act of forgetfulness, to which he was ever subject, he had sent *Stevinus* home, and his sermon to keep him company.

Ill-fated sermon! Thou wast lost, after this recovery of thee, a second time, dropp'd thro' an unsuspected fissure in thy master's pocket, down into a treacherous and a tatter'd lining,—trod deep into the dirt by the left hind foot of his Rosinante, inhumanly stepping upon thee as thou falledst;—buried ten days in the mire,—raised up out of it by a beggar, sold for a halfpenny to a parish-clerk,—transferred to his parson,—lost for ever to thy own, the remainder of his days,—nor restored to his restless MANES till this very moment, that I tell the world the story.

Can the reader believe, that this sermon of *Yorick*'s was preach'd at an assize, in the cathedral of *York*, before a thousand witnesses, ready to give oath of it, by a certain prebendary of that church, and actually printed by him when he had done, ——and within so short a space as two years and three months after *Yorick*'s death.—*Yorick*, indeed, was never better served in his life!——but it was a little hard to male-treat him after, and plunder him after he was laid in his grave.

However, as the gentleman who did it, was in perfect charity with *Yorick*,—and, in conscious justice, printed but a few copies to give away;—and that, I am told, he could moreover have made as good a one himself, had he thought fit,—I declare I would not have published this anecdote to the world;—nor do I publish it with an intent to hurt his character and advancement in the church;——I leave that to others;——but I find myself impell'd by two reasons, which I cannot withstand.

The first is, That, in doing justice, I may give rest to *Yorick*'s ghost;—which, as the country people,—and some others, believe,——*still walks*.

The second reason is, That, by laying open this story to the world, I gain an opportunity of informing it,——That in case the character of parson *Yorick*, and this sample of his sermons is liked,—that there are now in the possession of the *Shandy* Family, as many as will make a handsome volume, at the world's service,—and much good may they do it.

CHAPTER XVIII

OBADIAH gain'd the two crowns without dispute; for he came in jingling, with all the instruments in the green bays bag we spoke of, slung across his body, just as corporal *Trim* went out of the room.

It is now proper, I think, quoth Dr. *Slop*, (clearing up his looks) as we are in a condition to be of some service to Mrs. *Shandy*, to send up stairs to know how she goes on.

I have ordered, answered my father, the old midwife to come down to us upon the least difficulty;——for you must know, Dr. *Slop*, continued my father, with a perplexed kind of smile upon his countenance, that by express treaty, solemnly ratified between me and my wife, you are no more than an auxiliary in this affair,—and not so much as that,—unless the lean old mother of a midwife above stairs cannot do without you.— Women have their particular fancies, and in points of this nature, continued my father, where they bear the whole burden, and suffer so much acute pain for the advantage of our families, and the good of the species,—they claim a right of deciding, *en Soveraines*,[1] in whose hands, and in what fashion, they chuse to undergo it.

They are in the right of it,—quoth my uncle *Toby*. But, Sir, replied Dr. *Slop*, not taking notice of my uncle *Toby*'s opinion, but turning to my father,—they had better govern in other points;—and a father of a family, who wished its perpetuity, in my opinion, had better exchange this prerogative with them, and give up some other rights in lieu of it.—I know not, quoth my father, answering a little too testily, to be quite dispassionate in what he said,——I know not, quoth he, what we have left to give up, in lieu of who shall bring our children into the world,—unless that,—of who shall beget them.——One would almost give up any thing, replied Dr. *Slop*.—— I beg your pardon,—answered my uncle *Toby*.——Sir, replied Dr. *Slop*, it would astonish you to know what Improvements we have made of late years in all branches of obstetrical knowledge, but particularly in that one single point of the safe and expeditious extraction of the *fœtus*,——which has received such lights, that, for my part, (holding up his hands) I declare I wonder how the world has——I wish, quoth my uncle *Toby*, you had seen what prodigious armies we had in *Flanders*.

CHAPTER XIX

I HAVE dropp'd the curtain over this scene for a minute,—to remind you of one thing,—and to inform you of another.

What I have to inform you, comes, I own, a little out of its due course;—for it should have been told a hundred and fifty pages ago, but that I foresaw then 'twould come in pat hereafter, and be of more advantage here than elsewhere.----Writers had need look before them to keep up the spirit and connection of what they have in hand.

When these two things are done,—the curtain shall be drawn up again, and my uncle *Toby*, my father, and Dr. *Slop* shall go on with their discourse, without any more interruption.

First, then, the matter which I have to remind you of, is this;—that from the specimens of singularity in my father's notions in the point of Christian-names, and that other point previous thereto,—you was led, I think, into an opinion, (and I am sure I said as much) that my father was a gentleman altogether as odd and whimsical in fifty other opinions. In truth, there was not a stage in the life of man, from the very first act of his begetting,—down to the lean and slipper'd pantaloon in his second childishness,[1] but he had some favourite notion to himself, springing out of it, as sceptical, and as far out of the high-way of thinking, as these two which have been explained.

——Mr. *Shandy*, my father, Sir, would see nothing in the

light in which others placed it;—he placed things in his own light;—he would weigh nothing in common scales;—no,—he was too refined a researcher to lay open to so gross an imposition.—To come at the exact weight of things in the scientific steel-yard, the fulcrum, he would say, should be almost invisible, to avoid all friction from popular tenets;—without this the minutiæ of philosophy, which should always turn the balance, will have no weight at all.—Knowledge, like matter, he would affirm, was divisible *in infinitum*;[2]—that the grains and scruples were as much a part of it, as the gravitation of the whole world.—In a word, he would say, error was error,—no matter where it fell,—whether in a fraction,—or a pound,—'twas alike fatal to truth, and she was kept down at the bottom of her well as inevitably by a mistake in the dust of a butterfly's wing,—as in the disk of the sun, the moon, and all the stars of heaven put together.

He would often lament that it was for want of considering this properly, and of applying it skilfully to civil matters, as well as to speculative truths, that so many things in this world were out of joint;—that the political arch was giving way;—and that the very foundations of our excellent constitution in church and state, were so sapp'd as estimators had reported.

You cry out, he would say, we are a ruined, undone people.——Why?—he would ask, making use of the sorites or syllogism of *Zeno* and *Chrysippus*,[3] without knowing it belonged to them.—Why? why are we a ruined people?—Because we are corrupted.——Whence is it, dear Sir, that we are corrupted?—Because we are needy;—our poverty, and not our wills, consent.——And wherefore, he would add,—are we needy?——From the neglect, he would answer, of our pence and our halfpence:—Our bank-notes, Sir, our guineas--nay our shillings, take care of themselves.

'Tis the same, he would say, throughout the whole circle of the sciences;—the great, the established points of them, are not to be broke in upon.—The laws of nature will defend themselves;—but error—(he would add, looking earnestly at my mother)—error, Sir, creeps in thro' the minute-holes, and small crevices, which human nature leaves unguarded.

This turn of thinking in my father, is what I had to remind you of:——The point you are to be informed of, and which I have reserved for this place, is as follows:

Amongst the many and excellent reasons, with which my

father had urged my mother to accept of Dr. *Slop*'s assistance preferably to that of the old woman,—there was one of a very singular nature; which, when he had done arguing the matter with her as a Christian, and came to argue it over again with her as a philosopher,—he had put his whole strength to, depending indeed upon it as his sheet anchor.———It failed him; tho' from no defect in the argument itself; but that, do what he could, he was not able for his soul to make her comprehend the drift of it.———Cursed luck!—said he to himself, one afternoon, as he walk'd out of the room, after he had been stating it for an hour and a half to her, to no manner of purpose;—cursed luck! said he, biting his lip as he shut the door,—for a man to be master of one of the finest chains of reasoning in nature,—and have a wife at the same time with such a head-piece, that she cannot hang up a single inference within side of it, to save his soul from destruction.

This argument, though it was intirely lost upon my mother,—had more weight with him, than all his other arguments joined together:———I will therefore endeavour to do it justice,—and set it forth with all the perspicuity I am master of.

My father set out upon the strength of these two following axioms:

First, That an ounce of a man's own wit, was worth a tun of other people's; and,

Secondly, (Which, by the bye, was the ground-work of the first axiom,—tho' it comes last)—That every man's wit must come from every man's own soul,—and no other body's.

Now, as it was plain to my father, that all souls were by nature equal,—and that the great difference between the most acute and the most obtuse understanding,—was from no original sharpness or bluntness of one thinking substance above or below another,———but arose merely from the lucky or unlucky organization of the body, in that part where the soul principally took up her residence,—he had made it the subject of his enquiry to find out the identical place.

Now, from the best accounts he had been able to get of this matter, he was satisfied it could not be where *Des Cartes*[4] had fixed it, upon the top of the *pineal* gland of the brain; which, as he philosophised, form'd a cushion for her about the size of a marrow pea;—tho', to speak the truth, as so many nerves did terminate all in that one place,—'twas no bad conjecture;—and my father had certainly fallen with that great philosopher plumb into the center of the mistake, had it not been for my uncle *Toby*, who rescued him out of it, by a story he told him of a *Walloon* Officer at the battle of *Landen*, who had one part of his brain shot away by a musket-ball,—and another part of it taken out after by a *French* Surgeon; and, after all, recovered, and did his duty very well without it.

If death, said my father, reasoning with himself, is nothing but the separation of the soul from the body;—and if it is true that people can walk about and do their business without brains,—then certes the soul does not inhabit there. Q. E. D.

As for that certain very thin, subtle, and very fragrant juice which *Coglionissimo Borri*,[5] the great *Milaneze* physician, affirms, in a letter to *Bartholine*,[6] to have discovered in the cellulæ of the occipital parts of the cerebellum, and which he likewise affirms to be the principal seat of the reasonable soul (for, you must know, in these latter and more enlightened ages, there are two souls in every man living,—the one according to the great *Metheglingius*,[7] being called the *Animus*,[8] the other the *Anima*);—as for this opinion, I say, of *Borri*,——my father could never subscribe to it by any means; the very idea of so noble, so refined, so immaterial, and so exalted a being as the *Anima*, or even the *Animus*, taking up her residence, and sitting dabbling, like a tad-pole, all day long, both summer and winter, in a puddle,—or in a liquid of any kind, how thick or thin soever, he would say, shock'd his imagination; he would scarce give the doctrine a hearing.

What, therefore, seem'd the least liable to objections of any, was, that the chief sensorium, or head-quarters of the soul, and to which place all intelligences were referred, and from whence all her mandates were issued,—was in, or near, the cerebellum, --or rather some-where about the *medulla oblongata*, wherein it was generally agreed by *Dutch* anatomists, that all the minute nerves from all the organs of the seven senses concentered, like streets and winding alleys, into a square.

So far there was nothing singular in my father's opinion,—he had the best of philosophers, of all ages and climates, to go along with him.——But here he took a road of his own, setting up another *Shandean* hypothesis upon these corner-stones they had laid for him;—and which said hypothesis equally stood its ground; whether the subtilty and fineness of the soul depended upon the temperature and clearness of the said liquor, or of the finer net-work and texture in the cerebellum itself; which opinion he favoured.

He maintained, that next to the due care to be taken in the act of propagation of each individual, which required all the thought in the world, as it laid the foundation of this incomprehensible contexture in which wit, memory, fancy, eloquence, and what is usually meant by the name of good natural parts, do consist;—that next to this and his Christian-name, which were the two original and most efficacious causes of all;—that the third cause, or rather what logicians call the *Causa sine quâ non*,' and without which all that was done was of no manner of significance,--was the preservation of this delicate and fine-spun web, from the havock which was generally made in it by the violent compression and crush which the head was made to undergo, by the nonsensical method of bringing us into the world by that part foremost.

——This requires explanation.

My father, who dipp'd into all kinds of books, upon looking into *Lithopedus Senonesis de Partu difficili**, published by *Adrianus Smelvogt*, had found out, That the lax and pliable state of a child's head in parturition, the bones of the cranium having no sutures at that time, was such,—that by force of the woman's efforts, which, in strong labour-pains, was equal, upon an average, to a weight of 470 pounds averdupoise acting perpendicularly upon it;—it so happened that, in 49 instances out of 50, the said head was compressed and moulded into the shape of an oblong conical piece of dough, such as a pastry-cook generally rolls up in order to make a pye of.——Good God! cried my father, what havock and destruction must this make in the infinitely fine and tender texture of the cerebellum!—Or if there is such a juice as *Borri* pretends,—is it not enough to make the clearest liquor in the world both feculent and mothery?[11]

But how great was his apprehension, when he further understood, that this force, acting upon the very vertex of the head, not only injured the brain itself or cerebrum,——but that it

---

* The author is here twice mistaken;—for *Lithopædus* should be wrote thus, *Lithopædii Senonensis Icon*. The second mistake is, that this *Lithopædus* is not an author, but a drawing of a petrified child. The account of this, published by *Albosius*, 1580, may be seen at the end of *Cordæus*'s works in *Spachius*. Mr. *Tristram Shandy* has been led into this error, either from seeing *Lithopædus*'s name of late in a catalogue of learned writers in Dr.——, or by mistaking *Lithopædus* for *Trinecavellius*,—from the too great similitude of the names.[10]

necessarily squeez'd and propell'd the cerebrum towards the cerebellum, which was the immediate seat of the understanding.—Angels and Ministers of grace defend us! cried my father,—can any soul withstand this shock?—No wonder the intellectual web is so rent and tatter'd as we see it; and that so many of our best heads are no better than a puzzled skein of silk,---all perplexity,—all confusion within side.

But when my father read on, and was let into the secret, that when a child was turn'd topsy-turvy, which was easy for an operator to do, and was extracted by the feet;—that instead of the cerebrum being propell'd towards the cerebellum, the cerebellum, on the contrary, was propell'd simply towards the cerebrum where it could do no manner of hurt:—By heavens! cried he, the world is in a conspiracy to drive out what little wit God has given us,—and the professors of the obstetrick art are listed into the same conspiracy.—What is it to me which end of my son comes foremost into the world, provided all goes right after, and his cerebellum escapes uncrushed?

It is the nature of an hypothesis, when once a man has conceived it, that it assimulates every thing to itself as proper nourishment; and, from the first moment of your begetting it, it generally grows the stronger by every thing you see, hear, read, or understand. This is of great use.

When my father was gone with this about a month, there was scarce a phænomenon of stupidity or of genius, which he could not readily solve by it;—it accounted for the eldest son being the greatest blockhead in the family.--Poor Devil, he would say,--he made way for the capacity of his younger brothers.--It unriddled the observation of drivellers and monstrous heads,—shewing, *a priori*, it could not be otherwise,—unless **** I don't know what. It wonderfully explain'd and accounted for the acumen of the *Asiatick* genius, and that sprightlier turn, and a more penetrating intuition of minds, in warmer climates; not from the loose and common-place solution of a clearer sky, and a more perpetual sun-shine, &c.—which, for aught he knew, might as well rarify and dilute the faculties of the soul into nothing, by one extreme,—as they are condensed in colder climates by the other;—but he traced the affair up to its spring-head;—shew'd that, in warmer climates, nature had laid a lighter tax upon the fairest parts of the creation;---their pleasures more;—the necessity of their pains less, insomuch that the pressure and resistance upon the vertex was so slight, that the whole organization of the cerebellum was preserved;—nay, he did not believe, in natural births, that so much as a single thread of the net-work was broke or displaced,—so that the soul might just act as she liked.

When my father had got so far,—what a blaze of light did the accounts of the *Cæsarian* section, and of the towering geniuses who had come safe into the world by it, cast upon this hypothesis? Here you see, he would say, there was no injury done to the sensorium;—no pressure of the head against the pelvis;—no propulsion of the cerebrum towards the cerebellum, either by the *oss pubis* on this side, or the *oss coxcygis*[12] on that;—and, pray, what were the happy consequences? Why, Sir, your *Julius Cæsar*,[13] who gave the operation a name;—and your *Hermes Trismegistus*, who was born so before ever the operation had a name;—your *Scipio Africanus*; your *Manlius Torquatus*; our *Edward* the sixth,——who, had he lived, would have done the same honour to the hypothesis:——These, and many more, who figur'd high in the annals of fame,—all came *side-way*, Sir, into the world.

This incision of the *abdomen* and *uterus*, ran for six weeks together in my father's head;—he had read, and was satisfied, that wounds in the *epigastrium*, and those in the *matrix*, were not mortal;—so that the belly of the mother might be opened extremely well to give a passage to the child.—He mentioned the thing one afternoon to my mother,—merely as a matter of fact;—but seeing her turn as pale as ashes at the very mention of it, as much as the operation flattered his hopes,—he thought it as well to say no more of it,—contenting himself with admiring—what he thought was to no purpose to propose.[14]

This was my father Mr. *Shandy*'s hypothesis; concerning which I have only to add, that my brother *Bobby* did as great honour to it (whatever he did to the family) as any one of the great heroes we spoke of:—For happening not only to be christen'd, as I told you, but to be born too, when my father was at *Epsom*,--being moreover my mother's *first* child,--coming into the world with his head *foremost*,—and turning out afterwards a lad of wonderful slow parts,—my father spelt all these together into his opinion; and as he had failed at one end,—he was determined to try the other.

This was not to be expected from one of the sisterhood, who are not easily to be put out of their way,—and was therefore one of my father's great reasons in favour of a man of science, whom he could better deal with.

Of all men in the world, Dr. *Slop* was the fittest for my father's purpose;—for tho' his new-invented forceps was the armour he had proved, and what he maintained, to be the safest instrument of deliverance,—yet, it seems, he had scattered a word or two in his book, in favour of the very thing which ran in my father's fancy;—tho' not with a view to the soul's good in extracting by the feet, as was my father's system,—but for reasons merely obstetrical.

This will account for the coallition betwixt my father and Dr. *Slop*, in the ensuing discourse, which went a little hard against my uncle *Toby*.——In what manner a plain man, with nothing but common sense, could bear up against two such allies in science,—is hard to conceive.——You may conjecture upon it, if you please,—and whilst your imagination is in motion, you may encourage it to go on, and discover by what causes and effects in nature it could come to pass, that my uncle *Toby* got his modesty by the wound he received upon his groin.—You may raise a system to account for the loss of my nose by marriage articles,——and shew the world how it could happen, that I should have the misfortune to be called Tristram, in opposition to my father's hypothesis, and the wish of the whole family, God-fathers and God-mothers not excepted.—These, with fifty other points left yet unravelled, you may endeavour to solve if you have time;—but I tell you before-hand it will be in vain,—for not the sage *Alquife*, the magician in Don *Belianis* of *Greece*,[15] nor the no less famous *Urganda*, the sorceress his wife, (were they alive) could pretend to come within a league of the truth.

The reader will be content to wait for a full explanation of these matters till the next year,[16]—when a series of things will be laid open which he little expects.

END of the SECOND VOLUME.

THE

L I F E

A N D

O P I N I O N S

O F

TRISTRAM SHANDY,

G E N T L E M A N.

Multitudinis imperitæ non formido judicia; meis
tamen, rogo, parcant opusculis——in quibus
fuit propositi semper, a jocis ad seria, a seriis
vicissim ad jocos transire.

JOAN. SARESBERIENSIS,
Episcopus Lugdun.

V O L. I I I.

L O N D O N :
Printed for R. and J. DODSLEY in *Pall-Mall.*
M.DCC.LXI.

CHAPTER I

——"*I wish*, Dr. *Slop*," quoth my uncle *Toby* (repeating his wish for Dr. *Slop* a second time, and with a degree of more zeal and earnestness in his manner of wishing, than he had wished it at first*)——"*I wish*, Dr. *Slop*," *quoth* my uncle *Toby*, "*you had seen what prodigious armies we had in Flanders.*"

My uncle *Toby*'s wish did Dr. *Slop* a disservice which his heart never intended any man,——Sir, it confounded him—and thereby putting his ideas first into confusion, and then to flight, he could not rally them again for the soul of him.

In all disputes,——male or female,——whether for honour, for profit or for love,—it makes no difference in the case;—nothing is more dangerous, madam, than a wish coming sideways in this unexpected manner upon a man: the safest way in general to take off the force of the wish, is, for the party wished at, instantly to get up upon his legs—and wish the *wisher* something in return, of pretty near the same value,——so balancing the account upon the spot, you stand as you were—nay sometimes gain the advantage of the attack by it.

This will be fully illustrated to the world in my chapter of wishes.——

Dr. *Slop* did not understand the nature of this defence;——he was puzzled with it, and it put an entire stop to the dispute for four minutes and a half;——five had been fatal to it:—my father saw the danger——the dispute was one of the most interesting disputes in the world, "Whether the child of his prayers and endeavours should be born without a head or with one:"——he waited to the last moment to allow Dr. *Slop*, in whose behalf the wish was made, his right of returning it; but perceiving, I say, that he was confounded, and continued looking with that perplexed vacuity of eye which puzzled souls generally stare with,——first in my uncle *Toby*'s face——then in his——then up——then down——then east——east and by east, and so on,——coasting it along by the plinth of the wainscot till he had got to the opposite point of the compass,—and that he had actually begun to count the brass nails upon the arm of his chair——my father thought there was no time to be lost with my uncle *Toby*, so took up the discourse as follows.

* Vid. Vol. II. p. 159.[1]

CHAPTER II

"—WHAT prodigious armies you had in *Flanders!*"——

Brother *Toby*, replied my father, taking his wig from off his head with his right hand, and with his *left* pulling out a striped *India* handkerchief[1] from his right coat pocket, in order to rub his head, as he argued the point with my uncle *Toby*.——

——Now, in this I think my father was much to blame; and I will give you my reasons for it.

Matters of no more seeming consequence in themselves than, "*Whether my father should have taken off his wig with his right hand or with his left,*"——have divided the greatest kingdoms, and made the crowns of the monarchs who governed them, to totter upon their heads.—But need I tell you, Sir, that the circumstances with which every thing in this world is begirt, give every thing in this world its size and shape;——and by tightening it, or relaxing it, this way or that, make the thing to be, what it is—great—little—good—bad—indifferent or not indifferent, just as the case happens.

As my father's *India* handkerchief was in his right coat pocket, he should by no means have suffered his right hand to have got engaged: on the contrary, instead of taking off his wig with it, as he did, he ought to have committed that entirely to the left; and then, when the natural exigency my father was under of rubbing his head, call'd out for his handkerchief, he would have had nothing in the world to have done, but to have put his right hand into his right coat pocket and taken it out;—which he might have done without any violence, or the least ungraceful twist in any one tendon or muscle of his whole body.

In this case, (unless indeed, my father had been resolved to make a fool of himself by holding the wig stiff in his left hand—or by making some nonsensical angle or other at his elbow joint, or armpit)—his whole attitude had been easy—natural—unforced: *Reynolds*[2] himself, as great and gracefully as he paints, might have painted him as he sat.

Now, as my father managed this matter,——consider what a devil of a figure my father made of himself.

—In the latter end of Queen *Anne*'s reign, and in the beginning of the reign of King *George* the first—"*Coat pockets were cut very low down in the skirt.*"——I need say no more——the father of mischief, had he been hammering at it a month, could not have contrived a worse fashion for one in my father's situation.

CHAPTER III

IT was not an easy matter in any king's reign, (unless you were as lean a subject as myself)[1] to have forced your hand diagonally, quite across your whole body, so as to gain the bottom of your opposite coat-pocket.—In the year, one thousand seven hundred and eighteen, when this happened, it was extremely difficult; so that when my uncle *Toby* discovered the transverse zig-zaggery of my father's approaches towards it, it instantly brought into his mind those he had done duty in, before the gate of St. *Nicholas*;——the idea of which drew off his attention so entirely from the subject in debate, that he had got his right hand to the bell to ring up *Trim*, to go and fetch his map of *Namur*, and his compasses and sector along with it, to measure the returning angles of the traverses of that attack,—but particularly of that one, where he received his wound upon his groin.

My father knit his brows, and as he knit them, all the blood in his body seemed to rush up into his face——my uncle *Toby* dismounted immediately.

—I did not apprehend your uncle *Toby* was o' horse-back.——

CHAPTER IV

A MAN's body and his mind, with the utmost reverence to both I speak it, are exactly like a jerkin, and a jerkin's lining;—rumple the one—you rumple the other. There is one certain exception however in this case, and that is, when you are so fortunate a fellow, as to have had your jerkin made of a gum-taffeta,[1] and the body-lining to it, of a sarcenet or thin persian.[2].

Zeno,[3] *Cleanthes*, *Diogenes Babylonius*, *Dyonisius Heracleotes*, *Antipater*, *Panætius* and *Possidonius* amongst the *Greeks*;—*Cato*[4] and *Varro* and *Seneca* amongst the *Romans*;—*Pantenus*[5] and *Clemens Alexandrinus* and *Montaigne* amongst the *Christians*; and a score and a half of good honest, unthinking, *Shandean* people as ever lived, whose names I can't recollect,—all pretended that their jerkins were made after this fashion,——you might have rumpled and crumpled, and doubled and creased, and fretted and fridged the outsides of them all to pieces;—in short, you might have played the very devil with them, and at the same time, not one of the insides of 'em would have one button the worse, for all you had done to them.

I believe in my conscience that mine is made up somewhat after this sort:—for never poor jerkin has been tickled off, at such a rate as it has been these last nine months together, ——and yet I declare the lining to it,—as far as I am a judge of the matter, it is not a three-penny piece the worse;—pell mell, helter skelter, ding dong, cut and thrust, back stroke and fore stroke, side way and long way, have they been trimming it for me:—had there been the least gumminess in my lining,——by heaven! it had all of it long ago been fray'd and fretted to a thread.

—You Messrs. the monthly Reviewers![6]——how could you cut and slash my jerkin as you did?——how did you know, but you would cut my lining too?

Heartily and from my soul, to the protection of that Being who will injure none of us, do I recommend you and your affairs,—so God bless you;—only next month, if any one of you should gnash his teeth, and storm and rage at me, as some of you did last MAY, (in which I remember the weather was very hot)—don't be exasperated, if I pass it by again with good temper,——being determined as long as I live or write (which in my case means the same thing) never to give the honest gentleman a worse word or a worse wish, than my uncle *Toby* gave the fly which buzz'd about his nose all *dinner time*,——"Go, ——go poor devil," quoth he, "——get thee gone,——why should I hurt thee? This world is surely wide enough to hold both thee and me."

CHAPTER V

ANY man, madam, reasoning upwards, and observing the prodigious suffusion of blood in my father's countenance,—by means of which, (as all the blood in his body seemed to rush up into his face, as I told you) he must have redden'd, pictorially and scientintically speaking, six whole tints and a half, if not a full octave above his natural colour:——any man, madam, but my uncle *Toby*, who had observed this, together with the violent knitting of my father's brows, and the extravagant contortion of his body during the whole affair,—would have concluded my father in a rage; and taking that for granted,——had he been a lover of such kind of concord as arises from two such instruments being put into exact tune,—he would instantly have skrew'd up his, to the same pitch;——and then the devil and all had broke loose—the whole piece, madam, must have been played off like the sixth of Avison Scarlatti[1]—*con furia*,[2]—like mad.——Grant me patience!——What has *con furia*,—*con strepito*,[3]—or any other hurlyburly word whatever to do with harmony?

Any man, I say, madam, but my uncle *Toby*, the benignity of whose heart interpreted every motion of the body in the kindest sense the motion would admit of, would have concluded my father angry and blamed him too. My uncle *Toby* blamed nothing but the taylor who cut the pocket-hole;——so sitting still, till my father had got his handkerchief out of it, and looking all the time up in his face with inexpressible good will—my father at length went on as follows.

CHAPTER VI

——"WHAT prodigious armies you had in *Flanders!*"

—Brother *Toby*, quoth my father, I do believe thee to be as honest a man, and with as good and as upright a heart as ever God created;——nor is it thy fault, if all the children which have been, may, can, shall, will or ought to be begotten, come with their heads foremost into the world:—but believe me, dear *Toby*, the accidents which unavoidably way-lay them, not only in the article of our begetting 'em,—though these in my opinion, are well worth considering,——but the dangers and difficulties our children are beset with, after they are got forth into the world, are enow,—little need is there to expose them to unnecessary ones in their passage to it.——Are these dangers, quoth my uncle *Toby*, laying his hand upon my father's knee, and looking up seriously in his face for an answer,——are these dangers greater now o' days, brother, than in times past? Brother *Toby*, answered my father, if a child was but fairly begot, and born alive, and healthy, and the mother did well after it,——our forefathers never looked further.——My uncle *Toby* instantly withdrew his hand from off my father's knee, reclined his body gently back in his chair, raised his head till he could just see the cornish[1] of the room, and then directing the buccinatory muscles along his cheeks, and the orbicular muscles around his lips to do their duty——he whistled *Lillabullero*.

CHAPTER VII

WHILST my uncle *Toby* was whistling Lillabullero to my father,——Dr. *Slop* was stamping, and cursing and damning at *Obadiah* at a most dreadful rate;——it would have done your heart good, and cured you, Sir, for ever, of the vile sin of swearing to have heard him.—I am determined therefore to relate the whole affair to you.

When Dr. *Slop*'s maid delivered the green bays bag, with her master's instruments in it, to *Obadiah*, she very sensibly exhorted him to put his head and one arm through the strings, and ride with it slung across his body: so undoing the bow-knot, to lengthen the strings for him, without any more ado, she helped him on with it. However, as this, in some measure, unguarded the mouth of the bag, lest any thing should bolt out in galloping back at the speed *Obadiah* threatened, they consulted to take it off again; and in the great care and caution of their hearts, they had taken the two strings and tied them close (pursing up the mouth of the bag first) with half a dozen hard knots, each of which, *Obadiah*, to make all safe, had twitched and drawn together with all the strength of his body.

This answered all that *Obadiah* and the maid intended; but was no remedy against some evils which neither he or she foresaw. The instruments, it seems, as tight as the bag was tied above, had so much room to play in it, towards the bottom, (the shape of the bag being conical) that *Obadiah* could not make a trot of it, but with such a terrible jingle, what with the *tire-tête*, *forceps* and *squirt*, as would have been enough, had *Hymen*[1] been taking a jaunt that way, to have frightened him out of the country; but when *Obadiah* accelerated this motion, and from a plain trot assayed to prick his coach-horse into a full gallop—by heaven! Sir,—the jingle was incredible.

As *Obadiah* had a wife and three children—the turpitude of fornication, and the many other political ill consequences of this jingling, never once entered his brain,——he had however his objection, which came home to himself, and weighed with him, as it has oft-times done with the greatest patriots.——"*The poor fellow, Sir, was not able to hear himself whistle.*"

CHAPTER VIII

As *Obadiah* loved wind musick preferably to all the instrumental musick he carried with him,—he very considerately set his imagination to work, to contrive and to invent by what means he should put himself in a condition of enjoying it.

In all distresses (except musical) where small cords are wanted,——nothing is so apt to enter a man's head, as his hat-band:——the philosophy of this is so near the surface—I scorn to enter into it.

As *Obadiah*'s was a mix'd case,——mark, Sirs,—I say, a mix'd case; for it was obstretical,—*scrip*-tical,—squirtical, papistical,—and as far as the coach-horse was concerned in it,—caball-istical—and only partly musical;—*Obadiah* made no scruple of availing himself of the first expedient which offered;—so taking hold of the bag and instruments, and gripeing them hard together with one hand, and with the finger and thumb of the other, putting the end of the hat-band betwixt his teeth, and then slipping his hand down to the middle of it,—he tied and cross-tied them all fast together from one end to the other (as you would cord a trunk) with such a multiplicity of round-abouts and intricate cross turns, with a hard knot at every intersection or point where the strings met,—that Dr. *Slop* must have had three fifths of *Job*'s patience at least to have unloosed them.—I think in my conscience, that had NATURE been in one of her nimble moods, and in humour for such a contest——and she and Dr. *Slop* both fairly started together—there is no man living who had seen the bag with all that *Obadiah* had done to it,—and known likewise, the great speed the goddess can make when she thinks proper, who would have had the least doubt remaining in his mind——which of the two would have carried off the prize. My mother, madam, had been delivered sooner than the green bag infallibly—at least by twenty *knots*.——Sport of small accidents, *Tristram Shandy!* that thou art, and ever will be! had that trial been made for thee, and it was fifty to one but it had,——thy affairs had not been so depress'd—(at least by the depression of thy nose) as they have been; nor had the fortunes of thy house and the occasions of making them, which have so often presented themselves in the course of thy life, to thee, been so often, so vexatiously, so tamely, so irrecoverably abandoned—as thou hast been forced to leave them!—but 'tis over,—all but the account of 'em, which cannot be given to the curious till I am got out into the world.

CHAPTER IX

GREAT wits jump: for the moment Dr. *Slop* cast his eyes upon his bag (which he had not done till the dispute with my uncle *Toby* about midwifery put him in mind of it)—the very same thought occurred.—'Tis God's mercy, quoth he, (to himself) that Mrs. *Shandy* has had so bad a time of it,—else she might have been brought to bed seven times told, before one half of these knots could have got untied.——But here, you must distinguish——the thought floated only in Dr. *Slop*'s mind, without sail or ballast to it, as a simple proposition; millions of which, as your worship knows, are every day swiming quietly in the middle of the thin juice of a man's understanding, without being carried backwards or forwards, till some little gusts of passion or interest drive them to one side.

A sudden trampling in the room above, near my mother's bed, did the proposition the very service I am speaking of. By all that's unfortunate, quoth Dr. *Slop*, unless I make haste, the thing will actually befall me as it is.

CHAPTER X

IN the case of *knots*,——by which, in the first place, I would not be understood to mean slip-knots,——because in the course of my life and opinions,——my opinions concerning them will come in more properly when I mention the catastrophe of my great uncle Mr. *Hammond Shandy*,——a little man,——but of high fancy:——he rushed into the duke of *Monmouth*'s affair:'——nor, secondly, in this place, do I mean that particular species of knots, called bow-knots;——there is so little address, or skill, or patience, required in the unloosing them, that they are below my giving any opinion at all about them.—But by the knots I am speaking of, may it please your reverences to believe, that I mean good, honest, devilish tight, hard knots, made *bona fide*, as *Obadiah* made his;—in which there is no quibbling provision made by the duplication and return of the two ends of the strings through the annulus or noose made by the second *implication* of them—to get them slipp'd and undone by ————I hope you apprehend me.

In the case of these *knots* then, and of the several obstructions, which, may it please your reverences, such knots cast in our way in getting through life——every hasty man can whip out his penknife and cut through them.——'Tis wrong. Believe me, Sirs, the most virtuous way, and which both reason and conscience dictate—is to take our teeth or our fingers to them.——Dr. *Slop* had lost his teeth—his favourite instrument, by extracting in a wrong direction, or by some misapplication of it, unfortunately slipping, he had formerly in a hard labour, knock'd out three of the best of them, with the handle of it:—he tried his fingers—alas! the nails of his fingers and thumbs were cut close.—The deuce take it! I can make nothing of it either way, cried Dr. *Slop*.——The trampling over head near my mother's bed side increased.—Pox take the fellow! I shall never get the knots untied as long as I live.—My mother gave a groan—Lend me your penknife—I must e'en cut the knots at last-----pugh!---psha!---Lord! I have cut my thumb quite across to the very bone——curse the fellow——if there was not another man midwife within fifty miles—I am undone for this bout——I wish the scoundrel hang'd—I wish he was shot—I wish all the devils in hell had him for a block-head——

My father had a great respect for *Obadiah*, and could not bear to hear him disposed of in such a manner——he had moreover some little respect for himself——and could as ill bear with the indignity offer'd to himself in it.

Had Dr. *Slop* cut any part about him, but his thumb——my

father had pass'd it by——his prudence had triumphed: as it was, he was determined to have his revenge.

Small curses, Dr. *Slop*, upon great occasions, quoth my father, (condoling with him first upon the accident) are but so much waste of our strength and soul's health to no manner of purpose.—I own it, replied Dr. *Slop*.——They are like sparrow shot, quoth my uncle *Toby*, (suspending his whistling) fired against a bastion.——They serve, continued my father, to stir the humours—but carry off none of their acrimony:—for my own part, I seldom swear or curse at all——I hold it bad—but if I fall into it, by surprize, I generally retain so much presence of mind (right, quoth my uncle *Toby*) as to make it answer my purpose—that is, I swear on, till I find myself easy. A wise and a just man however would always endeavour to proportion the vent given to these humours, not only to the degree of them stirring within himself—but to the size and ill intent of the offence upon which they are to fall.——"*Injuries come only from the heart*,"——quoth my uncle *Toby*. For this reason, continued my father, with the most *Cervantick* gravity, I have the greatest veneration in the world for that gentleman, who, in distrust of his own discretion in this point, sat down and composed (that is at his leisure) fit forms of swearing suitable to all cases, from the lowest to the highest provocations which could possibly happen to him,—which forms being well consider'd by him, and such moreover as he could stand to, he kept them ever by him on the chimney piece, within his reach, ready for use.——I never apprehended, replied Dr. *Slop*, that such a thing was ever thought of,——much less executed. I beg your pardon—answered my father; I was reading, though not using, one of them to my brother *Toby* this morning, whilst he pour'd out the tea—'tis here upon the shelf over my head;—but if I remember right, 'tis too violent for a cut of the thumb.——Not at all, quoth Dr. *Slop*—the devil take the fellow.—Then answered my father, 'Tis much at your service, Dr. *Slop*——on condition you will read it aloud;——so rising up and reaching down a form of excommunication of the church of *Rome*, a copy of which, my father (who was curious in his collections) had procured out of the leger-book of the church of *Rochester*, writ by ERNULPHUS[2] the bishop—with a most affected seriousness of look and voice, which might have cajoled ERNULPHUS himself,—he put it into Dr. *Slop*'s hands,—Dr. *Slop* wrapt his thumb up in the corner of his handkerchief, and with a wry face, though without any suspicion, read aloud, as follows,—my uncle *Toby* whistling *Lillabullero*, as loud as he could, all the time.

Textus de Ecclesiâ Roffensi, per Ernulfum Episcopum.

CAP. XXV.

EXCOMMUNICATIO.

Ex auctoritate Dei omnipotentis, Patris, et Filij, et Spiritus Sancti, et sanctorum canonum, sanctæque et intemeratæ Virginis Dei genetricis Mariæ,

——Atque omnium cœlestium virtutum, angelorum, archangelorum, thronorum, dominationum, potestatuum, cherubin ac seraphin, & sanctorum patriarchum, prophetarum, & omnium apostolorum et evangelistarum, & sanctorum innocentum, qui in conspectu Agni soli digni inventi sunt canticum cantare novum, et sanctorum martyrum, et sanctorum confessorum, et sanctarum virginum, atque omnium simul sanctorum et electorum Dei,—Excommunicamus, et anathe-
matizamus hunc furem, vel hunc malefactorem, N. N. et a
liminibus sanctae Dei ecclesiæ sequestramus ut æternis suppli-
ciis excruciandus, mancipetur, cum Dathan et Abiram, et cum his qui dixerunt Domino Deo, Recede à nobis, scientiam viarum tuarum nolumus: et sicut aquâ ignis extinguitur, sic extinguatur
lucerna ejus secula seculorum nisi resipuerit, et ad satisfac-
tionem venerit . Amen.

(interlinear glosses: vel os, s, vel os, s, vel i, n, vel eorum, n)

As the genuineness of the consultation of the *Sorbonne* upon the question of baptism, was doubted by some, and denied by others,——'twas thought proper to print the original of this excommunication; for the copy of which Mr. *Shandy* returns thanks to the chapter clerk of the dean and chapter of *Rochester*.[3]

CHAPTER XI

"By the authority of God Almighty, the Father, Son, and Holy Ghost, and of the holy canons, and of the undefiled Virgin *Mary*, mother and patroness of our Saviour," I think there is no necessity, quoth Dr. *Slop*, dropping the paper down to his knee, and addressing himself to my father,——as you have read it over, Sir, so lately, to read it aloud;—and as Captain *Shandy* seems to have no great inclination to hear it,——I may as well read it to myself. That's contrary to treaty, replied my father,—besides, there is something so whimsical, especially in the latter part of it, I should grieve to lose the pleasure of a second reading. Dr. *Slop* did not altogether like it,—but my uncle *Toby* offering at that instant to give over whistling, and read it himself to them;——Dr. *Slop* thought he might as well read it under the cover of my uncle *Toby*'s whistling,—as suffer my uncle *Toby* to read it alone;—so raising up the paper to his face, and holding it quite parallel to it, in order to hide his chagrin,—he read it aloud as follows,——my uncle *Toby* whistling Lillabullero, though not quite so loud as before.

"By the authority of God Almighty, the Father, Son, and Holy Ghost, and of the undefiled Virgin *Mary*, mother and patroness of our Saviour, and of all the celestial virtues, angels, archangels, thrones, dominions, powers, cherubins and seraphins, and of all the holy patriarchs, prophets, and of all the apostles and evangelists, and of the holy innocents, who in the sight of the holy Lamb, are found worthy to sing the new song of the holy martyrs and holy confessors, and of the holy virgins, and of all the saints together, with the holy and elect of God.——May he," (*Obadiah*) "be damn'd," (for tying these knots.)——"We excommunicate, and anathematise him, and from the thresholds of the holy church of God Almighty we sequester him, that he may be tormented, disposed and delivered over with *Dathan* and *Abiram*.[1] and with those who say unto the Lord God, Depart from us, we desire none of thy ways. And as fire is quenched with water, so let the light of him be put out for evermore, unless it shall repent him" (Obadiah, of the knots which he has tied) "and make satisfaction" (for them.) Amen.

Maledicat illum[os] Deus Pater qui hominem creavit. Maledicat illum[os] Dei Filius qui pro homine passus est. Maledicat illum Spiritus Sanctus qui in baptismo effusus est. Maledicat illum[os] sancta crux, quam Christus pro nostrâ salute hostem triumphans, ascendit.

Maledicat illum[os] sancta Dei genetrix et perpetua Virgo Maria. Maledicat illum[os] sanctus Michael, animarum susceptor sacrarum. Maledicant illum[os] omnes angeli et archangeli, principatus et potestates, omnisque militia cœlestis.

Maledicat illum[os] patriarcharum et prophetarum laudabilis numerus. Maledicat illum[os] sanctus Johannes præcursor et Baptista Christi, et sanctus Petrus, et sanctus Paulus, atque sanctus Andreas, omnesque Christi apostoli, simul et cæteri discipuli, quatuor quoque evangelistæ, qui sua prædicatione mundum universum converterunt. Maledicat illum[os] cuneus martyrum et confessorum mirificus, qui Deo bonis operibus placitus inventus est.

Maledicant illum[os] sacrarum virginum chori, quæ mundi vana causa honoris Christi respuenda contempserunt. Maledicant illum[os] omnes sancti qui ab initio mundi usque in finem seculi Deo dilecti inveniuntur.

Maledicant illum[os] cœli et terra, et omnia sancta in eis manentia.

Maledictus sit[n] ubicunque fuerit, sive in domo, sive in agro, sive in viâ, sive in semitâ, sive in silvâ, sive in aquâ, sive in ecclesiâ.

Maledictus sit vivendo, moriendo, ——————————

—————— ———— —————— —————— ———
—— ———— —————— —————— ————
—————— ———— —————— —————— ———
—————— ———— —————— ————

manducando, bibendo, esuriendo, sitiendo, jejunando, dormitando, dormiendo, vigilando, ambulando, stando, sedendo,

"May the Father who created man, curse him.—May the Son who suffered for us, curse him.——May the Holy Ghost who was given to us in baptism, curse him (Obadiah.)—May the holy cross which Christ for our salvation triumphing over his enemies, ascended,—curse him.

"May the holy and eternal *Virgin Mary*, mother of God, curse him.—May St. *Michael* the advocate of holy souls, curse him.—May all the angels and archangels, principalities and powers, and all the heavenly armies, curse him." [Our armies swore terribly in *Flanders*, cried my uncle *Toby*,—but nothing to this.—For my own part, I could not have a heart to curse my dog so.]

"May St. John the præ-cursor, and St. John the Baptist, and St. Peter and St. Paul, and St. Andrew, and all other Christ's apostles, together curse him. And may the rest of his disciples and four evangelists, who by their preaching converted the universal world,—and may the holy and wonderful company of martyrs and confessors, who by their holy works are found pleasing to God Almighty, curse him (Obadiah.)

"May the holy choir of the holy virgins, who for the honour of Christ have despised the things of the world, damn him.— May all the saints who from the beginning of the world to everlasting ages are found to be beloved of God, damn him.— May the heavens and earth, and all the holy things remaining therein, damn him," (Obadiah) "or her," (or whoever else had a hand in tying these knots.)

"May he (Obadiah) be damn'd where-ever he be,—whether in the house or the stables, the garden or the field, or the highway, or in the path, or in the wood, or in the water, or in the church.—May he be cursed in living, in dying." [Here my uncle *Toby* taking the advantage of a *minim* in the second barr of his tune, kept whistling one continual note to the end of the sentence——Dr. *Slop* with his division of curses moving under him, like a running bass all the way.] "May he be cursed in eating and drinking, in being hungry, in being thirsty, in fasting, in sleeping, in slumbering, in walking, in standing, in sitting, in

jacendo, operando, quiescendo, mingendo, cacando, fleboto-
mando.

Maledictus sit in totis viribus corporis.

Maledictus sit intus et exterius.

Maledictus sit in capillis; maledictus sit in cerebro. Maledictus sit in vertice, in temporibus, in fronte, in auriculis, in
superciliis, in oculis, in genis, in maxillis, in naribus, in dentibus,
mordacibus, in labris sive molibus, in labiis, in guttere, in
humeris, in harmis, in brachiis, in manubus, in digitis, in pec-
tore, in corde, et in omnibus interioribus stomacho tenus, in
renibus, in inguinibus, in femore, in genitalibus, in coxis, in
genubus, in cruribus, in pedibus, et in unguibus.

Maledictus sit in totis compagibus membrorum, a vertice
capitis, usque ad plantam pedis——non sit in eo sanitas.

Maledicat illum Christus Filius Dei vivi toto suæ majestatis
imperio

lying, in working, in resting, in pissing, in shitting, and in blood-letting."

"May he (*Obadiah*) be cursed in all the faculties of his body.

"May he be cursed inwardly and outwardly.—May he be cursed in the hair of his head.—May he be cursed in his brains, and in his vertex," (that is a sad curse, quoth my father) "in his temples, in his forehead, in his ears, in his eye-brows, in his cheeks, in his jaw-bones, in his nostrils, in his foreteeth and grinders, in his lips, in his throat, in his shoulders, in his wrists, in his arms, in his hands, in his fingers.

"May he be damn'd in his mouth, in his breast, in his heart and purtenance, down to the very stomach.

"May he be cursed in his reins, and in his groin," (God in heaven forbid, quoth my uncle *Toby*)—"in his thighs, in his genitals," (my father shook his head) "and in his hips, and in his knees, his legs, and feet, and toe-nails.

"May he be cursed in all the joints and articulations of his members, from the top of his head to the soal of his foot, may there be no soundness in him.

"May the Son of the living God, with all the glory of his Majesty"——[Here my uncle *Toby* throwing back his head, gave a monstrous long, loud Whew—w—w—— something betwixt the interjectional whistle of *Hey day!* and the word itself.——

—By the golden beard of *Jupiter*—and of *Juno*, (if her majesty wore one), and by the beards of the rest of your heathen worships, which by the bye was no small number, since what with the beards of your celestial gods, and gods aerial and acquatick,—to say nothing of the beards of town-gods and country-gods, or of the celestial goddesses your wives, or of the infernal goddesses your whores and concubines, (that is in case they wore 'em)——all which beards, as *Varro*[2] tells me, upon his word and honour, when mustered up together, made no less than thirty thousand effective beards upon the pagan establishment;——every beard of which claimed the rights and privileges of being stroked and sworn by,—by all these beards together then,——I vow and protest, that of the two bad cassocks I am worth in the world, I would have given the better of them, as freely as ever *Cid Hamet*[3] offered his,——only to have stood by, and heard my uncle *Toby*'s accompanyment.]

——et insurgat adversus illum cœlum cum omnibus virtutibus quæ in eo moventur ad *damnandum* eum, nisi penituerit et ad satisfactionem venerit. Amen. Fiat, fiat. Amen.

——"Curse him,"——continued Dr. *Slop*,——"and may heaven with all the powers which move therein, rise up against him, curse and damn him (Obadiah) unless he repent and make satisfaction. Amen. So be it,—so be it. Amen."

I declare, quoth my uncle *Toby*, my heart would not let me curse the devil himself with so much bitterness.——He is the father of curses, replied Dr. *Slop*.——So am not I, replied my uncle.——But he is cursed, and damn'd already, to all eternity,——replied Dr. *Slop*.

I am sorry for it, quoth my uncle *Toby*.

Dr. *Slop* drew up his mouth, and was just beginning to return my uncle *Toby* the compliment of his Whu—u—u——or interjectional whistle,——when the door hastily opening in the next chapter but one——put an end to the affair.

CHAPTER XII

Now don't let us give ourselves a parcel of airs, and pretend that the oaths we make free with in this land of liberty of ours are our own; and because we have the spirit to swear them,——imagine that we have had the wit to invent them too.

I'll undertake this moment to prove it to any man in the world, except to a connoisseur;——though I declare I object only to a connoisseur in swearing,—as I would do to a connoisseur in painting, &c. &c. the whole set of 'em are so hung round and *befetish'd* with the bobs and trinkets of criticism,——or to drop my metaphor, which by the bye is a pity,——for I have fetch'd it as far as from the coast of *Guinea*;——their heads, Sir, are stuck so full of rules and compasses, and have that eternal propensity to apply them upon all occasions, that a work of genius had better go to the devil at once, than stand to be prick'd and tortured to death by 'em.

——And how did *Garrick*[1] speak the soliloquy last night?—Oh, against all rule, my Lord,—most ungrammatically! betwixt the substantive and the adjective, which should agree together in *number*, *case* and *gender*, he made a breach thus,—stopping, as if the point wanted settling;——and betwixt the nominative case, which your lordship knows should govern the verb, he suspended his voice in the epilogue a dozen times, three seconds and three fifths by a stop-watch, my Lord, each time.——Admirable grammarian!——But in suspending his voice

——was the sense suspended likewise? Did no expression of attitude or countenance fill up the chasm?—Was the eye silent? Did you narrowly look?—I look'd only at the stop-watch, my Lord.——Excellent observer!

And what of this new book the whole world makes such a rout about?—Oh! 'tis out of all plumb, my Lord,——quite an irregular thing!—not one of the angles at the four corners was a right angle.—I had my rule and compasses, &c. my Lord, in my pocket.——Excellent critic!

—And for the epick poem, your lordship bid me look at;—upon taking the length, breadth, height, and depth of it, and trying them at home upon an exact scale of *Bossu*'s,[2]—'tis out, my Lord, in every one of its dimensions.——Admirable connoisseur!

—And did you step in, to take a look at the grand picture, in your way back?——'Tis a melancholy daub! my Lord; not one principle of the *pyramid* in any one group!——and what a price!——for there is nothing of the colouring of *Titian*,[3] ——the expression of *Rubens*,—the grace of *Raphael*,——the purity of *Dominichino*,—the *corregiescity* of *Corregio*,—the learning of *Poussin*,—the airs of *Guido*,—the taste of the *Carrachi*'s,—or the grand contour of *Angelo*.——Grant me patience, just heaven!——Of all the cants which are canted in this canting world,——though the cant of hypocrites may be the worst,—the cant of criticism is the most tormenting!

I would go fifty miles on foot, for I have not a horse worth riding on, to kiss the hand of that man whose generous heart will give up the reins of his imagination into his author's hands,——be pleased he knows not why, and cares not wherefore.

Great *Apollo!*[4] if thou art in a giving humour,——give me, ——I ask no more, but one stroke of native humour, with a single spark of thy own fire along with it,——and send *Mercury*,[5] with the *rules and compasses*, if he can be spared, with my compliments to——no matter.

Now to any one else, I will undertake to prove, that all the oaths and imprecations, which we have been puffing off upon the world for these two hundred and fifty years last past, as originals,——except St. *Paul*'s *thumb*,——*God's flesh and God's fish*, which were oaths monarchical, and, considering who made them, not much amiss; and as kings oaths, 'tis not much matter whether they were fish or flesh;——else, I say, there is not an oath, or at least a curse amongst them, which has not been copied over and over again out of *Ernulphus*, a thousand times: but, like all other copies, how infinitely short of the force and spirit of the original!—It is thought to be no bad oath,——and by itself passes very well——"*G---d damn you.*"——Set it beside *Ernulphus's*——'God Almighty the Father damn you,—God the Son damn you,—God the Holy Ghost damn you,"—you see 'tis nothing.—There is an orientality in his, we cannot rise up to: besides, he is more copious in his invention,——possess'd more of the excellencies of a swearer,——had such a thorough knowledge of the human frame, its membranes, nerves, ligaments, knittings of the joints, and articulations,—that when *Ernulphus* cursed,—no part escaped him.—'Tis true, there is something of a *hardness* in his manner,—and, as in *Michael Angelo*, a want of *grace*,——but then there is such a greatness of *gusto!*—

My father, who generally look'd upon every thing in a light very different from all mankind,——would, after all, never allow this to be an original.——He consider'd rather *Ernulphus's* anathema, as an institute of swearing, in which, as he suspected, upon the decline of *swearing* in some milder pontificate, *Ernulphus*, by order of the succeeding pope, had with great learning and diligence collected together all the laws of it;——for the same reason that *Justinian*,[6] in the decline of the empire, had ordered his chancellor *Tribonian*[7] to collect the *Roman* or civil laws all together into one code or digest,—lest through the rust of time,—and the fatality of all things committed to oral tradition, they should be lost to the world for ever.

For this reason my father would oft-times affirm, there was not an oath, from the great and tremendous oath of *William* the Conqueror, (*By the splendour of God*) down to the lowest oath of a scavenger, (*Damn your eyes*) which was not to be found in *Ernulphus*.——In short, he would add,—I defy a man to swear *out* of it.

The hypothesis is, like most of my father's, singular and ingenious too;——nor have I any objection to it, but that it overturns my own.

CHAPTER XIII

——BLESS my soul!——my poor mistress is ready to faint,
——and her pains are gone,——and the drops are done,
——and the bottle of julap is broke,——and the nurse has cut
her arm,——(and I, my thumb, cried Dr. *Slop*) and the child is
where it was, continued *Susannah*,——and the midwife has
fallen backwards upon the edge of the fender, and bruised her
hip as black as your hat.——I'll look at it, quoth Dr. *Slop*.
——There is no need of that, replied *Susannah*,——you had
better look at my mistress,——but the midwife would gladly
first give you an account how things are, so desires you would
go up stairs and speak to her this moment.

Human nature is the same in all professions.

The midwife had just before been put over Dr. *Slop*'s head.—
He had not digested it.—No, replied Dr. *Slop*, 'twould be full as
proper, if the midwife came down to me.—I like subordination,
quoth my uncle *Toby*,—and but for it, after the reduction of
Lisle,[1] I know not what might have become of the garrison of
Ghent, in the mutiny for bread, in the year Ten.———Nor,
replied Dr. *Slop*, (parodying my uncle *Toby*'s hobby-horsical
reflection, though full as hobby-horsically himself)—do I
know, Captain *Shandy*, what might have become of the garrison above stairs, in the mutiny and confusion I find all things are
in at present, but for the subordination of fingers and thumbs to
******——the application of which, Sir, under this accident of
mine, comes in so *a propos*, that without it, the cut upon my
thumb might have been felt by the *Shandy* family, as long as the
Shandy family had a name.

CHAPTER XIV

LET us go back to the ******——in the last chapter.

It is a singular stroke of eloquence (at least it was so, when
eloquence flourished at *Athens* and *Rome*, and would be so
now, did orators wear mantles) not to mention the name of a
thing, when you had the thing about you, *in petto*, ready to
produce, pop, in the place you want it. A scar, an axe, a sword, a
pink'd-doublet, a rusty helmet, a pound and a half of pot-ashes
in an urn, or a three-halfpenny pickle pot,——but above all, a

tender infant royally accoutred.—Tho' if it was too young, and the oration as long as *Tully*'s second *Philippick*.¹—it must certainly have beshit the orator's mantle.——And then again, if too old,—it must have been unwieldy and incommodious to his action,—so as to make him lose by his child almost as much as he could gain by it.—Otherwise, when a state orator has hit the precise age to a minute,—hid his BAMBINO² in his mantle so cunningly that no mortal could smell it,—and produced it so critically, that no soul could say, it came in by head and shoulders,——Oh, Sirs! it has done wonders.——It has open'd the sluices, and turn'd the brains, and shook the principles, and unhinged the politicks of half a nation.

These feats however are not to be done, except in those states and times, I say, where orators wore mantles,—and pretty large ones too, my brethren, with some twenty or five and twenty yards of good purple, superfine, marketable cloth in them, ——with large flowing folds and doubles, and in a great stile of design.——All which plainly shews, may it please your worships, that the decay of eloquence, and the little good service it does at present, both within, and without doors, is owing to nothing else in the world, but short coats, and the disuse of *trunk-hose*.——We can conceal nothing under ours, Madam, worth shewing.

CHAPTER XV

DR. *Slop* was within an ace of being an exception to all this argumentation: for happening to have his green bays bag upon his knees, when he began to parody my uncle *Toby*,——'twas as good as the best mantle in the world to him: for which purpose, when he foresaw the sentence would end in his new invented *forceps*, he thrust his hand into the bag in order to have them ready to clap in, where your reverences took so much notice of the ******, which had he managed,—my uncle *Toby* had certainly been overthrown: the sentence and the argument in that case jumping closely in one point, so like the two lines which form the salient angle of a raveline,—Dr. *Slop* would never have given them up;——and my uncle *Toby* would as soon thought of flying, as taking them by force: but Dr. *Slop* fumbled so vilely in pulling them out, it took off the whole effect, and what was a ten times worse evil (for they seldom come alone in this life) in pulling out his *forceps*, his *forceps* unfortunately drew out the *squirt* along with it.

When a proposition can be taken in two senses,——'tis a law in disputation That the respondent may reply to which of the two he pleases, or finds most convenient for him.——This threw the advantage of the argument quite on my uncle *Toby's* side.——"Good God!" cried my uncle *Toby*, "*are children brought into the world with a squirt?*"

CHAPTER XVI

——Upon my honour, Sir, you have tore every bit of the skin quite off the back of both my hands with your forceps, cried my uncle *Toby*,—and you have crush'd all my knuckles into the bargain with them, to a jelly. 'Tis your own fault, said Dr. *Slop*,——you should have clinch'd your two fists together into the form of a child's head, as I told you, and sat firm.——I did so, answered my uncle *Toby*.——Then the points of my forceps have not been sufficiently arm'd, or the rivet wants closing—or else the cut on my thumb has made me a little aukward,——or possibly—'Tis well, quoth my father, interrupting the detail of possibilities,——that the experiment was not first made upon my child's head piece.——It would not have been a cherry stone the worse, answered Dr. *Slop*. I maintain it, said my uncle *Toby*, it would have broke the cerebellum, (unless indeed the skull had been as hard as a granado)[1] and turned it all into a perfect posset. Pshaw! replied Dr. *Slop*, a child's head is naturally as soft as the pap of an apple;——the sutures give way,——and besides, I could have extracted by the feet after. ——Not you, said she.—I rather wish you would begin that way, quoth my father.

Pray do, added my uncle *Toby*.

CHAPTER XVII

——And pray, good woman, after all, will you take upon you to say, it may not be the child's hip, as well as the child's head?——'Tis most certainly the head, replied the midwife. Because, continued Dr. *Slop*, (turning to my father) as positive as these old ladies generally are,——'tis a point very difficult to

know,—and yet of the greatest consequence to be known;——because, Sir, if the hip is mistaken for the head,—there is a possibility (if it is a boy) that the forceps * * * * * * *
* .

——What the possibility was, Dr. *Slop* whispered very low to my father, and then to my uncle *Toby*.——There is no such danger, continued he, with the head.—No, in truth, quoth my father,—but when your possibility has taken place at the hip,——you may as well take off the head too.

—It is morally impossible the reader should understand this,——'tis enough Dr. *Slop* understood it;——so taking the green bays bag in his hand, with the help of *Obadiah*'s pumps, he tripp'd pretty nimbly, for a man of his size, across the room to the door,——and from the door was shewn the way, by the good old midwife, to my mother's apartment.

CHAPTER XVIII

IT is two hours, and ten minutes,—and no more,——cried my father, looking at his watch, since Dr. *Slop* and *Obadiah* arrived,——and I know not how it happens, brother *Toby*,——but to my imagination it seems almost an age.

——Here——pray, Sir, take hold of my cap,—nay, take the bell along with it, and my pantoufles[1] too.——

Now, Sir, they are all at your service; and I freely make you a present of 'em, on condition, you give me all your attention to this chapter.

Though my father said, "*he knew not how it happen'd*,"—yet he knew very well, how it happen'd;——and at the instant he spoke it, was pre-determined in his mind, to give my uncle *Toby* a clear account of the matter by a metaphysical dissertation upon the subject of *duration and its simple modes*, in order to shew my uncle *Toby*, by what mechanism and mensurations in the brain it came to pass, that the rapid succession of their ideas, and the eternal scampering of discourse from one thing to another, since Dr. *Slop* had come into the room, had lengthened out so short a period, to so inconceivable an extent.——"I know not how it happens,——cried my father,——"but it seems an age."

—'Tis owing, entirely, quoth my uncle *Toby*, to the succession of our ideas.

My father, who had an itch in common with all philosophers, of reasoning upon every thing which happened, and accounting for it too,—proposed infinite pleasure to himself in this, of the succession of ideas, and had not the least apprehension of having it snatch'd out of his hands by my uncle *Toby*, who (honest man!) generally took every thing as it happened; ——and who, of all things in the world, troubled his brain the least with abstruse thinking;—the ideas of time and space, ——or how we came by those ideas,——or of what stuff they were made,—or whether they were born with us,——or we pick'd them up afterwards as we went along,—or whether we did it in frocks,—or not till we had got into breeches,—with a thousand other inquiries and disputes about INFINITY, PRESCIENCE, LIBERTY, NECESSITY, and so forth, upon whose desperate and unconquerable theories, so many fine heads have been turned and crack'd,—never did my uncle *Toby*'s the least injury at all; my father knew it,—and was no less surprised, than he was disappointed with my uncle's fortuitous solution.

Do you understand the theory of that affair? replied my father.

Not I, quoth my uncle.

——But you have some ideas, said my father, of what you talk about.——

No more than my horse, replied my uncle *Toby*.

Gracious heaven! cried my father, looking upwards, and clasping his two hands together,—there is a worth in thy honest ignorance, brother *Toby*,—'twere almost a pity to exchange it for a knowledge.——But I'll tell thee.——

To understand what *time* is aright, without which we never can comprehend *infinity*, insomuch as one is a portion of the other,——we ought seriously to sit down and consider what idea it is, we have of *duration*, so as to give a satisfactory account, how we came by it.—What is that to any body? quoth my uncle *Toby*. *For if you will turn your eyes inwards upon your mind, continued my father, and observe attentively, you will perceive, brother, that whilst you and I are talking together, and thinking and smoking our pipes: or whilst we receive successively ideas in our minds, we know that we do exist, and so we estimate the existence, or the continuation of the existence of ourselves, or any thing else commensurate to the succession of*

* Vid. Locke.[2]

any ideas in our minds, the duration of ourselves, or any such other thing co-existing with our thinking,——*and so according to that preconceived*——You puzzle me to death, cried my uncle *Toby*.—

——'Tis owing to this, replied my father, that in our computations of *time*, we are so used to minutes, hours, weeks, and months,——and of clocks (I wish there was a not a clock in the kingdom)[3] to measure out their several portions to us, and to those who belong to us,——that 'twill be well, if in time to come, the *succession of our ideas* be of any use or service to us at all.

Now, whether we observe it or no, continued my father, in every sound man's head, there is a regular succession of ideas of one sort or other, which follow each other in train just like ——A train of artillery? said my uncle *Toby*.—A train of a fiddle stick!—quoth my father,—which follow and succeed one another in our minds at certain distances, just like the images in the inside of a lanthorn turned round by the heat of a candle.—I declare, quoth my uncle *Toby*, mine are more like a smoak-jack.[4]——Then, brother *Toby*, I have nothing more to say to you upon the subject, said my father.

CHAPTER XIX

——WHAT a conjuncture was here lost!——My father in one of his best explanatory moods,—in eager pursuit of a metaphysic point into the very regions where clouds and thick darkness would soon have encompassed it about;——my uncle *Toby* in one of the finest dispositions for it in the world;—his head like a smoak-jack;——the funnel unswept, and the ideas whirling round and round about in it, all obfuscated and darkened over with fuliginous matter!——By the tomb stone of *Lucian*[1]——if it is in being,——if not, why then, by his ashes! by the ashes of my dear *Rabelais*,[2] and dearer *Cervantes*,[3] ——my father and my uncle *Toby*'s discourse upon TIME and ETERNITY,—was a discourse devoutly to be wished for! and the petulancy of my father's humour in putting a stop to it, as he did, was a robbery of the *Ontologic treasury*,[4] of such a jewel, as no coalition of great occasions and great men, are ever likely to restore to it again.

CHAPTER XX

THO' my father persisted in not going on with the discourse,—yet he could not get my uncle *Toby*'s smoak-jack out of his head,—piqued as he was as first with it;——there was something in the comparison at the bottom, which hit his fancy; for which purpose resting his elbow upon the table, and reclining the right side of his head upon the palm of his hand,—but looking first stedfastly in the fire,——he began to commune with himself and philosophize about it: but his spirits being wore out with the fatigues of investigating new tracts, and the constant exertion of his faculties upon that variety of subjects which had taken their turn in the discourse,—the idea of the smoak-jack soon turned all his ideas upside down,—so that he fell asleep almost before he knew what he was about.

As for my uncle *Toby*, his smoak-jack had not made a dozen revolutions, before he fell asleep also.——Peace be with them both.——Dr. *Slop* is engaged with the midwife, and my mother above stairs.—*Trim* is busy in turning an old pair of jack-boots into a couple of mortars to be employed in the siege of *Messina*[1] next summer,——and is this instant boring the touch holes with the point of a hot poker.——All my heroes are off my hands; ——'tis the first time I have had a moment to spare,—and I'll make use of it, and write my preface.

THE
AUTHOR'S PREFACE

No, I'll not say a word about it,—here it is;——in publishing it,——I have appealed to the world,——and to the world I leave it;——it must speak for itself.

All I know of the matter is,——when I sat down, my intent was to write a good book; and as far as the tenuity of my understanding would hold out,—a wise, aye, and a discreet,——taking care only, as I went along, to put into it all the wit and the judgment (be it more or less) which the great author and bestower of them had thought fit originally to give me,——so that, as your worships see,—'tis just as God pleases.

Now, *Agelastes*[2] (speaking dispraisingly) sayeth, That there may be some wit in it, for aught he knows,——but no judgment at all. And *Triptolemus* and *Phutatorius* agreeing thereto, ask, How is it possible there should? for that wit and judgment in this world never go together; inasmuch as they are two operations differing from each other as wide as east is from west.—So, says *Locke*,—so are farting and hickuping, say I. But in answer to this, *Didius* the great church lawyer, in his code *de fartandi et illustrandi fallaciis*,[3] doth maintain and make fully appear, That an illustration is no argument,—nor do I maintain the wiping of a looking-glass clean, to be a syllogism;——but you all, may it please your worships, see the better for it,——so that the main good these things do, is only to clarify the understanding, previous to the application of the argument itself, in order to free it from any little motes, or specks of opacular matter, which if left swiming therein, might hinder a conception and spoil all.

Now, my dear Anti-Shandeans, and thrice able critics,[4] and fellow-labourers, (for to you I write this Preface)——and to you, most subtle statesmen and discreet doctors (do—pull off your beards) renowned for gravity and wisdom;—*Monopolos*[5] my politician,—*Didius*, my counsel; *Kysarcius*, my friend;—*Phutatorius*, my guide;—*Gastripheres*, the preserver of my life; *Somnolentius*, the balm and repose of it,—not forgetting all others as well sleeping as waking,—ecclesiastical as civil, whom for brevity, but out of no resentment to you, I lump all together.———Believe me, right worthy,

My most zealous wish and fervent prayer in your behalf, and in my own too, in case the thing is not done already for us,———is, that the great gifts and endowments both of wit and judgment, with every thing which usually goes along with them,———such as memory, fancy, genius, eloquence, quick parts, and what not, may this precious moment without stint or measure, let or hinderance, be poured down warm as each of us could bear it,—scum and sediment an' all; (for I would not have a drop lost) into the several receptacles, cells, cellules, domiciles, dormitories, refectories, and spare places of our brains,—in such sort, that they might continue to be injected and tunn'd into, according to the true intent and meaning of my wish, until every vessel of them, both great and small, be so replenished, saturated and fill'd up therewith, that no more, would it save a man's life, could possibly be got either in or out.

Bless us!—what noble work we should make!—how should I tickle it off!———and what spirits should I find myself in, to be writing away for such readers!—and you,—just heaven!—with what raptures would you sit and read,—but oh!—'tis too much,———I am sick,———I faint away deliciously at the thoughts of it!———'tis more than nature can bear!———lay hold of me,—I am giddy,—I am stone blind,———I'm dying,———I am gone.———Help! Help! Help!—But hold,—I grow something better again, for I am beginning to foresee, when this is over, that as we shall all of us continue to be great wits,—we should never agree amongst ourselves, one day to an end:———there would be so much satire and sarcasm,———scoffing and flouting, with raillying and reparteeing of it,———thrusting and parrying in one corner or another,———there would be nothing but mischief amongst us.—Chaste stars! what biting and scratching, and what a racket and a clatter we should make, what with breaking of heads, and rapping of knuckles, and hitting of sore places,—there would be no such thing as living for us.

But then again, as we should all of us be men of great judgment, we should make up matters as fast as ever they went wrong; and though we should abominate each other, ten times worse than so many devils or devilesses, we should nevertheless, my dear creatures, be all courtesy and kindness,———milk and honey,———'twould be a second land of promise,———a paradise upon earth, if there was such a thing to be had,—so that upon the whole we should have done well enough.

All I fret and fume at, and what most distresses my invention at present, is how to bring the point itself to bear; for as your worships well know, that of these heavenly emanations of *wit* and *judgment*, which I have so bountifully wished both for your worships and myself,—there is but a certain *quantum* stored up for us all, for the use and behoof of the whole race of mankind; and such small *modicums* of 'em are only sent forth into this wide world, circulating here and there in one by corner or another,—and in such narrow streams, and at such prodigious intervals from each other, that one would wonder how it holds out, or could be sufficient for the wants and emergencies of so many great states, and populous empires.

Indeed there is one thing to be considered, that in *Nova Zembla*,[6] *North Lapland*, and in all those cold and dreary tracts of the globe, which lie more directly under the artick and antartick circles,——where the whole province of a man's concernments lies for near nine months together, within the narrow compass of his cave,——where the spirits are compressed almost to nothing,——and where the passions of a man, with every thing which belongs to them, are as frigid as the zone itself;—there the least quantity of *judgment*[7] imaginable does the business,—and of *wit*,—there is a total and an absolute saving,—for as not one spark is wanted,——so not one spark is given. Angels and ministers of grace defend us![8] What a dismal thing would it have been to have governed a kingdom, to have fought a battle, or made a treaty, or run a match, or wrote a book, or got a child, or held a provincial chapter there, with so *plentiful a lack* of wit and judgment about us! for mercy's sake! let us think no more about it, but travel on as fast as we can southwards into *Norway*,——crossing over *Swedeland*,[9] if you please, through the small triangular province of *Angermania*[10] to the lake of *Bothnia*; coasting along it through east and west *Bothnia*, down to *Carelia*,[11] and so on, through all those states and provinces which border upon the far side of the *Gulf* of *Finland*, and the north east of the *Baltick*, up to *Petersbourg*,[12] and just stepping into *Ingria*;[13]——then stretching over directly from thence through the north parts of the *Russian* empire—leaving *Siberia* a little upon the left hand till we get into the very heart of *Russian* and *Asiatick Tartary*.[14]

Now throughout this long tour which I have led you, you observe the good people are better off by far, than in the polar countries which we have just left:—for if you hold your hand over your eyes, and look very attentively, you may perceive some small glimmerings (as it were) of wit, with a comfortable provision of good plain *houshold* judgment, which taking the quality and quantity of it together, they make a very good shift with,—and had they more of either the one or the other, it would destroy the proper ballance betwixt them, and I am satisfied moreover they would want occasions to put them to use.

Now, Sir, if I conduct you home again into this warmer and more luxuriant island, where you perceive the spring tide of our blood and humours runs high,—where we have more ambition, and pride, and envy, and lechery, and other whoreson passions upon our hands to govern and subject to reason,—the *height* of our wit and the *depth* of our judgment, you see, are exactly proportioned to the *length* and *breadth* of our necessities,—and accordingly, we have them sent down amongst us in such a flowing kind of decent and creditable plenty, that no one thinks he has any cause to complain.

It must however be confessed on this head, that, as our air blows hot and cold,——wet and dry, ten times in a day, we have them in no regular and settled way;——so that sometimes for near half a century together, there shall be very little wit or judgment, either to be seen or heard of amongst us:——the small channels of them shall seem quite dried up,—then all of a sudden the sluices shall break out, and take a fit of running again like fury,—you would think they would never stop:——and then it is, that in writing and fighting, and twenty other gallant things, we drive all the world before us.

It is by these observations, and a wary reasoning by analogy in that kind of argumentative process, which *Suidas*[15] calls *dialectick induction*,—that I draw and set up this position as most true and veritable.

That of these two luminaries, so much of their irradiations are suffered from time to time to shine down upon us; as he, whose infinite wisdom which dispenses every thing in exact weight and measure, knows will just serve to light us on our way in this night of our obscurity; so that your reverences and worships now find out, nor is it a moment longer in my power to conceal it from you, That the fervent wish in your behalf with which I set out, was no more than the first insinuating *How d'ye* of a caressing prefacer stifling his reader, as a lover sometimes does a coy mistress into silence. For alas! could this effusion of light have been as easily procured, as the exordium wished it—I tremble to think how many thousands for it, of benighted travellers (in the learned sciences at least) must have groped and blundered on in the dark, all the nights of their lives, —running their heads against posts, and knocking out their brains without ever getting to their journies end;—some falling with their noses perpendicularly into stinks,—others horizontally with their tails into kennels.[16] Here one half of a learned profession tilting full butt against the other half of it, and then tumbling and rolling one over the other in the dirt like hogs.——Here the brethren, of another profession, who should have run in opposition to each other, flying on the contrary like a flock of wild geese, all in a row the same way.—What confusion!—what mistakes!—fiddlers and painters judging by their eyes and ears,—admirable!—trusting to the passions excited in an air sung, by a story painted to the heart,——instead of measuring them by a quadrant.

In the foreground of this picture, a *statesman* turning the political wheel, like a brute, the wrong way round against the stream of corruption,—by heaven!—instead of *with* it.

In this corner, a son of the divine *Esculapius*,[17] writing a book against predestination; perhaps worse,—feeling his patient's pulse, instead of his apothecary's—a brother of the faculty in the back ground upon his knees in tears,—drawing the curtains of a mangled victim to beg his forgiveness;—offering a fee,— instead of taking one.

In that spacious HALL, a coalition of the gown, from all the barrs of it, driving a damn'd, dirty, vexatious cause before them, with all their might and main, the wrong way;——kicking it *out* of the great doors, instead of, *in*,——and with such fury in their looks, and such a degree of inveteracy in their manner of kicking it, as if the laws had been originally made for the peace and preservation of mankind:—perhaps a more enormous mistake committed by them still,—a litigated point fairly hung up; ——for instance, Whether *John o'Nokes*[18] his nose, could stand in *Tom o'Stiles* his face, without a trespass, or not,—rashly determined by them in five and twenty minutes, which, with the cautious pro's and con's required in so intricate a proceeding, might have taken up as many months,— and if carried on upon a military plan, as your honours know, an ACTION should be, with all the stratagems practicable therein,—such as feints,— forced marches,—surprizes,—ambuscades,—mask-batteries, and a thousand other strokes of generalship which consist in catching at all advantages on both sides,——might reasonably have lasted them as many years, finding food and raiment all that term for a centumvirate[19] of the profession.

As for the clergy————No——If I say a word against them, I'll be shot.— I have no desire,—and besides, if I had, ——I durst not for my soul touch upon the subject,——with such weak nerves and spirits, and in the condition I am in at present, 'twould be as much as my life was worth, to deject and contrist myself with so sad and melancholy an account,—and therefore, 'tis safer to draw a curtain across, and hasten from it, as fast as I can, to the main and principal point I have undertaken to clear up,——and that is, How it comes to pass, that your men of least *wit* are reported to be men of most *judgment*.——But mark,—I say, *reported to be*,——for it is no more, my dear Sirs, than a report, and which like twenty others taken up every day upon trust, I maintain to be a vile and a malicious report into the bargain.

This by the help of the observations already premised, and I hope already weighed and perpended by your reverences and worships, I shall forthwith make appear.

I hate set dissertations,——and above all things in the world, 'tis one of the silliest things in one of them, to darken your hypothesis by placing a number of tall, opake words, one before another, in a right line, betwixt your own and your readers conception,——when in all likelihood, if you had looked about, you might have seen something standing, or hanging up, which would have cleared the point at once,—"for what hinderance, hurt or harm, doth the laudable desire of knowledge bring to any man, if even from a sot, a pot, a fool, a stool, a winter-mittain, a truckle for a pully, the lid of a goldsmith's crucible, an oyl bottle, an old slipper, or a cane chair,"[20]——I am this moment sitting upon one. Will you give me leave to illustrate this affair of wit and judgment, by the two knobs on the top of the back of it,——they are fasten'd on, you see, with two pegs stuck slightly into two gimlet-holes, and will place what I have to say in so clear a light, as to let you see through the drift and meaning of my whole preface, as plainly as if every point and particle of it was made up of sun beams.

I enter now directly upon the point.

——Here stands *wit*, ——and there stands *judgment*, close beside it, just like the two knobbs I'm speaking of, upon the back of this self same chair on which I am sitting.

——You see, they are the highest and most ornamental parts of its *frame*,——as wit and judgment are of *ours*,——and like them too, indubitably both made and fitted to go together, in order as we say in all such cases of duplicated embellishments, ——*to answer one another*.

Now for the sake of an experiment, and for the clearer illustrating this matter,—let us for a moment, take off one of these two curious ornaments (I care not which) from the point or pinnacle of the chair it now stands on;——nay, don't laugh at it.——But did you ever see in the whole course of your lives such a ridiculous business as this has made of it?——Why, 'tis as miserable a sight as a sow with one ear; and there is just as much sense and symmetry in the one, as in the other:—do,—pray, get off your seats, only to take a view of it.——Now would any man who valued his character a straw, have turned a piece of work out of his hand in such a condition?——nay, lay your hands upon your hearts, and answer this plain question, Whether this one single knobb which now stands here like a blockhead by itself, can serve any purpose upon earth, but to put one in mind of the want of the other;——and let me further ask, in case the chair was your own, if you would not in your consciences think, rather than be as it is, that it would be ten times better without any knobb at all.

Now these two knobs——or top ornaments of the mind of man, which crown the whole entablature,—being, as I said, wit and judgment, which of all others, as I have proved it, are the most needful,—the most priz'd,——the most calamitous to be without, and consequently the hardest to come at,——for all these reasons put together, there is not a mortal amongst us, so destitute of a love of good fame or feeding,——or so ignorant of what will do him good therein,—who does not wish and stedfastly resolve in his own mind, to be, or to be thought at least master of the one or the other, and indeed of both of them, if the thing seems any way feasible, or likely to be brought to pass.

Now your graver gentry having little or no kind of chance in aiming at the one,—unless they laid hold of the other,——pray what do you think would become of them?—Why, Sirs, in spight of all their *gravities*, they must e'en have been contented to have gone with their insides naked:—this was not to be borne, but by an effort of philosophy not to be supposed in the case we are upon,——so that no one could well have been angry with them, had they been satisfied with what little they could have snatched up and secreted under their cloaks and great perrywigs, had they not raised a *hue* and *cry* at the same time against the lawful owners.

I need not tell your worships, that this was done with so much cunning and artifice,—that the great *Locke*, who was seldom outwitted by false sounds,——was nevertheless bubbled here. The cry, it seems, was so deep and solemn a one, and what with the help of great wigs, grave faces, and other implements of deceit, was rendered so general a one against the *poor wits* in this matter, that the philosopher himself was deceived by it,—it was his glory to free the world from the lumber of a thousand vulgar errors;—— but this was not of the number; so that instead of sitting down cooly, as such a philosopher should have done, to have examined the matter of fact before he philosophised upon it;——on the contrary, he took the fact for granted, and so joined in with the cry, and halloo'd it as boisterously as the rest.

This has been made the *Magna Charta* of stupidity ever since,—but your reverences plainly see, it has been obtained in such a manner, that the title to it is not worth a groat;——which by the bye is one of the many and vile impositions which gravity and grave folks have to answer for hereafter.

As for great wigs, upon which I may be thought to have spoken my mind too freely,——I beg leave to qualify whatever has been unguardedly said to their dispraise or prejudice, by one general declaration——That I have no abhorrence whatever, nor do I detest and abjure either great wigs or long beards,—— any further than when I see they are bespoke and let grow on purpose to carry on this self-same imposture——for any purpose,—peace be with them;—☞ mark only,—I write not for them.

CHAPTER XXI

EVERY day for at least ten years together did my father resolve to have it mended,——'tis not mended yet;——no family but ours would have borne with it an hour,—and what is most astonishing, there was not a subject in the world upon which my father was so eloquent, as upon that of door-hinges.——And yet at the same time, he was certainly one of the greatest bubbles to them, I think, that history can produce: his rhetoric and conduct were at perpetual handy-cuffs.——Never did the parlour-door open—but his philosophy or his principles fell a victim to it;——three drops of oyl with a feather, and a smart stroke of a hammer, had saved his honour for ever.

——Inconsistent soul that man is!—languishing under wounds, which he has the power to heal!—his whole life a contradiction to his knowledge!—his reason, that precious gift of God to him—(instead of pouring in oyl) serving but to sharpen his sensibilities,——to multiply his pains and render him more melancholy and uneasy under them!—poor unhappy creature, that he should do so!——are not the necessary causes of misery in this life enow, but he must add voluntary ones to his stock of sorrow;——struggle against evils which cannot be avoided, and submit to others, which a tenth part of the trouble they create him, would remove from his heart for ever?

By all that is good and virtuous! if there are three drops of oyl to be got, and a hammer to be found within ten miles of *Shandy-Hall*,—the parlour-door hinge shall be mended this reign.

CHAPTER XXII

WHEN corporal *Trim* had brought his two mortars to bear, he was delighted with his handy-work above measure; and knowing what a pleasure it would be to his master to see them, he was not able to resist the desire he had of carrying them directly into his parlour.

Now next to the moral lesson I had in view in mentioning the affair of *hinges*, I had a speculative consideration arising out of it, and it is this.

Had the parlour-door open'd and turn'd upon its hinges, as a door should do———

——Or for example, as cleverly as our government has been turning upon its hinges,———(that is, in case things have all along gone well with your worship,—otherwise I give up my simile)—in this case, I say, there had been no danger either to master or man, in corporal *Trim*'s peeping in: the moment, he had beheld my father and my uncle *Toby* fast asleep,———the respectfulness of his carriage was such, he would have retired as silent as death, and left them both in their arm-chairs, dreaming as happy as he had found them: but the thing was morally speaking so very impracticable, that for the many years in which this hinge was suffered to be out of order, and amongst the hourly grievances my father submitted to upon its account,—this was one; that he never folded his arms to take his nap after dinner, but the thoughts of being unavoidably awakened by the first person who should open the door, was always uppermost in his imagination, and so incessantly step'd in betwixt him and the first balmy presage of his repose, as to rob him, as he often declared, of the whole sweets of it.

"*When things move upon bad hinges*, an' please your lordships, *how can it be otherwise?*"

Pray what's the matter? Who is there? cried my father, waking, the moment the door began to creak.———I wish the smith would give a peep at that confounded hinge.———'Tis nothing, an' please your honour, said *Trim*, but two mortars I am bringing in.———They shan't make a clatter with them here, cried my father hastily.———If Dr. *Slop* has any drugs to pound, let him do it in the kitchen.———May it please your honour, cried *Trim*,—they are two mortar-pieces for a siege next summer, which I have been making out of a pair of jack-boots, which *Obadiah* told me your honour had left off wearing.——— By heaven! cried my father, springing out of his chair, as he swore,—I have not one appointment belonging to me, which I set so much store by, as I do by these jack-boots,———they were our great-grandfather's, brother *Toby*,———they were *hereditary*. Then I fear, quoth my uncle *Toby*, *Trim* has cut off the entail.———I have only cut off the tops, an' please your honour, cried *Trim*.———I hate *perpetuities* as much as any man alive, cried my father,———but these jack-boots, continued he, (smiling, though very angry at the same time) have been in the family, brother, ever since the civil wars;——Sir *Roger Shandy* wore them at the battle of *Marston-Moor*.[1]—I declare I would not have taken ten pounds for them.——I'll pay you the money, brother *Shandy*, quoth my uncle *Toby*, looking at the two mortars with infinite pleasure, and putting his hand into his breeches-pocket, as he viewed them.——I'll pay you the ten pounds this moment with all my heart and soul.——

Brother *Toby*, replied my father, altering his tone, you care not what money you dissipate and throw away, provided, continued he, 'tis but upon a SIEGE.—Have I not a hundred and twenty pounds a year, besides my half-pay? cried my uncle *Toby*.——What is that, replied my father, hastily,—to ten pounds for a pair of jack-boots?——twelve guineas for your *pontoons*;——half as much for your *Dutch*-draw-bridge;—to say nothing of the train of little brass-artillery you bespoke last week, with twenty other preparations for the siege of *Messina*; believe me, dear brother *Toby*, continued my father, taking him kindly by the hand,—these military operations of yours are above your strength;—you mean well, brother,—but they carry you into greater expences than you were first aware of, ——and take my word,——dear *Toby*, they will in the end quite ruin your fortune, and make a beggar of you.——What signifies it if they do, brother, replied my uncle *Toby*, so long as we know 'tis for the good of the nation.—

My father could not help smiling for his soul;—his anger at the worst was never more than a spark,—and the zeal and simplicity of *Trim*,——and the generous (tho' hobby-horsical) gallantry of my uncle *Toby*, brought him into perfect good humour with them in an instant.

Generous souls!—God prosper you both, and your mortar-pieces too, quoth my father to himself.

CHAPTER XXIII

ALL is quiet and hush, cried my father, at least above stairs,—I hear not one foot stirring.——Prithee, *Trim*, who is in the kitchen? There is no one soul in the kitchen, answered *Trim*, making a low bow as he spoke, except Dr. *Slop*.—Confusion! cried my father, (getting up upon his legs a second time)——not one single thing has gone right this day! had I faith in astrology, brother, (which by the bye, my father had) I would have sworn some retrograde planet[1] was hanging over this unfortunate house of mine, and turning every individual thing in it out of its place.———Why, I thought Dr. *Slop* had been above stairs with my wife, and so said you.—What can the fellow be puzzling about in the kitchen?———He is busy, an' please your honour, replied *Trim*, in making a bridge.———'Tis very obliging in him, quoth my uncle *Toby*;———pray give my humble service to Dr. *Slop*, *Trim*, and tell him I thank him heartily.

You must know, my uncle *Toby* mistook the bridge as widely as my father mistook the mortars;———but to understand how my uncle *Toby* could mistake the bridge,— I fear I must give you an exact account of the road which led to it;———or to drop my metaphor, (for there is nothing more dishonest in an historian, than the use of one,)———in order to conceive the probability of this error in my uncle *Toby* aright, I must give you some account of an adventure of *Trim*'s, though much against my will. I say much against my will, only because the story, in one sense, is certainly out of its place here; for by right it should come in, either amongst the anecdotes of my uncle *Toby*'s amours with widow *Wadman*, in which corporal *Trim* was no mean actor,—or else in the middle of his and my uncle *Toby*'s campaigns on the bowling green,———for it will do very well in either place;———but then if I reserve it for either of those parts of my story,—I ruin the story I'm upon,—and if I tell it here—I anticipate matters, and ruin it there.

—What would your worships have me to do in this case?

—Tell it, Mr. *Shandy*, by all means.———You are a fool, *Tristram*, if you do.

O ye POWERS! (for powers ye are, and great ones too)— which enable mortal man to tell a story worth the hearing,— that kindly shew him, where he is to begin it,—and where he is to end it,—what he is to put into it,—and what he is to leave out,—how much of it he is to cast into shade,—and whereabouts he is to throw his light!———Ye, who preside over this vast empire of biographical freebooters, and see how many scrapes and plunges your subjects hourly fall into;—will you do one thing?

I beg and beseech you, (in case you will do nothing better for us) that where-ever, in any part of your dominions it so falls out, that three several roads meet in one point, as they have done just here,—that at least you set up a guide-post, in the center of them, in mere charity to direct an uncertain devil, which of the three he is to take.

CHAPTER XXIV

THO' the shock my uncle *Toby* received the year after the demolition of *Dunkirk*,[1] in his affair with widow *Wadman*, had fixed him in a resolution, never more to think of the sex,——or of aught which belonged to it;—yet corporal *Trim* had made no such bargain with himself. Indeed in my uncle *Toby*'s case there was a strange and unaccountable concurrence of circumstances which insensibly drew him in, to lay siege to that fair and strong citadel.——In *Trim*'s case there was a concurrence of nothing in the world, but of him and *Bridget* in the kitchen;—though in truth, the love and veneration he bore his master was such, and so fond was he of imitating him in all he did, that had my uncle *Toby* employed his time and genius in tagging of points,——I am persuaded the honest corporal would have laid down his arms, and followed his example with pleasure. When therefore my uncle *Toby* sat down before the mistress,—corporal *Trim* incontinently took ground before the maid.

Now, my dear friend *Garrick*, whom I have so much cause to esteem and honour,—(why, or wherefore, 'tis no matter)—can it escape your penetration,—I defy it,—that so many play-wrights, and opificers[2] of chit chat have ever since been working upon *Trim*'s and my uncle *Toby*'s pattern.—I care not what *Aristotle*,[3] or *Pacuvius*,[4] or *Bossu*,[5] or *Riccoboni*[6] say,—(though I never read one of them)——there is not a greater difference between a single-horse chair and madam *Pompadour*'s *vis a vis*,[7] than betwixt a single amour, and an amour thus nobly doubled, and going upon all four, prancing throughout a grand drama.—Sir, a simple, single, silly affair of that kind,——is quite lost in five acts,——but that is neither here or there.

After a series of attacks and repulses in a course of nine months on my uncle *Toby*'s quarter, a most minute account of every particular of which shall be given in its proper place, my uncle *Toby*, honest man! found it necessary to draw off his forces, and raise the siege somewhat indignantly.

Corporal *Trim*, as I said, had made no such bargain either with himself——or with any one else,—the fidelity however of his heart not suffering him to go into a house which his master had forsaken with disgust,——he contented himself with turning his part of the siege into a blockade;——that is, he kept others off,—for though he never after went to the house, yet he never met *Bridget* in the village, but he would either nod or wink, or smile, or look kindly at her,—or (as circumstances directed), he would shake her by the hand,——or ask her lovingly how she did,—or would give her a ribban,——and now and then, though never but when it could be done with decorum, would give *Bridget* a——

Precisely in this situation, did these things stand for five years; that is, from the demolition of *Dunkirk* in the year 13, to the latter end of my uncle *Toby*'s campaign in the year 18, which was about six or seven weeks before the time I'm speaking of.—When *Trim*, as his custom was, after he had put my uncle *Toby* to bed, going down one moon-shiny night to see that every thing was right at his fortifications,——in the lane separated from the bowling-green with flowering shrubs and holly,—he espied his *Bridget*.

As the corporal thought there was nothing in the world so well worth shewing as the glorious works which he and my uncle *Toby* had made, *Trim* courteously and gallantly took her by the hand, and led her in: this was not done so privately, but that the foul-mouth'd trumpet of Fame carried it from ear to ear, till at length it reached my father's, with this untoward circumstance along with it, that my uncle *Toby*'s curious drawbridge, constructed and painted after the *Dutch* fashion, and which went quite across the ditch,—was broke down, and some how or other crush'd all to pieces that very night.

My father, as you have observed, had no great esteem for my uncle *Toby*'s hobby-horse,—he thought it the most ridiculous horse that ever gentleman mounted, and indeed unless my uncle *Toby* vexed him about it, could never think of it once, without smiling at it,——so that it never could get lame or happen any mischance, but it tickled my father's imagination beyond measure; but this being an accident much more to his humour than any one which had yet befall'n it, it proved an inexhaustible fund of entertainment to him.——Well,—but dear *Toby!* my father would say, do tell us seriously how this affair of the bridge happened.——How can you teaze me so much about it? my uncle *Toby* would reply,—I have told it you twenty times, word for word as *Trim* told it me.—Prithee, how was it then, corporal? my father would cry, turning to *Trim*.—It was a mere misfortune, an' please your honour,——I was shewing Mrs. *Bridget*[8] our fortifications, and in going too near the edge of the fossè, I unfortunately slip'd in.——Very well *Trim!* my father would cry,—(smiling mysteriously, and giving a nod,——but without interrupting him)——and being link'd fast, an' please your honour, arm in arm with Mrs. *Bridget*, I dragg'd her after me, by means of which she fell backwards soss[9] against the bridge,——and *Trim*'s foot, (my uncle *Toby* would cry, taking the story out of his mouth) getting into the cuvette, he tumbled full against the bridge too.—It was a thousand to one, my uncle *Toby* would add, that the poor fellow did not break his leg.— Ay truly! my father would say,——a limb is soon broke, brother *Toby*, in such encounters.——And so, an' please your honour, the bridge, which your honour knows was a very slight one, was broke down betwixt us, and splintered all to pieces.

At other times, but especially when my uncle *Toby* was so unfortunate as to say a syllable about cannons, bombs or petards,—my father would exhaust all the stores of his eloquence (which indeed were very great) in a panegyric upon the BATTERING-RAMS of the ancients,—the VINEA[10] which *Alexander* made use of at the siege of *Tyre*.[11]——He would tell my uncle *Toby* of the CATAPULTÆ of the *Syrians* which threw such monstrous stones so many hundred feet, and shook the strongest bulwarks from their very foundation;—he would go on and describe the wonderful mechanism of the BALLISTA,[12] which *Marcellinus*[13] makes so much rout about,—the terrible effects of the PYRABOLI,—which cast fire,——the danger of the TEREBRA and SCORPIO, which cast javelins.—But what are these, he would say, to the destructive machinery of corporal *Trim?*—Believe me, brother *Toby*, no bridge, or bastion, or sally port that ever was constructed in this world, can hold out against such artillery.

My uncle *Toby* would never attempt any defence against the force of this ridicule, but that of redoubling the vehemence of smoaking his pipe; in doing which, he raised so dense a vapour one night after supper, that it set my father, who was a little phthisical, into a suffocating fit of violent coughing: my uncle *Toby* leap'd up without feeling the pain upon his groin,——and, with infinite pity, stood beside his brother's chair, tapping his back with one hand, and holding his head with the other, and from time to time, wiping his eyes with a clean cambrick handkerchief, which he pull'd out of his pocket.——The affectionate and endearing manner in which my uncle *Toby* did these little offices,——cut my father thro' his reins, for the pain he had just been giving him.——May my brains be knock'd out with a battering ram or a catapulta, I care not which, quoth my father to himself,——if ever I insult this worthy soul more.

CHAPTER XXV

THE draw-bridge being held irreparable, *Trim* was ordered directly to set about another,——but not upon the same model; for cardinal *Alberoni*'s[1] intrigues at that time being discovered, and my uncle *Toby* rightly foreseeing that a flame would inevitably break out betwixt *Spain* and the Empire, and that the operations of the ensuing campaign must in all likelihood be either in *Naples* or *Scicily*,——he determined upon an *Italian* bridge,—(my uncle *Toby*, by the bye, was not far out in his conjectures)——but my father, who was infinitely the better politician, and took the lead as far of my uncle *Toby* in the cabinet, as my uncle *Toby* took it of him in the field,—convinced him, that if the King of *Spain* and the Emperor went together by the ears, that *England* and *France* and *Holland* must, by force of their pre-engagements, all enter the lists too;——and if so, he would say, the combatants, brother *Toby*, as sure as we are alive, will fall to it again, pell-mell, upon the old prize-fighting stage of *Flanders*;——then what will you do with your *Italian* bridge?

——We will go on with it then, upon the old model, cried my uncle *Toby*.

When corporal *Trim* had about half finished it in that stile, ——my uncle *Toby* found out a capital defect in it, which he had never thoroughly considered before. It turned, it seems, upon hinges at both ends of it, opening in the middle, one half of which turning to one side of the fossè, and the other, to the other; the advantage of which was this, that by dividing the weight of the bridge into two equal portions, it impowered my uncle *Toby* to raise it up or let it down with the end of his crutch, and with one hand, which, as his garrison was weak, was as much as he could well spare,—but the disadvantages of such a construction were insurmountable,——for by this means, he would say, I leave one half of my bridge in my enemy's possession,——and pray of what use is the other?

The natural remedy for this, was no doubt to have his bridge fast only at one end with hinges, so that the whole might be lifted up together, and stand bolt upright,——but that was rejected for the reason given above.

For a whole week after he was determined in his mind to have one of that particular construction which is made to draw back horizontally, to hinder a passage;——and to thrust forwards again to gain a passage,——of which sorts your worships might have seen three famous ones at *Spires*[2] before its destruction,—and one now at *Brisac*,[3] if I mistake not;——but my father advising my uncle *Toby*, with great earnestness, to have nothing more to do with thrusting bridges,—and my uncle foreseeing moreover that it would but perpetuate the memory of the corporal's misfortune,—he changed his mind, for that of the marquis *d'Hôpital*'s[4] invention, which the younger *Bernouilli* has so well and learnedly described, as your worships may see,—*Act. Erud. Lips.* an. 1695,—to these a lead weight is an eternal ballance, and keeps watch as well as a couple of centinels, inasmuch as the construction of them was a curve-line approximating to a cycloid,—if not a cycloid itself.

My uncle *Toby* understood the nature of a parabola as well as any man in *England*,—but was not quite such a master of the cycloid;—he talked however about it every day;——the bridge went not forwards.——We'll ask somebody about it, cried my uncle *Toby* to *Trim*.

CHAPTER XXVI

WHEN *Trim* came in and told my father, that Dr. *Slop* was in the kitchen, and busy in making a bridge,—my uncle *Toby*,—the affair of the jack-boots having just then raised a train of military ideas in his brain,—took it instantly for granted that Dr. *Slop* was making a model of the marquis *d'Hôpital*'s bridge.——'Tis very obliging in him, quoth my uncle *Toby*;——pray give my humble service to Dr. *Slop*, *Trim*, and tell him I thank him heartily.

Had my uncle *Toby*'s head been a *Savoyard*'s box,[1] and my father peeping in all the time at one end of it,——it could not have given him a more distinct conception of the operations in my uncle *Toby*'s imagination, than what he had; so notwithstanding the catapulta and battering-ram, and his bitter imprecation about them, he was just beginning to triumph——

When *Trim*'s answer, in an instant, tore the laurel from his brows, and twisted it to pieces.

CHAPTER XXVII

——THIS unfortunate draw-bridge of yours, quoth my father—God bless your honour, cried *Trim*, 'tis a bridge for master's nose.——In bringing him into the world with his vile instruments, he has crush'd his nose, *Susannah* says, as flat as a pancake to his face, and he is making a false bridge with a piece of cotton and a thin piece of whalebone out of *Susannah*'s stays, to raise it up.

——Lead me, brother *Toby*, cried my father, to my room this instant.

CHAPTER XXVIII

FROM the first moment I sat down to write my life for the amusement of the world, and my opinions for its instruction, has a cloud insensibly been gathering over my father.——A tide of little evils and distresses has been setting in against him. ——Not one thing, as he observed himself, has gone right: and now is the storm thicken'd, and going to break, and pour down full upon his head.

I enter upon this part of my story in the most pensive and melancholy frame of mind, that ever sympathetic breast was touched with.——My nerves relax as I tell it.——Every line I write, I feel an abatement of the quickness of my pulse, and of that careless alacrity with it, which every day of my life prompts me to say and write a thousand things I should not. ——And this moment that I last dipp'd my pen into my ink, I could not help taking notice what a cautious air of sad composure and solemnity there appear'd in my manner of doing it.——Lord! how different from the rash jerks, and harebrain'd squirts thou art wont, *Tristram!* to transact it with in other humours,——dropping thy pen,—spurting thy ink about thy table and thy books,——as if thy pen and thy ink, thy books and thy furniture cost thee nothing.

CHAPTER XXIX

——I WON'T go about to argue the point with you,—'tis so,— and I am persuaded of it, madam, as much as can be, "That both man and woman bear pain or sorrow, (and, for aught I know, pleasure too) best in a horizontal position."

The moment my father got up into his chamber, he threw himself prostrate across his bed in the wildest disorder imaginable, but at the same time, in the most lamentable attitude of a man borne down with sorrows, that ever the eye of pity dropp'd a tear for.——The palm of his right hand, as he fell upon the bed, receiving his forehead, and covering the greatest part of both his eyes gently sunk down with his head (his elbow giving way backwards) till his nose touch'd the quilt;——his left arm hung insensible over the side of the bed, his knuckles reclining upon the handle of the chamber pot, which peep'd out beyond the valance,—his right leg (his left being drawn up towards his body) hung half over the side of the bed, the edge of it pressing upon his shin-bone.——He felt it not. A fix'd, inflexible sorrow took possession of every line of his face.— He sigh'd once,—heaved his breast often,—but utter'd not a word.

An old set-stitch'd chair, valanced and fringed around with party-colour'd worsted bobs, stood at the bed's head, opposite to the side where my father's head reclined.——My uncle *Toby* sat him down in it.

Before an affliction is digested,——consolation ever comes
too soon;——and after it is digested,—it comes too late: so that
you see, madam, there is but a mark between these two, as fine
almost as a hair, for a comforter to take aim at: my uncle *Toby*
was always either on this side, or on that of it, and would often
say, He believed in his heart, he could as soon hit the longitude;[1]
for this reason, when he sat down in the chair, he drew the
curtain a little forwards, and having a tear at every one's service,—he pull'd out a cambrick handkerchief,——gave a low
sigh,——but held his peace.

CHAPTER XXX

——"ALL *is not gain that is got into the purse.*"[1]——So that
notwithstanding my father had the happiness of reading the
oddest books in the universe, and had moreover, in himself, the
oddest way of thinking, that ever man in it was bless'd with, yet
it had this drawback upon him after all,——that it laid him open
to some of the oddest and most whimsical distresses; of which
this particular one which he sunk under at present is as strong an
example as can be given.

No doubt, the breaking down of the bridge of a child's nose,
by the edge of a pair of forceps,—however scientifically
applied,——would vex any man in the world, who was at so
much pains in begetting a child, as my father was,——yet it will
not account for the extravagance of his affliction, or will it
justify the unchristian manner he abandoned and surrender'd
himself up to it.

To explain this, I must leave him upon the bed for half an
hour,——and my good uncle *Toby* in his old fringed chair
sitting beside him.

CHAPTER XXXI

——I THINK it a very unreasonable demand,——cried my great
grandfather, twisting up the paper, and throwing it upon the
table.——By this account, madam, you have but two thousand
pounds fortune, and not a shilling more,——and you insist
upon having three hundred pounds a year jointure for it.——

—"Because," replied my great grandmother, "you have little or no nose, Sir."——

Now, before I venture to make use of the word *Nose* a second time,—to avoid all confusion in what will be said upon it, in this interesting part of my story, it may not be amiss to explain my own meaning, and define, with all possible exactness and precision, what I would willingly be understood to mean by the term: being of opinion, that 'tis owing to the negligence and perverseness of writers, in despising this precaution, and to nothing else,——That all the polemical writings in divinity, are not as clear and demonstrative as those upon *a Will o' the Wisp*, or any other sound part of philosophy, and natural pursuit; in order to which, what have you to do, before you set out, unless you intend to go puzzling on to the day of judgment,——but to give the world a good definition, and stand to it, of the main word you have most occasion for,—changing it, Sir, as you would a guinea, into small coin?—which done,—let the father of confusion puzzle you, if he can; or put a different idea either into your head, or your reader's head, if he knows how.

In books of strict morality and close reasoning, such as this I am engaged in,—the neglect is inexcusable; and heaven is witness, how the world has revenged itself upon me for leaving so many openings to equivocal strictures,—and for depending so much as I have done, all along, upon the cleanliness of my reader's imaginations.

——Here are two senses, cried *Eugenius*, as we walk'd along, pointing with the fore finger of his right hand to the word *Crevice*, in the fifty second page of the second volume[1] of this book of books,—here are two senses,——quoth he.—And here are two roads, replied I, turning short upon him,——a dirty and a clean one,——which shall we take?——The clean,—by all means, replied *Eugenius*. *Eugenius*, said I, stepping before him, and laying my hand upon his breast,——to define——is to distrust.——Thus I triumph'd over *Eugenius*; but I triumph'd over him as I always do, like a fool.——'Tis my comfort however, I am not an obstinate one; therefore

I define a nose, as follows,——intreating only beforehand, and beseeching my readers, both male and female, of what age, complexion, and condition soever, for the love of God and their own souls, to guard against the temptations and suggestions of the devil, and suffer him by no art or wile to put any other ideas into their minds, than what I put into my definition.——For by the word *Nose*, throughout all this long chapter of noses, and in every other part of my work, where the word *Nose* occurs,—I declare, by that word I mean a Nose, and nothing more, or less.

CHAPTER XXXII

——"Because," quoth my great grandmother, repeating the words again,——"you have little or no nose, Sir"——

S'death! cried my great grandfather, clapping his hand upon his nose,—'tis not so small as that comes to;—'tis a full inch longer than my father's.——Now, my great grandfather's nose was for all the world like unto the noses of all the men, women, and children, whom *Pantagruel*[1] found dwelling upon the island of ENNASIN.[2]——By the way, if you would know the strange way of getting a-kin amongst so flat-nosed a people, ——you must read the book;—find it out yourself, you never can.——

——'Twas shaped, Sir, like an ace of clubs.

——'Tis a full inch, continued my great grandfather, pressing up the ridge of his nose with his finger and thumb; and repeating his assertion,——'tis a full inch longer, madam, than my father's—. You must mean your uncle's, replied my great grandmother.

——My great grandfather was convinced.—He untwisted the paper, and signed the article.

CHAPTER XXXIII

——WHAT an unconscionable jointure, my dear, do we pay out of this small estate of ours, quoth my grandmother to my grandfather.

My father, replied my grandfather, had no more nose, my dear, saving the mark, than there is upon the back of my hand.——

——Now, you must know, that my great grandmother outlived my grandfather twelve years; so that my father had the jointure to pay, a hundred and fifty pounds half yearly——(on *Michaelmas* and *Lady day*)—during all that time.

No man discharged pecuniary obligations with a better grace than my father.——And as far as the hundred pounds went, he would fling it upon the table, guinea by guinea, with that spirited jerk of an honest welcome, which generous souls, and generous souls only, are able to fling down money: but as soon as ever he enter'd upon the odd fifty,—he generally gave a loud *Hem!*—rubb'd the side of his nose leisurely with the flat part of his fore finger,—inserted his hand cautiously betwixt his head and the cawl[1] of his wig,—look'd at both sides of every guinea, as he parted with it,—and seldom could get to the end of the fifty pounds, without pulling out his handkerchief, and wiping his temples.

Defend me, gracious heaven! from those persecuting spirits who make no allowances for these workings within us.—Never,—O never may I lay down in their tents, who cannot relax the engine, and feel pity for the force of education, and the prevalence of opinions long derived from ancestors!

For three generations at least, this *tenet* in favour of long noses had gradually been taking root in our family.——TRADI- TION was all along on its side, and INTEREST was every half year stepping in to strengthen it; so that the whimsicality of my father's brain was far from having the whole honour of this, as it had of almost all his other strange notions.—For in a great measure he might be said to have suck'd this in, with his mother's milk. He did his part however.——If education planted the mistake, (in case it was one) my father watered it, and ripened it to perfection.

He would often declare, in speaking his thoughts upon the subject, that he did not conceive how the greatest family in *England* could stand it out against an uninterrupted succession of six or seven short noses.—And for the contrary reason, he would generally add, That it must be one of the greatest prob- lems in civil life, where the same number of long and jolly noses following one another in a direct line, did not raise and hoist it up into the best vacancies in the kingdom.——He would often boast that the *Shandy* family rank'd very high in king *Harry* the VIIIth's time, but owed its rise to no state engine,—he would say,—but to that only;—but that, like other families, he would add,—it had felt the turn of the wheel, and had never recovered the blow of my great grandfather's nose.——It was an ace of clubs indeed, he would cry, shaking his head,——and as vile a one for an unfortunate family, as ever turn'd up trumps.

——Fair and softly, gentle reader!——where is thy fancy carrying thee?——If there is truth in man, by my great grandfather's nose, I mean the external organ of smelling, or that part of man which stands prominent in his face,—and which painters say, in good jolly noses and well-proportioned faces, should comprehend a full third,—that is, measuring downwards from the setting on of the hair.——

——What a life of it has an author, at this pass!

CHAPTER XXXIV

IT is a singular blessing, that nature has form'd the mind of man with the same happy backwardness and renitency[1] against conviction, which is observed in old dogs,—— "of not learning new tricks."

What a shuttlecock of a fellow would the greatest philosopher that ever existed, be whisk'd into at once, did he read such books, and observe such facts, and think such thoughts, as would eternally be making him change sides!

Now, my father, as I told you last year, detested all this.—He pick'd up an opinion, Sir, as a man in a state of nature picks up an apple.—It becomes his own,—and if he is a man of spirit, he would lose his life rather than give it up.——

I am aware, that *Didius* the great civilian, will contest this point; and cry out against me, Whence comes this man's right to this apple? *ex confesso*,[2] he will say,——things were in a state of nature.—The apple, as much *Frank*'s apple, as *John*'s. Pray, Mr. *Shandy*, what patent has he to shew for it? and how did it begin to be his? was it, when he set his heart upon it? or when he gather'd it? or when he chew'd it? or when he roasted it? or when he peel'd? or when he brought it home? or when he digested?——or when he——?——. For 'tis plain, Sir, if the first picking up of the apple, made it not his,——that no subsequent act could.

Brother *Didius*, *Tribonius*[3] will answer,—(now *Tribonius* the civilian and church lawyer's beard being three inches and a half and three eighths longer than *Didius* his beard,—I'm glad he takes up the cudgels for me, so I give myself no further trouble about the answer.)—Brother *Didius*, *Tribonius* will say, it is a decreed case, as you may find it in the fragments of *Gregorius*[4] and *Hermogenes*'s codes, and in all the codes from *Justinian*'s down to the codes of *Louis*[5] and *Des Eaux*,—That the sweat of a man's brows, and the exsudations[6] of a man's brains, are as much a man's own property, as the breeches upon his backside;——which said exsudations, &c. being dropp'd upon the said apple by the labour of finding it, and picking it up; and being moreover indissolubly wasted, and as indissolubly annex'd by the picker up, to the thing pick'd up, carried home, roasted, peel'd, eaten, digested, and so on;——'tis evident that the gatherer of the apple, in so doing, has mix'd up something which was his own, with the apple which was not his own, by which means he has acquired a property;—or, in other words, the apple is *John*'s apple.

By the same learned chain of reasoning my father stood up for all his opinions: he had spared no pains in picking them up, and the more they lay out of the common way, the better still was his title.——No mortal claim'd them: they had cost him moreover as much labour in cooking and digesting as in the case above, so that they might well and truely be said to be his own goods and chattles.——Accordingly he held fast by 'em, both by teeth and claws,——would fly to whatever he could lay his hands on,——and in a word, would intrench and fortify them round with as many circumvallations and breast-works, as my uncle *Toby* would a citadel.

There was one plaguy rub in the way of this,—the scarcity of materials to make any thing of a defence with, in case of a smart attack; inasmuch as few men of great genius had exercised their parts in writing books upon the subject of great noses: by the trotting of my lean horse, the thing is incredible! and I am quite lost in my understanding when I am considering what a treasure of precious time and talents together has been wasted upon worse subjects,——and how many millions of books in all languages, and in all possible types and bindings, have been fabricated upon points not half so much tending to the unity and peace-making of the world. What was to be had, however, he set the greater store by; and though my father would oft-times sport with my uncle *Toby*'s library,——which, by the bye, was ridiculous enough,—yet at the very same time he did it, he collected every book and treatise which had been systematically wrote upon noses, with as much care as my honest uncle *Toby* had done those upon military architecture.——'Tis true, a much less table would have held them,—but that was not thy transgression, my dear uncle.——

Here,——but why here,——rather than in any other part of my story,——I am not able to tell;——but here it is,——my heart stops me to pay to thee, my dear uncle *Toby*, once for all, the tribute I owe thy goodness.—Here let me thrust my chair aside, and kneel down upon the ground, whilst I am pouring forth the warmest sentiments of love for thee, and veneration for the excellency of thy character, that ever virtue and nature kindled in a nephew's bosom.——Peace and comfort rest for evermore upon thy head!—Thou envied'st no man's comforts,——insulted'st no man's opinions.——Thou blackened'st no man's character,——devoured'st no man's bread: gently with faithful *Trim* behind thee, didst thou amble round the little circle of thy pleasures, jostling no creature in thy way;——for each one's service, thou hadst a tear,——for each man's need, thou hadst a shilling.

Whilst I am worth one, to pay a weeder,——thy path from thy door to thy bowling green shall never be grown up.—— Whilst there is a rood and a half of land in the *Shandy* family, thy fortifications, my dear uncle *Toby*, shall never be demolish'd.

CHAPTER XXXV

MY father's collection was not great, but to make amends, it was curious; and consequently, he was some time in making it; he had the great good fortune however to set off well, in getting *Bruscambille*'s[1] prologue upon long noses, almost for nothing,—for he gave no more for *Bruscambille* than three half crowns; owing indeed to the strong fancy which the stall-man saw my father had for the book the moment he laid his hands upon it.—There are not three *Bruscambilles* in *Christendom*, ——said the stall-man, except what are chain'd up in the libraries of the curious. My father flung down the money as quick as lightening,—took *Bruscambille* into his bosom,——hyed home from *Piccadilly* to *Coleman*-street with it, as he would have hyed home with a treasure, without taking his hand once off from *Bruscambille* all the way.

To those who do not yet know of which gender *Bruscambille* is,——inasmuch as a prologue upon long noses might easily be done by either,——'twill be no objection against the simile,—to say, That when my father got home, he solaced himself with *Bruscambille* after the manner, in which, 'tis ten to one, your worship solaced yourself with your first mistress,——that is, from morning even unto night: which by the bye, how delightful soever it may prove to the inamorato,—is of little, or no entertainment at all, to by-standers.—Take notice, I go no farther with the simile,—my father's eye was greater than his appetite,—his zeal greater than his knowledge,—he cool'd—his affections became divided,——he got hold of *Prignitz*,[2]—purchased *Scroderus*, *Andrea Paræus*,[3] *Bouchet*'s Evening Conferences,[4] and above all, the great and learned *Hafen Slawkenbergius*;[5] of which, as I shall have much to say by and bye,——I will say nothing now.

CHAPTER XXXVI

OF all the tracts my father was at the pains to procure and study in support of his hypothesis, there was not any one wherein he felt a more cruel disappointment at first, than in the celebrated dialogue between *Pamphagus* and *Cocles*, written by the chaste pen of the great and venerable *Erasmus*,[1] upon the various uses and seasonable applications of long noses.——Now don't let Satan, my dear girl, in this chapter, take advantage of any one spot of rising-ground to get astride of your imagination, if you can any ways help it; or if he is so nimble as to slip on,——let me beg of you, like an unback'd filly, *to frisk it, to squirt it, to jump it, to rear it, to bound it,—and to kick it, with long kicks and short kicks*, till like *Tickletoby*'s mare,[2] you break a strap or a crupper, and throw his worship into the dirt.——You need not kill him.——

——And pray who was *Tickletoby*'s mare?—'tis just as discreditable and unscholar-like a question, Sir, as to have asked

what year (*ab urb. con.*)³ the second Punic war⁴ broke out.—
Who was *Tickletoby*'s mare!—Read, read, read, read, my unlearned reader! read,—or by the knowledge of the great saint
*Paraleipomenon*⁵—I tell you before-hand, you had better throw
down the book at once; for without *much reading*, by which
your reverence knows, I mean *much knowledge*, you will no
more be able to penetrate the moral of the next marbled page⁶
(motly emblem of my work!) than the world with all its sagacity
has been able to unravel the many opinions, transactions and
truths which still lie mystically hid under the dark veil of the
black one.

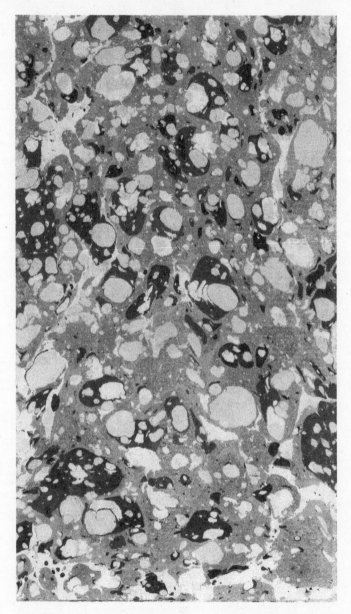

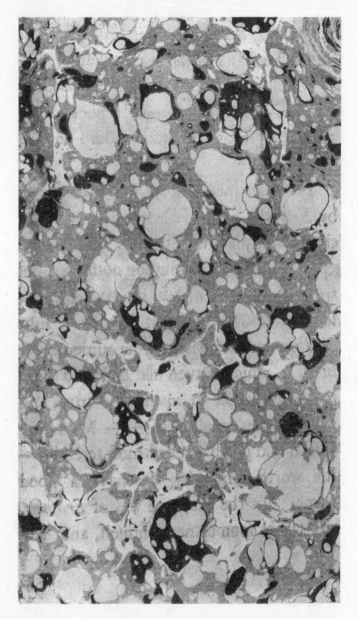

CHAPTER XXXVII

"*NIHIL me pœnitet hujus nasi*,"[1] quoth *Pamphagus*;—that is,
——"My nose has been the making of me."——"*Nec est cur pœniteat*,"[2] replies *Cocles*; that is, "How the duce should such a nose fail?"

The doctrine, you see, was laid down by *Erasmus*, as my father wished it, with the utmost plainness; but my father's disappointment was, in finding nothing more from so able a pen, but the bare fact itself; without any of that speculative subtilty or ambidexterity of argumentation upon it, which heaven had bestow'd upon man on purpose to investigate truth and fight for her on all sides.——My father pish'd and pugh'd at first most terribly,—'tis worth something to have a good name. As the dialogue was of *Erasmus*, my father soon came to himself, and read it over and over again with great application, studying every word and every syllable of it thro' and thro' in its most strict and literal interpretation,—he could still make nothing of it, that way. Mayhaps there is more meant, than is said in it, quoth my father.—Learned men, brother *Toby*, don't write dialogues upon long noses for nothing.——I'll study the mystic and the allegoric sense,——here is some room to turn a man's self in, brother.

My father read on.——

Now, I find it needful to inform your reverences and worships, that besides the many nautical uses of long noses enumerated by *Erasmus*, the dialogist affirmeth that a long nose is not without its domestic conveniences also, for that in a case of distress,—and for want of a pair of bellows, it will do excellently well, *ad excitandum focum*, (to stir up the fire.)

Nature had been prodigal in her gifts to my father beyond measure, and had sown the seeds of verbal criticism as deep within him, as she had done the seeds of all other knowledge,—so that he had got out his penknife, and was trying experiments upon the sentence, to see if he could not scratch some better sense into it.—I've got within a single letter, brother *Toby*, cried my father, of *Erasmus* his mystic meaning.—You are near enough, brother, replied my uncle, in all conscience.——Pshaw! cried my father, scratching on,—I might as well be seven miles off.—I've done it,——said my father, snapping his fingers.—See, my dear brother *Toby*, how I have mended the

sense.—But you have marr'd a word, replied my uncle *Toby*.—
My father put on his spectacles,—bit his lip,—and tore out the
leaf in a passion.

CHAPTER XXXVIII

O *SLAWKENBERGIUS!* thou faithful analyzer of my
Disgrázias,[1]——thou sad foreteller of so many of the whips and
short turns, which in one stage or other of my life have come slap
upon me from the shortness of my nose, and no other cause,
that I am conscious of.——Tell me, *Slawkenbergius!* what secret impulse was it? what intonation of voice? whence came it?
how did it sound in thy ears?—art thou sure thou heard'st
it?—which first cried out to thee,—go,—go, *Slawkenbergius!*
dedicate the labours of thy life,—neglect thy pastimes,—call
forth all the powers and faculties of thy nature,——macerate
thyself in the service of mankind, and write a grand FOLIO for
them, upon the subject of their noses.

How the communication was conveyed into *Slawkenbergius's* sensorium,——so that *Slawkenbergius* should know
whose finger touch'd the key,——and whose hand it was that
blew the bellows,——as *Hafen Slawkenbergius* has been dead
and laid in his grave above fourscore and ten years,——we can
only raise conjectures.

Slawkenbergius was play'd upon, for aught I know, like one
of *Whitfield's*[2] disciples,——that is, with such a distinct intelligence, Sir, of which of the two *masters* it was, that had been
practising upon his *instrument*,——as to make all reasoning
upon it needless.

——For in the account which *Hafen Slawkenbergius* gives
the world of his motives and occasions for writing, and spending so many years of his life upon this one work,——towards
the end of his prologomena, which by the bye should have come
first,——but the bookbinder has most injudiciously placed it
betwixt the analitical contents of the book, and the book itself,——he informs his reader, that ever since he had arrived at
the age of discernment, and was able to sit down coolly, and
consider within himself the true state and condition of man, and
distinguish the main end and design of his being;——or,——to
shorten my translation, for *Slawkenbergius's* book is in *Latin*,
and not a little prolix in this passage,——ever since I under-

stood, quoth *Slawkenbergius*, any thing,——or rather *what was what*,——and could perceive that the point of long noses had been too loosely handled by all who had gone before;——have I, *Slawkenbergius*, felt a strong impulse, with a mighty and an unresistible call within me, to gird up myself to this undertaking.

And to do justice to *Slawkenbergius*, he has entered the list with a stronger lance, and taken a much larger career in it, than any one man who had ever entered it before him,——and indeed, in many respects, deserves to be *en-nich'd* as a prototype for all writers, of voluminous works at least, to model their books by,——for he has taken in, Sir, the whole subject,—examined every part of it, *dialectically*,—then brought it into full day; dilucidating³ it with all the light which either the collision of his own natural parts could strike,——or the profoundest knowledge of the sciences had impowered him to cast upon it,——collating, collecting and compiling,—begging, borrowing, and stealing, as he went along, all that had been wrote or wrangled thereupon in the schools and porticos of the learned: so that *Slawkenbergius* his book may properly be considered, not only as a model,—but as a thorough-stitch'd DIGEST and regular institute of *noses*; comprehending in it, all that is, or can be needful to be known about them.

For this cause it is, that I forbear to speak of so many (otherwise) valuable books and treatises of my father's collecting, wrote either, plump upon noses,—or collaterally touching them;——such for instance as *Prignitz*, now lying upon the table before me, who with infinite learning, and from the most candid and scholar-like examination of above four thousand different skulls, in upwards of twenty charnel houses in *Silesia*, which he had rummaged,—has informed us, that the mensuration and configuration of the osseous or boney parts of human noses, in any *given* tract of country, except *Crim Tartary*,⁴ where they are all crush'd down by the thumb, so that no judgment can be formed upon them,——are much nearer alike, than the world imagines;——the difference amongst them, being, he says, a mere trifle, not worth taking notice of,——but that the size and jollity of every individual nose, and by which one nose ranks above another, and bears a higher price, is owing to the cartilagenous and muscular parts of it, into whose ducts and sinuses the blood and animal spirits being impell'd, and driven by the warmth and force of the imagination, which is but a step from it, (bating the case of ideots, whom *Prignitz*, who had lived many years in *Turky*, supposes under the more immediate tutelage of heaven)——it so happens, and ever must, says *Prignitz*, that the excellency of the nose is in a direct arithmetical proportion to the excellency of the wearer's fancy.

It is for the same reason, that is, because 'tis all comprehended in *Slawkenbergius*, that I say nothing likewise of *Scroderus (Andrea)* who all the world knows, set himself to oppugn *Prignitz* with great violence,——proving it in his own way, first, *logically* and then by a series of stubborn facts, "That so far was *Prignitz* from the truth, in affirming that the fancy begat the nose, that on the contrary,—the nose begat the fancy."

—The learned suspected *Scroderus*, of an indecent sophism in this,—and *Prignitz* cried out aloud in the dispute, that *Scroderus* had shifted the idea upon him,—but *Scroderus* went on, maintaining his thesis.——

My father was just balancing within himself, which of the two sides he should take in this affair; when *Ambrose Paræus* decided it in a moment, and by overthrowing the systems, both of *Prignitz* and *Scroderus*, drove my father out of both sides of the controversy at once.

Be witness——

I don't acquaint the learned reader,—in saying it, I mention it only to shew the learned, I know the fact myself.——

That this *Ambrose Paræus* was chief surgeon and nose-mender to *Francis* the ninth of *France*,[5] and in high credit with him and the two preceding, or succeeding kings (I know not which)—and that except in the slip he made in his story of *Taliacotius*'s noses,[6] and his manner of setting them on, ——was esteemed by the whole college of physicians at that time, as more knowing in matters of noses, than any one who had ever taken them in hand.

Now *Ambrose Paræus* convinced my father, that the true and efficient cause of what had engaged so much the attention of the world, and upon which *Prignitz* and *Scroderus* had wasted so much learning and fine parts,—was neither this nor that,——but that the length and goodness of the nose was owing simply to the softness and flaccidity in the nurse's breast,——as the flatness and shortness of *puisne*[7] noses was, to the firmness and elastic reputation of the same organ of nutrition in the hale and lively,—which, tho' happy for the woman, was the undoing of the child, inasmuch as his nose was so snubb'd, so rebuff'd, so rebated, and so refrigerated thereby, as never to arrive *ad mensuram suam legitimam*;[8]——but that in case of the flaccidity and softness of the nurse or mother's breast,—by sinking into it, quoth *Paræus*, as into so much butter, the nose was comforted, nourish'd, plump'd up, refresh'd, refocillated,[9] and set a growing for ever.

I have but two things to observe of *Paræus*; first, that he proves and explains all this with the utmost chastity and decorum of expression:—for which may his soul for ever rest in peace!

And, secondly, that besides the systems of *Prignitz* and *Scroderus*, which *Ambrose Paræus* his hypothesis effectually overthrew,——it overthrew at the same time the system of peace and harmony of our family; and for three days together, not only embroiled matters between my father and my mother, but turn'd likewise the whole house and every thing in it, except my uncle *Toby*, quite upside down.

Such a ridiculous tale of a dispute between a man and his wife, never surely in any age or country got vent through the key-hole of a street door!

My mother, you must know,——but I have fifty things more necessary to let you know first,—I have a hundred difficulties which I have promised to clear up, and a thousand distresses and domestic misadventures crouding in upon me thick and three-fold, one upon the neck of another,——a cow broke in (tomorrow morning) to my uncle *Toby*'s fortifications, and eat up two ratios[10] and half of dried grass, tearing up the sods with it, which faced his horn-work and covered way.—*Trim* insists upon being tried by a court-martial,—the cow to be shot,—*Slop* to be *crucifix'd*,—myself to be *tristram'd*, and at my very baptism made a martyr of; ——poor unhappy devils that we all are!—I want swaddling,——but there is no time to be lost in exclamations.——I have left my father lying across his bed, and my uncle *Toby* in his old fringed chair, sitting beside him, and promised I would go back to them in half an hour, and five and thirty minutes are laps'd already.——Of all the perplexities a mortal author was ever seen in,—this certainly is the greatest,—for I have *Hafen Slawkenbergius*'s folio, Sir, to finish——a dialogue between my father and my uncle *Toby*, upon the solution of *Prignitz, Scroderus, Ambrose Paræus, Ponocrates* and *Grangousier*[11] to relate,—a tale out of *Slawkenbergius* to translate, and all this in five minutes less, than no time at all; ——such a head!—would to heaven! my enemies only saw the inside of it!

CHAPTER XXXIX

THERE was not any one scene more entertaining in our family,—and to do it justice in this point;——and I here put off my cap and lay it upon the table close beside my ink-horn, on purpose to make my declaration to the world concerning this one article, the more solemn,——that I believe in my soul, (unless my love and partiality to my understanding blinds me) the hand of the supreme Maker and first Designer of all things, never made or put a family together, (in that period at least of it, which I have sat down to write the story of)——where the characters of it were cast or contrasted with so dramatic a felicity as ours was, for this end; or in which the capacities of affording such exquisite scenes, and the powers of shifting them perpetually from morning to night, were lodged and intrusted with so unlimited a confidence, as in the SHANDY-FAMILY.

Not any one of these was more diverting, I say, in this whimsical theatre of ours,—than what frequently arose out of this self-same chapter of long noses,——especially when my father's imagination was heated with the enquiry, and nothing would serve him but to heat my uncle *Toby*'s too.

My uncle *Toby* would give my father all possible fair play in this attempt; and with infinite patience would sit smoking his pipe for whole hours together, whilst my father was practising upon his head, and trying every accessible avenue to drive *Prignitz* and *Scroderus*'s solutions into it.

Whether they were above my uncle *Toby*'s reason——or contrary to it,——or that his brain was like *damp* tinder,[1] and no spark could possibly take hold,—or that it was so full of saps, mines, blinds, curtins, and such military disqualifications to his seeing clearly into *Prignitz* and *Scroderus*'s doctrines,—I say not,—let school men—scullions, anatomists, and engineers, fight for it amongst themselves.——

'Twas some misfortune, I make no doubt, in this affair, that my father had every word of it to translate for the benefit of my uncle *Toby*, and render out of *Slawkenbergius*'s *Latin*, of which, as he was no great master, his translation was not always of the purest,—and generally least so where 'twas most wanted,—this naturally open'd a door to a second misfortune;—that in the warmer paroxisms of his zeal to open my uncle *Toby*'s eyes——my father's ideas run on, as much faster than the translation, as the translation outmoved my uncle *Toby*'s;——neither the one or the other added much to the perspicuity of my father's lecture.

CHAPTER XL

THE gift of ratiocination and making syllogisms,—I mean in man,—for in superior classes of beings, such as angels and spirits,—'tis all done, may it please your worships, as they tell me, by INTUITION;—and beings inferior, as your worships all know,——syllogize by their noses: though there is an island swiming in the sea, though not altogether at its ease, whose inhabitants, if my intelligence deceives me not, are so wonderfully gifted, as to syllogize after the same fashion, and oft-times to make very well out too:——but that's neither here nor there——

The gift of doing it as it should be, amongst us,—or the great and principal act of ratiocination in man, as logicians tell us, is the finding out the agreement or disagreement of two ideas one with another, by the intervention of a third; (called the *medius terminus*)[1] just as a man, as *Locke*[2] well observes, by a yard, finds two mens nine-pin-alleys to be of the same length, which could not be brought together, to measure their equality, by *juxtaposition*.

Had the same great reasoner looked on, as my father illustrated his systems of noses, and observed my uncle *Toby*'s deportment,—what great attention he gave to every word,—and as oft as he took his pipe from his mouth, with what wonderful seriousness he contemplated the length of it,—surveying it transversely as he held it betwixt his finger and his thumb,——then foreright,—then this way, and then that, in all its possible directions and foreshortenings,——he would have concluded my uncle *Toby* had got hold of the *medius terminus*; and was syllogizing and measuring with it the truth of each hypothesis of long noses, in order as my father laid them before him. This by the bye, was more than my father wanted,—his aim in all the pains he was at in these philosophic lectures,—was to enable my uncle *Toby* not to *discuss*,——but *comprehend*——to *hold* the grains and scruples of learning,—not to *weigh* them.—My uncle *Toby*, as you will read in the next chapter, did neither the one or the other.

CHAPTER XLI

'Tis a pity, cried my father one winter's night, after a three hours painful translation of *Slawkenbergius*,—'tis a pity, cried my father, putting my mother's thread-paper into the book for a mark, as he spoke——that truth, brother *Toby*, should shut herself up in such impregnable fastnesses, and be so obstinate as not to surrender herself sometimes up upon the closest siege.——

Now it happened then, as indeed it had often done before, that my uncle *Toby*'s fancy, during the time of my father's explanation of *Prignitz* to him,——having nothing to stay it there, had taken a short flight to the bowling-green;——his body might as well have taken a turn there too,——so that with all the semblance of a deep school-man intent upon the *medius terminus*,——my uncle *Toby* was in fact as ignorant of the whole lecture, and all its pro's and con's, as if my father had been translating *Hafen Slawkenbergius* from the *Latin* tongue into the *Cherokeè*. But the word *siege*, like a talismanic power, in my father's metaphor, wafting back my uncle *Toby*'s fancy, quick as a note could follow the touch,—he open'd his ears,—and my father observing that he took his pipe out of his mouth, and shuffled his chair nearer the table, as with a desire to profit,—my father with great pleasure began his sentence again,——changing only the plan, and dropping the metaphor of the siege of it, to keep clear of some dangers my father apprehended from it.

'Tis a pity, said my father, that truth can only be on one side, brother *Toby*,—considering what ingenuity these learned men have all shewn in their solutions of noses.——Can noses be dissolved? replied my uncle *Toby*.——

——My father thrust back his chair,——rose up,——put on his hat,——took four long strides to the door,—jerked it open,—thrust his head half way out,—shut the door again,—took no notice of the bad hinge,—returned to the table,—

pluck'd my mother's thread-paper out of *Slawkenbergius's* book,—went hastily to his bureau,—walk'd slowly back, twisting my mother's thread-paper about his thumb,—unbutton'd his waistcoat,——threw my mother's thread-paper into the fire,—bit her sattin pin-cushion in two, fill'd his mouth with bran,—confounded it;—but mark!—the oath of confusion was levell'd at my uncle *Toby's* brain,——which was e'en confused enough already,——the curse came charged only with the bran,—the bran, may it please your honours,—was no more than powder to the ball.

'Twas well my father's passions lasted not long; for so long as they did last, they led him a busy life on't, and it is one of the most unaccountable problems that ever I met with in my observations of human nature, that nothing should prove my father's mettle so much, or make his passions go off so like gun-powder, as the unexpected strokes his science met with from the quaint simplicity of my uncle *Toby's* questions. ——Had ten dozen of hornets stung him behind in so many different places all at one time,—he could not have exerted more mechanical functions in fewer seconds,—or started half so much, as with one single *quære* of three words unseasonably popping in full upon him in his hobbyhorsical career.

'Twas all one to my uncle *Toby*,—he smoaked his pipe on, with unvaried composure,—his heart never intended offence to his brother,—and as his head could seldom find out where the sting of it lay,——he always gave my father the credit of cooling by himself.——He was five minutes and thirty-five seconds about it in the present case.

By all that's good! said my father, swearing, as he came to himself, and taking the oath out of *Ernulphus's* digest of curses,—(though to do my father justice it was a fault (as he told Dr. *Slop* in the affair of *Ernulphus*) which he as seldom committed as any man upon earth.)——By all that's good and great! brother *Toby*, said my father, if it was not for the aids of philosophy, which befriend one so much as they do,—you would put a man beside all temper.—Why, by the *solutions* of noses, of which I was telling you, I meant as you might have known, had you favoured me with one grain of attention, the various accounts which learned men of different kinds of knowledge have given the world, of the causes of short and long noses. —There is no cause but one, replied my uncle *Toby*,—why one man's nose is longer than another's, but because that God pleases to have it so.—That is *Grangousier*'s solution,[1] said my father.—'Tis he, continued my uncle *Toby*, looking up, and not regarding my father's interruption, who makes us all, and frames and puts us together in such forms and proportions, and for such ends, as is agreeable to his infinite wisdom.——'Tis a pious account, cried my father, but not philosophical,—there is more religion in it than sound science. 'Twas no inconsistent part of my uncle *Toby*'s character,——that he feared God, and reverenced religion.——So the moment my father finished his remark,—my uncle *Toby* fell a whistling *Lillabullero*, with more zeal (though more out of tune) than usual.——

What is become of my wife's thread-paper?

CHAPTER XLII

No matter,——as an appendage to seamstressy, the thread-paper might be of some consequence to my mother,—of none to my father, as a mark in *Slawkenbergius*. *Slawkenbergius* in every page of him was a rich treasury of inexhaustible knowledge to my father,—he could not open him amiss; and he would often say in closing the book, that if all the arts and sciences in the world, with the books which treated of them, were lost,——should the wisdom and policies of governments, he would say, through disuse, ever happen to be forgot, and all that statesmen had wrote, or caused to be written, upon the strong or the weak sides of courts and kingdoms, should they be forgot also,—and *Slawkenbergius* only left,—there would be enough in him in all conscience, he would say, to set the world a-going again. A treasure therefore was he indeed! an institute of all that was necessary to be known of noses, and every thing else,——at *matin*, noon, and vespers was *Hafen Slawkenbergius* his recreation and delight: 'twas for ever in his hands,—you would have sworn, Sir, it had been a canon's prayer-book,—so worn, so glazed, so contrited and attrited was it with fingers and with thumbs in all its parts, from one end even unto the other.

I am not such a bigot to *Slawkenbergius*, as my father;—there is a fund in him, no doubt; but in my opinion, the best, I don't say the most profitable, but the most amusing part of *Hafen Slawkenbergius*, is his tales,——and, considering he was a *German*, many of them told not without fancy:——these take up his second book, containing nearly one half of his folio, and are

comprehended in ten decads, each decad containing ten tales.
——Philosophy is not built upon tales; and therefore 'twas
certainly wrong in *Slawkenbergius* to send them into the world
by that name;—there are a few of them in his eighth, ninth, and
tenth decads, which I own seem rather playful and sportive,
than speculative,—but in general they are to be looked upon by
the learned as a detail of so many independent facts, all of them
turning round somehow or other upon the main hinges of his
subject, and collected by him with great fidelity, and added to
his work as so many illustrations upon the doctrines of noses.

As we have leisure enough upon our hands,—if you give me
leave, madam, I'll tell you the ninth tale of his tenth decad.

THE END OF THE THIRD VOLUME.

W. Hogarth inv.   *F. Ravanet sculp.*

THE
LIFE
AND
OPINIONS
OF
TRISTRAM SHANDY,
GENTLEMAN.

Multitudinis imperitæ non formido judicia; meis
tamen, rogo, parcant opusculis——in quibus
fuit propositi semper, a jocis ad seria, a seriis
vicissim ad jocos transire.

JOAN. SARESBERIENSIS,
Episcopus Lugdun.

VOL. IV.

LONDON:

Printed for R. and J. DODSLEY in *Pall-Mall.*
M. DCC. LXI.

SLAWKENBERGII
Fabella.*

Vespera quâdam frigidulâ, posteriori in parte mensis Augusti, peregrinus, mulo fusco colore insidens, manticâ a tergo, paucis indusijs, binis calceis, braccisque sericis coccinejs repletâ Argentoratum ingressus est.

Militi eum percontanti, quum portus intraret, dixit, se apud Nasorum promontorium fuisse, Francofurtum proficisci, et Argentoratum, transitu ad fines Sarmatiæ mensis intervallo, reversurum.

Miles peregrini in faciem suspexit—Di boni, nova forma nasi!

At multum mihi profuit, inquit peregrinus, carpum amento extrahens, e quo pependit acinaces: Loculo manum inseruit; & magnâ cum urbanitate, pilei parte anteriore tactâ manu sinistrâ, ut extendit dextram, militi florinum dedit et processit.

Dolet mihi, ait miles, tympanistam nanum et valgum alloquens, virum adeo urbanum vaginam perdidisse; itinerari haud poterit nudâ acinaci, neque vaginam toto Argentorato, habilem inveniet.—Nullam unquam habui, respondit peregrinus respiciens,—seque comiter inclinans—hoc more gesto, nudam acinacem elevans, mulo lentò progrediente, ut nasum tueri possim.

Non immerito, benigne peregrine, respondit miles.
Nihili æstimo, ait ille tympanista, e pergamenâ factitius est.

Prout christianus sum, inquit miles, nasus ille, ni sexties major sit, meo esset conformis.
Crepitare audivi ait tympanista.
Mehercule! sanguinem emisit, respondit miles.
Miseret me, inquit tympanista, qui non ambo tetigimus!

* As *Hafen Slawkenbergius de Nasis* is extremely scarce, it may not be unacceptable to the learned reader to see the specimen of a few pages of his original; I will make no reflection upon it, but that his story-telling Latin is much more concise than his philosophic—and, I think, has more of Latinity in it.

SLAWKENBERGIUS's
TALE.

IT was one cool refreshing evening, at the close of a very sultry day, in the latter end of the month of *August*, when a stranger, mounted upon a dark mule, with a small cloak-bag behind him, containing a few shirts, a pair of shoes, and a crimson-sattin pair of breeches, entered the town of *Strasburg*.

He told the centinel, who questioned him as he entered the gates, that he had been at the promontory of NOSES—was going on to *Frankfort*—and should be back again at *Strasburg* that day month, in his way to the borders of *Crim-Tartary*.

The centinel looked up into the stranger's face—never saw such a nose in his life!

—I have made a very good venture of it, quoth the stranger—so slipping his wrist out of the loop of a black ribban, to which a short scymetar was hung: He put his hand into his pocket, and with great courtesy touching the forepart of his cap with his left-hand, as he extended his right—he put a florin into the centinel's hand, and passed on.

It grieves me, said the centinel, speaking to a little dwarfish bandy-leg'd drummer, that so courteous a soul should have lost his scabbard—he cannot travel without one to his scymetar, and will not be able to get a scabbard to fit it in all *Strasburg*.——I never had one, replied the stranger, looking back to the centinel, and putting his hand up to his cap as he spoke——I carry it, continued he thus—holding up his naked scymetar, his mule moving on slowly all the time, on purpose to defend my nose.

It is well worth it, gentle stranger, replied the centinel.

—'Tis not worth a single stiver, said the bandy-leg'd drummer—'tis a nose of parchment.

As I am a true catholic—except that it is six times as big—'tis a nose, said the centinel, like my own.

—I heard it crackle, said the drummer.

By dunder, said the centinel, I saw it bleed.

What a pity, cried the bandy-legg'd drummer, we did not both touch it!

Eodem temporis puncto, quo hæc res argumentata fuit inter militem et tympanistam, disceptabatur ibidem tubicine & uxore suâ, qui tunc accesserunt, et peregrino prætereunte, restiterunt.

Quantus nasus! æque longus est, ait tubicina, ac tuba.

Et ex eodem metallo, ait tubicen, velut sternutamento audias.

Tantum abest, respondit illa, quod fistulam dulcedine vincit. Æneus est, ait tubicen.
Nequaquam, respondit uxor.
Rursum affirmo, ait tubicen, quod æneus est.
Rem penitus explorabo; prius, enim digito tangam, ait uxor, quam dormivero.
Mulus peregrini, gradu lento progressus est, ut unumquodque verbum controversiæ, non tantum inter militem et tympanistam, verum etiam inter tubicinem et uxorem ejus, audiret.
Nequaquam, ait ille, in muli collum fræna demittens, & manibus ambabus in pectus positis, (mulo lentè progrediente) nequaquam ait ille, respiciens, non necesse est ut res isthæc dilucidata foret. Minime gentium! meus nasus nunquam tangetur, dum spiritus hos reget artus—ad quid agendum? ait uxor burgomagistri.

Peregrinus illi non respondit. Votum faciebat tunc temporis sancto Nicolao, quo facto, sinum dextram inserens, e quâ negligenter pependit acinaces, lento gradu processit per plateam Argentorati latam quæ ad diversorium templo ex adversum ducit.

Peregrinus mulo descendens stabulo includi, & manticam inferri jussit: quâ apertâ et coccineis sericis femoralibus extractis cum argenteo laciniato Περιζωματὲ, his sese induit, statimque, acinaci in manu, ad forum deambulavit.

Quod ubi peregrinus esset ingressus, uxorem tubicinis obviam

At the very time that this dispute was maintaining by the centinel and the drummer—was the same point debating betwixt a trumpeter and a trumpeter's wife, who were just then coming up, and had stopped to see the stranger pass by.

Benedicity![1]——What a nose! 'tis as long, said the trumpeter's wife, as a trumpet.

And of the same mettle, said the trumpeter, as you hear by its sneezing.

—'Tis as soft as a flute, said she.

—'Tis brass, said the trumpeter.

—'Tis a pudding's end—said his wife.

I tell thee again, said the trumpeter, 'tis a brazen nose.

I'll know the bottom of it, said the trumpeter's wife, for I will touch it with my finger before I sleep.

The stranger's mule moved on at so slow a rate, that he heard every word of the dispute, not only betwixt the centinel and the drummer; but betwixt the trumpeter and the trumpeter's wife.

No! said he, dropping his reins upon his mule's neck, and laying both his hands upon his breast, the one over the other in a saint-like position (his mule going on easily all the time) No! said he, looking up,—I am not such a debtor to the world—slandered and disappointed as I have been——as to give it that conviction—no! said he, my nose shall never be touched whilst heaven gives me strength—To do what? said a burgomaster's wife.

The stranger took no notice of the burgomaster's wife—he was making a vow to saint *Nicolas*; which done, having uncrossed his arms with the same solemnity with which he crossed them, he took up the reins of his bridle with his left-hand, and putting his right-hand into his bosom, with his scymetar hanging loosely to the wrist of it, he rode on as slowly as one foot of the mule could follow another thro' the principal streets of *Strasburg*, till chance brought him to the great inn in the market-place over-against the church.

The moment the stranger alighted, he ordered his mule to be led into the stable, and his cloak-bag to be brought in; then opening, and taking out of it, his crimson-sattin breeches, with a silver-fringed—(appendage to them, which I dare not translate)—he put his breeches, with his fringed cod-piece on, and forthwith with his short scymetar in his hand, walked out to the grand parade.

The stranger had just taken three turns upon the parade,

euntem aspicit; illico cursum flectit, metuens ne nasus suus exploraretur, atque ad diversorium regressus est—exuit se vestibus; braccas coccineas sericas manticæ imposuit mulumque educi jussit.

Francofurtum proficiscor, ait ille, et Argentoratum quatuor abhinc hebdomadis revertar.

Bene curasti hoc jumentum (ait) muli faciem manu demulcens ——me, manticamque meam, plus sexcentis mille passibus portavit.

Longa via est! respondit hospes, nisi plurimum esset negoti. ——Enimvero ait peregrinus a nasorum promontorio redij, et nasum speciosissimum egregiosissimumque quem unquam quisquam sortitus est, acquisivi!

Dum peregrinus hanc miram rationem, de seipso reddit, hospes et uxor ejus, oculis intentis, peregrini nasum contemplantur—Per sanctos, sanctasque omnes, ait hospitis uxor, nasis duodecim maximis, in toto Argentorato major est!—estne ait illa mariti in aurem insusurrans, nonne est nasus prægrandis?

Dolus inest, anime mi, ait hospes—nasus est falsus.—

Verus est, respondit uxor.—
Ex abiete factus est, ait ille, terebinthinum olet——
Carbunculus inest, ait uxor.
Mortuus est nasus, respondit hospes.
Vivus est, ait illa, ——& si ipsa vivam tangam.

Votum feci sancto Nicolao, ait peregrinus, nasum meum intactum fore usque ad—Quodnam tempus? illico respondit illa.

Minime tangetur, inquit ille (manibus in pectus compositis) usque ad illam horam—Quam horam? ait illa.—Nullam, respondit peregrinus, donec pervenio, ad—Quem locum,—obsecro? ait illa—Peregrinus nil respondens mulo conscenso discessit.

when he perceived the trumpeter's wife at the opposite side of it—so turning short, in pain lest his nose should be attempted, he instantly went back to his inn——undressed himself, packed up his crimson-sattin breeches, &c. in his cloak-bag, and called for his mule.

I am going forwards, said the stranger, for *Franckfort*——and shall be back at *Strasburg* this day month.

I hope, continued the stranger, stroking down the face of his mule with his left-hand as he was going to mount it, that you have been kind to this faithful slave of mine——it has carried me and my cloak-bag, continued he, tapping the mule's back, above six hundred leagues.

—'Tis a long journey, Sir, replied the master of the inn—— unless a man has great business.—Tut! tut! said the stranger, I have been at the promontory of Noses; and have got me one of the goodliest and jolliest, thank heaven, that ever fell to a single man's lot.

Whilst the stranger was giving this odd account of himself, the master of the inn and his wife kept both their eyes fixed full upon the stranger's nose—By saint *Radagunda*,[2] said the inn-keeper's wife to herself, there is more of it than in any dozen of the largest noses put together in all *Strasburg!* is it not, said she, whispering her husband in his ear, is it not a noble nose?

'Tis an imposture, my dear, said the master of the inn—'tis a false nose.—

'Tis a true nose, said his wife.—

'Tis made of fir-tree, said he,—I smell the turpentine.—

There's a pimple on it, said she.

'Tis a dead nose, replied the inn-keeper.

'Tis a live nose, and if I am alive myself, said the inn-keeper's wife, I will touch it.

I have made a vow to saint *Nicolas* this day, said the stranger, that my nose shall not be touched till—Here the stranger, suspending his voice, looked up—Till when? said she hastily.

It shall never be touched, said he, clasping his hands and bringing them close to his breast, till that hour.——What hour? cried the inn-keeper's wife.——Never!—never!—said the stranger, never till I am got—For heaven sake into what place? said she.—The stranger rode away without saying a word.

The stranger had not got half a league on his way towards *Frankfort*, before all the city of *Strasburg* was in an uproar about his nose. The *Compline*-bells were just ringing to call the *Strasburgers* to their devotions, and shut up the duties of the day in prayer:——no soul in all *Strasburg* heard 'em—the city was like a swarm of bees——men, women, and children (the *Compline*-bells tinkling all the time) flying here and there—in at one door, out at another—this way and that way—long ways and cross ways—up one street, down another street—in at this ally, out at that——did you see it? did you see it? did you see it? O! did you see it?—who saw it? who did see it? for mercy's sake, who saw it?

Alack o'day! I was at vespers!——I was washing, I was starching, I was scouring, I was quilting—GOD help me! I never saw it—I never touch'd it!——would I had been a centinel, a bandy-leg'd drummer, a trumpeter, a trumpeter's wife, was the general cry and lamentation in every street and corner of *Strasburg*.

Whilst all this confusion and disorder triumphed throughout the great city of *Strasburg*, was the courteous stranger going on as gently upon his mule in his way to *Frankfort*, as if he had had no concern at all in the affair—talking all the way he rode in broken sentences, sometimes to his mule—sometimes to himself——sometimes to his Julia.

O Julia, my lovely Julia!—nay I cannot stop to let thee bite that thistle—that ever the suspected tongue of a rival should have robbed me of enjoyment when I was upon the point of tasting it.—

—Pugh!—'tis nothing but a thistle—never mind it—thou shalt have a better supper at night.—

——Banish'd from my country—my friends—from thee.—

Poor devil, thou'rt sadly tired with thy journey!—come—get on a little faster—there's nothing in my cloak-bag but two shirts —a crimson-sattin pair of breeches, and a fringed—Dear Julia!

—But why to *Frankfort*?—is it that there is a hand unfelt, which secretly is conducting me through these meanders and unsuspected tracts?—

—Stumbling! by saint *Nicolas*! every step——why at this rate we shall be all night in getting in——

—To happiness—or am I to be the sport of fortune and slander—destined to be driven forth unconvicted—unheard— untouched——if so, why did I not stay at *Strasburg*, where justice——but I had sworn!—Come, thou shalt drink—to *St. Nicolas*—O *Julia!*——What dost thou prick up thy ears at?—'tis nothing but a man, &c.——

The stranger rode on communing in this manner with his mule and *Julia*—till he arrived at his inn, where, as soon as he arrived, he alighted—saw his mule, as he had promised it, taken good care of——took off his cloak-bag, with his crimson-sattin breeches, &c. in it——called for an omelet to his supper, went to his bed about twelve o'clock, and in five minutes fell fast asleep.

It was about the same hour when the tumult in *Strasburg* being abated for that night,——the *Strasburgers* had all got quietly into their beds—but not like the stranger, for the rest either of their minds or bodies; queen *Mab*,[3] like an elf as she was, had taken the stranger's nose, and without reduction of its bulk, had that night been at the pains of slitting and dividing it into as many noses of different cuts and fashions, as there were heads in *Strasburg* to hold them. The abbess of *Quedlingberg*,[4] who, with the four great dignitaries of her chapter, the prioress, the deaness, the sub-chantress, and senior canoness, had that week come to *Strasburg* to consult the university upon a case of conscience relating to their placket holes—was ill all the night.

The courteous stranger's nose had got perched upon the top of the pineal gland of her brain, and made such rousing work in the fancies of the four great dignitaries of her chapter, they could not get a wink of sleep the whole night thro' for it ——there was no keeping a limb still amongst them—in short, they got up like so many ghosts.

The penitentiaries of the third order of saint *Francis*[5]——the nuns of mount *Calvary*[6]—the *Præmonstratenses*[7]——the *Clunienses**[8]—the *Carthusians*,[9] and all the severer orders of nuns who lay that night in blankets or hair-cloth, were still in a worse condition than the abbess of *Quedlingberg*—by tumbling and tossing, and tossing and tumbling from one side of their beds to the other the whole night long—the several sisterhoods had scratch'd and mawl'd themselves all to death—they got out of their beds almost flead alive—every body thought saint *Anthony*[10] had visited them for probation with his fire——they had never once, in short, shut their eyes the whole night long from vespers to matins.

* *Hafen Slawkenbergius* means the Benedictine nuns of *Cluny*, founded in the year 940, by *Odo*, abbé de *Cluny*.

The nuns of saint *Ursula*[11] acted the wisest—they never attempted to go to bed at all.

The dean of *Strasburg*, the prebendaries, the capitulars[12] and domiciliars[13] (capitularly assembled in the morning to consider the case of butter'd buns)[14] all wished they had followed the nuns of saint *Ursula*'s example.——In the hurry and confusion every thing had been in the night before, the bakers had all forgot to lay their leaven—there were no butter'd buns to be had for breakfast in all *Strasburg*—the whole close of the cathedral was in one eternal commotion—such a cause of restlessness and disquietude, and such a zealous inquiry into the cause of that restlessness, had never happened in *Strasburg*, since *Martin Luther*,[15] with his doctrines, had turned the city up-side down.

If the stranger's nose took this liberty of thrusting itself thus into the dishes* of religious orders, &c. what a carnival did his nose make of it, in those of the laity!—'tis more than my pen, worn to the stump as it is, has power to describe; tho' I acknowledge, (*cries* Slawkenbergius, *with more gaiety of thought than I could have expected from him*) that there is many a good simile now subsisting in the world which might give my countrymen some idea of it; but at the close of such a folio as this, wrote for their sakes, and in which I have spent the greatest part of my life—tho' I own to them the simile is in being, yet would it not be unreasonable in them to expect I should have either time or inclination to search for it? Let it suffice to say, that the riot and disorder it occasioned in the *Strasburgers* fantacies was so general—such an overpowering mastership had it got of all the faculties of the *Strasburgers* minds—so many strange things, with equal confidence on all sides, and with equal eloquence in all places, were spoken and sworn to concerning it, that turned the whole stream of all discourse and wonder towards it—every soul, good and bad—rich and poor—learned and unlearned— doctor and student—mistress and maid—gentle and simple— nun's flesh and woman's flesh in *Strasburg* spent their time in hearing tidings about it—every eye in *Strasburg* languished to see it——every finger—every thumb in *Strasburg* burned to touch it.

* Mr. *Shandy's* compliments to orators—is very sensible that *Slawkenbergius* has here changed his metaphor—which he is very guilty of;—that as a translator, Mr. *Shandy* has all along done what he could to make him stick to it—but that here 'twas impossible.

Now what might add, if any thing may be thought necessary to add to so vehement a desire—was this, that the centinel, the bandy-legg'd drummer, the trumpeter, the trumpeter's wife, the burgo-master's widow, the master of the inn, and the master of the inn's wife, how widely soever they all differed every one from another in their testimonies and descriptions of the stranger's nose—they all agreed together in two points—namely, that he was gone to *Frankfort*, and would not return to *Strasburg* till that day month; and secondly, whether his nose was true or false, that the stranger himself was one of the most perfect paragons of beauty--the finest made man!—the most genteel!—the most generous of his purse—the most courteous in his carriage that had ever entered the gates of *Strasburg*—that as he rode, with his scymetar slung loosely to his wrist, thro' the streets—and walked with his crimson-sattin breeches across the parade—'twas with so sweet an air of careless modesty, and so manly withal—as would have put the heart in jeopardy (had his nose not stood in his way) of every virgin who had cast her eyes upon him.

I call not upon that heart which is a stranger to the throbs and yearnings of curiosity, so excited to justify the abbess of *Quedlingberg*, the prioress, the deaness and subchantress for sending at noon-day for the trumpeter's wife: she went through the streets of *Strasburg* with her husband's trumpet in her hand;—the best apparatus the straitness of the time would allow her, for the illustration of her theory—she staid no longer than three days.

The centinel and the bandy-legg'd drummer!—nothing on this side of old *Athens* could equal them! they read their lectures under the city gates to comers and goers, with all the pomp of a *Chrysippus*[16] and a *Crantor*[17] in their porticos.

The master of the inn, with his ostler on his left-hand, read his also in the same stile,—under the portico or gateway of his stable-yard—his wife, hers more privately in a back room: all flocked to their lectures; not promiscuously—but to this or that, as is ever the way, as faith and credulity marshal'd them—in a word, each *Strasburger* came crouding for intelligence—and every *Strasburger* had the intelligence he wanted.

Tis worth remarking, for the benefit of all demonstrators in natural philosophy, &c. that as soon as the trumpeter's wife had finished the abbess of *Quedlinberg*'s private lecture, and had begun to read in public, which she did upon a stool in the middle of the great parade—she incommoded the other demonstrators mainly, by gaining incontinently the most fashionable part of the city of *Strasburg* for her auditory—But when a demonstrator in philosophy (cries *Slawkenbergius*) has a *trumpet* for an apparatus, pray what rival in science can pretend to be heard besides him?

Whilst the unlearned, thro' these conduits of intelligence, were all busied in getting down to the bottom of the well, where TRUTH keeps her little court—were the learned in their way as busy in pumping her up thro' the conduits of dialect induction—they concerned themselves not with facts—they reasoned—

Not one profession had thrown more light upon this subject than the faculty[18]—had not all their disputes about it run into the affair of *Wens* and œdematous swellings, they could not keep clear of them for their bloods and souls—the stranger's nose had nothing to do either with wens or œdematous swellings.

It was demonstrated however very satisfactorily, that such a ponderous mass of heterogenious matter could not be congested and conglomerated to the nose, whilst the infant was *in Utero*,[19] without destroying the statical balance of the fœtus, and throwing it plump upon its head nine months before the time.——

—The opponents granted the theory—they denied the consequences.

And if a suitable provision of veins, arteries, &c. said they, was not laid in, for the due nourishment of such a nose, in the very first stamina and rudiments of its formation before it came into the world (bating the case of Wens) it could not regularly grow and be sustained afterwards.

This was all answered by a dissertation upon nutriment, and the effect which nutriment had in extending the vessels, and in the increase and prolongation of the muscular parts to the greatest growth and expansion imaginable—In the triumph of which theory, they went so far as to affirm, that there was no cause in nature, why a nose might not grow to the size of the man himself.

The respondents satisfied the world this event could never happen to them so long as a man had but one stomach and one pair of lungs—For the stomach, said they, being the only organ destined for the reception of food, and turning it into chyle,—

and the lungs the only engine of sanguification—it could possibly work off no more, than what the appetite brought it: or admitting the possibility of a man's overloading his stomach, nature had set bounds however to his lungs—the engine was of a determined size and strength, and could elaborate but a certain quantity in a given time—that is, it could produce just as much blood as was sufficient for one single man, and no more; so that, if there was as much nose as man—they proved a mortification must necessarily ensue; and forasmuch as there could not be a support for both, that the nose must either fall off from the man, or the man inevitably fall off from his nose.

Nature accommodates herself to these emergencies, cried the opponents—else what do you say to the case of a whole stomach—a whole pair of lungs, and but *half* a man, when both his legs have been unfortunately shot off?—

He dies of a plethora, said they—or must spit blood, and in a fortnight or three weeks go off in a consumption—

—It happens otherways—replied the opponents.——

It ought not, said they.

The more curious and intimate inquirers after nature and her doings, though they went hand in hand a good way together, yet they all divided about the nose at last, almost as much as the faculty itself.

They amicably laid it down, that there was a just and geometrical arrangement and proportion of the several parts of the human frame to its several destinations, offices, and functions, which could not be transgressed but within certain limits—that nature, though she sported—she sported within a certain circle;—and they could not agree about the diameter of it.

The logicians stuck much closer to the point before them than any of the classes of the literati;—they began and ended with the word nose; and had it not been for a *petitio principii*,[20] which one of the ablest of them ran his head against in the beginning of the combat, the whole controversy had been settled at once.

A nose, argued the logician, cannot bleed without blood—and not only blood—but blood circulating in it to supply the phænomenon with a succession of drops—(a stream being but a quicker succession of drops, that is included, said he)—Now death, continued the logician, being nothing but the stagnation of the blood—

I deny the definition—Death is the separation of the soul from the body, said his antagonist—Then we don't agree about our weapon, said the logician—Then there is an end of the dispute, replied the antagonist.

The civilians[21] were still more concise; what they offered being more in the nature of a decree—than a dispute.

—Such a monstrous nose, said they, had it been a true nose, could not possibly have been suffered in civil society—and if false—to impose upon society with such false signs and tokens, was a still greater violation of its rights, and must have had still less mercy shewn it.

The only objection to this was, that if it proved any thing, it proved the stranger's nose was neither true nor false.

This left room for the controversy to go on. It was maintained by the advocates of the ecclesiastic court, that there was nothing to inhibit a decree, since the stranger *ex mero motu*[22] had confessed he had been at the Promontory of Noses, and had got one of the goodliest, &c. &c.—To this it was answered, it was impossible there should be such a place as the Promontory of Noses, and the learned be ignorant where it lay. The commissary of the bishop of *Strasburg* undertook the advocates, explained this matter in a treatise upon proverbial phrases, shewing them, that the Promontory of Noses was a mere allegoric expression, importing no more than that nature had given him a long nose: in proof of which, with great learning, he cited the underwritten authorities*, which had decided the point incontestably, had it not appeared that a dispute about some franchises of dean and chapter-lands had been determined by it nineteen years before.

It happened—I must not say unluckily for Truth, because they were giving her a lift another way in so doing; that the two universities of *Strasburg*—the *Lutheran*, founded in the year 1538 by *Jacobus Sturmius*,[24] counsellor of the senate,—and the *Popish*, founded by *Leopold*, arch-duke of *Austria*,[25] were, dur-

---

* Nonnulli ex nostratibus eadem loquendi formulâ utun. Quinimo et Logistae & Canonistae—Vid. Parce Bar e Jas in d. L. Provincial. Constitut. de conjec. vid. Vol. Lib 4. Titul. 1. N. 7. quâ etiam in re conspir. Om. de Promontorio Nas. Tichmak. ff. d. tit. 3. fol. 189. passim. Vid. Glos. de contrahend. empt. &c. nec non J. Scrudr. in cap. §. refut. ff. per totum. cum his conf. Rever. J. Tubal, Sentent. & Prov. cap. 9. ff. 11, 12. obiter. V. et Librum, cui Tit. de Terris & Phras. Belg. ad finem cum, Comment. N. Bardy Belg. Vid. Scrip. Argentotarens. de Antiq. Ecc. in Episc. Archiv. fid. coll. per Von Jacobum Koinshoven Folio Argent. 1583, præcip. ad finem. Quibus add. Rebuff in L. obvenire de Signif. Nom. ff. fol. & de Jure, Gent. & Civil. de protib. aliena feud. per federa, test. Joha. Luxius in prolegom. quem velim videas, de Analy. Cap. 1, 2, 3. Vid. Idea.[23]

ing all this time, employing the whole depth of their knowledge (except just what the affair of the abbess of *Quedlinburg*'s placket-holes required)—in determining the point of *Martin Luther*'s damnation.

The *Popish* doctors had undertaken to demonstrate *a priori*; that from the necessary influence of the planets on the twenty-second day of *October* 1483——when the moon was in the twelfth house—*Jupiter, Mars*, and *Venus* in the third, the *Sun, Saturn*, and *Mercury* all got together in the fourth—that he must in course, and unavoidably be a damn'd man—and that his doctrines, by a direct corollary, must be damn'd doctrines too.

By inspection into his horoscope, where five planets were in coition[26] all at once with scorpio* (in reading this my father would always shake his head) in the ninth house which the *Arabians* allotted to religion—it appeared that *Martin Luther* did not care one stiver about the matter—and that from the horoscope directed to the conjunction of *Mars*—they made it plain likewise he must die cursing and blaspheming—with the blast of which his soul (being steep'd in guilt) sailed before the wind, into the lake of hell fire.

The little objection of the *Lutheran* doctors to this, was, that it must certainly be the soul of another man, born *Oct.* 22, 1483,[28] which was forced to sail down before the wind in that manner—inasmuch as it appeared from the register of *Islaben* in the county of *Mansfelt*, that *Luther* was not born in the year 1483, but in 84; and not on the 22d day of *October*, but on the 10th of *November*, the eve of *Martinmas*-day, from whence he had the name of *Martin*.

[—I must break off my translation for a moment; for if I did not, I know I should no more be able to shut my eyes in bed, than the abbess of *Quedlinburg*—It is to tell the reader, that my father never read this passage of *Slawkenbergius* to my uncle *Toby* but with triumph—not over my uncle *Toby*, for he never opposed him in it—but over the whole world.

—Now you see, brother *Toby*, he would say, looking up,

* Hæc mira, satisque horrenda. Planetarum coitio sub Scorpio Asterismo in nonâ cœli statione, quam Arabes religioni deputabant, efficit *Martinum Lutherum* sacrilegum hereticum, christianæ religionis hostem acerrimum atque prophanum, ex horoscopi directione ad Martis coitum, religiosissimus obiit, ejus Anima scelestissima ad infernos navigavit—ab Alecto, Tisiphone et Magera flagellis igneis cruciata pereniter.

—Lucas Gauricus in Tractatu astrologico de præteritis multorum hominum accidentibus per genituras examinatis.[27]

"that christian names are not such indifferent things;"— had *Luther* here been called by any other name but *Martin*, he would have been damned to all eternity—Not that I look upon *Martin*, he would add, as a good name—far from it—'tis something better than a neutral, and but a little—yet little as it is, you see it was of some service to him.

My father knew the weakness of this prop to his hypothesis, as well as the best logician could shew him—yet so strange is the weakness of man at the same time, as it fell in his way, he could not for his life but make use of it; and it was certainly for this reason, that though there are many stories in *Hafen Slawkenbergius's* Decads full as entertaining as this I am translating, yet there is not one amongst them which my father read over with half the delight—it flattered two of his strangest hypotheses together—his NAMES and his NOSES—I will be bold to say, he might have read all the books in the *Alexandrian* library,[29] had not fate taken other care of them, and not have met with a book or a passage in one, which hit two such nails as these upon the head at one stroke.]

The two universities of *Strasburg* were hard tugging at this affair of *Luther's* navigation. The Protestant doctors had demonstrated, that he had not sailed right before the wind, as the Popish doctors had pretended; and as every one knew there was no sailing full in the teeth of it,—they were going to settle, in case he had sailed, how many points he was off; whether *Martin* had doubled the cape, or had fallen upon a lee-shore; and no doubt, as it was an enquiry of much edification, at least to those who understood this sort of NAVIGATION, they had gone on with it in spite of the size of the stranger's nose, had not the size of the stranger's nose drawn off the attention of the world from what they were about—it was their business to follow.——

The abbess of *Quedlinburg* and her four dignitaries was no stop; for the enormity of the stranger's nose running full as much in their fancies as their case of conscience—The affair of their placket-holes kept cold—In a word, the printers were ordered to distribute their types—all controversies dropp'd.

'Twas a square cap with a silk tassel upon the crown of it—to a nut shell—to have guessed on which side of the nose the two universities would split.

'Tis above reason, cried the doctors on one side.

'Tis below reason, cried the others.

'Tis faith, cried the one.

'Tis a fiddle-stick, said the other.

'Tis possible, cried the one.

'Tis impossible, said the other.

God's power is infinite, cried the Nosarians, he can do any thing.

He can do nothing, replied the Anti-nosarians, which implies contradictions.

He can make matter think, said the Nosarians.

As certainly as you can make a velvet cap out of a sow's ear, replied the Antinosarians.

He can make two and two five, replied the Popish doctors.— 'Tis false, said their opponents.—

Infinite power is infinite power, said the doctors who maintained the *reality* of the nose.——It extends only to all possible things, replied the *Lutherans*.

By God in heaven, cried the Popish doctors, he can make a nose, if he thinks fit, as big as the steeple of *Strasburg*.

Now the steeple of *Strasburg* being the biggest and the tallest church-steeple to be seen in the whole world, the Antinosarians denied that a nose of 575 geometrical feet in length could be worn, at least by a middle-siz'd man—The Popish doctors swore it could—The *Lutheran* doctors said No;—it could not.

This at once started a new dispute, which they pursued a great way upon the extent and limitation of the moral and natural attributes of God—That controversy led them naturally into *Thomas Aquinas*,[30] and *Thomas Aquinas* to the devil.

The stranger's nose was no more heard of in the dispute—it just served as a frigate to launch them into the gulph of school-divinity,—and then they all sailed before the wind.

Heat is in proportion to the want of true knowledge.

The controversy about the attributes, &c. instead of cooling, on the contrary had inflamed the *Strasburgers* imaginations to a most inordinate degree—The less they understood of the matter, the greater was their wonder about it—they were left in all the distresses of desire unsatisfied—saw their doctors, the *Parchmentarians*, the *Brassarians*, the *Turpentarians*, on one side—the Popish doctors on the other, like *Pantagruel* and his companions[31] in quest of the oracle of the bottle, all embarked and out of sight.

——The poor *Strasburgers* left upon the beach!

—What was to be done?—No delay—the uproar increased—
every one in disorder—the city gates set open.—

Unfortunate *Strasburgers!* was there in the store-house of
nature—was there in the lumber-rooms of learning—was there
in the great arsenal of chance, one single engine left undrawn
forth to torture your curiosities, and stretch your desires, which
was not pointed by the hand of fate to play upon your hearts?—
I dip not my pen into my ink to excuse the surrender of
yourselves—'tis to write your panegyrick. Shew me a city so
macerated with expectation—who neither eat, or drank, or
slept, or prayed, or hearkened to the calls either of religion or
nature for seven and twenty days together, who could have held
out one day longer.

On the twenty-eighth the courteous stranger had promised
to return to *Strasburg*.

Seven thousand coaches (*Slawkenbergius* must certainly have
made some mistake in his numerical characters) 7000 coaches—
15000 single horse chairs——20000 waggons, crouded as full as
they could all hold with senators, counsellors, syndicks—
beguines, widows, wives, virgins, canons, concubines, all in
their coaches—The abbess of *Quedlinburg*, with the prioress,
the deaness and sub-chantress leading the procession in one
coach, and the dean of *Strasburg*, with the four great dignitaries
of his chapter on her left-hand—the rest following higglety-
pigglety as they could; some on horseback——some on foot—
some led—some driven—some down the *Rhine*—some this
way—some that—all set out at sun-rise to meet the courteous
stranger on the road.

Haste we now towards the catastrophe of my tale—I say
Catastrophe[32] (cries *Slawkenbergius*) inasmuch as a tale, with
parts rightly disposed, not only rejoiceth (*gaudet*) in the *Catastrophe* and *Peripeitia*[33] of a DRAMA, but rejoiceth moreover in
all the essential and integrant parts of it—it has its *Protasis*,[34]
Epitasis,[35] *Catastasis*,[36] its *Catastrophe* or *Peripeitia* growing one
out of the other in it, in the order *Aristotle* first planted them—
without which a tale had better never be told at all, says *Slawkenbergius*, but be kept to a man's self.

In all my ten tales, in all my ten decads, have I, *Slawkenbergius*, tied down every tale of them as tightly to this rule, as I have
done this of the stranger and his nose.

—From his first parley with the centinel, to his leaving the city
of *Strasburg*, after pulling off his crimson-sattin pair of breeches,

is the *Protasis* or first entrance——where the characters of the *Personæ Dramatis* are just touched in, and the subject slightly begun.

The *Epitasis*, wherein the action is more fully entered upon and heightened, till it arrives at its state or height called the *Catastasis*, and which usually takes up the 2d and 3d act, is included within that busy period of my tale, betwixt the first night's uproar about the nose, to the conclusion of the trumpeter's wife's lectures upon it in the middle of the grand parade; and from the first embarking of the learned in the dispute—to the doctors finally sailing away, and leaving the *Strasburgers* upon the beach in distress, is the *Catastasis* or the ripening of the incidents and passions for their bursting forth in the fifth act.

This commences with the setting out of the *Strasburgers* in the *Frankfort* road, and terminates in unwinding the labyrinth and bringing the hero out of a state of agitation (as *Aristotle* calls it) to a state of rest and quietness.

This, says *Hafen Slawkenbergius*, constitutes the catastrophe or peripeitia of my tale—and that is the part of it I am going to relate.

We left the stranger behind the curtain asleep—he enters now upon the stage.

—What dost thou prick up thy ears at?—'tis nothing but a man upon a horse—was the last word the stranger uttered to his mule. It was not proper then to tell the reader, that the mule took his master's word for it; and without any more *ifs* or *ands*, let the traveller and his horse pass by.

The traveller was hastening with all diligence to get to *Strasburg* that night—What a fool am I, said the traveller to himself, when he had rode about a league farther, to think of getting into *Strasburg* this night—*Strasburg!*—the great *Strasburg!*—*Strasburg*, the capital of all *Alsatia! Strasburg*, an imperial city! *Strasburg*, a sovereign state! *Strasburg*, garrisoned with five thousand of the best troops in all the world!—Alas! if I was at the gates of *Strasburg* this moment, I could not gain admittance into it for a ducat,—nay a ducat and half—'tis too much—better go back to the last inn I have passed—than lie I know not where—or give I know not what. The traveller, as he made these reflections in his mind, turned his horse's head about, and three minutes after the stranger had been conducted into his chamber, he arrived at the same inn.

—We have bacon in the house, said the host, and bread ——and till eleven o'clock this night had three eggs in it—but a stranger, who arrived an hour ago, has had them dressed into an omlet, and we have nothing.——

Alas! said the traveller, harrassed as I am, I want nothing but a bed—I have one as soft as is in *Alsatia*, said the host.

—The stranger, continued he, should have slept in it, for 'tis my best bed, but upon the score of his nose—He has got a defluxion,[37] said the traveller—Not that I know, cried the host—But 'tis a camp-bed, and *Jacinta*, said he, looking towards the maid, imagined there was not room in it to turn his nose in—Why so? cried the traveller starting back—It is so long a nose, replied the host—The traveller fixed his eyes upon *Jacinta*, then upon the ground—kneeled upon his right knee—had just got his hand laid upon his breast—Trifle not with my anxiety, said he, rising up again—'Tis no trifle, said *Jacinta*, 'tis the most glorious nose!—The traveller fell upon his knee again—laid his hand upon his breast—then said he, looking up to heaven! thou hast conducted me to the end of my pilgrim-age——'Tis *Diego!*

The traveller was the brother of the Julia, so often invoked that night by the stranger as he rode from *Strasburg* upon his mule; and was come, on her part, in quest of him. He had accompanied his sister from *Valadolid*[38] across the *Pyrenean* mountains thro' *France*, and had many an entangled skein to wind off in pursuit of him thro' the many meanders and abrupt turnings of a lover's thorny tracks.

—Julia had sunk under it—and had not been able to go a step farther than to *Lyons*, where, with the many disquietudes of a tender heart, which all talk of—but few feel—she sicken'd, but had just strength to write a letter to *Diego*; and having conjured her brother never to see her face till he had found him out, and put the letter into his hands, Julia took to her bed.

Fernandez (for that was her brother's name)—tho' the camp-bed was as soft as any one in *Alsace*, yet he could not shut his eyes in it.—As soon as it was day he rose, and hearing *Diego* was risen too, he enter'd his chamber, and discharged his sister's commission.

The letter was as follows:

Seig. DIEGO.

"Whether my suspicions of your nose were justly excited or

not—'tis not now to inquire—it is enough I have not had firmness to put them to farther tryal.

"How could I know so little of myself, when I sent my *Duena* to forbid your coming more under my lattice? or how could I know so little of you, *Diego*, as to imagine you would not have staid one day in *Valadolid* to have given ease to my doubts?—Was I to be abandoned, *Diego*, because I was deceived? or was it kind to take me at my word, whether my suspicions were just or no, and leave me, as you did, a prey to much uncertainty and sorrow.

"In what manner Julia has resented this—my brother, when he puts this letter into your hands, will tell you: He will tell you in how few moments she repented of the rash message she had sent you—in what frantic haste she flew to her lattice, and how many days and nights together she leaned immoveably upon her elbow, looking thro' it towards the way which *Diego* was wont to come.

"He will tell you, when she heard of your departure—how her spirits deserted her—how her heart sicken'd—how piteously she mourn'd—how low she hung her head. O *Diego!* how many weary steps has my brother's pity led me by the hand languishing to trace out yours! how far has desire carried me beyond strength—and how oft have I fainted by the way, and sunk into his arms, with only power to cry out—O my *Diego!*

"If the gentleness of your carriage has not belied your heart, you will fly to me, almost as fast as you fled from me—haste as you will, you will arrive but to see me expire.—'Tis a bitter draught, *Diego*, but oh! 'tis embitter'd still more by dying *un——*."

She could proceed no farther.

Slawkenbergius supposes the word intended was *unconvinced*, but her strength would not enable her to finish her letter.

The heart of the courteous *Diego* overflowed as he read the letter—he ordered his mule forthwith and *Fernandez*'s horse to be saddled; and as no vent in prose is equal to that of poetry in such conflicts—chance, which as often directs us to remedies as to *diseases*, having thrown a piece of charcoal into the window—*Diego* availed himself of it, and whilst the ostler was getting ready his mule, he eased his mind against the wall as follows.

ODE.

Harsh and untuneful are the notes of love,
  Unless my Julia strikes the key,
Her hand alone can touch the part,
  Whose dulcet move-
-ment charms the heart,
  And governs all the man with sympathetic sway.

2d.

  O Julia!

The lines were very natural—for they were nothing at all to
the purpose, says *Slawkenbergius*, and 'tis a pity there were no
more of them; but whether it was that Seig. *Diego* was slow in
composing verses—or the ostler quick in saddling mules—is
not averred; certain it was, that *Diego*'s mule and *Fernandez*'s
horse were ready at the door of the inn, before *Diego* was ready
for his second stanza; so without staying to finish his ode, they
both mounted, sallied forth, passed the *Rhine*, traversed *Alsace*,
shaped their course towards *Lyons*, and before the *Strasburgers*
and the abbess of *Quedlingberg* had set out on their cavalcade,
had *Fernandez*, *Diego*, and his *Julia*, crossed the *Pyrenean*
mountains, and got safe to *Valadolid*.

'Tis needless to inform the geographical reader, that when
Diego was in *Spain*, it was not possible to meet the courteous
stranger in the *Frankfort* road; it is enough to say, that of all
restless desires, curiosity being the strongest—the *Strasburgers*
felt the full force of it; and that for three days and nights they
were tossed to and fro in the *Frankfort* road, with the tempestuous fury of this passion, before they could submit to return
home—When alas! an event was prepared for them, of all others
the most grievous that could befal a free people.

As this revolution of the *Strasburgers* affairs is often spoken
of, and little understood, I will, in ten words, says *Slawkenbergius*, give the world an explanation of it, and with it put an end
to my tale.

Every body knows of the grand system of Universal Monar-
chy, wrote by order of Mons. *Colbert*,[39] and put in manuscript
into the hands of *Lewis* the fourteenth, in the year 1664.

'Tis as well known, that one branch out of many of that
system, was the getting possession of *Strasburg*, to favour an

entrance at all times into *Suabia*,[40] in order to disturb the quiet of *Germany*—and that in consequence of this plan, *Strasburg* unhappily fell at length into their hands.

It is the lot of few to trace out the true springs of this and such like revolutions—The vulgar look too high for them—Statesmen look too low—Truth (for once) lies in the middle.

What a fatal thing is the popular pride of a free city! cries one historian—The *Strasburgers* deemed it a diminution of their freedom to receive an imperial garrison—and so fell a prey to a *French* one.

The fate, says another, of the *Strasburgers*, may be a warning to all free people to save their money—They anticipated their revenues—brought themselves under taxes, exhausted their strength, and in the end became so weak a people, they had not strength to keep their gates shut, and so the *French* pushed them open.

Alas! alas! cries *Slawkenbergius*, 'twas not the *French*—'twas CURIOSITY pushed them open—The *French* indeed, who are ever upon the catch, when they saw the *Strasburgers*, men, women, and children, all marched out to follow the stranger's nose—each man followed his own, and marched in.

Trade and manufactures have decayed and gradually grown down ever since—but not from any cause which commercial heads have assigned; for it is owing to this only, that Noses have ever so run in their heads, that the *Strasburgers* could not follow their business.

Alas! alas! cries *Slawkenbergius*, making an exclamation—it is not the first—and I fear will not be the last fortress that has been either won——or lost by NOSES.

The E N D of
Slawkenbergius's TALE.

CHAPTER I

WITH all this learning upon Noses running perpetually in my father's fancy—with so many family prejudices—and ten decads of such tales running on for ever along with them—how was it possible with such exquisite—was it a true nose?—That a man with such exquisite feelings as my father had, could bear the shock at all below stairs—or indeed above stairs, in any other posture, but the very posture I have described.

—Throw yourself down upon the bed, a dozen times—taking care only to place a looking-glass first in a chair on one side of it, before you do it.——But was the stranger's nose a true nose—or was it a false one?

To tell that before-hand, madam, would be to do injury to one of the best tales in the christian world; and that is the tenth of the tenth decad which immediately follows this.

This tale, crieth *Slawkenbergius* somewhat exultingly, has been reserved by me for the concluding tale of my whole work; knowing right well, that when I shall have told it, and my reader shall have read it thro'—'twould be even high time for both of us to shut up the book; inasmuch, continues *Slawkenbergius*, as I know of no tale which could possibly ever go down after it.

—'Tis a tale indeed!

This sets out with the first interview in the inn at *Lyons*, when *Fernandez* left the courteous stranger and his sister *Julia* alone in her chamber, and is overwritten,

The INTRICACIES
of
Diego and *Julia*.

Heavens! thou art a strange creature *Slawkenbergius!* what a whimsical view of the involutions of the heart of woman hast thou opened! how this can ever be translated, and yet if this specimen of *Slawkenbergius*'s tales, and the exquisitiveness of his moral should please the world—translated shall a couple of volumes be.—Else, how this can ever be translated into good *English*, I have no sort of conception.—There seems in some passages to want a sixth sense to do it rightly.——What can he mean by the lambent pupilability of slow, low, dry chat, five notes below the natural tone,—which you know, madam, is little more than a whisper? The moment I pronounced the words, I could perceive an attempt towards a vibration in the strings, about the region of the heart.—The brain made no acknowledgment.—There's often no good understanding betwixt 'em.—I felt as if I understood it.——I had no ideas.—The movement could not be without cause.—I'm lost. I can make nothing of it,—unless, may it please your worships, the voice, in that case being little more than a whisper, unavoidably forces the eyes to approach not only within six inches of each other—but to look into the pupils—is not that dangerous?—But it can't be avoided—for to look up to the cieling, in that case the two chins unavoidably meet—and to look down into each others laps, the foreheads come into immediate contact, which at once puts an end to the conference—I mean to the sentimental part of it.——What is left, madam, is not worth stooping for.

CHAPTER II

My father lay stretched across the bed as still as if the hand of death had pushed him down, for a full hour and a half, before he began to play upon the floor with the toe of that foot which hung over the bed-side; my uncle *Toby*'s heart was a pound lighter for it.—In a few moments, his left-hand, the knuckles of which had all the time reclined upon the handle of the chamber-pot, came to its feeling—he thrust it a little more within the valance—drew up his hand, when he had done, into his bosom—gave a hem!—My good uncle *Toby*, with infinite pleasure, answered it; and full gladly would have ingrafted a sentence of consolation upon the opening it afforded; but having no talents, as I said, that way, and fearing moreover that he might set out with something which might make a bad matter worse, he contented himself with resting his chin placidly upon the cross of his crutch.

Now whether the compression shortened my uncle *Toby*'s face into a more pleasurable oval,—or that the philanthropy of his heart, in seeing his brother beginning to emerge out of the sea of his afflictions, had braced up his muscles,—so that the compression upon his chin only doubled the benignity which was there before, is not hard to decide.—My father, in turning his eyes, was struck with such a gleam of sun-shine in his face, as melted down the sullenness of his grief in a moment.

He broke silence as follows.

CHAPTER III

Did ever man, brother *Toby*, cried my father, raising himself up upon his elbow, and turning himself round to the opposite side of the bed where my uncle *Toby* was sitting in his old fringed chair, with his chin resting upon his crutch—did ever a poor unfortunate man, brother *Toby*, cried my father, receive so many lashes?——The most I ever saw given, quoth my uncle *Toby*, (ringing the bell at the bed's head for *Trim*) was to a grenadier, I think in *Makay*'s regiment.[1]

—Had my uncle *Toby* shot a bullet thro' my father's heart, he could not have fallen down with his nose upon the quilt more suddenly.

Bless me! said my uncle *Toby*.

CHAPTER IV

WAS it *Makay*'s regiment, quoth my uncle *Toby*, where the poor grenadier was so unmercifully whipp'd at *Bruges* about the ducats.—O Christ! he was innocent! cried *Trim* with a deep sigh.——And he was whipp'd, may it please your honour, almost to death's door.—They had better have shot him outright as he begg'd, and he had gone directly to heaven, for he was as innocent as your honour.——I thank thee, *Trim*, quoth my uncle *Toby*. I never think of his, continued *Trim*, and my poor brother *Tom*'s misfortunes, for we were all three schoolfellows, but I cry like a coward.—Tears are no proof of cowardice, *Trim*.—I drop them oft-times myself, cried my uncle *Toby*.—I know your honour does, replied *Trim*, and so am not ashamed of it myself.—But to think, may it please your honour, continued *Trim*, a tear stealing into the corner of his eye as he spoke—to think of two virtuous lads with hearts as warm in their bodies, and as honest as God could make them—the children of honest people, going forth with gallant spirits to seek their fortunes in the world—and fall into such evils!—poor *Tom!* to be tortured upon a rack for nothing—but marrying a *Jew*'s widow who sold sausages—honest *Dick Johnson*'s soul to be scourged out of his body, for the ducats another man put into his knapsack!—O!—these are misfortunes, cried *Trim*, pulling out his handkerchief—these are misfortunes, may it please your honour, worth lying down and crying over.

—My father could not help blushing.

—'Twould be a pity, *Trim*, quoth my uncle *Toby*, thou shouldst ever feel sorrow of thy own—thou feelest it so tenderly for others.—Alack-o-day, replied the corporal, brightening up his face—your honour knows I have neither wife or child——I can have no sorrows in this world.——My father could not help smiling.——As few as any man, *Trim*, replied my uncle *Toby*; nor can I see how a fellow of thy light heart can suffer, but from the distress of poverty in thy old age—when thou art passed all services, *Trim*,—and hast out-lived thy friends—An'please your honour, never fear, replied *Trim* chearily—But I would have thee never fear, *Trim*, replied my uncle; and therefore, continued my uncle *Toby*, throwing down his crutch, and getting up upon his legs as he uttered the word *therefore*—in recompence, *Trim*, of thy long fidelity to me, and that goodness of thy heart I have had such proofs of—whilst thy master is worth a shilling—thou shalt never ask elsewhere, *Trim*, for a penny. *Trim* attempted to thank my uncle *Toby*,—but had not power—tears trickled down his cheeks faster than he could wipe them off—He laid his hands upon his breast—made a bow to the ground, and shut the door.

——I have left *Trim* my bowling-green, cried my uncle *Toby*—My father smiled—I have left him moreover a pension, continued my uncle *Toby*—My father looked grave.

CHAPTER V

Is this a fit time, said my father to himself, to talk of PENSIONS and GRENADIERS?

CHAPTER VI

WHEN my uncle *Toby* first mentioned the grenadier, my father, I said, fell down with his nose flat to the quilt, and as suddenly as if my uncle *Toby* had shot him; but it was not added, that every other limb and member of my father instantly relapsed with his nose into the same precise attitude in which he lay first described; so that when corporal *Trim* left the room, and my father found himself disposed to rise off the bed,—he had all the little preparatory movements to run over again, before he could do it.—Attitudes are nothing, madam,—'tis the transition from one attitude to another—like the preparation and resolution of the discord into harmony, which is all in all.

For which reason my father played the same jig over again with his toe upon the floor—pushed the chamber-pot still a little farther within the valance—gave a hem—raised himself up upon his elbow—and was just beginning to address himself to my uncle *Toby*—when recollecting the unsuccessfulness of his first effort in that attitude,—he got upon his legs, and in making the third turn across the room, he stopped short before my uncle *Toby*; and laying the three first fingers of his right-hand in the palm of his left, and stooping a little, he addressed himself to my uncle *Toby* as follows.

CHAPTER VII

WHEN I reflect, brother *Toby*, upon MAN; and take a view of that dark side of him which represents his life as open to so many causes of trouble—when I consider, brother *Toby*, how oft we eat the bread of affliction, and that we are born to it, as to the portion of our inheritance—I was born to nothing, quoth my uncle *Toby*, interrupting my father—but my commission. Zooks![1] said my father, did not my uncle leave you a hundred and twenty pounds a year?—What could I have done without it? replied my uncle *Toby*.—That's another concern, said my father testily—But I say, *Toby*, when one runs over the catalogue of all the cross reckonings and sorrowful *items* with which the heart of man is overcharged, 'tis wonderful by what hidden resources the mind is enabled to stand it out, and bear itself up, as it does against the impositions laid upon our nature.——'Tis by the assistance of Almighty God, cried my uncle *Toby*, looking up, and pressing the palms of his hands close together—'tis not from our own strength, brother *Shandy*—a sentinel in a wooden centry-box, might as well pretend to stand it out against a detachment of fifty men,—we are upheld by the grace and the assistance of the best of Beings.

—That is cutting the knot, said my father, instead of untying it.—But give me leave to lead you, brother *Toby*, a little deeper into this mystery.

With all my heart, replied my uncle *Toby*.

My father instantly exchanged the attitude he was in, for that in which *Socrates* is so finely painted by *Raffael* in his school of *Athens*;[2] which your connoisseurship knows is so exquisitely imagined, that even the particular manner of the reasoning of *Socrates* is expressed by it—for he holds the fore-finger of his left-hand between the fore-finger and the thumb of his right,

and seems as if he was saying to the libertine he is reclaiming—
"*You grant me* this—and this: and this, and this, I don't ask of
you—they follow of themselves in course."

So stood my father, holding fast his fore-finger betwixt his
finger and his thumb, and reasoning with my uncle *Toby* as he
sat in his old fringed chair, valanced around with party-
coloured worsted bobs—O *Garrick!* what a rich scene of this
would thy exquisite powers make! and how gladly would I
write such another to avail myself of thy immortality, and
secure my own behind it.

CHAPTER VIII

THOUGH man is of all others the most curious vehicle, said my
father, yet at the same time 'tis of so slight a frame and so
totteringly put together, that the sudden jerks and hard jostlings
it unavoidably meets with in this rugged journey, would overset
and tear it to pieces a dozen times a day—was it not, brother
Toby, that there is a secret spring within us—Which spring, said
my uncle *Toby*, I take to be Religion.—Will that set my child's
nose on? cried my father, letting go his finger, and striking one
hand against the other—It makes every thing straight for us,
answered my uncle *Toby*—Figuratively speaking, dear *Toby*, it
may, for aught I know, said my father; but the spring I am
speaking of, is that great and elastic power within us of counter-
balancing evil, which like a secret spring in a well-ordered
machine, though it can't prevent the shock—at least it imposes
upon our sense of it.

Now, my dear brother, said my father, replacing his forefinger, as he was coming closer to the point,—had my child
arrived safe into the world, unmartyr'd in that precious part of
him—fanciful and extravagant as I may appear to the world in
my opinion of christian names, and of that magic bias which
good or bad names irresistably impress upon our characters and
conducts—heaven is witness! that in the warmest transports of
my wishes for the prosperity of my child, I never once wished to
crown his head with more glory and honour, than what
GEORGE or EDWARD[1] would have spread around it.

But alas! continued my father, as the greatest evil has befallen him—I must counteract and undo it with the greatest
good.

He shall be christened *Trismegistus*, brother.

I wish it may answer—replied my uncle *Toby*, rising up.

CHAPTER IX

WHAT a chapter of chances, said my father, turning himself about upon the first landing, as he and my uncle *Toby* were going down stairs——what a long chapter of chances do the events of this world lay open to us! Take pen and ink in hand, brother *Toby*, and calculate it fairly—I know no more of calculations than this balluster,[1] said my uncle *Toby*, (striking short of it with his crutch, and hitting my father a desperate blow souse upon his shin-bone)—'Twas a hundred to one—cried my uncle *Toby*.——I thought, quoth my father, (rubbing his shin) you had known nothing of calculations, brother *Toby*.—'Twas a meer chance, said my uncle *Toby*—Then it adds one to the chapter—replied my father.

The double success of my father's repartees tickled off the pain of his shin at once—it was well it so fell out—(chance! again)—or the world to this day had never known the subject of my father's calculation—to guess it—there was no chance—What a lucky chapter of chances has this turned out! for it has saved me the trouble of writing one express, and in truth I have anew[2] already upon my hands without it——Have not I promised the world a chapter of knots? two chapters upon the right and the wrong end of a woman? a chapter upon whiskers? a chapter upon wishes?—a chapter of noses?—No, I have done that—a chapter upon my uncle *Toby's* modesty: to say nothing of a chapter upon chapters, which I will finish before I sleep—by my great grandfather's whiskers, I shall never get half of 'em through this year.

Take pen and ink in hand, and calculate it fairly, brother *Toby*, said my father, and it will turn out a million to one, that of all the parts of the body, the edge of the forceps should have the ill luck just to fall upon and break down that one part, which should break down the fortunes of our house with it.

It might have been worse, replied my uncle *Toby*—I don't comprehend, said my father—Suppose the hip had presented, replied my uncle *Toby*, as Dr. *Slop* foreboded.

My father reflected half a minute—looked down—touched the middle of his forehead slightly with his finger—

—True, said he.

CHAPTER X

Is it not a shame to make two chapters of what passed in going down one pair of stairs? for we are got no farther yet than to the first landing, and there are fifteen more steps down to the bottom; and for aught I know, as my father and my uncle *Toby* are in a talking humour, there may be as many chapters as steps;—let that be as it will, Sir, I can no more help it than my destiny:—A sudden impulse comes across me—— drop the curtain, *Shandy*—I drop it——Strike a line here across the paper, *Tristram*—I strike it—and hey for a new chapter!

The duce of any other rule have I to govern myself by in this affair—and if I had one—as I do all things out of all rule—I would twist it and tear it to pieces, and throw it into the fire when I had done—Am I warm? I am, and the cause demands it—a pretty story! is a man to follow rules—or rules to follow him?

Now this, you must know, being my chapter upon chapters, which I promised to write before I went to sleep, I thought it meet to ease my conscience entirely before I lay'd down, by telling the world all I knew about the matter at once: Is not this ten times better than to set out dogmatically with a sententious parade of wisdom, and telling the world a story of a roasted horse[1]—that chapters relieve the mind—that they assist—or impose upon the imagination—and that in a work of this dramatic cast they are as necessary as the shifting of scenes—with fifty other cold conceits, enough to extinguish the fire which roasted him.—O! but to understand this, which is a puff at the fire of *Diana*'s temple[2]—you must read *Longinus*[3]—read away—if you are not a jot the wiser by reading him the first time over—never fear—read him again—*Avicenna*[4] and *Licetus*,[5] read *Aristotle*'s metaphysicks forty times through a piece, and never understood a single word.—But mark the consequence— *Avicenna* turned out a desperate writer at all kinds of writing— for he wrote books *de omni scribili*;[6] and for *Licetus* (*Fortunio*) though all the world knows he was born a fœtus*, of no more than five inches and a half in length, yet he grew to that astonishing height in literature, as to write a book with a title as long as himself——the learned know I mean his *Gonopsychanthropologia*, upon the origin of the human soul.

So much for my chapter upon chapters, which I hold to be the best chapter in my whole work; and take my word, whoever reads it, is full as well employed, as in picking straws.

CHAPTER XI

WE shall bring all things to rights, said my father, setting his foot upon the first step from the landing——This *Trismegistus*, continued my father, drawing his leg back, and turning to my uncle *Toby*—was the greatest (*Toby*) of all earthly beings—he was the greatest king—the greatest lawgiver—the greatest philosopher—and the greatest priest——and engineer—said my uncle *Toby*.—

—In course, said my father.

* *Ce Fœtus* n'etoit pas plus grand que la paúme de la main; mais son pere l'ayant éxaminè en qualitè de Médecin, & ayant trouvé que c'etoit quelque chose de plus qu'un Embryon, le fit transporter tout vivant à Rapallo, ou il le fit voir à Jerôme Bardi & à d'autres Medecins du lieu. On trouva qu'il ne lui manquoit rien d'essentiel a la vie; & son pere pour faire voir un essai de son expérience, entreprit d'achever l'ouvrage de la Nature, & de travailler a la formation de l'Enfant avec le même artifice que celui dont on se sert pour faire éclorre les Poulets en Egypte. Il instruisit une Nourisse de tout ce qu'elle avoit à faire, & ayant fait mettre son fils dans un four proprement accommodè, il reuissit à l'élever et a lui faire prendre ses accroissemens necessaires, par l'uniformité d'une chaleur étrangère mesurée exactement sur les dégrés d'un Thermométre, ou d'un autre instrument équivalent. (Vide Mich. Giustinian, ne gli Scritt, Liguri á. Cart 223. 488.)

On auroit toujours été très-satisfait de l'industrie d'un Pere si experimenté dans l'Art de la Generation, quand il n'auroit pû prolonger la vie a son fils que pour quelques mois, ou pour peu d'années.

Mais quand on se represente que l'Enfant a vecu pres de quatre-vingts ans, & que il a composé quatre-vingts Ouvrages differents tous fruits d'une longue lecture,—il faut convenir que tout ce qui est incroyable n'est pas toujours faux, & que la *Vraisemblance n'est pas toujours du coté de la Verité*.

Il n'avoit que dix-neuf ans lors qu'il composa Gonopsychanthropologia de Origine Animæ humanæ.

(Les Enfans celebres, revûs & corriges par M. De la Monnoye de l'Academie Françoise.)[7]

CHAPTER XII

—And how does your mistress? cried my father, taking the
same step over again from the landing, and calling to *Susannah*,
whom he saw passing by the foot of the stairs with a huge
pin-cushion in her hand—how does your mistress? As well,
said *Susannah*, tripping by, but without looking up, as can be
expected—What a fool am I, said my father! drawing his leg
back again—let things be as they will, brother *Toby*, 'tis ever
the precise answer—And how is the child, pray?—No answer.
And where is doctor *Slop*? added my father, raising his voice
aloud, and looking over the ballusters—*Susannah* was out of
hearing.

Of all the riddles of a married life, said my father, crossing the
landing, in order to set his back against the wall, whilst he
propounded it to my uncle *Toby*—of all the puzzling riddles,
said he, in a marriage state,—of which you may trust me,
brother *Toby*, there are more asses loads than all *Job*'s stock of
asses[1] could have carried—there is not one that has more intrica-
cies in it than this—that from the very moment the mistress of
the house is brought to bed, every female in it, from my lady's
gentlewoman down to the cinder-wench, becomes an inch taller
for it; and give themselves more airs upon that single inch, than
all their other inches put together.

I think rather, replied my uncle *Toby*, that 'tis we who sink an
inch lower.——If I meet but a woman with child—I do it—'Tis
a heavy tax upon that half of our fellow-creatures, brother
Shandy, said my uncle *Toby*—'Tis a piteous burden upon 'em,
continued he, shaking his head.—Yes, yes, 'tis a painful thing—
said my father, shaking his head too—but certainly since shaking of heads came into fashion, never did two heads shake
together, in concert, from two such different springs.

God bless ⎫ 'em all—said my uncle
Duce take ⎭ *Toby* and my father, each to himself.

CHAPTER XIII

Holla!—you chairman!—here's sixpence—do step into that
bookseller's shop, and call me a *day-tall* critick.[1] I am very
willing to give any one of 'em a crown to help me with his

tackling, to get my father and my uncle *Toby* off the stairs, and
to put them to bed.—

—'Tis even high time; for except a short nap, which they both
got whilst *Trim* was boring the jack-boots—and which, by the
bye, did my father no sort of good upon the score of the bad
hinge—they have not else shut their eyes, since nine hours
before the time that doctor *Slop* was led into the back parlour in
that dirty pickle by *Obadiah*.

Was every day of my life to be as busy a day as this,—and to
take up,—truce—

I will not finish that sentence till I have made an observation
upon the strange state of affairs between the reader and myself,
just as things stand at present—an observation never applicable
before to any one biographical writer since the creation of the
world, but to myself—and I believe will never hold good to any
other, until its final destruction——and therefore, for the very
novelty of it alone, it must be worth your worships attending to.

I am this month one whole year older than I was this time
twelve-month; and having got, as you perceive, almost into the
middle of my fourth volume—and no farther than to my first
day's life—'tis demonstrative that I have three hundred and
sixty-four days more life to write just now, than when I first set
out; so that instead of advancing, as a common writer, in my
work with what I have been doing at it—on the contrary, I am
just thrown so many volumes back—was every day of my life to
be as busy a day as this—And why not?—and the transactions
and opinions of it to take up as much description—And for
what reason should they be cut short? as at this rate I should just
live 364 times faster than I should write—It must follow, an'
please your worships, that the more I write, the more I shall
have to write—and consequently, the more your worships read,
the more your worships will have to read.

Will this be good for your worships eyes?

It will do well for mine; and, was it not that my OPINIONS
will be the death of me, I perceive I shall lead a fine life of it out
of this self-same life of mine; or, in other words, shall lead a
couple of fine lives together.

As for the proposal of twelve volumes a year, or a volume a
month, it no way alters my prospect—write as I will, and rush as
I may into the middle of things, as *Horace* advises,[2]—I shall
never overtake myself—whipp'd and driven to the last pinch, at
the worst I shall have one day the start of my pen—and one day

is enough for two volumes—and two volumes will be enough for one year.—

Heaven prosper the manufactures of paper under this propitious reign, which is now open'd to us,—as I trust its providence will prosper every thing else in it that is taken in hand.—

As for the propagation of Geese[3]—I give myself no concern—Nature is all bountiful—I shall never want tools to work with.

—So then, friend! you have got my father and my uncle *Toby* off the stairs, and seen them to bed?—And how did you manage it?—You dropp'd a curtain at the stairs foot—I thought you had no other way for it—Here's a crown for your trouble.

CHAPTER XIV

—THEN reach me my breeches off the chair, said my father to *Susannah*—There is not a moment's time to dress you, Sir, cried *Susannah*—the child is as black in the face as my—As your, what? said my father, for like all orators, he was a dear searcher into comparisons—Bless me, Sir, said *Susannah*, the child's in a fit—And where's Mr. *Yorick*—Never where he should be, said *Susannah*, but his curate's in the dressing-room, with the child upon his arm, waiting for the name——and my mistress bid me run as fast as I could to know, as captain *Shandy* is the god-father, whether it should not be called after him.

Were one sure, said my father to himself, scratching his eye-brow, that the child was expiring, one might as well compliment my brother *Toby* as not—and 'twould be a pity, in such a case, to throw away so great a name as *Trismegistus* upon him—But he may recover.

No, no,—said my father to *Susannah*, I'll get up——There is no time, cried *Susannah*, the child's as black as my shoe. *Trismegistus*, said my father—But stay—thou art a leaky vessel, *Susannah*, added my father; canst thou carry *Trismegistus* in thy head, the length of the gallery without scattering—Can I? cried *Susannah*, shutting the door in a huff—If she can, I'll be shot, said my father, bouncing out of bed in the dark, and groping for his breeches.

Susannah ran with all speed along the gallery.

My father made all possible speed to find his breeches.

Susannah got the start, and kept it—'Tis *Tris*—something, cried *Susannah*—There is no christian name in the world, said the curate, beginning with *Tris*—but *Tristram*. Then 'tis *Tristram-gistus*, quoth *Susannah*.

—There is no *gistus* to it, noodle!—'tis my own name, replied the curate, dipping his hand as he spoke into the bason—*Tristram!* said he, &c. &c. &c. &c. so *Tristram* was I called, and *Tristram* shall I be to the day of my death.

My father followed *Susannah* with his night-gown across his arm, with nothing more than his breeches on, fastened through haste with but a single button, and that button through haste thrust only half into the button-hole.

—She has not forgot the name, cried my father, half opening the door—No, no, said the curate, with a tone of intelligence—And the child is better, cried *Susannah*—And how does your mistress? As well, said *Susannah*, as can be expected—Pish! said my father, the button of his breeches slipping out of the button-hole—So that whether the interjection was levelled at *Susannah*, or the button-hole,—whether pish was an interjection of contempt or an interjection of modesty, is a doubt, and must be a doubt till I shall have time to write the three following favorite chapters, that is, my chapter of *chamber-maids*—my chapter of *pishes*, and my chapter of *button-holes*.

All the light I am able to give the reader at present is this, that the moment my father cried Pish! he whisk'd himself about—and with his breeches held up by one hand, and his night-gown thrown across the arm of the other, he returned along the gallery to bed, something slower than he came.

CHAPTER XV

I WISH I could write a chapter upon sleep.

A fitter occasion could never have presented itself, than what this moment offers, when all the curtains of the family are drawn—the candles put out—and no creature's eyes are open but a single one, for the other has been shut these twenty years, of my mother's nurse.

It is a fine subject!

And yet, as fine as it is, I would undertake to write a dozen chapters upon button-holes, both quicker and with more fame than a single chapter upon this.

Button-holes!——there is something lively in the very idea of 'em—and trust me, when I get amongst 'em—You gentry with great beards—look as grave as you will—I'll make merry work with my button-holes—I shall have 'em all to myself—'tis a maiden subject—I shall run foul of no man's wisdom or fine sayings in it.

But for sleep—I know I shall make nothing of it before I begin—I am no dab at your fine sayings in the first place—and in the next, I cannot for my soul set a grave face upon a bad matter, and tell the world—'tis the refuge of the unfortunate—the enfranchisement of the prisoner—the downy lap of the hopeless, the weary and the broken-hearted; nor could I set out with a lye in my mouth, by affirming, that of all the soft and delicious functions of our nature, by which the great Author of it, in his bounty, has been pleased to recompence the sufferings wherewith his justice and his good pleasure has wearied us,—that this is the chiefest (I know pleasures worth ten of it) or what a happiness it is to man, when the anxieties and passions of the day are over, and he lays down upon his back, that his soul shall be so seated within him, that which ever way she turns her eyes, the heavens shall look calm and sweet above her—no desire—or fear—or doubt that troubles the air, nor any difficulty pass'd, present, or to come, that the imagination may not pass over without offence, in that sweet secession.

—"God's blessing, said *Sancho Panca*,[1] be upon the man who first invented this self-same thing called sleep——it covers a man all over like a cloak." Now there is more to me in this, and it speaks warmer to my heart and affections, than all the dissertations squeez'd out of the heads of the learned together upon the subject.

—Not that I altogether disapprove of what *Montaigne* advances upon it[2]—'tis admirable in its way.——(I quote by memory.)

The world enjoys other pleasures, says he, as they do that of sleep, without tasting or feeling it as it slips and passes by—We should study and ruminate upon it, in order to render proper thanks to him who grants it to us—for this end I cause myself to be disturbed in my sleep, that I may the better and more sensibly relish it—And yet I see few, says he again, who live with less sleep when need requires; my body is capable of a firm, but not of a violent and sudden agitation—I evade of late all violent exercises—I am never weary with walking—but from my youth, I never liked to ride upon pavements. I love to lie hard and alone, and even without my wife—This last word may stagger the faith of the world—but remember, "La Vraisemblance (as *Baylet* says in the affair of *Liceti*) n'est pas toujours du Cotè de la Verité."³ And so much for sleep.

CHAPTER XVI

IF my wife will but venture him—brother *Toby, Trismegistus* shall be dress'd and brought down to us, whilst you and I are getting our breakfasts together.—

—Go, tell *Susanna, Obadiah*, to step here.

She is run up stairs, answered *Obadiah*, this very instant, sobbing and crying, and wringing her hands as if her heart would break.—

We shall have a rare month of it, said my father, turning his head from *Obadiah*, and looking wistfully in my uncle *Toby*'s face for some time—we shall have a devilish month of it, brother *Toby*, said my father, setting his arms a-kimbo, and shaking his head; fire, water, women, wind—brother *Toby!*—'Tis some misfortune, quoth my uncle *Toby*—That it is, cried my father,—to have so many jarring elements breaking loose, and riding triumph in every corner of a gentleman's house—Little boots it to the peace of a family, brother *Toby*, that you and I possess ourselves, and sit here silent and unmoved,—whilst such a storm is whistling over our heads——

—And what's the matter, *Susannah?* They have called the child *Tristram*——and my mistress is just got out of an hysterick fit about it—No!—'tis not my fault, said *Susannah*—I told him it was *Tristram-gistus.*

——Make tea for yourself, brother *Toby*, said my father, taking down his hat—but how different from the sallies and agitations of voice and members which a common reader would imagine!

—For he spake in the sweetest modulation—and took down his hat with the gentlest movement of limbs, that ever affliction harmonized and attuned together.

—Go to the bowling-green for corporal *Trim*, said my uncle *Toby*, speaking to *Obadiah*, as soon as my father left the room.

CHAPTER XVII

WHEN the misfortune of my NOSE fell so heavily upon my father's head,—the reader remembers that he walked instantly up stairs, and cast himself down upon his bed; and from hence, unless he has a great insight into human nature, he will be apt to expect a rotation of the same ascending and descending movements from him, upon this misfortune of my NAME;——no.

The different weight, dear Sir,—nay even the different package of two vexations of the same weight,—makes a very wide difference in our manners of bearing and getting through with them.—It is not half an hour ago, when (in the great hurry and precipitation of a poor devil's writing for daily bread) I threw a fair sheet, which I had just finished, and carefully wrote out, slap into the fire, instead of the foul one.

Instantly I snatch'd off my wig, and threw it perpendicularly, with all imaginable violence, up to the top of the room—indeed I caught it as it fell—but there was an end of the matter; nor do I think any thing else in *Nature*, would have given such immediate ease: She, dear Goddess, by an instantaneous impulse, in all *provoking cases*, determines us to a sally of this or that member—or else she thrusts us into this or that place, or posture of body, we know not why—But mark, madam, we live amongst riddles and mysteries—the most obvious things, which come in our way, have dark sides, which the quickest sight cannot penetrate into; and even the clearest and most exalted understandings amongst us find ourselves puzzled and at a loss in almost every cranny of nature's works; so that this, like a thousand other things, falls out for us in a way, which tho' we cannot reason upon it,—yet we find the good of it, may it please your reverences and your worships—and that's enough for us.

Now, my father could not lie down with this affliction for his life—nor could he carry it up stairs like the other—He walked composedly out with it to the fish-pond.

Had my father leaned his head upon his hand, and reasoned an hour which way to have gone—reason, with all her force, could not have directed him to any thing like it: there is something, Sir, in fish-ponds—but what it is, I leave to system builders and fish-pond diggers betwixt 'em to find out—but there is something, under the first disorderly transport of the humours, so unaccountably becalming in an orderly and a sober walk towards one of them, that I have often wondered that neither *Pythagoras*,[2] nor *Plato*,[3] nor *Solon*,[4] nor *Licurgus*,[5] nor *Mahomet*,[6] nor any of your noted lawgivers, ever gave order about them.

CHAPTER XVIII

YOUR honour, said *Trim*, shutting the parlour door before he began to speak, has heard, I imagine, of this unlucky accident ——O yes, *Trim!* said my uncle *Toby*, and it gives me great concern—I am heartily concerned too, but I hope your honour, replied *Trim*, will do me the justice to believe, that it was not in the least owing to me—To thee—*Trim!*—cried my uncle *Toby*, looking kindly in his face—'twas *Susannah*'s and the curate's folly betwixt them—What business could they have together, an'please your honour, in the garden?—In the gallery, thou meanest, replied my uncle *Toby*.

Trim found he was upon a wrong scent, and stopped short with a low bow—Two misfortunes, quoth the corporal to himself, are twice as many at least as are needful to be talked over at one time,—the mischief the cow has done in breaking into the fortifications, may be told his honour hereafter—*Trim*'s casuistry and address, under the cover of his low bow, prevented all suspicion in my uncle *Toby*, so he went on with what he had to say to *Trim* as follows.

—For my own part, *Trim*, though I can see little or no difference betwixt my nephew's being called *Tristram* or *Trismegistus*—yet as the thing sits so near my brother's heart, *Trim*,—I would freely have given a hundred pounds rather than it should have happened—A hundred pounds, an'please your honour, replied *Trim*,—I would not give a cherry-stone to boot—Nor would I, *Trim*, upon my own account, quoth my uncle *Toby*—but my brother, whom there is no arguing with in this case—maintains that a great deal more depends, *Trim*, upon christian names, than what ignorant people imagine;——for he says there never was a great or heroic action performed since the world began by one called *Tristram*—nay he will have it, *Trim*, that a man can neither be learned, or wise, or brave—'Tis all a fancy, an'please your honour—I fought just as well, replied the corporal, when the regiment called me *Trim*, as when they called me *James Butler*—And for my own part, said my uncle

Toby, though I should blush to boast of myself, *Trim*,—yet had my name been *Alexander*, I could have done no more at *Namur* than my duty—Bless your honour! cried *Trim*, advancing three steps as he spoke, does a man think of his christian name when he goes upon the attack?—Or when he stands in the trench, *Trim*? cried my uncle *Toby*, looking firm—Or when he enters a breach? said *Trim*, pushing in between two chairs—Or forces the lines? cried my uncle, rising up, and pushing his crutch like a pike—Or facing a platoon, cried *Trim*, presenting his stick like a firelock—Or when he marches up the glacis, cried my uncle *Toby*, looking warm and setting his foot upon his stool.——

CHAPTER XIX

My father was returned from his walk to the fish-pond—and opened the parlour-door in the very height of the attack, just as my uncle *Toby* was marching up the glacis—*Trim* recovered his arms—never was my uncle *Toby* caught riding at such a desperate rate in his life! Alas! my uncle *Toby*! had not a weightier matter called forth all the ready eloquence of my father—how hadst thou then and thy poor HOBBY-HORSE too have been insulted!

My father hung up his hat with the same air he took it down; and after giving a slight look at the disorder of the room, he took hold of one of the chairs which had formed the corporal's breach, and placing it over-against my uncle *Toby*, he sat down in it, and as soon as the tea-things were taken away and the door shut, he broke out in a lamentation as follows.

My FATHER'S LAMENTATION.

IT is in vain longer, said my father, addressing himself as much to *Ernulphus*'s curse, which was laid upon the corner of the chimney-piece,—as to my uncle *Toby* who sat under it—it is in vain longer, said my father, in the most querulous monotone imaginable, to struggle as I have done against this most uncomfortable of human persuasions—I see it plainly, that either for my own sins, brother *Toby*, or the sins and follies of the *Shandy*-family, heaven has thought fit to draw forth the heaviest of its artillery against me; and that the prosperity of my child is the point upon which the whole force of it is directed to play——Such a thing would batter the whole universe about our ears, brother *Shandy*, said my uncle *Toby*,—if it was so—Unhappy *Tristram!* child of wrath! child of decrepitude! interruption! mistake! and discontent! What one misfortune or disaster in the book of embryotic[1] evils, that could unmechanize thy frame, or entangle thy filaments! which has not fallen upon thy head, or ever thou camest into the world—what evils in thy passage into it!—What evils since!—produced into being, in the decline of thy father's days—when the powers of his imagination and of his body were waxing feeble—when radical heat and radical moisture, the elements which should have temper'd thine, were drying up; and nothing left to found thy stamina in, but negations—'tis pitiful—brother *Toby*, at the best, and called out for all the little helps that care and attention on both sides could give it. But how were we defeated! You know the event, brother *Toby*,—'tis too melancholy a one to be repeated now,—when the few animal spirits I was worth in the world, and with which memory, fancy, and quick parts should have been convey'd,—were all dispersed, confused, confounded, scattered, and sent to the devil.—

Here then was the time to have put a stop to this persecution against him;—and tried an experiment at least—whether calmness and serenity of mind in your sister, with a due attention, brother *Toby*, to her evacuations and repletions—and the rest of her non-naturals, might not, in a course of nine months gestation, have set all things to rights.—My child was bereft of these!—What a teazing life did she lead herself, and consequently her fœtus too, with that nonsensical anxiety of hers about lying in in town? I thought my sister submitted with the greatest patience, replied my uncle *Toby*——I never heard her utter one fretful word about it—She fumed inwardly, cried my father; and that, let me tell you, brother, was ten times worse for the child—and then! what battles did she fight with me, and what perpetual storms about the midwife—There she gave vent, said my uncle *Toby*—Vent! cried my father, looking up—

But what was all this, my dear *Toby*, to the injuries done us by my child's coming head foremost into the world, when all I wished in this general wreck of his frame, was to have saved this little casket unbroke, unrifled—

With all my precautions, how was my system turned topside turvy in the womb with my child! his head exposed to the hand of violence, and a pressure of 470 pounds averdupois weight acting so perpendicularly upon its apex—that at this hour 'tis ninety *per Cent.* insurance, that the fine network of the intellectual web be not rent and torn to a thousand tatters.

—Still we could have done.——Fool, coxcomb, puppy—give him but a NOSE—Cripple, Dwarf, Driviller, Goosecap[2]—(shape him as you will) the door of Fortune stands open—O *Licetus! Licetus!* had I been blest with a fœtus five inches long and a half, like thee—fate might have done her worst.

Still, brother *Toby*, there was one cast of the dye left for our child after all—O *Tristram! Tristram! Tristram!*

We will send for Mr. *Yorick*, said my uncle *Toby*.

—You may send for whom you will, replied my father.

CHAPTER XX

WHAT a rate have I gone on at, curvetting and frisking it away, two up and two down for four volumes together, without looking once behind, or even on one side of me, to see whom I trod upon!—I'll tread upon no one,—quoth I to myself when I mounted—I'll take a good rattling gallop; but I'll not hurt the poorest jack-ass upon the road—So off I set—up one lane—down another, through this turn-pike—over that, as if the arch-jockey of jockeys had got behind me.

Now ride at this rate with what good intention and resolution you may,—'tis a million to one you'll do some one a mischief, if not yourself—He's flung—he's off—he's lost his seat—he's down—he'll break his neck—see!—if he has not galloped full amongst the scaffolding of the undertaking criticks!—he'll knock his brains out against some of their posts—he's bounced out!—look—he's now riding like a madcap full tilt through a whole crowd of painters, fiddlers, poets, biographers, physicians, lawyers, logicians, players, schoolmen, churchmen, statesmen, soldiers, casuists, connoisseurs, prelates, popes, and engineers—Don't fear, said I—I'll not hurt the poorest jack-ass upon the king's high-way—But your horse throws dirt; see you've splash'd a bishop[1]—I hope in God, 'twas only *Ernulphus*, said I—But you have squirted full in the faces of Mess. *Le Moyne, De Romigny,* and *De Marcilly,* doctors of the Sorbonne[2]—That was last year, replied I—But you have trod this moment upon a king.——Kings have bad times on't, said I, to be trod upon by such people as me.

—You have done it, replied my accuser.

I deny it, quoth I, and so have got off, and here am I standing with my bridle in one hand, and with my cap in the other, to tell my story—And what is it? You shall hear in the next chapter.

CHAPTER XXI

As *Francis* the first of *France*[1] was one winterly night warming himself over the embers of a wood fire, and talking with his first minister of sundry things for the good of the state*—it would not be amiss, said the king, stirring up the embers with his cane, if this good understanding betwixt ourselves and *Switzerland* was a little strengthened—There is no end, Sire, replied the minister, in giving money to these people—they would swallow up the treasury of *France*—Poo! poo! answered the king——there are more ways, Mons. *le Premier*, of bribing states, besides that of giving money——I'll pay *Switzerland* the honour of standing godfather for my next child—Your majesty, said the minister, in so doing, would have all the grammarians in *Europe* upon your back;—*Switzerland*, as a republick, being a female, can in no construction be godfather—She may be godmother, replied *Francis*, hastily—so announce my intentions by a courier to morrow morning.

I am astonished, said *Francis* the First, (that day fortnight) speaking to his minister as he entered the closet, that we have had no answer from *Switzerland*—Sire, I wait upon you this moment, said Mons. *le Premier*, to lay before you my dispatches upon that business.—They take it kindly? said the king—They do, Sire, replied the minister, and have the highest sense of the honour your majesty has done them—but the republick, as godmother, claims her right in this case, of naming the child.

In all reason, quoth the king—she will christen him *Francis*, or *Henry*, or *Lewis*, or some name that she knows will be agreeable to us. Your majesty is deceived, replied the minister— I have this hour received a dispatch from our resident, with the determination of the republick on that point also—And what name has the republick fixed upon for the Dauphin?—*Shadrach, Mesech*, and *Abed-nego*,[3] replied the minister—By saint *Peter*'s girdle, I will have nothing to do with the *Swiss*, cried

* Vide Menagiana, vol. i.[2]

Francis the First, pulling up his breeches and walking hastily across the floor.

Your majesty, replied the minister calmly, cannot bring yourself off.

We'll pay them in money—said the king.

Sire, there are not sixty thousand crowns in the treasury, answered the minister——I'll pawn the best jewel in my crown, quoth *Francis* the First.

Your honour stands pawn'd already in this matter, answered Monsieur *le Premier*.

Then, Mons. *le Premier*, said the king, by——we'll go to war with 'em.

CHAPTER XXII

ALBEIT, gentle reader, I have lusted earnestly, and endeavoured carefully (according to the measure of such slender skill as God has vouchsafed me, and as convenient leisure from other occasions of needful profit and healthful pastime have permitted) that these little books, which I here put into thy hands, might stand instead of many bigger books—yet have I carried myself towards thee in such fanciful guise of careless disport, that right sore am I ashamed now to entreat thy lenity seriously—in beseeching thee to believe it of me, that in the story of my father and his christen-names,[1]—I had no thoughts of treading upon *Francis* the First—nor in the affair of the nose—upon *Francis* the Ninth[2]—nor in the character of my uncle *Toby*—of characterizing the militiating spirits of my country—the wound upon his groin, is a wound to every comparison of that kind,—nor by *Trim*,—that I meant the duke of *Ormond*[3]—or that my book is wrote against predestination, or free will, or taxes—If 'tis wrote against any thing,——'tis wrote, an'please your worships, against the spleen; in order, by a more frequent and a more convulsive elevation and depression of the diaphragm, and the succussations[4] of the intercostal and abdominal muscles in laughter, to drive the *gall* and other *bitter juices* from the gall bladder, liver and sweet-bread of his majesty's subjects, with all the inimicitious[5] passions which belong to them, down into their duodenums.

CHAPTER XXIII

—But can the thing be undone, *Yorick?* said my father—for in my opinion, continued he, it cannot. I am a vile canonist, replied *Yorick*—but of all evils, holding suspense to be the most tormenting, we shall at least know the worst of this matter. I hate these great dinners—said my father—The size of the dinner is not the point, answered *Yorick*— we want, Mr. *Shandy*, to dive into the bottom of this doubt, whether the name can be changed or not—and as the beards of so many commissaries, officials, advocates, proctors, registers, and of the most able of our school-divines, and others, are all to meet in the middle of one table, and *Didius* has so pressingly invited you,——who in your distress would miss such an occasion? All that is requisite, continued *Yorick*, is to apprize *Didius*, and let him manage a conversation after dinner so as to introduce the subject—Then my brother *Toby*, cried my father, clapping his two hands together, shall go with us.

—Let my old tye wig, quoth my uncle *Toby*, and my laced regimentals, be hung to the fire all night, *Trim*.

CHAPTER XXV

—No doubt, Sir—there is a whole chapter wanting here—and a chasm of ten pages[1] made in the book by it—but the book-binder is neither a fool, or a knave, or a puppy—nor is the book a jot more imperfect, (at least upon that score)—but, on the contrary, the book is more perfect and complete by wanting the chapter, than having it, as I shall demonstrate to your reverences in this manner—I question first by the bye, whether the same experiment might not be made as successfully upon sundry other chapters——but there is no end, an'please your reverences, in trying experiments upon chapters—we have had enough of it—So there's an end of that matter.

But before I begin my demonstration, let me only tell you, that the chapter which I have torn out, and which otherwise you would all have been reading just now, instead of this,—was the description of my father's, my uncle *Toby*'s, *Trim*'s and *Obadiah*'s setting out and journeying to the visitations[2] at ****.

We'll go in the coach, said my father—Prithee, have the arms been altered, *Obadiah?*—It would have made my story much better, to have begun with telling you, that at the time my mother's arms were added to the *Shandy*'s, when the coach was repainted upon my father's marriage, it had so fallen out, that the coach-painter, whether by performing all his works with the left-hand, like *Turpilius*[3] the *Roman*, or *Hans Holbein*[4] of *Basil*—or whether 'twas more from the blunder of his head than hand—or whether, lastly, it was from the sinister turn, which every thing relating to our family was apt to take—It so fell out, however, to our reproach, that instead of the *bend dexter*,[5] which since *Harry* the Eighth's reign was honestly our due—— a *bend sinister*, by some of these fatalities, had been drawn quite across the field of the *Shandy*-arms. 'Tis scarce credible that the mind of so wise a man as my father was, could be so much incommoded with so small a matter. The word coach—let it be whose it would—or coach-man, or coach-horse, or coach-hire, could never be named in the family, but he constantly complained of carrying this vile mark of Illegitimacy upon the door of his own; he never once was able to step into the coach, or out of it, without turning round to take a view of the arms, and making a vow at the same time, that it was the last time he would ever set his foot in it again, till the *bend-sinister* was taken out—but like the affair of the hinge, it was one of the many things which the *Destinies* had set down in their books—ever to be grumbled at (and in wiser families than ours)—but never to be mended.

—Has the *bend-sinister* been brush'd out, I say? said my father—There has been nothing brush'd out, Sir, answered *Obadiah*, but the lining. We'll go o'horse-back, said my father, turning to *Yorick*—Of all things in the world, except politicks, the clergy know the least of heraldry, said *Yorick*—No matter for that, cried my father—I should be sorry to appear with a blot in my escutcheon before them——Never mind the *bend-sinister*, said my uncle *Toby*, putting on his tye-wig—No, indeed, said my father,—you may go with my aunt *Dinah* to a visitation with a *bend-sinister*, if you think fit—My poor uncle *Toby* blush'd. My father was vexed at himself—No—my dear brother *Toby*, said my father, changing his tone—but the damp of the coach-lining about my loins, may give me the Sciatica again, as it did *December, January,* and *Febuary* last winter—so if you please you shall ride my wife's pad—and as you are to preach, *Yorick*, you had better make the best of your way before,—and leave me to take care of my brother *Toby*, and to follow at our own rates.

Now the chapter I was obliged to tear out, was the description of this cavalcade, in which corporal *Trim* and *Obadiah*, upon two coach-horses a-breast, led the way as slow as a patrole—whilst my uncle *Toby*, in his laced regimentals and tye-wig, kept his rank with my father, in deep roads and dissertations alternately upon the advantage of learning and arms, as each could get the start.

—But the painting of this journey, upon reviewing it, appears to be so much above the stile and manner of any thing else I have been able to paint in this book, that it could not have remained in it, without depreciating every other scene; and destroying at the same time that necessary equipoise and balance, (whether of good or bad) betwixt chapter and chapter, from whence the just proportions and harmony of the whole work results. For my own part, I am but just set up in the business, so know little about it—but, in my opinion, to write a book is for all the world like humming a song—be but in tune with yourself, madam, 'tis no matter how high or how low you take it.—

—This is the reason, may it please your reverences, that some of the lowest and flattest compositions pass off very well—(as

Yorick told my uncle *Toby* one night) by siege—My uncle *Toby* looked brisk at the sound of the word *siege*,[6] but could make neither head or tail of it.

I'm to preach at court next Sunday, said *Homenas*[7]—run over my notes—so I humm'd over doctor *Homenas*'s notes—the modulation's very well—'twill do, *Homenas*, if it holds on at this rate—so on I humm'd—and a tolerable tune I thought it was; and to this hour, may it please your reverences, had never found out how low, how flat, how spiritless and jejune it was, but that all of a sudden, up started an air in the middle of it, so fine, so rich, so heavenly—it carried my soul up with it into the other world; now had I, (as *Montaigne*[8] complained in a parallel accident)—had I found the declivity easy, or the ascent accessible—certes I had been outwitted—Your notes, *Homenas*, I should have said, are good notes,—but it was so perpendicular a precipice—so wholly cut off from the rest of the work, that by the first note I humm'd, I found myself flying into the other world, and from thence discovered the vale from whence I came, so deep, so low, and dismal, that I shall never have the heart to descend into it again.

☞ A dwarf who brings a standard along with him to measure his own size—take my word, is a dwarf in more articles than one—And so much for tearing out of chapters.

CHAPTER XXVI

—SEE if he is not cutting it all into slips, and giving them about him to light their pipes!—'Tis abominable, answered *Didius*; it should not go unnoticed, said doctor *Kysarcius*—☞ he was of the *Kysarcij* of the low countries.

Methinks, said *Didius*, half rising from his chair, in order to remove a bottle and a tall decanter, which stood in a direct line betwixt him and *Yorick*—you might have spared this sarcastick stroke, and have hit upon a more proper place, Mr. *Yorick*—or at least upon a more proper occasion to have shewn your contempt of what we have been about: If the Sermon is of no better worth than to light pipes with—'twas certainly, Sir, not good enough to be preached before so learned a body; and if 'twas good enough to be preached before so learned a body— 'twas certainly, Sir, too good to light their pipes with afterwards.

—I have got him fast hung up, quoth *Didius* to himself, upon one of the two horns of my dilemma—let him get off as he can.

I have undergone such unspeakable torments, in bringing forth this sermon, quoth *Yorick*, upon this occasion,—that I declare, *Didius*, I would suffer martyrdom—and if it was possible my horse with me, a thousand times over, before I would sit down and make such another: I was delivered of it at the wrong end of me—it came from my head instead of my heart—and it is for the pain it gave me, both in the writing and preaching of it, that I revenge myself of it, in this manner.—To preach, to shew the extent of our reading, or the subtleties of our wit—to parade it in the eyes of the vulgar with the beggarly accounts of a little learning, tinseled over with a few words which glitter, but convey little light and less warmth—is a dishonest use of the poor single half hour in a week which is put into our hands—'Tis not preaching the gospel—but ourselves—For my own part, continued *Yorick*, I had rather direct five words point blank to the heart—

As *Yorick* pronounced the word *point blank*, my uncle *Toby* rose up to say something upon projectiles——when a single word, and no more, uttered from the opposite side of the table, drew every one's ears towards it—a word of all others in the dictionary the last in that place to be expected—a word I am ashamed to write—yet must be written—must be read;—illegal—uncanonical—guess ten thousand guesses, multiplied into themselves—rack—torture your invention for ever, you're where you was—In short, I'll tell it in the next chapter.

CHAPTER XXVII

ZOUNDS! ————————————————————

——————————————Z——ds! cried *Phutatorius*,[1] partly to himself—and yet high enough to be heard—and what seemed odd, 'twas uttered in a construction of look, and in a tone of voice, somewhat between that of a man in amazement, and of one in bodily pain.

One or two who had very nice ears, and could distinguish the expression and mixture of the two tones as plainly as a *third* or a *fifth*, or any other chord in musick—were the most puzzled and perplexed with it—the *concord* was good in itself—but then 'twas quite out of the key, and no way applicable to the subject started;—so that with all their knowledge, they could not tell what in the world to make of it.

Others who knew nothing of musical expression, and merely lent their ears to the plain import of the *word*, imagined that *Phutatorius*, who was somewhat of a cholerick spirit, was just going to snatch the cudgels out of *Didius*'s hands, in order to bemawl *Yorick* to some purpose—and that the desperate monosyllable Z——ds was the exordium to an oration, which, as they judged from the sample, presaged but a rough kind of handling of him; so that my uncle *Toby*'s good nature felt a pang for what *Yorick* was about to undergo. But seeing *Phutatorius* stop short, without any attempt or desire to go on—a third party began to suppose, that it was no more than an involuntary respiration, casually forming itself into the shape of a twelve-penny oath[2]—without the sin or substance of one.

Others, and especially one or two who sat next him, looked upon it on the contrary, as a real and substantial oath propensly formed against *Yorick*, to whom he was known to bear no good liking—which said oath, as my father philosophized upon it, actually lay fretting and fuming at that very time in the upper regions of *Phutatorius*'s purtenance; and so was naturally, and according to the due course of things, first squeezed out by the sudden influx of blood, which was driven into the right ventricle of *Phutatorius*'s heart, by the stroke of surprize which so strange a theory of preaching had excited.

How finely we argue upon mistaken facts!

There was not a soul busied in all these various reasonings upon the monosyllable which *Phutatorius* uttered,—who did not take this for granted, proceeding upon it as from an axiom, namely, that *Phutatorius*'s mind was intent upon the subject of debate which was arising between *Didius* and *Yorick*; and indeed as he looked first towards the one, and then towards the other, with the air of a man listening to what was going forwards,—who would not have thought the same? But the truth was, that *Phutatorius* knew not one word or one syllable of what was passing—but his whole thoughts and attention were taken up with a transaction which was going forwards at that very instant within the precincts of his own *Galligaskins*, and in a part of them, where of all others he stood most interested to watch accidents: So that notwithstanding he looked with all the attention in the world, and had gradually skrewed up every nerve and muscle in his face, to the utmost pitch the instrument would bear, in order, as it was thought, to give a sharp reply to *Yorick*, who sat over-against him—Yet I say, was *Yorick* never once in any one domicile of *Phutatorius*'s brain—but the true cause of his exclamation lay at least a yard below.

This I will endeavour to explain to you with all imaginable decency.

You must be informed then, that *Gastripheres*, who had taken a turn into the kitchen a little before dinner, to see how things went on—observing a wicker-basket of fine chesnuts standing upon the dresser, had ordered that a hundred or two of them might be roasted and sent in, as soon as dinner was over—*Gastripheres* inforcing his orders about them, that *Didius*, but *Phutatorius* especially, were particularly fond of 'em.

About two minutes before the time that my uncle *Toby* interrupted *Yorick*'s harangue—*Gastripheres*'s chesnuts were brought in—and as *Phutatorius*'s fondness for 'em, was uppermost in the waiter's head, he laid them directly before *Phutatorius*, wrapt up hot in a clean damask napkin.

Now whether it was physically impossible, with half a dozen hands all thrust into the napkin at a time—but that some one chesnut, of more life and rotundity than the rest, must be put in motion—it so fell out, however, that one was actually sent rolling off the table; and as *Phutatorius* sat straddling under—it fell perpendicularly into that particular aperture of *Phutatorius*'s breeches, for which, to the shame and indelicacy of our language be it spoke, there is no chaste word throughout all *Johnson*'s dictionary—let it suffice to say—it was that particular aperture, which in all good societies, the laws of decorum do strictly require, like the temple of *Janus*³ (in peace at least) to be universally shut up.

The neglect of this punctilio in *Phutatorius* (which by the bye should be a warning to all mankind) had opened a door to this accident.—

—Accident, I call it, in compliance to a received mode of speaking,—but in no opposition to the opinion either of *Acrites*⁴ or *Mythogeras* in this matter; I know they were both prepossessed and fully persuaded of it—and are so to this hour, That there was nothing of accident in the whole event—but that the chesnut's taking that particular course, and in a manner of its accord—and then falling with all its heat directly into that one particular place, and no other——was a real judgment upon *Phutatorius*, for that filthy and obscene treatise *de Concubinis retinendis*,[5] which *Phutatorius* had published about twenty years ago—and was that identical week going to give the world a second edition of.

It is not my business to dip my pen in this controversy ——much undoubtedly may be wrote on both sides of the question—all that concerns me as an historian, is to represent the matter of fact, and render it credible to the reader, that the hiatus in *Phutatorius*'s breeches was sufficiently wide to receive the chesnut;—and that the chesnut, some how or other, did fall perpendicularly and piping hot into it, without *Phutatorius*'s perceiving it, or any one else at that time.

The genial warmth which the chesnut imparted, was not undelectable for the first twenty or five and twenty seconds,—and did no more than gently solicit *Phutatorius*'s attention towards the part:—But the heat gradually increasing, and in a few seconds more getting beyond the point of all sober pleasure, and then advancing with all speed into the regions of pain,—the soul of *Phutatorius*, together with all his ideas, his thoughts, his attention, his imagination, judgment, resolution, deliberation, ratiocination, memory, fancy, with ten batallions of animal spirits, all tumultuously crouded down, through different defiles and circuits, to the place in danger, leaving all his upper regions, as you may imagine, as empty as my purse.

With the best intelligence which all these messengers could bring him back, *Phutatorius* was not able to dive into the secret of what was going forwards below, nor could he make any kind of conjecture, what the devil was the matter with it: However, as he knew not what the true cause might turn out, he deemed it most prudent, in the situation he was in at present, to bear it, if possible, like a stoick; which, with the help of some wry faces and compursions[6] of the mouth, he had certainly accomplished, had his imagination continued neuter—but the sallies of the imagination are ungovernable in things of this kind—a thought instantly darted into his mind, that tho' the anguish had the sensation of glowing heat—it might, notwithstanding that, be a bite as well as a burn; and if so, that possibly a *Newt* or an *Asker*,[7] or some such detested reptile, had crept up, and was fastening his teeth—the horrid idea of which, with a fresh glow of pain arising that instant from the chesnut, seized *Phutatorius* with a sudden panick, and in the first terrifying disorder of the passion it threw him, as it has done the best generals upon earth, quite off his guard;—the effect of which was this, that he leapt incontinently up, uttering as he rose that interjection of surprise so much discanted upon, with the aposiopestick-break after it, marked thus, Z——ds—which, though not strictly canonical, was still as little as any man could have said upon the occasion;——and which, by the bye, whether canonical or not, *Phutatorius* could no more help than he could the cause of it.

Though this has taken up some time in the narrative, it took up little more time in the transaction, than just to allow time for *Phutatorius* to draw forth the chesnut, and throw it down with violence upon the floor—and for *Yorick*, to rise from his chair, and pick the chesnut up.

It is curious to observe the triumph of slight incidents over the mind:—What incredible weight they have in forming and governing our opinions, both of men and things,—that trifles light as air, shall waft a belief into the soul, and plant it so immoveably within it,—that *Euclid*'s[8] demonstrations, could they be brought to batter it in breach, should not all have power to overthrow it.

Yorick, I said, picked up the chesnut which *Phutatorius*'s wrath had flung down—the action was trifling—I am ashamed to account for it—he did it, for no reason, but that he thought the chesnut not a jot worse for the adventure—and that he held a good chesnut worth stooping for.—But this incident, trifling as it was, wrought differently in *Phutatorius*'s head: He considered this act of *Yorick*'s, in getting off his chair, and picking up the chesnut, as a plain acknowledgment in him, that the chesnut was originally his,—and in course, that it must have been the owner of the chesnut, and no one else, who could have plaid him such a prank with it: What greatly confirmed him in this opinion, was this, that the table being parallelogramical and very narrow, it afforded a fair opportunity for *Yorick*, who sat directly over-against *Phutatorius*, of slipping the chesnut in— and consequently that he did it. The look of something more than suspicion, which *Phutatorius* cast full upon *Yorick* as these thoughts arose, too evidently spoke his opinion—and as *Phutatorius* was naturally supposed to know more of the matter than any person besides, his opinion at once became the general one;—and for a reason very different from any which have been yet given—in a little time it was put out of all manner of dispute.

When great or unexpected events fall out upon the stage of this sublunary world—the mind of man, which is an inquisitive kind of a substance, naturally takes a flight, behind the scenes, to see what is the cause and first spring of them—The search was not long in this instance.

It was well known that *Yorick* had never a good opinion of the treatise which *Phutatorius* had wrote *de Concubinis retinendis*, as a thing which he feared had done hurt in the world—and 'twas easily found out, that there was a mystical meaning in *Yorick*'s prank—and that his chucking the chesnut hot into *Phutatorius*'s ***—*****, was a sarcastical fling at his book —the doctrines of which, they said, had inflamed many an honest man in the same place.

This conceit awaken'd *Semnolentus*—made *Agelastes* smile —and if you can recollect the precise look and air of a man's face intent in finding out a riddle—it threw *Gastripheres*'s into that form—and in short was thought by many to be a master-stroke of arch-wit.

This, as the reader has seen from one end to the other, was as groundless as the dreams of philosophy: *Yorick*, no doubt, as *Shakespear* said of his ancestor—"*was a man of jest,*'" but it was temper'd with something which withheld him from that, and many other ungracious pranks, of which he as undeservedly bore the blame;—but it was his misfortune all his life long to bear the imputation of saying and doing a thousand things of which (unless my esteem blinds me) his nature was incapable. All I blame him for—or rather, all I blame and alternately like him for, was that singularity of his temper, which would never suffer him to take pains to set a story right with the world, however in his power. In every ill usage of that sort, he acted precisely as in the affair of his lean horse—he could have explained it to his honour, but his spirit was above it; and besides he ever looked upon the inventor, the propagator and believer of an illiberal report alike so injurious to him,—he could not stoop to tell his story to them—and so trusted to time and truth to do it for him.

This heroic cast produced him inconveniences in many respects—in the present, it was followed by the fixed resentment of *Phutatorius*, who, as *Yorick* had just made an end of his chesnut, rose up from his chair a second time, to let him know it—which indeed he did with a smile; saying only—that he would endeavour not to forget the obligation.

But you must mark and carefully separate and distinguish these two things in your mind.

—The smile was for the company.

—The threat was for *Yorick*.

CHAPTER XXVIII

—CAN you tell me, quoth *Phutatorius*, speaking to *Gastripheres* who sat next to him,—for one would not apply to a surgeon in so foolish an affair,—can you tell me, *Gastripheres*, what is best to take out the fire?—Ask *Eugenius*, said *Gastripheres*—That greatly depends, said *Eugenius*, pretending ignorance of the adventure, upon the nature of the part—If it is a tender part, and a part which can conveniently be wrapt up—It is both the one and the other, replied *Phutatorius*, laying his hand as he spoke, with an emphatical nod of his head upon the part in question, and lifting up his right leg at the same time to ease and ventilate it—If that is the case, said *Eugenius*, I would advise you, *Phutatorius*, not to tamper with it by any means; but if you will send to the next printer, and trust your cure to such a simple thing as a soft sheet of paper just come off the press—you need do nothing more than twist it round—The damp paper, quoth *Yorick* (who sat next to his friend *Eugenius*) though I know it has a refreshing coolness in it—yet I presume is no more than the vehicle—and that the oil and lamp-black with which the paper is so strongly impregnated, does the business—Right, said *Eugenius*, and is of any outward application I would venture to recommend the most anodyne and safe.

Was it my case, said *Gastripheres*, as the main thing is the oil and lamp-black, I should spread them thick upon a rag, and clap it on directly. That would make a very devil of it, replied *Yorick*—And besides, added *Eugenius*, it would not answer the intention, which is the extreame neatness and elegance of the prescription, which the faculty hold to be half in half—for consider, if the type is a very small one, (which it should be) the sanative particles, which come into contact in this form, have the advantage of being spread so infinitely thin and with such a mathematical equality (fresh paragraphs and large capitals excepted) as no art or management of the spatula can come up to. It falls out very luckily, replied *Phutatorius*, that the second edition of my treatise *de Concubinis retinendis*, is at this instant in the press—You may take any leaf of it, said *Eugenius*—No matter which—provided, quoth *Yorick*, there is no bawdry in it—

They are just now, replied *Phutatorius*, printing off the ninth chapter—which is the last chapter but one in the book—Pray what is the title to that chapter, said *Yorick*, making a respectful bow to *Phutatorius* as he spoke—I think, answered *Phutatorius*,'tis that, *de re concubinariâ*.[1]

For heaven's sake keep out of that chapter, quoth *Yorick*. —By all means—added *Eugenius*.

CHAPTER XXIX

—Now, quoth *Didius*, rising up, and laying his right-hand with his fingers spread upon his breast—had such a blunder about a christian-name happened before the reformation—(It happened the day before yesterday, quoth my uncle *Toby* to himself) and when baptism was administer'd in *Latin* ——('Twas all in *English*, said my uncle)—Many things might have coincided with it, and upon the authority of sundry decreed cases, to have pronounced the baptism null, with a power of giving the child a new name—Had a priest, for instance, which was no uncommon thing, through ignorance of the *Latin* tongue, baptized a child of Tom-o'Stiles, *in nomino patriæ & filia & spiritum sanctos*,[1]—the baptism was held null—I beg your pardon, replied *Kysarcius*,—in that case, as the mistake was only in the *terminations*, the baptism was valid—and to have rendered it null, the blunder of the priest should have fallen upon the first syllable of each noun—and not, as in your case, upon the last.—

My father delighted in subtleties of this kind, and listen'd with infinite attention.

Gastripheres, for example, continued *Kysarcius*, baptizes a child of *John Stradling*'s, *in Gomine* gatris, *&c. &c.* instead of *in Nomine* patris, *&c.*—Is this a baptism? No,—say the ablest canonists; inasmuch as the radix of each word is hereby torn up, and the sense and meaning of them removed and changed quite to another object; for *Gomine* does not signify a name, nor *gatris* a father—What do they signify? said my uncle *Toby*—Nothing at all—quoth *Yorick*—Ergo, such a baptism is null, said *Kysarcius*—In course, answered *Yorick*, in a tone two parts jest and one part earnest—

But in the case cited, continued *Kysarcius*, where *patrim* is put for *patris*, *filia* for *filij*, and so on—as it is a fault only in the declension, and the roots of the words continue untouch'd, the inflexions of their branches, either this way or that, does not in any sort hinder the baptism, inasmuch as the same sense continues in the words as before—But then, said *Didius*, the intention of the priest's pronouncing them grammatically, must have been proved to have gone along with it—Right, answered *Kysarcius*; and of this, brother *Didius*, we have an instance in a decree of the decretals of Pope *Leo* the IIId.[2]—But my brother's child, cried my uncle *Toby*, has nothing to do with the Pope—'tis the plain child of a Protestant gentleman, christen'd *Tristram* against the wills and wishes both of its father and mother, and all who are a-kin to it—

If the wills and wishes, said *Kysarcius*, interrupting my uncle *Toby*, of those only who stand related to Mr. *Shandy*'s child, were to have weight in this matter, Mrs. *Shandy*, of all people, has the least to do in it—My uncle *Toby* lay'd down his pipe, and my father drew his chair still closer to the table to hear the conclusion of so strange an introduction.

It has not only been a question, captain *Shandy*, amongst the
* best lawyers and civilians in this land, continued *Kysarcius*, "*Whether the mother be of kin to her child*,"—but after much dispassionate enquiry and jactitation of the arguments on all sides,—it has been adjudged for the negative,—namely, "*That the mother is not of kin to her child*†." My father instantly clapp'd his hand upon my uncle *Toby*'s mouth, under colour of whispering in his ear—the truth was, he was alarmed for *Lillabullero*—and having a great desire to hear more of so curious an argument—he begg'd my uncle *Toby*, for heaven's sake, not to disappoint him in it—My uncle *Toby* gave a nod—resumed his pipe, and contenting himself with whistling *Lillabullero* inwardly—*Kysarcius*, *Didius*, and *Triptolemus* went on with the discourse as follows.

This determination, continued *Kysarcius*, how contrary soever it may seem to run to the stream of vulgar ideas, yet had reason strongly on its side; and has been put out of all manner of dispute from the famous case, known commonly by the name of

* Vid Swinburn on Testaments, Part 7. § 8.[3]
† Vid. Brook Abridg. Tit. Administr. N. 47.[4]

the Duke of *Suffolk*'s case:—It is cited in *Brook*, said *Trip-tolemus*—And taken notice of by Lord *Coke*,[5] added *Didius* —And you may find it in *Swinburn* on Testaments, said *Kysarcius*.

The case, Mr. *Shandy*, was this.

In the reign of *Edward* the Sixth,[6] *Charles* Duke of *Suffolk* having issue a son by one venter, and a daughter by another venter, made his last will, wherein he devised goods to his son, and died; after whose death the son died also—but without will, without wife, and without child—his mother and his sister by the father's side (for she was born of the former venter[7]) then living. The mother took the administration of her son's goods, according to the statute of the 21st of *Harry* the Eighth, where-by it is enacted, That in case any person die intestate, the administration of his goods shall be committed to the next of kin.

The administration being thus (surreptitiously) granted to the mother, the sister by the father's side commenced a suit before the Ecclesiastical Judge, alledging, 1st, That she herself was next of kin; and 2dly, That the mother was not of kin at all to the party deceased; and therefore pray'd the court, that the administration granted to the mother might be revoked, and be committed unto her, as next of kin to the deceased, by force of the said statute.

Hereupon, as it was a great cause, and much depending upon its issue—and many causes of great property likely to be de-cided in times to come, by the precedent to be then made—the most learned, as well in the laws of this realm, as in the civil law, were consulted together, whether the mother was of kin to her son, or no.—Whereunto not only the temporal lawyers—but the church-lawyers—the juris-consulti—the juris-prudentes[8]— the civilians—the advocates—the commissaries—the judges of the consistory and prerogative courts of *Canterbury* and *York*, with the master of the faculties, were all unanimously of opin-ion, That the mother was not of * kin to her child—

And what said the Duchess of *Suffolk* to it? said my uncle *Toby*.

The unexpectedness of my uncle *Toby*'s question, con-founded *Kysarcius* more than the ablest advocate——He stopp'd a full minute, looking in my uncle *Toby*'s face without

* Mater non numeratur inter consanguineos. Bald. in ult. C. de Verb. signific.[9]

replying——and in that single minute *Triptolemus* put by him, and took the lead as follows.

'Tis a ground and principle in the law, said *Triptolemus*, that things do not ascend, but descend in it; and I make no doubt 'tis for this cause, that however true it is, that the child may be of the blood or seed of its parents—that the parents, nevertheless, are not of the blood and seed of it; inasmuch as the parents are not begot by the child, but the child by the parents—For so they write, *Liberi sunt de sanguine patris & matris, sed pater et mater non sunt de sanguine liberorum.*[10]

——But this, *Triptolemus*, cried *Didius*, proves too much—for from this authority cited it would follow, not only what indeed is granted on all sides, that the mother is not of kin to her child—but the father likewise——It is held, said *Triptolemus*, the better opinion; because the father, the mother, and the child, though they be three persons, yet are they but (*una caro**) one flesh; and consequently no degree of kindred—or any method of acquiring one *in nature*—There you push the argument again too far, cried *Didius*—for there is no prohibition *in nature*, though there is in the levitical law,—but that a man may beget a child upon his grandmother—in which case, supposing the issue a daughter, she would stand in relation both of——But who ever thought, cried *Kysarcius*, of laying with his grand-mother?——The young gentleman, replied *Yorick*, whom *Selden*[11] speaks of—who not only thought of it, but justified his intention to his father by the argument drawn from the law of retaliation——"You lay'd, Sir, with my mother, said the lad—why may not I lay with yours?"——'Tis the *Argumentum commune*,[12] added *Yorick*.—'Tis as good, replied *Eugenius*, taking down his hat, as they deserve.

The company broke up——

CHAPTER XXX

——AND pray, said my uncle *Toby*, leaning upon *Yorick*, as he and my father were helping him leisurely down the stairs—don't be terrified, madam, this stair-case conversation is not so long as the last—And pray, *Yorick*, said my uncle *Toby*, which way is this said affair of *Tristram* at length settled by these

* Vide Brook Abridg. tit. Administr. N. 47.

learned men? Very satisfactorily, replied *Yorick*; no mortal, Sir, has any concern with it—for Mrs. *Shandy* the mother is nothing at all akin to him—and as the mother's is the surest side—Mr. *Shandy*, in course, is still less than nothing—In short, he is not as much akin to him, Sir, as I am—

—That may well be, said my father, shaking his head.

—Let the learned say what they will, there must certainly, quoth my uncle *Toby*, have been some sort of consanguinity betwixt the duchess of *Suffolk* and her son—

The vulgar are of the same opinion, quoth *Yorick*, to this hour.

CHAPTER XXXI

THOUGH my father was hugely tickled with the subtleties of these learned discourses—'twas still but like the anointing of a broken bone—The moment he got home, the weight of his afflictions returned upon him but so much the heavier, as is ever the case when the staff we lean on slips from under us—He became pensive—walked frequently forth to the fish-pond—let down one loop of his hat—sigh'd often—forbore to snap—and, as the hasty sparks of temper, which occasion snapping, so much assist perspiration and digestion, as *Hippocrates* tells us—he had certainly fallen ill with the extinction of them, had not his thoughts been critically drawn off, and his health rescued by a fresh train of disquietudes left him, with a legacy of a thousand pounds by my aunt *Dinah*—

My father had scarce read the letter, when taking the thing by the right end, he instantly begun to plague and puzzle his head how to lay it out mostly to the honour of his family—A hundred and fifty odd projects took possession of his brains by turns—he would do this, and that, and t'other—He would go to *Rome*—he would go to law—he would buy stock—he would buy *John Hobson*'s farm—he would new fore-front his house, and add a new wing to make it even—There was a fine water-mill on this side, and he would build a wind-mill on the other side of the river in full view to answer it—But above all things in the world, he would inclose the great *Ox-moor*, and send out my brother *Bobby* immediately upon his travels.

But as the sum was *finite*, and consequently could not do every thing—and in truth very few of these to any purpose,—of all the projects which offered themselves upon this occasion, the two last seemed to make the deepest impression; and he would infallibly have determined upon both at once, but for the small inconvenience hinted at above, which absolutely put him under a necessity of deciding in favour either of the one or the other.

This was not altogether so easy to be done; for though 'tis certain my father had long before set his heart upon this necessary part of my brother's education, and like a prudent man had actually determined to carry it into execution, with the first money that returned from the second creation of actions in the *Missisippi*-scheme,[1] in which he was an adventurer—yet the *Ox-moor*, which was a fine, large, whinny,[2] undrained, unimproved common, belonging to the *Shandy*-estate, had almost as old a claim upon him: He had long and affectionately set his heart upon turning it likewise to some account.

But having never hitherto been pressed with such a conjuncture of things, as made it necessary to settle either the priority or justice of their claims,—like a wise man he had refrained entering into any nice or critical examination about them: So that upon the dismission of every other project at this crisis,——the two old projects, the Ox-MOOR and my BROTHER, divided him again; and so equal a match were they for each other, as to become the occasion of no small contest in the old gentleman's mind,—which of the two should be set o'going first.

—People may laugh as they will——but the case was this.

It had ever been the custom of the family, and by length of time was almost become a matter of common right, that the eldest son of it should have free ingress, egress, and regress into foreign parts before marriage,—not only for the sake of bettering his own private parts, by the benefit of exercise and change of so much air—but simply for the mere delectation of his fancy, by the feather put into his cap, of having been abroad—*tantum valet*, my father would say, *quantum sonat*.[3]

Now as this was a reasonable, and in course a most christian indulgence—to deprive him of it, without why or wherefore,—and thereby make an example of him, as the first *Shandy* unwhirl'd about *Europe* in a post-chaise, and only because he was a heavy lad—would be using him ten times worse than a *Turk*.

On the other hand, the case of the *Ox-moor* was full as hard.

Exclusive of the original purchase-money, which was eight hundred pounds—it had cost the family eight hundred pounds more in a law-suit about fifteen years before—besides the Lord knows what trouble and vexation.

It had been moreover in possession of the *Shandy*-family ever since the middle of the last century; and though it lay full in view before the house, bounded on one extremity by the water-mill, and on the other by the projected wind-mill spoken of above,—and for all these reasons seemed to have the fairest title of any part of the estate to the care and protection of the family—yet by an unaccountable fatality, common to men, as well as the ground they tread on,—it had all along most shamefully been overlook'd; and to speak the truth of it, had suffered so much by it, that it would have made any man's heart have bled (*Obadiah* said) who understood the value of land, to have rode over it, and only seen the condition it was in.

However, as neither the purchasing this tract of ground—nor indeed the placing of it where it lay, were either of them, properly speaking, of my father's doing—he had never thought himself any way concerned in the affair—till the fifteen years before, when the breaking out of that cursed law-suit mentioned above (and which had arose about its boundaries)—which being altogether my father's own act and deed, it naturally awakened every other argument in its favour; and upon summing them all up together, he saw, not merely in interest, but in honour, he was bound to do something for it—and that now or never was the time.

I think there must certainly have been a mixture of ill-luck in it, that the reasons on both sides should happen to be so equally balanced by each other; for though my father weigh'd them in all humours and conditions—spent many an anxious hour in the most profound and abstracted meditation upon what was best to be done——reading books of farming one day—books of travels another—laying aside all passion whatever—viewing the arguments on both sides in all their lights and circumstances ——communing every day with my uncle *Toby*—arguing with *Yorick*, and talking over the whole affair of the *Ox-moor* with *Obadiah*—yet nothing in all that time appeared so strongly in behalf of the one, which was not either strictly applicable to the other, or at least so far counterbalanced by some consideration of equal weight, as to keep the scales even.

For to be sure, with proper helps, and in the hands of some people, tho' the *Ox-moor* would undoubtedly have made a different appearance in the world from what it did, or ever would do in the condition it lay—yet every tittle of this was true, with regard to my brother *Bobby*—let *Obadiah* say what he would.——

In point of interest—the contest, I own, at first sight, did not appear so undecisive betwixt them; for whenever my father took pen and ink in hand, and set about calculating the simple expence of paring and burning, and fenceing in the *Ox-moor*, &c. &c.—with the certain profit it would bring him in return—the latter turned out so prodigiously in his way of working the account, that you would have sworn the *Ox-moor* would have carried all before it. For it was plain he should reap a hundred lasts of rape, at twenty pounds a last, the very first year—besides an excellent crop of wheat the year following—and the year after that, to speak within bounds, a hundred——but, in all likelihood, a hundred and fifty—if not two hundred quarters of pease and beans—besides potatoes without end—But then, to think he was all this while breeding up my brother like a hog to eat them—knocked all on the head again, and generally left the old gentleman in such a state of suspence—that, as he often declared to my uncle *Toby*—he knew no more than his heels what to do.

No body, but he who has felt it, can conceive what a plaguing thing it is to have a man's mind torn asunder by two projects of equal strength, both obstinately pulling in a contrary direction at the same time: For to say nothing of the havock, which by a certain consequence is unavoidably made by it all over the finer system of the nerves, which you know convey the animal spirits and more subtle juices from the heart to the head, and so on ——It is not to be told in what a degree such a wayward kind of friction works upon the more gross and solid parts, wasting the fat and impairing the strength of a man every time as it goes backwards and forwards.

My father had certainly sunk under this evil, as certainly as he had done under that of my CHRISTIAN NAME—had he not been rescued out of it as he was out of that, by a fresh evil—the misfortune of my brother *Bobby*'s death.

What is the life of man! Is it not to shift from side to side?—from sorrow to sorrow?——to button up one cause of vexation!—and unbutton another!

CHAPTER XXXII

FROM this moment I am to be considered as heir-apparent to the *Shandy* family—and it is from this point properly, that the story of my LIFE and my OPINIONS sets out; with all my hurry and precipitation I have but been clearing the ground to raise the building——and such a building do I foresee it will turn out, as never was planned, and as never was executed since *Adam*. In less than five minutes I shall have thrown my pen into the fire, and the little drop of thick ink which is left remaining at the bottom of my ink-horn, after it—I have but half a score things to do in the time——I have a thing to name—a thing to lament—a thing to hope—a thing to promise, and a thing to threaten—I have a thing to suppose—a thing to declare—a thing to conceal—a thing to chuse, and a thing to pray for.—This chapter, therefore, I *name* the chapter of THINGS—and my next chapter to it, that is, the first chapter of my next volume, if I live, shall be my chapter upon WHISKERS, in order to keep up some sort of connection in my works.

The thing I lament is, that things have crowded in so thick upon me, that I have not been able to get into that part of my work, towards which, I have all the way, looked forwards, with so much earnest desire; and that is the campaigns, but especially the amours of my uncle *Toby*, the events of which are of so singular a nature, and so Cervantick a cast, that if I can so manage it, as to convey but the same impressions to every other brain, which the occurrences themselves excite in my own——I will answer for it the book shall make its way in the world, much better than its master has done before it——Oh *Tristram! Tristram!* can this but be once brought about——the credit, which will attend thee as an author, shall counterbalance the many evils which have befallen thee as a man—thou wilt feast upon the one—when thou hast lost all sense and remembrance of the other!——

No wonder I itch so much as I do, to get at these amours—They are the choicest morsel of my whole story! and when I do get at 'em—assure yourselves, good folks,—(nor do I value whose squeamish stomach takes offence at it) I shall not be at all nice in the choice of my words;——and that's the thing I have to *declare*.—I shall never get all through in five minutes, that I fear—and the thing I *hope* is, that your worships and reverences are not offended—if you are, depend upon't I'll give you something, my good gentry, next year, to be offended at——that's my dear *Jenny*'s way—but who my *Jenny* is—and which is the right and which the wrong end of a woman, is the thing to be *concealed*—it shall be told you the next chapter but one, to my chapter of button-holes,—and not one chapter before.

And now that you have just got to the end of these four volumes——the thing I have to *ask* is, how do you feel your heads? my own akes dismally—as for your healths, I know, they are much better——True *Shandeism*, think what you will against it, opens the heart and lungs, and like all those affections which partake of its nature, it forces the blood and other vital fluids of the body to run freely thro' its channels, and makes the wheel of life run long and chearfully round.

Was I left like *Sancho Pança*,[2] to chuse my kingdom, it should not be maritime—or a kingdom of blacks to make a penny of——no, it should be a kingdom of hearty laughing subjects: And as the bilious and more saturnine passions, by creating disorders in the blood and humours, have as bad an influence, I see, upon the body politick as body natural—and as nothing but a habit of virtue can fully govern those passions, and subject them to reason—I should add to my prayer—that God would give my subjects grace to be as WISE as they were MERRY; and then should I be the happiest monarch, and they the happiest people under heaven—

And so, with this moral for the present, may it please your worships and your reverences, I take my leave of you till this time twelve-month, when (unless this vile cough kills me in the mean time) I'll have another pluck at your beards, and lay open a story to the world you little dream of.

FINIS.

THE
LIFE
AND
OPINIONS
OF
TRISTRAM SHANDY,
GENTLEMAN.

Dixero si quid fortè jocosius, hoc mihi juris
Cum venia dabis.————[1]   HOR.

—*Si quis calumnietur levius esse quam decet theo-*
logum, aut mordacius quam deceat Christia-
num—non Ego, sed Democritus dixit.—[2]

ERASMUS.

VOL. V.

LONDON:

Printed for T. BECKET and P. A. DEHONDT,
in the Strand.   M DCC LXII.

THE

L I F E

AND

O P I N I O N S

OF

TRISTRAM SHANDY,

GENTLEMAN.

Dixero si quid fortè jocosius, hoc mihi juris
Cum venia dabis.——   HOR.

—Si quis calumnietur levius esse quam decet theologum,
aut mordacius quam deceat Christianum—non Ego,
sed Democritus dixit——

                                    ERASMUS.

Si quis Clericus, aut Monachus, verba joculatoria, risum
moventia sciebat anathema esto.[3]
                    Second Council of CARTHAGE.

The SECOND EDITION.

VOL. V.

L O N D O N.

Printed for T. BECKET and P. A. DEHONDT,
in the Strand.   M DCC LXVII.

To the Right Honourable
JOHN,
Lord Viscount SPENCER.[1]

My Lord,

I HUMBLY beg leave to offer you these two Volumes; they are the best my talents, with such bad health as I have, could produce:—had providence granted me a larger stock of either, they had been a much more proper present to your Lordship.

I beg your Lordship will forgive me, if, at the same time I dedicate this work to you, I join Lady SPENCER, in the liberty I take of inscribing the story of *Le Fever* in the sixth volume to her name; for which I have no other motive, which my heart has informed me of, but that the story is a humane one.

> *I am,*
> *My Lord,*
> *Your Lordship's*
> *Most devoted,*
> *And most humble Servant,*
> LAUR. STERNE.

CHAPTER I

If it had not been for those two mettlesome tits, and that madcap of a postilion, who drove them from Stilton to Stamford,[1] the thought had never entered my head. He flew like lightning——there was a slope of three miles and a half——we scarce touched the ground——the motion was most rapid—most impetuous—'twas communicated to my brain—my heart partook of it——By the great God of day, said I, looking towards the sun, and thrusting my arm out of the fore-window of the chaise, as I made my vow, "I will lock up my study door the moment I get home, and throw the key of it ninety feet below the surface of the earth, into the draw-well at the back of my house."

The London waggon confirmed me in my resolution: it hung tottering upon the hill, scarce progressive, drag'd—drag'd up by eight *heavy beasts*——"by main strength!—quoth I, nodding— but your betters draw the same way—and something of every bodies!——O rare!"

Tell me, ye learned, shall we for ever be adding so much to the *bulk*—so little to the *stock?*[2]

Shall we for ever make new books, as apothecaries make new mixtures, by pouring only out of one vessel into another?

Are we for ever to be twisting, and untwisting the same rope? for ever in the same track—for ever at the same pace?

Shall we be destined to the days of eternity, on holy-days, as well as working-days, to be shewing the *relicks of learning*, as monks do the relicks of their saints—without working one— one single miracle with them?

Who made MAN, with powers which dart him from earth to heaven in a moment—that great, that most excellent, and most noble creature of the world—the *miracle* of nature, as Zoroaster[3] in his book περὶ φύσεως called him—the SHEKINAH[4] of the divine presence, as Chrysostom—the *image* of God, as Moses— the *ray* of divinity, as Plato—the *marvel* of marvels, as Aristotle——to go sneaking on at this pitiful— pimping—pettifogging rate?

I scorn to be as abusive as Horace[5] upon the occasion——but if there is no catachresis in the wish, and no sin in it, I wish from my soul, that every imitator in *Great Britain*, *France*, and

Ireland, had the farcy for his pains; and that there was a good farcical house, large enough to hold—aye—and sublimate them, *shag-rag and bob-tail*, male and female, all together: and this leads me to the affair of *Whiskers*——but, by what chain of ideas—I leave as a legacy in *mort main*[6] to Prudes and Tartufs,[7] to enjoy and make the most of.

Upon Whiskers.

I'm sorry I made it——'twas as inconsiderate a promise as ever entered a man's head——A chapter upon whiskers! alas! the world will not bear it——'tis a delicate world—but I knew not of what mettle it was made—nor had I ever seen the under-written fragment; otherwise, as surely as noses are noses, and whiskers are whiskers still; (let the world say what it will to the contrary) so surely would I have steered clear of this dangerous chapter.

The Fragment.

* * * * * * * * * * * * * *
* * * * * * * * * * * * *
* *——You are half asleep, my good lady, said the old gentleman, taking hold of the old lady's hand and giving it a gentle squeeze, as he pronounced the word *Whiskers*——shall we change the subject? By no means, replied the old lady—I like your account of these matters: so throwing a thin gauze handkerchief over her head, and leaning it back upon the chair with her face turned towards him, and advancing her two feet as she reclined herself—I desire, continued she, you will go on.

The old gentleman went on as follows.——Whiskers! cried the queen of *Navarre*,[8] dropping her knotting-ball, as *La Fosseuse* uttered the word——Whiskers; madam, said *La Fosseuse*, pinning the ball to the queen's apron, and making a courtesy as she repeated it.

La Fosseuse's voice was naturally soft and low, yet 'twas an articulate voice: and every letter of the word *whiskers* fell distinctly upon the queen of *Navarre*'s ear—Whiskers! cried the queen, laying a greater stress upon the word, and as if she had still distrusted her ears—Whiskers; replied *La Fosseuse*, repeating the word a third time—There is not a cavalier, madam, of his age in *Navarre*, continued the maid of honour, pressing the page's interest upon the queen, that has so gallant a pair—Of what? cried *Margaret*, smiling——Of whiskers, said *La Fosseuse*, with infinite modesty.

The word whiskers still stood its ground, and continued to be made use of in most of the best companies throughout the little kingdom of *Navarre*, notwithstanding the indiscreet use which *La Fosseuse* had made of it: the truth was, *La Fosseuse* had pronounced the word, not only before the queen, but upon sundry other occasions at court, with an accent which always implied something of a mystery——And as the court of *Margaret*, as all the world knows, was at that time a mixture of gallantry and devotion——and whiskers being as applicable to the one, as the other, the word naturally stood its ground—it gain'd full as much as it lost; that is, the clergy were for it—the laity were against it—and for the women,——*they* were divided.——

The excellency of the figure and mien of the young Sieur *de Croix*, was at that time beginning to draw the attention of the maids of honour towards the terras before the palace gate, where the guard was mounted. The Lady *de Baussiere* fell deeply in love with him,—*La Battarelle* did the same—it was the finest weather for it, that ever was remembered in *Navarre*—*La Guyol, La Maronette, La Sabatiere*, fell in love with the Sieur *de Croix* also—*La Rebours* and *La Fosseuse* knew better—*De Croix* had failed in an attempt to recommend himself to *La Rebours*; and *La Rebours* and *La Fosseuse* were inseparable.

The queen of *Navarre* was sitting with her ladies in the painted bow-window, facing the gate of the second court, as *De Croix* passed through it—He is handsome, said the Lady *Baussiere*.—He has a good mien, said *La Battarelle*.—He is finely shaped, said *La Guyol*.—I never saw an officer of the horse-guards in my life, said *La Maronette*, with two such legs—Or who stood so well upon them, said *La Sabatiere*——But he has no whiskers, cried *La Fosseuse*—Not a pile, said *La Rebours*.

The queen went directly to her oratory, musing all the way, as she walked through the gallery, upon the subject; turning it this way and that way in her fancy——*Ave Maria!*—what can *La Fosseuse* mean? said she, kneeling down upon the cushion.

La Guyol, La Batterelle, La Maronette, La Sabatiere, retired instantly to their chambers—Whiskers! said all four of them to themselves, as they bolted their doors on the inside.

The Lady *Carnavallette* was counting her beads with both

hands, unsuspected under her farthingal—from St. *Antony* down to St. *Ursula* inclusive, not a saint passed through her fingers without whiskers; St. *Francis*,[9] St. *Dominick*, St. *Bennet*, St. *Basil*, St. *Bridget*, had all whiskers.

The Lady *Baussiere* had got into a wilderness of conceits, with moralizing too intricately upon *La Fosseuse*'s text—She mounted her palfry, her page followed her—the host passed by—the lady *Baussiere* rode on.

One denier, cried the order of mercy—one single denier, in behalf of a thousand patient captives, whose eyes look towards heaven and you for their redemption.

—The Lady *Baussiere* rode on.

Pity the unhappy, said a devout, venerable, hoary-headed man, meekly holding up a box, begirt with iron, in his withered hands——I beg for the unfortunate—good, my lady, 'tis for a prison—for an hospital—'tis for an old man—a poor man undone by shipwreck, by suretyship, by fire——I call God and all his angels to witness—'tis to cloath the naked—to feed the hungry—'tis to comfort the sick and the broken hearted.

—The Lady *Baussiere* rode on.

A decayed kinsman bowed himself to the ground.

—The Lady *Baussiere* rode on.

He ran begging bare-headed on one side of her palfry, conjuring her by the former bonds of friendship, alliance, consanguinity, &c.—Cousin, aunt, sister, mother—for virtue's sake, for your own, for mine, for Christ's sake remember me—pity me.

—The Lady *Baussiere* rode on.

Take hold of my whiskers, said the Lady *Baussiere*——The page took hold of her palfry. She dismounted at the end of the terrace.

There are some trains of certain ideas which leave prints of themselves about our eyes and eye-brows; and there is a consciousness of it, somewhere about the heart, which serves but to make these etchings the stronger—we see, spell, and put them together without a dictionary.

Ha, ha! hee, hee! cried *La Guyol* and *La Sabatiere*, looking close at each others prints——Ho, ho! cried *La Batterelle* and *Maronette*, doing the same:—Whist! cried one—st, st,—said a second,—hush, quoth a third——poo, poo, replied a fourth—gramercy! cried the Lady *Carnavallette*;—'twas she who bewhisker'd St. *Bridget*.

La Fosseuse drew her bodkin from the knot of her hair, and having traced the outline of a small whisker, with the blunt end of it, upon one side of her upper lip, put it into *La Rebours*'s hand—*La Rebours* shook her head.

The Lady *Baussiere* cough'd thrice into the inside of her muff—*La Guyol* smiled—Fy, said the Lady *Baussiere*. The queen of *Navarre* touched her eye with the tip of her fore finger—as much as to say, I understand you all.

'Twas plain to the whole court the word was ruined: *La Fosseuse* had given it a wound, and it was not the better for passing through all these defiles——It made a faint stand, however, for a few months; by the expiration of which, the Sieur *de Croix*, finding it high time to leave *Navarre* for want of whiskers—the word in course became indecent, and (after a few efforts) absolutely unfit for use.

The best word, in the best language of the best world, must have suffered under such combinations.—The curate of *d'Estella*[10] wrote a book against them, setting forth the dangers of accessory ideas, and warning the *Navarois* against them.

Does not all the world know, said the curate *d'Estella* at the conclusion of his work, that Noses ran the same fate some centuries ago in most parts of *Europe*, which Whiskers have now done in the kingdom of *Navarre*—The evil indeed spread no further then—, but have not beds and bolsters, and night-caps and chamber-pots stood upon the brink of destruction ever since? Are not trouse,[11] and placket-holes, and pump-handles—and spigots and faucets, in danger still, from the same association?—Chastity, by nature the gentlest of all affections—give it but its head—'tis like a ramping and a roaring lion.

The drift of the curate *d'Estella*'s argument was not under-stood.—They ran the scent the wrong way.—The world bridled his ass at the tail.—And when the *extreams* of DELICACY, and the *beginnings* of CONCUPISCENCE, hold their next provincial chapter together, they may decree that bawdy also.

CHAPTER II

WHEN my father received the letter which brought him the melancholy account of my brother *Bobby*'s death, he was busy calculating the expence of his riding post from *Calais* to *Paris*, and so on to *Lyons*.

'Twas a most inauspicious journey; my father having had

every foot of it to travel over again, and his calculation to begin afresh, when he had almost got to the end of it, by *Obadiah*'s opening the door to acquaint him the family was out of yeast—and to ask whether he might not take the great coach-horse early in the morning, and ride in search of some.—With all my heart, *Obadiah*, said my father, (pursuing his journey)—take the coach-horse, and welcome.—But he wants a shoe, poor creature! said *Obadiah*.—Poor creature! said my uncle *Toby*, vibrating the note back again, like a string in unison. Then ride the *Scotch* horse,[1] quoth my father hastily.—He cannot bear a saddle upon his back, quoth *Obadiah*, for the whole world. ——The devil's in that horse; then take PATRIOT,[2] cried my father, and shut the door.——PATRIOT is sold, said *Obadiah*. —Here's for you! cried my father, making a pause, and looking in my uncle *Toby*'s face, as if the thing had not been a matter of fact.—Your worship ordered me to sell him last *April*, said *Obadiah*.—Then go on foot for your pains, cried my father.—I had much rather walk than ride, said *Obadiah*, shutting the door.

What plagues! cried my father, going on with his calculation.—But the waters are out, said *Obadiah*,—opening the door again.

Till that moment, my father, who had a map of *Sanson*'s,[3] and a book of the post roads before him, had kept his hand upon the head of his compasses, with one foot of them fixed upon *Nevers*, the last stage he had paid for—purposing to go on from that point with his journey and calculation, as soon as *Obadiah* quitted the room; but this second attack of *Obadiah*'s, in opening the door and laying the whole country under water, was too much.—He let go his compasses—or rather with a mixed motion betwixt accident and anger, he threw them upon the table; and then there was nothing for him to do, but to return back to *Calais* (like many others) as wise as he had set out.

When the letter was brought into the parlour, which contained the news of my brother's death, my father had got forwards again upon his journey to within a stride of the compasses of the very same stage of *Nevers*.—By your leave, Mons. *Sanson*, cried my father, striking the point of his compasses through *Nevers* into the table,—and nodding to my uncle *Toby*, to see what was in the letter,—twice of one night is too much for an *English* gentleman and his son, Mons. *Sanson*, to be

turned back from so lousy a town as *Nevers*,—what think'st
thou, *Toby*, added my father in a sprightly tone.—Unless it be a
garrison town, said my uncle *Toby*,—for then—I shall be a fool,
said my father, smiling to himself, as long as I live.—So giving a
second nod—and keeping his compasses still upon *Nevers* with
one hand, and holding his book of the post-roads in the other—
half calculating and half listening, he leaned forwards upon the
table with both elbows, as my uncle *Toby* hummed over the
letter.

——   ——   ——   ——   ——   ——   ——

——   ——   ——   ——   ——   ——

——   ——   ——   ——   ——   ——

——   ——   ——   ——   ——   —— he's gone!
said my uncle *Toby*.—Where—Who? cried my father.—My
nephew, said my uncle *Toby*.——What—without leave—
without money——without governor? cried my father in
amazement. No:—he is dead, my dear brother, quoth my uncle
Toby.—Without being ill? cried my father again.—I dare say
not, said my uncle *Toby*, in a low voice, and fetching a deep sigh
from the bottom of his heart, he has been ill enough, poor lad!
I'll answer for him—for he is dead.

When *Agrippina*[4] was told of her son's death, *Tacitus* informs
us, that not being able to moderate the violence of her passions,
she abruptly broke off her work—My father stuck his compasses into *Nevers*, but so much the faster.—What contrarieties!
his, indeed, was matter of calculation—*Agrippina*'s must have
been quite a different affair; who else could pretend to reason
from history?

How my father went on, in my opinion, deserves a chapter to
itself.—

CHAPTER III

—— —— And a chapter it shall have, and a devil of a
one too—so look to yourselves.

'Tis either *Plato*,[1] or *Plutarch*,[2] or *Seneca*,[3] or *Xenophon*,[4] or
Epictetus,[5] or *Theophrastus*,[6] or *Lucian*[7]—or some one perhaps
of later date—either *Cardan*,[8] or *Budæus*,[9] or *Petrarch*,[10] or
Stella[11]—or possibly it may be some divine or father of the
church, St. *Austin*,[12] or St. *Cyprian*,[13] or *Barnard*,[14] who affirms
that it is an irresistable and natural passion to weep for the loss

of our friends or children—and *Seneca*[15] (I'm positive) tells us somewhere, that such griefs evacuate themselves best by that particular channel.—And accordingly we find, that *David* wept for his son *Absolom*[16]—*Adrian* for his *Antinous*[17]—*Niobe*[18] for her children, and that *Apollodorus* and *Crito*[19] both shed tears for *Socrates* before his death.

My father managed his affliction otherwise; and indeed differently from most men either ancient or modern; for he neither wept it away, as the *Hebrews* and the *Romans*—or slept it off, as the *Laplanders*—or hang'd it, as the *English*, or drowned it, as the *Germans*—nor did he curse it, or damn it, or excommunicate it, or rhyme it, or lillabullero it.——

——He got rid of it, however.

Will your worships give me leave to squeeze in a story between these two pages?

When *Tully*[20] was bereft of his dear daughter *Tullia*, at first he laid it to his heart,—he listened to the voice of nature, and modulated his own unto it.—O my *Tullia!* my daughter! my child!—still, still, still,——'twas O my *Tullia!*——my *Tullia!* Methinks I see my *Tullia*, I hear my *Tullia*, I talk with my *Tullia*.—But as soon as he began to look into the stores of philosophy, and consider how many excellent things might be said upon the occasion—no body upon earth can conceive, says the great orator, how happy, how joyful it made me.

My father was as proud of his eloquence as MARCUS TULLIUS CICERO could be for his life, and for aught I am convinced of to the contrary at present, with as much reason: it was indeed his strength—and his weakness too.——His strength—for he was by nature eloquent,—and his weakness—for he was hourly a dupe to it; and provided an occasion in life would but permit him to shew his talents, or say either a wise thing, a witty, or a shrewd one—(bating the case of a systematick misfortune)—he had all he wanted.—A blessing which tied up my father's tongue, and a misfortune which set it loose with a good grace, were pretty equal: sometimes, indeed, the misfortune was the better of the two; for instance, where the pleasure of the harangue was as *ten*, and the pain of the misfortune but as *five*—my father gained half in half, and consequently was as well again off, as it never had befallen him.

This clue will unravel, what otherwise would seem very inconsistent in my father's domestick character; and it is this, that in the provocations arising from the neglects and blunders of servants, or other mishaps unavoidable in a family, his anger, or rather the duration of it, eternally ran counter to all conjecture.

My father had a favourite little mare, which he had consigned over to a most beautiful Arabian horse, in order to have a pad out of her for his own riding: he was sanguine in all his projects; so talked about his pad every day with as absolute a security, as if it had been reared, broke,—and bridled and saddled at his door ready for mounting. By some neglect or other in *Obadiah*, it so fell out, that my father's expectations were answered with nothing better than a mule, and as ugly a beast of the kind as ever was produced.

My mother and my uncle *Toby* expected my father would be the death of *Obadiah*—and that there never would be an end of the disaster.——See here! you rascal, cried my father, pointing to the mule, what you have done!—It was not me, said *Obadiah*.—How do I know that? replied my father.

Triumph swam in my father's eyes, at the repartee—the *Attic* salt brought water into them—and so *Obadiah* heard no more about it.

Now let us go back to my brother's death.

Philosophy has a fine saying for every thing.—For *Death* it has an entire set; the misery was, they all at once rushed into my father's head, that 'twas difficult to string them together, so as to make any thing of a consistent show out of them.—He took them as they came.

" 'Tis an inevitable chance—the first statute in *Magnâ Chartâ*—it is an everlasting act of parliament, my dear brother,—*All must die.*

"If my son could not have died, it had been matter of wonder,—not that he is dead."

"Monarchs and princes dance in the same ring with us."[21]

"—*To die*, is the great debt and tribute due unto nature: tombs and monuments, which should perpetuate our memories, pay it themselves; and the proudest pyramid of them all, which wealth and science have erected, has lost its apex, and stands obtruncated in the traveller's horizon." (My father found he got great ease, and went on)—"Kingdoms and provinces, and towns and cities, have they not their periods? and when those principles and powers, which at first cemented and put them together, have performed their several evolutions, they fall back."—Brother *Shandy*, said my uncle *Toby*, laying down his pipe at the word *evolutions*—Revolutions, I meant, quoth my father,—by heaven! I meant revolutions, brother *Toby*—evolutions is nonsense.—'Tis not nonsense—said my uncle *Toby*.——But is it not nonsense to break the thread of such a discourse, upon such an occasion? cried my father—do not—dear *Toby*, continued he, taking him by the hand, do not—do not, I beseech thee, interrupt me at this crisis.—My uncle *Toby* put his pipe into his mouth.

"Where is *Troy*[22] and *Mycenæ*,[23] and *Thebes*[24] and *Delos*,[25] and *Persepolis*,[26] and *Agrigentum*"[27]—continued my father, taking up his book of post-roads, which he had laid down.—"What is become, brother *Toby*, of *Nineveh*[28] and *Babylon*,[29] of *Cizicum*[30] and *Mitylenæ*?[31] The fairest towns that ever the sun rose upon, are now no more: the names only are left, and those (for many of them are wrong spelt) are falling themselves by piece-meals to decay, and in length of time will be forgotten, and involved with every thing in a perpetual night: the world itself, brother *Toby*, must—must come to an end.

"Returning out of *Asia*, when I sailed from *Ægina* towards *Megara*,"[32] (*when can this have been? thought my uncle Toby*) "I began to view the country round about. *Ægina* was behind me, *Megara* was before, *Pyræus* on the right hand, *Corinth* on the left.—What flourishing towns now prostrate upon the earth! Alas! alas! said I to myself, that man should disturb his soul for the loss of a child, when so much as this lies awfully buried in his presence——Remember, said I to myself again— remember thou art a man."—

Now my uncle *Toby* knew not that this last paragraph was an extract of *Servius Sulpicius*'s consolatory letter to *Tully*.—He had as little skill, honest man, in the fragments, as he had in the whole pieces of antiquity.—And as my father, whilst he was concerned in the *Turky* trade, had been three or four different times in the *Levant*, in one of which he had staid a whole year and a half at *Zant*,[33] my uncle *Toby* naturally concluded, that in some one of these periods he had taken a trip across the *Archipelago* into *Asia*; and that all this sailing affair with *Ægina* behind, and *Megara* before, and *Pyræus* on the right hand, &c. &c. was nothing more than the true course of my father's voyage and reflections.—'Twas certainly in his *manner*, and many an undertaking critick would have built two stories higher upon worse foundations.—And pray, brother, quoth my uncle *Toby*, laying the end of his pipe upon my father's hand in a kindly way of interruption—but waiting till he finished the account—what year of our Lord was this?—'Twas no year of our Lord, replied my father.—That's impossible, cried my uncle *Toby*.—Simpleton! said my father,—'twas forty years before Christ was born.

My uncle *Toby* had but two things for it; either to suppose his brother to be the wandering *Jew*, or that his misfortunes had disordered his brain.—"May the Lord God of heaven and earth protect him and restore him," said my uncle *Toby*, praying silently for my father, and with tears in his eyes.

—My father placed the tears to a proper account, and went on with his harangue with great spirit.

"There is not such great odds, brother *Toby*, betwixt good and evil, as the world imagines"——(this way of setting off, by the bye, was not likely to cure my uncle *Toby*'s suspicions.)—"Labour, sorrow, grief, sickness, want, and woe, are the sauces of life."—Much good may it do them—said my uncle *Toby* to himself.——

"My son is dead!—so much the better;—'tis a shame in such a tempest to have but one anchor."

"But he is gone for ever from us!—be it so. He is got from under the hands of his barber before he was bald—he is but risen from a feast before he was surfeited—from a banquet before he had got drunken."

"The *Thracians* wept when a child was born"—(and we were very near it, quoth my uncle *Toby*)—"and feasted and made merry when a man went out of the world; and with reason.—Death opens the gate of fame, and shuts the gate of envy after it,—it unlooses the chain of the captive, and puts the bonds-man's task into another man's hands."

"Shew me the man, who knows what life is, who dreads it, and I'll shew thee a prisoner who dreads his liberty."

Is it not better, my dear brother *Toby*, (for mark—our appetites are but diseases)—is it not better not to hunger at all, than to eat?—not to thirst, than to take physick to cure it?

Is it not better to be freed from cares and agues, from love and melancholy, and the other hot and cold fits of life, than like a galled traveller, who comes weary to his inn, to be bound to begin his journey afresh?

There is no terror, brother *Toby*, in its looks, but what it borrows from groans and convulsions—and the blowing of noses, and the wiping away of tears with the bottoms of curtains

in a dying man's room.—Strip it of these, what is it—'Tis better
in battle than in bed, said my uncle *Toby*.—Take away its
herses, its mutes, and its mourning,—its plumes, scutcheons,
and other mechanic aids—What is it?—*Better in battle!* continued my father, smiling, for he had absolutely forgot my
brother *Bobby*—'tis terrible no way—for consider, brother
Toby,—when we *are*—death is *not*;—and when death *is*—we
are *not*. My uncle *Toby* laid down his pipe to consider the
proposition; my father's eloquence was too rapid to stay for any
man—away it went,—and hurried my uncle *Toby*'s ideas along
with it.——

For this reason, continued my father, 'tis worthy to recollect,
how little alteration in great men, the approaches of death have
made.—*Vespasian*[34] died in a jest upon his close stool—*Galba*[35]
with a sentence—*Septimius Severus*[36] in a dispatch—*Tiberius*[37]
in dissimulation, and *Cæsar Augustus*[38] in a compliment.—I
hope, 'twas a sincere one—quoth my uncle *Toby*.

—'Twas to his wife,—said my father.

CHAPTER IV

——And lastly—for of all the choice anecdotes which history can produce of this matter, continued my father,—this,
like the gilded dome which covers in the fabrick—crowns all.—
'Tis of *Cornelius Gallus*,[1] the prætor—which I dare say,
brother *Toby*, you have read.—I dare say I have not, replied my
uncle.—He died, said my father, as
* * * * * * * * * * * * * *
—And if it was with his wife, said my uncle *Toby*—there could
be no hurt in it.—That's more than I know—replied my father.

CHAPTER V

MY mother was going very gingerly in the dark along the
passage which led to the parlour, as my uncle *Toby* pronounced
the word *wife*.—'Tis a shrill, penetrating sound of itself, and
Obadiah had helped it by leaving the door a little a-jar, so that
my mother heard enough of it, to imagine herself the subject of
the conversation: so laying the edge of her finger across her two
lips—holding in her breath, and bending her head a little down-

wards, with a twist of her neck—(not towards the door, but from it, by which means her ear was brought to the chink)—she listened with all her powers:——the listening slave,[1] with the Goddess of Silence at his back,[2] could not have given a finer thought for an intaglio.

In this attitude I am determined to let her stand for five minutes: till I bring up the affairs of the kitchen (as *Rapin*[3] does those of the church) to the same period.

CHAPTER VI

THOUGH in one sense, our family was certainly a simple machine, as it consisted of a few wheels; yet there was thus much to be said for it, that these wheels were set in motion by so many different springs, and acted one upon the other from such a variety of strange principles and impulses,——that though it was a simple machine, it had all the honour and advantages of a complex one,——and a number of as odd movements within it, as ever were beheld in the inside of a *Dutch* silk-mill.

Amongst these there was one, I am going to speak of, in which, perhaps, it was not altogether so singular, as in many others; and it was this, that whatever motion, debate, harangue, dialogue, project, or dissertation, was going forwards in the parlour, there was generally another at the same time, and upon the same subject, running parallel along with it in the kitchen.

Now to bring this about, whenever an extraordinary message, or letter, was delivered in the parlour,—or a discourse suspended till a servant went out—or the lines of discontent were observed to hang upon the brows of my father or mother—or, in short, when any thing was supposed to be upon the tapis worth knowing or listening to, 'twas the rule to leave the door, not absolutely shut, but somewhat a-jar—as it stands just now,—which, under covert of the bad hinge, (and that possibly might be one of the many reasons why it was never mended) it was not difficult to manage; by which means, in all these cases, a passage was generally left, not indeed as wide as the *Dardanells*, but wide enough, for all that, to carry on as much of this windward trade, as was sufficient to save my father the trouble of governing his house;—my mother at this moment stands profiting by it.—*Obadiah* did the same thing, as soon as he had left the letter upon the table which brought the news of my brother's death; so that before my father had well got over his surprize, and entered upon his harangue,—had *Trim* got upon his legs, to speak his sentiments upon the subject.

A curious observer of nature, had he been worth the inventory of all *Job*'s stock—though, by the bye, *your curious observers are seldom worth a groat*—would have given the half of it, to have heard Corporal *Trim* and my father, two orators so contrasted by nature and education, haranguing over the same bier.

My father a man of deep reading—prompt memory—with *Cato*, and *Seneca*, and *Epictetus*, at his fingers ends.—

The corporal—with nothing—to remember—of no deeper reading than his muster-roll—or greater names at his finger's end, than the contents of it.

The one proceeding from period to period, by metaphor and allusion, and striking the fancy as he went along, (as men of wit and fancy do) with the entertainment and pleasantry of his pictures and images.

The other, without wit or antithesis, or point, or turn, this way or that; but leaving the images on one side, and the pictures on the other, going strait forwards as nature could lead him, to the heart. O *Trim!* would to heaven thou had'st a better historian!—would!—thy historian had a better pair of breeches! ——O ye criticks! will nothing melt you?

CHAPTER VII

———My young master in *London* is dead! said *Obadiah*.——

——A green sattin night-gown of my mother's, which had been twice scoured, was the first idea which *Obadiah*'s exclamation brought into *Susannah*'s head.—Well might *Locke*[1] write a chapter upon the imperfections of words.—Then, quoth *Susannah*, we must all go into mourning.—But note a second time: the word *mourning*, notwithstanding *Susannah* made use of it herself—failed also of doing its office; it excited not one single idea, tinged either with grey or black,—all was green.——The green sattin night-gown hung there still.

——O! 'twill be the death of my poor mistress, cried *Susannah*.—My mother's whole wardrobe followed.—What a procession! her red damask,—her orange-tawny,—her white and yellow lutestrings,—her brown taffata,—her bone-laced caps, her bed-gowns, and comfortable under-petticoats.—Not a rag was left behind.—"*No,—she will never look up again,*" said *Susannah*.

We had a fat foolish scullion—my father, I think, kept her for her simplicity;—she had been all autumn struggling with a dropsy.—He is dead! said *Obadiah*,—he is certainly dead!—So am not I, said the foolish scullion.

———Here is sad news, *Trim!* cried *Susannah*, wiping her eyes as *Trim* step'd into the kitchen,—master *Bobby* is dead and *buried*,—the funeral was an interpolation of *Susannah*'s,—we shall have all to go into mourning, said *Susannah*.

I hope not, said *Trim*.—You hope not! cried *Susannah* earnestly.—The mourning ran not in *Trim*'s head, whatever it did in *Susannah*'s.—I hope—said *Trim*, explaining himself, I hope in God the news is not true. I heard the letter read with my own ears, answered *Obadiah*; and we shall have a terrible piece of work of it in stubbing the ox-moor.—Oh! he's dead, said *Susannah*.—As sure, said the scullion, as I am alive.

I lament for him from my heart and my soul, said *Trim*, fetching a sigh.—Poor creature!—poor boy! poor gentleman!

—He was alive last *Whitsontide*, said the coachman.—*Whitsontide!* alas! cried *Trim*, extending his right arm, and falling instantly into the same attitude in which he read the sermon,— what is *Whitsontide, Jonathan*, (for that was the coachman's name) or *Shrovetide*, or any tide or time past, to this? Are we not here now, continued the corporal, (striking the end of his stick perpendicularly upon the floor, so as to give an idea of health and stability)—and are we not—(dropping his hat upon the ground) gone! in a moment!—'Twas infinitely striking! *Susannah* burst into a flood of tears.—We are not stocks and stones.—*Jonathan, Obadiah*, the cook-maid, all melted.—The foolish fat scullion herself, who was scouring a fish-kettle upon her knees, was rous'd with it.—The whole kitchen crouded about the corporal.

Now as I perceive plainly, that the preservation of our constitution in church and state,—and possibly the preservation of the whole world—or what is the same thing, the distribution and balance of its property and power, may in time to come depend greatly upon the right understanding of this stroke of the corporal's eloquence—I do demand your attention,—your worships and reverences, for any ten pages together, take them where you will in any other part of the work, shall sleep for it at your ease.

I said, "we were not stocks and stones"—'tis very well. I should have added, nor are we angels, I wish we were,—but men cloathed with bodies, and governed by our imaginations;—and what a junketting piece of work of it there is, betwixt these and our seven senses, especially some of them, for my own part, I own it, I am ashamed to confess. Let it suffice to affirm, that of all the senses, the eye, (for I absolutely deny the touch, though most of your *Barbati*,[2] I know, are for it) has the quickest commerce with the soul,—gives a smarter stroke, and leaves something more inexpressible upon the fancy, than words can either convey—or sometimes get rid of.

—I've gone a little about—no matter, 'tis for health—let us only carry it back in our mind to the mortality of *Trim*'s hat.—"Are we not here now,—and gone in a moment?"— There was nothing in the sentence—'twas one of your self-evident truths we have the advantage of hearing every day; and if *Trim* had not trusted more to his hat than his head—he had made nothing at all of it.

———"Are we not here now;"—continued the corporal, "and are we not"—(dropping his hat plumb upon the ground— and pausing, before he pronounced the word)—"gone! in a moment?" The descent of the hat was as if a heavy lump of clay had been kneaded into the crown of it.———Nothing could have expressed the sentiment of mortality, of which it was the type and fore-runner, like it,—his hand seemed to vanish from under it,—it fell dead,—the corporal's eye fix'd upon it, as upon a corps,—and *Susannah* burst into a flood of tears.

Now—Ten thousand, and ten thousand times ten thousand (for matter and motion are infinite) are the ways by which a hat may be dropped upon the ground, without any effect.———Had he flung it, or thrown it, or cast it, or skimmed it, or squirted, or let it slip or fall in any possible direction under heaven,—or in the best direction that could be given to it,—had he dropped it like a goose—like a puppy—like an ass—or in doing it, or even after he had done, had he looked like a fool,—like a ninny—like a nicompoop—it had fail'd, and the effect upon the heart had been lost.

Ye who govern this mighty world and its mighty concerns with the *engines* of eloquence,—who heat it, and cool it, and melt it, and mollify it,——and then harden it again to *your purpose*——

Ye who wind and turn the passions with this great wind-lass,—and, having done it, lead the owners of them, whither ye think meet—

Ye, lastly, who drive— —and why not, Ye also who are driven, like turkeys to market, with a stick and a red clout—meditate—meditate, I beseech you, upon *Trim's* hat.

CHAPTER VIII

STAY——I have a small account to settle with the reader, before *Trim* can go on with his harangue.—It shall be done in two minutes.

Amongst many other book-debts, all of which I shall discharge in due time,—I own myself a debtor to the world for two items,—a chapter upon *chamber-maids and button holes*, which, in the former part of my work, I promised and fully intended to pay off this year: but some of your worships and reverences telling me, that the two subjects, especially so connected together, might endanger the morals of the world,—I pray the chapter upon chamber-maids and button-holes may be forgiven me,—and that they will accept of the last chapter in lieu of it; which is nothing, an't please your reverences, but a chapter of *chamber-maids, green-gowns, and old hats*.[1]

Trim took his off the ground,—put it upon his head,—and then went on with his oration upon death, in manner and form following.

CHAPTER IX

——To us, *Jonathan*, who know not what want or care is—who live here in the service of two of the best of masters—(bating in my own case his majesty King *William* the Third, whom I had the honour to serve both in *Ireland* and *Flanders*)—I own it, that from *Whitsontide* to within three weeks of *Christmas*,—'tis not long—'tis like nothing;—but to those, *Jonathan*, who know what death is, and what havock and destruction he can make, before a man can well wheel about—'tis like a whole age.—O *Jonathan!* 'twould make a good-natured man's heart

bleed, to consider, continued the corporal, (standing perpendicularly) how low many a brave and upright fellow has been laid
since that time!—And trust me, *Susy*, added the corporal, turning to *Susannah*, whose eyes were swiming in water,—before
that time comes round again,—many a bright eye will be dim.—
Susannah placed it to the right side of the page—she wept—but
she court'sied too.—Are we not, continued *Trim*, looking still
at *Susannah*—are we not like a flower of the field—a tear of
pride stole in betwixt every two tears of humiliation—else no
tongue could have described *Susannah*'s affliction—is not all
flesh grass?—'Tis clay,—'tis dirt.—They all looked directly at
the scullion,—the scullion had just been scouring a fish-
kettle.—It was not fair.——

—What is the finest face that ever man looked at!—I could
hear *Trim* talk so for ever, cried *Susannah*,—what is it! (*Susannah* laid her hand upon *Trim*'s shoulder)—but corruption?
——*Susannah* took it off.

—Now I love you for this—and 'tis this delicious mixture
within you which makes you dear creatures what you are—and
he who hates you for it——all I can say of the matter,
is—That he has either a pumkin for his head—or a pippin for his
heart,—and whenever he is dissected 'twill be found so.

CHAPTER X

WHETHER *Susannah*, by taking her hand too suddenly from off
the corporal's shoulder, (by the whisking about of her passions)——broke a little the chain of his reflections——

Or whether the corporal began to be suspicious, he had got
into the doctor's quarters, and was talking more like the chaplain than himself——

Or whether -
Or whether——for in all such cases a man of invention and
parts may with pleasure fill a couple of pages with supposi-
tions——which of all these was the cause, let the curious phy-
siologist, or the curious any body determine—'tis certain, at
least, the corporal went on thus with his harangue.

For my own part, I declare it, that out of doors, I value not
death at all:—not this . . added the corporal, snapping his
fingers,—but with an air which no one but the corporal could
have given to the sentiment.—In battle, I value death not

this . . . and let him not take me cowardly, like poor *Joe Gibbins*, in scouring his gun.—What is he? A pull of a trigger—a push of a bayonet an inch this way or that—makes the difference.—Look along the line—to the right—see! *Jack*'s down! well,—'tis worth a regiment of horse to him.—No—'tis *Dick*. Then *Jack*'s no worse.—Never mind which,—we pass on,—in hot pursuit the wound itself which brings him is not felt,—the best way is to stand up to him,—the man who flies, is in ten times more danger than the man who marches up into his jaws.—I've look'd him, added the corporal, an hundred times in the face,—and know what he is.—He's nothing, *Obadiah*, at all in the field.—But he's very frightful in a house, quoth *Obadiah*.——I never mind it myself, said *Jonathan*, upon a coach-box.—It must, in my opinion, be most natural in bed, replied *Susannah*.—And could I escape him by creeping into the worst calf's skin that ever was made into a knapsack, I would do it there—said *Trim*—but that is nature.

——Nature is nature, said *Jonathan*—And that is the reason, cried *Susannah*, I so much pity my mistress.—She will never get the better of it.—Now I pity the captain the most of any one in the family, answered *Trim*.——Madam will get ease of heart in weeping,—and the Squire in talking about it,—but my poor master will keep it all in silence to himself.—I shall hear him sigh in his bed for a whole month together, as he did for lieutenant *Le Fever*. An' please your honour, do not sigh so piteously, I would say to him as I laid besides him. I cannot help it, *Trim*, my master would say,——'tis so melancholy an accident—I cannot get it off my heart.—Your honour fears not death yourself.—I hope, *Trim*, I fear nothing, he would say, but the doing a wrong thing.——Well, he would add, whatever betides, I will take care of *Le Fever*'s boy.—And with that, like a quieting draught, his honour would fall asleep.

I like to hear *Trim*'s stories about the captain, said *Susannah*.—He is a kindly-hearted gentleman, said *Obadiah*, as ever lived.—Aye,—and as brave a one too, said the corporal, as ever stept before a platoon.—There never was a better officer in the king's army,—or a better man in God's world; for he would march up to the mouth of a cannon, though he saw the lighted match at the very touch-hole,—and yet, for all that, he has a heart as soft as a child for other people.——He would not hurt a chicken.——I would sooner, quoth *Jonathan*, drive such a gentleman for seven pounds a year—than some for eight.—

Thank thee, *Jonathan!* for thy twenty shillings,—as much, *Jonathan,* said the corporal, shaking him by the hand, as if thou hadst put the money into my own pocket.——I would serve him to the day of my death out of love. He is a friend and a brother to me,—and could I be sure my poor brother *Tom* was dead,—continued the corporal, taking out his handkerchief,—was I worth ten thousand pounds, I would leave every shilling of it to the captain.——*Trim* could not refrain from tears at this testamentary proof he gave of his affection to his master.——The whole kitchen was affected.——Do tell us this story of the poor lieutenant, said *Susannah.*——With all my heart, answered the corporal.

Susannah, the cook, *Jonathan, Obadiah,* and corporal *Trim,* formed a circle about the fire; and as soon as the scullion had shut the kitchen door,—the corporal begun.

CHAPTER XI

I AM a *Turk* if I had not as much forgot my mother, as if Nature had plaistered me up, and set me down naked upon the banks of the river *Nile,*[1] without one.——Your most obedient servant, Madam—I've cost you a great deal of trouble,—I wish it may answer;—but you have left a crack in my back,—and here's a great piece fallen off here before,—and what must I do with this foot?——I shall never reach *England* with it.

For my own part I never wonder at any thing;—and so often has my judgment deceived me in my life, that I always suspect it, right or wrong,—at least I am seldom hot upon cold subjects. For all this, I reverence truth as much as any body; and when it has slipped us, if a man will but take me by the hand, and go quietly and search for it, as for a thing we have both lost, and can neither of us do well without,—I'll go to the world's end with him:——But I hate disputes,—and therefore (bating religious points, or such as touch society) I would almost subscribe to any thing which does not choak me in the first passage, rather than be drawn into one——But I cannot bear suffocation,——and bad smells worst of all.——For which reasons, I resolved from the beginning, That if ever the army of martyrs was to be augmented,—or a new one raised,—I would have no hand in it, one way or t'other.

CHAPTER XII

——But to return to my mother.

My uncle *Toby*'s opinion, Madam, "that there could be no harm in *Cornelius Gallus,* the *Roman* prætor's lying with his wife;"——or rather the last word of that opinion,—(for it was all my mother heard of it) caught hold of her by the weak part of the whole sex:——You shall not mistake me,—I mean her curiosity,—she instantly concluded herself the subject of the conversation, and with that prepossession upon her fancy, you will readily conceive every word my father said, was accommodated either to herself, or her family concerns.

——Pray, Madam, in what street does the lady live, who would not have done the same?

From the strange mode of *Cornelius*'s death, my father had made a transition to that of *Socrates,* and was giving my uncle *Toby* an abstract of his pleading before his judges;——'twas irresistable:——not the oration of *Socrates,*—but my father's temptation to it.——He had wrote the *Life of *Socrates* himself the year before he left off trade, which, I fear, was the means of hastening him out of it;——so that no one was able to set out with so full a sail, and in so swelling a tide of heroic loftiness upon the occasion, as my father was. Not a period in *Socrates*'s oration, which closed with a shorter word than *transmigration,* or *annihilation,*—or a worse thought in the middle of it than *to be—or not to be,*—the entering upon a new and untried state of things,—or, upon a long, a profound and peaceful sleep, without dreams, without disturbance;——*That we and our children were born to die,—but neither of us born to be slaves.*——No— there I mistake; that was part of *Eleazer*'s oration, as recorded by *Josephus*[1] (*de Bell. Judaic.*)——*Eleazer* owns he had it from the philosophers of *India;* in all likelihood *Alexander* the Great, in his irruption into *India,* after he had over-run *Persia,* amongst the many things he stole,—stole that sentiment also; by which means it was carried, if not all the way by himself, (for we all know he died at *Babylon*) at least by some of his maroders,[2] into *Greece,*—from *Greece* it got to *Rome,*—from *Rome* to

---

* This book my father would never consent to publish; 'tis in manuscript, with some other tracts of his, in the family, all, or most of which will be printed in due time.

France,—and from *France* to *England:*——So things come round.——

By land carriage I can conceive no other way.——

By water the sentiment might easily have come down the *Ganges* into the *Sinus Gangeticus*, or *Bay of Bengal*, and so into the *Indian Sea*; and following the course of trade, (the way from *India* by the *Cape of Good Hope* being then unknown) might be carried with other drugs and spices up the *Red Sea* to *Joddah*, the port of *Mekka*, or else to *Tor* or *Sues*, towns at the bottom of the gulf; and from thence by karrawans[3] to *Coptos*, but three days journey distant, so down the *Nile* directly to *Alexandria*, where the SENTIMENT would be landed at the very foot of the great stair-case of the *Alexandrian* library,—and from that store-house it would be fetched.——Bless me! what a trade was driven by the learned in those days!

CHAPTER XIII

——Now my father had a way, a little like that of *Job*'s (in case there ever was such a man——if not, there's an end of the matter.——

Though, by the bye, because your learned men find some difficulty in fixing the precise æra in which so great a man lived;—whether, for instance, before or after the patriarchs, &c.—— to vote, therefore, that he never lived *at all*, is a little cruel,—'tis not doing as they would be done by— happen that as it may)——My father, I say, had a way, when things went extremely wrong with him, especially upon the first sally of his impatience,—of wondering why he was begot,—wishing himself dead;—sometimes worse:——And when the provocation ran high, and grief touched his lips with more than ordinary powers,—Sir, you scarce could have distinguished him from *Socrates* himself.——Every word would breathe the sentiments of a soul disdaining life, and careless about all its issues; for which reason, though my mother was a woman of no deep reading, yet the abstract of *Socrates*'s oration, which my father was giving my uncle *Toby*, was not altogether new to her.—She listened to it with composed intelligence, and would have done so to the end of the chapter, had not my father plunged (which he had no occasion to have done) into that part of the pleading where the great philosopher reckons up his connections, his alliances, and children; but renounces a security to be so won by working upon the passions of his judges.—"I have friends—I have relations,—I have three desolate children,"—says *Socrates*.—

——Then, cried my mother, opening the door,——you have one more, Mr. *Shandy*, than I know of.

By heaven! I have one less,—said my father, getting up and walking out of the room.

CHAPTER XIV

——They are *Socrates*'s children, said my uncle *Toby*. He has been dead a hundred years ago, replied my mother.

My uncle *Toby* was no chronologer—so not caring to advance a step but upon safe ground, he laid down his pipe deliberately upon the table, and rising up, and taking my mother most kindly by the hand, without saying another word, either good or bad, to her, he led her out after my father, that he might finish the ecclaircissment himself.

CHAPTER XV

HAD this volume been a farce, which, unless every one's life and opinions are to be looked upon as a farce as well as mine, I see no reason to suppose—the last chapter, Sir, had finished the first act of it, and then this chapter must have set off thus.

Ptr..rr..ing—twing—twang—prut—trut——'tis a cursed bad fiddle.—Do you know whether my fiddle's in tune or no?—trut..prut..—They should be *fifths*.——'Tis wickedly strung—tr...a.e.i.o.u.-twang.—The bridge is a mile too high, and the sound-post absolutely down,—else—trut . . prut—hark! 'tis not so bad a tone.—Diddle diddle, diddle diddle, diddle diddle, dum. There is nothing in playing before good judges,—but there's a man there—no—not him with the bundle under his arm—the grave man in black.—S'death! not the gentleman with the sword on.—Sir, I had rather play a *Caprichio*[1] to *Calliope*[2] herself, than draw my bow across my fiddle before that very man; and yet, I'll stake my *Cremona*[3] to a *Jew*'s trump,[4] which is the greatest musical odds that ever were laid, that I will this moment stop three hundred and fifty leagues out of tune upon my fiddle, without punishing one single nerve that belongs to him.—Twaddle diddle, tweddle diddle,—twiddle diddle,——twoddle diddle,—twuddle diddle,——pruttrut—krish—krash—krush.—I've undone you, Sir,—but you see he is no worse,—and was *Apollo* to take his fiddle after me, he can make him no better.

Diddle diddle, diddle diddle, diddle diddle—hum—dum—drum.

—Your worships and your reverences love musick—and God has made you all with good ears—and some of you play delightfully yourselves——trut-prut,—prut-trut.

O! there is—whom I could sit and hear whole days,—whose talents lie in making what he fiddles to be felt,—who inspires me with his joys and hopes, and puts the most hidden springs of my heart into motion.——If you would borrow five guineas of me, Sir,—which is generally ten guineas more than I have to spare—or you, Messrs. Apothecary and Taylor, want your bills paying,—that's your time.

CHAPTER XVI

THE first thing which entered my father's head, after affairs were a little settled in the family, and *Susannah* had got posses-sion of my mother's green sattin night-gown,—was to sit down coolly, after the example of *Xenophon*,[1] and write a TRISTRA-*pædia*, or system of education for me; collecting first for that purpose his own scattered thoughts, counsels, and notions; and binding them together, so as to form an INSTITUTE for the government of my childhood and adolescence. I was my father's last stake—he had lost my brother *Bobby* entirely,—he had lost, by his own computation, full three fourths of me—that is, he had been unfortunate in his three first great casts for me—my geniture, nose, and name,—there was but this one left; and accordingly my father gave himself up to it with as much devotion as ever my uncle *Toby* had done to his doctrine of projectils.—The difference between them was, that my uncle *Toby* drew his whole knowledge of projectils from *Nicholas Tartaglia*—My father spun his, every thread of it, out of his own brain,—or reeled and cross-twisted what all other spinners and spinsters had spun before him, that 'twas pretty near the same torture to him.

In about three years, or something more, my father had got advanced almost into the middle of his work.—Like all other writers, he met with disappointments.—He imagined he should be able to bring whatever he had to say, into so small a compass, that when it was finished and bound, it might be rolled up in my mother's hussive.[2]—Matter grows under our hands.—Let no man say,—"Come—I'll write a *duodecimo*."

My father gave himself up to it, however, with the most painful diligence, proceeding step by step in every line, with the same kind of caution and circumspection (though I cannot say upon quite so religious a principle) as was used by *John de la Casse*,[3] the lord archbishop of *Benevento*, in compassing his *Galatea*; in which his Grace of *Benevento* spent near forty years of his life; and when the thing came out, it was not of above half the size or the thickness of a *Rider*'s Almanack.[4]—How the holy man managed the affair, unless he spent the greatest part of his time in combing his whiskers, or playing at *primero* with his chaplain,—would pose any mortal not let into the true secret;—and therefore 'tis worth explaining to the world, was it only for the encouragement of those few in it, who write not so much to be fed—as to be famous.[5]

I own had *John de la Casse*, the archbishop of *Benevento*, for whose memory (notwithstanding his *Galatea*) I retain the highest veneration,—had he been, Sir, a slender clerk—of dull wit—slow parts—costive head, and so forth,—he and his *Galatea* might have jogged on together to the age of *Methusalah* for me,—the phænomenon had not been worth a parenthesis.—

But the reverse of this was the truth: *John de la Casse* was a genius of fine parts and fertile fancy; and yet with all these great advantages of nature, which should have pricked him forwards with his *Galatea*, he lay under an impuissance at the same time of advancing above a line and an half in the compass of a whole summer's day: this disability in his Grace arose from an opinion he was afflicted with,—which opinion was this,—*viz.* that whenever a Christian was writing a book (not for his private amusement, but) where his intent and purpose was *bonâ fide*, to print and publish it to the world, his first thoughts were always the temptations of the evil one.—This was the state of ordinary writers: but when a personage of venerable character and high station, either in church or state, once turned author,—he maintained, that from the very moment he took pen in hand—all the devils in hell broke out of their holes to cajole him.—'Twas

Term-time with them,—every thought, first and last, was cap-
tious;—how specious and good soever,—'twas all one;—in
whatever form or colour it presented itself to the imagination,—
'twas still a stroke of one or other of 'em levelled at him, and was
to be fenced off.—So that the life of a writer, whatever he might
fancy to the contrary, was not so much a state of *composition*, as
a state of *warfare*; and his probation in it, precisely that of any
other man militant upon earth,—both depending alike, not half
so much upon the degrees of his WIT—as his RESISTANCE.

My father was hugely pleased with this theory of *John de la
Casse*, archbishop of *Benevento*; and (had it not cramped him a
little in his creed) I believe would have given ten of the best acres
in the *Shandy* estate, to have been the broacher of it.—How far
my father actually believed in the devil, will be seen, when I
come to speak of my father's religious notions, in the progress
of this work: 'tis enough to say here, as he could not have the
honour of it, in the literal sense of the doctrine—he took up
with the allegory of it;—and would often say, especially when
his pen was a little retrograde, there was as much good meaning,
truth, and knowledge, couched under the veil of *John de la
Casse*'s parabolical representation,—as was to be found in any
one poetic fiction, or mystick record of antiquity.—Prejudice
of education, he would say, *is the devil,*—and the multitudes of
them which we suck in with our mother's milk—*are the devil
and all.*——We are haunted with them, brother *Toby*, in all our
lucubrations and researches; and was a man fool enough to
submit tamely to what they obtruded upon him,—what would
his book be? Nothing,—he would add, throwing his pen away
with a vengeance,—nothing but a farrago of the clack of nurses,
and of the nonsense of the old women (of both sexes) throughout the kingdom.

This is the best account I am determined to give of the slow
progress my father made in his *Tristra-pædia*; at which (as I
said) he was three years and something more, indefatigably at
work, and at last, had scarce compleated, by his own reckoning,
one half of his undertaking: the misfortune was, that I was all
that time totally neglected and abandoned to my mother; and
what was almost as bad, by the very delay, the first part of the
work, upon which my father had spent the most of his pains,
was rendered entirely useless,——every day a page or two
became of no consequence.——

——Certainly it was ordained as a scourge upon the pride of

human wisdom, That the wisest of us all, should thus outwit ourselves, and eternally forego our purposes in the intemperate act of pursuing them.

In short, my father was so long in all his acts of resistance,—or in other words,—he advanced so very slow with his work, and I began to live and get forwards at such a rate, that if an event had not happened,——which, when we get to it, if it can be told with decency, shall not be concealed a moment from the reader——I verily believe, I had put by my father, and left him drawing a sun-dial, for no better purpose than to be buried under ground.

CHAPTER XVII

——'Twas nothing,—I did not lose two drops of blood by it——'twas not worth calling in a surgeon, had he lived next door to us——thousands suffer by choice, what I did by accident.——Doctor *Slop* made ten times more of it, than there was occasion:——some men rise, by the art of hanging great weights upon small wires,—and I am this day (*August* the 10th, 1761) paying part of the price of this man's reputation.——O 'twould provoke a stone, to see how things are carried on in this world!——The chamber-maid had left no ******* *** under the bed:——Cannot you contrive, master, quoth *Susannah*, lifting up the sash with one hand, as she spoke, and helping me up into the window seat with the other,—cannot you manage, my dear, for a single time to **** *** ** *** ******?

I was five years old.——*Susannah* did not consider that nothing was well hung in our family,——so slap came the sash down like lightening upon us;—Nothing is left,—cried *Susannah*,—nothing is left—for me, but to run my country.——

My uncle *Toby*'s house was a much kinder sanctuary; and so *Susannah* fled to it.

CHAPTER XVIII

WHEN *Susannah* told the corporal the misadventure of the sash, with all the circumstances which attended the *murder* of me,—(as she called it)—the blood forsook his cheeks;—all accessaries in murder, being principals,—*Trim*'s conscience told him he was as much to blame as *Susannah*,—and if the doctrine had been true, my uncle *Toby* had as much of the blood-shed to answer for to heaven, as either of 'em;—so that neither reason or instinct, separate or together, could possibly have guided *Susannah*'s steps to so proper an asylum. It is in vain to leave this to the Reader's imagination:——to form any kind of hypothesis that will render these propositions feasible, he must cudgel his brains sore,—and to do it without,—he must have such brains as no reader ever had before him.——Why should I put them either to tryal or to torture? 'Tis my own affair: I'll explain it myself.

CHAPTER XIX

'TIS a pity, *Trim*, said my uncle *Toby*, resting with his hand upon the corporal's shoulder, as they both stood surveying their works,—that we have not a couple of field pieces to mount in the gorge of that new redoubt;——'twould secure the lines all along there, and make the attack on that side quite complete:——get me a couple cast, *Trim*.

Your honour shall have them, replied *Trim*, before to-morrow morning.

It was the joy of *Trim*'s heart,—nor was his fertile head ever at a loss for expedients in doing it, to supply my uncle *Toby* in his campaigns, with whatever his fancy called for; had it been his last crown, he would have sate down and hammered it into a paderero[1] to have prevented a single wish in his Master. The corporal had already,—what with cutting off the ends of my uncle *Toby*'s spouts—hacking and chiseling up the sides of his leaden gutters,—melting down his pewter shaving bason,—and going at last, like *Lewis* the fourteenth, on to the top of the church, for spare ends, &c.——he had that very campaign brought no less than eight new battering cannons, besides three demi-culverins[2] into the field; my uncle *Toby*'s demand for two more pieces for the redoubt, had set the corporal at work again; and no better resource offering, he had taken the two leaden weights from the nursery window: and as the sash pullies, when the lead was gone, were of no kind of use, he had taken them away also, to make a couple of wheels for one of their carriages.

He had dismantled every sash window in my uncle *Toby*'s house long before, in the very same way,—though not always in the same order; for sometimes the pullies had been wanted, and not the lead,—so then he began with the pullies,—and the pullies being picked out, then the lead became useless,—and so the lead went to pot too.

——A great MORAL might be picked handsomely out of this, but I have not time—'tis enough to say, wherever the demolition began, 'twas equally fatal to the sash window.

CHAPTER XX

THE corporal had not taken his measures so badly in this stroke of artilleryship, but that he might have kept the matter entirely to himself, and left *Susannah* to have sustained the whole weight of the attack, as she could;—true courage is not content with coming off so.——The corporal, whether as general or comptroller of the train,—'twas no matter,——had done that, without which, as he imagined, the misfortune could never have happened,—*at least in* Susannah's *hands*;——How would your honours have behaved?——He determined at once, not to take shelter behind *Susannah*,—but to give it; and with this resolution upon his mind, he marched upright into the parlour, to lay the whole *manœuvre* before my uncle *Toby*.

My uncle *Toby* had just then been giving *Yorick* an account of the Battle of *Steenkirk*, and of the strange conduct of count *Solmes*[1] in ordering the foot to halt, and the horse to march where it could not act; which was directly contrary to the king's commands, and proved the loss of the day.

There are incidents in some families so pat to the purpose of what is going to follow,—they are scarce exceeded by the invention of a dramatic writer;—I mean of ancient days.——

Trim, by the help of his forefinger, laid flat upon the table, and the edge of his hand striking a-cross it at right angles, made a shift to tell his story so, that priests and virgins might have listened to it;—and the story being told,—the dialogue went on as follows.

CHAPTER XXI

——I would be picquetted to death, cried the corporal, as he concluded *Susannah*'s story, before I would suffer the woman to come to any harm,—'twas my fault, an please your honour,—not hers.

Corporal *Trim*, replied my uncle *Toby*, putting on his hat which lay upon the table,——if any thing can be said to be a fault, when the service absolutely requires it should be done,—'tis I certainly who deserve the blame,——you obeyed your orders.

Had count *Solmes*, *Trim*, done the same at the battle of *Steenkirk*, said *Yorick*, drolling a little upon the corporal, who had been run over by a dragoon in the retreat,——he had saved thee;——Saved! cried *Trim*, interrupting *Yorick*, and finishing the sentence for him after his own fashion,——he had saved five battalions, an please your reverence, every soul of them:——there was *Cutts's*[1]—continued the corporal, clapping the forefinger of his right hand up on the thumb of his left, and counting round his hand,——there was *Cutts's*,——*Mackay's*——*Angus's*,——*Graham's*——and *Leven's*, all cut to pieces;——and so had the *English* life-guards too, had it not been for some regiments upon the right, who marched up boldly to their relief, and received the enemy's fire in their faces, before any one of their own platoons discharged a musket,——they'll go to heaven for it,—added *Trim*.—*Trim* is right, said my uncle *Toby*, nodding to *Yorick*,——he's perfectly right. What signified his marching the horse, continued the corporal, where the ground was so strait, and the *French* had such a nation of hedges, and copses, and ditches, and fell'd trees laid this way and that to cover them; (as they always have.)——Count *Solmes* should have sent us,——we would have fired muzzle to muzzle with them for their lives.——There was nothing to be done for the horse:——he had his foot shot off however for his pains, continued the corporal, the very next campaign at *Landen*.—Poor *Trim* got his wound there, quoth my uncle *Toby*.——'Twas owing, an please your honour, entirely to count *Solmes*,——had we drub'd them soundly at *Steenkirk*, they would not have fought us at *Landen*.——Possibly not,——*Trim*, said my uncle *Toby*;——though if they have the advantage of a wood, or you give them a moment's time to intrench themselves, they are a nation which will pop and pop for ever at you.——There is no way but to march cooly up to them,——receive their fire, and fall in upon them, pell-mell——Ding dong, added *Trim*.——Horse and foot, said my uncle *Toby*.——Helter skelter, said *Trim*.——Right and left, cried my uncle *Toby*.——Blood an' ounds, shouted the corporal;——the battle raged,——*Yorick* drew his chair a little to one side for safety, and after a moment's pause, my uncle *Toby* sinking his voice a note,—resumed the discourse as follows.

CHAPTER XXII

KING *William*, said my uncle *Toby*, addressing himself to *Yorick*, was so terribly provoked at count *Solmes* for disobeying his orders, that he would not suffer him to come into his presence for many months after.——I fear, answered *Yorick*, the squire will be as much provoked at the corporal, as the King at the count.——But 'twould be singularly hard in this case, continued he, if corporal *Trim*, who has behaved so diametrically opposite to count *Solmes*, should have the fate to be rewarded with the same disgrace;——too oft in this world, do things take that train.——I would spring a mine, cried my uncle *Toby*, rising up,——and blow up my fortifications, and my house with them, and we would perish under their ruins, ere I would stand by and see it.——*Trim* directed a slight,——but a grateful bow towards his master,——and so the chapter ends.

CHAPTER XXIII

——Then, *Yorick*, replied my uncle *Toby*, you and I will lead the way abreast,——and do you, corporal, follow a few paces behind us.——And *Susannah*, an please your honour, said *Trim*, shall be put in the rear.——'Twas an excellent disposition,—and in this order, without either drums beating, or colours flying, they marched slowly from my uncle *Toby*'s house to *Shandy-hall*.

——I wish, said *Trim*, as they entered the door,—instead of the sash-weights, I had cut off the church-spout, as I once thought to have done.—You have cut off spouts enow, replied *Yorick*.——

CHAPTER XXIV

As many pictures as have been given of my father, how like him soever in different airs and attitudes,—not one, or all of them, can ever help the reader to any kind of preconception of how my father would think, speak, or act, upon any untried occasion or occurrence of life.—There was that infinitude of oddities in him, and of chances along with it, by which handle he would take a thing,—it baffled, Sir, all calculations.——The truth was, his road lay so very far on one side, from that wherein most men travelled,—that every object before him presented a face and section of itself to his eye, altogether different from the plan and elevation of it seen by the rest of mankind.—In other words, 'twas a different object,—and in course was differently considered:

This is the true reason, that my dear *Jenny* and I, as well as all the world besides us, have such eternal squabbles about nothing.—She looks at her outside,—I, at her in—. How is it possible we should agree about her value?

CHAPTER XXV

'TIS a point settled,—and I mention it for the comfort of *Confucius*, who is apt to get entangled in telling a plain story —that provided he keeps along the line of his story,—he may go backwards and forwards as he will,—'tis still held to be no digression.

This being premised, I take the benefit of the *act of going backwards* myself.

CHAPTER XXVI

FIFTY thousand pannier loads of devils—(not of the Archbishop of *Benevento*'s—I mean of *Rabelais*'s devils) with their tails chopped off by their rumps, could not have made so diabolical a scream of it, as I did—when the accident befell me: it summoned up my mother instantly into the nursery,—so that

* Mr. *Shandy* is supposed to mean ***** *** ***, Esq; member for ******,——and not the *Chinese* Legislator.

Susannah had but just time to make her escape down the back stairs, as my mother came up the fore.

Now, though I was old enough to have told the story myself,—and young enough, I hope, to have done it without malignity; yet *Susannah*, in passing by the kitchen, for fear of accidents, had left it in short-hand with the cook—the cook had told it with a commentary to *Jonathan*, and *Jonathan* to *Obadiah*; so that by the time my father had rung the bell half a dozen times, to know what was the matter above,—was *Obadiah* enabled to give him a particular account of it, just as it had happened.—I thought as much, said my father, tucking up his night-gown;—and so walked up stairs.

One would imagine from this——(though for my own part I somewhat question it)—that my father before that time, had actually wrote that remarkable chapter in the *Tristrapædia*, which to me is the most original and entertaining one in the whole book;—and that is the *chapter upon sash-windows*, with a bitter *Philippick* at the end of it, upon the forgetfulness of chamber-maids.—I have but two reasons for thinking otherwise.

First, Had the matter been taken into consideration, before the event happened, my father certainly would have nailed up the sash-window for good an' all;—which, considering with what difficulty he composed books,—he might have done with ten times less trouble, than he could have wrote the chapter: this argument I foresee holds good against his writing the chapter, even after the event; but 'tis obviated under the second reason, which I have the honour to offer to the world in support of my opinion, that my father did not write the chapter upon sash-windows and chamber-pots, at the time supposed,—and it is this.

——That, in order to render the *Tristrapædia* complete,—I wrote the chapter myself.

CHAPTER XXVII

My father put on his spectacles—looked,—took them off,—put them into the case—all in less than a statutable minute; and without opening his lips, turned about, and walked precipitately down stairs: my mother imagined he had stepped down for lint and basilicon; but seeing him return with a couple of folios under his arm, and *Obadiah* following him with a large reading desk, she took it for granted 'twas an herbal, and so drew him a chair to the bed side, that he might consult upon the case at his ease.

—If it be but right done,—said my father, turning to the Section—*de sede vel subjecto circumcisionis*,[1]——for he had brought up *Spencer de Legibus Hebræorum Ritualibus*[2]—and *Maimonides*,[3] in order to confront and examine us altogether.——

——If it be but right done, quoth he:—Only tell us, cried my mother, interrupting him, what herbs.——For that, replied my father, you must send for Dr. *Slop*.

My mother went down, and my father went on, reading the section as follows.

* * * * * * * * * *
* * * * * * * * * *
* * * * * ——Very well,—said my father,
* * * * * * * * * *
* * * * * * * * * *

****—nay, if it has that convenience——and so without stopping a moment to settle it first in his mind, whether the *Jews* had it from the *Egyptians*, or the *Egyptians* from the *Jews*,—he rose up, and rubbing his forehead two or three times across with the palm of his hand, in the manner we rub out the footsteps of care, when evil has trod lighter upon us than we foreboded,—he shut the book, and walked down stairs.—Nay, said he, mentioning the name of a different great nation upon every step as he set his foot upon it—if the EGYPTIANS,—the SYRIANS,—the PHOENICIANS,—the ARABIANS,—the CAPADOCIANS,——if the COLCHI,[4] and TROGLODYTES did it——if SOLON and PYTHAGORAS submitted,—what is TRISTRAM?——Who am I, that I should fret or fume one moment about the matter?

CHAPTER XXVIII

DEAR *Yorick*, said my father smiling, (for *Yorick* had broke his rank with my uncle *Toby* in coming through the narrow entry, and so had stept first into the parlour)—this *Tristram* of ours, I find, comes very hardly by all his religious rites.—Never was the son of *Jew, Christian, Turk*, or *Infidel* initiated into them in so oblique and slovenly a manner.—But he is no worse, I trust, said *Yorick*.—There has been certainly, continued my father, the duce and all to do in some part or other of the ecliptic, when this offspring of mine was formed.—That, you are a better judge of than I, replied *Yorick*.—Astrologers, quoth my father, know better than us both:—the trine and sextil aspects[1] have jumped awry,—or the opposite of their ascendents have not hit it, as they should,—or the lords of the genitures (as they call them) have been at *bo-peep*,[2]—or something has been wrong above, or below with us.

'Tis possible, answered *Yorick*.—But is the child, cried my uncle *Toby*, the worse?—The *Troglodytes* say not, replied my father.—And your theologists, *Yorick*, tell us—Theologically? said *Yorick*,—or speaking after the manner of * apothecaries?— † statesmen?—or ‡ washer-women?

——I'm not sure, replied my father,—but they tell us, brother *Toby*, he's the better for it.——Provided, said *Yorick*, you travel him into *Egypt*.——Of that, answered my father, he will have the advantage, when he sees the *Pyramids*.——

Now every word of this, quoth my uncle *Toby*, is *Arabick* to me.——I wish, said *Yorick*, 'twas so, to half the world.

—*ILUS, continued my father, circumcised his whole army one morning.—Not without a court martial? cried my uncle *Toby*.——Though the learned, continued he, taking no notice of my uncle *Toby*'s remark, but turning to *Yorick*,—are greatly divided still who *Ilus* was;—some say *Saturn*;—some the supream Being;—others, no more than a brigadier general under *Pharoah-neco*.——Let him be who he will, said my uncle *Toby*, I know not by what article of war he could justify it.

The controvertists, answered my father, assign two and twenty different reasons for it:—others indeed, who have drawn their pens on the opposite side of the question, have shewn the world the futility of the greatest part of them.—But then again, our best polemic divines—I wish there was not a polemic divine, said *Yorick*, in the kingdom;—one ounce of practical divinity—is worth a painted ship load of all their reverences have imported these fifty years.—Pray, Mr. *Yorick*, quoth my uncle *Toby*,—do tell me what a polemic divine is.

---

* Χαλεπῆς νόσου, καὶ δυσιάτου ἀπαλλαγὴ, ἣν ἄνθρακα καλοῦσιν.

PHILO.[3]

† Τὰ τεμνόμενα τῶν ἐθνῶν πολυγονώτατα, καὶ πολυανθρωπότατα εἶναι.[4]
‡ Καθαφιότητος εινεκεν.   BOCHART.[5]
* Ὁ Ιλος, τὰ ἀιδοῖα πεφιτέμνεται, ταυτὸ ποιῆσαι καὶ τοὺς ἅμ' αυτῷ συμμάχους καταναγκάσας.   SANCHUNIATHO.[6]

———The best description, captain *Shandy*, I have ever read, is of a couple of 'em, replied *Yorick*, in the account of the battle fought single hands betwixt *Gymnast* and captain *Tripet*;[7] which I have in my pocket.———I beg I may hear it, quoth my uncle *Toby* earnestly.—You shall, said *Yorick*.—And as the corporal is waiting for me at the door,—and I know the description of a battle, will do the poor fellow more good than his supper,—I beg, brother, you'll give him leave to come in.— With all my soul, said my father.———*Trim* came in, erect and happy as an emperour; and having shut the door, *Yorick* took a book from his right-hand coat pocket, and read, or pretended to read, as follows.

CHAPTER XXIX

———"which words being heard by all the soldiers which were there, divers of them being inwardly terrified, did shrink back and make room for the assailant: all this did *Gymnast* very well remark and consider; and therefore, making as if he would have alighted from off his horse, as he was poising himself on the mounting side, he most nimbly (with his short sword by his thigh) shifting his feet in the stirrup and performing the stirrup-leather feat, whereby, after the inclining of his body down-wards, he forthwith launched himself aloft into the air, and placed both his feet together upon the saddle, standing upright, with his back turned towards his horse's head,—Now (said he) my case goes forward. Then suddenly in the same posture wherein he was, he fetched a gambol upon one foot, and turning to the left-hand, failed not to carry his body perfectly round, just into his former position, without missing one jot.———Ha! said *Tripet*, I will not do that at this time,—and not without cause. Well, said *Gymnast*, I have failed,—I will undo this leap; then with a marvellous strength and agility, turning towards the right-hand, he fetched another frisking gambol as before; which done, he set his right-hand thumb upon the bow of the saddle, raised himself up, and sprung into the air, poising and uphold-ing his whole weight upon the muscle and nerve of the said thumb, and so turned and whirled himself about three times: at the fourth, reversing his body and overturning it upside-down, and foreside back, without *touching any thing*, he brought

himself betwixt the horse's two ears, and then giving himself a
jerking swing, he seated himself upon the crupper——"
    (This can't be fighting, said my uncle *Toby*.——The corporal
shook his head at it.——Have patience, said *Yorick*.)
    "Then (*Tripet*) pass'd his right leg over his saddle, and placed
himself *en croup*.¹——But, said he, 'twere better for me to get into
the saddle; then putting the thumbs of both hands upon the
crupper before him, and thereupon leaning himself, as upon the
only supporters of his body, he incontinently turned heels over
head in the air, and straight found himself betwixt the bow of
the saddle in a tolerable seat; then springing into the air with a
summerset, he turned him about like a wind-mill, and made
above a hundred frisks, turns and demi-pommadas."²——Good
God! cried *Trim*, losing all patience,—one home thrust of a
bayonet is worth it all.——I think so too, replied *Yorick*.——
——I am of a contrary opinion, quoth my father.

CHAPTER XXX

——No,—I think I have advanced nothing, replied my
father, making answer to a question which *Yorick* had taken the
liberty to put to him,—I have advanced nothing in the *Tristra-
pædia*, but what is as clear as any one proposition in *Euclid*.——
Reach me, *Trim*, that book from off the scrutoir:¹——it has oft
times been in my mind, continued my father, to have read it
over both to you, *Yorick*, and to my brother *Toby*, and I think it
a little unfriendly in myself, in not having done it long ago:
——shall we have a short chapter or two now,—and a chapter
or two hereafter, as occasions serve; and so on, till we get
through the whole? My uncle *Toby* and *Yorick* made the
obeisance which was proper; and the corporal, though he was
not included in the compliment, laid his hand upon his breast,
and made his bow at the same time.——The company smiled.
Trim, quoth my father, has paid the full price for staying out
the *entertainment*.——He did not seem to relish the play,
replied *Yorick*.——'Twas a Tom-fool-battle, an' please your
reverence, of captain *Tripet*'s and that other officer, making so
many summersets, as they advanced;——the *French* come on
capering now and then in that way,—but not quite so much.
    My uncle *Toby* never felt the consciousness of his existence
with more complacency than what the corporal's, and his own

reflections, made him do at that moment;——he lighted his pipe,——*Yorick* drew his chair closer to the table,—*Trim* snuff'd the candle,—my father stir'd up the fire,—took up the book,—cough'd twice, and begun.

CHAPTER XXXI

THE first thirty pages, said my father, turning over the leaves,— are a little dry; and as they are not closely connected with the subject,——for the present we'll pass them by: 'tis a prefatory introduction, continued my father, or an introductory preface (for I am not determined which name to give it) upon political or civil government; the foundation of which being laid in the first conjunction betwixt male and female, for procreation of the species——I was insensibly led into it.——'Twas natural, said *Yorick*.

The original of society, continued my father, I'm satisfied is, what *Politian*[1] tells us, *i. e.* merely conjugal; and nothing more than the getting together of one man and one woman;—to which, (according to *Hesiod*)[2] the philosopher adds a servant: ——but supposing in the first beginning there were no men servants born——he lays the foundation of it, in a man,—a woman—and a bull.——I believe 'tis an ox, quoth *Yorick*, quoting the passage (οἶκον μὲν πρώτιστα, γυναῖκά τε, βοῦν τ' ἀροτῆρα.)——A bull must have given more trouble than his head was worth.——But there is a better reason still, said my father, (dipping his pen into his ink) for, the ox being the most patient of animals, and the most useful withal in tilling the ground for their nourishment,—was the properest instrument, and emblem too, for the new joined couple, that the creation could have associated with them.—And there is a stronger reason, added my uncle *Toby*, than them all for the ox.—My father had not power to take his pen out of his ink-horn, till he had heard my uncle *Toby*'s reason.—For when the ground was tilled, said my uncle *Toby*, and made worth inclosing, then they began to secure it by walls and ditches, which was the origin of fortification.——True, true; dear *Toby*, cried my father, strik-ing out the bull, and putting the ox in his place.

My father gave *Trim* a nod, to snuff the candle, and resumed his discourse.

——I enter upon this speculation, said my father carelessly,

and half shutting the book, as he went on,—merely to shew the foundation of the natural relation between a father and his child; the right and jurisdiction over whom he acquires these several ways—

1st, by marriage.

2d, by adoption.

3d, by legitimation.

And 4th, by procreation; all which I consider in their order.

I lay a slight stress upon one of them; replied *Yorick*——the act, especially where it ends there, in my opinion lays as little obligation upon the child, as it conveys power to the father.— You are wrong,—said my father argutely, and for this plain reason *.—I own, added my father, that the offspring, upon this account, is not so under the power and jurisdiction of the *mother*.—But the reason, replied *Yorick*, equally holds good for her.——She is under authority herself, said my father:—and besides, continued my father, nodding his head and laying his finger upon the side of his nose, as he assigned his reason,—*she is not the principal agent*, Yorick.—In what? quoth my uncle *Toby*, stopping his pipe.—Though by all means, added my father (not attending to my uncle *Toby*) "*The son ought to pay her respect*," as you may read, *Yorick*, at large in the first book of the Institutes of *Justinian*, at the eleventh title and the tenth section.—I can read it as well, replied *Yorick*, in the Catechism.

CHAPTER XXXII

*T*RIM can repeat every word of it by heart, quoth my uncle *Toby*.—Pugh! said my father, not caring to be interrupted with *Trim*'s saying his Catechism. He can upon my honour, replied my uncle *Toby*.—Ask him, Mr. *Yorick*, any question you please.——

—The fifth Commandment, *Trim*—said *Yorick*, speaking mildly, and with a gentle nod, as to a modest Catechumen. The corporal stood silent.—You don't ask him right, said my uncle *Toby*, raising his voice, and giving it rapidly like the word of command;——The fifth——cried my uncle *Toby*.—I must begin with the first, an' please your honour, said the corporal.——

—*Yorick* could not forbear smiling.—Your reverence does not consider, said the corporal, shouldering his stick like a musket, and marching into the middle of the room, to illustrate his position,—that 'tis exactly the same thing, as doing one's exercise in the field.—

"*Join your right hand to your firelock,*" cried the corporal, giving the word of command, and performing the motion.—

"*Poise your firelock,*" cried the corporal, doing the duty still of both adjutant and private man.—

"*Rest your firelock;*"—one motion, an' please your reverence, you see leads into another.—If his honour will begin but with the *first*—

THE FIRST—cried my uncle *Toby*, setting his hand upon his side— * .

THE SECOND—cried my uncle *Toby*, waving his tobacco-pipe, as he would have done his sword at the head of a regiment.—The corporal went through his *manual* with exactness; and having *honoured his father and mother*, made a low bow, and fell back to the side of the room.

Every thing in this world, said my father, is big with jest,—and has wit in it, and instruction too,—if we can but find it out.[1]

—Here is the *scaffold work* of INSTRUCTION, its true point of folly, without the BUILDING behind it.—

—Here is the glass for pedagogues, preceptors, tutors, governours, gerund-grinders and bear-leaders[2] to view themselves in, in their true dimensions.—

Oh! there is a husk and shell, *Yorick,* which grows up with learning, which their unskilfulness knows not how to fling away!

—SCIENCES MAY BE LEARNED BY ROTE, BUT WISDOM NOT.

Yorick thought my father inspired.—I will enter into obligations this moment, said my father, to lay out all my aunt *Dinah*'s legacy, in charitable uses (of which, by the bye, my father had no high opinion) if the corporal has any one determinate idea annexed to any one word he has repeated.—Prythee, *Trim*, quoth my father, turning round to him,—What do'st thou mean, by "*honouring thy father and mother?*"

Allowing them, an' please your honour, three halfpence a day out of my pay, when they grew old.—And didst thou do that, *Trim?* said *Yorick*.—He did indeed, replied my uncle *Toby*.— Then, *Trim*, said *Yorick*, springing out of his chair, and taking the corporal by the hand, thou art the best commentator upon that part of the *Decalogue*; and I honour thee more for it, corporal *Trim*, than if thou hadst had a hand in the *Talmud* itself.

CHAPTER XXXIII

O BLESSED health! cried my father, making an exclamation, as he turned over the leaves to the next chapter,—thou art above all gold and treasure; 'tis thou who enlargest the soul,—and openest all it's powers to receive instruction and to relish virtue.—He that has thee, has little more to wish for;—and he that is so wretched as to want thee,—wants every thing with thee.

I have concentrated all that can be said upon this important head, said my father, into a very little room, therefore we'll read the chapter quite thro'.

My father read as follows.

"The whole secret of health depending upon the due contention for mastery betwixt the radical heat and the radical moisture"—You have proved that matter of fact, I suppose, above, said *Yorick*. Sufficiently, replied my father.

In saying this, my father shut the book,—not as if he resolved to read no more of it, for he kept his forefinger in the chapter: ——nor pettishly,—for he shut the book slowly; his thumb resting, when he had done it, upon the upper-side of the cover, as his three fingers supported the lower-side of it, without the least compressive violence.——

I have demonstrated the truth of that point, quoth my father, nodding to *Yorick*, most sufficiently in the preceding chapter.

Now could the man in the moon be told, that a man in the earth had wrote a chapter, sufficiently demonstrating, That the secret of all health depended upon the due contention for mastery betwixt the *radical heat* and the *radical moisture*,—and that he had managed the point so well, that there was not one single word wet or dry upon radical heat or radical moisture, throughout the whole chapter,—or a single syllable in it, *pro* or *con*, directly or indirectly, upon the contention betwixt these two powers in any part of the animal œconomy——

"O thou eternal maker of all beings!"—he would cry,

striking his breast with his right hand, (in case he had one)—
"Thou whose power and goodness can enlarge the faculties of
thy creatures to this infinite degree of excellence and
perfection,—What have we MOONITES done?"

CHAPTER XXXIV

WITH two strokes, the one at *Hippocrates*, the other at Lord
Verulam,[1] did my father atchieve it.

The stroke at the prince of physicians, with which he began,
was no more than a short insult upon his sorrowful complaint of
the *Ars longa*,—and *Vita brevis*.[2]——Life short, cried my
father,—and the art of healing tedious! And who are we to
thank for both, the one and the other, but the ignorance of
quacks themselves,—and the stage-loads of chymical nostrums,
and peripatetic lumber, with which in all ages, they have first
flatter'd the world, and at last deceived it.

——O my lord *Verulam!* cried my father, turning from
Hippocrates, and making his second stroke at him, as the principal of nostrum-mongers, and the fittest to be made an example
of to the rest,——What shall I say to thee, my great lord
Verulam? What shall I say to thy internal spirit,—thy opium,—
thy salt-petre,——thy greasy unctions,—thy daily purges,—
thy nightly glisters, and succedaneums?

——My father was never at a loss what to say to any man,
upon any subject; and had the least occasion for the exordium of
any man breathing: how he dealt with his lordship's opinion,
——you shall see;——but when—I know not:——we must
first see what his lordship's opinion was.

CHAPTER XXXV

"THE two great causes, which conspire with each other to
shorten life, says lord *Verulam*, are first——

"The internal spirit, which like a gentle flame, wastes the
body down to death:—And secondly, the external air, that
parches the body up to ashes:—which two enemies attacking us
on both sides of our bodies together, at length destroy our
organs, and render them unfit to carry on the functions of life."

This being the state of the case; the road to Longevity was

plain; nothing more being required, says his lordship, but to repair the waste committed by the internal spirit, by making the substance of it more thick and dense, by a regular course of opiates on one side, and by refrigerating the heat of it on the other, by three grains and a half of salt-petre every morning before you got up.——

Still this frame of ours was left exposed to the inimical assaults of the air without;—but this was fenced off again by a course of greasy unctions, which so fully saturated the pores of the skin, that no spicula could enter;——nor could any one get out. ——This put a stop to all perspiration, sensible and insensible, which being the cause of so many scurvy distempers—a course of glisters was requisite to carry off redundant humours,—and render the system compleat.

What my father had to say to my lord of *Verulam*'s opiates, his salt-petre, and greasy unctions and glisters, you shall read,— but not to day—or to morrow: time presses upon me,—my reader is impatient—I must get forwards.——You shall read the chapter at your leisure, (if you chuse it) as soon as ever the *Tristrapædia* is published.——

Sufficeth it at present, to say, my father levelled the hypothesis with the ground, and in doing that, the learned know, he built up and established his own.——

CHAPTER XXXVI

THE whole secret of health, said my father, beginning the sentence again, depending evidently upon the due contention betwixt the radical heat and radical moisture within us;—the least imaginable skill had been sufficient to have maintained it, had not the school-men confounded the task, merely (as *Van Helmont*,[1] the famous chymist, has proved) by all along mistaking the radical moisture for the tallow and fat of animal bodies.

Now the radical moisture is not the tallow or fat of animals, but an oily and balsamous substance; for the fat and tallow, as also the phlegm or watery parts are cold; whereas the oily and balsamous parts are of a lively heat and spirit, which accounts for the observation of *Aristotle*, "*Quod omne animal post coitum est* triste."[2]

Now it is certain, that the radical heat lives in the radical moisture, but whether *vice versâ*, is a doubt: however, when the one decays, the other decays also; and then is produced, either an unnatural heat, which causes an unnatural dryness——or an unnatural moisture, which causes dropsies.——So that if a child, as he grows up, can but be taught to avoid running into fire or water, as either of 'em threaten his destruction,——'twill be all that is needful to be done upon that head.——

CHAPTER XXXVII

THE description of the siege of *Jerico*[1] itself, could not have engaged the attention of my uncle *Toby* more powerfully than the last chapter;—his eyes were fixed upon my father, throughout it;—he never mentioned radical heat and radical moisture, but my uncle *Toby* took his pipe out of his mouth, and shook his head; and as soon as the chapter was finished, he beckoned to the corporal to come close to his chair, to ask him the following question,—*aside.*——* * * * * * * * * * * * * * * * * * * *. It was at the siege of *Limerick*,[2] an' please your honour, replied the corporal, making a bow.

The poor fellow and I, quoth my uncle *Toby*, addressing himself to my father, were scarce able to crawl out of our tents, at the time the siege of *Limerick* was raised, upon the very account you mention.——Now what can have got into that precious noddle of thine, my dear brother *Toby?* cried my father, mentally.——By Heaven! continued he, communing still with himself, it would puzzle an *Œdipus*[3] to bring it in point.——

I believe, an' please your honour, quoth the corporal, that if it had not been for the quantity of brandy we set fire to every night, and the claret and cinnamon with which I plyed your honour off;—And the geneva, *Trim*, added my uncle *Toby*, which did us more good than all——I verily believe, continued the corporal, we had both, an' please your honour, left our lives in the trenches, and been buried in them too.——The noblest grave, corporal! cried my uncle *Toby*, his eyes sparkling as he spoke, that a soldier could wish to lie down in.——But a pitiful death for him! an' please your honour, replied the corporal.

All this was as much *Arabick* to my father, as the rites of the *Colchi* and *Troglodites* had been before to my uncle *Toby*; my father could not determine whether he was to frown or smile.——

My uncle *Toby*, turning to *Yorick*, resumed the case at *Limerick*, more intelligibly than he had begun it,—and so settled the point for my father at once.

CHAPTER XXXVIII

It was undoubtedly, said my uncle *Toby*, a great happiness for myself and the corporal, that we had all along a burning fever, attended with a most raging thirst, during the whole five and twenty days the flux was upon us in the camp; otherwise what my brother calls the radical moisture, must, as I conceive it, inevitably have got the better.——My father drew in his lungs top-full of air, and looking up, blew it forth again, as slowly as he possibly could.——

——It was heaven's mercy to us, continued my uncle *Toby*, which put it into the corporal's head to maintain that due contention betwixt the radical heat and the radical moisture, by reinforceing the fever, as he did all along, with hot wine and spices; whereby the corporal kept up (as it were) a continual firing, so that the radical heat stood its ground from the beginning to the end, and was a fair match for the moisture, terrible as it was.——Upon my honour, added my uncle *Toby*, you might have heard the contention within our bodies, brother *Shandy*, twenty toises.—If there was no firing, said *Yorick*.

Well—said my father, with a full aspiration, and pausing a while after the word——Was I a judge, and the laws of the country which made me one permitted it, I would condemn some of the worst malefactors, provided they had had their clergy ——————— *Yorick* foreseeing the sentence was likely to end with no sort of mercy, laid his hand upon my father's breast, and begged he would respite it for a few minutes, till he asked the corporal a question.——Prithee, *Trim*, said *Yorick*, without staying for my father's leave,—tell us honestly—what is thy opinion concerning this self-same radical heat and radical moisture?

With humble submission to his honour's better judgment, quoth the corporal, making a bow to my uncle *Toby*—Speak thy opinion freely, corporal, said my uncle *Toby*.—The poor fellow is my servant,—not my slave,—added my uncle *Toby*, turning to my father.——

The corporal put his hat under his left arm, and with his stick hanging upon the wrist of it, by a black thong split into a tassel about the knot, he marched up to the ground where he had performed his catechism; then touching his under jaw with the thumb and fingers of his right hand before he opened his mouth,——he delivered his notion thus.

CHAPTER XXXIX

JUST as the corporal was humming, to begin—in waddled Dr. Slop.—'Tis not two-pence matter—the corporal shall go on in the next chapter, let who will come in.——

Well, my good doctor, cried my father sportively, for the transitions of his passions were unaccountably sudden,—and what has this whelp of mine to say to the matter?——

Had my father been asking after the amputation of the tail of a puppy-dog—he could not have done it in a more careless air: the system which Dr. Slop had laid down, to treat the accident by, no way allowed of such a mode of enquiry.—He sat down.

Pray, Sir, quoth my uncle Toby, in a manner which could not go unanswered,—in what condition is the boy?—'Twill end in a phimosis,[1] replied Dr. Slop.

I am no wiser than I was, quoth my uncle Toby,—returning his pipe into his mouth.——Then let the corporal go on, said my father, with his medical lecture.—The corporal made a bow to his old friend, Dr. Slop, and then delivered his opinion concerning radical heat and radical moisture, in the following words.

CHAPTER XL

THE city of Limerick, the siege of which was begun under his majesty king William himself, the year after I went into the army—lies, an' please your honours, in the middle of a devilish wet, swampy country.—'Tis quite surrounded, said my uncle Toby, with the Shannon, and is, by its situation, one of the strongest fortified places in Ireland.——

I think this is a new fashion, quoth Dr. Slop, of beginning a medical lecture.—'Tis all true, answered Trim.—Then I wish the faculty would follow the cut of it, said Yorick.—'Tis all cut through, an' please your reverence, said the corporal, with drains and bogs; and besides, there was such a quantity of rain fell during the siege, the whole country was like a puddle,— 'twas that, and nothing else, which brought on the flux, and which had like to have killed both his honour and myself; now there was no such thing, after the first ten days, continued the corporal, for a soldier to lie dry in his tent, without cutting a ditch round it, to draw off the water;—nor was that enough, for those who could afford it, as his honour could, without setting fire every night to a pewter dish full of brandy, which took off the damp of the air, and made the inside of the tent as warm as a stove.——

And what conclusion dost thou draw, Corporal *Trim*, cried my father, from all these premises?

I infer, an' please your worship, replied *Trim*, that the radical moisture is nothing in the world but ditch-water—and that the radical heat, of those who can go to the expence of it, is burnt brandy—the radical heat and moisture of a private man, an' please your honours, is nothing but ditch-water—and a dram of geneva——and give us but enough of it, with a pipe of tobacco, to give us spirits, and drive away the vapours—we know not what it is to fear death.

I am at a loss, Captain *Shandy*, quoth Doctor *Slop*, to determine in which branch of learning your servant shines most, whether in physiology, or divinity.—*Slop* had not forgot *Trim*'s comment upon the sermon.—

It is but an hour ago, replied *Yorick*, since the corporal was examined in the latter, and pass'd muster with great honour.——

The radical heat and moisture, quoth Doctor *Slop*, turning to my father, you must know, is the basis and foundation of our being,—as the root of a tree is the source and principle of its vegetation.—It is inherent in the seeds of all animals, and may be preserved sundry ways, but principally in my opinion by *consubstantials*,[1] *impriments*, and *occludents*.——Now this poor fellow, continued Dr. *Slop*, pointing to the corporal, has had the misfortune to have heard some superficial emperic discourse upon this nice point.——That he has,—said my father.——Very likely, said my uncle.—I'm sure of it—quoth *Yorick*.——

CHAPTER XLI

DOCTOR *Slop* being called out to look at a cataplasm he had ordered, it gave my father an opportunity of going on with another chapter in the *Tristra-pædia*.——Come! chear up, my lads; I'll shew you land———for when we have tugged through that chapter, the book shall not be opened again this twelve-month.—Huzza!—

CHAPTER XLII

——FIVE years with a bib under his chin;
   Four years in travelling from Christ-cross-row to *Malachi*;[1]
   A year and a half in learning to write his own name;
   Seven long years and more τυπτω-ing it,[2] at Greek and Latin;
   Four years at his *probations* and his *negations*—the fine statue still lying in the middle of the marble block,—and nothing done, but his tools sharpened to hew it out!—'Tis a piteous delay!—Was not the great *Julius Scaliger*[3] within an ace of never getting his tools sharpened at all?———Forty-four years old was he before he could manage his Greek;—and *Peter Damianus*,[4] lord bishop of *Ostia*, as all the world knows, could not so much as read, when he was of man's estate.—And *Baldus*[5] himself, as eminent as he turned out after, entered upon the law so late in life, that every body imagined he intended to be an advocate in the other world: no wonder, when *Eudamidas*,[6] the son of *Archidamas*, heard *Xenocrates* at seventy-five disputing about *wisdom*, that he asked gravely,—*If the old man be yet disputing and enquiring concerning wisdom,—what time will he have to make use of it?*

Yorick listened to my father with great attention; there was a seasoning of wisdom unaccountably mixed up with his strangest whims, and he had sometimes such illuminations in the darkest of his eclipses, as almost attoned for them:—be wary, Sir, when you imitate him.

I am convinced, *Yorick*, continued my father, half reading and half discoursing, that there is a North west passage to the intellectual world; and that the soul of man has shorter ways of going to work, in furnishing itself with knowledge and instruction, than we generally take with it.——But alack! all fields have not a river or a spring running besides them;—every child, *Yorick!* has not a parent to point it out.

——The whole entirely depends, added my father, in a low voice, upon the *auxiliary verbs*, Mr. *Yorick.*

Had *Yorick* trod upon *Virgil's* snake,[7] he could not have looked more surprised.—I am surprised too, cried my father, observing it,—and I reckon it as one of the greatest calamities which ever befell the republick of letters, That those who have been entrusted with the education of our children, and whose business it was to open their minds, and stock them early with ideas, in order to set the imagination loose upon them, have made so little use of the auxiliary verbs in doing it, as they have done——So that, except *Raymond Lullius*,[8] and the elder *Pelegrini*,[9] the last of which arrived to such perfection in the use of 'em, with his topics, that in a few lessons, he could teach a young gentleman to discourse with plausibility upon any subject, *pro* and *con*, and to say and write all that could be spoken or written concerning it, without blotting a word, to the admiration of all who beheld him.—I should be glad, said *Yorick,* interrupting my father, to be made to comprehend this matter. You shall, said my father.

The highest stretch of improvement a single word is capable of, is a high metaphor,——for which, in my opinion, the idea is generally the worse, and not the better;——but be that as it may,—when the mind has done that with it—there is an end,—the mind and the idea are at rest,—until a second idea enters;——and so on.

Now the use of the *Auxiliaries* is, at once to set the soul a going by herself upon the materials as they are brought her; and by the versability of this great engine, round which they are twisted, to open new tracks of enquiry, and make every idea engender millions.

You excite my curiosity greatly, said *Yorick.*

For my own part, quoth my uncle *Toby,* I have given it up.——The *Danes*,[10] an' please your honour, quoth the corporal, who were on the left at the siege of *Limerick*, were all auxiliaries.——And very good ones, said my uncle *Toby.*—And your honour rou'd with them, captains with captains.—Very well, said the corporal.[11]—But the auxiliaries, my brother is talking about, answered my uncle *Toby*,—I conceive to be different things.——

——You do? said my father rising up.

CHAPTER XLIII

My father took a single turn across the room, then sat down and finished the chapter.

The verbs auxiliary we are concerned in here, continued my father, are, *am*; *was*; *have*; *had*; *do*; *did*; *make*; *made*; *suffer*; *shall*; *should*; *will*; *would*; *can*; *could*; *owe*; *ought*; *used*; or *is wont*.—And these varied with tenses, *present, past, future,* and conjugated with the verb *see*,—or with these questions added to them;—*Is it? Was it? Will it be? Would it be? May it be? Might it be?* And these again put negatively, *Is it not? Was it not? Ought it not?*—Or affirmatively,—*It is; It was; It ought to be.* Or chronologically,—*Has it been always? Lately? How long ago?*—Or hypothetically,—*If it was; If it was not?* What would follow?——If the *French* should beat the *English?* If the *Sun* go out of the *Zodiac?*[1]

Now, by the right use and application of these, continued my father, in which a child's memory should be exercised, there is no one idea can enter his brain how barren soever, but a magazine of conceptions and conclusions may be drawn forth from it.——Did'st thou ever see a white bear?[2] cried my father, turning his head round to *Trim*, who stood at the back of his chair:—No, an' please your honour, replied the corporal.—— But thou could'st discourse about one, *Trim*, said my father, in case of need?——How is it possible, brother, quoth my uncle *Toby*, if the corporal never saw one?——'Tis the fact I want; replied my father,—and the possibility of it, is as follows.

A WHITE BEAR! Very well. Have I ever seen one? Might I ever have seen one? Am I ever to see one? Ought I ever to have seen one? Or can I ever see one?

Would I had seen a white bear? (for how can I imagine it?)

If I should see a white bear, what should I say? If I should never see a white bear, what then?

If I never have, can, must or shall see a white bear alive; have I ever seen the skin of one? Did I ever see one painted?—described? Have I never dreamed of one?

Did my father, mother, uncle, aunt, brothers or sisters, ever see a white bear? What would they give? How would they behave? How would the white bear have behaved? Is he wild? Tame? Terrible? Rough? Smooth?

—Is the white bear worth seeing?—

—Is there no sin in it?—
Is it better than a BLACK ONE?

END of the FIFTH VOLUME.

THE
L I F E
A N D
O P I N I O N S
O F
TRISTRAM SHANDY,
G E N T L E M A N.

Dixero si quid fortè jocosius, hoc mihi juris
Cum venia dabis.   Hor.

-----*Si quis calumnietur levius esse quam decet theolo-*
gum, aut mordacius quam deceat Christianum----
non Ego, sed Democritus dixit.----

Erasmus.

VOL. VI.

L O N D O N:
Printed for T. Becket and P. A. Dehondt,
in the Strand. MDCCLXII.

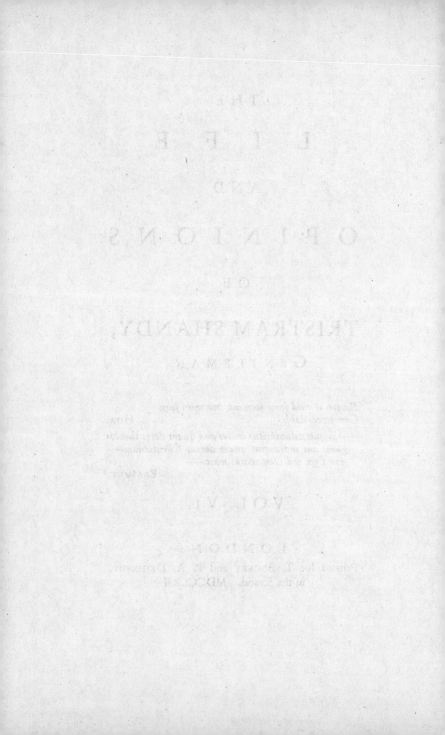

CHAPTER I

——WE'LL not stop two moments, my dear Sir,—only, as we have got thro' these five volumes, (do, Sir, sit down upon a set——they are better than nothing) let us just look back upon the country we have pass'd through.——

——What a wilderness has it been! and what a mercy that we have not both of us been lost, or devoured by wild beasts in it.

Did you think the world itself, Sir, had contained such a number of Jack Asses?——How they view'd and review'd us as we passed over the rivulet at the bottom of that little valley! ——and when we climbed over that hill, and were just getting out of sight—good God! what a braying did they all set up together!

——Prithee, shepherd! who keeps all those Jack Asses? * * *

——Heaven be their comforter——What! are they never curried?——Are they never taken in in winter?——Bray bray—bray. Bray on,—the world is deeply your debtor; ——louder still—that's nothing;—in good sooth, you are ill-used:——Was I a Jack Asse, I solemnly declare, I would bray in G-sol-re-ut from morning, even unto night.

CHAPTER II

WHEN my father had danced his white bear backwards and forwards through half a dozen pages, he closed the book for good an' all,—and in a kind of triumph redelivered it into *Trim*'s hand, with a nod to lay it upon the 'scrutoire where he found it.——*Tristram*, said he, shall be made to conjugate every word in the dictionary, backwards and forwards the same way;——every word, *Yorick*, by this means, you see, is converted into a thesis or an hypothesis;—every thesis and hypothesis have an offspring of propositions;—and each proposition has its own consequences and conclusions; every one of which leads the mind on again, into fresh tracks of enquiries and doubtings.——The force of this engine, added my father, is incredible, in opening a child's head.——'Tis enough, brother

Shandy, cried my uncle *Toby*, to burst it into a thousand splinters.——

I presume, said *Yorick*, smiling,—it must be owing to this, ——(for let logicians say what they will, it is not to be accounted for sufficiently from the bare use of the ten predicaments[1])——That the famous *Vincent Quirino*,[2] amongst the many other astonishing feats of his childhood, of which the Cardinal *Bembo*[3] has given the world so exact a story,—should be able to paste up in the publick schools at *Rome*, so early as in the eighth year of his age, no less than four thousand, five hundred, and sixty different theses, upon the most abstruse points of the most abstruse theology;—and to defend and maintain them in such sort, as to cramp and dumbfound his opponents.——What is that, cried my father, to what is told us of *Alphonsus Tostatus*,[4] who, almost in his nurse's arms, learned all the sciences and liberal arts without being taught any one of them?——What shall we say of the great *Piereskius?*[5]—That's the very man, cried my uncle *Toby*, I once told you of, brother *Shandy*, who walked a matter of five hundred miles, reckoning from *Paris* to *Schevling*, and from *Schevling* back again, merely to see *Stevinus*'s flying chariot.——He was a very great man! added my uncle *Toby*; (meaning *Stevinus*)—He was so; brother *Toby*, said my father, (meaning *Piereskius*)——and had multiplied his ideas so fast, and increased his knowlege to such a prodigious stock, that, if we may give credit to an anecdote concerning him, which we cannot with-hold here, without shaking the authority of all anecdotes whatever—at seven years of age, his father committed entirely to his care the education of his younger brother, a boy of five years old,—with the sole management of all his concerns.—Was the father as wise as the son? quoth my uncle *Toby:*—I should think not, said *Yorick:*—But what are these, continued my father—(breaking out in a kind of enthusiasm)—what are these, to those prodigies of childhood in *Grotius*,[6] *Scioppius*, *Heinsius*, *Politian*, *Pascal*, *Joseph Scaliger*, *Ferdinand de Cordouè*, and others—some of which left off their *substantial forms*[7] at nine years old, or sooner, and went on reasoning without them;—others went through their classics at seven;—wrote tragedies at eight;—*Ferdinand de Cordouè* was so wise at nine,—'twas thought the Devil was in him;——and at *Venice* gave such proofs of his knowlege and goodness, that the monks imagined he was *Antichrist*, or nothing.——Others were masters of fourteen languages at ten,—finished the course of their rhetoric, poetry, logic, and ethics at eleven,—put forth their commentaries upon *Servius*[8] and *Martianus Capella*[9] at twelve,—and at thirteen received their degrees in philosophy, laws, and divinity:——But you forget the great *Lipsius*,[10] quoth *Yorick*, who composed a work* the day he was born;——They should have wiped it up, said my uncle *Toby*, and said no more about it.

CHAPTER III

WHEN the cataplasm was ready, a scruple of *decorum* had unseasonably rose up in *Susannah*'s conscience, about holding the candle, whilst *Slop* tied it on; *Slop* had not treated *Susannah*'s distemper with anodines,—and so a quarrel had ensued betwixt them.

——Oh! oh!——said *Slop*, casting a glance of undue freedom in *Susannah*'s face, as she declined the office;——then, I think I know you, madam——You know me, Sir! cried *Susannah* fastidiously, and with a toss of her head, levelled evidently, not at his profession, but at the doctor himself,——you know me! cried *Susannah* again.——Doctor *Slop* clapped his finger and his thumb instantly upon his nostrils;——*Susannah*'s spleen was ready to burst at it;——'Tis false, said *Susannah*.—Come, come, Mrs. Modesty, said *Slop*, not a little elated with the success of his last thrust,——if you won't hold the candle, and look—you may hold it and shut your eyes:—That's one of your popish shifts, cried *Susannah*:——'Tis better, said *Slop*, with a nod, than no shift at all, young woman;——I defy you, Sir, cried *Susannah*, pulling her shift sleeve below her elbow.

It was almost impossible for two persons to assist each other in a surgical case with a more splenetic cordiality.

Slop snatched up the cataplasm,——*Susannah* snatched up the candle;——A little this way, said *Slop*; *Susannah* looking

---

* Nous aurions quelque interêt, says *Baillet*, de montrer qu'il n'a rien de ridicule s'il étoit véritable, au moins dans le sens énigmatique que *Nicius Erythræus* a tâché de lui donner. Cet auteur dit que pour comprendre comme *Lipse*, a pû composer un ouvrage le premier jour de sa vie, il faut s'imaginer, que ce premier jour n'est pas celui de sa naissance charnelle, mais celui au quel il a commencé d'user de la raison; il veut que ç'ait été à l'age de *neuf* ans; et il nous veut persuader que ce fut en cet âge, que *Lipse* fit un poem.——Le tour est ingenieux, &c. &c.[11]

one way, and rowing another, instantly set fire to *Slop*'s wig, which being somewhat bushy and unctuous withal, was burnt out before it was well kindled.——You impudent whore! cried *Slop*,—(for what is passion, but a wild beast)—you impudent whore, cried *Slop*, getting upright, with the cataplasm in his hand;——I never was the destruction of any body's nose, said *Susannah*,—which is more than you can say:——Is it? cried *Slop*, throwing the cataplasm in her face;——Yes, it is, cried *Susannah*, returning the compliment with what was left in the pan.——

CHAPTER IV

DOCTOR *Slop* and *Susannah* filed cross-bills against each other in the parlour; which done, as the cataplasm had failed, they retired into the kitchen to prepare a fomentation for me;—and whilst that was doing, my father determined the point as you will read.

CHAPTER V

YOU see 'tis high time, said my father, addressing himself equally to my uncle *Toby* and *Yorick*, to take this young creature out of these women's hands, and put him into those of a private governor. *Marcus Antoninus*[1] provided fourteen governors all at once to superintend his son *Commodus*'s education,—and in six weeks he cashiered five of them;—I know very well, continued my father, that *Commodus*'s mother was in love with a gladiator at the time of her conception, which accounts for a great many of *Commodus*'s cruelties when he became emperor;—but still I am of opinion, that those five whom *Antoninus* dismissed, did *Commodus*'s temper in that short time, more hurt than the other nine were able to rectify all their lives long.

Now as I consider the person who is to be about my son, as the mirror in which he is to view himself from morning to night, and by which he is to adjust his looks, his carriage, and perhaps the inmost sentiments of his heart;—I would have one, *Yorick*, if possible, polished at all points, fit for my child to look into.——This is very good sense, quoth my uncle *Toby* to himself.

——There is, continued my father, a certain mien and motion of the body and all its parts, both in acting and speaking, which argues a man *well within*; and I am not at all surprized that *Gregory* of *Nazianzum*,[2] upon observing the hasty and unto-ward gestures of *Julian*, should foretel he would one day become an apostate;——or that St. *Ambrose*[3] should turn his *Amanuensis* out of doors, because of an indecent motion of his head, which went backwards and forwards like a flail;——or that *Democritus*[4] should conceive *Protagoras*[5] to be a scholar, from seeing him bind up a faggot, and thrusting, as he did it, the small twigs inwards.——There are a thousand unnoticed open-ings, continued my father, which let a penetrating eye at once into a man's soul; and I maintain it, added he, that a man of sense does not lay down his hat in coming into a room,—or take it up in going out of it, but something escapes, which discovers him.

It is for these reasons, continued my father, that the governor I make choice of shall neither* lisp, or squint, or wink, or talk loud, or look fierce, or foolish;——or bite his lips, or grind his teeth, or speak through his nose, or pick it, or blow it with his fingers.——

He shall neither walk fast,—or slow, or fold his arms,—for that is laziness;—or hang them down,—for that is folly; or hide them in his pocket, for that is nonsense.——

He shall neither strike, or pinch, or tickle,—or bite, or cut his nails, or hawk, or spit, or snift, or drum with his feet or fingers in company;——nor (according to *Erasmus*) shall he speak to any one in making water,—nor shall he point to carrion or excrement.——Now this is all nonsense again, quoth my uncle *Toby* to himself.——

I will have him, continued my father, cheerful, faceté,[7] jovial; at the same time, prudent, attentive to business, vigilant, acute, argute, inventive, quick in resolving doubts and speculative questions;——he shall be wise and judicious, and learned:——And why not humble, and moderate, and gentle tempered, and good? said *Yorick:*——And why not, cried my uncle *Toby*, free, and generous, and bountiful, and brave?——He shall, my dear *Toby*, replied my father, getting up and shaking him by his hand.—Then, brother *Shandy*, answered my uncle *Toby*, rais-

* Vid. *Pellegrina*.[6]

ing himself off the chair, and laying down his pipe to take hold of my father's other hand,—I humbly beg I may recommend poor *Le Fever*'s son to you;——a tear of joy of the first water sparkled in my uncle *Toby*'s eye,—and another, the fellow to it, in the corporal's, as the proposition was made;——you will see why when you read *Le Fever*'s story:——fool that I was! nor can I recollect, (nor perhaps you) without turning back to the place, what it was that hindered me from letting the corporal tell it in his own words;—but the occasion is lost,—I must tell it now in my own.

CHAPTER VI

The Story of LE FEVER.

IT was some time in the summer of that year in which *Dendermond*[1] was taken by the allies,—which was about seven years before my father came into the country,—and about as many, after the time, that my uncle *Toby* and *Trim* had privately decamped from my father's house in town, in order to lay some of the finest sieges to some of the finest fortified cities in *Europe*——when my uncle *Toby* was one evening getting his supper, with *Trim* sitting behind him at a small sideboard,—I say, sitting—for in consideration of the corporal's lame knee (which sometimes gave him exquisite pain)—when my uncle *Toby* dined or supped alone, he would never suffer the corporal to stand; and the poor fellow's veneration for his master was such, that, with a proper artillery, my uncle *Toby* could have taken *Dendermond* itself, with less trouble than he was able to gain this point over him; for many a time when my uncle *Toby* supposed the corporal's leg was at rest, he would look back, and detect him standing behind him with the most dutiful respect: this bred more little squabbles betwixt them, than all other causes for five and twenty years together——But this is neither here nor there—why do I mention it?——Ask my pen,—it governs me,—I govern not it.

He was one evening sitting thus at his supper, when the landlord of a little inn in the village came into the parlour with an empty phial in his hand, to beg a glass or two of sack; 'Tis for a poor gentleman,—I think, of the army, said the landlord, who has been taken ill at my house four days ago, and has never held up his head since, or had a desire to taste any thing, till just now, that he has a fancy for a glass of sack and a thin toast,——*I think*, says he, taking his hand from his forehead, *it would comfort me.*——

——If I could neither beg, borrow, or buy such a thing,—added the landlord,—I would almost steal it for the poor gentleman, he is so ill.——I hope in God he will still mend, continued he,—we are all of us concerned for him.

Thou art a good natured soul, I will answer for thee, cried my uncle *Toby*; and thou shalt drink the poor gentleman's health in a glass of sack thyself,—and take a couple of bottles with my service, and tell him he is heartily welcome to them, and to a dozen more if they will do him good.

Though I am persuaded, said my uncle *Toby*, as the landlord shut the door, he is a very compassionate fellow—*Trim*,—yet I cannot help entertaining a high opinion of his guest too; there must be something more than common in him, that in so short a time should win so much upon the affections of his host; ——And of his whole family, added the corporal, for they are all concerned for him.——Step after him, said my uncle *Toby*,—do *Trim*,—and ask if he knows his name.

——I have quite forgot it, truly, said the landlord, coming back into the parlour with the corporal,—but I can ask his son again:——Has he a son with him then? said my uncle *Toby*.—A boy, replied the landlord, of about eleven or twelve years of age;—but the poor creature has tasted almost as little as his father; he does nothing but mourn and lament for him night and day:——He has not stirred from the bedside these two days.

My uncle *Toby* laid down his knife and fork, and thrust his plate from before him, as the landlord gave him the account; and *Trim*, without being ordered, took away without saying one word, and in a few minutes after brought him his pipe and tobacco.

——Stay in the room a little, said my uncle *Toby*.——

Trim!——said my uncle *Toby*, after he lighted his pipe, and smoak'd about a dozen whiffs.——*Trim* came in front of his master and made his bow;—my uncle *Toby* smoak'd on, and said no more.——Corporal! said my uncle *Toby*——the corporal made his bow.——My uncle *Toby* proceeded no farther, but finished his pipe.

Trim! said my uncle *Toby*, I have a project in my head, as it is a bad night, of wrapping myself up warm in my roquelaure, and paying a visit to this poor gentleman.——Your honour's roquelaure, replied the corporal, has not once been had on, since the night before your honour received your wound, when we mounted guard in the trenches before the gate of St. *Nicholas*; ——and besides it is so cold and rainy a night, that what with the roquelaure, and what with the weather, 'twill be enough to give your honour your death, and bring on your honour's torment in your groin. I fear so; replied my uncle *Toby*, but I am not at rest in my mind, *Trim*, since the account the landlord has given me.——I wish I had not known so much of this affair,— added my uncle *Toby*,—or that I had known more of it:—— How shall we manage it? Leave it, an't please your honour, to me, quoth the corporal;——I'll take my hat and stick and go to the house and reconnoitre, and act accordingly; and I will bring your honour a full account in an hour.——Thou shalt go, *Trim*, said my uncle *Toby*, and here's a shilling for thee to drink with his servant.——I shall get it all out of him, said the corporal, shutting the door.

My uncle *Toby* filled his second pipe; and had it not been, that he now and then wandered from the point, with considering whether it was not full as well to have the curtain of the tennaile[2] a straight line, as a crooked one,—he might be said to have thought of nothing else but poor *Le Fever* and his boy the whole time he smoaked it.

CHAPTER VII

The Story of LE FEVER *continued.*

IT was not till my uncle *Toby* had knocked the ashes out of his third pipe, that corporal *Trim* returned from the inn, and gave him the following account.

I despaired at first, said the corporal, of being able to bring back your honour any kind of intelligence concerning the poor sick lieutenant—Is he in the army then? said my uncle *Toby* ——He is: said the corporal——And in what regiment? said my uncle *Toby*——I'll tell your honour, replied the corporal, every thing straight forwards, as I learnt it.—Then, *Trim*, I'll fill another pipe, said my uncle *Toby*, and not interrupt thee till thou hast done; so sit down at thy ease, *Trim*, in the window seat, and begin thy story again. The corporal made his old bow, which generally spoke as plain as a bow could speak it—*Your honour is good:*——And having done that, he sat down, as he was ordered,—and begun the story to my uncle *Toby* over again in pretty near the same words.

I despaired at first, said the corporal, of being able to bring back any intelligence to your honour, about the lieutenant and his son; for when I asked where his servant was, from whom I made myself sure of knowing every thing which was proper to be asked,—That's a right distinction, *Trim*, said my uncle *Toby*—I was answered, an' please your honour, that he had no servant with him;——that he had come to the inn with hired horses, which, upon finding himself unable to proceed, (to join, I suppose, the regiment) he had dismissed the morning after he came.—If I get better, my dear, said he, as he gave his purse to his son to pay the man,—we can hire horses from hence. ——But alas! the poor gentleman will never get from hence, said the landlady to me,—for I heard the death-watch[1] all night long;——and when he dies, the youth, his son, will certainly die with him; for he is broken-hearted already.

I was hearing this account, continued the corporal, when the youth came into the kitchen, to order the thin toast the landlord spoke of;——but I will do it for my father myself, said the youth.——Pray let me save you the trouble, young gentleman, said I, taking up a fork for the purpose, and offering him my chair to sit down upon by the fire, whilst I did it.——I believe, Sir, said he, very modestly, I can please him best myself.——I am sure, said I, his honour will not like the toast the worse for being toasted by an old soldier.——The youth took hold of my hand, and instantly burst into tears.——Poor youth! said my uncle *Toby*,—he has been bred up from an infant in the army, and the name of a soldier, *Trim*, sounded in his ears like the name of a friend;—I wish I had him here.

——I never in the longest march, said the corporal, had so great a mind to my dinner, as I had to cry with him for company:—What could be the matter with me, an' please your honour? Nothing in the world, *Trim*, said my uncle *Toby*, blowing his nose,—but that thou art a good natured fellow.

When I gave him the toast, continued the corporal, I thought it was proper to tell him I was Captain *Shandy*'s servant, and that your honour (though a stranger) was extremely concerned for his father;—and that if there was any thing in your house or cellar——(And thou might'st have added my purse too, said my uncle *Toby*)——he was heartily welcome to it:——He made a very low bow, (which was meant to your honour) but no answer,—for his heart was full—so he went up stairs with the toast;—I warrant you, my dear, said I, as I opened the kitchen door, your father will be well again.——Mr. *Yorick*'s curate was smoaking a pipe by the kitchen fire,—but said not a word good or bad to comfort the youth.——I thought it wrong; added the corporal——I think so too, said my uncle *Toby*.

When the lieutenant had taken his glass of sack and toast, he felt himself a little revived, and sent down into the kitchen, to let me know, that in about ten minutes he should be glad if I would step up stairs.——I believe, said the landlord, he is going to say his prayers,——for there was a book laid upon the chair by his bedside, and as I shut the door, I saw his son take up a cushion.——

I thought, said the curate, that you gentlemen of the army, Mr. *Trim*, never said your prayers at all.——I heard the poor gentleman say his prayers last night, said the landlady, very devoutly, and with my own ears, or I could not have believed it.——Are your sure of it? replied the curate.——A soldier, an' please your reverence, said I, prays as often (of his own accord) as a parson;——and when he is fighting for his king, and for his own life, and for his honour too, he has the most reason to pray to God, of any one in the whole world——'Twas well said of thee, *Trim*, said my uncle *Toby*.——But when a soldier, said I, an' please your reverence, has been standing for twelve hours together in the trenches, up to his knees in cold water,—or engaged, said I, for months together in long and dangerous marches—harrassed, perhaps, in his rear to-day;—harrassing others to-morrow;—detached here;—countermanded there;—resting this night out upon his arms;—beat up in his shirt the next;—benumbed in his joints;—perhaps without straw in his tent to kneel on;—must say his prayers *how* and *when* he can.—I believe, said I,—for I was piqued, quoth the corporal, for the reputation of the army,—I believe, an' please your reverence, said I, that when a soldier gets time to pray,—he prays as heartily as a parson,—though not with all his fuss and hypocrisy.——Thou shouldst not have said that, *Trim*, said my uncle *Toby*,—for God only knows who is a hypocrite, and who is not:——At the great and general review of us all, corporal, at the day of judgment, (and not till then)—it will be seen who has done their duties in this world,—and who has not; and we shall be advanced, *Trim*, accordingly.——I hope we shall, said *Trim*.——It is in the Scripture, said my uncle *Toby*; and I will shew it thee to-morrow:—In the mean time we may depend upon it, *Trim*, for our comfort, said my uncle *Toby*, that God Almighty is so good and just a governor of the world, that if we have but done our duties in it,—it will never be enquired into, whether we have done them in a red coat or a black one:——I hope not; said the corporal——But go on, *Trim*, said my uncle *Toby*, with thy story.

When I went up, continued the corporal, into the lieutenant's room, which I did not do till the expiration of the ten minutes,—he was lying in his bed with his head raised upon his hand, with his elbow upon the pillow, and a clean white cambrick handkerchief beside it:——The youth was just stooping down to take up the cushion, upon which I supposed he had been kneeling,—the book was laid upon the bed,—and as he rose, in taking up the cushion with one hand, he reached out his other to take it away at the same time.——Let it remain there, my dear, said the lieutenant.

He did not offer to speak to me, till I had walked up close to his bed-side:—If you are Captain *Shandy*'s servant, said he, you must present my thanks to your master, with my little boy's thanks along with them, for his courtesy to me;—if he was of *Leven*'s—said the lieutenant.—I told him your honour was—Then, said he, I served three campaigns with him in *Flanders*, and remember him,—but 'tis most likely, as I had not the honour of any acquaintance with him, that he knows nothing of me.——You will tell him, however, that the person his good nature has laid under obligations to him, is one *Le Fever*, a lieutenant in *Angus*'s——but he knows me not,—said he, a second time, musing;——possibly he may my story—added he—pray tell the captain, I was the ensign at *Breda*,[2] whose wife was most unfortunately killed with a musket shot, as she lay in my arms in my tent.——I remember the story, an't please your honour, said I, very well.——Do you so? said he, wiping his eyes with his handkerchief,—then well may I.—In saying this, he drew a little ring out of his bosom, which seemed tied with a black ribband about his neck, and kiss'd it twice——Here, *Billy*, said he,——the boy flew across the room to the bed-side,—and falling down upon his knee, took the ring in his hand, and kissed it too,—then kissed his father, and sat down upon the bed and wept.

I wish, said my uncle *Toby*, with a deep sigh,—I wish, *Trim*, I was asleep.

Your honour, replied the corporal, is too much concerned;—shall I pour your honour out a glass of sack to your pipe?——Do, *Trim*, said my uncle *Toby*.

I remember, said my uncle *Toby*, sighing again, the story of the ensign and his wife, with a circumstance his modesty omitted;—and particularly well that he, as well as she, upon some account or other, (I forget what) was universally pitied by the whole regiment;—but finish the story thou art upon:—'Tis finished already, said the corporal,—for I could stay no longer,—so wished his honour a good night; young *Le Fever* rose from off the bed, and saw me to the bottom of the stairs; and as we went down together, told me, they had come from *Ireland*, and were on their route to join the regiment in *Flanders*.——But alas! said the corporal,—the lieutenant's last day's march is over.—Then what is to become of his poor boy? cried my uncle *Toby*.

CHAPTER VIII

The Story of LE FEVER *continued.*

IT was to my uncle *Toby*'s eternal honour,——though I tell it only for the sake of those, who, when coop'd in betwixt a natural and a positive law,[1] know not for their souls, which way in the world to turn themselves——That notwithstanding my uncle *Toby* was warmly engaged at that time in carrying on the siege of *Dendermond*, parallel with the allies, who pressed theirs on so vigorously, that they scarce allowed him time to get his dinner——that nevertheless he gave up *Dendermond*, though he had already made a lodgment upon the counterscarp;—and bent his whole thoughts towards the private distresses at the inn; and, except that he ordered the garden gate to be bolted up, by which he might be said to have turned the siege of *Dendermond* into a blockade,—he left *Dendermond* to itself,—to be relieved or not by the *French* king, as the *French* king thought good; and only considered how he himself should relieve the poor lieutenant and his son.

——That kind BEING, who is a friend to the friendless, shall recompence thee for this.

Thou hast left this matter short, said my uncle *Toby* to the corporal, as he was putting him to bed,——and I will tell thee in what, *Trim*.——In the first place, when thou madest an offer of my services to *Le Fever*,—as sickness and travelling are both expensive, and thou knowest he was but a poor lieutenant, with a son to subsist as well as himself, out of his pay,—that thou didst not make an offer to him of my purse; because, had he stood in need, thou knowest, *Trim*, he had been as welcome to it as myself.——Your honour knows, said the corporal, I had no orders;——True, quoth my uncle *Toby*,—thou didst very right, *Trim*, as a soldier,—but certainly very wrong as a man.

In the second place, for which, indeed, thou hast the same excuse, continued my uncle *Toby*,——when thou offeredst him whatever was in my house,—thou shouldst have offered him my house too:——A sick brother officer should have the best quarters, *Trim*, and if we had him with us,—we could tend and look to him:——Thou art an excellent nurse thyself, *Trim*,—and what with thy care of him, and the old woman's, and his boy's, and mine together, we might recruit him again at once, and set him upon his legs.——

——In a fortnight or three weeks, added my uncle *Toby*, smiling,—he might march.——He will never march, an' please your honour, in this world, said the corporal:——He will march; said my uncle *Toby*, rising up from the side of the bed, with one shoe off:——An' please your honour, said the corporal, he will never march, but to his grave:——He shall march, cried my uncle *Toby*, marching the foot which had a shoe on, though without advancing an inch,—he shall march to his regiment.——He cannot stand it, said the corporal;——He shall be supported, said my uncle *Toby*;——He'll drop at last, said the corporal, and what will become of his boy?——He shall not drop, said my uncle *Toby*, firmly.——A-well-o'day,—do what we can for him, said *Trim*, maintaining his point,—the poor soul will die:——He shall not die, by G—, cried my uncle *Toby*.

——The ACCUSING SPIRIT which flew up to heaven's chancery with the oath, blush'd as he gave it in;—and the RECORDING ANGEL as he wrote it down, dropp'd a tear upon the word, and blotted it out for ever.

CHAPTER IX

——My uncle *Toby* went to his bureau,—put his purse into his breeches pocket, and having ordered the corporal to go early in the morning for a physician,—he went to bed, and fell asleep.

CHAPTER X

The Story of LE FEVER *concluded.*

THE sun looked bright the morning after, to every eye in the village but *Le Fever's* and his afflicted son's; the hand of death press'd heavy upon his eye-lids,——and hardly could the wheel at the cistern turn round its circle,—when my uncle *Toby*, who had rose up an hour before his wonted time, entered the lieutenant's room, and without preface or apology, sat himself down upon the chair by the bed-side, and independantly of all modes and customs, opened the curtain in the manner an old friend and brother officer would have done it, and asked him how he did,—how he had rested in the night,—what was his complaint,—where was his pain,—and what he could do to help him:——and without giving him time to answer any one of the enquiries, went on and told him of the little plan which he had been concerting with the corporal the night before for him.——

——You shall go home directly, *Le Fever*, said my uncle *Toby*, to my house,—and we'll send for a doctor to see what's the matter,—and we'll have an apothecary,—and the corporal shall be your nurse;——and I'll be your servant, *Le Fever*.

There was a frankness in my uncle *Toby*,—not the *effect* of familiarity,—but the *cause* of it,—which let you at once into his soul, and shewed you the goodness of his nature; to this, there was something in his looks, and voice, and manner, superadded, which eternally beckoned to the unfortunate to come and take shelter under him; so that before my uncle *Toby* had half finished the kind offers he was making to the father, had the son insensibly pressed up close to his knees, and had taken hold of the breast of his coat, and was pulling it towards him.——The blood and spirits of *Le Fever*, which were waxing cold and slow within him, and were retreating to their last citadel, the heart,—rallied back,—the film forsook his eyes for a moment,—he looked up wishfully[1] in my uncle *Toby*'s face,—then cast a look upon his boy,——and that *ligament*, fine as it was,—was never broken.——

Nature instantly ebb'd again,——the film returned to its place,——the   pulse   fluttered——stopp'd——went   on ——throb'd——stopp'd   again——moved——stopp'd—— shall I go on?——No.

CHAPTER XI

I AM so impatient to return to my own story, that what remains of young *Le Fever*'s, that is, from this turn of his fortune, to the time my uncle *Toby* recommended him for my preceptor, shall be told in a very few words, in the next chapter.—All that is necessary to be added to this chapter is as follows.—

That my uncle *Toby*, with young *Le Fever* in his hand, attended the poor lieutenant, as chief mourners, to his grave.

That the governor of *Dendermond* paid his obsequies all military honours,—and that *Yorick*, not to be behind hand— paid him all ecclesiastic—for he buried him in his chancel:— And it appears likewise, he preached a funeral sermon over him——I say it *appears*,—for it was *Yorick*'s custom, which I suppose a general one with those of his profession, on the first leaf of every sermon which he composed, to chronicle down the time, the place, and the occasion of its being preached: to this, he was ever wont to add some short comment or stricture upon the sermon itself, seldom, indeed, much to its credit:—For instance, *This sermon upon the jewish dispensation—I don't like it at all;—Though I own there is a world of* WATER-LANDISH[1] *knowledge in it,—but 'tis all tritical,[2] and most tritically put together.*——*This is but a flimsy kind of a composition; what was in my head when I made it?*

——*N.B. The excellency of this text is, that it will suit any sermon,—and of this sermon,——that it will suit any text.*

——*For this sermon I shall be hanged,—for I have stolen the greatest part of it. Doctor* Paidagunes *found me out.* ☞ *Set a thief to catch a thief.*——[3]

On the back of half a dozen I find written, *So, so,* and no more——and upon a couple *Moderato*;[4] by which, as far as one may gather from *Altieri*'s *Italian* dictionary,[5]—but mostly from the authority of a piece of green whipcord, which seemed to have been the unravelling of *Yorick*'s whip-lash, with which he has left us the two sermons marked *Moderato*, and the half dozen of *So, so*, tied fast together in one bundle by themselves,—one may safely suppose he meant pretty near the same thing.

There is but one difficulty in the way of this conjecture, which is this, that the *moderato*'s are five times better than the *so, so*'s;—shew ten times more knowlege of the human heart;—have seventy times more wit and spirit in them;—(and, to rise properly in my climax)—discover a thousand times more genius;—and to crown all, are infinitely more entertaining than those tied up with them;—for which reason, whene'er *Yorick*'s *dramatic* sermons are offered to the world, though I shall admit but one out of the whole number of the *so, so*'s, I shall, nevertheless, adventure to print the two *moderato*'s without any sort of scruple.

What *Yorick* could mean by the words *lentamente*,[6]—*tenutè*,[7]—*grave*,[8]—and sometimes *adagio*,[9]—as applied to theological compositions, and with which he has characterized some of these sermons, I dare not venture to guess.——I am more puzzled still upon finding *a l'octava alta!*[10] upon one;——*Con strepito*[11] upon the back of another;——*Scicilliana*[12] upon a third;——*Alla capella*[13] upon a fourth;——*Con l'arco*[14] upon this;——*Senza l'arco*[15] upon that.——All I know is, that they are musical terms, and have a meaning;——and as he was a musical man, I will make no doubt, but that by some quaint application of such metaphors to the compositions in hand, they impressed very distinct ideas of their several characters upon his fancy,—whatever they may do upon that of others.

Amongst these, there is that particular sermon which has unaccountably led me into this digression——The funeral sermon upon poor *Le Fever*, wrote out very fairly, as if from a hasty copy.—I take notice of it the more, because it seems to have been his favourite composition——It is upon mortality; and is tied length-ways and cross-ways with a yarn thrum, and then rolled up and twisted round with a half sheet of dirty blue paper, which seems to have been once the cast cover of a general review,[16] which to this day smells horribly of horse-drugs.——Whether these marks of humiliation were designed,—I something doubt;——because at the end of the sermon, (and not at the beginning of it)—very different from his way of treating the rest, he had wrote——

Bravo!

——Though not very offensively,——for it is at two inches, at least, and a half's distance from, and below the concluding line of the sermon, at the very extremity of the page, and in that right hand corner of it, which, you know, is generally covered with your thumb; and, to do it justice, it is wrote besides with a crow's quill so faintly in a small *Italian* hand, as scarce to sollicit the eye towards the place, whether your thumb is there or not,—so that from the *manner of it*, it stands half excused; and being wrote moreover with very pale ink, diluted almost to nothing,—'tis more like a *ritratto*[17] of the shadow of vanity, than of VANITY herself—of the two; resembling rather a faint thought of transient applause, secretly stirring up in the heart of the composer, than a gross mark of it, coarsely obtruded upon the world.

With all these extenuations, I am aware, that in publishing this, I do no service to *Yorick*'s character as a modest man;—but all men have their failings! and what lessens this still farther, and almost wipes it away, is this; that the word was struck through sometime afterwards (as appears from a different tint of the ink) with a line quite across it in this manner, ~~BRAVO~~——as if he had retracted, or was ashamed of the opinion he had once entertained of it.

These short characters of his sermons were always written, excepting in this one instance, upon the first leaf of his sermon, which served as a cover to it; and usually upon the inside of it, which was turned towards the text;—but at the end of his discourse, where, perhaps, he had five or six pages, and some-times, perhaps, a whole score to turn himself in,—he took a larger circuit, and indeed, a much more mettlesome one;—as if he had snatched the occasion of unlacing himself with a few more frolicksome strokes at vice, than the straitness of the pulpit allowed.—These, though hussar-like, they skirmish lightly and out of all order, are still auxiliaries on the side of virtue—; tell me then, Mynheer Vander Blonederdondergewdenstronke,[18] why they should not be printed together?

CHAPTER XII

WHEN my uncle *Toby* had turned every thing into money, and settled all accounts betwixt the agent of the regiment and *Le Fever*, and betwixt *Le Fever* and all mankind,——there remained nothing more in my uncle *Toby*'s hands, than an old regimental coat and a sword; so that my uncle *Toby* found little or no opposition from the world in taking administration. The coat my uncle *Toby* gave the corporal;——Wear it, *Trim*, said my uncle *Toby*, as long as it will hold together, for the sake of the poor lieutenant——And this,——said my uncle *Toby*, taking up the sword in his hand, and drawing it out of the scabbard as he spoke——and this, *Le Fever*, I'll save for thee,—'tis all the fortune, continued my uncle *Toby*, hanging it up upon a crook, and pointing to it,—'tis all the fortune, my dear *Le Fever*, which God has left thee; but if he has given thee a heart to fight thy way with it in the world,—and thou doest it like a man of honour,—'tis enough for us.

As soon as my uncle *Toby* had laid a foundation, and taught him to inscribe a regular polygon in a circle, he sent him to a public school, where, excepting *Whitsontide* and *Christmas*, at which times the corporal was punctually dispatched for him,—he remained to the spring of the year, seventeen; when the stories of the emperor's sending his army into *Hungary* against the *Turks*, kindling a spark of fire in his bosom, he left his *Greek* and *Latin* without leave, and throwing himself upon his knees before my uncle *Toby*, begged his father's sword, and my uncle *Toby*'s leave along with it, to go and try his fortune under *Eugene*.[1]—Twice did my uncle *Toby* forget his wound, and cry out, *Le Fever!* I will go with thee, and thou shalt fight beside me——And twice he laid his hand upon his groin, and hung down his head in sorrow and disconsolation.——

My uncle *Toby* took down the sword from the crook, where it had hung untouched ever since the lieutenant's death, and delivered it to the corporal to brighten up;——and having detained *Le Fever* a single fortnight to equip him, and contract for his passage to *Leghorn*,—he put the sword into his hand, ——If thou art brave, *Le Fever*, said my uncle *Toby*, this will not fail thee,——but Fortune, said he, (musing a little)——Fortune may——And if she does,—added my uncle *Toby*, embracing him, come back again to me, *Le Fever*, and we will shape thee another course.

The greatest injury could not have oppressed the heart of *Le Fever* more than my uncle *Toby*'s paternal kindness;——he parted from my uncle *Toby*, as the best of sons from the best of fathers——both dropped tears——and as my uncle *Toby* gave him his last kiss, he slipped sixty guineas, tied up in an old purse of his father's, in which was his mother's ring, into his hand,—and bid God bless him.

CHAPTER XIII

Le Fever got up to the Imperial army just time enough to try what metal his sword was made of, at the defeat of the *Turks* before *Belgrade*;[1] but a series of unmerited mischances had pursued him from that moment, and trod close upon his heels for four years together after: he had withstood these buffetings to the last, till sickness overtook him at *Marseilles*, from whence he wrote my uncle *Toby* word, he had lost his time, his services, his health, and, in short, every thing but his sword;——and was waiting for the first ship to return back to him.

As this letter came to hand about six weeks before *Susannah*'s accident, *Le Fever* was hourly expected; and was uppermost in my uncle *Toby*'s mind all the time my father was giving him and *Yorick* a description of what kind of a person he would chuse for a preceptor to me: but as my uncle *Toby* thought my father at first somewhat fanciful in the accomplishments he required, he forbore mentioning *Le Fever*'s name,——till the character, by *Yorick*'s interposition, ending unexpectedly, in one, who should be gentle tempered, and generous, and good, it impressed the image of *Le Fever*, and his interest upon my uncle *Toby* so forceably, he rose instantly off his chair; and laying down his pipe, in order to take hold of both my father's hands——I beg, brother *Shandy*, said my uncle *Toby*, I may recommend poor *Le Fever*'s son to you——I beseech you, do, added *Yorick*——He has a good heart, said my uncle *Toby*——And a brave one too, an' please your honour, said the corporal.

——The best hearts, *Trim*, are ever the bravest, replied my uncle *Toby*.——And the greatest cowards, an' please your

honour, in our regiment, were the greatest rascals in it.——
There was serjeant *Kumbur*, and ensign——.

——We'll talk of them, said my father, another time.

CHAPTER XIV

WHAT a jovial and a merry world would this be, may it please
your worships, but for that inextricable labyrinth of debts,
cares, woes, want, grief, discontent, melancholy, large join-
tures, impositions, and lies!

Doctor *Slop*, like a son of a w——, as my father called him for
it,—to exalt himself,—debased me to death,—and made ten
thousand times more of *Susannah*'s accident, than there was any
grounds for; so that in a week's time, or less, it was in every
body's mouth, *That poor Master Shandy* *   *   *   *
*   *   *   *   *   *   *   *   entirely.——
And FAME, who loves to double every thing,—in three days
more, had sworn positively she saw it,—and all the world, as
usual, gave credit to her evidence——"That the nursery window had not only *   *   *   *   *   *   *   *
*   *   *   *   *   *   *   *   *
*   *   *   *   *;——but that   *   *   *   *
*   *   *   *   *   *   *   *   *
*   *   *'s also."

Could the world have been sued like a BODY-CORPORATE,—
my father had brought an action upon the case, and trounced it
sufficiently; but to fall foul of individuals about it——as every
soul who had mentioned the affair, did it with the greatest pity
imaginable;——'twas like flying in the very face of his best
friends:——And yet to acquiesce under the report, in silence—
was to acknowledge it openly,—at least in the opinion of one
half of the world; and to make a bustle again, in contradicting
it,—was to confirm it as strongly in the opinion of the other
half.——

——Was ever poor devil of a country gentleman so ham-
pered? said my father.

I would shew him publickly, said my uncle *Toby*, at the
market cross.

——'Twill have no effect, said my father.

CHAPTER XV

——I'll put him, however, into breeches said my father,——let the world say what it will.

CHAPTER XVI

THERE are a thousand resolutions, Sir, both in church and state, as well as in matters, Madam, of a more private concern;—which, though they have carried all the appearance in the world of being taken, and entered upon in a hasty, hare-brained, and unadvised manner, were, notwithstanding this, (and could you or I have got into the cabinet, or stood behind the curtain, we should have found it was so) weighed, poized, and perpended ——argued upon——canvassed through——entered into, and examined on all sides with so much coolness, that the GODDESS of COOLNESS herself (I do not take upon me to prove her existence) could neither have wished it, or done it better.

Of the number of these was my father's resolution of putting me into breeches; which, though determined at once,—in a kind of huff, and a defiance of all mankind, had, nevertheless, been *pro'd* and *conn'd*, and judicially talked over betwixt him and my mother about a month before, in two several *beds of justice*,[1] which my father had held for that purpose. I shall explain the nature of these beds of justice in my next chapter; and in the chapter following that, you shall step with me, Madam, behind the curtain, only to hear in what kind of manner my father and my mother debated between themselves, this affair of the breeches,—from which you may form an idea, how they debated all lesser matters.

CHAPTER XVII

THE ancient *Goths* of *Germany*, who (the learned *Cluverius*[1] is positive) were first seated in the country between the *Vistula* and the *Oder*, and who afterwards incorporated the *Herculi*, the *Bugians*, and some other *Vandallick* clans to 'em,—had all of them a wise custom of debating every thing of importance to their state, twice; that is,—once drunk, and once sober:

——Drunk—that their counsels might not want vigour; ——and sober—that they might not want discretion.

Now my father being entirely a water-drinker,—was a long time gravelled almost to death, in turning this as much to his advantage, as he did every other thing, which the ancients did or said; and it was not till the seventh year of his marriage, after a thousand fruitless experiments and devices, that he hit upon an expedient which answered the purpose;——and that was when any difficult and momentous point was to be settled in the family, which required great sobriety, and great spirit too, in its determination,——he fixed and set apart the first *Sunday* night in the month, and the *Saturday* night which immediately preceded it, to argue it over, in bed with my mother: By which contrivance, if you consider, Sir, with yourself,   *   *   *
*   *   *   *   *   *   *   *   *   *   *   *
*   *   *   *   *   *   *   *   *   *   *   *
*   *   *   *   *   *   *   *   *   *   *   *
*   *   *   *   *   *.

These my father, humourously enough, called his *beds of justice*;——for from the two different counsels taken in these two different humours, a middle one was generally found out, which touched the point of wisdom as well, as if he had got drunk and sober a hundred times.

It must not be made a secret of to the world, that this answers full as well in literary discussions, as either in military or conjugal; but it is not every author that can try the experiment as the *Goths* and *Vandals* did it——or if he can, may it be always for his body's health; and to do it, as my father did it,— am I sure it would be always for his soul's.——

My way is this:——

In all nice and ticklish discussions,—(of which, heaven knows, there are but too many in my book)—where I find I cannot take a step without the danger of having either their worships or their reverences upon my back——I write one half *full*,—and t'other *fasting*;—or write it all full,—and correct it fasting;——or write it fasting,— and correct it full, for they all come to the same thing:—So that with a less variation from my father's plan, than my father's from the *Gothick*——I feel myself upon a par with him in his first bed of justice,—and no way inferior to him in his second.——These different and almost irreconcileable effects, flow uniformly from the wise and wonderful mechanism of nature,—of which,—be her's the honour.——All that we can do, is to turn and work the machine to the improvement and better manufactury of the arts and sciences.——

Now, when I write full,—I write as if I was never to write fasting again as long as I live;——that is, I write free from the cares, as well as the terrors of the world.——I count not the number of my scars,—nor does my fancy go forth into dark entries and bye corners to antedate my stabs.——In a word, my pen takes its course; and I write on as much from the fullness of my heart, as my stomach.——

But when, an' please your honours, I indite fasting, 'tis a different history.——I pay the world all possible attention and respect,—and have as great a share (whilst it lasts) of that understrapping virtue of discretion, as the best of you.——So that betwixt both, I write a careless kind of a civil, nonsensical, good humoured *Shandean* book, which will do all your hearts good——

——And all your heads too,—provided you understand it.

CHAPTER XVIII

WE should begin, said my father, turning himself half round in bed, and shifting his pillow a little towards my mother's, as he opened the debate——We should begin to think, Mrs. *Shandy*, of putting this boy into breeches.——

We should so,—said my mother.——We defer it, my dear, quoth my father, shamefully.——

I think we do, Mr. *Shandy*,—said my mother.

——Not but the child looks extremely well, said my father, in his vests and tunicks.——

——He does look very well in them,—replied my mother.——

——And for that reason it would be almost a sin, added my father, to take him out of 'em.——

——It would so,—said my mother:——But indeed he is growing a very tall lad,—rejoin'd my father.

——He is very tall for his age, indeed,—said my mother.——

——I can not (making two syllables of it) imagine, quoth my father, who the duce he takes after.——

I cannot conceive, for my life,—said my mother.——

Humph!——said my father.

(The dialogue ceased for a moment.)

——I am very short myself,——continued my father, gravely.

You are very short, Mr. *Shandy*,——said my mother.

Humph! quoth my father to himself, a second time: in muttering which, he plucked his pillow a little further from my mother's,——and turning about again, there was an end of the debate for three minutes and a half.

——When he gets these breeches made, cried my father in a higher tone, he'll look like a beast in 'em.

He will be very aukward in them at first, replied my mother.——

——And 'twill be lucky, if that's the worst on't, added my father.

It will be very lucky, answered my mother.

I suppose, replied my father,——making some pause first,——he'll be exactly like other people's children.——

Exactly, said my mother.——

——Though I should be sorry for that, added my father: and so the debate stopped again.

——They should be of leather, said my father, turning him about again.—

They will last him, said my mother, the longest.

But he can have no linings to 'em, replied my father.——

He cannot, said my mother.

'Twere better to have them of fustian, quoth my father.

Nothing can be better, quoth my mother.——

——Except dimity,——replied my father:——'Tis best of all,——replied my mother.

——One must not give him his death, however,——interrupted my father.

By no means, said my mother:——and so the dialogue stood still again.

I am resolved, however, quoth my father, breaking silence the fourth time, he shall have no pockets in them.——

——There is no occasion for any, said my mother.——

I mean in his coat and waistcoat,——cried my father.

——I mean so too,——replied my mother.

——Though if he gets a gig¹ or a top——Poor souls! it is a crown and a scepter to them,——they should have where to secure it.——

Order it as you please, Mr. *Shandy*, replied my mother.

——————

——But don't you think it right? added my father, pressing the point home to her.

Perfectly, said my mother, if it pleases you, Mr. *Shandy*.

——There's for you! cried my father, losing temper—— Pleases me!——You never will distinguish, Mrs. *Shandy*, nor shall I ever teach you to do it, betwixt a point of pleasure and a point of convenience.——This was on the *Sunday* night; ——and further this chapter sayeth not.

CHAPTER XIX

AFTER my father had debated the affair of the breeches with my mother,—he consulted *Albertus Rubenius*[1] upon it; and *Albertus Rubenius* used my father ten times worse in the consultation (if possible) than even my father had used my mother: For as *Rubenius* had wrote a quarto *express, De re Vestiaria Veterum*,— it was *Rubenius*'s business to have given my father some lights.—On the contrary, my father might as well have thought of extracting the seven cardinal virtues out of a long beard,—as of extracting a single word out of *Rubenius* upon the subject.

Upon every other article of ancient dress, *Rubenius* was very communicative to my father;—gave him a full and satisfactory account of

The Toga, or loose gown.

The Chlamys.[2]

The Ephod.

The Tunica, or Jacket.

The Synthesis.

The Pænula.

The Lacema, with its Cucullus.

The Paludamentum.

The Prætexta.

The Sagum, or soldier's jerkin.

The Trabea: of which, according to *Suetonius*,[3] there were three kinds.—

——But what are all these to the breeches? said my father.

Rubenius threw him down upon the counter all kinds of shoes which had been in fashion with the *Romans*.——There was,

The open shoe.

> The close shoe.
> The slip shoe.
> The wooden shoe.
> The soc.
> The buskin.

And The military shoe with hobnails in it, which Juvenal[4] takes notice of.

There were, The clogs.
> The patins.
> The pantoufles.
> The brogues.
> The sandals, with latchets to them.

There was, The felt shoe.
> The linen shoe.
> The laced shoe.
> The braided shoe.
> The calceus incisus.[5]

And The calceus rostratus.

Rubenius shewed my father how well they all fitted,—in what manner they laced on,—with what points, straps, thongs, lachets, ribands, jaggs, and ends.——

——But I want to be informed about the breeches, said my father.

Albertus Rubenius informed my father that the *Romans* manufactured stuffs of various fabricks,——some plain,—some striped,—others diapered throughout the whole contexture of the wool, with silk and gold——That linen did not begin to be in common use, till towards the declension of the empire, when the *Egyptians* coming to settle amongst them, brought it into vogue.

——That persons of quality and fortune distinguished themselves by the fineness and whiteness of their cloaths; which colour (next to purple, which was appropriated to the great offices) they most affected and wore on their birth-days and public rejoicings.——That it appeared from the best historians of those times, that they frequently sent their cloaths to the fuller, to be cleaned and whitened;——but that the inferior people, to avoid that expence, generally wore brown cloaths, and of a something coarser texture,—till towards the beginning of *Augustus*'s reign, when the slave dressed like his master, and almost every distinction of habiliment was lost, but the *Latus Clavus.*[6]

And what was the *Latus Clavus?* said my father.

Rubenius told him, that the point was still litigating amongst the learned:——That *Egnatius,*[7] *Sigonius, Bossius Ticinensis, Bayfius, Budæus, Salmasius, Lipsius, Lazius, Isaac Causabon,* and *Joseph Scaliger,* all differed from each other,—and he from them: That some took it to be the button,—some the coat itself,—others only the colour of it:—That the great *Bayfius,* in his Wardrobe of the ancients, chap. 12.—honestly said, he knew not what it was,—whether a tibula,[8]—a stud,—a button,—a loop,—a buckle,—or clasps and keepers.——

——My father lost the horse, but not the saddle——They are *hooks and eyes,* said my father——and with hooks and eyes he ordered my breeches to be made.

CHAPTER XX

WE are now going to enter upon a new scene of events.——

——Leave we then the breeches in the taylor's hands, with my father standing over him with his cane, reading him as he sat at work a lecture upon the *latus clavus,* and pointing to the precise part of the waistband, where he was determined to have it sewed on.——

Leave we my mother—(truest of all the *Poco-curante's*[1] of her sex!)—careless about it, as about every thing else in the world which concerned her;—that is,—indifferent whether it was done this way or that,—provided it was but done at all.——

Leave we *Slop* likewise to the full profits of all my dishonours.——

Leave we poor *Le Fever* to recover, and get home from *Marseilles* as he can.——And last of all,—because the hardest of all——

Let us leave, if possible, *myself:*——But 'tis impossible,—I must go along with you to the end of the work.

CHAPTER XXI

IF the reader has not a clear conception of the rood and the half of ground which lay at the bottom of my uncle *Toby's* kitchen garden, and which was the scene of so many of his delicious hours,—the fault is not in me,—but in his imagination;—for I am sure I gave him so minute a description, I was almost ashamed of it.

When FATE was looking forwards one afternoon, into the great transactions of future times,—and recollected for what purposes, this little plot, by a decree fast bound down in iron, had been destined,—she gave a nod to NATURE—'twas enough—Nature threw half a spade full of her kindliest compost upon it, with just so *much* clay in it, as to retain the forms of angles and indentings,—and so *little* of it too, as not to cling to the spade, and render works of so much glory, nasty in foul weather.

My uncle *Toby* came down, as the reader has been informed, with plans along with him, of almost every fortified town in *Italy* and *Flanders*; so let the Duke of *Marlborough*,[1] or the allies, have set down before what town they pleased, my uncle *Toby* was prepared for them.

His way, which was the simplest one in the world, was this; as soon as ever a town was invested—(but sooner when the design was known) to take the plan of it, (let it be what town it would) and enlarge it upon a scale to the exact size of his bowling-green; upon the surface of which, by means of a large role of packthread, and a number of small piquets driven into the ground, at the several angles and redans, he transferred the lines from his paper; then taking the profile of the place, with its works, to determine the depths and slopes of the ditches,—the talus of the glacis, and the precise height of the several banquets, parapets, &c.—he set the corporal to work——and sweetly went it on: ——The nature of the soil,—the nature of the work itself,—and above all, the good nature of my uncle *Toby* sitting by from morning to night, and chatting kindly with the corporal upon past-done deeds,—left LABOUR little else but the ceremony of the name.

When the place was finished in this manner, and put into a proper posture of defence,—it was invested,—and my uncle *Toby* and the corporal began to run their first parallel.[2]——I beg I may not be interrupted in my story, by being told, *That the first parallel should be at least three hundred toises distant from the main body of the place,—and that I have not left a single inch for it;*——for my uncle *Toby* took the liberty of incroaching upon his kitchen garden, for the sake of enlarging his works on the bowling green, and for that reason generally ran his first and second parallels betwixt two rows of his cabbages

and his collyflowers; the conveniences and inconveniences of
which will be considered at large in the history of my uncle
Toby's and the corporal's campaigns, of which, this I'm now
writing is but a sketch, and will be finished, if I conjecture right,
in three pages (but there is no guessing)——The campaigns
themselves will take up as many books; and therefore I
apprehend it would be hanging too great a weight of one kind of
matter in so flimsy a performance as this, to rhapsodize them, as
I once intended, into the body of the work——surely they had
better be printed apart,——we'll consider the affair——so take
the following sketch of them in the mean time.

CHAPTER XXII

WHEN the town, with its works, was finished, my uncle *Toby*
and the corporal began to run their first parallel——not at
random, or any how——but from the same points and distances
the allies had begun to run theirs; and regulating their
approaches and attacks, by the accounts my uncle *Toby* received from the daily papers,—they went on, during the whole
siege, step by step with the allies.

When the duke of *Marlborough* made a lodgment,——my
uncle *Toby* made a lodgment too.——And when the face of a
bastion was battered down, or a defence ruined,—the corporal
took his mattock and did as much,—and so on;——gaining
ground, and making themselves masters of the works one after
another, till the town fell into their hands.

To one who took pleasure in the happy state of others,—
there could not have been a greater sight in the world, than, on a
post-morning, in which a practicable breach had been made by
the duke of *Marlborough*, in the main body of the place,—to
have stood behind the horn-beam hedge, and observed the spirit
with which my uncle *Toby*, with *Trim* behind him, sallied
forth;——the one with the *Gazette*[1] in his hand,—the other
with a spade on his shoulder to execute the contents.——What
an honest triumph in my uncle *Toby*'s looks as he marched up to
the ramparts! What intense pleasure swimming in his eye as he
stood over the corporal, reading the paragraph ten times over to
him, as he was at work, lest, peradventure, he should make the
breach an inch too wide,—or leave it an inch too narrow
——But when the *chamade*[2] was beat, and the corporal helped

my uncle up it, and followed with the colours in his hand, to fix them upon the ramparts——Heaven! Earth! Sea!——but what avails apostrophes?——with all your elements, wet or dry, ye never compounded so intoxicating a draught.

In this track of happiness for many years, without one interruption to it, except now and then when the wind continued to blow due west for a week or ten days together, which detained the *Flanders* mail, and kept them so long in torture,——but still 'twas the torture of the happy——In this track, I say, did my uncle *Toby* and *Trim* move for many years, every year of which, and sometimes every month, from the invention of either the one or the other of them, adding some new conceit or quirk of improvement to their operations, which always opened fresh springs of delight in carrying them on.

The first year's campaign was carried on from beginning to end, in the plain and simple method I've related.

In the second year, in which my uncle *Toby* took *Liege* and *Ruremond*,³ he thought he might afford the expence of four handsome draw-bridges, of two of which I have given an exact description, in the former part of my work.

At the latter end of the same year he added a couple of gates with portcullises:——These last were converted afterwards in orgues,⁴ as the better thing; and during the winter of the same year, my uncle *Toby*, instead of a new suit of cloaths, which he always had at *Christmas*, treated himself with a handsome sentry-box, to stand at the corner of the bowling-green, betwixt which point and the foot of the glacis, there was left a little kind of an esplanade for him and the corporal to confer and hold councils of war upon.

——The sentry-box was in case of rain.

All these were painted white three times over the ensuing spring, which enabled my uncle *Toby* to take the field with great splendour.

My father would often say to *Yorick*, that if any mortal in the whole universe had done such a thing, except his brother *Toby*, it would have been looked upon by the world as one of the most refined satyrs upon the parade and prancing manner, in which *Lewis* XIV. from the beginning of the war, but particularly that very year, had taken the field——But 'tis not my brother *Toby*'s nature, kind soul! my father would add, to insult any one.

——But let us go on.

CHAPTER XXIII

I must observe, that although in the first year's campaign, the word *town* is often mentioned,—yet there was no town at that time within the polygon; that addition was not made till the summer following the spring in which the bridges and sentry-box were painted, which was the third year of my uncle *Toby*'s campaigns,—when upon his taking *Amberg*, *Bonn*, and *Rhinberg*, and *Huy* and *Limbourg*,[1] one after another, a thought came into the corporal's head, that to talk of taking so many towns, *without one* TOWN *to show for it*,—was a very nonsensical way of going to work, and so proposed to my uncle *Toby*, that they should have a little model of a town built for them,—to be run up together of slit deals, and then painted, and clapped within the interior polygon to serve for all.

My uncle *Toby* felt the good of the project instantly, and instantly agreed to it, but with the addition of two singular improvements, of which he was almost as proud, as if he had been the original inventor of the project itself.

The one was to have the town built exactly in the stile of those, of which it was most likely to be the representative:——with grated windows, and the gable ends of the houses, facing the streets, &c. &c.—as those in *Ghent* and *Bruges*, and the rest of the towns in *Brabant* and *Flanders*.

The other was, not to have the houses run up together, as the corporal proposed, but to have every house independant, to hook on, or off, so as to form into the plan of whatever town they pleased. This was put directly into hand, and many and many a look of mutual congratulation was exchanged between my uncle *Toby* and the corporal, as the carpenter did the work.

——It answered prodigiously the next summer——the town was a perfect *Proteus*[2]——It was *Landen*, and *Trerebach*, and *Santvliet*, and *Drusen*, and *Hagenau*,—and then it was *Ostend* and *Menin*, and *Aeth* and *Dendermond*.[3]——

——Surely never did any TOWN act so many parts, since *Sodom* and *Gomorrah*, as my uncle *Toby*'s town did.

In the fourth year, my uncle *Toby* thinking a town looked foolishly without a church, added a very fine one with a steeple.——*Trim* was for having bells in it;——my uncle *Toby* said, the mettle had better be cast into cannon.

This led the way the next campaign for half a dozen brass field pieces,—to be planted three and three on each side of my uncle *Toby*'s sentry-box; and in a short time, these led the way for a train of somewhat larger,—and so on—(as must always be the case in hobby-horsical affairs) from pieces of half an inch bore, till it came at last to my father's jack boots.

The next year, which was that in which *Lisle* was besieged, and at the close of which both *Ghent* and *Bruges* fell into our hands,—my uncle *Toby* was sadly put to it for *proper* ammunition;——I say proper ammunition——because his great artillery would not bear powder; and 'twas well for the *Shandy* family they would not——For so full were the papers, from the beginning to the end of the siege, of the incessant firings kept up by the besiegers,——and so heated was my uncle *Toby*'s imagination with the accounts of them, that he had infallibly shot away all his estate.

SOMETHING therefore was wanting, as a *succedaneum*, especially in one or two of the more violent paroxysms of the siege, to keep up something like a continual firing in the imagination,——and this *something*, the corporal, whose principal strength lay in invention, supplied by an entire new system of battering of his own,—without which, this had been objected to by military critics, to the end of the world, as one of the great *desiderata* of my uncle *Toby*'s apparatus.

This will not be explained the worse, for setting off, as I generally do, at a little distance from the subject.

CHAPTER XXIV

WITH two or three other trinkets, small in themselves, but of great regard, which poor *Tom*, the corporal's unfortunate brother, had sent him over, with the account of his marriage with the *Jew*'s widow——there was

A *Montero*-cap[1] and two *Turkish* tobacco pipes.

The *Montero*-cap I shall describe by and bye.——The *Turkish* tobacco pipes had nothing particular in them, they were fitted up and ornamented as usual, with flexible tubes of *Morocco* leather and gold wire, and mounted at their ends, the one of them with ivory,—the other with black ebony, tipp'd with silver.

My father, who saw all things in lights different from the rest of the world, would say to the corporal, that he ought to look upon these two presents more as tokens of his brother's nicety, than his affection.——*Tom* did not care, *Trim*, he would say, to put on the cap, or to smoak in the tobacco-pipe of a *Jew*. ——God bless your honour, the corporal would say, (giving a strong reason to the contrary)—how can that be.——

The Montero-cap was scarlet, of a superfine *Spanish* cloth, died in grain, and mounted all round with furr, except about four inches in the front, which was faced with a light blue, slightly embroidered,—and seemed to have been the property of a *Portuguese* quarter-master, not of foot, but of horse, as the word denotes.

The corporal was not a little proud of it, as well for its own sake, as the sake of the giver, so seldom or never put it on but upon GALA-days; and yet never was a Montero-cap put to so many uses; for in all controverted points, whether military or culinary, provided the corporal was sure he was in the right,—it was either his *oath*,—his *wager*,—or his *gift*.

——'Twas his gift in the present case.

I'll be bound, said the corporal, speaking to himself, to *give* away my Montero-cap to the first beggar who comes to the door, if I do not manage this matter to his honour's satisfaction.

The completion was no further off, than the very next morning; which was that of the storm of the counterscarp betwixt the *Lower Deule*, to the right, and the gate St. *Andrew*,—and on the left, between St. *Magdalen*'s and the river.

As this was the most memorable attack in the whole war,— the most gallant and obstinate on both sides,—and I must add the most bloody too, for it cost the allies themselves that morning above eleven hundred men,—my uncle *Toby* prepared himself for it with a more than ordinary solemnity.

The eve which preceded, as my uncle *Toby* went to bed, he ordered his ramallie wig,[2] which had laid inside out for many years in the corner of an old campaigning trunk, which stood by his bedside, to be taken out and laid upon the lid of it, ready for the morning;—and the very first thing he did in his shirt, when he had stepped out of bed, my uncle *Toby*, after he had turned the rough side outwards,—put it on:——This done, he proceeded next to his breeches, and having buttoned the waist-band, he forthwith buckled on his sword belt, and had got his sword half way in,—when he considered he should want shaving, and that it would be very inconvenient doing it with his sword on,—so took it off:——In assaying to put on his regimental coat and waistcoat, my uncle *Toby* found the same objection in his wig,—so that went off too:—So that what with one thing, and what with another, as always falls out when a man is in the most haste,—'twas ten o'clock, which was half an hour later than his usual time, before my uncle *Toby* sallied out.

CHAPTER XXV

MY uncle *Toby* had scarce turned the corner of his yew hedge, which separated his kitchen garden from his bowling green, when he perceived the corporal had began the attack without him.——

Let me stop and give you a picture of the corporal's apparatus; and of the corporal himself in the height of this attack just as it struck my uncle *Toby*, as he turned towards the sentry box, where the corporal was at work,——for in nature there is not such another,——nor can any combination of all that is grotesque and whimsical in her works produce its equal.

The corporal——

——Tread lightly on his ashes, ye men of genius,——for he was your kinsman:

Weed his grave clean, ye men of goodness,—for he was your brother.—Oh corporal! had I thee, but now,—now, that I am able to give thee a dinner and protection,—how would I cherish thee! thou should'st wear thy Montero-cap every hour of the day, and every day of the week,—and when it was worn out, I would purchase thee a couple like it:——But alas! alas! alas! now that I can do this, in spight of their reverences—the occasion is lost—for thou art gone;—thy genius fled up to the stars from whence it came;—and that warm heart of thine, with all its generous and open vessels, compressed into a *clod of the valley!*[1]

——But what——what is this, to that future and dreaded page, where I look towards the velvet pall, decorated with the military ensigns of thy master—the first—the foremost of created beings;——where, I shall see thee, faithful servant! laying his sword and scabbard with a trembling hand across his coffin, and then returning pale as ashes to the door, to take his mourning horse by the bridle, to follow his hearse, as he directed thee;——where—all my father's systems shall be baffled by his sorrows; and, in spight of his philosophy, I shall behold him, as he inspects the lackered plate, twice taking his spectacles from off his nose, to wipe away the dew which nature has shed upon them———When I see him cast in the rosemary[2] with an air of disconsolation, which cries through my ears,———O *Toby!* in what corner of the world shall I seek thy fellow?

———Gracious powers! which erst have opened the lips of the dumb in his distress, and made the tongue of the stammerer speak plain———when I shall arrive at this dreaded page, deal not with me, then, with a stinted hand.

CHAPTER XXVI

THE corporal, who the night before had resolved in his mind, to supply the grand *desideratum*, of keeping up something like an incessant firing upon the enemy during the heat of the attack,— had no further idea in his fancy at that time, than a contrivance of smoaking tobacco against the town, out of one of my uncle *Toby*'s six field pieces, which were planted on each side of his sentry-box; the means of effecting which occurring to his fancy at the same time, though he had pledged his cap, he thought it in no danger from the miscarriage of his projects.

Upon turning it this way, and that, a little in his mind, he soon began to find out, that by means of his two *Turkish* tobacco-pipes, with the supplement of three smaller tubes of wash-leather at each of their lower ends, to be tagg'd by the same number of tin pipes fitted to the touch holes, and sealed with clay next the cannon, and then tied hermetically with waxed silk at their several insertions into the *Morocco* tube,—he should be able to fire the six field pieces all together, and with the same ease as to fire one.———

———Let no man say from what taggs and jaggs hints may not be cut out for the advancement of human knowlege. Let no man who has read my father's first and second *beds of justice*, ever rise up and say again, from collision of what kinds of bodies, light may, or may not be struck out, to carry the arts and sciences up to perfection.———Heaven! thou knowest how I love them;———thou knowest the secrets of my heart, and that I would this moment give my shirt———Thou art a fool, *Shandy*, says *Eugenius*,—for thou hast but a dozen in the world,—and 'twill break thy set.———

No matter for that, *Eugenius*; I would give the shirt off my back to be burnt into tinder, were it only to satisfy one feverish enquirer, how many sparks at one good stroke, a good flint and steel could strike into the tail of it.——Think ye not that in striking these *in*,—he might, peradventure, strike something *out*? as sure as a gun.——

——But this project, by the bye.

The corporal sat up the best part of the night in bringing *his* to perfection; and having made a sufficient proof of his cannon, with charging them to the top with tobacco,—he went with contentment to bed.

CHAPTER XXVII

THE corporal had slipped out about ten minutes before my uncle *Toby*, in order to fix his apparatus, and just give the enemy a shot or two before my uncle *Toby* came.

He had drawn the six field-pieces for this end, all close up together in front of my uncle *Toby's* sentry-box, leaving only an interval of about a yard and a half betwixt the three, on the right and left, for the convenience of charging, &c.—and the sake possibly of two batteries, which he might think double the honour of one.

In the rear, and facing this opening, with his back to the door of the sentry-box, for fear of being flanked, had the corporal wisely taken his post:——He held the ivory pipe, appertaining to the battery on the right, betwixt the finger and thumb of his right hand,—and the ebony pipe tipp'd with silver, which appertained to the battery on the left, betwixt the finger and thumb of the other——and with his right knee fixed firm upon the ground, as if in the front rank of his platoon, was the corporal, with his montero-cap upon his head, furiously playing off his two cross batteries at the same time against the counterguard, which faced the counterscarp, where the attack was to be made that morning. His first intention, as I said, was no more than giving the enemy a single puff or two;—but the pleasure of the *puffs*, as well as the *puffing*, had insensibly got hold of the corporal, and drawn him on from puff to puff, into the very height of the attack, by the time my uncle *Toby* joined him.

'Twas well for my father, that my uncle *Toby* had not his will to make that day.

CHAPTER XXVIII

MY uncle *Toby* took the ivory pipe out of the corporal's hand,—looked at it for half a minute, and returned it.

In less than two minutes my uncle *Toby* took the pipe from the corporal again, and raised it half way to his mouth——then hastily gave it back a second time.

The corporal redoubled the attack,——my uncle *Toby* smiled,——then looked grave,——then smiled for a moment,——then looked serious for a long time;——Give me hold of the ivory pipe, *Trim*, said my uncle *Toby*——my uncle *Toby* put it to his lips,——drew it back directly,——gave a peep over the horn-beam hedge;——never did my uncle *Toby*'s mouth water so much for a pipe in his life.——My uncle *Toby* retired into the sentry-box with the pipe in his hand.——

——Dear uncle *Toby!* don't go into the sentry-box with the pipe,—there's no trusting a man's self with such a thing in such a corner.

CHAPTER XXIX

I BEG the reader will assist me here, to wheel off my uncle *Toby*'s ordnance behind the scenes,——to remove his sentry-box, and clear the theatre, *if possible*, of horn-works and half moons, and get the rest of his military apparatus out of the way;——that done, my dear friend *Garrick*, we'll snuff the candles bright,— sweep the stage with a new broom,—draw up the curtain, and exhibit my uncle *Toby* dressed in a new character, throughout which the world can have no idea how he will act: and yet, if pity be akin to love,—and bravery no alien to it, you have seen enough of my uncle *Toby* in these, to trace these family likenesses, betwixt the two passions (in case there is one) to your heart's content.

Vain science! thou assists us in no case of this kind—and thou puzzlest us in every one.

There was, Madam, in my uncle *Toby*, a singleness of heart which misled him so far out of the little serpentine tracks in which things of this nature usually go on; you can—you can have no conception of it: with this, there was a plainness and simplicity of thinking, with such an unmistrusting ignorance of the plies and foldings of the heart of woman;——and so naked and defenceless did he stand before you, (when a siege was out of his head) that you might have stood behind any one of your serpentine walks, and shot my uncle *Toby* ten times in a day, through his liver,[1] if nine times in a day, Madam, had not served your purpose.[2]

With all this, Madam,—and what confounded every thing as much on the other hand, my uncle *Toby* had that unparalleled modesty of nature I once told you of, and which, by the bye, stood eternal sentry upon his feelings, that you might as soon ——But where am I going? these reflections croud in upon me ten pages at least too soon, and take up that time, which I ought to bestow upon facts.

CHAPTER XXX

OF the few legitimate sons of *Adam*, whose breasts never felt what the sting of love was,—(maintaining first, all mysogynists to be bastards)—the greatest heroes of ancient and modern story have carried off amongst them, nine parts in ten of the honour; and I wish for their sakes I had the key of my study out of my draw-well,[1] only for five minutes, to tell you their names—recollect them I cannot—so be content to accept of these, for the present, in their stead.——

There was the great king *Aldrovandus*,[2] and *Bosphorus*, and *Capadocius*, and *Dardanus*, and *Pontus*, and *Asius*,——to say nothing of the iron-hearted *Charles* the XIIth, whom the Countess of K***** herself could make nothing of.——There was *Babylonicus*, and *Mediterraneus*, and *Polixenes*, and *Persicus*, and *Prusicus*, not one of whom (except *Capadocius* and *Pontus*, who were both a little suspected) ever once bowed down his breast to the goddess——The truth is, they had all of them something else to do—and so had my uncle *Toby*—till Fate—till Fate I say, envying his name the glory of being handed down to posterity with *Aldrovandus*'s and the rest,—she basely patched up the peace of *Utrecht*.[3]

——Believe me, Sirs, 'twas the worst deed she did that year.

CHAPTER XXXI

AMONGST the many ill consequences of the treaty of *Utrecht*, it was within a point of giving my uncle *Toby* a surfeit of sieges; and though he recovered his appetite afterwards, yet *Calais* itself left not a deeper scar in *Mary*'s heart,[1] than *Utrecht* upon my uncle *Toby*'s. To the end of his life he never could hear *Utrecht* mentioned upon any account whatever,—or so much as read an article of news extracted out of the *Utrecht Gazette*, without fetching a sigh, as if his heart would break in twain.

My father, who was a great MOTIVE-MONGER, and consequently a very dangerous person for a man to sit by, either laughing or crying,—for he generally knew your motive for doing both, much better than you knew it yourself—would always console my uncle *Toby* upon these occasions, in a way, which shewed plainly, he imagined my uncle *Toby* grieved for nothing in the whole affair, so much as the loss of his *hobby-horse*.——Never mind, brother *Toby*, he would say,—by God's blessing we shall have another war break out again some of these days; and when it does,—the belligerent powers, if they would hang themselves, cannot keep us out of play.——I defy 'em, my dear *Toby*, he would add, to take countries without taking towns,——or towns without sieges.

My uncle *Toby* never took this back-stroke of my father's at his hobby horse kindly.——He thought the stroke ungenerous; and the more so, because in striking the horse, he hit the rider too, and in the most dishonourable part a blow could fall; so that upon these occasions, he always laid down his pipe upon the table with more fire to defend himself than common.

I told the reader, this time two years, that my uncle *Toby* was not eloquent; and in the very same page gave an instance to the contrary:——I repeat the observation, and a fact which contradicts it again.—He was not eloquent,—it was not easy to my uncle *Toby* to make long harangues,—and he hated florid ones; but there were occasions where the stream overflowed the man, and ran so counter to its usual course, that in some parts my uncle *Toby*, for a time, was at least equal to *Tertullus*[2]——but in others, in my own opinion, infinitely above him.

My father was so highly pleased with one of these apologetical orations of my uncle *Toby*'s, which he had delivered one evening before him and *Yorick*, that he wrote it down before he went to bed.

I have had the good fortune to meet with it amongst my father's papers, with here and there an insertion of his own, betwixt two crooks, thus [   ], and is endorsed,

My brother TOBY's *justification of his own principles and conduct in wishing to continue the war.*

I may safely say, I have read over this apologetical oration of my uncle *Toby*'s a hundred times, and think it so fine a model of defence,—and shews so sweet a temperament of gallantry and good principles in him, that I give it the world, word for word, (interlineations and all) as I find it.

CHAPTER XXXII

My uncle TOBY's *apologetical oration.*

I AM not insensible, brother *Shandy*, that when a man, whose profession is arms, wishes, as I have done, for war,—it has an ill aspect to the world;——and that, how just and right soever his motives and intentions may be,—he stands in an uneasy posture in vindicating himself from private views in doing it.

For this cause, if a soldier is a prudent man, which he may be, without being a jot the less brave, he will be sure not to utter his wish in the hearing of an enemy; for say what he will, an enemy will not believe him.——He will be cautious of doing it even to a friend,—lest he may suffer in his esteem:——But if his heart is overcharged, and a secret sigh for arms must have its vent, he will reserve it for the ear of a brother, who knows his character to the bottom, and what his true notions, dispositions, and principles of honour are: What, I *hope*, I have been in all these, brother *Shandy*, would be unbecoming in me to say:——much worse, I know, have I been than I ought,—and something worse, perhaps, than I think: But such as I am, you, my dear brother *Shandy*, who have sucked the same breasts with me,—and with whom I have been brought up from my cradle,—and from whose knowlege, from the first hours of our boyish pastimes, down to this, I have concealed no one action of my life, and scarce a thought in it——Such as I am, brother, you must by this time know me, with all my vices, and with all my weaknesses too, whether of my age, my temper, my passions, or my understanding.

Tell me then, my dear brother *Shandy*, upon which of them it is, that when I condemned the peace of *Utrecht*, and grieved the war was not carried on with vigour a little longer, you should think your brother did it upon unworthy views; or that in wishing for war, he should be bad enough to wish more of his fellow creatures slain,—more slaves made, and more families driven from their peaceful habitations, merely for his own pleasure:——Tell me, brother *Shandy*, upon what one deed of mine do you ground it? [*The devil a deed do I know of, dear* Toby, *but one for a hundred pounds, which I lent thee to carry on these cursed sieges.*]

If, when I was a school-boy, I could not hear a drum beat, but my heart beat with it—was it my fault?——Did I plant the propensity there?——did I sound the alarm within, or Nature?

When *Guy*, Earl of *Warwick*,[1] and *Parismus* and *Parismenus*, and *Valentine* and *Orson*, and the *Seven Champions of England* were handed around the school,—were they not all purchased with my own pocket money? Was that selfish, brother *Shandy*? When we read over the siege of *Troy*, which lasted ten years and eight months,——though with such a train of artillery as we had at *Namur*, the town might have been carried in a week—was I not as much concerned for the destruction of the *Greeks* and *Trojans* as any boy of the whole school? Had I not three strokes of a ferula given me, two on my right hand and one on my left, for calling *Helena*[2] a bitch for it? Did any one of you shed more tears for *Hector*? And when king *Priam* came to the camp to beg his body,[3] and returned weeping back to *Troy* without it,—you know, brother, I could not eat my dinner.——

——Did that bespeak me cruel? Or because, brother *Shandy*, my blood flew out into the camp, and my heart panted for war,—was it a proof it could not ache for the distresses of war too?

O brother! 'tis one thing for a soldier to gather laurels,—and 'tis another to scatter cypress.——[*Who told thee, my dear* Toby, *that cypress was used by the ancients on mournful occasions?*]

——'Tis one thing, brother *Shandy*, for a soldier to hazard his own life—to leap first down into the trench, where he is sure to be cut in pieces:——'Tis one thing, from public spirit and a thirst of glory, to enter the breach the first man,—to stand in the foremost rank, and march bravely on with drums and trumpets, and colours flying about his ears:——'Tis one thing, I say, brother *Shandy*, to do this—and 'tis another thing to reflect on the miseries of war;—to view the desolations of whole countries, and consider the intolerable fatigues and hardships which the soldier himself, the instrument who works them, is forced (for six-pence a day, if he can get it) to undergo.

Need I be told, dear *Yorick*, as I was by you, in *Le Fever's* funeral sermon, *That so soft and gentle a creature, born to love, to mercy, and kindness, as man is, was not shaped for this?* ——But why did you not add, *Yorick*,—if not by NATURE— that he is so by NECESSITY?——For what is war? what is it, *Yorick*, when fought as ours has been, upon principles of *liberty*, and upon principles of *honour*——what is it, but the getting together of quiet and harmless people, with their swords in their hands, to keep the ambitious and the turbulent within bounds? And heaven is my witness, brother *Shandy*, that the pleasure I have taken in these things,—and that infinite delight, in particular, which has attended my sieges in my bowling green, has arose within me, and I hope in the corporal too, from the consciousness we both had that in carrying them on, we were answering the great ends of our creation.

CHAPTER XXXIII

I told the Christian reader——I say *Christian*——hoping he is one——and if he is not, I am sorry for it——and only beg he will consider the matter with himself, and not lay the blame entirely upon this book,——

I told him, Sir——for in good truth, when a man is telling a story in the strange way I do mine, he is obliged continually to be going backwards and forwards to keep all tight together in the reader's fancy——which, for my own part, if I did not take heed to do more than at first, there is so much unfixed and equivocal matter starting up, with so many breaks and gaps in it,—and so little service do the stars afford, which, nevertheless, I hang up in some of the darkest passages, knowing that the world is apt to lose its way, with all the lights the sun itself at noon day can give it——and now, you see, I am lost myself!——

——But 'tis my father's fault; and whenever my brains come

to be dissected, you will perceive, without spectacles, that he has left a large uneven thread, as you sometimes see in an unsaleable piece of cambrick, running along the whole length of the web, and so untowardly, you cannot so much as cut out a **, (here I hang up a couple of lights again)——or a fillet, or a thumb-stall, but it is seen or felt.——

Quanto id diligentius in liberis procreandis cavendum,[1] sayeth *Cardan*. All which being considered, and that you see 'tis morally impracticable for me to wind this round to where I set out——

I begin the chapter over again.

CHAPTER XXXIV

I TOLD the Christian reader in the beginning of the chapter which preceded my uncle *Toby*'s apologetical oration,— though in a different trope from what I shall make use of now, That the peace of *Utrecht* was within an ace of creating the same shyness betwixt my uncle *Toby* and his hobby-horse, as it did betwixt the queen and the rest of the confederating powers.[1]

There is an indignant way in which a man sometimes dismounts his horse, which as good as says to him, "I'll go afoot, Sir, all the days of my life, before I would ride a single mile upon your back again." Now my uncle *Toby* could not be said to dismount his horse in this manner; for in strictness of language, he could not be said to dismount his horse at all——his horse rather flung him——and somewhat *viciously*, which made my uncle *Toby* take it ten times more unkindly. Let this matter be settled by state jockies as they like.——It created, I say, a sort of shyness betwixt my uncle *Toby* and his hobby-horse.——He had no occasion for him from the month of *March* to *November*, which was the summer after the articles were signed, except it was now and then to take a short ride out, just to see that the fortifications and harbour of *Dunkirk* were demolished, according to stipulation.

The *French* were so backwards all that summer in setting about that affair, and Monsieur *Tugghe*,[2] the deputy from the magistrates of *Dunkirk*, presented so many affecting petitions to the queen,—beseeching her majesty to cause only her thunderbolts to fall upon the martial works, which might have incurred her displeasure,—but to spare—to spare the mole, for the mole's sake; which, in its naked situation, could be no more than an object of pity——and the queen (who was but a woman) being of a pitiful disposition,—and her ministers also, they not wishing in their hearts to have the town dismantled, for these private reasons, *   *   *   *   *   *   *

*   *   *   *   *   *   *____

*   *   *   *   *   *   *   *   *   *   *   *

*   *   *   *   *   *   *   *   *   *   *   *

*   *   *; so that the whole went heavily on with my uncle *Toby*; insomuch, that it was not within three full months, after he and the corporal had constructed the town, and put it in a condition to be destroyed, that the several commandants, commissaries, deputies, negotiators, and intendants, would permit him to set about it.——Fatal interval of inactivity!

The corporal was for beginning the demolition, by making a breach in the ramparts, or main fortifications of the town ——No,—that will never do, corporal, said my uncle *Toby*, for in going that way to work with the town, the *English* garrison will not be safe in it an hour; because if the *French* are treacherous——They are as treacherous as devils, an' please your honour, said the corporal——It gives me concern always when I hear it, *Trim*, said my uncle *Toby*,—for they don't want personal bravery; and if a breach is made in the ramparts, they may enter it, and make themselves masters of the place when they please:——Let them enter it, said the corporal, lifting up his pioneer's spade in both his hands, as if he was going to lay about him with it,—let them enter, an' please your honour, if they dare.——In cases like this, corporal, said my uncle *Toby*, slipping his right hand down to the middle of his cane, and holding it afterwards truncheon-wise, with his forefinger extended,——'tis no part of the consideration of a commandant, what the enemy dare,—or what they dare not do; he must act with prudence. We will begin with the outworks both towards the sea and the land, and particularly with fort *Louis*, the most distant of them all, and demolish it first,—and the rest, one by one, both on our right and left, as we retreat towards the town;——then we'll demolish the mole,—next fill up the harbour,—then retire into the citadel, and blow it up into the air; and having done that, corporal, we'll embark for *England*. ——We are there, quoth the corporal, recollecting himself ——Very true, said my uncle *Toby*—looking at the church.

CHAPTER XXXV

A DELUSIVE, delicious consultation or two of this kind, betwixt my uncle *Toby* and *Trim*, upon the demolition of *Dunkirk*,—for a moment rallied back the ideas of those pleasures,
which were slipping from under him:——still—still all went on
heavily——the magic left the mind the weaker—STILLNESS,
with SILENCE at her back, entered the solitary parlour, and
drew their gauzy mantle over my uncle *Toby*'s head;——and
LISTLESSNESS, with her lax fibre and undirected eye, sat quietly
down beside him in his arm chair.——No longer *Amberg*, and
Rhinberg, and *Limbourg*, and *Huy*, and *Bonn*, in one year,—
and the prospect of *Landen*, and *Trerebach*, and *Drusen*, and
Dendermond, the next,—hurried on the blood:—No longer
did saps, and mines, and blinds, and gabions, and palisadoes,
keep out this fair enemy of man's repose:——No more could
my uncle *Toby*, after passing the *French* lines, as he eat his egg at
supper, from thence break into the heart of *France*,—cross over
the *Oyes*, and with all *Picardie* open behind him, march up to
the gates of *Paris*, and fall asleep with nothing but ideas of
glory:——No more was he to dream, he had fixed the royal
standard upon the tower of the *Bastile*, and awake with it
streaming in his head.

——Softer visions,—gentler vibrations stole sweetly in upon
his slumbers;—the trumpet of war fell out of his hands,—he
took up the lute, sweet instrument! of all others the most
delicate! the most difficult!——how wilt thou touch it, my dear
uncle *Toby*?

CHAPTER XXXVI

NOW, because I have once or twice said, in my inconsiderate
way of talking, That I was confident the following memoirs of
my uncle *Toby*'s courtship of widow *Wadman*, whenever I got
time to write them, would turn out one of the most compleat
systems, both of the elementary and practical part of love and
love-making, that ever was addressed to the world——are you
to imagine from thence, that I shall set out with a description of
what love is? whether part God and part Devil, as *Plotinus*[1] will
have it——

———Or by a more critical equation, and supposing the whole of love to be as ten———to determine, with *Ficinus*,[2] "*How many parts of it—the one,—and how many the other*;"—or whether it is *all of it one great Devil*, from head to tail, as *Plato* has taken upon him to pronounce; concerning which conceit of his, I shall not offer my opinion:—but my opinion of *Plato* is this; that he appears, from this instance, to have been a man of much the same temper and way of reasoning with doctor *Baynyard*,[3] who being a great enemy to blisters, as imagining that half a dozen of 'em on at once, would draw a man as surely to his grave, as a herse and six—rashly concluded, that the Devil himself was nothing in the world, but one great bouncing *Cantharidis*.[4]

———

I have nothing to say to people who allow themselves this monstrous liberty in arguing, but what *Nazianzen* cried out (*that is polemically*) to *Philagrius*[5]———

"῎Ευγε!" *O rare!* '*tis fine reasoning, Sir, indeed!*—"ὅτι φιλοσοφεῖς ἐν Πάθεσι"—*and most nobly do you aim at truth, when you philosophize about it in your moods and passions.*

Nor is it to be imagined, for the same reason, I should stop to enquire, whether love is a disease,———or embroil myself with *Rhasis*[6] and *Dioscorides*,[7] whether the seat of it is in the brain or liver;—because this would lead me on, to an examination of the two very opposite manners, in which patients have been treated———the one, of *Aætius*,[8] who always begun with a cooling glyster of hempseed and bruised cucumbers;—and followed on with thin potations of water lillies and purslane—to which he added a pinch of snuff, of the herb *Hanea*;[9]—and where *Aætius* durst venture it,—his topaz-ring.[10]

———The other, that of *Gordonius*,[11] who (in his cap. 15. *de Amore*) directs they should be thrashed, "*ad putorem usque*," ———till they stink again.

These are disquisitions, which my father, who had laid in a great stock of knowledge of this kind, will be very busy with, in the progress of my uncle *Toby*'s affairs: I must anticipate thus much, That from his theories of love, (with which, by the way, he contrived to crucify my uncle *Toby*'s mind, almost as much as his amours themselves)—he took a single step into practice;—and by means of a camphorated cerecloth, which he found means to impose upon the taylor for buckram, whilst he was making my uncle *Toby* a new pair of breeches, he produced *Gordonius's* effect upon my uncle *Toby* without the disgrace.

What changes this produced, will be read in its proper place: all that is needful to be added to the anecdote, is this,——That whatever effect it had upon my uncle *Toby*,——it had a vile effect upon the house;——and if my uncle *Toby* had not smoaked it down as he did, it might have had a vile effect upon my father too.

CHAPTER XXXVII

——'TWILL come out of itself by and bye.——All I contend for is, that I am not *obliged* to set out with a definition of what love is; and so long as I can go on with my story intelligibly, with the help of the word itself, without any other idea to it, than what I have in common with the rest of the world, why should I differ from it a moment before the time?——When I can get on no further,—and find myself entangled on all sides of this mystick labyrinth,—my Opinion will then come in, in course,—and lead me out.

At present, I hope I shall be sufficiently understood, in telling the reader, my uncle *Toby fell in love:*

—Not that the phrase is at all to my liking: for to say a man is *fallen* in love,—or that he is *deeply* in love,—or up to the ears in love,—and sometimes even *over head and ears in it*,—carries an idiomatical kind of implication, that love is a thing *below* a man:—this is recurring again to *Plato's* opinion, which, with all his divinityship,—I hold to be damnable and heretical;—and so much for that.

Let love therefore be what it will,—my uncle *Toby* fell into it.

——And possibly, gentle reader, with such a temptation—so wouldst thou: For never did thy eyes behold, or thy concupiscence covet any thing in this world, more concupiscible than widow *Wadman*.

CHAPTER XXXVIII

To conceive this right,—call for pen and ink—here's paper
ready to your hand.——Sit down, Sir, paint her to your own
mind——as like your mistress as you can——as unlike your
wife as your conscience will let you—'tis all one to me
——please but your own fancy in it.

———Was ever any thing in Nature so sweet!—so exquisite!
———Then, dear Sir, how could my uncle *Toby* resist it?

Thrice happy book! thou wilt have one page, at least, within thy covers, which MALICE will not blacken, and which IGNOR-ANCE cannot misrepresent.[1]

CHAPTER XXXIX

As *Susannah* was informed by an express from Mrs. *Bridget*, of my uncle *Toby*'s falling in love with her mistress, fifteen days before it happened,—the contents of which express, *Susannah* communicated to my mother the next day,—it has just given me an opportunity of entering upon my uncle *Toby*'s amours a fortnight before their existence.

I have an article of news to tell you, Mr. *Shandy*, quoth my mother, which will surprise you greatly.———

Now my father was then holding one of his second beds of justice, and was musing within himself about the hardships of matrimony, as my mother broke silence.———

"———My brother *Toby*, quoth she, is going to be married to Mrs. *Wadman*."

———Then he will never, quoth my father, be able to lie *diagonally* in his bed again as long as he lives.

It was a consuming vexation to my father, that my mother never asked the meaning of a thing she did not understand.

———That she is not a woman of science, my father would say—is her misfortune—but she might ask a question.—

My mother never did.———In short, she went out of the world at last without knowing whether it turned *round*, or stood *still*.———My father had officiously told her above a thousand times which way it was,—but she always forgot.

For these reasons a discourse seldom went on much further betwixt them, than a proposition,—a reply, and a rejoinder; at the end of which, it generally took breath for a few minutes, (as in the affair of the breeches) and then went on again.

If he marries, 'twill be the worse for us,—quoth my mother.

Not a cherry-stone, said my father,—he may as well batter away his means upon that, as any thing else.

———To be sure, said my mother: so here ended the proposi-tion,—the reply,—and the rejoinder, I told you of.

It will be some amusement to him, too,———said my father.

A very great one, answered my mother, if he should have children.——

——Lord have mercy upon me,——said my father to himself

* * * * * * * * * * *
* * * * * * * * * * *
* * * * * * * * * * *
* * * * * * * * * * *
* * * * * * .

CHAPTER XL

I AM now beginning to get fairly into my work; and by the help of a vegitable diet, with a few of the cold feeds, I make no doubt but I shall be able to go on with my uncle *Toby*'s story, and my own, in a tolerable straight line. Now,

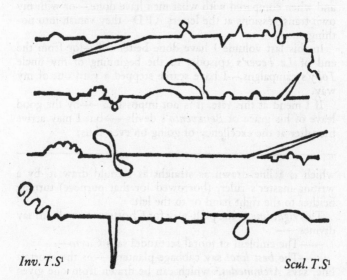

Inv. T.S[1]   *Scul. T.S*[1]

These were the four lines I moved in through my first, second, third, and fourth volumes.——In the fifth volume I have been very good,——the precise line I have described in it being this:

By which it appears, that except at the curve, marked A. where I took a trip to *Navarre*,—and the indented curve B. which is the short airing when I was there with the Lady *Baussiere* and her page,—I have not taken the least frisk of a digression, till *John de la Casse*'s devils led me the round you see marked D.—for as for *c c c c c* they are nothing but parentheses, and the common *ins* and *outs* incident to the lives of the greatest ministers of state; and when compared with what men have done,—or with my own transgressions at the letters A B D—they vanish into nothing.

In this last volume I have done better still—for from the end of *Le Fever*'s episode, to the beginning of my uncle *Toby*'s campaigns,—I have scarce stepped a yard out of my way.

If I mend at this rate, it is not impossible——by the good leave of his grace of *Benevento*'s devils——but I may arrive hereafter at the excellency of going on even thus;

---

which is a line drawn as straight as I could draw it, by a writing-master's ruler, (borrowed for that purpose) turning neither to the right hand or to the left.

This *right line*,—the path-way for Christians to walk in! say divines——

——The emblem of moral rectitude! says *Cicero*——

——The *best line!* say cabbage-planters——is the shortest line, says *Archimedes*,[2] which can be drawn from one given point to another.——

I wish your ladyships would lay this matter to heart in your next birthday suits![3]

——What a journey!

Pray can you tell me,—that is, without anger, before I write my chapter upon straight lines——by what mistake——who told them so——or how it has come to pass, that your men of wit and genius have all along confounded this line, with the line of GRAVITATION.

END of the SIXTH VOLUME.

THE

L I F E

AND

O P I N I O N S

OF

TRISTRAM SHANDY,

GENTLEMAN.

Non enim excursus hic ejus, sed opus ipsum est.
PLIN. Lib. quintus Epistola sexta.[1]

VOL. VII.

LONDON:

Printed for T. BECKET and P. A. DEHONT,
in the Strand.   MDCCLXV.

CHAPTER I

No——I think, I said, I would write two volumes every year, provided the vile cough which then tormented me, and which to this hour I dread worse than the devil, would but give me leave——and in another place—(but where, I can't recollect now) speaking of my book as a *machine*, and laying my pen and ruler down cross-wise upon the table, in order to gain the greater credit to it—I swore it should be kept a going at that rate these forty years if it pleased but the fountain of life to bless me so long with health and good spirits.

Now as for my spirits, little have I to lay to their charge—nay so very little (unless the mounting me upon a long stick, and playing the fool with me nineteen hours out of the twenty-four, be accusations) that on the contrary, I have much—much to thank 'em for: cheerily have ye made me tread the path of life with all the burdens of it (except its cares) upon my back; in no one moment of my existence, that I remember, have ye once deserted me, or tinged the objects which came in my way, either with sable, or with a sickly green; in dangers ye gilded my horizon with hope, and when DEATH himself knocked at my door—ye bad him come again; and in so gay a tone of careless indifference, did ye do it, that he doubted of his commission

——

"—There must certainly be some mistake in this matter," quoth he.

Now there is nothing in this world I abominate worse, than to be interrupted in a story——and I was that moment telling Eugenius a most tawdry one in my way, of a nun who fancied herself a shell-fish, and of a monk damn'd for eating a muscle,[1] and was shewing him the grounds and justice of the procedure——

"—Did ever so grave a personage get into so vile a scrape?" quoth Death. Thou hast had a narrow escape, Tristram, said Eugenius, taking hold of my hand as I finish'd my story——

But there is no *living*, Eugenius, replied I, at this rate; for as this *son of a whore* has found out my lodgings——

—You call him rightly, said Eugenius,—for by sin, we are told, he enter'd the world——I care not which way he enter'd, quoth I, provided he be not in such a hurry to take me out with him—for I have forty volumes to write, and forty thousand things to say and do, which no body in the world will say and do for me, except thyself; and as thou seest he has got me by the throat (for Eugenius could scarce hear me speak across the table) and that I am no match for him in the open field, had I not better, whilst these few scatter'd spirits remain, and these two spider legs of mine (holding one of them up to him) are able to support me—had I not better, Eugenius, fly for my life? 'tis my advice, my dear Tristram, said Eugenius——then by heaven! I will lead him a dance he little thinks of—for I will gallop, quoth I, without looking once behind me to the banks of the Garonne; and if I hear him clattering at my heels——I'll scamper away to mount Vesuvius——from thence to Joppa, and from Joppa to the world's end, where, if he follows me, I pray God he may break his neck——

—He runs more risk *there*, said Eugenius, than thou.

Eugenius's wit and affection brought blood into the cheek from whence it had been some months banish'd—'twas a vile moment to bid adieu in; he led me to my chaise——*Allons!* said I; the post boy gave a crack with his whip——off I went like a cannon, and in half a dozen bounds got into Dover.

CHAPTER II

Now hang it! quoth I, as I look'd towards the French coast—a man should know something of his own country too, before he goes abroad——and I never gave a peep into Rochester church, or took notice of the dock of Chatham,[1] or visited St. Thomas[2] at Canterbury, though they all three laid in my way——

—But mine, indeed, is a particular case——

So without arguing the matter further with Thomas o'Becket, or any one else—I skip'd into the boat, and in five minutes we got under sail and scudded away like the wind.

Pray captain, quoth I, as I was going down into the cabin, is a man never overtaken by *Death* in this passage?

Why, there is not time for a man to be sick in it, replied he——What a cursed lyar! for I am sick as a horse, quoth I, already——what a brain!——upside down!——hey dey! the cells are broke loose one into another, and the blood, and the lymph, and the nervous juices, with the fix'd and volatile salts, are all jumbled into one mass——good g—! every thing turns

round in it like a thousand whirlpools——I'd give a shilling to
know if I shan't write the clearer for it——

Sick! sick! sick! sick!——

——When shall we get to land? captain——they have hearts like
stones——O I am deadly sick!——reach me that thing, boy
——'tis the most discomfiting sickness——I wish I was at the
bottom—Madam! how is it with you? Undone! undone!
un——O! undone! sir—What the first time?——No, 'tis the
second, third, sixth, tenth time, sir,—hey-day——what a
trampling over head!—hollo! cabin boy! what's the matter—

The wind chopp'd about! s'Death!—then I shall meet him
full in the face.

What luck!—'tis chopp'd about again, master——O the devil
chop it——

Captain, quoth she, for heaven's sake, let us get ashore.

CHAPTER III

It is a great inconvenience to a man in a haste, that there are
three distinct roads between Calais and Paris, in behalf of which
there is so much to be said by the several deputies from the
towns which lie along them, that half a day is easily lost in
settling which you'll take.

First, the road by Lisle and Arras, which is the most
about——but most interesting, and instructing.

The second that by Amiens, which you may go, if you would
see Chantilly——

And that by Beauvais, which you may go, if you will.

For this reason a great many chuse to go by Beauvais.

CHAPTER IV

"Now before I quit Calais," a travel-writer would say, "it
would not be amiss to give some account of it."—Now I think it
very much amiss—that a man cannot go quietly through a town,
and let it alone, when it does not meddle with him, but that he
must be turning about and drawing his pen at every kennel he
crosses over, merely o' my conscience, for the sake of drawing
it; because, if we may judge from what has been wrote of these
things, by all who have *wrote and gallop'd*—or who have

gallop'd and wrote, which is a different way still; or who for more expedition than the rest, have *wrote-galloping*, which is the way I do at present——from the great Addison[1] who did it with his satchel of school-books hanging at his a— and galling his beast's crupper at every stroke—there is not a galloper of us all who might not have gone on ambling quietly in his own ground (in case he had any) and have wrote all he had to write, dry shod, as well as not.

For my own part, as heaven is my judge, and to which I shall ever make my last appeal—I know no more of Calais, (except the little my barber told me of it, as he was whetting his razor) than I do this moment of *Grand Cairo*; for it was dusky in the evening when I landed, and dark as pitch in the morning when I set out, and yet by merely knowing what is what, and by drawing this from that in one part of the town, and by spelling and putting this and that together in another—I would lay any travelling odds, that I this moment write a chapter upon Calais as long as my arm; and with so distinct and satisfactory a detail of every item, which is worth a stranger's curiosity in the town—that you would take me for the town clerk of Calais itself—and where, sir, would be the wonder? was not Democritus, who laughed ten times more than I—town-clerk of *Abdera?* and was not (I forget his name) who had more discretion than us both, town-clerk of Ephesus?[2]——it should be penn'd moreover, Sir, with so much knowledge and good sense, and truth, and precision——

—Nay—if you don't believe me, you may read the chapter for your pains.

CHAPTER V

Calais, *Calatium, Calusium, Calesium*.[1]

This town, if we may trust it's archives, the authority of which I see no reason to call in question in this place—was *once* no more than a small village belonging to one of the first Counts de Guines; and as it boasts at present of no less than fourteen thousand inhabitants, exclusive of four hundred and twenty distinct families in the *basse ville*, or suburbs——it must have grown up little by little, I suppose, to it's present size.

Though there are four convents, there is but one parochial church in the whole town; I had not an opportunity of taking its exact dimensions, but it is pretty easy to make a tolerable conjecture of 'em—for as there are fourteen thousand inhabitants in the town, if the church holds them all, it must be considerably large—and if it will not—'tis a very great pity they have not another—it is built in form of a cross, and dedicated to the Virgin Mary; the steeple which has a spire to it, is placed in the middle of the church, and stands upon four pillars elegant and light enough, but sufficiently strong at the same time—it is decorated with eleven altars, most of which are rather fine than beautiful. The great altar is a masterpiece in its kind; 'tis of white marble, and as I was told near sixty feet high—had it been much higher, it had been as high as mount Calvary itself—therefore, I suppose it must be high enough in all conscience.

There was nothing struck me more than the great *Square*; tho' I cannot say 'tis either well paved or well built; but 'tis in the heart of the town, and most of the streets, especially those in that quarter, all terminate in it; could there have been a fountain in all Calais, which it seems there cannot, as such an object would have been a great ornament, it is not to be doubted, but that the inhabitants would have had it in the very centre of this square,—not that it is properly a square,—because 'tis forty feet longer from east to west, than from north to south; so that the French in general have more reason on their side in calling them *Places* than *Squares*, which strictly speaking, to be sure they are not.

The town-house[2] seems to be but a sorry building, and not to be kept in the best repair; otherwise it had been a second great ornament to this place; it answers however its destination, and serves very well for the reception of the magistrates, who assemble in it from time to time; so that 'tis presumable, justice is regularly distributed.

I had heard much of it, but there is nothing at all curious in the *Courgain*; 'tis a distinct quarter of the town inhabited solely by sailors and fishermen; it consists of a number of small streets, neatly built and mostly of brick; 'tis extremely populous, but as that may be accounted for, from the principles of their diet,—there is nothing curious in that neither.——A traveller may see it to satisfy himself—he must not omit however taking notice of *La Tour de Guet*,[3] upon any account; 'tis so called from its particular destination, because in war it serves to discover and give notice of the enemies which approach the place, either by sea or land;——but 'tis monstrous high, and catches the eye so continually, you cannot avoid taking notice of it, if you would.

It was a singular disappointment to me, that I could not have permission to take an exact survey of the fortifications, which are the strongest in the world, and which, from first to last, that is, from the time they were set about by Philip of France Count of Bologne, to the present war, wherein many reparations were made, have cost (as I learned afterwards from an engineer in Gascony)—above a hundred millions of livres. It is very remarkable that at the *Tête de Gravelenes*,[4] and where the town is naturally the weakest, they have expended the most money; so that the outworks stretch a great way into the campaign, and consequently occupy a large tract of ground.—However, after all that is *said* and *done*, it must be acknowledged that Calais was never upon any account so considerable from itself, as from its situation, and that easy enterance which it gave our ancestors upon all occasions into France: it was not without its inconveniences also; being no less troublesome to the English in those times, than Dunkirk has been to us, in ours; so that it was deservedly looked upon as the key to both kingdoms, which no doubt is the reason that there have arisen so many contentions who should keep it: of these, the siege of Calais, or rather the blockade (for it was shut up both by land and sea) was the most memorable, as it withstood the efforts of Edward the third a whole year, and was not terminated at last but by famine and extream misery; the gallantry of *Eustace de St. Pierre*,[5] who first offered himself a victim for his fellow citizens, has rank'd his name with heroes. As it will not take up above fifty pages, it would be injustice to the reader, not to give him a minute account of that romantic transaction, as well as of the siege itself, in Rapin's own words:[6]

CHAPTER VI

——BUT courage! gentle reader!——I scorn it——'tis enough to have thee in my power——but to make use of the advantage which the fortune of the pen has now gained over thee, would be too much——No——! by that all powerful fire which warms the visionary brain, and lights the spirits through un-worldly tracts! ere I would force a helpless creature upon this hard service, and make thee pay, poor soul! for fifty pages which I have no right to sell thee,—naked as I am, I would browse upon the mountains, and smile that the north wind brought me neither my tent or my supper.

—So put on, my brave boy! and make the best of thy way to Boulogne.

CHAPTER VII

——BOULOGNE!——hah!—so we are all got together—debtors and sinners before heaven; a jolly set of us—but I can't stay and quaff it off with you—I'm pursued myself like a hundred devils, and shall be overtaken before I can well change horses:——for heaven's sake, make haste——'Tis for high treason, quoth a very little man, whispering as low as he could to a very tall man that stood next him——Or else for murder; quoth the tall man——Well thrown size-ace!¹ quoth I. No; quoth a third, the gentleman has been committing—— ——.

Ah! ma chere fille! said I, as she tripp'd by, from her matins—you look as rosy as the morning (for the sun was rising, and it made the compliment the more gracious)——No; it can't be that, quoth a fourth——(she made a curt'sy to me—I kiss'd my hand) 'tis debt; continued he: 'Tis certainly for debt; quoth a fifth; I would not pay that gentleman's debts, quoth *Ace*, for a thousand pounds; Nor would I, quoth *Size*, for six times the sum—Well thrown, Size-Ace, again! quoth I;—but I have no debt but the debt of NATURE, and I want but patience of her, and I will pay her every farthing I owe her——How can you be so hard-hearted, MADAM, to arrest a poor traveller going along without molestation to any one, upon his lawful occasions? do stop that death-looking, long-striding scoundrel of a scare-sinner, who is posting after me——he never would have followed me but for you——if it be but for a stage, or two, just to give me start of him, I beseech you, madam—— ——do, dear lady——.

——Now, in troth, 'tis a great pity, quoth mine Irish host,² that all this good courtship should be lost; for the young gentlewoman has been after going out of hearing of it all along——.

——Simpleton! quoth I.

——So you have nothing *else* in Boulogne worth seeing?

—By Jasus! there is the finest Seminary for the Humani-
ties——.

—There cannot be a finer; quoth I.

CHAPTER VIII

When the precipitancy of a man's wishes hurries on his ideas
ninety times faster than the vehicle he rides in—woe be to truth!
and woe be to the vehicle and its tackling (let 'em be made of
what stuff you will) upon which he breathes forth the disappointment of his soul!

As I never give general characters either of men or things in
choler, "*the most haste, the worst speed*;" was all the reflection I
made upon the affair, the first time it happen'd;—the second,
third, fourth, and fifth time, I confined it respectively to those
times, and accordingly blamed only the second, third, fourth,
and fifth post-boy for it, without carrying my reflections further; but the event continuing to befall me from the fifth, to the
sixth, seventh, eighth, ninth, and tenth time, and without one
exception, I then could not avoid making a national reflection of
it, which I do in these words;

*That something is always wrong in a French post-chaise upon
first setting out.*

Or the proposition may stand thus.

*A French postilion has always to alight before he has got three
hundred yards out of town.*

What's wrong now?——Diable!——a rope's broke!——a
knot has slipt!——a staple's drawn!——a bolt's to whittle!
——a tag, a rag, a jag, a strap, a buckle, or a buckle's tongue,
want altering.——

Now true as all this is, I never think myself impower'd to
excommunicate thereupon either the post-chaise, or its driver——nor do I take it into my head to swear by the living G—,
I would rather go a foot ten thousand times——or that I will be
damn'd if ever I get into another——but I take the matter coolly
before me, and consider, that some tag, or rag, or jag, or bolt, or
buckle, or buckle's tongue, will ever be a wanting, or want
altering, travel where I will——so I never chaff, but take the
good and the bad as they fall in my road, and get on:——Do so,
my lad! said I; he had lost five minutes already, in alighting in

order to get at a luncheon of black bread which he had cramm'd
into the chaise-pocket, and was remounted and going leisurely
on, to relish it the better——Get on, my lad, said I, briskly—
but in the most persuasive tone imaginable, for I jingled a four
and twenty sous piece against the glass, taking care to hold the
flat side towards him, as he look'd back: the dog grinn'd intelligence from his right ear to his left, and behind his sooty
muzzle discover'd such a pearly row of teeth, that *Sovereignty*
would have pawn'd her jewels for them.——

Just heaven! { What masticators!——
              { What bread!——

and so, as he finish'd the last mouthful of it, we enter'd the town
of Montreuil.

CHAPTER IX.

THERE is not a town in all France, which in my opinion, looks
better in the map, than MONTREUIL;——I own, it does not
look so well in the book of post roads; but when you come to
see it—to be sure it looks most pitifully.

There is one thing however in it at present very handsome;
and that is the inn-keeper's daughter: She has been eighteen
months at Amiens, and six at Paris, in going through her classes;
so knits, and sews, and dances, and does the little coquetries
very well.——

—A slut!¹ in running them over within these five minutes that
I have stood looking at her, she has let fall at least a dozen loops
in a white thread stocking——Yes, yes—I see, you cunning
gipsy!—'tis long, and taper—you need not pin it to your knee—
and that 'tis your own—and fits you exactly.——

——That Nature should have told this creature a word about
a *statue's thumb!*——

—But as this sample is worth all their thumbs——besides I
have her thumbs and fingers in at the bargain if they can be any
guide to me,—and as *Janatone* withal (for that is her name)
stands so well for a drawing——may I never draw more, or
rather may I draw like a draught-horse, by main strength all the
days of my life,—if I do not draw her in all her proportions, and
with as determin'd a pencil, as if I had her in the wettest
drapery.——

—But your worships chuse rather that I give you the length,

breadth, and perpendicular height of the great parish church, or a drawing of the fascade of the abbey of Saint Austreberte[2] which has been transported from Artois hither—every thing is just I suppose as the masons and carpenters left them,—and if the belief in Christ continues so long, will be so these fifty years to come—so your worships and reverences, may all measure them at your leisures——but he who measures thee, Janatone, must do it now—thou carriest the principles of change within thy frame; and considering the chances of a transitory life, I would not answer for thee a moment; e'er twice twelve months are pass'd and gone, thou mayest grow out like a pumkin, and lose thy shapes——or, thou mayest go off like a flower, and lose thy beauty——nay, thou mayest go off like a hussy—and lose thyself.——I would not answer for my aunt Dinah, was she alive——'faith, scarce for her picture——were it but painted by Reynolds—

—But if I go on with my drawing, after naming that son of Apollo, I'll be shot——

So you must e'en be content with the original; which if the evening is fine in passing thro' Montreuil, you will see at your chaise door, as you change horses: but unless you have as bad a reason for haste as I have—you had better stop:—She has a little of the *devote*:[3] but that, sir, is a terce to a nine[4] in your favour ——

—L— help me! I could not count a single point: so had been piqued, and repiqued, and capotted[5] to the devil.

CHAPTER X

ALL which being considered, and that Death moreover might be much nearer me than I imagined——I wish I was at Abbeville, quoth I, were it only to see how they card and spin——so off we set.

de Montreuil a Nampont - poste et demi de Nampont a Bernay - - - poste

de Bernay a Nouvion - - - poste

de Nouvion a ABBEVILLE   poste

——but the carders and spinners were all gone to bed.

* Vid. Book of French post-roads, page 36. edition of 1762.

CHAPTER XI

WHAT a vast advantage is travelling! only it heats one; but there is a remedy for that, which you may pick out of the next chapter.

CHAPTER XII

WAS I in a condition to stipulate with death, as I am this moment with my apothecary, how and where I will take his glister¹——I should certainly declare against submitting to it before my friends; and therefore, I never seriously think upon the mode and manner of this great catastrophe, which generally takes up and torments my thoughts as much as the catastrophe itself, but I constantly draw the curtain across it with this wish, that the Disposer of all things may so order it, that it happen not to me in my own house——but rather in some decent inn——at home, I know it,——the concern of my friends, and the last services of wiping my brows and smoothing my pillow, which the quivering hand of pale affection shall pay me, will so crucify my soul, that I shall die of a distemper which my physician is not aware of: but in an inn, the few cold offices I wanted, would be purchased with a few guineas, and paid me with an undisturbed, but punctual attention——but mark. This inn, should not be the inn at Abbeville——if there was not another inn in the universe, I would strike that inn out of the capitulation: so

Let the horses be in the chaise exactly by four in the morning——Yes, by four, Sir,——or by Genevieve! I'll raise a clatter in the house, shall wake the dead.

CHAPTER XIII

"MAKE them like unto a wheel,"¹ is a bitter sarcasm, as all the learned know, against the *grand tour*,² and that restless spirit for making it, which David prophetically foresaw would haunt the children of men in the latter days; and therefore, as thinketh the great bishop Hall, 'tis one of the severest imprecations which David ever utter'd against the enemies of the Lord—and, as if he had said, "I wish them no worse luck than always to be rolling about"—So much motion, continues he, (for he was very corpulent)—is so much unquietness; and so much of rest, by the same analogy, is so much of heaven.

Now, I (being very thin) think differently; and that so much of motion, is so much of life, and so much of joy——and that to stand still, or get on but slowly, is death and the devil——

Hollo! Ho!——the whole world's asleep!——bring out the horses——grease the wheels——tie on the mail——and drive a nail into that moulding——I'll not lose a moment——

Now the wheel we are talking of, and *whereinto* (but not *whereonto*, for that would make an Ixion's wheel[3] of it) he curseth his enemies, according to the bishop's habit of body, should certainly be a post-chaise wheel, whether they were set up in Palestine at that time or not——and my wheel, for the contrary reasons, must as certainly be a cart-wheel groaning round its revolution once in an age; and of which sort, were I to turn commentator, I should make no scruple to affirm, they had great store in that hilly country.

I love the Pythagoreans[4] (much more than ever I dare tell my dear Jenny) for their "χωρισμὸν ἀπὸ τοῦ Σώματος, εἰς το Καλῶς Φιλοσοφεῖν"——[their] "*getting out of the body, in order to think well.*" No man thinks right whilst he is in it; blinded as he must be, with his congenial humours, and drawn differently aside, as the bishop and myself have been, with too lax or too tense a fibre——REASON, is half of it, SENSE; and the measure of heaven itself is but the measure of our present appetites and concoctions——

——But which of the two, in the present case, do you think to be mostly in the wrong?

You, certainly: quoth she, to disturb a whole family so early.

CHAPTER XIV

——But she did not know I was under a vow not to shave my beard till I got to Paris;——yet I hate to make mysteries of nothing;——'tis the cold cautiousness of one of those little souls from which *Lessius*[1] (*lib.* 13. *de moribus divinis, cap.* 24.) hath made his estimate, wherein he setteth forth, That one Dutch mile,[2] cubically multiplied, will allow room enough, and to spare, for eight hundred thousand millions, which he supposes to be as great a number of souls (counting from the fall of

Adam) as can possibly be damn'd to the end of the world.

From what he has made this second estimate——unless from the parental goodness of God—I don't know——I am much more at a loss what could be in Franciscus Ribbera's[3] head, who pretends that no less a space than one of two hundred Italian miles[4] multiplied into itself, will be sufficient to hold the like number——he certainly must have gone upon some of the old Roman souls, of which he had read, without reflecting how much, by a gradual and most tabid[5] decline, in a course of eighteen hundred years, they must unavoidably have shrunk, so as to have come, when he wrote, almost to nothing.

In Lessius's time, who seems the cooler man, they were as little as can be imagined——

——We find them less *now*——

And next winter we shall find them less again; so that if we go on from little to less, and from less to nothing, I hesitate not one moment to affirm, that in half a century, at this rate, we shall have no souls at all; which being the period beyond which I doubt likewise of the existence of the Christian faith, 'twill be one advantage that both of 'em will be exactly worn out together——

Blessed Jupiter! and blessed every other heathen god and goddess! for now ye will all come into play again, and with Priapus[6] at your tails——what jovial times!——but where am I? and into what a delicious riot of things am I rushing? I——I who must be cut short in the midst of my days, and taste no more of 'em than what I borrow from my imagination ——peace to thee, generous fool! and let me go on.

CHAPTER XV

——"So hating, I say, to make mysteries of *nothing*"——I intrusted it with the post-boy, as soon as ever I got off the stones; he gave a crack with his whip to balance the compliment; and with the thill-horse[1] trotting, and a sort of an up and a down of the other, we danced it along to *Ailly au clochers*, famed in days of yore for the finest chimes in the world; but we danced through it without music——the chimes being greatly out of order—(as in truth they were through all France).[2]

And so making all possible speed, from
Ailly au clochers, I got to Hixcourt,

from Hixcourt, I got to Pequignay, and
from Pequignay, I got to AMIENS,
concerning which town I have nothing to inform you, but what
I have informed you once before——and that was——that
Janatone went there to school.

CHAPTER XVI

IN the whole catalogue of those whiffling vexations which come
puffing across a man's canvass, there is not one of a more teasing
and tormenting nature, than this particular one which I am
going to describe——and for which, (unless you travel with an
avance-courier,[1] which numbers do in order to prevent it)
——there is no help: and it is this.

That be you in never so kindly a propensity to sleep——tho'
you are passing perhaps through the finest country—upon the
best roads,—and in the easiest carriage for doing it in the
world——nay was you sure you could sleep fifty miles straight
forwards, without once opening your eyes——nay what is
more, was you as demonstratively satisfied as you can be of any
truth in Euclid, that you should upon all accounts be full as well
asleep as awake——nay perhaps better——Yet the incessant
returns of paying for the horses at every stage,——with the
necessity thereupon of putting your hand into your pocket, and
counting out from thence, three livres fifteen sous (sous by
sous) puts an end to so much of the project, that you cannot
execute above six miles of it (or supposing it is a post and a half,
that is but nine)——were it to save your soul from destruction.

—I'll be even with 'em, quoth I, for I'll put the precise sum
into a piece of paper, and hold it ready in my hand all the way:
"Now I shall have nothing to do" said I (composing myself to
rest) "but to drop this gently into the post-boy's hat, and not
say a word."——Then there wants two sous more to drink
——or there is a twelve sous piece of Louis XIV. which will not
pass[2]—or a livre and some odd liards[3] to be brought over from
the last stage, which Monsieur had forgot; which altercations
(as a man cannot dispute very well asleep) rouse him: still is
sweet sleep retrievable; and still might the flesh weigh down the
spirit, and recover itself of these blows—but then, by heaven!
you have paid but for a single post—whereas 'tis a post and a
half; and this obliges you to pull out your book of post-roads,

the print of which is so very small, it forces you to open your eyes, whether you will or no: then Monsieur le Curè offers you a pinch of snuff——or a poor soldier shews you his leg——or a shaveling[4] his box——or the priestesse of the cistern will water your wheels——they do not want it——but she swears by her *priesthood* (throwing it back) that they do:——then you have all these points to argue, or consider over in your mind; in doing of which, the rational powers get so thoroughly awakened ——you may get 'em to sleep again as you can.

It was entirely owing to one of these misfortunes, or I had pass'd clean by the stables of Chantilly[5]——

——But the postillion first affirming, and then persisting in it to my face, that there was no mark upon the two sous piece, I open'd my eyes to be convinced—and seeing the mark upon it, as plain as my nose—I leap'd out of the chaise in a passion, and so saw every thing at Chantilly in spite.—I tried it but for three posts and a half, but believe 'tis the best principle in the world to travel speedily upon; for as few objects look very inviting in that mood—you have little or nothing to stop you; by which means it was that I pass'd through St. Dennis, without turning my head so much as on side towards the Abby——

——Richness of their treasury! stuff and nonsense!—bating their jewels, which are all false, I would not give three sous for any one thing in it, but *Jaidas's lantern*[6]——nor for that either, only as it grows dark, it might be of use.

CHAPTER XVII

CRACK, crack——crack, crack——crack, crack——so this is Paris! quoth I (continuing in the same mood)——and this is Paris!——humph!——Paris! cried I, repeating the name the third time——

The first, the finest, the most brilliant——

—The streets however are nasty;

But it looks, I suppose, better than it smells——crack, crack——crack, crack——What a fuss thou makest!—as if it concern'd the good people to be inform'd, That a man with pale face, and clad in black, had the honour to be driven into Paris at nine o'clock at night, by a postilion in a tawny yellow jerkin turned up with red calamanco——crack, crack——crack, crack——crack, crack——I wish thy whip——

——But 'tis the spirit of thy nation; so crack—crack on.

Ha!——and no one gives the wall!¹——but in the SCHOOL OF URBANITY herself, if the walls are besh—t—how can you do otherwise?

And prithee when do they light the lamps? What?—never in the summer months!——Ho! 'tis the time of sallads.——O rare! sallad and soup—soup and sallad—sallad and soup, *encore*——

——'Tis *too much* for sinners.

Now I cannot bear the barbarity of it; how can that unconscionable coachman talk so much bawdy to that lean horse? don't you see, friend, the streets are so villainously narrow, that there is not room in all Paris to turn a wheel-barrow? In the grandest city of the whole world, it would not have been amiss, if they had been left a thought wider; nay were it only so much in every single street, as that a man might know (was it only for satisfaction) on which side of it he was walking.

One—two—three—four—five—six—seven—eight—nine—ten.—Ten cook's shops! and twice the number of barber's! and all within three minutes driving! one would think that all the cooks in the world on some great merry-meeting with the barbers, by joint consent had said—Come, let us all go live at Paris: the French love good eating——they are all *gourmands* ——we shall rank high; if their god is their belly——their cooks must be gentlemen: and forasmuch as *the periwig maketh the man*, and the periwig-maker maketh the periwig—— ergo, would the barbers say, we shall rank higher still—we shall be above you all—we shall be * Capitouls at least—pardi! we shall all wear swords²——

—And so, one would swear, (that is by candle-light,—but there is no depending upon it) they continue to do, to this day.

CHAPTER XVIII

THE French are certainly misunderstood:——but whether the fault is theirs, in not sufficiently explaining themselves; or speaking with that exact limitation and precision which one would expect on a point of such importance, and which moreover, is so likely to be contested by us——or whether the

---

* Chief Magistrate in Toulouse, &c. &c. &c.

fault may not be altogether on our side, in not understanding their language always so critically as to know "what they would be at"——I shall not decide; but 'tis evident to me, when they affirm, "*That they who have seen Paris, have seen every thing,*" they must mean to speak of those who have seen it by day-light.[1]

As for candle-light—I give it up——I have said before, there was no depending upon it—and I repeat it again; but not because the lights and shades are too sharp—or the tints confounded—or that there is neither beauty or keeping, &c. . . . for that's not truth—but it is an uncertain light in this respect, That in all the five hundred grand Hôtels, which they number up to you in Paris—and the five hundred good things, at a modest computation (for 'tis only allowing one good thing to a Hôtel[2]) which by candle-light are best to be *seen, felt, heard, and understood* (which, by the bye is a quotation from Lilly[3])——the devil a one of us out of fifty, can get our heads fairly thrust in amongst them.

This is no part of the French computation: 'tis simply this.

That by the last survey taken in the year one thousand seven hundred and sixteen, since which time there have been considerable augmentations, Paris doth contain nine hundred streets; (viz.)

In the quarter called the *City*—there are fifty three streets.

In St. *James* of the Shambles, fifty five streets.

In St. *Oportune*, thirty four streets.

In the quarter of the *Louvre*, twenty five streets.

In the *Palace Royal*, or St. *Honorius*, forty nine streets.

In *Mont. Martyr*, forty one streets.

In St. *Eustace*, twenty nine streets.

In the *Halles*, twenty seven streets.

In St. *Dennis*, fifty five streets.

In St. *Martin*, fifty four streets.

In St. *Paul*, or the *Mortellerie*, twenty seven streets.

The *Greve*, thirty eight streets.

In St. *Avoy*, or the *Verrerie*, nineteen streets.

In the *Marais*, or the *Temple*, fifty two streets.

In St. *Antony*'s, sixty eight streets.

In the *Place Maubert*, eighty one streets.

In St. *Bennet*, sixty streets.

In St. *Andrews de Arcs*, fifty one streets.

In the quarter of the *Luxembourg*, sixty two streets.

And in that of St. Germain, fifty five streets, into any of which you may walk; and that when you have seen them with all that belongs to them, fairly by daylight—their gates, their bridges, their squares, their statues----and have crusaded it moreover through all their parish churches, by no means omitting St. *Roche* and *Sulplice*---and to crown all, have taken a walk to the four palaces, which you may see either with or without the statues and pictures, just as you chuse—

——Then you will have seen——

——but, 'tis what no one needeth to tell you, for you will read it yourself upon the portico of the Louvre, in these words,

*EARTH NO SUCH FOLKS!—NO FOLKS E'ER SUCH A TOWN As PARIS IS!—SING, DERRY, DERRY, DOWN.

The French have a *gay* way of treating every thing that is Great; and that is all can be said upon it.

CHAPTER XIX

IN mentioning the word *gay* (as in the close of the last chapter) it puts one (*i.e.* an author) in mind of the word *spleen*——especially if he has any thing to say upon it: not that by any analysis—or that from any table of interest or genealogy, there appears much more ground of alliance betwixt them, than betwixt light and darkness, or any two of the most unfriendly opposites in nature——only 'tis an undercraft of authors to keep up a good understanding amongst words, as politicians do amongst men—not knowing how near they may be under a necessity of placing them to each other—which point being now gain'd, and that I may place mine exactly to my mind, I write it down here—

SPLEEN.

This, upon leaving Chantilly, I declared to be the best principle in the world to travel speedily upon; but I gave it only as matter of opinion, I still continue in the same sentiments—only I had not then experience enough of its working to add this, that though you do get on at a tearing rate, yet you get on but uneasily to yourself at the same time; for which reason I here quit it entirely, and for ever, and 'tis heartily at one's service—it

---

* Non Orbis gentem, non urbem gens habet ullam
——————————ulla parem.[4]

has spoiled me the digestion of a good supper, and brought on a bilious diarrhæa, which has brought me back again to my first principle on which I set out——and with which I shall now scamper it away to the banks of the Garonne——

——No;——I cannot stop a moment to give you the character of the people—their genius—their manners—their customs—their laws—their religion—their government—their manufactures—their commerce—their finances, with all the resources and hidden springs which sustain them: qualified as I may be, by spending three days and two nights amongst them, and during all that time, making these things the entire subject of my enquiries and reflections——

Still—still I must away——the roads are paved—the posts are short—the days are long—'tis no more than noon—I shall be at Fontainbleau[1] before the king——

—Was he going there? not that I know——

CHAPTER XX

Now I hate to hear a person, especially if he be a traveller, complain that we do not get on so fast in France as we do in England; whereas we get on much faster, *consideratis*, *considerandis*;[1] thereby always meaning, that if you weigh their vehicles with the mountains of baggage which you lay both before and behind upon them—and then consider their puny horses, with the very little they give them—'tis a wonder they get on at all: their suffering is most unchristian, and 'tis evident thereupon to me, that a French post-horse would not know what in the world to do, was it not for the two words ******
and ****** in which there is as much sustenance, as if you gave him a peck of corn: now as these words cost nothing, I long from my soul to tell the reader what they are; but here is the question—they must be told him plainly, and with the most distinct articulation, or it will answer no end—and yet to do it in that plain way—though their reverences may laugh at it in the bed-chamber—full well I wot, they will abuse it in the parlour: for which cause, I have been volving and revolving in my fancy some time, but to no purpose, by what clean device or facete contrivance I might so modulate them, that whilst I satisfy *that ear* which the reader chuses to *lend* me—I might not dissatisfy the other which he keeps to himself.

——My ink burns my finger to try——and when I have
——'twill have a worse consequence——it will burn (I fear)
my paper.

——No;——I dare not——

But if you wish to know how the *abbess* of Andoüillets,[2] and a
novice of her convent got over the difficulty (only first wishing
myself all imaginable success)—I'll tell you without the least
scruple.

CHAPTER XXI

THE abbess of Andoüillets, which if you look into the large set
of provincial maps now publishing at Paris, you will find situated amongst the hills which divide Burgundy from Savoy,
being in danger of an *Anchylosis* or stiff joint (the *sinovia*[1] of her
knee becoming hard by long matins) and having tried every
remedy——first, prayers and thanksgiving; then invocations to
all the saints in heaven promiscuously——then particularly to
every saint who had ever had a stiff leg before her——then
touching it with all the reliques of the convent, principally with
the thigh-bone of the man of Lystra,[2] who had been impotent
from his youth——then wrapping it up in her veil when she
went to bed——then cross-wise her rosary——then bringing in
to her aid the secular arm, and anointing it with oils and hot fat
of animals——then treating it with emollient and resolving
fomentations——then with poultices of marsh-mallows, mal-
lows, bonus Henricus, white lillies and fenugreek——then taking the woods, I mean the smoak of 'em, holding her scapulary
across her lap——then decoctions of wild chicory, water cres-
ses, chervil, sweet cecily and cochlearia——and nothing all this
while answering, was prevailed on at last to try the hot baths
of Bourbon[3]——so having first obtain'd leave of the visitor-
general to take care of her existence—she ordered all to be got
ready for her journey: a novice of the convent of about seventeen, who had been troubled with a whitloe in her middle finger,
by sticking it constantly into the abbess's cast poultices, &c.—
had gained such an interest, that overlooking a sciatical old nun,
who might have been set up for ever by the hot baths of
Bourbon, Margarita, the little novice, was elected as the companion of the journey.

An old calesh,[4] belonging to the abbesse, lined with green frize, was ordered to be drawn out into the sun—the gardener of the convent being chosen muleteer, led out the two old mules to clip the hair from the rump-ends of their tails, whilst a couple of lay-sisters were busied, the one in darning the lining, and the other in sewing on the shreds of yellow binding, which the teeth of time had unravelled——the under-gardener dress'd the muleteer's hat in hot wine-lees——and a taylor sat musically at it, in a shed overagainst the convent, in assorting four dozen of bells for the harness, whistling to each bell as he tied it on with a thong——

——The carpenter and the smith of Andoüillets held a council of wheels; and by seven, the morning after, all look'd spruce, and was ready at the gate of the convent for the hot-baths of Bourbon—two rows of the unfortunate stood ready there an hour before.

The abbess of Andoüillets, supported by Margarita the novice, advanced slowly to the calesh, both clad in white, with their black rosaries hanging at their breasts——

——There was a simple solemnity in the contrast: they entered the calesh; the nuns in the same uniform, sweet emblem of innocence, each occupied a window, and as the abbess and Margarita look'd up—each (the sciatical poor nun excepted)—each stream'd out the end of her veil in the air—then kiss'd the lilly hand which let it go: the good abbess and Margarita laid their hands saint-wise upon their breasts—look'd up to heaven—then to them—and look'd "God bless you, dear sisters."

I declare I am interested in this story, and wish I had been there.

The gardener, who I shall now call the muleteer, was a little, hearty, broad-set, good natured, chattering, toping kind of a fellow, who troubled his head very little with the *hows* and *whens* of life; so had mortgaged a month of his conventical wages in a borrachio, or leathern cask of wine, which he had disposed behind the calesh, with a large russet coloured riding coat over it, to guard it from the sun; and as the weather was hot, and he, not a niggard of his labours, walking ten times more than he rode—he found more occasions than those of nature, to fall back to the rear of his carriage; till by frequent coming and going, it had so happen'd, that all his wine had leak'd out at the *legal* vent of the borrachio, before one half of the journey was finish'd.

Man is a creature born to habitudes. The day had been sultry—the evening was delicious—the wine was generous—the Burgundian hill on which it grew was steep—a little tempting bush[5] over the door of a cool cottage at the foot of it, hung vibrating in full harmony with the passions—a gentle air rustled distinctly through the leaves—"Come—come, thirsty muleteer—come in."

——The muleteer was a son of Adam. I need not say one word more. He gave the mules, each of 'em, a sound lash, and looking in the abbess's and Margarita's faces (as he did it)—as much as to say, "here I am"—he gave a second good crack—as much as to say to his mules, "get on"——so slinking behind, he enter'd the little inn at the foot of the hill.

The muleteer, as I told you, was a little, joyous, chirping fellow, who thought not of to-morrow, nor of what had gone before, or what was to follow it, provided he got but his scantling of Burgundy, and a little chit-chat along with it; so entering into a long conversation, as how he was chief gardener to the convent of Andoüillets, &c. &c. and out of friendship for the abbess and Mademoiselle Margarita, who was only in her noviciate, he had come along with them from the confines of Savoy, &c.--&c.-- and as how she had got a white swelling by her devotions——and what a nation of herbs he had procured to mollify her humours, &c. &c. and that if the waters of Bourbon did not mend that leg—she might as well be lame of both—&c. &c. &c.—He so contrived his story as absolutely to forget the heroine of it—and with her, the little novice, and what was a more ticklish point to be forgot than both—the two mules; who being creatures that take advantage of the world, inasmuch as their parents took it of them—and they not being in a condition to return the obligation *downwards*[6] (as men and women and beasts are)—they do it side-ways, and long-ways, and back-ways—and up hill, and down hill, and which way they can.——Philosophers, with all their ethics, have never considered this rightly—how should the poor muleteer then, in his cups, consider it at all? he did not in the least—'tis time we do; let us leave him then in the vortex of his element, the happiest and most thoughtless of mortal men——and for a moment let us look after the mules, the abbess, and Margarita.

By virtue of the muleteer's two last strokes, the mules had gone quietly on, following their own consciences up the hill, till they had conquer'd about one half of it; when the elder of them, a shrewd crafty old devil, at the turn of an angle, giving a side glance, and no muleteer behind them——

By my fig! said she, swearing, I'll go no further——And if I do, replied the other—they shall make a drum of my hide.——

And so with one consent they stopp'd thus——

CHAPTER XXII

——Get on with you, said the abbess.

——Wh----ysh——ysh——cried Margarita.

Sh---a——shu-u——shu--u--sh--aw——shaw'd the abbess.

——Whu—v—w——whew—w—w—whuv'd Margarita, pursing up her sweet lips betwixt a hoot and a whistle.

Thump—thump—thump—obstreperated the abbess of Andoüillets with the end of her gold-headed cane against the bottom of the calesh——

——The old mule let a f—

CHAPTER XXIII

WE are ruin'd and undone, my child, said the abbess to Margarita——we shall be here all night——we shall be plunder'd ——we shall be ravish'd——

——We shall be ravish'd, said Margarita, as sure as a gun.

Sancta Maria! cried the abbess (forgetting the O!)—why was I govern'd by this wicked stiff joint? why did I leave the convent of Andoüillets? and why didst thou not suffer thy servant to go unpolluted to her tomb?

O my finger! my finger! cried the novice, catching fire at the word *servant*—why was I not content to put it here, or there, any where rather than be in this strait?

——Strait! said the abbess.

Strait——said the novice; for terrour had struck their understandings——the one knew not what she said——the other what she answer'd.

O my virginity! virginity! cried the abbess.

——inity!——inity! said the novice, sobbing.

CHAPTER XXIV

MY dear mother, quoth the novice, coming a little to herself,
——there are two certain words, which I have been told will
force any horse, or ass, or mule, to go up a hill whether he will or
no; be he never so obstinate or ill-will'd, the moment he hears
them utter'd, he obeys. They are words magic! cried the abbess,
in the utmost horrour—No; replied Margarita calmly—but
they are words sinful—What are they? quoth the abbess, interrupting her: They are sinful in the first degree, answered Margarita,—they are mortal—and if we are ravish'd and die un-
absolved of them, we shall both——but you may pronounce
them to me, quoth the abbess of Andouillets——They cannot,
my dear mother, said the novice, be pronounced at all; they will
make all the blood in one's body fly up into one's face——But
you may whisper them in my ear, quoth the abbess.

Heaven! hadst thou no guardian angel to delegate to the inn at
the bottom of the hill? was there no generous and friendly spirit
unemploy'd——no agent in nature, by some monitory shivering, creeping along the artery which led to his heart, to rouze the
muleteer from his banquet?——no sweet minstrelsy to bring
back the fair idea of the abbess and Margarita, with their black
rosaries!

Rouse! rouse!——but 'tis too late—the horrid words are
pronounced this moment——

——and how to tell them—Ye, who can speak of every thing
existing, with unpolluted lips——instruct me——guide
me——

CHAPTER XXV

ALL sins whatever, quoth the abbess, turning casuist in the
distress they were under, are held by the confessor of our
convent to be either mortal or venial: there is no further division. Now a venial sin being the slightest and least of all sins,—
being halved—by taking, either only the half of it, and leaving
the rest—or, by taking it all, and amicably halving it betwixt
yourself and another person—in course becomes diluted into
no sin at all.

Now I see no sin in saying, *bou, bou, bou, bou, bou,*[1] a

hundred times together; nor is there any turpitude in pronouncing the syllable *ger*, *ger*, *ger*, *ger*, *ger*, were it from our matins to our vespers: Therefore, my dear daughter, continued the abbess of Andouillets—I will say *bou*, and thou shalt say *ger*; and then alternately, as there is no more sin in *fou* than in *bou*—Thou shalt say *fou*—and I will come in (like fa, sol, la, re, mi, ut, at our complines) with *ter*. And accordingly the abbess, giving the pitch note, set off thus:

Abbess, } Bou--bou--bou--
Margarita, } ──ger,--ger,--ger
Margarita, } Fou--fou--fou--
Abbess,   } ──ter,--ter,--ter.

The two mules acknowledged the notes by a mutual lash of their tails; but it went no further.——'Twill answer by an' by, said the novice.

Abbess, } Bou-bou-bou-bou-bou-bou-
Margarita, } ──ger, ger, ger, ger, ger, ger.

Quicker still, cried Margarita.

Fou, fou, fou, fou, fou, fou, fou, fou, fou.

Quicker still, cried Margarita.

Bou, bou, bou, bou, bou, bou, bou, bou, bou.

Quicker still—God preserve me! said the abbess—They do not understand us, cried Margarita—But the Devil does, said the abbess of Andouillets.

CHAPTER XXVI

WHAT a tract of country have I run!—how many degrees nearer to the warm sun am I advanced, and how many fair and goodly cities have I seen, during the time you have been reading, and reflecting, Madam, upon this story! There's FONTAINBLEAU, and SENS, and JOIGNY, and AUXERRE, and DIJON the capital of Burgundy, and CHALLON, and Mâcon the capital of the Mâconese, and a score more upon the road to LYONS——and now I have run them over——I might as well talk to you of so many market-towns in the moon, as tell you one word about them: it will be this chapter at the least, if not both this and the next entirely lost, do what I will——

—Why, 'tis a strange story! Tristram.

　　　　　　　　　　　　—Alas! Madam,
had it been upon some melancholy lecture of the cross—the
peace of meekness, or the contentment of resignation——I had
not been incommoded: or had I thought of writing it upon the
purer abstractions of the soul, and that food of wisdom, and
holiness, and contemplation, upon which the spirit of man
(when separated from the body) is to subsist for ever——You
would have come with a better appetite from it——

　　——I wish I never had wrote it: but as I never blot any thing
out——let us use some honest means to get it out of our heads
directly.

　　——Pray reach me my fool's cap——I fear you sit upon it,
Madam——'tis under the cushion——I'll put it on——

Bless me! you have had it upon your head this half
hour.——There then let it stay, with a

Fa-ra diddle di

and a fa-ri diddle d

and a high-dum—dye-dum

　　fiddle---dumb-c.

And now, Madam, we may venture, I hope, a little to go on.

CHAPTER XXVII

　　——All you need say of *Fontainbleau* (in case you are ask'd)
is, that it stands about forty miles (south *something*) from Paris,
in the middle of a large forest——That there is something great
in it——That the king goes there once, every two or three years,
with his whole court, for the pleasure of the chase—and that
during that carnival of sporting, any English gentleman of
fashion (you need not forget yourself) may be accommodated
with a nag or two, to partake of the sport, taking care only not to
out-gallop the king——

Though there are two reasons why you need not talk loud of
this to every one.

First, Because 'twill make the said nags the harder to be got;
and

Secondly, 'Tis not a word of it true.——*Allons!*

As for SENS——you may dispatch it in a word——— "*'Tis
an archiepiscopal see.*"

　　——For JOIGNY—the less, I think, one says of it, the better.

But for AUXERRE—I could go on for ever: for in my *grand tour* through Europe, in which, after all, my father (not caring to trust me with any one) attended me himself, with my uncle Toby, and Trim, and Obadiah, and indeed most of the family, except my mother, who being taken up with a project of knitting my father a pair of large worsted breeches—(the thing is common sense)—and she not caring to be put out of her way, she staid at home at SHANDY HALL, to keep things right during the expedition; in which, I say, my father stopping us two days at Auxerre, and his researches being ever of such a nature, that they would have found fruit even in a desert——he has left me enough to say upon AUXERRE: in short, wherever my father went——but 'twas more remarkably so, in this journey through France and Italy, than in any other stages of his life ——his road seemed to lie so much on one side of that, wherein all other travellers had gone before him—he saw kings and courts and silks of all colours, in such strange lights——and his remarks and reasonings upon the characters, the manners and customs of the countries we pass'd over, were so opposite to those of all other mortal men, particularly those of my uncle Toby and Trim—(to say nothing of myself)—and to crown all—the occurrences and scrapes which we were perpetually meeting and getting into, in consequence of his systems and opiniatry—they were of so odd, so mixed and tragicomical a contexture—That the whole put together, it appears of so different a shade and tint from any tour of Europe, which was ever executed—That I will venture to pronounce—the fault must be mine and mine only—if it be not read by all travellers and travel-readers, till travelling is no more,—or which comes to the same point—till the world, finally, takes it into it's head to stand still.——

——But this rich bale is not to be open'd now; except a small thread or two of it, merely to unravel the mystery of my father's stay at AUXERRE.

——As I have mentioned it—'tis too slight to be kept suspended; and when 'tis wove in, there's an end of it.

We'll go, brother Toby, said my father, whilst dinner is coddling[1]—to the abby of Saint Germain, if it be only to see these bodies, of which monsieur Sequier[2] has given such a recommendation.——I'll go see any body; quoth my uncle Toby; for he was all compliance thro' every step of the journey—— Defend me! said my father—they are all mummies——Then one need not shave; quoth my uncle Toby——Shave! no—cried my father—'twill be more like relations to go with our beards on—So out we sallied, the corporal lending his master his arm, and bringing up the rear, to the abby of Saint Germain.

Every thing is very fine, and very rich, and very superb, and very magnificent, said my father, addressing himself to the sacristan, who was a young brother of the order of Benedictines—but our curiosity has led us to see the bodies of which monsieur Sequier has given the world so exact a description.—— The sacristan made a bow, and lighting a torch first, which he had always in the vestry ready for the purpose; he led us into the tomb of St. Heribald[3]——This, said the sacristan, laying his hand upon the tomb, was a renowned prince of the house of Bavaria, who under the successive reigns of Charlemagne,[4] Louis le Debonair, and Charles the Bald, bore a great sway in the government, and had a principal hand in bringing every thing into order and discipline——

Then he has been as great, said my uncle, in the field, as in the cabinet——I dare say he has been a gallant soldier——He was a monk—said the sacristan.

My uncle Toby and Trim sought comfort in each others faces—but found it not: my father clapp'd both his hands upon his cod-piece, which was a way he had when any thing hugely tickled him; for though he hated a monk and the very smell of a monk worse than all the devils in hell——Yet the shot hitting my uncle Toby and Trim so much harder than him, 'twas a relative triumph; and put him into the gayest humour in the world.

——And pray what do you call this gentleman? quoth my father, rather sportingly: This tomb, said the young Benedictine, looking downwards, contains the bones of Saint MAXIMA,[5] who came from Ravenna on purpose to touch the body——

——Of Saint MAXIMUS, said my father, popping in with his saint before him—they were two of the greatest saints in the whole martyrology, added my father——Excuse me, said the sacristan——'twas to touch the bones of Saint Germain the builder of the abby——And what did she get by it? said my uncle Toby——What does any woman get by it? said my father——MARTYRDOME; replied the young Benedictine, making a bow down to the ground, and uttering the word with so humble, but decisive a cadence, it disarmed my father for a moment. 'Tis supposed, continued the Benedictine, that St. Maxima has lain in this tomb four hundred years, and two hundred before her canonization——'Tis but a slow rise, brother Toby; quoth my father, in this self same army of martyrs.——A desperate slow one, an' please your honour, said Trim, unless one could purchase——I should rather sell out entirely, quoth my uncle Toby——I am pretty much of your opinion, brother Toby, said my father.

——Poor St. Maxima! said my uncle Toby low to himself, as we turn'd from her tomb: She was one of the fairest and most beautiful ladies either of Italy or France, continued the sacristan——But who the duce has got lain down here, besides her, quoth my father, pointing with his cane to a large tomb as we walked on——It is Saint *Optat*,[6] Sir, answered the sacristan ——And properly is Saint Optat plac'd! said my father: And what is Saint Optat's story? continued he. Saint *Optat*, replied the sacristan, was a bishop——

——I thought so, by heaven! cried my father, interrupting him——Saint Optat!——how should Saint *Optat* fail? so snatching out his pocket-book, and the young Benedictine holding him the torch as he wrote, he set it down as a new prop to his system of christian names, and I will be bold to say, so disinterested was he in the search of truth, that had he found a treasure in St. Optat's tomb, it would not have made him half so rich: 'Twas as successful a short visit as ever was paid to the dead; and so highly was his fancy pleas'd with all that had passed in it,—that he determined at once to stay another day in Auxerre.

——I'll see the rest of these good gentry to-morrow, said my father, as we cross'd over the square—And while you are paying that visit, brother Shandy, quoth my uncle Toby—the corporal and I will mount the ramparts.

CHAPTER XXVIII

——Now this is the most puzzled skein of all——for in this last chapter, as far at least as it has help'd me through *Auxerre*, I have been getting forwards in two different journies together, and with the same dash of the pen—for I have got entirely out of Auxerre in this journey which I am writing now, and I am got half way out of Auxerre in that which I shall write hereafter

——There is but a certain degree of perfection in every thing; and by pushing at something beyond that, I have brought myself into such a situation, as no traveller ever stood before me; for I am this moment walking across the market-place of Auxerre with my father and my uncle Toby, in our way back to dinner——and I am this moment also entering Lyons with my post-chaise broke into a thousand pieces——and I am moreover this moment in a handsome pavillion built by Pringello*, upon the banks of the Garonne, which Mons. Sligniac has lent me, and where I now sit rhapsodizing all these affairs.

——Let me collect myself, and pursue my journey.

CHAPTER XXIX

I am glad of it, said I, settling the account with myself as I walk'd into Lyons——my chaise being all laid higgledy-piggledy with my baggage in a cart, which was moving slowly before me——I am heartily glad, said I, that 'tis all broke to pieces; for now I can go directly by water to Avignon, which will carry me on a hundred and twenty miles of my journey, and not cost me seven livres——and from thence, continued I, bringing forwards the account, I can hire a couple of mules—or asses, if I like, (for no body knows me) and cross the plains of Languedoc, for almost nothing——I shall gain four hundred livres by the misfortune clear into my purse; and pleasure! worth—worth double the money by it. With what velocity, continued I, clapping my two hands together, shall I fly down the rapid Rhone, with the VIVARES on my right-hand, and DAUPHINY on my left, scarce seeing the ancient cities of VIENNE, *Valence*, and Vivieres. What a flame will it rekindle in the lamp, to snatch a blushing grape from the Hermitage and Cotê roti,[1] as I shoot by the foot of them? and what a fresh spring in the blood! to behold upon the banks advancing and retiring, the castles of romance, whence courteous knights have whilome rescued the distress'd——and see vertiginous, the rocks, the mountains, the cataracts, and all the hurry which Nature is in with all her great works about her——

* The same Don Pringello, the celebrated Spanish architect, of whom my cousin Antony has made such honourable mention in a scholium to the Tale inscribed to his name.

Vid. p. 129, small edit.[1]

As I went on thus, methought my chaise, the wreck of which look'd stately enough at the first, insensibly grew less and less in its size; the freshness of the painting was no more—the gilding lost its lustre—and the whole affair appeared so poor in my eyes—so sorry!—so contemptible! and, in a word, so much worse than the abbess of Andoüillet's itself—that I was just opening my mouth to give it to the devil—when a pert vamping chaise-undertaker, stepping nimbly across the street, demanded if Monsieur would have his chaise refitted——No, no, said I, shaking my head sideways—Would Monsieur chuse to sell it? rejoin'd the undertaker—With all my soul, said I—the iron work is worth forty livres—and the glasses worth forty more—and the leather you may take to live on.

—What a mine of wealth, quoth I, as he counted me the money, has this post chaise brought me in? And this is my usual method of book-keeping, at least with the disasters of life—making a penny of every one of 'em as they happen to me——

——Do, my dear Jenny, tell the world for me, how I behaved under one, the most oppressive of its kind which could befall me as a man, proud, as he ought to be, of his manhood——

'Tis enough, said'st thou, coming close up to me, as I stood with my garters in my hand, reflecting upon what had *not* pass'd——'Tis enough, Tristram, and I am satisfied, said'st thou, whispering these words in my ear, **** ** **** *** ******;—**** ** ****——any other man would have sunk down to the center——

——Every thing is good for something, quoth I.

——I'll go into Wales for six weeks, and drink goat's-whey—and I'll gain seven years longer life for the accident. For which reason I think myself inexcusable, for blaming Fortune so often as I have done, for pelting me all my life long, like an ungracious dutchess, as I call'd her, with so many small evils: surely if I have any cause to be angry with her, 'tis that she has not sent me great ones—a score of good cursed, bouncing losses, would have been as good as a pension to me.

——One of a hundred a year, or so, is all I wish—I would not be at the plague of paying land tax for a larger.

CHAPTER XXX

To those who call vexations, VEXATIONS, as knowing what they are, there could not be a greater, than to be the best part of a day in Lyons, the most opulent and flourishing city in France, enriched with the most fragments of antiquity—and not be able to see it. To be withheld upon *any* account, must be a vexation; but to be withheld *by* a vexation——must certainly be, what philosophy justly calls

VEXATION
upon
VEXATION.

I had got my two dishes of milk coffee (which by the bye is excellently good for a consumption, but you must boil the milk and coffee together—otherwise 'tis only coffee and milk)—and as it was no more than eight in the morning, and the boat did not go off till noon, I had time to see enough of Lyons to tire the patience of all the friends I had in the world with it. I will take a walk to the cathedral, said I, looking at my list, and see the wonderful mechanism of this great clock of Lippius of Basil,[1] in the first place——

Now, of all things in the world, I understand the least of mechanism——I have neither genius, or taste, or fancy—and have a brain so entirely unapt for every thing of that kind, that I solemnly declare I was never yet able to comprehend the principles of motion of a squirrel cage,[2] or a common knife-grinder's wheel—tho' I have many an hour of my life look'd up with great devotion at the one—and stood by with as much patience as any christian ever could do, at the other——

I'll go see the surprising movements of this great clock, said I, the very first thing I do: and then I will pay a visit to the great library of the Jesuits,[3] and procure, if possible, a sight of the thirty volumes of the general history of China, wrote (not in the Tartarian but) in the Chinese language, and in the Chinese character too.

Now I almost know as little of the Chinese language, as I do of the mechanism of Lippius's clock-work; so, why these should have jostled themselves into the two first articles of my list——I leave to the curious as a problem of Nature. I own it looks like one of her ladyship's obliquities; and they who court her, are interested in finding out her humour as much as I.

When these curiosities are seen, quoth I, half addressing myself to my *valet de place*,[4] who stood behind me——'twill be no hurt if WE go to the church of St. Ireneus,[5] and see the pillar to which Christ was tied——and after that, the house where Pontius Pilate lived[6]——'Twas at the next town, said the *valet de place*—at Vienne; I am glad of it, said I, rising briskly from my chair, and walking across the room with strides twice as long as my usual pace——"for so much the sooner shall I be at the *Tomb of the two lovers*."'

What was the cause of this movement, and why I took such long strides in uttering this——I might leave to the curious too; but as no principle of clock-work is concern'd in it——'twill be as well for the reader if I explain it myself.

CHAPTER XXXI

O! THERE is a sweet æra in the life of man, when, (the brain being tender and fibrillous,[1] and more like pap than any thing else)——a story read of two fond lovers, separated from each other by cruel parents, and by still more cruel destiny——

> Amandus——He
> Amanda——She

each ignorant of the other's course,

> He——east
> She——west

Amandus taken captive by the Turks, and carried to the emperor of Morocco's court, where the princess of Morocco falling in love with him, keeps him twenty years in prison, for the love of his Amanda——

She—(Amanda) all the time wandering barefoot, and with dishevell'd hair, o'er rocks and mountains enquiring for Amandus——Amandus! Amandus!—making every hill and vally to echo back his name——

> Amandus! Amandus!

at every town and city sitting down forlorn at the gate——Has Amandus!—has my Amandus enter'd?——till,——going round, and round, and round the world——chance unexpected bringing them at the same moment of the night, though by different ways, to the gate of Lyons their native city, and each in well known accents calling out aloud,

Is Amandus
Is my Amanda } still alive?

they fly into each others arms, and both drop down dead for joy.

There is a soft æra in every gentle mortal's life, where such a story affords more *pabulum* to the brain, than all the *Frusts*,[2] and *Crusts*, and *Rusts* of antiquity, which travellers can cook up for it.

——'Twas all that stuck on the right side of the cullender[3] in my own, of what Spon[4] and others, in their accounts of Lyons, had *strained* into it; and finding, moreover, in some Itinerary, but in what God knows——That sacred to the fidelity of Amandus and Amanda, a tomb was built without the gates, where to this hour, lovers call'd upon them to attest their truths,——I never could get into a scrape of that kind in my life, but this *tomb of the lovers*, would some how or other, come in at the close——nay such a kind of empire had it establish'd over me, that I could seldom think or speak of Lyons—and sometimes not so much as see even a *Lyons-waistcoat*, but this remnant of antiquity would present itself to my fancy; and I have often said in my wild way of running on——tho' I fear with some irreverence——"I thought this shrine (neglected as it was) as valuable as that of Mecca, and so little short, except in wealth, of the Santa Casa[5] itself, that some time or other, I would go a pilgrimage (though I had no other business at Lyons) on purpose to pay it a visit."

In my list, therefore, of *Videnda*[6] at Lyons, this, tho' *last*—was not, you see, *least*; so taking a dozen or two of longer strides than usual across my room, just whilst it passed my brain, I walked down calmly into the *Basse Cour*,[7] in order to sally forth; and having called for my bill—as it was uncertain whether I should return to my inn, I had paid it——had moreover given the maid ten sous, and was just receiving the dernier compliments of Monsieur Le Blanc, for a pleasant voyage down the Rhône——when I was stopped at the gate——

CHAPTER XXXII

——'Twas by a poor ass who had just turned in with a couple of large panniers upon his back, to collect eleemosunary turnip tops and cabbage leaves; and stood dubious, with his two forefeet on the inside of the threshold, and with his two hinder feet towards the street, as not knowing very well whether he was to go in, or no.

Now, 'tis an animal (be in what hurry I may) I cannot bear to strike——there is a patient endurance of sufferings, wrote so unaffectedly in his looks and carriage, which pleads so mightily for him, that it always disarms me; and to that degree, that I do not like to speak unkindly to him: on the contrary, meet him where I will——whether in town or country—in cart or under panniers—whether in liberty or bondage——I have ever something civil to say to him on my part; and as one word begets another (if he has as little to do as I)——I generally fall into conversation with him; and surely never is my imagination so busy as in framing his responses from the etchings of his countenance—and where those carry me not deep enough——in flying from my own heart into his, and seeing what is natural for an ass to think—as well as a man, upon the occasion. In truth, it is the only creature of all the classes of beings below me, with whom I can do this: for parrots, jackdaws, &c.——I never exchange a word with them——nor with the apes, &c. for pretty near the same reason; they act by rote, as the others speak by it, and equally make me silent: nay my dog and my cat, though I value them both——(and for my dog he would speak if he could)—yet some how or other, they neither of them possess the talents for conversation——I can make nothing of a discourse with them, beyond the *proposition*, the *reply*, and *rejoinder*, which terminated my father's and my mother's conversations, in his beds of justice——and those utter'd—there's an end of the dialogue——

—But with an ass, I can commune for ever.

Come Honesty! said I,—seeing it was impracticable to pass betwixt him and the gate——art thou for coming in, or going out?

The ass twisted his head round to look up the street——

Well—replied I—we'll wait a minute for thy driver:

——He turned his head thoughtful about, and looked wistfully the opposite way——

I understand thee perfectly; answered I——if thou takest a wrong step in this affair, he will cudgel thee to death——Well! a minute is but a minute, and if it saves a fellow creature a drubbing, it shall not be set down as ill-spent.

He was eating the stem of an artichoke as this discourse went on, and in the little peevish contentions of nature betwixt hunger and unsavouriness, had dropt it out of his mouth half a dozen times, and pick'd it up again——God help thee, Jack! said I, thou hast a bitter breakfast on't—and many a bitter day's labour--and many a bitter blow, I fear, for its wages——'tis all—all bitterness to thee, whatever life is to others.——And now thy mouth, if one knew the truth of it, is as bitter, I dare say, as soot—(for he had cast aside the stem) and thou hast not a friend perhaps in all this world, that will give thee a macaroon.——In saying this, I pull'd out a paper of 'em, which I had just purchased, and gave him one—and at this moment that I am telling it, my heart smites me, that there was more of pleasantry in the conceit, of seeing *how* an ass would eat a macaroon ——than of benevolence in giving him one, which presided in the act.

When the ass had eaten his macaroon, I press'd him to come in——the poor beast was heavy loaded——his legs seem'd to tremble under him——he hung rather backwards, and as I pull'd at his halter, it broke short in my hand——he look'd up pensive in my face—"Don't thrash me with it—but if you will, you may"——If I do, said I, I'll be d——d.

The word was but one half of it pronounced, like the abbess of Andoüillet's—(so there was no sin in it)—when a person coming in, let fall a thundering bastinado upon the poor devil's crupper, which put an end to the ceremony.

     Out upon it!

cried I——but the interjection was equivocal——and, I think, wrong placed too—for the end of an osier which had started out from the contexture of the ass's pannier, had caught hold of my breeches pocket as he rush'd by me, and rent it in the most disasterous direction you can imagine——so that the

    Out upon it! in my opinion, should have come in here——but this I leave to be settled by

The
REVIEWERS
of
MY BREECHES.

which I have brought over along with me for that purpose.

CHAPTER XXXIII[1]

WHEN all was set to rights, I came down stairs again into the *basse cour* with my valet de place, in order to sally out towards the tomb of the two lovers, *&c.*—and was a second time stopp'd at the gate——not by the ass—but by the person who struck him; and who, by that time, had taken possession (as is not uncommon after a defeat) of the very spot of ground where the ass stood.

It was a commissary sent to me from the post-office, with a rescript in his hand for the payment of some six livres odd sous.

Upon what account? said I.——'Tis upon the part of the king, replied the commissary, heaving up both his shoulders——

——My good friend, quoth I——as sure as I am I—and you are you——

——And who are you? said he.——Don't puzzle me; said I.

CHAPTER XXXIV

——But it is an indubitable verity, continued I, addressing myself to the commissary, changing only the form of my asseveration——that I owe the king of France nothing but my good-will; for he is a very honest man, and I wish him all health and pastime in the world——

Pardonnez moi—replied the commissary, you are indebted to him six livres four sous, for the next post from hence to St. Fons, in your rout to Avignion—which being a post royal, you pay double for the horses and postillion——otherwise 'twould have amounted to no more than three livres, two sous——

——But I don't go by land; said I.

——You may if you please; replied the commissary——

Your most obedient servant——said I, making him a low
bow——

The commissary, with all the sincerity of grave good breeding—made me one, as low again.——I never was more dis-
concerted with a bow in my life.

——The devil take the serious character of these people!
quoth I—(aside) they understand no more of IRONY than
this——

The comparison was standing close by with his panniers—
but something seal'd up my lips—I could not pronounce the
name——

Sir, said I, collecting myself—it is not my intention to take
post——

—But you may—said he, persisting in his first reply—you
may take post if you chuse——

—And I may take salt to my pickled herring, said I, if I
chuse——

—But I do not chuse——

—But you must pay for it, whether you do or no——

Aye! for the salt; said I (I know)——

—And for the post too; added he. Defend me; cried
I——

I travel by water—I am going down the Rhône this very
afternoon—my baggage is in the boat—and I have actually paid
nine livres for my passage——

C'est tout egal—'tis all one; said he.

Bon Dieu! what, pay for the way I go! and for the way I do
not go!

——C'est tout egal; replied the commissary——

——The devil it is! said I—but I will go to ten thousand
Bastiles first——

O England! England! thou land of liberty, and climate of
good sense, thou tenderest of mothers—and gentlest of nurses,
cried I, kneeling upon one knee, as I was beginning my apos-
trophè——

When the director of Madam Le Blanc's conscience coming
in at that instant, and seeing a person in black, with a face as pale
as ashes, at his devotions—looking still paler by the contrast and
distress of his drapery—ask'd, if I stood in want of the aids of
the church——

I go by WATER—said I—and here's another will be for making me pay for going by OYL.

CHAPTER XXXV

As I perceived the commissary of the post-office would have his six livres four sous, I had nothing else for it, but to say some smart thing upon the occasion, worth the money:

And so I set off thus——

——And pray Mr. commissary, by what law of courtesy is a defenceless stranger to be used just the reverse from what you use a Frenchman in this matter?

By no means; said he.

Excuse me; said I—for you have begun, sir, with first tearing off my breeches—and now you want my pocket——

Whereas—had you first taken my pocket, as you do with your own people—and then left me bare a—'d after—I had been a beast to have complain'd——

As it is——

——'Tis contrary to the *law of nature*.

——'Tis contrary to *reason*.

——'Tis contrary to the GOSPEL.

But not to this——said he—putting a printed paper into my hand.

PAR LE ROY.[1]

—— ——'Tis a pithy prolegomenon, quoth I—and so read on — — — — — — — — — — — — — —
— — — — — — — — — — — — — —
— — — — — — — — — — — — — —
— — — — — — — — — — — — — —
— — — — — — — — — — — — — —

——By all which it appears, quoth I, having read it over, a little too rapidly, that if a man sets out in a post-chaise from Paris—he must go on travelling in one, all the days of his life—or pay for it.——Excuse me, said the commissary, the spirit of the ordinance is this—That if you set out with an intention of running post from Paris to Avignion, &c. you shall not change that intention or mode of travelling, without first satisfying the fermiers[2] for two posts further than the place you repent at—and 'tis founded, continued he, upon this, that the REVENUES are not to fall short through your *fickleness*——

——O by heavens! cried I—if fickleness is taxable in France—we have nothing to do but to make the best peace with you we can——

AND SO THE PEACE WAS MADE;[3]

——And if it is a bad one—as Tristram Shandy laid the corner stone of it—nobody but Tristram Shandy ought to be hanged.

CHAPTER XXXVI

THOUGH I was sensible I had said as many clever things to the commissary as came to six livres four sous, yet I was determined to note down the imposition amongst my remarks before I retir'd from the place; so putting my hand into my coat pocket for my remarks—(which by the bye, may be a caution to travellers to take a little more care of *their* remarks for the future) "my remarks were *stolen*"——Never did sorry traveller make such a pother and racket about his remarks as I did about mine, upon the occasion.

Heaven! earth! sea! fire! cried I, calling in every thing to my aid but what I should——My remarks are stolen!—what shall I do?—Mr. commissary! pray did I drop any remarks as I stood besides you?——

You dropp'd a good many very singular ones; replied he——Pugh! said I, those were but a few, not worth above six livres two sous—but these are a large parcel——He shook his head——Monsieur Le Blanc! Madam Le Blanc! did you see any papers of mine?—you maid of the house! run up stairs—François! run up after her——

——I must have my remarks——they were the best remarks, cried I, that ever were made—the wisest—the wittiest——What shall I do?—which way shall I turn myself?

Sancho Pança, when he lost his ass's FURNITURE,[1] did not exclaim more bitterly.

CHAPTER XXXVII

WHEN the first transport was over, and the registers of the brain were beginning to get a little out of the confusion into which this jumble of cross accidents had cast them—it then presently occurr'd to me, that I had left my remarks in the pocket of the chaise—and that in selling my chaise, I had sold my remarks along with it, to the chaise-vamper.   I leave this void space that the reader may swear into it, any oath that he is most accustomed to——For my own part, if ever I swore a *whole* oath into a vacancy in my life, I think it was into that—— *** **** **, said I—and so my remarks through France, which were as full of wit, as an egg is full of meat, and as well worth four hundred guineas, as the said egg is worth a penny—Have I been selling here to a chaise-vamper—for four Louis d'Ors—and giving him a post-chaise (by heaven) worth six into the bargain; had it been to Dodsley, or Becket,[1] or any creditable bookseller, who was either leaving off business, and wanted a post-chaise—or who was beginning it—and wanted my remarks, and two or three guineas along with them—I could have borne it——but to a chaise-vamper!—shew me to him this moment François—said I—the valet de place put on his hat, and led the way—and I pull'd off mine, as I pass'd the commissary, and followed him.

CHAPTER XXXVIII

WHEN we arrived at the chaise-vamper's house, both the house and the shop were shut up; it was the eighth of September, the nativity of the blessed Virgin Mary, mother of God—

——Tantarra-ra-tan-tivi——the whole world was going out a May-poling—frisking here—capering there—no body cared a button for me or my remarks; so I sat me down upon a bench by the door, philosophating upon my condition: by a better fate than usually attends me, I had not waited half an hour, when the mistress came in, to take the papilliotes[1] from off her hair, before she went to the May-poles——

The French women, by the bye, love May-poles, *a la folie*[2]— that is, as much as their matins——give 'em but a May-pole, whether in May, June, July, or September—they never count the times——down it goes——'tis meat, drink, washing, and lodging to 'em——and had we but the policy, an' please your worships (as wood is a little scarce in France) to send them but plenty of May-poles——

The women would set them up; and when they had done, they would dance round them (and the men for company) till they were all blind.

The wife of the chaise-vamper step'd in, I told you, to take the papilliotes from off her hair——the toilet stands still for no man——so she jerk'd off her cap, to begin with them as she open'd the door, in doing which, one of them fell upon the ground——I instantly saw it was my own writing——

——O Seignieur! cried I—you have got all my remarks upon your head, Madam!——*J'en suis bien mortifiée*, said she—— 'tis well, thinks I, they have stuck there—for could they have gone deeper, they would have made such confusion in a French woman's noddle—She had better have gone with it unfrizled, to the day of eternity.

Tenez—said she—so without any idea of the nature of my suffering, she took them from her curls, and put them gravely one by one into my hat——one was twisted this way—— another twisted that——ay! by my faith; and when they are published, quoth I,——

They will be worse twisted still.

CHAPTER XXXIX

AND now for Lippius's clock! said I, with the air of a man, who had got thro' all his difficulties——nothing can prevent us seeing that, and the Chinese history, &c. except the time, said François——for 'tis almost eleven—then we must speed the faster, said I, striding it away to the cathedral.

I cannot say, in my heart, that it gave me any concern in being told by one of the minor canons, as I was entering the west door,—That Lippius's great clock was all out of joints, and had not gone for some years——It will give me the more time, thought I, to peruse the Chinese history; and besides I shall be able to give the world a better account of the clock in it's decay, than I could have done in its flourishing condition——

——And so away I posted to the college of the Jesuits.

Now it is with the project of getting a peep at the history of China in Chinese characters—as with many others I could mention, which strike the fancy only at a distance; for as I came nearer and nearer to the point—my blood cool'd—the freak gradually went off, till, at length I would not have given a cherry-stone to have it gratified——The truth was, my time was short, and my heart was at the Tomb of the Lovers——I wish to God, said I, as I got the rapper in my hand, that the key of the library may be but lost; it fell out as well——

For all the JESUITS *had got the cholic*[1]—and to that degree, as never was known in the memory of the oldest practitioner.

CHAPTER XL

As I knew the geography of the Tomb of the Lovers, as well as if I had lived twenty years in Lyons, namely, that it was upon the turning of my right hand, just without the gate, leading to the Fauxbourg de Vaise——I dispatch'd François to the boat, that I might pay the homage I so long ow'd it, without a witness of my weakness.—I walk'd with all imaginable joy towards the place——when I saw the gate which intercepted the tomb, my heart glowed within me——

—Tender and faithful spirits! cried I, addressing myself to Amandus and Amanda—long—long have I tarried to drop this tear upon your tomb——I come——I come——

When I came—there was no tomb to drop it upon.

What would I have given for my uncle Toby to have whistled, Lillo bullero!

CHAPTER XLI

No matter how, or in what mood—but I flew from the tomb of the lovers—or rather I did not fly *from* it—(for there was no such thing existing) and just got time enough to the boat to save my passage;—and e'er I had sailed a hundred yards, the Rhône and the Saôn met together, and carried me down merrily betwixt them.

But I have described this voyage down the Rhône, before I made it——

——So now I am at Avignion—and as there is nothing to see[1] but the old house, in which the duke of Ormond[2] resided, and nothing to stop me but a short remark upon the place, in three minutes you will see me crossing the bridge upon a mule, with François upon a horse with my portmanteau behind him, and the owner of both, striding the way before us with a long gun upon his shoulder, and a sword under his arm, least peradventure we should run away with his cattle. Had you seen my breeches in entering Avignon,——Though you'd have seen them better, I think, as I mounted—you would not have thought the precaution amiss, or found in your heart to have taken it, in dudgeon: for my own part, I took it most kindly; and determined to make him a present of them, when we got to the end of our journey, for the trouble they had put him to, of arming himself at all points against them.

Before I go further, let me get rid of my remark upon Avignon, which is this; That I think it wrong, merely because a man's hat has been blown off his head by chance the first night he comes to Avignion,——that he should therefore say, "Avignion is more subject to high winds than any town in all France:" for which reason I laid no stress upon the accident till I had inquired of the master of the inn about it, who telling me seriously it was so——and hearing moreover, the windyness of Avignion spoke of in the country about as a proverb——I set it down, merely to ask the learned what can be the cause——the consequence I saw—for they are all Dukes, Marquisses, and Counts, there³——the duce a Baron, in all Avignion——so that there is scarce any talking to them, on a windy day.

Prithee friend, said I, take hold of my mule for a moment ——for I wanted to pull off one of my jack-boots, which hurt my heel—the man was standing quite idle at the door of the inn, and as I had taken it into my head, he was someway concerned about the house or stable, I put the bridle into his hand—so begun with my boot:—when I had finished the affair, I turned about to take the mule from the man, and thank him——

——*But Monsieur le Marquis* had walked in——

CHAPTER XLII

I HAD now the whole south of France, from the banks of the Rhône to those of the Garonne to traverse upon my mule at my own leisure—*at my own leisure*——for I had left Death, the lord knows——and He only—how far behind me——"I have followed many a man thro' France, quoth he—but never at this mettlesome rate"——Still he followed,——and still I fled him——but I fled him chearfully——still he pursued—but like one who pursued his prey without hope——as he lag'd, every step he lost, softened his looks——why should I fly him at this rate?

So notwithstanding all the commissary of the post-office had said, I changed the *mode* of my travelling once more; and after so precipitate and rattling a course as I had run, I flattered my fancy with thinking of my mule, and that I should traverse the rich plains of Languedoc upon his back, as slowly as foot could fall.

There is nothing more pleasing to a traveller——or more terrible to travel-writers, than a large rich plain; especially if it is without great rivers or bridges; and presents nothing to the eye, but one unvaried picture of plenty: for after they have once told you that 'tis delicious! or delightful! (as the case happens)—that the soil was grateful, and that nature pours out all her abundance, &c. . . . they have then a large plain upon their hands, which they know not what to do with—and which is of little or no use to them but to carry them to some town; and that town, perhaps of little more; but a new place to start from to the next plain——and so on.

—This is most terrible work; judge if I don't manage my plains better.

CHAPTER XLIII

I HAD not gone above two leagues and a half, before the man with his gun, began to look at his priming.

I had three several times loiter'd *terribly* behind; half a mile at least every time: once, in deep conference with a drum-maker, who was making drums for the fairs of *Baucaira* and *Tarascone*—I did not understand the principles——

The second time, I cannot so properly say, I stopp'd——for meeting a couple of Franciscans straiten'd more for time than myself, and not being able to get to the bottom of what I was about——I had turn'd back with them——

The third, was an affair of trade with a gossip, for a hand basket of Provence figs for four sous; this would have been transacted at once; but for a case of conscience at the close of it; for when the figs were paid for, it turn'd out, that there were two dozen of eggs cover'd over with vine-leaves at the bottom of the basket—as I had no intention of buying eggs—I made no sort of claim of them—as for the space they had occupied—what signified it? I had figs enow for my money——

—But it was my intention to have the basket—it was the gossip's intention to keep it, without which, she could do nothing with her eggs——and unless I had the basket, I could do as little with my figs, which were too ripe already, and most of 'em burst at the side: this brought on a short contention, which terminated in sundry proposals, what we should both do——

—How we disposed of our eggs and figs, I defy you, or the Devil himself, had he not been there (which I am persuaded he was) to form the least probable conjecture: You will read the whole of it————not this year, for I am hastening to the story of my uncle Toby's amours—but you will read it in the collection of those which have arose out of the journey across this plain———and which, therefore, I call my

PLAIN STORIES.

How far my pen has been fatigued like those of other travellers, in this journey of it, over so barren a track—the world must judge—but the traces of it, which are now all set o' vibrating together this moment, tell me 'tis the most fruitful and busy period of my life; for as I had made no convention with my man with the gun as to time—by stopping and talking to every soul I met who was not in a full trot—joining all parties before me—waiting for every soul behind—hailing all those who were coming through cross roads—arresting all kinds of beggars, pilgrims, fiddlers, fryars—not passing by a woman in a mulberry-tree without commending her legs, and tempting her into conversation with a pinch of snuff————In short, by seizing every handle, of what size or shape soever, which chance held out to me in this journey—I turned my *plain* into a *city*—I was always in company, and with great variety too; and as my mule loved society as much as myself, and had some proposals always on his part to offer to every beast he met—I am confident we could have passed through Pall-Mall or St. James's-Street for a month together, with fewer adventures—and seen less of human nature.

O! there is that sprightly frankness which at once unpins every plait of a Languedocian's dress—that whatever is beneath it, it looks so like the simplicity which poets sing of in better days—I will delude my fancy, and believe it is so.

'Twàs in the road betwixt Nismes[1] and Lunel, where there is the best Muscatto[2] wine in all France, and which by the bye belongs to the honest canons of MONTPELLIER—and foul befall the man who has drank it at their table, who grudges them a drop of it.

————The sun was set—they had done their work; the nymphs had tied up their hair afresh—and the swains were preparing for a carousal————My mule made a dead point————'Tis the fife and tabourin,[3] said I————I'm frighten'd to death, quoth he————They

are running at the ring of pleasure, said I, giving him a prick
——By saint Boogar, and all the saints at the backside of the
door of purgatory, said he—(making the same resolution with
the abbesse of Andoüillets) I'll not go a step further——'Tis very
well, sir, said I—I never will argue a point with one of your
family, as long as I live; so leaping off his back, and kicking off
one boot into this ditch, and t'other into that—I'll take a dance,
said I——so stay you here.

A sun-burnt daughter of Labour rose up from the groupe to
meet me as I advanced towards them; her hair, which was a dark
chesnut, approaching rather to a black, was tied up in a knot, all
but a single tress.

We want a cavalier, said she, holding out both her hands, as if
to offer them——And a cavalier ye shall have; said I, taking
hold of both of them.

Hadst thou, Nannette, been array'd like a dutchesse!

——But that cursed slit in thy petticoat!

Nannette cared not for it.

We could not have done without you, said she, letting go one
hand, with self-taught politeness, leading me up with the other.

A lame youth, whom Apollo had recompenced with a pipe,
and to which he had added a tabourin of his own accord, ran
sweetly over the prelude, as he sat upon the bank——Tie me up
this tress instantly, said Nannette, putting a piece of string into
my hand——It taught me to forget I was a stranger——The
whole knot fell down——We had been seven years acquainted.

The youth struck the note upon the tabourin—his pipe followed, and off we bounded——"the duce take that slit!"

The sister of the youth who had stolen her voice from heaven,
sung alternately with her brother——'twas a Gascoigne round-
elay.

VIVA LA JOIA!

FIDON LA TRISTESSA![4]

The nymphs join'd in unison, and their swains an octave below
them——

I would have given a crown to have it sew'd up—Nannette
would not have given a sous—*Viva la joia!* was in her lips—
Viva la joia! was in her eyes. A transient spark of amity shot
across the space betwixt us——She look'd amiable!——Why
could I not live and end my days thus! Just disposer of our joys
and sorrows, cried I, why could not a man sit down in the lap of

content here—and dance, and sing, and say his prayers, and go
to heaven with this nut brown maid? capriciously did she bend
her head on one side, and dance up insiduous——Then 'tis time
to dance off, quoth I; so changing only partners and tunes, I
danced it away from Lunel to Montpellier——from thence to
Pesçnas, Beziers——I danced it along through Narbonne, Car-
casson, and Castle Naudairy, till at last I danced myself into
Perdrillo's pavillion,[5] where pulling a paper of black lines, that I
might go on straight forwards, without digression or parenthesis, in my uncle Toby's amours——

I begun thus——

END of the SEVENTH VOLUME.

THE

L I F E

AND

O P I N I O N S

OF

TRISTRAM SHANDY,

GENTLEMAN.

Non enim excursus hic ejus, sed opus ipsum est.
PLIN. Lib. quintus Epistola sexta.

VOL. VIII.

L O N D O N:

Printed for T. BECKET and P. A. DEHONT,
in the Strand.   M DCC LXV.

CHAPTER I.

——But softly——for in these sportive plains, and under this genial sun, where at this instant all flesh is running out piping, fiddling, and dancing to the vintage, and every step that's taken, the judgment is surprised by the imagination, I defy, notwithstanding all that has been said upon *straight lines** in sundry pages of my book—I defy the best cabbage planter that ever existed, whether he plants backwards or forwards, it makes little difference in the account (except that he will have more to answer for in the one case than in the other)—I defy him to go on cooly, critically, and canonically, planting his cabbages one by one, in straight lines, and stoical distances, especially if slits in petticoats are unsew'd up—without ever and anon straddling out, or sidling into some bastardly digression——In *Freeze-land*, *Fog-land* and some other lands I wot of—it may be done——

But in this clear climate of fantasy and perspiration, where every idea, sensible and insensible, gets vent—in this land, my dear Eugenius—in this fertile land of chivalry and romance, where I now sit, unskrewing my ink-horn to write my uncle Toby's amours, and with all the meanders of JULIA's track in quest of her DIEGO, in full view of my study window—if thou comest not and takest me by the hand——

What a work is it likely to turn out!

Let us begin it.

CHAPTER II

IT is with LOVE as with CUCKOLDOM——

——But now I am talking of beginning a book, and have long had a thing upon my mind to be imparted to the reader, which if not imparted now, can never be imparted to him as long as I live (whereas the COMPARISON may be imparted to him any hour in the day)——I'll just mention it, and begin in good earnest.

The thing is this.

That of all the several ways of beginning a book which are now in practice throughout the known world, I am confident

* Vid. Vol. VI. p. 152.[1]

my own way of doing it is the best——I'm sure it is the most religious——for I begin with writing the first sentence——and trusting to Almighty God for the second.

'Twould cure an author for ever of the fuss and folly of opening his street-door, and calling in his neighbours and friends, and kinsfolk, with the devil and all his imps, with their hammers and engines, &c. only to observe how one sentence of mine follows another, and how the plan follows the whole.

I wish you saw me half starting out of my chair, with what confidence, as I grasp the elbow of it, I look up——catching the idea, even sometimes before it half way reaches me——

I believe in my conscience I intercept many a thought which heaven intended for another man.

Pope and his Portrait* are fools to me——no martyr is ever so full of faith or fire——I wish I could say of good works too——but I have no

Zeal or Anger——or

Anger or Zeal——

And till gods and men agree together to call it by the same name——the errantest TARTUFFE, in science—in politics—or in religion, shall never kindle a spark within me, or have a worse word, or a more unkind greeting, than what he will read in the next chapter.

CHAPTER III.

——Bon jour!——good-morrow!——so you have got your cloak on betimes!——but 'tis a cold morning, and you judge the matter rightly——'tis better to be well mounted, than go o'foot——and obstructions in the glands are dangerous—— And how goes it with thy concubine—thy wife—and thy little ones o'both sides? and when did you hear from the old gentleman and lady—your sister, aunt, uncle and cousins——I hope they have got better of their colds, coughs, claps, tooth-aches, fevers, stranguries, sciaticas, swellings, and sore-eyes.

——What a devil of an apothecary! to take so much blood—give such a vile purge—puke—poultice—plaister—night-draught—glister—blister?——And why so many grains of calomel? santa Maria! and such a dose of opium! periclitating,[1] pardi! the whole family of ye, from head to tail——By my great

* Vid. Pope's Portrait.[1]

aunt Dinah's old black velvet mask! I think there was no occasion for it.

Now this being a little bald about the chin, by frequently putting off and on, *before* she was got with child by the coachman—not one of our family would wear it after. To cover the MASK afresh, was more than the mask was worth——and to wear a mask which was bald, or which could be half seen through, was as bad as having no mask at all——

This is the reason, may it please your reverences, that in all our numerous family, for these four generations, we count no more than one archbishop, a Welch judge, some three or four aldermen, and a single mountebank——

In the sixteenth century, we boast of no less than a dozen alchymists.

CHAPTER IV

"It is with Love as with Cuckoldom"——the suffering party is at least the *third*, but generally the last in the house who knows any thing about the matter: this comes, as all the world knows, from having half a dozen words for one thing; and so long, as what in this vessel of the human frame, is *Love*—may be *Hatred*, in that——*Sentiment* half a yard higher——and *Non-sense*————no Madam,—not there——I mean at the part I am now pointing to with my forefinger——how can we help ourselves?

Of all mortal, and immortal men too, if you please, who ever soliloquized upon this mystic subject, my uncle Toby was the worst fitted, to have push'd his researches, thro' such a contention of feelings; and he had infallibly let them all run on, as we do worse matters, to see what they would turn out——had not Bridget's pre-notification of them to Susannah, and Susannah's repeated manifesto's thereupon to all the world, made it necessary for my uncle Toby to look into the affair.

CHAPTER V

Why weavers, gardeners, and gladiators—or a man with a pined leg (proceeding from some ailment in the *foot*)—should ever have had some tender nymph breaking her heart in secret for them, are points well and duely settled and accounted for, by ancient and modern physiologists.

A water-drinker, provided he is a profess'd one, and does it without fraud or covin, is precisely in the same predicament: not that, at first sight, there is any consequence, or shew of logic in it, "That a rill of cold water dribbling through my inward parts, should light up a torch in my Jenny's——

——The proposition does not strike one; on the contrary it seems to run opposite to the natural workings of causes and effects——

But it shews the weakness and imbecility of human reason.

——"And in perfect good health with it?"

—The most perfect—Madam, that friendship herself could wish me——

—"And drink nothing!—nothing but water?"

—Impetuous fluid! the moment thou presses against the flood-gates of the brain——see how they give way!——

In swims CURIOSITY, beckoning to her damsels to follow—they dive into the centre of the current——

FANCY sits musing upon the bank, and with her eyes following the stream, turns straws and bulrushes into masts and bowsprits——And DESIRE, with vest held up to the knee in one hand, snatches at them, as they swim by her, with the other——

O ye water-drinkers! is it then by this delusive fountain, that ye have so often governed and turn'd this world about like a mill-wheel—grinding the faces of the impotent—be-powdering their ribs—be-peppering their noses, and changing sometimes even the very frame and face of nature——

—If I was you, quoth Yorick, I would drink more water, Eugenius.—And, if I was you, Yorick, replied Eugenius, so would I.

Which shews they had both read Longinus[1]——

For my own part, I am resolved never to read any book but my own, as long as I live.

CHAPTER VI

I wish my uncle Toby had been a water-drinker; for then the thing had been accounted for, That the first moment Widow

Wadman saw him, she felt something stirring within her in his favour—Something!—something.

—Something perhaps more than friendship—less than love—something—no matter what—no matter where—I would not give a single hair off my mule's tail, and be obliged to pluck it off myself (indeed the villain has not many to spare, and is not a little vicious into the bargain) to be let by your worships into the secret——

But the truth is, my uncle Toby was not a water-drinker; he drank it neither pure nor mix'd, or any how, or any where, except fortuitously upon some advanced posts, where better liquor was not to be had——or during the time he was under cure; when the surgeon telling him it would extend the fibres, and bring them sooner into contact——my uncle Toby drank it for quietness sake.

Now as all the world knows, that no effect in nature can be produced without a cause and as it is as well known, that my uncle Toby, was neither a weaver—a gardener, or a gladiator—unless as a captain, you will needs have him one—but then he was only a captain of foot—and besides the whole is an equivocation——There is nothing left for us to suppose, but that my uncle Toby's leg——but that will avail us little in the present hypothesis, unless it had proceeded from some ailment *in the foot*—whereas his leg was not emaciated from any disorder in his foot—for my uncle Toby's leg was not emaciated at all. It was a little stiff and awkward, from a total disuse of it, for the three years he lay confined at my father's house in town; but it was plump and muscular, and in all other respects as good and promising a leg as the other.

I declare, I do not recollect any one opinion or passage of my life, where my understanding was more at a loss to make ends meet, and torture the chapter I had been writing, to the service of the chapter following it, than in the present case: one would think I took a pleasure in running into difficulties of this kind, merely to make fresh experiments of getting out of 'em—— Inconsiderate soul that thou art! What! are not the unavoidable distresses with which, as an author and a man, thou art hemm'd in on every side of thee——are they, Tristram, not sufficient, but thou must entangle thyself still more?

Is it not enough that thou art in debt, and that thou hast ten cart-loads of thy fifth and sixth volumes still[1]—still unsold, and art almost at thy wit's ends, how to get them off thy hands.

To this hour art thou not tormented with the vile asthma thou gattest in skating against the wind in Flanders? and is it but two months ago, that in a fit of laughter, on seeing a cardinal make water like a quirister[2] (with both hands) thou brakest a vessel in thy lungs, whereby, in two hours, thou lost as many quarts of blood; and hadst thou lost as much more, did not the faculty tell thee————it would have amounted to a gallon?————

CHAPTER VII

————But for heaven's sake, let us not talk of quarts or gallons————let us take the story straight before us; it is so nice and intricate a one, it will scarce bear the transposition of a single tittle; and some how or other, you have got me thrust almost into the middle of it—

—I beg we may take more care.

CHAPTER VIII

MY uncle Toby and the corporal had posted down with so much heat and precipitation, to take possession of the spot of ground we have so often spoke of, in order to open their campaign as early as the rest of the allies; that they had forgot one of the most necessary articles of the whole affair; it was neither a pioneer's spade, a pick-ax, or a shovel—

—It was a bed to lie on: so that as Shandy Hall was at that time unfurnished; and the little inn where poor Le Fever died, not yet built; my uncle Toby was constrained to accept of a bed at Mrs. Wadman's, for a night or two, till corporal Trim (who to the character of an excellent valet, groom, cook, sempster, surgeon and engineer, super-added that of an excellent upholsterer too) with the help of a carpenter and a couple of taylors, constructed one in my uncle Toby's house.

A daughter of Eve, for such was widow Wadman, and 'tis all the character I intend to give of her—

—"*That she was a perfect woman;*" had better be fifty leagues off—or in her warm bed—or playing with a case-knife[1]—or any thing you please—than make a man the object of her attention, when the house and all the furniture is her own.

There is nothing in it out of doors and in broad day-light,

where a woman has a power, physically speaking, of viewing a man in more lights than one—but here, for her soul, she can see him in no light without mixing something of her own goods and chattels along with him——till by reiterated acts of such combinations, he gets foisted into her inventory——

—And then good night.

But this is not matter of SYSTEM; for I have delivered that above——nor is it matter of BREVIARY——for I make no man's creed but my own——nor matter of FACT——at least that I know of; but 'tis matter copulative and introductory to what follows.

CHAPTER IX

I DO not speak it with regard to the coarseness or cleanness of them—or the strength of their gussets——but pray do not night-shifts differ from day-shifts as much in this particular, as in any thing else in the world; That they so far exceed the others in length, that when you are laid down in them, they fall almost as much below the feet, as the day-shifts fall short of them?

Widow Wadman's night-shifts (as was the mode I suppose in King William's and Queen Anne's reigns) were cut however after this fashion; and if the fashion is changed, (for in Italy they are come to nothing)——so much the worse for the public; they were two Flemish ells[1] and a half in length; so that allowing a moderate woman two ells, she had half an ell to spare, to do what she would with.

Now from one little indulgence gain'd after another, in the many bleak and decemberly nights of a seven years widowhood, things had insensibly come to this pass, and for the two last years had got establish'd into one of the ordinances of the bed-chamber—That as soon as Mrs. Wadman was put to bed, and had got her legs stretched down to the bottom of it, of which she always gave Bridget notice—Bridget with all suitable decorum, having first open'd the bed-cloaths at the feet, took hold of the half ell of cloath we are speaking of, and having gently, and with both her hands, drawn it downwards to its furthest extension, and then contracted it again side long by four or five even plaits, she took a large corking pin out of her sleeve, and with the point directed towards her, pin'd the plaits all fast together a little above the hem; which done she tuck'd all in tight at the feet, and wish'd her mistress a good night.

This was constant, and without any other variation than this; that on shivering and tempestuous nights, when Bridget un-tuck'd the feet of the bed, &c. to do this——she consulted no thermometer but that of her own passions; and so performed it standing——kneeling——or squatting, according to the different degrees of faith, hope, and charity, she was in, and bore towards her mistress that night. In every other respect the *etiquette* was sacred, and might have vied with the most mechanical one of the most inflexible bed-chamber in Christendom.

The first night, as soon as the corporal had conducted my uncle Toby up stairs, which was about ten——Mrs. Wadman threw herself into her arm chair, and crossing her left knee with her right, which formed a resting-place for her elbow, she reclin'd her cheek upon the palm of her hand, and leaning forwards, ruminated till midnight upon both sides of the question.

The second night she went to her bureau, and having ordered Bridget to bring her up a couple of fresh candles and leave them upon the table, she took out her marriage-settlement, and read it over with great devotion: and the third night (which was the last of my uncle Toby's stay) when Bridget had pull'd down the night-shift, and was assaying to stick in the corking pin——

——With a kick of both heels at once, but at the same time the most natural kick that could be kick'd in her situation——for supposing * * * * * * * * * to be the sun in its meridian, it was a north-east kick——she kick'd the pin out of her fingers—— the *etiquette* which hung upon it, down——down it fell to the ground, and was shivered into a thousand atoms.

From all which it was plain that widow Wadman was in love with my uncle Toby.

CHAPTER X

MY uncle Toby's head at that time was full of other matters, so that it was not till the demolition of Dunkirk, when all the other civilities of Europe were settled, that he found leisure to return this.

This made an armistice (that is speaking with regard to my uncle Toby——but with respect to Mrs. Wadman, a vacancy)——of almost eleven years. But in all cases of this nature, as it is the second blow, happen at what distance of time it will, which makes the fray——I chuse for that reason to call these the amours of my uncle Toby with Mrs. Wadman, rather than the amours of Mrs. Wadman with my uncle Toby.

This is not a distinction without a difference.

It is not like the affair of *an old hat cock'd*——and *a cock'd old hat*, about which your reverences have so often been at odds with one another——but there is a difference here in the nature of things——

And let me tell you, gentry, a wide one too.

CHAPTER XI

Now as widow Wadman did love my uncle Toby——and my uncle Toby did not love widow Wadman, there was nothing for widow Wadman to do, but to go on and love my uncle Toby——or let it alone.

Widow Wadman would do neither the one or the other——

——Gracious heaven!——but I forget I am a little of her temper myself; for whenever it so falls out, which it sometimes does about the equinoxes, that an earthly goddess is so much this, and that, and t'other, that I cannot eat my breakfast for her——and that she careth not three halfpence whether I eat my breakfast or no——

——Curse on her! and so I send her to Tartary, and from Tartary to *Terra del Fuogo*,[1] and so on to the devil: in short there is not an infernal nitch where I do not take her divinityship and stick it.

But as the heart is tender, and the passions in these tides ebb and flow ten times in a minute, I instantly bring her back again; and as I do all things in extremes, I place her in the very centre of the milky-way——

Brightest of stars! thou wilt shed thy influence upon some one——

——The duce take her and her influence too——for at that word I lose all patience——much good may it do him!——By all that is hirsute and gashly![2] I cry, taking off my furr'd cap, and twisting it round my finger——I would not give sixpence for a dozen such!

——But 'tis an excellent cap too (putting it upon my head,

and pressing it close to my ears)—and warm—and soft; especially if you stroke it the right way—but alas! that will
never be my luck——(so here my philosophy is shipwreck'd
again)

——No; I shall never have a finger in the pye (so here I break
my metaphor)——

    Crust and crumb
    Inside and out
    Top and bottom——I detest it, I hate it, I repudiate it——I'm
sick at the sight of it——

    'Tis all pepper,
        garlick,
        staragen,³
        salt, and
        devil's dung——by the great arch cook of cooks, who
does nothing, I think, from morning to night, but sit down by
the fire-side and invent inflammatory dishes for us, I would not
touch it for the world——

——O Tristam! Tristram! cried Jenny.

O Jenny! Jenny! replied I, and so went on with the twelfth
chapter.

CHAPTER XII

——"Not touch it for the world" did I say——

Lord, how I have heated my imagination with this metaphor!

CHAPTER XIII

WHICH shews, let your reverences and worships say what you
will of it (for as for *thinking*——all who *do* think—think pretty
much alike, both upon it and other matters)——LOVE is certainly, at least alphabetically speaking, one of the most

    A gitating
    B ewitching
    C onfounded
    D evilish affairs of life——the most
    E xtravagant
    F utilitous
    G alligaskinish

H andy-dandyish

I racundulous (there is not K to it) and

L yrical of all human passions: at the same time, the most

M isgiving

N innyhammering

O bstipating

P ragmatical

S tridulous

R idiculous—though by the bye the R should have gone first—But in short 'tis of such a nature, as my father once told my uncle Toby upon the close of a long dissertation upon the subject——"You can scarce," said he, "combine two ideas together upon it, brother Toby, without an hypallage"—— What's that? cried my uncle Toby.

The cart before the horse, replied my father——

——And what has he to do there? cried my uncle Toby—— Nothing, quoth my father, but to get in——or let it alone.

Now widow Wadman, as I told you before, would do neither the one or the other.

She stood however ready harnessed and caparisoned at all points to watch accidents.

CHAPTER XIV

THE Fates, who certainly all foreknew of these amours of widow Wadman and my uncle Toby, had, from the first creation of matter and motion (and with more courtesy than they usually do things of this kind) established such a chain of causes and effects hanging so fast to one another, that it was scarce possible for my uncle Toby to have dwelt in any other house in the world, or to have occupied any other garden in Christendom, but the very house and garden which join'd and laid parallel to Mrs. Wadman's; this, with the advantage of a thickset arbour in Mrs. Wadman's garden, but planted in the hedge-row of my uncle Toby's, put all the occasions into her hands which Love-militancy wanted; she could observe my uncle Toby's motions, and was mistress likewise of his councils of war; and as his unsuspecting heart had given leave to the corporal, through the mediation of Bridget, to make her a wicker gate of communication to enlarge her walks, it enabled her to carry on her approaches to the very door of the sentry-box; and sometimes out of gratitude, to make the attack, and endeavour to blow my uncle Toby up in the very sentry-box itself.

CHAPTER XV

IT is a great pity——but 'tis certain from every day's observation of man, that he may be set on fire like a candle, at either end——provided there is a sufficient wick standing out; if there is not——there's an end of the affair; and if there is——by lighting it at the bottom, as the flame in that case has the misfortune generally to put out itself——there's an end of the affair again.

For my part, could I always have the ordering of it which way I would be burnt myself——for I cannot bear the thoughts of being burnt like a beast——I would oblige a housewife constantly to light me at the top; for then I should burn down decently to the socket; that is, from my head to my heart, from my heart to my liver, from my liver to my bowels, and so on by the meseraick[1] veins and arteries, through all the turns and lateral insertions of the intestines and their tunicles, to the blind gut——

——I beseech you, doctor Slop, quoth my uncle Toby, interrupting him as he mentioned the *blind gut*, in a discourse with my father the night my mother was brought to bed of me——I beseech you, quoth my uncle Toby, to tell me which is the blind gut; for, old as I am, I vow I do not know to this day where it lies.

The *blind gut*, answered doctor Slop, lies betwixt the *Illion*[2] and *Colon*——

——In a man? said my father.

——'Tis precisely the same, cried doctor Slop, in a woman——

That's more than I know; quoth my father.

CHAPTER XVI

——And so to make sure of both systems, Mrs. Wadman predetermined to light my uncle Toby neither at this end or that; but like a prodigal's candle, to light him, if possible, at both ends at once.

Now, through all the lumber rooms of military furniture, including both of horse and foot, from the great arsenal of Venice to the Tower of London (exclusive) if Mrs. Wadman had been rummaging for seven years together, and with Bridget to help her, she could not have found any one *blind* or *mantelet* so fit for her purpose, as that which the expediency of my uncle Toby's affairs had fix'd up ready to her hands.

I believe I have not told you——but I don't know——possibly I have——be it as it will, 'tis one of the number of those many things, which a man had better do over again, than dispute about it——That whatever town or fortress the corporal was at work upon, during the course of their campaign, my uncle Toby always took care on the inside of his sentry-box, which was towards his left hand, to have a plan of the place, fasten'd up with two or three pins at the top, but loose at the bottom, for the conveniency of holding it up to the eye, &c. . . . as occasions required; so that when an attack was resolved upon, Mrs. Wadman had nothing more to do, when she had got advanced to the door of the sentry-box, but to extend her right hand; and edging in her left foot at the same movement, to take hold of the map or plan, or upright, or whatever it was, and with outstretched neck meeting it half way,—to advance it towards her; on which my uncle Toby's passions were sure to catch fire—for he would instantly take hold of the other corner of the map in his left hand, and with the end of his pipe, in the other, begin an explanation.

When the attack was advanced to this point;——the world will naturally enter into the reasons of Mrs. Wadman's next stroke of generalship——which was, to take my uncle Toby's tobacco-pipe out of his hand as soon as she possibly could; which, under one pretence or other, but generally that of pointing more distinctly at some redoubt or breast-work in the map, she would effect before my uncle Toby (poor soul!) had well march'd above half a dozen toises with it.

—It obliged my uncle Toby to make use of his forefinger.

The difference it made in the attack was this; That in going upon it, as in the first case, with the end of her forefinger against the end of my uncle Toby's tobacco-pipe, she might have travelled with it, along the lines, from Dan to Beersheba, had my uncle Toby's lines reach'd so far, without any effect: For as there was no arterial or vital heat in the end of the tobacco-pipe, it could excite no sentiment——it could neither give fire by pulsation——or receive it by sympathy——'twas nothing but smoak.

Whereas, in following my uncle Toby's forefinger with hers, close thro' all the little turns and indentings of his works—— pressing sometimes against the side of it——then treading upon it's nail——then tripping it up——then touching it here—— then there, and so on——it set something at least in motion.

This, tho' slight skirmishing, and at a distance from the main body, yet drew on the rest; for here, the map usually falling with the back of it, close to the side of the sentry-box, my uncle Toby, in the simplicity of his soul, would lay his hand flat upon it, in order to go on with his explanation; and Mrs. Wadman, by a manœuvre as quick as thought, would as certainly place her's close besides it; this at once opened a communication large enough for any sentiment to pass or repass, which a person skill'd in the elementary and practical part of love-making, has occasion for——

By bringing up her forefinger parallel (as before) to my uncle Toby's——it unavoidably brought the thumb into action—— and the forefinger and thumb being once engaged, as naturally brought in the whole hand. Thine, dear uncle Toby! was never now in it's right place——Mrs. Wadman had it ever to take up, or, with the gentlest pushings, protrusions, and equivocal compressions, that a hand to be removed is capable of receiving——to get it press'd a hair breadth of one side out of her way.

Whilst this was doing, how could she forget to make him sensible, that it was her leg (and no one's else) at the bottom of the sentry-box, which slightly press'd against the calf of his ——So that my uncle Toby being thus attacked and sore push'd on both his wings——was it a wonder, if now and then, it put his centre into disorder?——

——The duce take it! said my uncle Toby.

CHAPTER XVII

THESE attacks of Mrs. Wadman, you will readily conceive to be of different kinds; varying from each other, like the attacks which history is full of, and from the same reasons. A general looker on, would scarce allow them to be attacks at all——or if he did, would confound them all together——but I write not to them: it will be time enough to be a little more exact in my descriptions of them, as I come up to them, which will not be for some chapters; having nothing more to add in this, but that in a bundle of original papers and drawings which my father took care to roll up by themselves, there is a plan of Bouchain[1] in perfect preservation (and shall be kept so, whilst I have power to preserve any thing) upon the lower corner of which, on the right hand side, there is still remaining the marks of a snuffy finger and thumb, which there is all the reason in the world to imagine, were Mrs. Wadman's; for the opposite side of the margin, which I suppose to have been my uncle Toby's, is absolutely clean: This seems an authenticated record of one of these attacks; for there are vestigia of the two punctures partly grown up, but still visible on the opposite corner of the map, which are unquestionably the very holes, through which it has been pricked up in the sentry-box——

By all that is priestly! I value this precious relick, with it's *stigmata* and *pricks*, more than all the relicks of the Romish church——always excepting, when I am writing upon these matters, the pricks which enter'd the flesh of St. *Radagunda*[2] in the desert, which in your road from FESSE to CLUNY, the nuns of that name will shew you for love.

CHAPTER XVIII

I THINK, an' please your honour, quoth Trim, the fortifications are quite destroyed——and the bason is upon a level with the mole——I think so too; replied my uncle Toby with a sigh half suppress'd——but step into the parlour, Trim, for the stipulation——it lies upon the table.

It has lain there these six weeks, replied the corporal, till this very morning that the old woman kindled the fire with it—

——Then, said my uncle Toby, there is no further occasion for our services. The more, an' please your honour, the pity, said the corporal; in uttering which he cast his spade into the wheel-barrow, which was beside him, with an air the most expressive of disconsolation that can be imagined, and was heavily turning about to look for his pick-ax, his pioneer's shovel, his picquets and other little military stores, in order to carry them off the field——when a heigh ho! from the sentry-box, which, being made of thin slit deal, reverberated the sound more sorrowfully to his ear, forbad him.

——No; said the corporal to himself, I'll do it before his honour rises to-morrow morning; so taking his spade out of the wheel-barrow again, with a little earth in it, as if to level something at the foot of the glacis——but with a real intent to approach nearer to his master, in order to divert him——he loosen'd a sod or two——pared their edges with his spade, and having given them a gentle blow or two with the back of it, he sat himself down close by my uncle Toby's feet, and began as follows.

CHAPTER XIX

IT was a thousand pities——though I believe, an' please your honour, I am going to say but a foolish kind of a thing for a soldier——

A soldier, cried my uncle Toby, interrupting the corporal, is no more exempt from saying a foolish thing, Trim, than a man of letters——But not so often; and please your honour, replied the corporal——My uncle Toby gave a nod.

It was a thousand pities then, said the corporal, casting his eye upon Dunkirk, and the mole, as *Servius Sulpicius*, in returning out of Asia (when he sailed from Ægina towards Megara) did upon Corinth and Pyreus——

——"It was a thousand pities, an' please your honour, to destroy these works——and a thousand pities to have let them stood."——

——Thou art right, Trim, in both cases: said my uncle Toby——This, continued the corporal, is the reason, that from the beginning of their demolition to the end——I have never once whistled, or sung, or laugh'd, or cry'd, or talk'd of pass'd done deeds, or told your honour one story good or bad——

——Thou hast many excellencies, Trim, said my uncle Toby, and I hold it not the least of them, as thou happenest to be a story-teller, that of the number thou hast told me, either to amuse me in my painful hours, or divert me in my grave ones—thou hast seldom told me a bad one——

——Because, an' please your honour, except one of a *King of Bohemia and his seven castles*,—they are all true; for they are about myself——

I do not like the subject the worse, Trim, said my uncle Toby, on that score: But prithee what is this story? thou hast excited my curiosity.

I'll tell it your honour, quoth the corporal directly——Provided, said my uncle Toby, looking earnestly towards Dunkirk and the mole again——provided it is not a merry one; to such, Trim, a man should ever bring one half of the entertainment along with him; and the disposition I am in at present would wrong both thee, Trim, and thy story——It is not a merry one by any means, replied the corporal—Nor would I have it altogether a grave one, added my uncle Toby——It is neither the one nor the other, replied the corporal, but will suit your honour exactly——Then I'll thank thee for it with all my heart, cried my uncle Toby, so prithee begin it, Trim.

The corporal made his reverence; and though it is not so easy a matter as the world imagines, to pull off a lank montero cap with grace——or a whit less difficult, in my conceptions, when a man is sitting squat upon the ground, to make a bow so teeming with respect as the corporal was wont, yet by suffering the palm of his right hand, which was towards his master, to slip backward upon the grass, a little beyond his body, in order to allow it the greater sweep——and by an unforced compression, at the same time, of his cap with the thumb and the two forefingers of his left, by which the diameter of the cap became reduced, so that it might be said, rather to be insensibly squeez'd—than pull'd off with a flatus[1]——the corporal acquitted himself of both, in a better manner than the posture of his affairs promised; and having hemmed twice, to find in what key his story would best go, and best suit his master's humour—he exchanged a single look of kindness with him, and set off thus.

The Story of the king of Bohemia
and his seven castles.

THERE was a certain king of Bo--he——

As the corporal was entering the confines of Bohemia, my uncle Toby obliged him to halt for a single moment; he had set out bare-headed, having since he pull'd off his Montero-cap in the latter end of the last chapter, left it lying beside him on the ground.

——The eye of Goodness espieth all things——so that before the corporal had well got through the first five words of his story, had my uncle Toby twice touch'd his Montero-cap with the end of his cane, interrogatively——as much as to say, Why don't you put it on, Trim? Trim took it up with the most respectful slowness, and casting a glance of humiliation as he did it, upon the embroidery of the fore-part, which being dismally tarnish'd and fray'd moreover in some of the principal leaves and boldest parts of the pattern, he lay'd it down again betwixt his two feet, in order to moralize upon the subject.

——'Tis every word of it but too true, cried my uncle Toby, that thou art about to observe——

"*Nothing in this world, Trim, is made to last for ever.*"

——But when tokens, dear Tom, of thy love and remembrance wear out, said Trim, what shall we say?

There is no occasion, Trim, quoth my uncle Toby, to say any thing else; and was a man to puzzle his brains till Doom's day, I believe, Trim, it would be impossible.

The corporal perceiving my uncle Toby was in the right, and that it would be in vain for the wit of man to think of extracting a purer moral from his cap, without further attempting it, he put it on; and passing his hand across his forehead to rub out a pensive wrinkle, which the text and the doctrine between them had engender'd, he return'd, with the same look and tone of voice, to his story of the king of Bohemia and his seven castles.

The story of the king of Bohemia and
his seven castles, continued.

THERE was a certain king of Bohemia, but in whose reign, except his own, I am not able to inform your honour——

I do not desire it of thee, Trim, by any means, cried my uncle Toby.

——It was a little before the time, an' please your honour, when giants were beginning to leave off breeding;—but in what year of our Lord that was——

——I would not give a half-penny to know, said my uncle Toby.

——Only, an' please your honour, it makes a story look the better in the face——

——'Tis thy own, Trim, so ornament it after thy own fashion; and take any date, continued my uncle Toby, looking pleasantly upon him—take any date in the whole world thou choosest, and put it to—thou art heartily welcome——

The corporal bowed; for of every century, and of every year

of that century, from the first creation of the world down to Noah's flood; and from Noah's flood to the birth of Abraham; through all the pilgrimages of the patriarchs, to the departure of the Israelites out of Egypt——and throughout all the Dynasties, Olympiads, Urbecondita's,[2] and other memorable epochas of the different nations of the world, down to the coming of Christ, and from thence to the very moment in which the corporal was telling his story——had my uncle Toby subjected this vast empire of time and all its abysses at his feet; but as MODESTY scarce touches with a finger what LIBERALITY offers her with both hands open—the corporal contented himself with the very *worst year* of the whole bunch; which, to prevent your honours of the Majority and Minority from tearing the very flesh off your bones in contestation, 'Whether that year is not always the last cast-year of the last cast-almanack'——I tell you plainly it was; but from a different reason than you wot of——

——It was the year next him——which being the year of our Lord seventeen hundred and twelve, when the duke of Ormond was playing the devil in Flanders——the corporal took it, and set out with it afresh on his expedition to Bohemia.

The story of the king of Bohemia and
his seven castles, continued.

IN the year of our Lord one thousand seven hundred and twelve, there was, an' please your honour——

——To tell thee truly, Trim, quoth my uncle Toby, any other date would have pleased me much better, not only on account of the sad stain upon our history that year, in marching off our troops, and refusing to cover the siege of Quesnoi, though Fagel[3] was carrying on the works with such incredible vigour—but likewise on the score, Trim, of thy own story; because if there are—and which, from what thou hast dropt, I partly suspect to be the fact—if there are giants in it——

There is but one, an' please your honour——

——'Tis as bad as twenty, replied my uncle Toby——thou should'st have carried him back some seven or eight hundred years out of harm's way, both of criticks and other people; and therefore I would advise thee, if ever thou tellest it again——

——If I live, an' please your honour, but once to get through it, I will never tell it again, quoth Trim, either to man, woman, or child——Poo—poo! said my uncle Toby—but with accents of such sweet encouragement did he utter it, that the corporal went on with his story with more alacrity than ever.

The story of the king of Bohemia and
his seven castles, continued.

THERE was, an' please your honour, said the corporal, raising his voice and rubbing the palms of his two hands cheerily together as he begun, a certain king of Bohemia——

——Leave out the date entirely, Trim, quoth my uncle Toby, leaning forwards, and laying his hand gently upon the corporal's shoulder to temper the interruption—leave it out entirely, Trim; a story passes very well without these niceties, unless one is pretty sure of 'em——Sure of 'em! said the corporal, shaking his head——

Right; answered my uncle Toby, it is not easy, Trim, for one, bred up as thou and I have been to arms, who seldom looks further forward than to the end of his musket, or backwards beyond his knapsack, to know much about this matter——God bless your honour! said the corporal, won by the *manner* of my uncle Toby's reasoning, as much as by the reasoning itself, he has something else to do; if not on action, or a march, or upon duty in his garrison—he has his firelock, an' please your honour, to furbish—his accoutrements to take care of—his regimentals to mend—himself to shave and keep clean, so as to appear always like what he is upon the parade; what business, added the corporal triumphantly, has a soldier, an' please your honour, to know any thing at all of *geography?*

——Thou would'st have said *chronology*, Trim, said my uncle Toby; for as for geography, 'tis of absolute use to him; he must be acquainted intimately with every country and its boundaries where his profession carries him; he should know every town and city, and village and hamlet, with the canals, the roads, and hollow ways which lead up to them; there is not a river or a rivulet he passes, Trim, but he should be able at first sight to tell thee what is its name—in what mountains it takes its rise—what is its course—how far it is navigable—where fordable—where not; he should know the fertility of every valley, as well as the hind who ploughs it; and be able to describe, or, if it is required, to give thee an exact map of all the plains and defiles, the forts, the acclivities, the woods and morasses, thro' and by which his army is to march; he should know their produce, their plants, their minerals, their waters, their animals, their seasons, their climates, their heats and cold, their inhabitants, their customs, their language, their policy, and even their religion.

Is it else to be conceived, corporal, continued my uncle Toby, rising up in his sentry-box, as he began to warm in this part of his discourse—how Marlborough could have marched his army from the banks of the Maes to Belburg; from Belburg to Kerpenord—(here the corporal could sit no longer) from Kerpenord, Trim, to Kalsaken; from Kalsaken to Newdorf; from Newdorf to Landenbourg; from Landenbourg to Mildenheim; from Mildenheim to Elchingen; from Elchingen to Gingen; from Gingen to Balmerchoffen; from Balmerchoffen to Skellenburg, where he broke in upon the enemy's works; forced his passage over the *Danube*; cross'd the *Lech*—pushed on his troops into the heart of the empire, marching at the head of them through Friburg, Hokenwert, and Schonevelt, to the plains of Blenheim and Hochstet?——Great as he was, corporal, he could not have advanced a step, or made one single day's march without the aids of *Geography*——As for *Chronology*, I own, Trim, continued my uncle Toby, sitting down again coolly in his sentry-box, that of all others, it seems a science which the soldier might best spare, was it not for the lights which that science must one day give him, in determining the invention of powder; the furious execution of which, renversing every thing like thunder before it, has become a new æra to us of military improvements, changing so totally the nature of attacks and defences both by sea and land, and awakening so much art and skill in doing it, that the world cannot be too exact in ascertaining the precise time of its discovery, or too inquisitive in knowing what great man was the discoverer, and what occasions gave birth to it.

I am far from controverting, continued my uncle Toby, what historians agree in, that in the year of our Lord 1380, under the reign of Wencelaus,[4] son of Charles the fourth——a certain priest, whose name was Schwartz,[5] shew'd the use of powder to the Venetians, in their wars against the Genoese; but 'tis certain he was not the first; because if we are to believe Don Pedro the bishop of Leon[6]—How came priests and bishops, an' please your honour, to trouble their heads so much about gunpowder? God knows, said my uncle Toby——his providence brings good out of every thing—and he avers, in his chronicle of King Alphonsus,[7] who reduced Toledo, That in the year 1343, which was full thirty seven years before that time, the secret of powder was well known, and employed with success, both by

Moors and Christians, not only in their sea-combats, at that period, but in many of their most memorable sieges in Spain and Barbary—And all the world knows, that Friar Bacon[8] had wrote expressly about it, and had generously given the world a receipt to make it by, above a hundred and fifty years before even Schwartz was born—And that the Chinese, added my uncle Toby, embarass us, and all accounts of it still more, by boasting of the invention some hundreds of years even before him——

—They are a pack of liars, I believe, cried Trim——

——They are some how or other deceived, said my uncle Toby, in this matter, as is plain to me from the present miserable state of military architecture amongst them; which consists of nothing more than a fossè with a brick wall without flanks—and for what they give us as a bastion at each angle of it, 'tis so barbarously constructed, that it looks for all the world————Like one of my seven castles, an' please your honour, quoth Trim.

My uncle Toby, tho' in the utmost distress for a comparison, most courteously refused Trim's offer—till Trim telling him, he had half a dozen more in Bohemia, which he knew not how to get off his hands——my uncle Toby was so touch'd with the pleasantry of heart of the corporal——that he discontinued his dissertation upon gunpowder——and begged the corporal forthwith to go on with his story of the King of Bohemia and his seven castles.

The story of the King of Bohemia and
his seven castles, continued.

This *unfortunate* King of Bohemia, said Trim——Was he unfortunate then? cried my uncle Toby, for he had been so wrapt up in his dissertation upon gun-powder and other military affairs, that tho' he had desired the corporal to go on, yet the many interruptions he had given, dwelt not so strong upon his fancy, as to account for the epithet——Was he *unfortunate* then, Trim? said my uncle Toby, pathetically——The corporal, wishing first the *word* and all its synonimas at the devil, forthwith began to run back in his mind, the principal events in the King of Bohemia's story; from every one of which, it appearing that he was the most fortunate man that ever existed in the world——it put the corporal to a stand: for not caring to retract

his epithet——and less, to explain it——and least of all, to twist
his tale (like men of lore) to serve a system——he looked up in
my uncle Toby's face for assistance——but seeing it was the
very thing, my uncle Toby sat in expectation of himself——
after a hum and a haw, he went on——

The King of Bohemia, an' please your honour, replied the
corporal, was *unfortunate*, as thus——That taking great pleasure and delight in navigation and all sort of sea-affairs——and
there *happening* throughout the whole kingdom of Bohemia, to
be no sea-port town whatever——

How the duce should there—Trim? cried my uncle Toby; for
Bohemia being totally inland, it could have happen'd no otherwise——It might; said Trim, if it had pleased God——

My uncle Toby never spoke of the being and natural attributes of God, but with diffidence and hesitation——

——I believe not, replied my uncle Toby, after some pause
——for being inland, as I said, and having Silesia and Moravia
to the east; Lusatia and Upper Saxony to the north; Franconia
to the west; and Bavaria to the south: Bohemia could not have
been propell'd to the sea, without ceasing to be Bohemia
——nor could the sea, on the other hand, have come up to
Bohemia, without overflowing a great part of Germany, and
destroying millions of unfortunate inhabitants who could make
no defence against it——Scandalous! cried Trim—Which
would bespeak, added my uncle Toby, mildly, such a want of
compassion in him who is the father of it——that, I think,
Trim——the thing could have happen'd no way.

The corporal made the bow of unfeigned conviction; and
went on.

Now the King of Bohemia with his queen and courtiers
happening one fine summer's evening to walk out——Aye!
there the word *happening* is right, Trim, cried my uncle Toby;
for the King of Bohemia and his queen might have walk'd out,
or let it alone;——'twas a matter of contingency, which might
happen, or not, just as chance ordered it.

King William was of an opinion, an' please your honour,
quoth Trim, that every thing was predestined for us in this
world; insomuch, that he would often say to his soldiers, that
"every ball had it's billet." He was a great man, said my uncle
Toby——And I believe, continued Trim, to this day, that the
shot which disabled me at the battle of Landen, was pointed at
my knee for no other purpose, but to take me out of his service,

and place me in your honour's, where I should be taken so much better care of in my old age——It shall never, Trim, be construed otherwise, said my uncle Toby.

The heart, both of the master and the man, were alike subject to sudden overflowings;——a short silence ensued.

Besides, said the corporal, resuming the discourse—but in a gayer accent——if it had not been for that single shot, I had never, an' please your honour, been in love——

So, thou wast once in love, Trim! said my uncle Toby, smiling——

Souse! replied the corporal—over head and ears! an' please your honour. Prithee when? where?—and how came it to pass?——I never heard one word of it before; quoth my uncle Toby:——I dare say, answered Trim, that every drummer and serjeant's son in the regiment knew of it——Its high time I should——said my uncle Toby.

Your honour remembers with concern, said the corporal, the total rout and confusion of our camp and army at the affair of Landen; every one was left to shift for himself; and if it had not been for the regiments of Wyndham, Lumley, and Galway,[9] which covered the retreat over the bridge of Neerspeeken, the king himself could scarce have gain'd it——he was press'd hard, as your honour knows, on every side of him——

Gallant mortal! cried my uncle Toby, caught up with enthusiasm—this moment, now that all is lost, I see him galloping across me, corporal, to the left, to bring up the remains of the English horse along with him to support the right, and tear the laurel from Luxembourg's brows,[10] if yet 'tis possible——I see him with the knot of his scarfe just shot off, infusing fresh spirits into poor Galway's regiment—riding along the line—then wheeling about, and charging Conti[11] at the head of it——Brave! brave by heaven! cried my uncle Toby—he deserves a crown——As richly, as a thief a halter; shouted Trim.

My uncle Toby knew the corporal's loyalty;—otherwise the comparison was not at all to his mind——it did not altogether strike the corporal's fancy when he had made it——but it could not be recall'd——so he had nothing to do, but proceed.

As the number of wounded was prodigious, and no one had time to think of any thing, but his own safety—Though Talmash,[12] said my uncle Toby, brought off the foot with great prudence——But I was left upon the field, said the corporal. Thou wast so; poor fellow! replied my uncle Toby——So that it was noon the next day, continued the corporal, before I was exchanged, and put into a cart with thirteen or fourteen more, in order to be convey'd to our hospital.

There is no part of the body, an' please your honour, where a wound occasions more intolerable anguish than upon the knee——

Except the groin; said my uncle Toby. An' please your honour, replied the corporal, the knee, in my opinion, must certainly be the most acute, there being so many tendons and what-d'ye-call-'ems all about it.

It is for that reason, quoth my uncle Toby, that the groin is infinitely more sensible——there being not only as many tendons and what-d'ye-call-'ems (for I know their names as little as thou do'st)——about it——but moreover * * *——

Mrs. Wadman, who had been all the time in her arbour—instantly stopp'd her breath—unpinn'd her mob at the chin, and stood up upon one leg——

The dispute was maintained with amicable and equal force betwixt my uncle Toby and Trim for some time; till Trim at length recollecting that he had often cried at his master's sufferings, but never shed a tear at his own—was for giving up the point, which my uncle Toby would not allow——'Tis a proof of nothing, Trim, said he, but the generosity of thy temper——

So that whether the pain of a wound in the groin (cæteris paribus[13]) is greater than the pain of a wound in the knee—— or

Whether the pain of a wound in the knee is not greater than the pain of a wound in the groin——are points which to this day remain unsettled.

CHAPTER XX

THE anguish of my knee, continued the corporal, was excessive in itself; and the uneasiness of the cart, with the roughness of the roads which were terribly cut up—making bad still worse—every step was death to me: so that with the loss of blood, and the want of care-taking of me, and a fever I felt coming on besides——(Poor soul! said my uncle Toby) all together, an' please your honour, was more than I could sustain.

I was telling my sufferings to a young woman at a peasant's house, where our cart, which was the last of the line, had halted;

they had help'd me in, and the young woman had taken a cordial out of her pocket and dropp'd it upon some sugar, and seeing it had cheer'd me, she had given it me a second and a third time——So I was telling her, an' please your honour, the anguish I was in, and was saying it was so intolerable to me, that I had much rather lie down upon the bed, turning my face towards one which was in the corner of the room—and die, than go on——when, upon her attempting to lead me to it, I fainted away in her arms. She was a good soul! as your honour, said the corporal, wiping his eyes, will hear.

I thought *love* had been a joyous thing, quoth my uncle Toby.

'Tis the most serious thing, an' please your honour (sometimes) that is in the world.

By the persuasion of the young woman, continued the corporal, the cart with the wounded men set off without me: she had assured them I should expire immediately if I was put into the cart. So when I came to myself——I found myself in a still quiet cottage, with no one but the young woman, and the peasant and his wife. I was laid across the bed in the corner of the room, with my wounded leg upon a chair, and the young woman beside me, holding the corner of her handkerchief dipp'd in vinegar to my nose with one hand, and rubbing my temples with the other.

I took her at first for the daughter of the peasant (for it was no inn)—so had offer'd her a little purse with eighteen florins, which my poor brother Tom (here Trim wip'd his eyes) had sent me as a token, by a recruit, just before he set out for Lisbon——

——I never told your honour that piteous story yet——here Trim wiped his eyes a third time.

The young woman call'd the old man and his wife into the room, to shew them the money, in order to gain me credit for a bed and what little necessaries I should want, till I should be in a condition to be got to the hospital——Come then! said she, tying up the little purse—I'll be your banker—but as that office alone will not keep me employ'd, I'll be your nurse too.

I thought by her manner of speaking this, as well as by her dress, which I then began to consider more attentively—that the young woman could not be the daughter of the peasant.

She was in black down to her toes, with her hair conceal'd under a cambrick border, laid close to her forehead: she was one of those kind of nuns, an' please your honour, of which, your honour knows, there are a good many in Flanders which they let go loose——By thy description, Trim, said my uncle Toby, I dare say she was a young Beguine, of which there are none to be found any where but in the Spanish Netherlands—except at Amsterdam—they differ from nuns in this, that they can quit their cloister if they choose to marry; they visit and take care of the sick by profession——I had rather, for my own part, they did it out of good-nature.

——She often told me, quoth Trim, she did it for the love of Christ—I did not like it.——I believe, Trim, we are both wrong, said my uncle Toby—we'll ask Mr. Yorick about it to-night at my brother Shandy's——so put me in mind; added my uncle Toby.

The young Beguine, continued the corporal, had scarce given herself time to tell me "she would be my nurse," when she hastily turned about to begin the office of one, and prepare something for me——and in a short time—though I thought it a long one—she came back with flannels, &c. &c. and having fomented my knee soundly for a couple of hours, &c. and made me a thin basin of gruel for my supper—she wish'd me rest, and promised to be with me early in the morning.——She wish'd me, an' please your honour, what was not to be had. My fever ran very high that night—her figure made sad disturbance within me—I was every moment cutting the world in two—to give her half of it—and every moment was I crying, That I had nothing but a knapsack and eighteen florins to share with her——The whole night long was the fair Beguine, like an angel, close by my bedside, holding back my curtain and offering me cordials—and I was only awakened from my dream by her coming there at the hour promised, and giving them in reality. In truth, she was scarce ever from me, and so accustomed was I to receive life from her hands, that my heart sickened, and I lost colour when she left the room: and yet, continued the corporal, (making one of the strangest reflections upon it in the world)——

——"*It was not love*"——for during the three weeks she was almost constantly with me, fomenting my knee with her hand, night and day—I can honestly say, an' please your honour— that * * * * * * * * * *
* * * * * * * once.

That was very odd, Trim, quoth my uncle Toby——

I think so too—said Mrs. Wadman.

It never did, said the corporal.

CHAPTER XXI

——But 'tis no marvel, continued the corporal—seeing my uncle Toby musing upon it—for Love, an' please your honour, is exactly like war, in this; that a soldier, though he has escaped three weeks compleat o'Saturday-night,—may nevertheless be shot through his heart on Sunday morning——*It happened so here*, an' please your honour, with this difference only—that it was on Sunday in the afternoon, when I fell in love all at once with a sisserara[1]——it burst upon me, an' please your honour, like a bomb——scarce giving me time to say, "God bless me."

I thought, Trim, said my uncle Toby, a man never fell in love so very suddenly.

Yes, an' please your honour, if he is in the way of it ——replied Trim.

I prithee, quoth my uncle Toby, inform me how this matter happened.

——With all pleasure, said the corporal, making a bow.

CHAPTER XXII

I had escaped, continued the corporal, all that time from falling in love, and had gone on to the end of the chapter, had it not been predestined otherwise——there is no resisting our fate.

It was on a Sunday, in the afternoon, as I told your honour——

The old man and his wife had walked out——

Every thing was still and hush as midnight about the house——

There was not so much as a duck or a duckling about the yard——

——When the fair Beguine came in to see me.

My wound was then in a fair way of doing well——the inflammation had been gone off for some time, but it was succeeded with an itching both above and below my knee, so insufferable, that I had not shut my eyes the whole night for it.

Let me see it, said she, kneeling down upon the ground parallel to my knee, and laying her hand upon the part below it——It only wants rubbing a little, said the Beguine; so covering it with the bed cloaths, she began with the forefinger of her right-hand to rub under my knee, guiding her fore-finger backwards and forwards by the edge of the flannel which kept on the dressing.

In five or six minutes I felt slightly the end of her second finger——and presently it was laid flat with the other, and she continued rubbing in that way round and round for a good while; it then came into my head, that I should fall in love—I blush'd when I saw how white a hand she had—I shall never, an' please your honour, behold another hand so white whilst I live——

——Not in that place: said my uncle Toby——

Though it was the most serious despair in nature to the corporal—he could not forbear smiling.

The young Beguine, continued the corporal, perceiving it was of great service to me—from rubbing, for some time, with two fingers—proceeded to rub at length, with three—till by little and little she brought down the fourth, and then rubb'd with her whole hand: I will never say another word, an' please your honour, upon hands again—but it was softer than satin——

——Prithee, Trim, commend it as much as thou wilt, said my uncle Toby; I shall hear thy story with the more delight——The corporal thank'd his master most unfeignedly; but having nothing to say upon the Beguine's hand, but the same over again——he proceeded to the effects of it.

The fair Beguine, said the corporal, continued rubbing with her whole hand under my knee—till I fear'd her zeal would weary her——"I would do a thousand times more," said she, "for the love of Christ"—In saying which she pass'd her hand across the flannel, to the part above my knee, which I had equally complained of, and rubb'd it also.

I perceived, then, I was beginning to be in love——

As she continued rub-rub-rubbing—I felt it spread from under her hand, an' please your honour, to every part of my frame——

The more she rubb'd, and the longer strokes she took——the more the fire kindled in my veins——till at length, by two or three strokes longer than the rest——my passion rose to the highest pitch——I seiz'd her hand——

——And then, thou clapped'st it to thy lips, Trim, said my uncle Toby——and madest a speech.

Whether the corporal's amour terminated precisely in the way my uncle Toby described it, is not material; it is enough that it contain'd in it the essence of all the love-romances which ever have been wrote since the beginning of the world.

CHAPTER XXIII

As soon as the corporal had finished the story of his amour—or rather my uncle Toby for him—Mrs. Wadman silently sallied forth from her arbour, replaced the pin in her mob, pass'd the wicker gate, and advanced slowly towards my uncle Toby's sentry-box: the disposition which Trim had made in my uncle Toby's mind, was too favourable a crisis to be let slipp'd——

——The attack was determin'd upon: it was facilitated still more by my uncle Toby's having ordered the corporal to wheel off the pioneer's shovel, the spade, the pick-axe, the picquets, and other military stores which lay scatter'd upon the ground where Dunkirk stood—The corporal had march'd—the field was clear.

Now consider, sir, what nonsense it is, either in fighting, or writing, or any thing else (whether in rhyme to it, or not) which a man has occasion to do—to act by plan: for if ever Plan, independent of all circumstances, deserved registering in letters of gold (I mean in the archives of Gotham[1])—it was certainly the PLAN of Mrs. Wadman's attack of my uncle Toby in his sentry-box, BY PLAN——Now the Plan hanging up in it at this juncture, being the Plan of Dunkirk—and the tale of Dunkirk a tale of relaxation, it opposed every impression she could make: and besides, could she have gone upon it—the manœuvre of fingers and hands in the attack of the sentry-box, was so outdone by that of the fair Beguine's, in Trim's story—that just then, that particular attack, however successful before—became the most heartless attack that could be made——

O! let woman alone for this. Mrs. Wadman had scarce open'd the wicker-gate, when her genius sported with the change of circumstances.

——She formed a new attack in a moment.

CHAPTER XXIV

——I am half distracted, captain Shandy, said Mrs. Wadman,
holding up her cambrick handkerchief to her left eye, as she
approach'd the door of my uncle Toby's sentry-box——a
mote——or sand——or something——I know not what, has
got into this eye of mine——do look into it—it is not in the
white—

In saying which, Mrs. Wadman edged herself close in beside
my uncle Toby, and squeezing herself down upon the corner of
his bench, she gave him an opportunity of doing it without
rising up——Do look into it—said she.

Honest soul! thou didst look into it with as much innocency
of heart, as ever child look'd into a raree-shew-box; and 'twere
as much a sin to have hurt thee.

——If a man will be peeping of his own accord into things of
that nature——I've nothing to say to it——

My uncle Toby never did: and I will answer for him, that he
would have sat quietly upon a sopha from June to January,
(which, you know, takes in both the hot and cold months) with
an eye as fine as the Thracian* Rodope's beside him, without
being able to tell, whether it was a black or a blue one.

The difficulty was to get my uncle Toby, to look at one, at all.

'Tis surmounted. And

I see him yonder with his pipe pendulous in his hand, and the
ashes falling out of it—looking—and looking—then rubbing
his eyes——and looking again, with twice the good nature that
ever Gallileo look'd for a spot in the sun.[2]

——In vain! for by all the powers which animate the organ
——Widow Wadman's left eye shines this moment as lucid as
her right——there is neither mote, or sand, or dust, or chaff, or
speck, or particle of opake matter floating in it——there is
nothing, my dear paternal uncle! but one lambent delicious fire,
furtively shooting out from every part of it, in all directions,
into thine——

——If thou lookest, uncle Toby, in search of this mote one
moment longer——thou art undone.

* Rodope Thracia tam inevitabili fascino instructa, tam exacte oculis intuens
attraxit, ut si in illam quis incidesset, fieri non posset, quin caperetur.——I know
not who.[1]

CHAPTER XXV

AN eye is for all the world exactly like a cannon, in this respect; That it is not so much the eye or the cannon, in themselves, as it is the carriage of the eye——and the carriage of the cannon, by which both the one and the other are enabled to do so much execution. I don't think the comparison a bad one: However, as 'tis made and placed at the head of the chapter, as much for use as ornament, all I desire in return, is, that whenever I speak of Mrs. Wadman's eyes (except once in the next period) that you keep it in your fancy.

I protest, Madam, said my uncle Toby, I can see nothing whatever in your eye.

It is not in the white; said Mrs. Wadman: my uncle Toby look'd with might and main into the pupil——

Now of all the eyes, which ever were created——from your own, Madam, up to those of Venus herself, which certainly were as venereal a pair of eyes as ever stood in a head——there never was an eye of them all, so fitted to rob my uncle Toby of his repose, as the very eye, at which he was looking——it was not, Madam, a rolling eye——a romping or a wanton one—nor was it an eye sparkling—petulant or imperious—of high claims and terrifying exactions, which would have curdled at once that milk of human nature, of which my uncle Toby was made up——but 'twas an eye full of gentle salutations——and soft responses——speaking——not like the trumpet stop of some ill-made organ, in which many an eye I talk to, holds coarse converse——but whispering soft——like the last low accents of an expiring saint——"How can you live comfortless, captain Shandy, and alone, without a bosom to lean your head on—— or trust your cares to?"

It was an eye——

But I shall be in love with it myself, if I say another word about it.

——It did my uncle Toby's business.

CHAPTER XXVI

THERE is nothing shews the characters of my father and my uncle Toby, in a more entertaining light, than their different

manner of deportment, under the same accident——for I call
not love a misfortune, from a persuasion, that a man's heart is
ever the better for it——Great God! what must my uncle
Toby's have been, when 'twas all benignity without it.

My father, as appears from many of his papers, was very
subject to this passion, before he married——but from a little
subacid kind of drollish impatience in his nature, whenever it
befell him, he would never submit to it like a christian; but
would pish, and huff, and bounce, and kick, and play the Devil,
and write the bitterest Philippicks against the eye that ever man
wrote——there is one in verse upon some body's eye or other,
that for two or three nights together, had put him by his rest;
which in his first transport of resentment against it, he begins
thus:

> "A Devil 'tis——and mischief such doth work
> As never yet did Pagan, Jew, or Turk."*

In short during the whole paroxism, my father was all abuse
and foul language, approaching rather towards malediction
——only he did not do it with as much method as Ernulphus
——he was too impetuous; nor with Ernulphus's policy——
for tho' my father, with the most intolerant spirit, would
curse both this and that, and every thing under heaven, which
was either aiding or abetting to his love——yet never concluded
his chapter of curses upon it, without cursing himself in at the
bargain, as one of the most egregious fools and coxcombs, he
would say, that ever was let loose in the world.

My uncle Toby, on the contrary, took it like a lamb——sat
still and let the poison work in his veins without resistance——
in the sharpest exacerbations of his wound (like that on his
groin) he never dropt one fretful or discontented word——he
blamed neither heaven nor earth——or thought or spoke an
injurious thing of any body, or any part of it; he sat solitary and
pensive with his pipe——looking at his lame leg——then
whiffing out a sentimental heigh ho! which mixing with the
smoak, incommoded no one mortal.

He took it like a lamb——I say.

In truth he had mistook it at first; for having taken a ride with
my father, that very morning, to save if possible a beautiful
wood, which the dean and chapter were hewing down² to give

---

* This will be printed with my father's life of Socrates, &c. &c.¹

to the poor*; which said wood being in full view of my uncle Toby's house, and of singular service to him in his description of the battle of Wynnendale³—by trotting on too hastily to save it——upon an uneasy saddle——worse horse, &c. &c... it had so happened, that the serous part of the blood had got betwixt the two skins, in the nethermost part of my uncle Toby——the first shootings of which (as my uncle Toby had no experience of love) he had taken for a part of the passion—till the blister breaking in one case—and the other remaining—my uncle Toby was presently convinced, that his wound was not a skin-deep-wound——but that it had gone to his heart.

CHAPTER XXVII

THE world is ashamed of being virtuous——My uncle Toby knew little of the world; and therefore when he felt he was in love with widow Wadman, he had no conception that the thing was any more to be made a mystery of, than if Mrs. Wadman, had given him a cut with a gap'd knife¹ across his finger: Had it been otherwise——yet as he ever look'd upon Trim as a humble friend; and saw fresh reasons every day of his life, to treat him as such——it would have made no variation in the manner in which he informed him of the affair.

"I am in love, corporal!" quoth my uncle Toby.

CHAPTER XXVIII

IN love!——said the corporal—your honour was very well the day before yesterday, when I was telling your honour the story of the King of Bohemia—Bohemia! said my uncle Toby----musing a long time---What became of that story, Trim?

——We lost it, an' please your honour, somehow betwixt us—but your honour was as free from love then, as I am——'twas, just whilst thou went'st off with the wheel-barrow—with Mrs. Wadman, quoth my uncle Toby——She has left a ball here—added my uncle Toby—pointing to his breast——

——She can no more, an' please your honour, stand a siege, than she can fly—cried the corporal——

---

* Mr. Shandy must mean the poor *in spirit*; inasmuch as they divided the money amongst themselves.

——But as we are neighbours, Trim,—the best way I think is to let her know it civilly first—quoth my uncle Toby.

Now if I might presume, said the corporal, to differ from your honour——

—Why else, do I talk to thee Trim: said my uncle Toby, mildly——

—Then I would begin, an' please your honour, with making a good thundering attack upon her, in return—and telling her civilly afterwards—for if she knows any thing of your honour's being in love, before hand——L—d help her!—she knows no more at present of it, Trim, said my uncle Toby—than the child unborn——

Precious souls!——

Mrs. Wadman had told it with all its circumstances, to Mrs. Bridget twenty-four hours before; and was at that very moment sitting in council with her, touching some slight misgivings with regard to the issue of the affair, which the Devil, who never lies dead in a ditch, had put into her head—before he would allow half time, to get quietly through her *te Deum*——

I am terribly afraid, said widow Wadman, in case I should marry him, Bridget—that the poor captain will not enjoy his health, with the monstrous wound upon his groin——

It may not, Madam, be so very large, replied Bridget, as you think——and I believe besides, added she—that 'tis dried up——

——I could like to know—merely for his sake, said Mrs. Wadman——

—We'll know the long and the broad of it, in ten days—answered Mrs. Bridget, for whilst the captain is paying his addresses to you—I'm confident Mr. Trim will be for making love to me—and I'll let him as much as he will—added Bridget—to get it all out of him——

The measures were taken at once——and my uncle Toby and the corporal went on with theirs.

Now, quoth the corporal, setting his left hand a kimbo, and giving such a flourish with his right, as just promised success—and no more——if your honour will give me leave to lay down the plan of this attack——

——Thou wilt please me by it, Trim, said my uncle Toby, exceedingly—and as I foresee thou must act in it as my *aid de camp*, here's a crown, corporal, to begin with, to steep thy commission.

Then, an' please your honour, said the corporal (making a bow first for his commission)—we will begin with getting your honour's laced cloaths out of the great campaign trunk, to be well-air'd, and have the blue and gold taken up at the sleeves—and I'll put your white ramallie-wig fresh into pipes[1]—and send for a taylor, to have your honour's thin scarlet breeches turn'd——

—I had better take the red plush ones, quoth my uncle Toby——They will be too clumsy—said the corporal.

CHAPTER XXIX

——Thou wilt get a brush and a little chalk to my sword—— 'Twill be only in your honour's way, replied Trim.

CHAPTER XXX

——But your honour's two razors shall be new set—and I will get my Montero cap furbish'd up, and put on poor lieutenant Le Fever's regimental coat, which your honour gave me to wear for his sake—and as soon as your honour is clean shaved—and has got your clean shirt on, with your blue and gold, or your fine scarlet——sometimes one and sometimes t'other—and every thing is ready for the attack—we'll march up boldly, as if 'twas to the face of a bastion; and whilst your honour engages Mrs. Wadman in the parlour, to the right—— I'll attack Mrs. Bridget in the kitchen, to the left; and having seiz'd that pass, I'll answer for it, said the corporal, snapping his fingers over his head—that the day is our own.

I wish I may but manage it right; said my uncle Toby—but I declare, corporal I had rather march up to the very edge of a trench——

—A woman is quite a different thing—said the corporal.

—I suppose so, quoth my uncle Toby.

CHAPTER XXXI

IF any thing in this world, which my father said, could have provoked my uncle Toby, during the time he was in love, it was the perverse use my father was always making of an expression

of Hilarion[1] the hermit; who, in speaking of his abstinence, his
watchings, flagellations, and other instrumental parts of his
religion—would say—tho' with more facetiousness than
became an hermit—"That they were the means he used, to make
his *ass* (meaning his body) leave off kicking."

It pleased my father well; it was not only a laconick way of
expressing——but of libelling, at the same time, the desires and
appetites of the lower part of us; so that for many years of my
father's life, 'twas his constant mode of expression—he never
used the word *passions* once—but *ass* always instead of them
——So that he might be said truly, to have been upon the bones,
or the back of his own ass, or else of some other man's, during
all that time.

I must here observe to you, the difference betwixt

   My father's ass

   and my hobby-horse—in order to keep characters as separate as may be, in our fancies as we go along.

For my hobby-horse, if you recollect a little, is no way a
vicious beast; he has scarce one hair or lineament of the ass
about him——'Tis the sporting little filly-folly which carries
you out for the present hour—a maggot, a butterfly, a picture, a
fiddle-stick—an uncle Toby's siege—or an *any thing*, which a
man makes a shift to get a stride on, to canter it away from the
cares and solicitudes of life—'Tis as useful a beast as is in the
whole creation—nor do I really see how the world could do
without it——

——But for my father's ass——oh! mount him—mount
him—mount him—(that's three times, is it not?)—mount him
not:—'tis a beast concupiscent—and foul befall the man, who
does not hinder him from kicking.

CHAPTER XXXII

WELL! dear brother Toby, said my father, upon his first seeing
him after he fell in love—and how goes it with your ASSE?

Now my uncle Toby thinking more of the *part* where he had
had the blister, than of Hilarion's metaphor—and our pre-
conceptions having (you know) as great a power over the
sounds of words as the shapes of things, he had imagined, that
my father, who was not very ceremonious in his choice of
words, had enquired after the part by its proper name; so

notwithstanding my mother, doctor Slop, and Mr. Yorick, were sitting in the parlour, he thought it rather civil to conform to the term my father had made use of than not. When a man is hemm'd in by two indecorums, and must commit one of 'em—I always observe—let him choose which he will, the world will blame him—so I should not be astonished if it blames my uncle Toby.

My A—e, quoth my uncle Toby, is much better—brother Shandy——My father had formed great expectations from his Asse in this onset; and would have brought him on again; but doctor Slop setting up an intemperate laugh—and my mother crying out L— bless us!—it drove my father's Asse off the field—and the laugh then becoming general—there was no bringing him back to the charge, for some time——

And so the discourse went on without him.

Every body, said my mother, says you are in love, brother Toby—and we hope it is true.

I am as much in love, sister, I believe, replied my uncle Toby, as any man usually is——Humph! said my father——and when did you know it? quoth my mother——

——When the blister broke; replied my uncle Toby.

My uncle Toby's reply put my father into good temper—so he charged o'foot.

CHAPTER XXXIII

As the antients agree, brother Toby, said my father, that there are two different and distinct kinds of *love*, according to the different parts which are affected by it—the Brain or Liver——I think when a man is in love, it behoves him a little to consider which of the two he is fallen into.

What signifies it, brother Shandy, replied my uncle Toby, which of the two it is , provided it will but make a man marry, and love his wife, and get a few children.

——A few children! cried my father, rising out of his chair, and looking full in my mother's face, as he forced his way betwixt her's and doctor Slop's—a few children! cried my father, repeating my uncle Toby's words as he walk'd to and fro'——

——Not, my dear brother Toby, cried my father, recovering himself all at once, and coming close up to the back of my uncle

Toby's chair—not that I should be sorry had'st thou a score—on the contrary I should rejoice—and be as kind, Toby, to every one of them as a father—

My uncle Toby stole his hand unperceived behind his chair, to give my father's a squeeze——

——Nay, moreover, continued he, keeping hold of my uncle Toby's hand—so much do'st thou possess, my dear Toby, of the milk of human nature, and so little of its asperities—'tis piteous the world is not peopled by creatures which resemble thee; and was I an Asiatick monarch, added my father, heating himself with his new project—I would oblige thee, provided it would not impair thy strength—or dry up thy radical moisture too fast—or weaken thy memory or fancy, brother Toby, which these gymnicks[1] inordinately taken, are apt to do—else, dear Toby, I would procure thee the most beautiful women in my empire, and I would oblige thee, *nolens, volens*,[2] to beget for me one subject every *month*——

As my father pronounced the last word of the sentence—my mother took a pinch of snuff.

Now I would not, quoth my uncle Toby, get a child, *nolens, volens*, that is, whether I would or no, to please the greatest prince upon earth——

——And 'twould be cruel in me, brother Toby, to compell thee; said my father—but 'tis a case put to shew thee, that it is not thy begetting a child—in case thou should'st be able—but the system of Love and marriage thou goest upon, which I would set thee right in——

There is at least, said Yorick, a great deal of reason and plain sense in captain Shandy's opinion of love; and 'tis amongst the ill spent hours of my life which I have to answer for, that I have read so many flourishing poets and rhetoricians in my time, from whom I never could extract so much——

I wish, Yorick, said my father, you had read Plato;[3] for there you would have learnt that there are two LOVES—I know there were two RELIGIONS, replied Yorick, amongst the ancients——one—for the vulgar, and another for the learned; but I think ONE LOVE might have served both of them very well—

It could not; replied my father—and for the same reasons: for of these Loves, according to Ficinus's comment upon Velasius,[4] the one is *rational*——

——the other is *natural*——

the first ancient——without mother——where Venus had nothing to do: the second, begotten of Jupiter and Dione—

——Pray brother, quoth my uncle Toby, what has a man
who believes in God to do with this? My father could not stop
to answer, for fear of breaking the thread of his discourse——

This latter, continued he, partakes wholly of the nature of
Venus.

The first, which is the golden chain let down from heaven,
excites to love heroic, which comprehends in it, and excites to
the desire of philosophy and truth——the second, excites to
desire, simply——

——I think the procreation of children as beneficial to the
world, said Yorick, as the finding out the longitude[5]——

——To be sure, said my mother, *love* keeps peace in the
world——

——In the *house*—my dear, I own——It replenishes the
earth; said my mother——

But it keeps heaven empty—my dear; replied my father.

——'Tis Virginity, cried Slop, triumphantly, which fills paradise.

Well push'd nun! quoth my father.

CHAPTER XXXIV

My father had such a skirmishing, cutting kind of a slashing way
with him in his disputations, thrusting and ripping, and giving
every one a stroke to remember him by in his turn—that if there
were twenty people in company—in less than half an hour he
was sure to have every one of 'em against him.

What did not a little contribute to leave him thus without an
ally, was, that if there was any one post more untenable than the
rest, he would be sure to throw himself into it; and to do him
justice, when he was once there, he would defend it so gallantly,
that 'twould have been a concern, either to a brave man, or a
good-natured one, to have seen him driven out.

Yorick, for this reason, though he would often attack him—
yet could never bear to do it with all his force.

Doctor Slop's Virginity, in the close of the last chapter, had
got him for once on the right side of the rampart; and he was
beginning to blow up all the convents in Christendom about
Slop's ears, when corporal Trim came into the parlour to inform

my uncle Toby, that his thin scarlet breeches, in which the
attack was to be made upon Mrs. Wadman, would not do; for,
that the taylor, in ripping them up, in order to turn them, had
found they had been turn'd before——Then turn them again,
brother, said my father rapidly, for there will be many a turning
of 'em yet before all's done in the affair——They are as rotten as
dirt, said the corporal——Then by all means, said my father,
bespeak a new pair, brother——for though I know, continued
my father, turning himself to the company, that widow Wadman has been deeply in love with my brother Toby for many
years, and has used every art and circumvention of woman to
outwit him into the same passion, yet now that she has caught
him——her fever will be pass'd it's height——

——She has gain'd her point.

In this case, continued my father, which Plato, I am persuaded, never thought of——Love, you see, is not so much
a SENTIMENT as a SITUATION, into which a man enters,
as my brother Toby would do, into a *corps*——no matter
whether he loves the service or no——being once in it—he
acts as if he did; and takes every step to shew himself a man
of prowesse.

The hypothesis, like the rest of my father's, was plausible
enough, and my uncle Toby had but a single word to object to
it—in which Trim stood ready to second him——but my father
had not drawn his conclusion——

For this reason, continued my father (stating the case over
again) notwithstanding all the world knows, that Mrs. Wadman
affects my brother Toby—and my brother Toby contrariwise
affects Mrs. Wadman, and no obstacle in nature to forbid the
music striking up this very night, yet will I answer for it, that
this self-same tune will not be play'd this twelvemonth.

We have taken our measures badly, quoth my uncle Toby,
looking up interrogatively in Trim's face.

I would lay my Montero cap, said Trim——Now Trim's
Montero-cap, as I once told you, was his constant wager; and
having furbish'd it up that very night, in order to go upon the
attack—it made the odds look more considerable——I would
lay, an' please your honour, my Montero-cap to a shilling—was
it proper, continued Trim (making a bow) to offer a wager
before your honours——

——There is nothing improper in it, said my father—'tis a
mode of expression; for in saying thou would'st lay thy

Montero-cap to a shilling—all thou meanest is this—that thou believest——

——Now, What do'st thou believe?

That Widow Wadman, an' please your worship, cannot hold it out ten days——

And whence, cried Slop, jeeringly, hast thou all this knowledge of woman, friend?

By falling in love with a popish clergy-woman; said Trim.

'Twas a Beguine, said my uncle Toby.

Doctor Slop was too much in wrath to listen to the distinction; and my father taking that very crisis to fall in helter-skelter upon the whole order of Nuns and Beguines, a set of silly, fusty baggages——Slop could not stand it——and my uncle Toby having some measures to take about his breeches—and Yorick about his fourth general division[1]—in order for their several attacks next day—the company broke up: and my father being left alone, and having half an hour upon his hands betwixt that and bed-time; he called for pen, ink, and paper, and wrote my uncle Toby the following letter of instructions.

My dear brother Toby,

WHAT I am going to say to thee, is upon the nature of women, and of love-making to them; and perhaps it is as well for thee—tho' not so well for me—that thou hast occasion for a letter of instructions upon that head, and that I am able to write it to thee.

Had it been the good pleasure of him who disposes of our lots—and thou no sufferer by the knowledge, I had been well content that thou should'st have dipp'd the pen this moment into the ink, instead of myself; but that not being the case —————Mrs. Shandy being now close besides me, preparing for bed——I have thrown together without order, and just as they have come into my mind, such hints and documents as I deem may be of use to thee; intending, in this, to give thee a token of my love; not doubting, my dear Toby, of the manner in which it will be accepted.

In the first place, with regard to all which concerns religion in the affair——though I perceive from a glow in my cheek, that I blush as I begin to speak to thee upon the subject, as well knowing, notwithstanding thy unaffected secrecy, how few of its offices thou neglectest—yet I would remind thee of one (during the continuance of thy courtship) in a particular manner, which I would not have omitted; and that is, never to go forth upon the enterprize, whether it be in the morning or the afternoon, without first recommending thyself to the protection of Almighty God, that he may defend thee from the evil one.

Shave the whole top of thy crown clean, once at least every four or five days, but oftner if convenient; lest in taking off thy wig before her, thro' absence of mind, she should be able to discover how much has been cut away by Time——how much by Trim.

——'Twere better to keep ideas of baldness out of her fancy.

Always carry it in thy mind, and act upon it, as a sure maxim, Toby——

"*That women are timid:*" And 'tis well they are——else there would be no dealing with them.

Let not thy breeches be too tight, or hang too loose about thy thighs, like the trunk-hose of our ancestors.

——A just medium prevents all conclusions.

Whatever thou hast to say, be it more or less, forget not to utter it in a low soft tone of voice. Silence, and whatever approaches it, weaves dreams of midnight secrecy into the brain: For this cause, if thou canst help it, never throw down the tongs and poker.

Avoid all kinds of pleasantry and facetiousness in thy discourse with her, and do whatever lies in thy power at the same time, to keep from her all books and writings which tend thereto: there are some devotional tracts, which if thou canst entice her to read over—it will be well: but suffer her not to look into Rabelais, or Scarron,[2] or Don Quixote——

——They are all books which excite laughter; and thou knowest, dear Toby, that there is no passion so serious, as lust.

Stick a pin in the bosom of thy shirt, before thou enterest her parlour.

And if thou art permitted to sit upon the same sopha with her, and she gives thee occasion to lay thy hand upon hers—beware of taking it——thou can'st not lay thy hand on hers, but she will feel the temper of thine. Leave that and as many other things as thou canst, quite undetermined; by so doing, thou will have her curiosity on thy side; and if she is not conquer'd by that, and thy Asse continues still kicking, which there is great reason to suppose——Thou must begin, with first losing a few ounces of blood below the ears, according to the practice of the ancient

Scythians, who cured the most intemperate fits of the appetite by that means.

Avicenna, after this, is for having the part anointed with the syrrup of hellebore, using proper evacuations and purges——and I believe rightly. But thou must eat little or no goat's flesh, nor red deer——nor even foal's flesh by any means; and carefully abstain——that is, as much as thou canst, from peacocks, cranes, coots, didappers, and water hens——[3]

As for thy drink—I need not tell thee, it must be the infusion of VERVAIN,[4] and the herb HANEA, of which Ælian[5] relates such effects—but if thy stomach palls with it—discontinue it from time to time, taking cucumbers, melons, purslane, waterlillies, woodbine, and lettice, in the stead of them.

There is nothing further for thee, which occurs to me at present——

—Unless the breaking out of a fresh war——So wishing every thing, dear Toby, for the best,

I rest thy affectionate brother,

WALTER SHANDY.

CHAPTER XXXV

WHILST my father was writing his letter of instructions, my uncle Toby and the corporal were busy in preparing every thing for the attack. As the turning of the thin scarlet breeches was laid aside (at least for the present) there was nothing which should put it off beyond the next morning; so accordingly it was resolv'd upon, for eleven o'clock.

Come, my dear, said my father to my mother—'twill be but like a brother and sister, if you and I take a walk down to my brother Toby's——to countenance him in this attack of his.

My uncle Toby and the corporal had been accoutred both some time, when my father and mother enter'd, and the clock striking eleven, were that moment in motion to sally forth—but the account of this is worth more, than to be wove into the fag end of the eighth volume of such a work as this.——My father had no time but to put the letter of instructions into my uncle Toby's coat-pocket——and join with my mother in wishing his attack prosperous.

I could like, said my mother, to look through the key-hole

out of *curiosity*——Call it by it's right name, my dear, quoth my father—

And look through the key-hole as long as you will.

END of the EIGHTH VOLUME.

THE

L I F E

AND

O P I N I O N S

OF

TRISTRAM SHANDY,

GENTLEMAN.

Si quid urbaniusculè lusum a nobis, per Musas et Cha-
ritas et omnium poetarum Numina, Oro te, ne me
malè capias.[1]

VOL. IX.

LONDON:

Printed for T. BECKET and P. A. DEHONDT,
in the Strand.   MDCCLXVII.

THE

LIFE

AND

OPINIONS

OF

TRISTRAM SHANDY,

GENTLEMAN.

VOL. IX.

LONDON.

Printed for T. Becket and P. A. Dehondt,
in the Strand. MDCCLXVII.

VOLUME IX   111

my imagination. I shall inevitably give 't this turn to my passions and low-bred Contemplations, in the mean-time.

A

DEDICATION

TO A

GREAT MAN.[1]

HAVING, *a priori*, intended to dedicate *The Amours of my uncle Toby* to Mr. ***——I see more reasons, *a posteriori*, for doing it to Lord *******.

I should lament from my soul, if this exposed me to the jealousy of their Reverences; because, *a posteriori*, in Court-latin, signifies, the kissing hands for preferment—or any thing else—in order to get it.

My opinion of Lord ******* is neither better nor worse, than it was of Mr. ***. Honours, like impressions upon coin, may give an ideal and local value to a bit of base metal; but Gold and Silver will pass all the world over without any other recommendation than their own weight.

The same good will that made me think of offering up half an hour's amusement to Mr. *** when out of place—operates more forcibly at present, as half an hour's amusement will be more serviceable and refreshing after labour and sorrow, than after a philosophical repast.

Nothing is so perfectly *Amusement* as a total change of ideas; no ideas are so totally different as those of Ministers, and innocent Lovers: for which reason, when I come to talk of Statesmen and Patriots, and set such marks upon them as will prevent confusion and mistakes concerning them for the future—I propose to dedicate that Volume to some gentle Shepherd,

> Whose Thoughts proud Science never taught to stray,
> Far as the Statesman's walk or Patriot-way;
> Yet *simple Nature* to his hopes had given
> Out of a cloud-capp'd head a humbler heaven;
> Some *untam'd* World in depth of woods embraced—
> Some happier Island in the watry-waste—
> And where admitted to that equal sky,
> His *faithful Dogs* should bear him company.[2]

In a word, by thus introducing an entire new set of objects to

his Imagination, I shall unavoidably give a *Diversion* to his passionate and love-sick Contemplations. In the mean time,
I am
The AUTHOR.

CHAPTER I

I CALL all the powers of time and chance, which severally check us in our careers in this world, to bear me witness, that I could never yet get fairly to my uncle Toby's amours, till this very moment, that my mother's *curiosity*, as she stated the affair, — — or a different impulse in her, as my father would have it ——wished her to take a peep at them through the key-hole.

"Call it, my dear, by its right name, quoth my father, and look through the key-hole as long as you will."

Nothing but the fermentation of that little subacid humour, which I have often spoken of, in my father's habit, could have vented such an insinuation——he was however frank and generous in his nature, and at all times open to conviction; so that he had scarce got to the last word of this ungracious retort, when his conscience smote him.

My mother was then conjugally swinging with her left arm twisted under his right, in such wise, that the inside of her hand rested upon the back of his—she raised her fingers, and let them fall—it could scarce be call'd a tap; or if it was a tap——'twould have puzzled a casuist to say, whether 'twas a tap of remonstrance, or a tap of confession: my father, who was all sensibilities from head to foot, class'd it right—Conscience redoubled her blow—he turn'd his face suddenly the other way, and my mother supposing his body was about to turn with it in order to move homewards, by a cross movement of her right leg, keeping her left as its centre, brought herself so far in front, that as he turned his head, he met her eye——Confusion again! he saw a thousand reasons to wipe out the reproach, and as many to reproach himself——a thin, blue, chill, pellucid chrystal with all its humours so at rest, the least mote or speck of desire might have been seen at the bottom of it, had it existed——it did not——and how I happen to be so lewd myself, particularly a little before the vernal and autumnal equinoxes——Heaven above knows——My mother——madam——was so at no time, either by nature, by institution, or example.

A temperate current of blood ran orderly through her veins in all months of the year, and in all critical moments both of the day and night alike; nor did she superinduce the least heat into her humours from the manual effervescencies of devotional tracts, which having little or no meaning in them, nature is oft times obliged to find one——And as for my father's example! 'twas so far from being either aiding or abetting thereunto, that 'twas the whole business of his life to keep all fancies of that kind out of her head——Nature had done her part, to have spared him this trouble; and what was not a little inconsistent, my father knew it——And here am I sitting, this 12th day of August, 1766, in a purple jerkin and yellow pair of slippers, without either wig or cap on, a most tragicomical completion of his prediction, "That I should neither think, nor act like any other man's child, upon that very account."

The mistake of my father, was in attacking my mother's motive, instead of the act itself: for certainly key-holes were made for other purposes; and considering the act, as an act which interfered with a true proposition, and denied a key-hole to be what it was——it became a violation of nature; and was so far, you see, criminal.

It is for this reason, an' please your Reverences, That key-holes are the occasions of more sin and wickedness, than all other holes in this world put together.

——which leads me to my uncle Toby's amours.

CHAPTER II

THOUGH the Corporal had been as good as his word in putting my uncle Toby's great ramallie-wig into pipes, yet the time was too short to produce any great effects from it: it had lain many years squeezed up in the corner of his old campaign trunk; and as bad forms are not so easy to be got the better of, and the use of candle-ends not so well understood, it was not so pliable a business as one would have wished. The Corporal with cheary eye and both arms extended, had fallen back perpendicular from it a score times, to inspire it, if possible, with a better air——had SPLEEN given a look at it, 'twould have cost her ladyship a smile——it curl'd every where but where the Corporal would have it; and where a buckle or two, in his opinion, would have done it honour, he could as soon have raised the dead.

Such it was——or rather such would it have seem'd upon any other brow; but the sweet look of goodness which sat upon my uncle Toby's, assimulated every thing around it so sovereignly to itself, and Nature had moreover wrote GENTLEMAN with so fair a hand in every line of his countenance, that even his tarnish'd gold-laced hat and huge cockade of flimsy taffeta became him; and though not worth a button in themselves, yet the moment my uncle Toby put them on, they became serious objects, and altogether seem'd to have been picked up by the hand of Science to set him off to advantage.

Nothing in this world could have co-operated more powerfully towards this, than my uncle Toby's blue and gold——*had not Quantity in some measure been necessary to Grace:* in a period of fifteen or sixteen years since they had been made, by a total inactivity in my uncle Toby's life, for he seldom went further than the bowling-green—his blue and gold had become so miserably too strait for him, that it was with the utmost difficulty the Corporal was able to get him into them: the taking them up at the sleeves, was of no advantage.——They were laced however down the back, and at the seams of the sides, &c. in the mode of King William's reign; and to shorten all description, they shone so bright against the sun that morning, and had so metallick, and doughty an air with them, that had my uncle Toby thought of attacking in armour, nothing could have so well imposed upon his imagination.

As for the thin scarlet breeches, they had been unripp'd by the taylor between the legs, and left at *sixes and sevens*——

——Yes, Madam,——but let us govern our fancies. It is enough they were held impracticable the night before, and as there was no alternative in my uncle Toby's wardrobe, he sallied forth in the red plush.

The Corporal had array'd himself in poor Le Fevre's regimental coat; and with his hair tuck'd up under his Montero cap, which he had furbish'd up for the occasion, march'd three paces distant from his master: a whiff of military pride had puff'd out his shirt at the wrist; and upon that in a black leather thong clipp'd into a tassel beyond the knot, hung the Corporal's stick——My uncle Toby carried his cane like a pike.

——It looks well at least; quoth my father to himself.

CHAPTER III

My uncle Toby turn'd his head more than once behind him, to see how he was supported by the Corporal; and the Corporal as oft as he did it, gave a slight flourish with his stick—but not vapouringly; and with the sweetest accent of most respectful encouragement, bid his honour "never fear."

Now my uncle Toby did fear; and grievously too: he knew not (as my father had reproach'd him) so much as the right end of a Woman from the wrong, and therefore was never altogether at his ease near any one of them——unless in sorrow or distress; then infinite was his pity; nor would the most courteous knight of romance have gone further, at least upon one leg, to have wiped away a tear from a woman's eye; and yet excepting once that he was beguiled into it by Mrs. Wadman, he had never looked stedfastly into one; and would often tell my father in the simplicity of his heart, that it was almost (if not alout[1]) as bad as talking bawdy.——

——And suppose it is? my father would say.

CHAPTER IV

SHE cannot, quoth my uncle Toby, halting, when they had march'd up to within twenty paces of Mrs. Wadman's door—she cannot, Corporal, take it amiss.——

——She will take it, an' please your honour, said the Corporal, just as the Jew's widow at Lisbon took it of my brother Tom.——

——And how was that? quoth my uncle Toby, facing quite about to the Corporal.

Your honour, replied the Corporal, knows of Tom's misfortunes; but this affair has nothing to do with them any further than this, That if Tom had not married the widow——or had it pleased God after their marriage, that they had but put pork into their sausages, the honest soul had never been taken out of his warm bed, and dragg'd to the inquisition——'Tis a cursed place—added the Corporal, shaking his head,—when once a poor creature is in, he is in, an' please your honour, for ever.

'Tis very true; said my uncle Toby looking gravely at Mrs. Wadman's house, as he spoke.

Nothing, continued the Corporal, can be so sad as confinement for life—or so sweet, an' please your honour, as liberty.

Nothing, Trim——said my uncle Toby, musing——

Whilst a man is free—cried the Corporal, giving a flourish with his stick thus——

A thousand of my father's most subtle syllogisms could not have said more for celibacy.

My uncle Toby look'd earnestly towards his cottage and his bowling green.

The Corporal had unwarily conjured up the Spirit of calculation with his wand; and he had nothing to do, but to conjure him down again with his story, and in this form of Exorcism, most un-ecclesiastically did the Corporal do it.

CHAPTER V

As Tom's place, an' please your honour, was easy—and the weather warm—it put him upon thinking seriously of settling himself in the world; and as it fell out about that time, that a Jew who kept a sausage shop in the same street, had the ill luck to die of a strangury, and leave his widow in possession of a rousing trade——Tom thought (as every body in Lisbon was doing the best he could devise for himself) there could be no harm in offering her his service to carry it on: so without any introduction to the widow, except that of buying a pound of sausages at her shop—Tom set out—counting the matter thus within himself, as he walk'd along; that let the worst come of it that could, he should at least get a pound of sausages for their worth—but, if things went well, he should be set up; inasmuch as he should get not only a pound of sausages—but a wife—and a sausage-shop, an' please your honour, into the bargain.

Every servant in the family, from high to low, wish'd Tom success; and I can fancy, an' please your honour, I see him this moment with his white dimity waistcoat and breeches, and hat a little o' one side, passing jollily along the street, swinging his stick, with a smile and a chearful word for every body he met:——But alas! Tom! thou smilest no more, cried the Corporal, looking on one side of him upon the ground, as if he apostrophized him in his dungeon.

Poor fellow! said my uncle Toby, feelingly.

He was an honest, light-hearted lad, an' please your honour, as ever blood warm'd——

——Then he resembled thee, Trim, said my uncle Toby, rapidly.

The Corporal blush'd down to his fingers ends—a tear of sentimental bashfulness—another of gratitude to my uncle Toby—and a tear of sorrow for his brother's misfortunes, started into his eye and ran sweetly down his cheek together; my uncle Toby's kindled as one lamp does at another; and taking hold of the breast of Trim's coat (which had been that of Le Fevre's) as if to ease his lame leg, but in reality to gratify a finer feeling——he stood silent for a minute and a half; at the end of which he took his hand away, and the Corporal making a bow, went on with his story of his brother and the Jew's widow.

CHAPTER VI

WHEN Tom, an' please your honour, got to the shop, there was nobody in it, but a poor negro girl, with a bunch of white feathers slightly tied to the end of a long cane, flapping away flies—not killing them.——'Tis a pretty picture! said my uncle Toby—she had suffered persecution, Trim, and had learnt mercy——

——She was good, an' please your honour, from nature as well as from hardships; and there are circumstances in the story of that poor friendless slut that would melt a heart of stone, said Trim; and some dismal winter's evening, when your honour is in the humour, they shall be told you with the rest of Tom's story, for it makes a part of it——

Then do not forget, Trim, said my uncle Toby.

A Negro has a soul? an' please your honour, said the Corporal (doubtingly).

I am not much versed, Corporal, quoth my uncle Toby, in things of that kind; but I suppose, God would not leave him without one, any more than thee or me——

——It would be putting one sadly over the head of another, quoth the Corporal.

It would so; said my uncle Toby. Why then, an' please your honour, is a black wench to be used worse than a white one?

I can give no reason, said my uncle Toby——

——Only, cried the Corporal, shaking his head, because she has no one to stand up for her——

——'Tis that very thing, Trim, quoth my uncle Toby,——which recommends her to protection——and her brethren with her; 'tis the fortune of war which has put the whip into our hands *now*——where it may be hereafter, heaven knows! ——but be it where it will, the brave, Trim! will not use it unkindly.

——God forbid, said the Corporal.

Amen, responded my uncle Toby, laying his hand upon his heart.

The Corporal returned to his story, and went on——but with an embarrassment in doing it, which here and there a reader in this world will not be able to comprehend; for by the many sudden transitions all along, from one kind and cordial passion to another, in getting thus far on his way, he had lost the

sportable key of his voice which gave sense and spirit to his tale:
he attempted twice to resume it, but could not please himself; so
giving a stout hem! to rally back the retreating spirits, and aiding
Nature at the same time with his left arm a-kimbo on one side,
and with his right a little extended, supporting her on the
other—the Corporal got as near the note as he could; and in that
attitude, continued his story.

CHAPTER VII

As Tom, an' please your honour, had no business at that time with the Moorish girl, he passed on into the room beyond to talk to the Jew's widow about love——and his pound of sausages; and being, as I have told your honour, an open, cheary hearted lad, with his character wrote in his looks and carriage, he took a chair, and without much apology, but with great civility at the same time, placed it close to her at the table, and sat down.

There is nothing so awkward, as courting a woman, an' please your honour, whilst she is making sausages——So Tom began a discourse upon them; first gravely,——"as how they were made——with what meats, herbs and spices"——Then a little gayly—as, "With what skins——and if they never burst—— Whether the largest were not the best"——and so on—taking care only as he went along, to season what he had to say upon sausages, rather under, than over;——that he might have room to act in——

It was owing to the neglect of that very precaution, said my uncle Toby, laying his hand upon Trim's shoulder, That Count de la Motte lost the battle of Wynendale: he pressed too speedily into the wood; which if he had not done, Lisle had not fallen into our hands, nor Ghent and Bruges, which both followed her example; it was so late in the year, continued my uncle Toby, and so terrible a season came on, that if things had not fallen out as they did, our troops must have perished in the open field.——

——Why therefore, may not battles, an' please your honour, as well as marriages, be made in heaven?—My uncle Toby mused.——

Religion inclined him to say one thing, and his high idea of military skill tempted him to say another; so not being able to frame a reply exactly to his mind——my uncle Toby said nothing at all; and the Corporal finished his story.

As Tom perceived, an' please your honour, that he gained ground, and that all he had said upon the subject of sausages was kindly taken, he went on to help her a little in making them. ——First, by taking hold of the ring of the sausage whilst she stroked the forced meat down with her hand——then by cutting the strings into proper lengths, and holding them in his hand, whilst she took them out one by one——then, by putting them across her mouth, that she might take them out as she wanted them——and so on from little to more, till at last he adventured to tie the sausage himself, whilst she held the snout.——

——Now a widow, an' please your honour, always chuses a second husband as unlike the first as she can: so the affair was more than half settled in her mind before Tom mentioned it.

She made a feint however of defending herself, by snatching up a sausage:——Tom instantly laid hold of another——

But seeing Tom's had more gristle in it——

She signed the capitulation——and Tom sealed it; and there was an end of the matter.

CHAPTER VIII

ALL womankind, continued Trim, (commenting upon his story) from the highest to the lowest, an' please your honour, love jokes; the difficulty is to know how they chuse to have them cut; and there is no knowing that, but by trying as we do with our artillery in the field, by raising or letting down their breeches, till we hit the mark.——

——I like the comparison, said my uncle Toby, better than the thing itself——

——Because your honour, quoth the Corporal, loves glory, more than pleasure.

I hope, Trim, answered my uncle Toby, I love mankind more than either; and as the knowledge of arms tends so apparently to the good and quiet of the world——and particularly that branch of it which we have practised together in our bowling-green, has no object but to shorten the strides of AMBITION, and intrench the lives and fortunes of the *few*, from the plunderings of the *many*——whenever that drum beats in our ears, I trust, Corporal, we shall neither of us want so much humanity and fellow-feeling as to face about and march.

In pronouncing this, my uncle Toby faced about, and march'd firmly as at the head of his company——and the faithful Corporal, shouldering his stick, and striking his hand upon his coat-skirt as he took his first step——march'd close behind him down the avenue.

——Now what can their two noddles be about? cried my father to my mother——by all that's strange, they are besieging Mrs. Wadman in form, and are marching round her house to mark out the lines of circumvallation.

I dare say, quoth my mother——But stop, dear Sir——for what my mother dared to say upon the occasion——and what my father did say upon it—with her replies and his rejoinders, shall be read, perused, paraphrased, commented and discanted upon—or to say it all in a word, shall be thumb'd over by Posterity in a chapter apart——I say, by Posterity—and care not, if I repeat the word again—for what has this book done more than the Legation of Moses,[1] or the Tale of a Tub, that it may not swim down the gutter of Time along with them?

I will not argue the matter: Time wastes too fast: every letter I trace tells me with what rapidity Life follows my pen; the days and hours of it, more precious, my dear Jenny! than the rubies about thy neck, are flying over our heads like light clouds of a windy day, never to return more——every thing presses on—— whilst thou art twisting that lock,——see! it grows grey; and every time I kiss thy hand to bid adieu, and every absence which follows it, are preludes to that eternal separation which we are shortly to make.——

——Heaven have mercy upon us both!

CHAPTER IX

Now, for what the world thinks of that ejaculation——I would not give a groat.

CHAPTER X

My mother had gone with her left arm twisted in my father's right, till they had got to the fatal angle of the old garden wall, where Doctor Slop was overthrown by Obadiah on the coach-horse: as this was directly opposite to the front of Mrs. Wadman's house, when my father came to it, he gave a look across; and seeing my uncle Toby and the Corporal within ten paces of the door, he turn'd about— —"Let us just stop a moment, quoth my father, and see with what ceremonies my brother Toby and his man Trim make their first entry——it will not detain us, added my father, a single minute:"——No matter, if it be ten minutes, quoth my mother.

——It will not detain us half a one; said my father.

The Corporal was just then setting in with the story of his brother Tom and the Jew's widow: the story went on—and on——it had episodes in it——it came back, and went on—— and on again; there was no end of it——the reader found it very long——

——G— help my father! he pish'd fifty times at every new attitude, and gave the corporal's stick, with all its flourishings and danglings, to as many devils as chose to accept of them.

When issues of events like these my father is waiting for, are hanging in the scales of fate, the mind has the advantage of changing the principle of expectation three times, without which it would not have power to see it out.

Curiosity governs the *first moment*; and the second moment is all œconomy to justify the expence of the first——and for the third, fourth, fifth, and sixth moments, and so on to the day of judgment—'tis a point of Honour.

I need not be told, that the ethic writers have assigned this all to Patience; but that Virtue methinks, has extent of dominion sufficient of her own, and enough to do in it, without invading the few dismantled castles which Honour has left him upon the earth.

My father stood it out as well as he could with these three auxiliaries to the end of Trim's story; and from thence to the end of my uncle Toby's panegyrick upon arms, in the chapter following it; when seeing, that instead of marching up to Mrs. Wadman's door, they both faced about and march'd down the avenue diametrically opposite to his expectation—he broke out at once with that little subacid soreness of humour which, in certain situations, distinguished his character from that of all other men.

CHAPTER XI

——"Now what can their two noddles be about?" cried my
father--&c.----

I dare say, said my mother, they are making fortifications——

——Not on Mrs. Wadman's premises! cried my father, stepping back——

I suppose not: quoth my mother.

I wish, said my father, raising his voice, the whole science of
fortification at the devil, with all its trumpery of saps, mines,
blinds, gabions, fausse-brays[1] and cuvetts——

——They are foolish things——said my mother.

Now she had a way, which by the bye, I would this moment
give away my purple jerkin, and my yellow slippers into the
bargain, if some of your reverences would imitate—and that
was never to refuse her assent and consent to any proposition
my father laid before her, merely because she did not understand it, or had no ideas to the principal word or term of art,
upon which the tenet or proposition rolled. She contented
herself with doing all that her godfathers and godmothers promised for her—but no more; and so would go on using a hard
word twenty years together—and replying to it too, if it was a
verb, in all its moods and tenses, without giving herself any
trouble to enquire about it.

This was an eternal source of misery to my father, and broke
the neck, at the first setting out, of more good dialogues between them, than could have done the most petulant contradiction——the few which survived were the better for the
cuvetts——

—"They are foolish things;" said my mother.

——Particularly the *cuvetts*; replied my father.

'Twas enough—he tasted the sweet of triumph—and went
on.

—Not that they are, properly speaking, Mrs. Wadman's
premises, said my father, partly correcting himself—because
she is but tenant for life——

——That makes a great difference—said my mother——

—In a fool's head, replied my father——

Unless she should happen to have a child—said my
mother——

——But she must persuade my brother Toby first to get her one—

——To be sure, Mr. Shandy, quoth my mother.

——Though if it comes to persuasion—said my father—Lord have mercy upon them.

Amen: said my mother, *piano*.

Amen: cried my father, *fortissimè*.

Amen: said my mother again——but with such a sighing cadence of personal pity at the end of it, as discomfited every fibre about my father—he instantly took out his almanack; but before he could untie it, Yorick's congregation coming out of church, became a full answer to one half of his business with it—and my mother telling him it was a sacrament day[2]—left him as little in doubt, as to the other part—He put his almanack into his pocket.

The first Lord of the Treasury thinking of *ways and means*, could not have returned home, with a more embarrassed look.

CHAPTER XII

UPON looking back from the end of the last chapter and surveying the texture of what has been wrote, it is necessary, that upon this page and the five following, a good quantity of heterogeneous matter be inserted, to keep up that just balance betwixt wisdom and folly, without which a book would not hold together a single year: nor is it a poor creeping digression (which but for the name of, a man might continue as well going on in the king's highway) which will do the business——no; if it is to be a digression, it must be a good frisky one, and upon a frisky subject too, where neither the horse or his rider are to be caught, but by rebound.

The only difficulty, is raising powers suitable to the nature of the service: FANCY is capricious—WIT must not be searched for—and PLEASANTRY (good-natured slut as she is) will not come in at a call, was an empire to be laid at her feet.

——The best way for a man, is to say his prayers——

Only if it puts him in mind of his infirmities and defects as well ghostly as bodily—for that purpose, he will find himself rather worse after he has said them than before—for other purposes, better.

For my own part there is not a way either moral or mechanical under heaven that I could think of, which I have not taken with myself in this case: sometimes by addressing myself directly to the soul herself, and arguing the point over and over again with her upon the extent of her own faculties——

——I never could make them an inch the wider——

Then by changing my system, and trying what could be made of it upon the body, by temperance, soberness and chastity: These are good, quoth I, in themselves—they are good, absolutely;—they are good, relatively;—they are good for health—they are good for happiness in this world—they are good for happiness in the next——

In short, they were good for every thing but the thing wanted; and there they were good for nothing, but to leave the soul just as heaven made it: as for the theological virtues of faith and hope, they give it courage; but then that sniveling virtue of Meekness (as my father would always call it) takes it quite away again, so you are exactly where you started.

Now in all common and ordinary cases, there is nothing which I have found to answer so well as this——

——Certainly, if there is any dependence upon Logic, and that I am not blinded by self-love, there must be something of true genius about me, merely upon this symptom of it, that I do not know what envy is: for never do I hit upon any invention or device which tendeth to the furtherance of good writing, but I instantly make it public; willing that all mankind should write as well as myself.

——Which they certainly will, when they think as little.

CHAPTER XIII

Now in ordinary cases, that is, when I am only stupid, and the thoughts rise heavily and pass gummous[1] through my pen——

Or that I am got, I know not how, into a cold unmetaphorical vein of infamous writing, and cannot take a plumb-lift[2] out of it *for my soul*; so must be obliged to go on writing like a Dutch commentator to the end of the chapter, unless something be done——

——I never stand confering with pen and ink one moment; for if a pinch of snuff or a stride or two across the room will not do the business for me—I take a razor at once; and having tried the edge of it upon the palm of my hand, without further ceremony, except that of first lathering my beard, I shave it off; taking care only if I do leave a hair, that it be not a grey one: this done, I change my shirt—put on a better coat—send for my last wig—put my topaz ring[3] upon my finger; and in a word, dress myself from one end to the other of me, after my best fashion.

Now the devil in hell must be in it, if this does not do: for consider, Sir, as every man chuses to be present at the shaving of his own beard (though there is no rule without an exception) and unavoidably sits overagainst himself the whole time it is doing, in case he has a hand in it—the Situation, like all others, has notions of her own to put into the brain.——

——I maintain it, the conceits of a rough-bearded man, are seven years more terse and juvenile for one single operation; and if they did not run a risk of being quite shaved away, might be carried up by continual shavings, to the highest pitch of sublimity—How Homer could write with so long a beard, I don't know——and as it makes against my hypothesis, I as little care——But let us return to the Toilet.

Ludovicus Sorbonensis[4] makes this entirely an affair of the body (εξωτερικη πραξις)[5] as he calls it——but he is deceived: the soul and body are joint-sharers in every thing they get: A man cannot dress, but his ideas get cloath'd at the same time; and if he dresses like a gentleman, every one of them stands presented to his imagination, genteelized along with him—so that he has nothing to do, but take his pen, and write like himself.

For this cause, when your honours and reverences would know whether I writ clean and fit to be read, you will be able to judge full as well by looking into my Laundress's bill, as my book: there was one single month in which I can make it appear, that I dirtied one and thirty shirts with clean writing; and after all, was more abus'd, curs'd, criticis'd and confounded, and had more mystic heads shaken at me, for what I had wrote in that one month, than in all the other months of that year put together.

——But their honours and reverences had not seen my *bills*.

CHAPTER XIV

As I never had any intention of beginning the Digression, I am making all this preparation for, till I come to the 15th chapter——I have this chapter to put to whatever use I think proper——I have twenty this moment ready for it——I could write my chapter of Button-holes in it——

Or my chapter of *Pishes*, which should follow them——

Or my chapter of *Knots*, in case their reverences have done with them——they might lead me into mischief: the safest way is to follow the tract of the learned, and raise objections against what I have been writing, tho' I declare beforehand, I know no more than my heels how to answer them.

And first, it may be said, there is a pelting kind of *thersitical*[1] satire, as black as the very ink 'tis wrote with——(and by the bye, whoever says so, is indebted to the muster-master general of the Grecian army, for suffering the name of so ugly and foul-mouth'd a man as *Thersites* to continue upon his roll—— for it has furnished him with an epithet)——in these productions he will urge, all the personal washings and scrubbings upon earth do a sinking genius no sort of good——but just the contrary, inasmuch as the dirtier the fellow is, the better generally he succeeds in it.

To this, I have no other answer——at least ready——but that the Archbishop of Benevento wrote his *nasty* Romance of the Galatea,[2] as all the world knows, in a purple coat, waistcoat, and purple pair of breeches; and that the penance set him of writing a commentary upon the book of the Revelations, as severe as it was look'd upon by one part of the world, was far from being deem'd so, by the other, upon the single account of that *Investment*.

Another objection, to all this remedy, is its want of universality; forasmuch as the shaving part of it, upon which so much stress is laid, by an unalterable law of nature excludes one half of the species entirely from its use: all I can say is, that female writers, whether of England, or of France, must e'en go without it——

As for the Spanish ladies——I am in no sort of distress——

CHAPTER XV

THE fifteenth chapter is come at last; and brings nothing with it but a sad signature of "How our pleasures slip from under us in this world;"

For in talking of my digression——I declare before heaven I have made it! What a strange creature is mortal man! said she.

'Tis very true, said I——but 'twere better to get all these things out of our heads, and return to my uncle Toby.

CHAPTER XVI

WHEN my uncle Toby and the Corporal had marched down to the bottom of the avenue, they recollected their business lay the other way; so they faced about and marched up streight to Mrs. Wadman's door.

I warrant your honour; said the Corporal, touching his Montero-cap with his hand, as he passed him in order to give a knock at the door——My uncle Toby, contrary to his invariable way of treating his faithful servant, said nothing good or bad: the truth was, he had not altogether marshal'd his ideas; he wish'd for another conference, and as the Corporal was mounting up the three steps before the door—he hem'd twice—a portion of my uncle Toby's most modest spirits fled, at each expulsion, towards the Corporal; he stood with the rapper of the door suspended for a full minute in his hand, he scarce knew why. Bridget stood perdue within, with her finger and her thumb upon the latch, benumb'd with expectation; and Mrs. Wadman, with an eye ready to be deflowered again, sat breathless behind the window-curtain of her bed-chamber, watching their approach.

Trim! said my uncle Toby——but as he articulated the word, the minute expired, and Trim let fall the rapper.

My uncle Toby perceiving that all hopes of a conference were knock'd on the head by it——whistled Lillabullero.

CHAPTER XVII

As Mrs. Bridget's finger and thumb were upon the latch, the Corporal did not knock as oft as perchance your honour's taylor——I might have taken my example something nearer home; for I owe mine, some five and twenty pounds at least, and wonder at the man's patience——

——But this is nothing at all to the world: only 'tis a cursed thing to be in debt; and there seems to be fatality in the exchequers of some poor princes, particularly those of our house, which no Economy can bind down in irons: for my own part, I'm persuaded there is not any one prince, prelate, pope, or potentate, great or small upon earth, more desirous in his heart of keeping streight with the world than I am——or who takes more likely means for it. I never give above half a guinea——or walk with boots——or cheapen tooth-picks——or lay out a shilling upon a band-box the year round; and for the six months I'm in the country, I'm upon so small a scale, that with all the good temper in the world, I out-do Rousseau,[1] a bar length ——for I keep neither man or boy, or horse, or cow, or dog, or cat, or any thing that can eat or drink, except a thin poor piece of a Vestal[2] (to keep my fire in) and who has generally as bad an appetite as myself——but if you think this makes a philosopher of me——I would not, my good people! give a rush for your judgments.

True philosophy——but there is no treating the subject whilst my uncle is whistling Lillabullero.

——Let us go into the house.

CHAPTER XVIII

CHAPTER XIX

CHAPTER XX

_____* * * * * * * * * * * * **
* * * * * * * * * * * * * * * *
* * * * * * * *.
    * * * * * * * * * * * * *
* * * * * * * * * * * * * *
* * * * * * * * * * * * * *
* * *_____

——You shall see the very place, Madam; said my uncle
Toby.

Mrs. Wadman blush'd——look'd towards the door——
turn'd pale——blush'd slightly again——recovered her natural
colour——blush'd worse than ever; which for the sake of the
unlearned reader, I translate thus——

"_L—d! I cannot look at it——_
What would the world say if I look'd at it?
I should drop down, if I look'd at it—
I wish I could look at it——
There can be no sin in looking at it.
——_I will look at it._"

Whilst all this was running through Mrs. Wadman's imagination, my uncle Toby had risen from the sopha, and got to the
other side of the parlour-door, to give Trim an order about it in
the passage——

* * * * * * * * * * * * *
* * *——I believe it is in the garret, said my uncle Toby
——I saw it there, an' please your honour, this morning,
answered Trim——Then prithee, step directly for it, Trim,
said my uncle Toby, and bring it into the parlour.

The Corporal did not approve of the orders, but most chearfully obey'd them. The first was not an act of his will—the
second was; so he put on his Montero cap, and went as fast as his
lame knee would let him. My uncle Toby returned into the
parlour, and sat himself down again upon the sopha.

——You shall lay your finger upon the place—said my uncle
Toby.——I will not touch it, however, quoth Mrs. Wadman to
herself.

This requires a second translation:—it shews what little

knowledge is got by mere words—we must go up to the first springs.

Now in order to clear up the mist which hangs upon these three pages, I must endeavour to be as clear as possible myself.

Rub your hands thrice across your foreheads—blow your noses—cleanse your emunctories—sneeze, my good people!
——God bless you——

Now give me all the help you can.

CHAPTER XXI

As there are fifty different ends (counting all ends in——as well civil as religious) for which a woman takes a husband, she first sets about and carefully weighs, then separates and distinguishes in her mind, which of all that number of ends, is hers: then by discourse, enquiry, argumentation and inference, she investigates and finds out whether she has got hold of the right one——and if she has——then, by pulling it gently this way and that way, she further forms a judgment, whether it will not break in the drawing.

The imagery under which *Slawkenbergius* impresses this upon his reader's fancy, in the beginning of his third Decad, is so ludicrous, that the honour I bear the sex, will not suffer me to quote it——otherwise 'tis not destitute of humour.

"She first, saith Slawkenbergius, stops the asse, and holding his halter in her left hand (lest he should get away) she thrusts her right hand into the very bottom of his pannier to search for it—For what?—you'll not know the sooner, quoth Slawkenbergius, for interrupting me——

"I have nothing, good Lady, but empty bottles;" says the asse.

"I'm loaded with tripes," says the second.

——And thou art little better, quoth she to the third; for nothing is there in thy panniers but trunk-hose and pantofles— and so to the fourth and fifth, going on one by one through the whole string, till coming to the asse which carries it, she turns the pannier upside down, looks at it—considers it—samples it—measures it—stretches it—wets it—dries it—then takes her teeth both to the warp and weft of it——

——Of what? for the love of Christ!

I am determined, answered *Slawkenbergius*, that all the powers upon earth shall never wring that secret from my breast.

CHAPTER XXII

WE live in a world beset on all sides with mysteries and riddles—and so 'tis no matter——else it seems strange, that Nature, who makes every thing so well to answer its destination, and seldom or never errs, unless for pastime, in giving such forms and aptitudes to whatever passes through her hands, that whether she designs for the plough, the caravan, the cart—or whatever other creature she models, be it but an asse's foal, you are sure to have the thing you wanted; and yet at the same time should so eternally bungle it as she does, in making so simple a thing as a married man.

Whether it is in the choice of the clay——or that it is frequently spoiled in the baking; by an excess of which a husband may turn out too crusty (you know) on one hand——or not enough so, through defect of heat, on the other——or whether this great Artificer is not so attentive to the little Platonic exigences *of that part* of the species, for whose use she is fabricating *this*——or that her Ladyship sometimes scarce knows what sort of a husband will do——I know not: we will discourse about it after supper.

It is enough, that neither the observation itself, or the reasoning upon it, are at all to the purpose——but rather against it; since with regard to my uncle Toby's fitness for the marriage state, nothing was ever better: she had formed him of the best and kindliest clay——had temper'd it with her own milk, and breathed into it the sweetest spirit——she had made him all gentle, generous and humane——she had fill'd his heart with trust and confidence, and disposed every passage which led to it, for the communication of the tenderest offices——she had moreover considered the other causes for which matrimony was ordained——

And accordingly *   *   *   *   *   *   *   *   *   *
*   *   *   *   *   *   *   *   *   *   *   *   *   *
*   *   *   *   *   *   *   *   *   *   *   *   *   *
*   *   *   *.

The DONATION was not defeated by my uncle Toby's wound.

Now this last article was somewhat apocryphal; and the Devil, who is the great disturber of our faiths in this world, had raised scruples in Mrs. Wadman's brain about it; and like a true devil as he was, had done his own work at the same time, by turning my uncle Toby's Virtue thereupon into nothing but *empty bottles, tripes, trunk-hose,* and *pantofles.*

CHAPTER XXIII

Mrs. Bridget had pawn'd all the little stock of honour a poor chambermaid was worth in the world, that she would get to the bottom of the affair in ten days; and it was built upon one of the most concessible *postulatums*[1] in nature: namely, that whilst my uncle Toby was making love to her mistress, the Corporal could find nothing better to do, than make love to her——"*And I'll let him as much as he will,*" said Bridget, "*to get it out of him.*"

Friendship has two garments; an outer, and an under one. Bridget was serving her mistress's interests in the one—and doing the thing which most pleased herself in the other; so had as many stakes depending upon my uncle Toby's wound, as the Devil himself——Mrs. Wadman had but one—and as it possibly might be her last (without discouraging Mrs. Bridget, or discrediting her talents) was determined to play her cards herself.

She wanted not encouragement: a child might have look'd into his hand——there was such a plainness and simplicity in his playing out what trumps he had——with such an unmistrusting ignorance of the *ten-ace*[2]——and so naked and defenceless did he sit upon the same sopha with widow Wadman, that a generous heart would have wept to have won the game of him.

Let us drop the metaphor.

CHAPTER XXIV

——AND the story too—if you please: for though I have all along been hastening towards this part of it, with so much earnest desire, as well knowing it to be the choicest morsel of what I had to offer to the world, yet now that I am got to it, any one is welcome to take my pen, and go on with the story for me that will—I see the difficulties of the descriptions I'm going to give—and feel my want of powers.

It is one comfort at least to me, that I lost some fourscore ounces of blood this week in a most uncritical fever which attacked me at the beginning of this chapter; so that I have still some hopes remaining, it may be more in the serous or globular parts of the blood, than in the subtile *aura* of the brain——be it which it will—an Invocation can do no hurt——and I leave the affair entirely to the *invoked*, to inspire or to inject me according as he sees good.

THE INVOCATION.

GENTLE Spirit of sweetest humour, who erst didst sit upon the easy pen of my beloved CERVANTES; Thou who glided'st daily through his lattice, and turned'st the twilight of his prison into noon day brightness by thy presence——tinged'st his little urn of water with heaven-sent Nectar, and all the time he wrote of Sancho and his master, didst cast thy mystic mantle o'er his wither'd* stump, and wide extended it to all the evils of his life——

——Turn in hither, I beseech thee!——behold these breeches!——they are all I have in the world——that piteous rent was given them at Lyons——

My shirts! see what a deadly schism has happen'd amongst 'em—for the laps are in Lombardy, and the rest of 'em here—I never had but six, and a cunning gypsey of a laundress at Milan cut me off the *fore*-laps of five—To do her justice, she did it with some consideration—for I was returning *out* of Italy.

And yet, notwithstanding all this, and a pistol tinder-box which was moreover filched from me at Sienna, and twice that I pay'd five Pauls[1] for two hard eggs, once at Raddicoffini, and a second time at Capua—I do not think a journey through France and Italy,[2] provided a man keeps his temper all the way, so bad a thing as some people would make you believe: there must be *ups* and *downs*, or how the duce should we get into vallies where Nature spreads so many tables of entertainment.—'Tis non-sense to imagine they will lend you their voitures to be shaken to pieces for nothing; and unless you pay twelve sous for greasing your wheels, how should the poor peasant get butter to his bread?—We really expect too much—and for the livre or two above par for your suppers and bed—at the most they are but one shilling and ninepence halfpenny——who would embroil their philosophy for it? for heaven's and for your own sake, pay it——pay it with both hands open, rather than leave *Disappointment* sitting drooping upon the eye of your fair Hostess and her Damsels in the gate-way, at your departure ——and besides, my dear Sir, you get a sisterly kiss of each of 'em worth a pound——at least I did——

——For my uncle Toby's amours running all the way in my

* He lost his hand at the battle of Lepanto.[3]

head, they had the same effect upon me as if they had been my own——I was in the most perfect state of bounty and good will; and felt the kindliest harmony vibrating within me, with every oscillation of the chaise alike; so that whether the roads were rough or smooth, it made no difference; every thing I saw, or had to do with, touch'd upon some secret spring either of sentiment or rapture.

——They were the sweetest notes I ever heard; and I instantly let down the fore-glass to hear them more distinctly ——'Tis Maria; said the postilion, observing I was listening ——Poor Maria, continued he, (leaning his body on one side to let me see her, for he was in a line betwixt us) is sitting upon a bank playing her vespers upon her pipe, with her little goat beside her.

The young fellow utter'd this with an accent and a look so perfectly in tune to a feeling heart, that I instantly made a vow, I would give him a four and twenty sous piece, when I got to *Moulins*—

——And who is *poor Maria?* said I.

The love and pity of all the villages around us; said the postillion——it is but three years ago, that the sun did not shine upon so fair, so quick-witted and amiable a maid; and better fate did *Maria* deserve, than to have her Banns forbid, by the intrigues of the curate of the parish who published them——

He was going on, when Maria, who had made a short pause, put the pipe to her mouth and began the air again——they were the same notes;——yet were ten times sweeter: It is the evening service to the Virgin, said the young man——but who has taught her to play it—or how she came by her pipe, no one knows; we think that Heaven has assisted her in both; for ever since she has been unsettled in her mind, it seems her only consolation——she has never once had the pipe out of her hand, but plays that *service* upon it almost night and day.

The postillion delivered this with so much discretion and natural eloquence, that I could not help decyphering something in his face above his condition, and should have sifted out his history, had not poor Maria's taken such full possession of me.

We had got up by this time almost to the bank where Maria was sitting: she was in a thin white jacket with her hair, all but two tresses, drawn up into a silk net, with a few olive leaves twisted a little fantastically on one side——she was beautiful;

and if ever I felt the full force of an honest heart-ache, it was the moment I saw her——

——God help her! poor damsel! above a hundred masses, said the postillion, have been said in the several parish churches and convents around, for her,——but without effect; we have still hopes, as she is sensible for short intervals, that the Virgin at last will restore her to herself; but her parents, who know her best, are hopeless upon that score, and think her senses are lost for ever.

As the postillion spoke this, MARIA made a cadence so melancholy, so tender and querulous, that I sprung out of the chaise to help her, and found myself sitting betwixt her and her goat before I relapsed from my enthusiasm.

MARIA look'd wistfully for some time at me, and then at her goat——and then at me——and then at her goat again, and so on, alternately——

——Well, Maria, said I softly——What resemblance do you find?

I do intreat the candid reader to believe me, that it was from the humblest conviction of what a *Beast* man is,——that I ask'd the question; and that I would not have let fallen an unseasonable pleasantry in the venerable presence of Misery, to be entitled to all the wit that ever Rabelais scatter'd——and yet I own my heart smote me, and that I so smarted at the very idea of it, that I swore I would set up for Wisdom and utter grave sentences the rest of my days——and never——never attempt again to commit mirth with man, woman, or child, the longest day I had to live.

As for writing nonsense to them——I believe, there was a reserve—but that I leave to the world.

Adieu, Maria!—adieu, poor hapless damsel!——some time, but not *now*, I may hear thy sorrows from thy own lips——but I was deceived; for that moment she took her pipe and told me such a tale of woe with it, that I rose up, and with broken and irregular steps walk'd softly to my chaise.

——What an excellent inn at Moulins!

CHAPTER XXV

WHEN we have got to the end of this chapter (but not before) we must all turn back to the two blank chapters, on the account of which my honour has lain bleeding this half hour——I stop it, by pulling off one of my yellow slippers and throwing it with all my violence to the opposite side of my room, with a declaration at the heel of it——

——That whatever resemblance it may bear to half the chapters which are written in the world, or, for aught I know, may be now writing in it—that it was as casual as the foam of Zeuxis[1] his horse: besides, I look upon a chapter which has, *only nothing in it*, with respect; and considering what worse things there are in the world——That it is no way a proper subject for satire——

——Why then was it left so? And here, without staying for my reply, shall I be call'd as many blockheads, numsculs, doddypoles, dunderheads, ninnyhammers, goosecaps, joltheads, nicompoops, and sh--t-a-beds——and other unsavory appellations, as ever the cake-bakers of Lernè,[2] cast in the teeth of King Gargantua's shepherds——And I'll let them do it, as Bridget said, as much as they please; for how was it possible they should foresee the necessity I was under of writing the 25th chapter of my book, before the 18th, &c.

——So I don't take it amiss——All I wish is, that it may be a lesson to the world, "*to let people tell their stories their own way*."

The Eighteenth Chapter.

As Mrs. Bridget open'd the door before the Corporal had well given the rap, the interval betwixt that and my uncle Toby's introduction into the parlour, was so short, that Mrs. Wadman had but just time to get from behind the curtain——lay a Bible upon the table, and advance a step or two towards the door to receive him.

My uncle Toby saluted Mrs. Wadman, after the manner in which women were saluted by men in the year of our Lord God one thousand seven hundred and thirteen——then facing about, he march'd up abreast with her to the sopha, and in three plain words——though not before he was sat down——nor after he was sat down——but as he was sitting down, told her, "*he was in love*"——so that my uncle Toby strained himself more in the declaration than he needed.

Mrs. Wadman naturally looked down, upon a slit she had been darning up in her apron, in expectation every moment, that my uncle Toby would go on; but having no talents for amplification, and LOVE moreover of all others being a subject of which he was the least a master——When he had told Mrs. Wadman once that he loved her, he let it alone, and left the matter to work after its own way.

My father was always in raptures with this system of my uncle Toby's, as he falsely called it, and would often say, that could his brother Toby to his processe have added but a pipe of tobacco——he had wherewithal to have found his way, if there was faith in a Spanish proverb,[3] towards the hearts of half the women upon the globe.

My uncle Toby never understood what my father meant; nor will I presume to extract more from it, than a condemnation of an error which the bulk of the world lie under——but the French, every one of 'em to a man, who believe in it, almost as much as the REAL PRESENCE,[4] "*That talking of love, is making it.*"

——I would as soon set about making a black-pudding by the same receipt.

Let us go on: Mrs. Wadman sat in expectation my uncle Toby would do so, to almost the first pulsation of that minute, wherein silence on one side or the other, generally becomes indecent: so edging herself a little more towards him, and raising up her eyes, sub-blushing, as she did it——she took up the gauntlet——or the discourse (if you like it better) and communed with my uncle Toby, thus.

The cares and disquietudes of the marriage state, quoth Mrs. Wadman, are very great. I suppose so—said my uncle Toby: and therefore when a person, continued Mrs Wadman, is so much at his ease as you are—so happy, captain Shandy, in yourself, your friends and your amusements—I wonder, what reasons can incline you to the state——

——They are written, quoth my uncle Toby, in the Common-Prayer Book.[5]

Thus far my uncle Toby went on warily, and kept within his depth, leaving Mrs. Wadman to sail upon the gulph as she pleased.

——As for children—said Mrs. Wadman—though a principal end perhaps of the institution, and the natural wish, I suppose, of every parent—yet do not we all find, they are certain sorrows, and very uncertain comforts? and what is there, dear sir, to pay one for the heart-achs—what compensation for the many tender and disquieting apprehensions of a suffering and defenceless mother who brings them into life? I declare, said my uncle Toby, smit with pity, I know of none; unless it be the pleasure which it has pleased God——

——A fiddlestick! quoth she.

Chapter the Nineteenth.

Now there are such an infinitude of notes, tunes, cants, chants, airs, looks, and accents with which the word *fiddlestick* may be pronounced in all such causes as this, every one of 'em impressing a sense and meaning as different from the other, as *dirt* from *cleanliness*—That Casuists (for it is an affair of conscience on that score) reckon up no less than fourteen thousand in which you may do either right or wrong.

Mrs. Wadman hit upon the *fiddlestick*, which summoned up all my uncle Toby's modest blood into his cheeks—so feeling within himself that he had somehow or other got beyond his depth, he stopt short; and without entering further either into the pains or pleasures of matrimony, he laid his hand upon his heart, and made an offer to take them as they were, and share them along with her.

When my uncle Toby had said this, he did not care to say it again; so casting his eye upon the Bible which Mrs. Wadman had laid upon the table, he took it up; and popping, dear soul! upon a passage in it, of all others the most interesting to him— which was the siege of Jericho—he set himself to read it over— leaving his proposal of marriage, as he had done his declaration of love, to work with her after its own way. Now it wrought neither as an astringent or a loosener; nor like opium, or bark, or mercury, or buckthorn, or any one drug which nature had bestowed upon the world—in short, it work'd not at all in her; and the cause of that was, that there was something working there before——Babbler that I am! I have anticipated what it was a dozen times; but there is fire still in the subject——allons.

CHAPTER XXVI

IT is natural for a perfect stranger who is going from London to Edinburgh, to enquire before he sets out, how many miles to York; which is about the half way——nor does any body wonder, if he goes on and asks about the Corporation, &c. - -

It was just as natural for Mrs. Wadman, whose first husband was all his time afflicted with a Sciatica, to wish to know how far from the hip to the groin; and how far she was likely to suffer more or less in her feelings, in the one case than in the other.

She had accordingly read *Drake*'s anatomy[1] from one end to the other. She had peeped into *Wharton*[2] upon the brain, and borrowed * Graaf[3] upon the bones and muscles; but could make nothing of it.

She had reason'd likewise from her own powers——laid down theorems——drawn consequences, and come to no conclusion.

To clear up all, she had twice asked Doctor Slop, "if poor captain Shandy was ever likely to recover of his wound——?"

——He is recovered, Doctor Slop would say——

What! quite?

——Quite: madam——

But what do you mean by a recovery? Mrs. Wadman would say.

Doctor Slop was the worst man alive at definitions; and so Mrs. Wadman could get no knowledge: in short, there was no way to extract it, but from my uncle Toby himself.

There is an accent of humanity in an enquiry of this kind which lulls SUSPICION to rest——and I am half persuaded the serpent got pretty near it, in his discourse with Eve; for the propensity in the sex to be deceived could not be so great, that she should have boldness to hold chat with the devil, without it——But there is an accent of humanity——how shall I describe it?—'tis an accent which covers the part with a garment, and gives the enquirer a right to be as particular with it, as your body-surgeon.

"——Was it without remission?—

——Was it more tolerable in bed?

——Could he lie on both sides alike with it?

---

* This must be a mistake in Mr. Shandy; for Graaf wrote upon the pancreatick juice, and the parts of generation.

—Was he able to mount a horse?

—Was motion bad for it?" et cætera, were so tenderly spoke to, and so directed towards my uncle Toby's heart, that every item of them sunk ten times deeper into it than the evils themselves——but when Mrs. Wadman went round about by Namur to get at my uncle Toby's groin; and engaged him to attack the point of the advanced counterscarp, and *pêle mêle* with the Dutch to take the counterguard of St. Roch sword in hand—and then with tender notes playing upon his ear, led him all bleeding by the hand out of the trench, wiping her eye, as he was carried to his tent——Heaven! Earth! Sea!—all was lifted up—the springs of nature rose above their levels—an angel of mercy sat besides him on the sopha—his heart glow'd with fire—and had he been worth a thousand, he had lost every heart of them to Mrs. Wadman.

—And whereabouts, dear Sir, quoth Mrs. Wadman, a little categorically, did you receive this sad blow?——In asking this question, Mrs. Wadman gave a slight glance towards the waistband of my uncle Toby's red plush breeches, expecting naturally, as the shortest reply to it, that my uncle Toby would lay his fore-finger upon the place——It fell out otherwise—— for my uncle Toby having got his wound before the gate of St. Nicolas, in one of the traverses of the trench, opposite to the salient angle of the demi-bastion of St. Roch; he could at any time stick a pin upon the identical spot of ground where he was standing when the stone struck him: this struck instantly upon my uncle Toby's sensorium——and with it, struck his large map of the town and citadel of Namur and its environs, which he had purchased and pasted down upon a board by the Corporal's aid, during his long illness——it had lain with other military lumber in the garret ever since, and accordingly the Corporal was detached into the garret to fetch it.

My uncle Toby measured off thirty toises, with Mrs. Wadman's scissars, from the returning angle before the gate of St. Nicolas; and with such a virgin modesty laid her finger upon the place, that the goddess of Decency, if then in being—if not, 'twas her shade—shook her head, and with a finger wavering across her eyes—forbid her to explain the mistake.

Unhappy Mrs. Wadman!——

——For nothing can make this chapter go off with spirit but an apostrophe to thee——but my heart tells me, that in such a

crisis an apostrophe is but an insult in disguise, and ere I would
offer one to a woman in distress—let the chapter go to the devil;
provided any damn'd critick *in keeping* will be but at the trouble
to take it with him.

CHAPTER XXVII

My uncle Toby's Map is carried down into the kitchen.

CHAPTER XXVIII

——AND here is the *Maes*—and this is the *Sambre*; said the Corporal, pointing with his right hand extended a little towards the map, and his left upon Mrs. Bridget's shoulder—but not the shoulder next him—and this, said he, is the town of Namur—and this the citadel—and there lay the French—and here lay his honour and myself——and in this cursed trench, Mrs. Bridget, quoth the Corporal, taking her by the hand, did he receive the wound which crush'd him so miserably *here*——In pronouncing which he slightly press'd the back of her hand towards the part he felt for——and let it fall.

We thought, Mr. Trim, it had been more in the middle ——said Mrs. Bridget——

That would have undone us for ever—said the Corporal.

——And left my poor mistress undone too—said Bridget.

The Corporal made no reply to the repartee, but by giving Mrs. Bridget a kiss.

Come—come—said Bridget—holding the palm of her left-hand parallel to the plane of the horizon, and sliding the fingers of the other over it, in a way which could not have been done, had there been the least wart or protuberance——'Tis every syllable of it false, cried the Corporal, before she had half finished the sentence——

—I know it to be fact, said Bridget, from credible witnesses.

——Upon my honour, said the Corporal, laying his hand upon his heart, and blushing as he spoke with honest resentment—'tis a story, Mrs. Bridget, as false as hell——Not, said Bridget, interrupting him, that either I or my mistress care a halfpenny about it, whether 'tis so or no——only that when one is married, one would chuse to have such a thing by one at least——

It was somewhat unfortunate for Mrs. Bridget, that she had begun the attack with her manual exercise; for the Corporal instantly * * * * * * * * * * * * * *
* * * * * * * * * * * * * * *
* * * * * * * * * * * * * * *
* * *.

CHAPTER XXIX

It was like the momentary contest in the moist eye-lids of an April morning, "Whether Bridget should laugh or cry."

She snatch'd up a rolling-pin——'twas ten to one, she had laugh'd——

She laid it down——she cried; and had one single tear of 'em but tasted of bitterness, full sorrowful would the Corporal's heart have been that he had used the argument; but the Corporal understood the sex, a *quart major to a terce*[1] at least, better than my uncle Toby, and accordingly he assailed Mrs. Bridget after this manner.

I know, Mrs. Bridget, said the Corporal, giving her a most respectful kiss, that thou art good and modest by nature, and art withal so generous a girl in thyself, that if I know thee rightly, thou wouldst not wound an insect, much less the honour of so gallant and worthy a soul as my master, wast thou sure to be made a countess of——but thou has been set on, and deluded, dear Bridget, as is often a woman's case, "to please others more than themselves——"

Bridget's eyes poured down at the sensations the Corporal excited.

——Tell me——tell me then, my dear Bridget, continued the Corporal, taking hold of her hand, which hung down dead by her side,——and giving a second kiss——whose suspicion has misled thee?

Bridget sobb'd a sob or two——then open'd her eyes——the Corporal wiped 'em with the bottom of her apron——she then open'd her heart and told him all.

CHAPTER XXX

My uncle Toby and the Corporal had gone on separately with their operations the greatest part of the campaign, and as effectually cut off from all communication of what either the one or the other had been doing, as if they had been separated from each other by the *Maes* or the *Sambre*.

My uncle Toby, on his side, had presented himself every afternoon in his red and silver, and blue and gold alternately, and sustained an infinity of attacks in them, without knowing them to be attacks—and so had nothing to communicate——

The Corporal, on his side, in taking Bridget, by it had gain'd considerable advantages——and consequently had much to communicate——but what were the advantages——as well, as what was the manner by which he had seiz'd them, required so nice an historian that the Corporal durst not venture upon it; and as sensible as he was of glory, would rather have been contented to have gone barehead and without laurels for ever, than torture his master's modesty for a single moment——

——Best of honest and gallant servants!——But I have apostrophiz'd thee, Trim! once before——and could I apotheosize thee also (that is to say) with good company——I would do it *without ceremony* in the very next page.

CHAPTER XXXI

Now my uncle Toby had one evening laid down his pipe upon the table, and was counting over to himself upon his finger ends, (beginning at his thumb) all Mrs. Wadman's perfections one by one; and happening two or three times together, either by omitting some, or counting others twice over, to puzzle himself sadly before he could get beyond his middle finger——Prithee, Trim! said he, taking up his pipe again,——bring me a pen and ink: Trim brought paper also.

Take a full sheet——Trim! said my uncle Toby, making a sign with his pipe at the same time to take a chair and sit down close by him at the table. The Corporal obeyed——placed the paper directly before him——took a pen and dip'd it in the ink.

—She has a thousand virtues, Trim! said my uncle Toby——

Am I to set them down, an' please your honour? quoth the Corporal.

——But they must be taken in their ranks, replied my uncle Toby; for of them all, Trim, that which wins me most, and which is a security for all the rest, is the compassionate turn and singular humanity of her character—I protest, added my uncle Toby, looking up, as he protested it, towards the top of the ceiling——That was I her brother, Trim, a thousand fold, she could not make more constant or more tender enquiries after my sufferings——though now no more.

The Corporal made no reply to my uncle Toby's protestation, but by a short cough—he dip'd the pen a second time into the inkhorn; and my uncle Toby, pointing with the end of his pipe as close to the top of the sheet at the left hand corner of it, as he could get it——the Corporal wrote down word HUMANITY - - - - thus.

Prithee, Corporal, said my uncle Toby, as soon as Trim had done it——how often does Mrs. Bridget enquire after the wound on the cap of thy knee, which thou received'st at the battle of Landen?

She never, an' please your honour, enquires after it at all.

That, Corporal, said my uncle Toby, with all the triumph the goodness of his nature would permit——That shews the difference in the character of the mistress and maid——had the fortune of war allotted the same mischance to me, Mrs. Wadman would have enquired into every circumstance relating to it a hundred times——She would have enquired, an' please your honour, ten times as often about your honour's groin——The pain, Trim, is equally excruciating,——and Compassion has as much to do with the one as the other——

——God bless your honour! cried the Corporal——what has a woman's compassion to do with a wound upon the cap of a man's knee? had your honour's been shot into ten thousand splinters at the affair of Landen, Mrs. Wadman would have troubled her head as little about it as Bridget, because, added the Corporal, lowering his voice and speaking very distinctly, as he assigned his reason——

"The knee is such a distance from the main body—whereas the groin, your honour knows, is upon the very *curtin* of the *place*."

My uncle Toby gave a long whistle——but in a note which could scarce be heard across the table.

The Corporal had advanced too far to retire——in three words he told the rest——

My uncle Toby laid down his pipe as gently upon the fender, as if it had been spun from the unravellings of a spider's web——

——Let us go to my brother Shandy's, said he.

CHAPTER XXXII

THERE will be just time, whilst my uncle Toby and Trim are walking to my father's, to inform you, that Mrs. Wadman had, some moons before this, made a confident of my mother; and that Mrs. Bridget, who had the burden of her own, as well as her mistress's secret to carry, had got happily delivered of both to Susannah behind the garden-wall.

As for my mother, she saw nothing at all in it, to make the least bustle about——but Susannah was sufficient by herself for all the ends and purposes you could possibly have, in exporting a family secret; for she instantly imparted it by signs to Jonathan——and Jonathan by tokens to the cook, as she was basting a loin of mutton; the cook sold it with some kitchen-fat to the postilion for a groat, who truck'd it with the dairy-maid for something of about the same value——and though whis-per'd in the hay-loft, FAME caught the notes with her brazen trumpet and sounded them upon the house-top—In a word, not an old woman in the village or five miles round, who did not understand the difficulties of my uncle Toby's siege, and what were the secret articles which had delay'd the surrender.——

My father, whose way was to force every event in nature into an hypothesis, by which means never man crucified TRUTH at the rate he did——had but just heard of the report as my uncle Toby set out; and catching fire suddenly at the trespass done his brother by it, was demonstrating to Yorick, notwithstanding my mother was sitting by——not only, "That the devil was in women, and that the whole of the affair was lust;" but that every evil and disorder in the world of what kind or nature soever, from the first fall of Adam, down to my uncle Toby's (inclusive) was owing one way or other to the same unruly appetite.

Yorick was just bringing my father's hypothesis to some temper, when my uncle Toby entering the room with marks of infinite benevolence and forgiveness in his looks, my father's eloquence rekindled against the passion——and as he was not very nice in the choice of his words when he was wroth——as soon as my uncle Toby was seated by the fire, and had filled his pipe, my father broke out in this manner.

CHAPTER XXXIII

——That provision should be made for continuing the race of so great, so exalted and godlike a Being as man—I am far from denying—but philosophy speaks freely of every thing; and therefore I still think and do maintain it to be a pity, that it should be done by means of a passion which bends down the faculties, and turns all the wisdom, contemplations, and operations of the soul backwards——a passion, my dear, continued my father, addressing himself to my mother, which couples and equals wise men with fools, and makes us come out of our caverns and hiding-places more like satyrs and four-footed beasts than men.

I know it will be said, continued my father (availing himself of the *Prolepsis*) that in itself, and simply taken——like hunger, or thirst, or sleep——'tis an affair neither good or bad—or shameful or otherwise.——Why then did the delicacy of *Diogenes* and *Plato*[1] so recalcitrate against it? and wherefore, when we go about to make and plant a man, do we put out the candle? and for what reason is it, that all the parts thereof—the congredients—the preparations—the instruments, and whatever serves thereto, are so held as to be conveyed to a cleanly mind by no language, translation, or periphrasis whatever?

——The act of killing and destroying a man, continued my father raising his voice—and turning to my uncle Toby—you see, is glorious—and the weapons by which we do it are honourable——We march with them upon our shoulders——We strut with them by our sides——We gild them——We carve them——We in-lay them——We enrich them——Nay, if it be but a *scoundril* cannon, we cast an ornament upon the breech of it.——

——My uncle Toby laid down his pipe to intercede for a better epithet——and Yorick was rising up to batter the whole hypothesis to pieces——

——When Obadiah broke into the middle of the room with a complaint, which cried out for an immediate hearing.

The case was this:

My father, whether by ancient custom of the manor, or as improprietor of the great tythes,[2] was obliged to keep a Bull for the service of the Parish, and Obadiah had led his cow upon a *pop-visit*[3] to him one day or other the preceding summer——I say, one day or other—because as chance would have it, it was the day on which he was married to my father's house-maid ——so one was a reckoning to the other. Therefore when Obadiah's wife was brought to bed—Obadiah thanked God——

——Now, said Obadiah, I shall have a calf: so Obadiah went daily to visit his cow.

She'll calve on Monday—on Tuesday—or Wednesday at the farthest——

The cow did not calve——no—she'll not calve till next week——the cow put it off terribly——till at the end of the sixth week Obadiah's suspicions (like a good man's) fell upon the Bull.

Now the parish being very large, my father's Bull, to speak the truth of him, was no way equal to the department; he had, however, got himself, somehow or other, thrust into employment—and as he went through the business with a grave face, my father had a high opinion of him.

——Most of the townsmen, an' please your worship, quoth Obadiah, believe that 'tis all the Bull's fault——

——But may not a cow be barren? replied my father, turning to Doctor Slop.

It never happens: said Dr. Slop, but the man's wife may have come before her time naturally enough——Prithee has the child hair upon his head?—added Dr. Slop——

——It is as hairy as I am; said Obadiah.——Obadiah had not been shaved for three weeks——Wheu-- u ---- u -------- cried my father; beginning the sentence with an exclamatory whistle——and so, brother Toby, this poor Bull of mine, who is as good a Bull as ever p—ss'd, and might have done for Europa[4] herself in purer times——had he but two legs less, might have been driven into Doctors Commons[5] and lost his character—— which to a Town Bull, brother Toby, is the very same thing as his life——

L--d! said my mother, what is all this story about?——

A COCK and a BULL, said Yorick——And one of the best of its kind, I ever heard.

The END of the NINTH VOLUME.

EXPLANATORY NOTES

*Words have generally not been glossed when they appear in the
Concise Oxford Dictionary.*

*I am grateful to Dr Alex Lindsay for assistance with translations
from Latin and Greek.*

VOLUME I

title page   title: The mid-eighteenth century saw the publication of many
fictional 'lives', including the first part of Thomas Amory's *The Life
of John Buncle, Esq* (1756–66) and the anonymously authored *The
Life and Memoirs of Mr. Ephraim Tristram Bates* (1756). By calling
his book a 'life and opinions', Sterne challenges the very familiar
form of 'life and adventures', used in Francis Coventry's *The History
of Pompey the Little; or, the Life and Adventures of a Lap-Dog*
(1751); Edward Kimber's *The Life and Adventures of Joe Thompson*
(1751); or Robert Paltock's *The Life and Adventures of Peter Wilkins*
(1751). The tragi-comic overtones of the hero's name derive from the
combination of the chivalric 'Tristram' (or Tristan), best known in
English from *Le Morte Darthur*, a retelling of the Arthurian legends
by Sir Thomas Malory (1415/8–1471), and 'Shandy', a dialect term
implying 'wild', 'a little crack-brained', or 'somewhat crazy' (*OED*).

title page   epigraph: 'Not things, but opinions about things, trouble
men.' The motto is from the *Manual* of the Stoic philosopher Epictetus (AD *c*.55–*c*.135).

frontispiece   In a letter written early in March 1760, following the success of the small York-printed edition of the first two volumes of
Tristram Shandy, Sterne expressed the wish for an illustration by
William Hogarth (1697–1764) for the first London edition, to be
published the following month; as a result, the celebrated English
artist provided this illustration of Corporal Trim reading the sermon
to Walter Shandy, Uncle Toby, and a sleeping Dr. Slop (see II.xvii),
which was engraved by Simon François Ravenet (1721–74). Hogarth
would later provide a further illustration for the second instalment of
Tristram Shandy, published in 1761 (see below, n. to IV, frontispiece).

dedication   1. *Mr. PITT*: William Pitt, the Elder (1708–78) was at the
height of his popularity in 1759—the 'year of victories'—for his lead-
ership in the Seven Years War. Sterne included the dedication only in
the first London edition, the 'Second Edition' of *Tristram Shandy*,

after the book had proved a popular success. The dedication exists in two states, of which this is the first.

2. *bye corner of the kingdom*: When he wrote *Tristram Shandy*, Sterne was living at York, having recently moved to the city from the village of Sutton-on-the-Forest, eight miles away. The dedication, however, was almost certainly not written 'in a bye corner of the kingdom' but rather in London, where Sterne was enjoying the celebrity that followed the astonishing popular success of the first two volumes of his novel; see Sterne's letter to Pitt, requesting that he be permitted to dedicate the second edition to the prime minister; letter of [?28 March 1760], in *Letters of Laurence Sterne*, ed. Lewis Perry Curtis (Oxford: Clarendon, 1935), 103.

I 1. *humours*: In the ancient physiology still current in medieval Europe, the cardinal humours were blood, phlegm, choler (yellow bile), and melancholy (black bile); the ideal person had an equal mixture of the four, while a predominance of one would lead to a person who was sanguine, phlegmatic, choleric or melancholy, respectively.

2. *animal spirits*: Anciently, spirits were divided into three kinds: animal, vital, and vegetative; by the eighteenth century these had been reduced to animal spirits alone. Sterne here draws principally on John Locke's *An Essay Concerning Human Understanding* (4th edn. 1700), II. xxxiii. 6 (see note 5 to I.iv. below). However, the theory of animal spirits itself lost currency during the eighteenth century and Ephraim Chambers's *Cyclopaedia: or, an Universal Dictionary of Arts and Sciences* (2nd edn. 1738), from which Sterne derived much information on many topics, gave a sceptical account of their importance in human physiology, describing them as 'a fine subtile juice, or Humour in Animal Bodies; supposed to be the great instrument of muscular Motion, Sensation &c.', but pointing out that despite great controversy among anatomists as to their exact nature, 'their very existence has never been fairly proved'.

II 1. *HOMUNCULUS*: Dim. of Latin 'homo'—'little man'; here used to refer to the miniature human figure which early microscopists believed they saw in a spermatozoon.

2. *Tully*: Marcus Tullius Cicero (106–43 BC), author of e.g. *De republica* and the *Laws*, and Samuel Pufendorf (1632–94), author of *De Jure Naturae et Gentium* (1672), were both noted for their influence on the philosophy of natural law.

III 1. *natural philosopher*: The development of experimental science in the seventeenth century gave rise to a concept of natural philosophy which included astronomy, physics, and chemistry, as well as biology.

IV 1. *Pilgrim's Progress*: John Bunyan's *The Pilgrim's Progress* (1678) was one of the most widely read books in the eighteenth century, reaching at least its fortieth edition by 1760. Although Sterne's reference to his work being read by 'all ranks, professions, and denominations of men whatever' appears facetious, the anonymous author of a subsequent pamphlet concurred, saying that the book was 'dedicated to a minister, read by the clergy, approved of by the wits, studied by the merchants, gazed at by the ladies, and was become the pocket-companion of the nation' (*Alass! Poor Yorick* (1761)).

2. *Montaigne*: Michel de Montaigne (1533–92), French essayist; the reference is to the *Essays*, III. v, 'Upon Some Verses of Virgil'.

3. *Horace*: Quintus Horatius Flaccus (65–8 BC), author of *Ars Poetica* to which Tristram misleadingly refers; Horace, in fact, commends Homer for *not* starting his tale of the Trojan War *ab ovo*—that is, from the birth of Helen from Leda's egg (*Ars Poetica*, l. 147).

4. *Turky merchant*: i.e. a trader to Asia Minor.

5. *Locke*: John Locke (1632–1704), whose *An Essay Concerning Human Understanding* (4th edn. 1700) had great influence on eighteenth-century epistemology, or the theory of knowledge. Locke's view of the association of ideas, contained in book II, chapter xxxiii, gave rise, in a parodic form, to much of *Tristram Shandy*'s structure (see also n. 2 to I.1 above), though it remains uncertain whether Sterne had really studied the *Essay*, or was simply familiar with some of its principal ideas, gleaned from Chambers's *Cyclopaedia*, for example.

v 1. *fifth day of November*: 5 November had a double significance for eighteenth-century English Protestants, being both the anniversary of Guy Fawkes's Gunpowder Plot of 1605 and of the landing of the Dutch Protestant prince William of Orange, later William III (1650–1702), at Torbay in 1688, en route to claim the British and Irish crowns.

2. *Jupiter or Saturn*: The most distant of the seven anciently known planets of the solar system. Neptune was not discovered until 1846, while Pluto, discovered in 1930, is now considered a 'dwarf planet'.

3. *Fortune*: The Romans made Fortune a goddess; Sterne here distinguishes the pagan idea of Fortune from the Christian concept of Providence.

vi 1. O *diem præclarum!*: O splendid day!

vii 1. *ordinaries*: i.e. ordinary's licence.

2. *Didius*: In Didius, Sterne intended a loose, but immediately recognizable, satirical portrait of Dr. Francis Topham (*c*.1713–1770), one of his opponents in York ecclesiastical politics and a leading church lawyer.

3. *whim-wham*: Both an odd notion and a cant term for genitals; the faculties in which the 'neat *Formula*' of Didius appeared were documents relating to the licensing of midwives which, in the Northern Province of the Church, was under Topham's control.

4. *Dr. Kunastrokius*: A satirical allusion to the distinguished physician Dr. Richard Mead (1673–1754), whose patients included Queen Anne, George I, and George II besides Sir Robert Walpole and Alexander Pope.

5. *HOBBY-HORSES*: An important word for *Tristram Shandy*, generally denoting a hobby or favourite pastime but here including a pun on another meaning—prostitute.

VIII 1. *De gustibus non est disputandum*: There's no arguing about tastes.

IX 1. *tout ensemble*: Whole.

2. *Mr. Dodsley*: James Dodsley (1724–97), who took over the running of R. and J. Dodsley of Pall Mall from his more famous brother Robert (1703–64) in 1759, the year before the firm published the first London edition of the first two volumes of *Tristram Shandy*.

3. *CANDID and Miss CUNEGUND's affairs*: Voltaire's *Candide*, to which Sterne alludes, was published in 1759 and appeared in English translation as *Candid: or, All for the Best* that same year.

X 1. *Rosinante*: Don Quixote's horse, 'whose Bones stuck out like the Corners of a *Spanish* Real [coin]' (*The History of the Renowned Don Quixote de la Mancha*, I. i. 1). The novel, by Miguel de Cervantes, published 1605–15, was one of Sterne's favourites; see his comment on Don Quixote in I.IX, and n. 3 to III.XIX below. Here and subsequently, reference is made to the translation by Peter Motteux, revised by John Ozell, which Sterne knew. Yorick's 'lean, sorry, jack-ass of a horse', not being 'a horse at all points', is a gelding.

2. *Yanguesian carriers*: In the episode referred to, Rosinante is described as being 'chaste and modest' (*Don Quixote*, I. iii. 1).

3. *poudrè d'or*: Powdered with gold.

4. *chuck-farthing and shuffle-cap*: Chuck-farthing was a game of combined skill and chance in which coins were pitched at a mark, and then chucked at a hole by the player coming nearest the mark who won all the money that went into the hole; shuffle-cap was a game in which money was shaken in a hat.

5. *upon his own bones*: The gaunt, consumptive Sterne's description of Yorick is also a comic self-representation (see also n. 1 to III.III below).

6. *de vanitate mundi et fugâ sæculi*: On the vanity of the world and the flight of time.

7. *clapp'd . . . broken-winded*: Equine diseases: spavin and grease affect the hock-joint and heels respectively: a twitter-boned horse has a suppurating tumour on its foot.

8. *communibus annis*: In ordinary years.

9. *knight of La Mancha*: i.e. Don Quixote.

XI 1. *Horwendillus*: According to Saxo (see below), Horwendillus was the nineteenth Danish king and father of Amlethus (Hamlet).

2. *Saxo-Grammaticus's Danish history*: Saxo (*fl.* mid-twelfth century–early thirteenth century) was author of the *Gesta Danorum* which includes an account of Horwendillus (III. xxvii); his Latin eloquence led to his being called 'Grammaticus' in the early fourteenth century.

3. *crasis*: The combination of humours, constitution (see n. 1 to. I.1 above).

4. *gaité de cœur*: Cheerfulness of heart.

5. *a French wit*: François, duc de la Rochefoucauld (1613–80), one of whose Maxims this is.

XII 1. *Eugenius's*: The name 'Eugenius' derives from the Greek, and was widely employed in the eighteenth century to denote a character who was 'well-born' or 'noble'. Eugenius is often identified with John Hall, later Hall-Stevenson (1718–85), whom Sterne first knew as a fellow-student at Cambridge, and who was Master of Skelton Castle in Yorkshire. In later volumes of *Tristram Shandy* (VII.1 e.g.), the somewhat facetious identification of the irreverent Hall-Stevenson as Eugenius is probably correct. If Sterne had anyone particular in mind at this juncture, however, the prudent friend is more likely to have been Stephen Croft (1712–98), squire of Sterne's parish of Stillington.

2. *Sancho Pança*: The peasant who accompanies Don Quixote in the capacity of squire; the allusion is to *Don Quixote*, I. i. 7.

3. *flashes of his spirit . . . set the table in a roar!*: Slightly adapted from *Hamlet*, v. i. 192–3.

4. *epitaph and elegy*: Hamlet's words are spoken while he holds the skull of Yorick, the King's jester (*Hamlet*, v. i). The passage is also one that suggests the influence on Sterne's work of *The Life and Memoirs of Ephraim Tristram Bates* (see n. to I, title page), whose penultimate paragraph concludes:

scarce an Hour in the Day passes, but Strangers enquire for his Tomb; and, striking their Breasts, Cry!

Alas! poor Bates.

XIII 1. *gentlemen reviewers in Great-Britain*: Especially under the influence of the novelist Tobias Smollett (1721–71), founder of the *Critical Review* in 1756 and of the *British Magazine* in 1760, journal reviewing moved in the mid-eighteenth century from being the province of hack-writers to an activity no longer considered demeaning for those who were, or aspired to the status of, gentlemen; see also II.11 below.

XIV 1. *Jack Hickathrift*: The name more usually appears as 'Thomas': giant-killing hero of an English tale that appeared in chap-book form in the seventeenth century, under the title *The Pleasant History of Thomas Hickathrift*; Hickathrift is also mentioned in Henry Fielding's burlesque tragedy *Tom Thumb* (1730).

2. *two volumes of my life every year*: For the actual publication of *Tristram Shandy* in five instalments between 1759 and 1767, see Note on the Text.

XV 1. *femme sole*: Single woman.

2. *fee farms . . . free warrens*: *Fee-farms*—the rent paid for tenure by which land is held in fee simple subject to a perpetual fixed rent, without any other services; *knight's fees*—the amount of land for which the services of an armed knight were due to the sovereign; *views of frank-pledge*—courts held periodically for the production of the members of a hundred or manor; *put in exigent*—take a writ commanding the sheriff to summon the defendant to appear and deliver himself upon the pain of outlawry; *free warrens*—a right of keeping or hunting beasts and fowls of warren.

3. *toties quoties*: As often as the occasion demands.

4. *my poor mother . . . becomes me to decide*: Elizabeth Shandy's phantom pregnancy (or pseudocyesis) recalls the similarly delusive pregnancy of the wife of Commodore Trunnion, in Tobias Smollett's *The Adventures of Peregrine Pickle* (1751; rev. edn. 1758), ch. x.

XVI 1. *Stilton . . . to Grantham*: A distance of about thirty-five miles on the Great North Road.

XVIII 1. *Dr. Maningham*: Sir Richard Manningham (c. 1685–1759), a Fellow of the Royal Society by the age of 30 and knighted at 31, was the most famous man-midwife of his day.

2. *Jenny*: In the early part of *Tristram Shandy*, 'Jenny' most likely alludes to the singer Catherine (or Kitty) Fourmantel, to whom Sterne became sentimentally attached during the York music season of 1759–60; see also n. 1 to III.XII.

3. *Grand Monarch*: Louis XIV (1638–1715), the Sun-King.

4. *Sir Robert Filmer's*: Filmer (c. 1588–1653) was a political theorist best known for his *Patriarcha* (1680), which Locke attacked as the manifesto of the absolutist party in *Two Treatises on Government* (1690); Filmer's theories were largely discredited in the eighteenth century.

5. *tender and delicious sentiment*: The eighteenth-century cult of moral feeling—sentimentalism or sensibility—exploited the individual's capacity for sympathetic identification with another person, actual or imaginary, especially in their misfortunes. In *Tristram Shandy* and in his second fiction *A Sentimental Journey through France and Italy. By Mr. Yorick* (1768), Sterne treats the moral value of the cult with great seriousness but remains capable of responding with irony to its more extravagant excesses.

XIX 1. *DULCINEA'S*: In *Don Quixote*, the hero transforms in his imagination the peasant girl Aldonza Lorenzo into his ideal mistress, calling her Dulcinea del Toboso (*Don Quixote*), I. i. 1).

2. *TRISMEGISTUS*: Hermes Trismegistus (Trismegistos: Greek =

Thrice-Greatest) was the name given to the Egyptian god Thoth whom Socrates describes, in Plato's *Phaedrus*, as the inventor of writing (as well as arithmetic, calculation, geometry, astronomy, draughts, and dice); he was the supposed author of many thousands of works of theology, philosophy, astrology, and occult knowledge.

3. *ARCHIMEDES*: Archimedes (*c.*287–212 BC), mathematician and inventor.

4. *NYKY and SIMKIN*: Nyky—from Nick, the Devil; Simkin—a simpleton.

5. *NICODEMUS'D*: From Nicodemus, the ruler who came to see Jesus by night (John 3: 1–21); here, made timid.

6. *argumentum ad hominem*: Argument designed to appeal to the personal sentiments or prejudices of the listener.

7. Θεοδίδαχτος: Taught of God.

8. *Quintilian de Oratore*: The *Institutio oratoria* of Marcus Fabius Quintilianus (*c.*35–*c.* AD 95) was one of the most important works of classical rhetoric.

9. *Isocrates*: Isocrates (436–338 BC) was renowned as a Sophist teacher of rhetoric in Athens.

10. *Aristotle*: Aristotle (384–322 BC), philosopher and scientist, was author of the *Rhetoric*.

11. *Longinus*: Cassius Longinus (AD *c.*213–73), a rhetorician, philosopher, and—in the eighteenth century—supposed author of *On the Sublime*, now attributed to a Greek scholar of the first century AD of whom nothing else is known.

12. *Vossius*: Gerhard Johannes Voss (1577–1649), a Dutch theologian, whose works include the *Elementa rhetorica*.

13. *Skioppius*: Kaspar Schoppe (1576–1649), German controversialist and scholar.

14. *Ramus*: Pierre de la Ramée (1515–72), known as Petrus or Peter Ramus, logician and influence on Omer Talon (*c.*1510–1562), otherwise Audomarus Talaeus, who reformed Ciceronian rhetoric.

15. *Farnaby*: Thomas Farnaby (1574/5–1647), a schoolmaster and classical scholar who corresponded with Vossius between 1630 and 1642, was author of the *Index Rhetoricus*.

16. *Crackenthorp*: Richard Crakanthorpe (*c.*1568–1624), a puritan divine and controversialist.

17. *Burgersdicius*: Francis Burgersdyck (1590–1629), Dutch philosopher and logician.

18. *ad ignorantiam*: An argument designed to profit by the ignorance of the listener.

19. *Jesus College*: Sterne himself studied as an undergraduate at Jesus College, Cambridge, from 1733 to 1737, when he took his BA; he returned to take his MA in 1740.

20. *vive la Bagatelle*: Long live frivolity.

21. *Epsom*: In the eighteenth century, Epsom was famous both for

its mineral waters and for horse-racing; it was perhaps the former that brought Walter Shandy to this fashionable resort.

22. *Numps*: A fool or simpleton.

23. *TRISTRAM*: Walter Shandy has an aversion to the name, which derives from the French 'triste' or 'sad', and implies 'son of sorrow'.

24. *rerum naturâ*: The nature of things.

25. *EPIPHONEMA*: A rhetorical term expressing an exclamatory sentence or reflection intended to sum up a discourse or a passage in it.

26. *EROTESIS*: A rhetorical figure by which a speaker, in the form of a question, affirms the opposite of what is asked.

xx 1. *Pliny the younger*: Gaius Plinius Caecilius Secundus (AD c.61–c.112), adopted son of the elder Pliny, of whom he in fact made this remark.

2. *Parismenus*: *Parismus, The Renouned Prince of Bohemia* (1598) and *Parismenos* (1599) were the work of Emanuel Forde. They were frequently reprinted together.

3. *Seven Champions of England*: Sterne was most likely thinking of the Seven Champions of Christendom—Saints George, Denis, James, Anthony, Andrew, Patrick, and David—who figure in *The Famous History of the Seven Champions of Christendom*, by Richard Johnson (1573–?1659), much reprinted in the seventeenth century.

4. *If the reader ... it is as follows*: For St. Thomas Aquinas, see below, n. 30 to IV, Slawkenbergius's tale. 'Infantes ... *nullo modo*' translates: 'Children living in their mothers' wombs cannot be baptized by any means'. '*La chose impossible*' translates: 'the impossible thing'.

5. *MEMOIRE presenté ... de SORBONNE* etc: (translation of passage on pp. 49–51)

MEMORANDUM presented to Messrs. the Doctors of the SORBONNE

An obstetrical surgeon submits to the Doctors of the Sorbonne that there are cases, although very rare, where a mother cannot give birth, and even where the child is so enclosed in its mother's womb as to be unable to reveal any part of its body, which would be a case, following the Rites, to confer baptism on it, at least conditionally. The surgeon now consulting you aspires by means of a squirt, to baptize the child immediately, without doing any harm to the mother.——He asks if the means he has proposed are permissible and lawful and if they may serve in the case he has stated.

REPLY.

The Council opines that the question put forward labours under great difficulties. The theologians put on the one hand as a principle that baptism, which is a spiritual birth, supposes a preceding birth; one must be born into the world to be reborn in Jesus Christ, as they teach. St. Thomas, *part 3, question 88, article 11* follows this doctrine as a constant truth; one cannot, says this Holy Doctor, baptize children enclosed in their mothers' wombs, and St. Thomas's opinion is founded on the fact that the children are not born, and cannot be counted among other men; from whence he concludes that they cannot be the object of an external action, in order to receive through the ministry of men, the sacraments necessary to salvation: *Children living in their mothers' wombs have not yet come forth into the light to pass their lives with other men; wherefore they cannot be subjected to human action, that through men's ministry they may receive the sacraments necessary for salvation.* The rites prescribe in practice what theologians have established concerning these same matters, and they all uniformly prohibit the baptism of children enclosed in their mothers' wombs, if they do not reveal some part of their bodies. The concurrence of theologians, and of the rites, which are the rules of the dioceses, appears to constitute an authority which would terminate the present question; however the council conscientiously considering on the one hand that the reasoning of theologians is solely founded on reasons of expediency, and that the prohibition of the rites supposes that one cannot immediately baptize children thus enclosed in their mothers' wombs, which is contrary to the present supposition; and that on the other hand, considering that the same theologians teach that one may risk administering the sacraments that Jesus Christ established as easy but necessary means for men's sanctification; and furthermore considering that children enclosed in their mothers' wombs, should be capable of salvation because they are capable of damnation;—for these considerations, and having regard to what has been stated, according to which a certain means has been assuredly found of baptizing children thus enclosed, without doing any harm to the mother, the Council considers that one may avail oneself of the means proposed, in the confidence it has that God has not left such children without any succour and supposing as is stated, that the means in question is capable of procuring their baptism; however as it would mean in authorizing the proposed practice, changing a universally established rule, the Council considers that the enquirer should address himself to his bishop, and to whomever it falls to judge of the utility, and of the dangers of the means proposed, and how, under the approval of the bishop, the Council considers that it would be necessary to have recourse to the Pope, who has the right of explaining the rules of the church, and to derogate them in a case the law would not provide for, however wise and useful the manner of baptizing under discussion would appear, the Council could not approve it without the concurrence of these two authorities. The enquirer is advised at least to address himself to his bishop, and inform him of the present decision, so that, if the prelate agrees with the reasons on which the undersigned doctors base their arguments, he could be authorized in case of necessity, where it would be too risky to wait to ask and be granted permission to employ the proposed means, so advantageous to the salvation of the child. Moreover the Council, considering that one might make use of the method, nevertheless believes, that if the children concerned, should come into the world, against the expectations of those who had made use of the method, it would be necessary to baptize them *conditionally,* and in this the Council conforms to all the rites which in authorizing the baptism of a child who reveals some part of his body, none the less enjoins and orders the conditional baptism should it happily come into the world.

Deliberated at the Sorbonne, 10 April, 1733.

A. Le Moyne,
L. De Romigny,
De Marcilly.

6. **Vide Deventer. . . . p. 366*: The note first appeared in the second, London, edition, and was Sterne's response to criticism that the memorandum and reply were not genuine.

7. *aucun tort a le pere*: 'By means of a squirt and without doing any harm to the father'; Sterne's French, frequently faulty, was here corrected in the second edition to read '*au père*'.

XXI 1. *Dryden*: The idea occurs in *Of Dramatick Poesie, An Essay* (1668) by the poet John Dryden (1631–1700), but is not original to it.

2. *Addison*: In *The Spectator*, 371, Joseph Addison (1672–1719) argued that 'our English comedy excels that of all other nations in the novelty and variety of its characters' because of the number of 'Whims and Humorists' it contains. He comments on the influence of weather on character in, e.g., *the Spectator*, 83 and 162.

3. *Αχμὴ*: Acme.

4. *DINAH*: Dinah, daughter of Leah and Jacob, was abducted and raped by the Canaanite, Shechem, whom she subsequently married; the story is told in Gen. 34.

5. *Tacitus*: Cornelius Tacitus (*c.*56 AD–*c.*120 AD), Roman orator and historian, and exponent of a literary style admired for its compactness but at times criticized as elliptical.

6. *horn-work*: Terms from the science of fortification are annotated, here and subsequently, only when they do not appear in the *Concise Oxford Dictionary*. In *Tristram Shandy*, uncle Toby's use of such terms is partly intended to baffle the reader as it baffles other characters. Sterne's own knowledge of fortification derived almost exclusively from Chambers's *Cyclopaedia*. A horn-work is a

single-fronted outwork, the head of which consists of two demi-bastions connected by a curtain and joined to the main body of the work by two parallel wings. It is thrown out to occupy advantageous ground which it would have been inconvenient to include in the original enceinte (*OED*). A demi-bastion is a work in the form of half a bastion—a bastion being an irregular pentagon with its base in the line of the main works.

7. *Namur*: Strategically situated at the confluence of the Sambre and Meuse, to the south-east of Brussels, Namur was twice besieged in the 1690s; by the French in 1692 and again in 1695 by allied troops under William III. It was during the latter action that uncle Toby was wounded. The allied attackers finally took the citadel but at great cost and without gaining a decisive military advantage.

8. *Copernicus*: The retrogradation, or apparent retrogressive movement, of the planets was attributed by Nicolaus Copernicus (1473–1543) to the earth's daily rotation on its axis and annual revolution around the sun, in his *De hypothesibus motuum coelestium a se constitutis commentariolus*, a manuscript containing the earliest formulation of his belief in a heliocentric universe.

9. *sed magis amica veritas*: 'Plato is my friend but truth is a greater friend.'

10. *in Foro Scientiæ*: In the forum of knowledge.

11. *Lillabullero*: A song written in 1687, possibly by Thomas Wharton (1648–1715), later Marquess of Wharton, and intended to reflect discreditably on the Irish administration of Richard Talbot (1630–91), Earl of Tyrconnell, and Irish Viceroy under the Roman Catholic James II. The music had first appeared in 1686, and text and music were published in 1688, but the song's anti-Jacobite sentiments brought reprintings of *Lillabullero* in 1745, during the Jacobite Rebellion led by Prince Charles Edward Stuart, at a time when Sterne was himself engaged in writing anti-Jacobite journalism.

12. *Argumentum ad Verecundiam*: Argument to modesty.

13. *ex Absurdo*: Argument from absurdity.

14. *ex Fortiori*: Argument from an accepted conclusion to an even more evident one.

15. *Ars Logica*: Art of Logic.

16. *Argumentum Fistulatorium*: Argument of a player of the reed-pipe; unlike the previous terms of logic, this is Sterne's invention.

17. *Argumentum Baculinum*: Literally, argument of a staff, an argument depending on the threat of force.

18. *Argumentum ad Crumenam*: Argument to the purse; a *crumena* was a leather money-pouch worn around the neck.

19. *Argumentum Tripodium*: Argument to the third leg; another of Sterne's inventions.

20. *Argumentum ad Rem*: Argument addressed to the thing; an orthodox term of logic but here used punningly by Sterne.

XXII 1. *Bishop Hall*: Joseph Hall (1574–1656), cleric and moral philosopher, was made Bishop of Exeter in 1627 and of Norwich in 1641. Renowned as a satirist, he was a favourite author of Sterne who plagiarized his sermons, paraphrased him in *A Sentimental Journey*, and argued against him in *Tristram Shandy*. John Beal was a printer working in Aldersgate Street (occasionally Aldergate Street on contemporary title-pages) but just as the quotation does not appear in the *Decads*, so the edition to which Sterne refers has not been traced and may never have existed.

2. *like a bridegroom*: Ps. 19: 5.

XXIII 1. *Momus's glass*: Lucian of Samosata (b. *c.* AD 120) tells the story that when Hephaistos, the divine smith, made man, the god Momus blamed him for not putting a window in his breast; for his criticisms Momus was banished from heaven (*Hermotimus, or The Rival Philosophies*).

2. *window-money*: The tax on windows, a favourite eighteenth-century fiscal measure, had last been increased in 1758.

3. *dioptrical bee-hive*: Beehive with glass windows on opposite sides.

4. *Virgil*: In his *Aeneid* (iv. 173 ff.) Publius Vergilius Maro, Virgil (70–19 BC) describes how Rumour carries through the world the news of Dido's passion for Aeneas.

5. *Italians*: Probably a reference to the *castrati* who still enjoyed an eminent position among performers of vocal music in England.

6. *ad populum*: To the populace.

7. *Non-Naturals*: The six things necessary to health but liable, by abuse or accident, to become the cause of disease—air, meat and drink, sleep and waking, motion and rest, excretion and retention, the affections of the mind (for Sterne's interest in the Non-Naturals, see n. 1 to II.ix below).

8. *Camera*: Camera obscura, or chamber.

XXIV 1. *Philosopher*: To provide the falsity of the argument, attributed to Zeno of Elea (*fl.* early 5th *c.* BC), denying the existence of motion, Diogenes the Cynic (*c.*400 BC–*c.*325 BC) is supposed to have stood up and walked.

XXV 1. *oss pubis*: The pubic bone.

2. *coxendix*: Hip.

3. *oss illeum*: The iliac or flank bone.

VOLUME II

I 1. *King William's wars*: William III was continually engaged in a European war from 1691 to 1697. One of Sterne's principal sources of information about this period, and the siege of Namur in particu-

lar—so important to the chronology of *Tristram Shandy*, as well as to
uncle Toby—was Paul de Rapin de Thoyras, *The History of England*,
translated and continued Nicholas Tindal (3rd edn. 1743–7). Some of
the events had undoubtedly been familiar to him since boyhood,
however, since a relative who entertained the Sterne family in Co.
Westmeath in 1722–3, Brigadier-General Robert Stearne, had fought
with the Royal Regiment of Foot in Ireland, and had been present at
the siege of Namur, which he described as 'undoubtedly yᵉ Most
desperate that had been made in yᵉ Memory of man' (NLI MS 4166).

2. *counter-guard*: A narrow detached rampart, placed immediately
in front of an important work, to prevent its being breached.

3. *covered way*: Covert way, a way made in the counterscarp.

4. *half-moon*: Demilune, an outwork resembling a bastion with a
crescent-shaped gorge, constructed to protect a bastion and curtain.

5. *Hippocrates*: Hippocrates (c.460–c.377 BC), generally regarded as
the father of medicine, though little is known of his life and the
writings ascribed to him are certainly the work of several authors.

6. *Dr. James Mackenzie*: James Mackenzie (?1682–1761), physician
and author of *The History of Health and the Art of Preserving it*
(1758), in which he argues that the effects of fear, grief, and related
passions include the impairment of digestion (II. ii–'Of the Passions
and Affections of the Mind').

7. *toises*: French units of linear measurement, usually military, each
equivalent to 6¾ feet or 1.95 metres.

8. *returning angle*: An angle whose vertex is turned in towards the
centre of the fortification.

9. *salient angle*: An angle whose vertex points away from the centre
of the fortification.

10. *demi-bastion*: See n. 6 to I.xxi.

II 1. *cap and bell*: Traditional insignia of the jester.

2. *Malbranch*: Nicolas Malebranche (1638–1715), French Catholic
theologian and Cartesian philosopher, whose principal work was *De
la recherche de la vérité* ('Of the search for truth') (1674–8).

3. *Arthur's*: London club in St. James's Street, better known as
White's, and famous for heavy gambling.

4. *ink-shed*: Waste of ink.

5. *pudder*: Pother.

6. *οὐσία and ὑπόστασις*: Essence and substance, but in fact the
words are synonymous.

III 1. *Gobesius:* Probably an invention of Sterne's.

2. *Vauban's line*: After organizing the first siege of Namur (see n. 7
to I.xxi), Sébastian Le Prestre de Vauban (1633–1707), the foremost
military engineer of his day, improved the city's defences by rebuild-
ing the citadel.

3. *Ramelli*: The following list of names was taken, and at times

miscopied, by Sterne from the entry 'Fortifications' in Chambers's *Cyclopaedia*. Agostino Ramelli (*c.*1531–*c.*1590) published his *Le Diverse et artificiose machine* in Paris in 1588; Girolamo Cataneo (*fl.* mid-sixteenth century) was author of *Opera nuova di fortificare, offendere et defendere* (1564) and *Nuovo ragionamento del fabricare le fortezze* (1567); Simon Stevin or Stevinus (1548–1620) was a mathematician and author of the *Nouvelle Manière de Fortification*, published in Dutch in 1586 and translated into French in 1618; Samuel Marolois (?1572–?1627) was author of *Artis Muniendi*, translated into English as *The Art of Fortification, or architecture militaire as well offensive as defensive* (1638); Antoine Deville (1596–1656), a mathematician, published the *Fortifications d'Antoine Deville* (1629); Buonaiuto Lorini (?1540–?1611), a Florentine military engineer employed by the Venetian Republic, was the author of *Delle fortificationi* (1596); Baron Menno van Coehoorn (1641–1704), called the Dutch Vauban, after the French engineer against whom he vainly defended the citadel at Namur he had largely constructed, and which he retook in the second siege of the city, was author of a work on fortification (1685) translated into English in 1705; Johann Bernhard von Scheither (*fl.* seventeenth century) wrote the *Novissima Praxis Militaris* (1672); Blaise-François, comte de Pagan (1604–65), drew on his personal experience of numerous sieges to point to defects in existing systems of fortification, especially that of Deville, and to propose his own in the *Traité des fortifications* (1645); François Blondel (1618–86), tutor to the son of Louis XIV and author of several books on civil architecture, published his *Nouvelle Manière de fortifier les places* in 1684.

4. *invaded his library*: Don Quixote had 'above a hundred large Volumes neatly bound, and a good Number of small ones' (*Don Quixote*, I. i. 6).

5. *N. Tartaglia*: Niccolò Tartaglia (1500–57) was a geometrician whose *Quesiti ed invenzioni diverse* (1550) contained, in its later editions, a supplement on the art of fortification, including a section on the trajectory of missiles.

6. *Maltus*: Francis Malthus (d. 1658) was best known for his *Pratique de la guerre, contenant l'usage de l'artillerie, bombes & mortiers* (1650).

7. *Gallileo*: Galileo Galilei (1564–1642), astronomer and physicist, was also a mathematician who gave the law of parabolic fall—that a projectile follows a parabolic path.

8. *Torricellius*: Evangelista Torricelli (1608–47), a mathematician whose writings include work on the parabola.

9. *latus rectum*: Straight line.

10. *radical moister*: In medieval philosophy, the humour or moisture naturally inherent in all plants and animals, its presence being a necessary condition of their vitality.

IV 1. *cum grano salis:* With a grain of salt.

2. *Monsieur Ronjat:* Étienne (or Stephen) Ronjat (1657–1737), serjeant-surgeon to William III; Ronjat in fact only became serjeant-surgeon in 1701.

V 1. *incarnate:* To heal over.

2. *'Change:* The Royal Exchange, centre of England's commercial life.

3. *demigration:* Migration.

4. *Landen:* The Battle of Landen, or Neerwinden, was fought on 29 July 1693, and marked a significant allied defeat.

5. *broke no squares with 'em:* Made no mischief between them; an appropriately military metaphor based on the square formations employed by eighteenth-century infantry.

6. *Such was Corporal Trim:* Trim, properly James Butler, takes his more familiar name from the proverb 'Trim, *tram, like* master like man' (see John Ray, *A Compleat Collection of English Proverbs* (1737)), based on the 'similitude of their knowledge' that endears the 'man' to his 'master', uncle Toby. Sterne had used the name 'Trim' for the village Sexton and Dog-Whipper, a recognizable version of the church lawyer Dr. Francis Topham (see n. 2 to I.VII) in his satire on York ecclesiastical politics, *A Political Romance* (1759); here the grasping 'man', Topham, was all too similar to his 'master', the Archbishop of York, who took such offence at this characterization and those of other York Minster dignitaries that he ordered the whole edition of *A Political Romance* to be destroyed—though a very few copies survived the flames.

7. *fossé:* A ditch designed as a barrier against an advancing enemy.

8. *campaign:* Champaign, open country.

9. *something like a tansy:* Perfectly.

10. *epitasis:* The part of the play where the plot thickens.

VI 1. *Aposiopesis:* Rhetorical device in which the speaker stops suddenly as though unable or unwilling to go on.

2. *the Poco piu and the Poco meno:* (Ital.) the 'little more' and the 'little less', musical terms, the former used by Hogarth, see n. 3 below.

3. *the line of beauty in the sentence:* In the phrase 'line of beauty', Sterne applies to writing the idea of the 'serpentine line' that William Hogarth, in *The Analysis of Beauty* (1753), maintained to contain the essence of beauty; see n. 1 to II.XVII below.

VII 1. *the demolition of Dunkirk:* The demolition of the Dunkirk fortifications was a condition of the Treaty of Utrecht (see below, n. 3 to VI.xxx); it was partly effected in 1713. The present instance (see also e.g. p. 164) is a further indication of the importance of uncle Toby's military campaign as a unifying and elucidating time-scheme in the novel (see n. 1 to II.1 above).

2. *Aristotle's Master-Piece*: The quotation Sterne paraphrases is not from *Aristotle's Masterpiece: or, the Secrets of Generation Displayed* (1684)—a handbook on sex and pregnancy frequently reprinted in the late seventeenth and eighteenth centuries—but from *Aristotle's Book of Problems, with other Astronomers, Astrologers, Physicians and Philosophers* (1710), 'On the Head'; neither book, often bound together, is in fact by Aristotle.

VIII 1. *rung the bell*: Once regarded as a rare mistake in *Tristram Shandy*'s complex time-scheme, the passage of time that has elapsed since uncle Toby rang the bell is defended by John Sutherland in 'Slop Slip', in *The Literary Detective: 100 Puzzles in Classic Fiction* (Oxford: Oxford University Press, 2000), 271–6.

2. *duration and of its simple modes*: In the *Essay Concerning Human Understanding*, II xiv, 'Of duration and its simple modes', Locke speaks of the simple modes of duration as those 'whereof we have distinct *ideas*, as *hours, days, years*, etc., *time* and *eternity*'.

IX 1. *uncourtly figure of a Doctor Slop*: Dr. Slop is a caricature of the York man-midwife and suspected Jacobite Dr. John Burton (1710–71), whose Tory politics the Whig Sterne intensely disliked. Author of *Treatise of the Non-Naturals* (1738), to which Sterne had earlier alluded (see n. 7 to I.XXIII), Burton later wrote *An Essay towards a Complete New System of Midwifry* (1751), to which Sterne makes several references in the course of *Tristram Shandy*. If not distinguished, Burton was a much more competent obstetrician than Sterne would imply and was neither the 'little, squat, uncourtly figure' depicted, nor even, despite his alleged (and probable) Jacobitism, a Roman Catholic.

2. *sesquipedality*: Literally, being 'a foot and a half' long; here, great breadth.

3. *Hogarth's analysis of beauty*: Hogarth published *The Analysis of Beauty. Written with a view of fixing the fluctuating Ideas of Taste* in 1753 (see n. 3 to II.VI above). Returning the compliment, as the author had perhaps hoped, he presented Sterne with a drawing of the sermon-reading scene (II.XVII) which, engraved by Simon François Ravenet, appeared as frontispiece to the second edition of *Tristram Shandy* (see above, n. to I. frontispiece).

4. *Whiston's comets*: William Whiston (1667–1752), cleric and Isaac Newton's successor as Professor of Mathematics at Cambridge University, argued in his *New Theory of the Earth* (1696) that the Great Flood was caused by a comet colliding with the earth; after his Arianism caused him to lose his university appointment in 1710, he supported himself in part by lecturing on comets and other natural phenomena which he saw as fulfilments of biblical prophecies.

5. *beluted*: Covered with mud.

X   1. *unwiped, unappointed, unanealed*: 'Unanealed' is not having received extreme unction. Sterne here recalls the line 'Unhous'led, disappointed, unanel'd' spoken by the Ghost in *Hamlet*, I. v. 77, almost certainly—as a recent editor, Robert Folkenflik, has noticed—via Lewis Theobald's 1731 edition of Shakespeare, which has the reading 'unhousel'd, unappointed, unaneal'd'.

2. *majesty of mud*: Dr. Slop is compared to one of the contestants in the mud-diving competition in Alexander Pope's *The Dunciad* (1744), ii, l. 326.

3. *mental reservation*: A speaker employs a mental reservation if his statement is true only when qualified by an unspoken restrictive clause. A difference between Roman Catholic and Protestant concepts of falsehood led to mental reservations being associated with Catholics (like Dr. Slop).

XI   1. *Lucina*: A minor Roman deity, attendant on women, who makes the child see the light.

2. *Pilumnus!*: Pilumnus, or Picumnus, was one of three Roman deities who kept off the shadowy god Silvanus after childbirth, a task Pilumnus performed by pounding with a pestle.

3. *tire-tête*: The following list of new or recently popularized instruments suggests that Dr. Slop is an interventionist man-midwife; the *tire-tête* (from the French, *tirer*, to draw, and *tête*, head) was the invention of the great French obstetrician François Mauriceau (1637–1709); the *forceps*, developed in the early sixteenth century by the Chamberlen family, who kept them a trade secret, only came into common use in the eighteenth century, when they partly obviated the need, in obstructed deliveries, for wholly destructive implements such as the *crotchet*; for the *squirt* see n. 5 to I.xx above. The deployment of instruments in childbirth was a matter of considerable professional debate in the mid-eighteenth century though, like many of his contemporaries, Dr. John Burton argued against their unnecessary use.

XII   1. *Dennis*: John Dennis (1657–1734), English literary critic, to whom is attributed the remark: 'A man who could make so vile a pun would not scruple to pick a pocket.'

2. *Du Cange*: Charles Du Fresne Du Cange (1610–88), French polymath, best known as a philologist.

3. *epaulments*: Constructions designed as protection from enemy fire.

4. *double tenaille*: A small, low work consisting of two re-entering angles placed before the curtain between two bastions.

5. *Accoucheur*: Obstetrician; Dr. Slop prefers the French term as more dignified for his emergent profession; John Burton, who largely eschewed the term in his *Essay on Midwifry* (1751), used it frequently in his *A Letter to William Smellie, M.D., containing Critical and*

Practical Remarks upon his Treatise on the Theory and Practice of Midwifery (1753).

   6. *blinds*: Blindages, screens used as protection from enemy fire.

   7. *gabions*: Cylindrical wicker baskets, usually open at either end, filled with earth.

   8. *rash humour which my mother gave me*: *Julius Caesar*, IV. iii. 120.

XIV 1. *Brutus and Cassius at the close of the scene*: *Julius Caesar*, IV. ii. 52.

   2. *sailing chariot*: Stevinus (see above, n. 3 to II.III) was the inventor of a winged chariot, reputedly faster than any horse-drawn carriage.

   3. *Prince Maurice*: Maurice of Nassau, Prince of Orange (1567–1625), military and political leader of the Dutch Republic, was Stevinus's patron.

   4. *Peireskius*: Nicolas-Claude Fabri de Peiresc (1580–1637), a humanist of wide scientific and antiquarian interests, also encouraged the studies of the jurist Grotius whose work included verses celebrating Stevinus's chariot.

XV 1. *should have had the next Halberd*: Should have been promoted sergeant.

   2. *nothing doubting*: Acts 11: 12.

XVII 1. *the line of beauty*: Hogarth discussed the precise serpentine line he called the line of beauty, first published as a frontispiece to his engraved works in 1745, in *The Analysis of Beauty*, chapter vi (see n. 3 to II.VI above).

   2. *The SERMON*: The sermon, whose numerous admirers included Voltaire, was preached by Sterne himself on 29 July 1750, as the annual assize sermon in the Minster at York, where it was subsequently published that year. At the very end of the present chapter, Sterne advises his readers: 'in case the character of parson *Yorick*, and this sample of his sermons is liked,—that there are now in the possession of the *Shandy* Family, as many as will make a handsome volume, at the world's service,—and much good may they do it'. As a result of the successful inclusion of 'The Abuses of Conscience' in *Tristram Shandy*, two volumes of *The Sermons of Mr. Yorick* appeared from R. and J. Dodsley in London in May 1760. Sterne also published 'The Abuses of Conscience' again, in the second instalment of *The Sermons of Mr. Yorick* that appeared in January 1766. As it appears here—read aloud by Corporal Trim to Walter Shandy, his brother Toby, and a sleeping Dr. Slop, while preparations are being made for the birth of Tristram upstairs—the sermon reads very differently from its more conventional incarnations, and its very inclusion in the course of a bawdy novel occasioned moral outrage.

   3. *would have an old house over his head*: Would get into trouble.

4. *hardly do we guess aright . . . are before us*: Wisdom 9: 16; the Wise Man is Solomon.

5. *Elijah reproached the God Baal*: For Elijah's challenge to Baal, see 1 Kgs. 18; the verse paraphrased is v. 27.

6. *seven sacraments*: The seven sacraments of the Roman Catholic Church are baptism, eucharist, confirmation, penance, holy orders, marriage, extreme unction. As a good Anglican—i.e. member of the Church of England—uncle Toby admits only the first two.

7. *I pay every man . . . before me*: The passage recalls the parable of the pharisee and the tax collector, Luke 18: 9–14, esp. v. 11.

8. *bubble*: Cheat.

9. *David surprized Saul*: 1 Sam. 24: 4.

10. *Uriah*: The story of David and Uriah is told in 2 Sam. 11, and the rebuke of David by Nathan in 2 Sam. 12.

11. *thou wilt have confidence towards God*: 1 John 3: 21.

12. *Blessed is the man*: What follows is a loose paraphrase of Ecclesiasticus 14: 1–2 and 13: 25–6.

13. *Corps de Garde*: A small body of men acting as sentinels.

14. *cuvette*: Cunette; a trench sunk along the middle of a dry ditch or moat, serving as a drain and as an obstacle to the passage of the enemy.

15. *tables*: In Exod. 32: 19, Moses breaks the table of stone he has received from God on Mount Sinai.

16. *tricker*: Trigger.

17. *By their fruits ye shall know them*: Matt. 7: 20.

XVIII 1. *en Soveraines*: As sovereigns.

XIX 1. *the lean and slipper'd pantaloon in his second childishness*: Sterne conflates the sixth and seventh ages of man as described by Jaques in *As You Like It*, II. vii, 157–66.

2. *in infinitum*: Into infinite parts.

3. *Zeno and Chrysippus*: Zeno of Citium (*c*.335–263 BC) was founder of the Stoic school of philosophy; Chrysippus (*c*.280–207 BC) was successor to Cleanthes (see below, n. 3 to III.IV) as head of the Stoa.

4. *Des Cartes*: René Descartes (1596–1650), in the *Treatise on the Passions* (1649), considered the interaction of body and soul; the centre of interaction, he suggested, was the pineal gland.

5. *Coglionissimo Borri*: Giuseppe Francesco Borri, or Borro (1627–95), a celebrated alchemist and physician. 'Coglionissimo' is Sterne's coinage from the Italian 'coglioni' or testicles.

6. *Bartholine*: Thomas Bartholin (1616–80), a Danish anatomist.

7. *Metheglingius*: An invention of Sterne's from 'metheglinist', a maker of metheglin, a medicated or spiced mead—though perhaps Sterne once more had in mind Dr. Richard Mead (see n. 4 to I.VII).

8. *Animus*: The spiritual or rational soul; *anima* is the physical soul.

9. *Causa sine quâ non*: Indispensable cause.

10. *The author is here . . . great similitude of the names*: Sterne is again satirizing Dr. John Burton by reference to the latter's attack on Dr. William Smellie (Adrianus Smelvogt) whom he accused of having mistaken the title of a drawing of a petrified child for the name of an author. The attack occurs in Burton's *A Letter to William Smellie, M.D.*: 'A Catalogue of Several Authors omitted by Smellie' (the authors including Johann Adrian Slevogt, or Slevogtius, author of a work that discussed complications in childbirth: 'De Partu Difficili').

11. *mothery*: Feculent or mouldy.

12. *oss coxcygis*: Os coccygis, the small bone at the end of the spinal column.

13. *Julius Cæsar*: Sterne took this, and subsequent names, except Hermes Trismegistus, from the article 'Caesarian section' in Chambers's *Cyclopaedia*. Julius Caesar (100–44 BC) was almost certainly not born by section; Scipio Africanus (236–184/3 BC) was reputedly so born, as was Titus Manlius Torquatus (d. 203 BC); Edward VI (1537–53) was the son of Jane Seymour, who died twelve days after his birth.

14. *This incision . . . no purpose to propose*: Elizabeth Shandy might well have turned pale at the idea of undergoing a Caesarean section without anaesthetic but Sterne is once more satirizing John Burton, a rare example of a contemporary obstetrician not wholly opposed to section, and who mentions some eighteenth-century Irish examples of Caesarean births where both mother and child survived; see Burton, *An Essay towards a Complete New System of Midwifry* (1751), 266–72.

15. *Don Belianis of Greece*: The romance *The History of Don Belianis* first appeared in English in 1598.

16. *the next year*: Volumes III and IV of *Tristram Shandy* appeared in London on 28 January 1761.

VOLUME III

title page 1. *Multitudinis . . . jocos transire*: Sterne most likely took his motto, the conclusion of which he elaborated, from the final book of the *Policraticus* (1159) of John of Salisbury (1115/20–1180), Bishop of Chartres, via the preface to Rabelais by Peter Motteux (see n. 2 to III.xix below); it reads: 'I do not dread the judgements of the ignorant multitude; I ask, however, that they spare my little works in which it was always the design to pass in turn from jests to serious matters and from serious matters to jests.'

i 1. **Vid. Vol. II. p. 159*: In this edition p. 115.

ii 1. *India handkerchief*: India silk.

2. *Reynolds*: Sir Joshua Reynolds (1723–92), the greatest portrait artist of his day, painted Sterne three times; the most famous portrait was the first, done in 1760, an engraving of which appeared as frontispiece to the two volumes of *The Sermons of Mr. Yorick* published by Robert and James Dodsley in May 1760; it was followed by works done in 1764, and again in 1768, this last remaining unfinished at Sterne's death.

III 1. *as lean a subject as myself*: A further joke at Sterne's own expense (see n. 5 to I.x above). Though not the skeleton of later caricatures, Sterne was tall and thin, describing himself as 'tolerably strait made, and near six feet high'.

IV 1. *gum-taffeta*: Stiffened with gum.
   2. *persian*: Soft Persian silk.
   3. *Zeno*: In the passage that follows, Sterne alludes to the Stoic's endeavour to live in harmony with reason and consequent profession of indifference to change of fortune, pain, and death. For Zeno, see above, n. 3 to II.xix; Cleanthes of Assos (*c.*331–*c.*232 BC) succeeded Zeno as head of the Stoic school in 263; Diogenes of Babylon (*c.*240–152 BC) succeeded Zeno of Tarsus as head of the Stoic school; Dionysius of Heracleia (*c.*328–248 BC), a pupil of Zeno, who later abandoned Stoicism; Antipater of Tarsus (second century BC) was a pupil and successor of Diogenes of Babylon as head of the school at Athens; Panaetius (*c.*185–109 BC) succeeded Antipater as head of the Stoa; Posidonius (*c.*135–*c.*51/50 BC) was largely responsible for the emphasis on moral and religious elements within Stoic doctrine characteristic of the school at Rome, where he settled.
   4. *Cato*: Marcus Porcius Cato of Utica (95–46 BC), the statesman, was an adherent of Stoicism and was looked to as an example by later Roman Stoics; Marcus Terentius Varro (116–27 BC), prolific author, educated in Stoicism in Athens; Lucius Annaeus Seneca (4 BC–AD 65), the tragedian, was author of a number of works of Stoic philosophy.
   5. *Pantenus*: Pantenus (*fl. c.* AD 200), a Sicilian who settled in Alexandria and moved from Stoicism to Christianity; Titus Flavius Clemens (*c.*150–211/16), disciple of Pantenus and his successor as head of the Catechetical School at Alexandria; Montaigne (see above, n. 2 to I.iv) moved from a belief in Stoicism to an attack on it in the *Essays*.
   6. *You Messrs. the monthly Reviewers*: In 1760, in the wake of the enormous success of the first two volumes of *Tristram Shandy*, Sterne published a volume of his sermons under the title *The Sermons of Mr. Yorick* (see n. 2 to II.xvii). The *Monthly Review* for May 1760 praised the work but commented adversely on the method of publication: 'Must obscenity then be the handmaid to Religion—and must the exordium to a sermon, be a smutty tale?'

v 1. *Avison Scarlatti*: A collection of twelve *concerti grossi* published in 1744 by Charles Avison (bap. 1710–70) and arranged by him for strings from keyboard sonatas of Domenico Scarlatti (1685–1757).

2. *con furia*: Furiously; Sterne makes specific reference to the sixth concerto, one of whose movements is marked '*con furia*'.

3. *con strepito*: Noisily; the term is not Scarlatti's.

vi 1. *cornish*: Cornice.

vii 1. *Hymen*: Classical god of marriage.

x 1. *the duke of Monmouth's affair*: In 1685, the Duke of Monmouth, illegitimate son of Charles II, led a rebellion against his father's brother and successor James II; like many of his followers, he was subsequently tried and executed. Tristram's great-uncle Hammond may have been named for Thomas Hammond (c.1600–58), a parliamentarian army officer and one of those responsible for the execution of Charles I in 1649.

2. *ERNULPHUS*: Ernulf or Arnulf (1040–1124), French-born Bishop of Rochester.

3. *As the genuineness . . . of Rochester*: The text of the excommunication was given by Thomas Hearne (1678–1735) in his *Textus Roffensis* (1720), 35. An English translation of the curse appeared in the *Gentleman's Magazine* in 1745 and, during the Jacobite Rebellion of 1745–6, was also printed separately and sold in York for 3d., with the direction that it was 'fit to be framed and hung up in all Protestant Families' (*York Courant*, 19 Nov. 1745); the same number of the *Courant* offers a version of Lillabullero (see above, n. 11 to I.xxi).

xi 1. *Dathan and Abiram*: Together with Korah, and all their families, Dathan and Abiram were killed by an earthquake for their revolt against Moses and Aaron (Num. 16: 1–35).

2. *Varro*: It was not Varro (see above, n. 4 to III.iv) but Hesiod (*fl.* ?700 BC) who reckoned up 30,000 gods; Varro reckoned up 300 Jupiters. Sterne miscopied his source which here, as so often subsequently, was the *Anatomy of Melancholy* (1621; 6th ed. 1651) of Robert Burton (1577–1640); the present passage derives from Burton 3.4.1.3.

3. *Cid Hamet*: Cid Hamet Benengeli, supposed Arabic historian and alleged source of the history of Don Quixote (*Don Quixote*, 1. ii. 1).

xii 1. *Garrick*: The greatest English actor of his day, David Garrick (1717–79) was also an influential arbiter of London's literary taste. When the first volumes of *Tristram Shandy* appeared, Sterne composed a letter describing their success in York that his friend Catherine Fourmantel (see above, n. 2 to I.xviii) copied and sent to Garrick as her own. Garrick subsequently took up *Tristram Shandy* and a friendship developed between him and Sterne that ended only with the latter's death.

2. *Bossu's*: René Le Bossu (1631–80), author of the *Traité du poème épique* (1675), an influential work of neo-classical criticism whose reputation had undergone a considerable decline in England by the 1760s.

3. *Titian*: The qualities attributed to the following artists were those for which each was most conventionally celebrated in mid-eighteenth-century England, except *corregiescity*, which is Sterne's own coinage; Sterne was drawing on Sir Joshua Reynolds's essay on criticism and connoisseurship in *The Idler*, 61, where such terminology is dismissed as 'the cant of criticism'. *Titian*—Tiziano Vecellio (c.1485–1576); *Rubens*—Peter Paul Rubens (1577–1640); *Raphael*—Raffaello Sanzio (1483–1520); *Dominichino*—Domenico Zampieri, Domenichino (1581–1641); *Corregio*—Antonio Allegri, Correggio (c.1494–1534); *Poussin*—Nicolas Poussin (1594–1665); *Guido*—Guido Reni (1575–1642); *the Carrachi's*— Agostino (1557–1602), Annibale (1560–1609), and Lodovico (1555–1619) Carracci, the first two being brothers and the third their cousin; *Angelo*—Michelangelo Buonarroti (1475–1564).

4. *Apollo*: The most Greek of all the gods, often, though probably wrongly, identified with the sun.

5. *Mercury*: Roman god of traders but often indiscriminately identified with the Greek Hermes, messenger to the gods.

6. *Justinian*: Flavius Petrus Sabbatius Justinianus (AD c.482–565) became emperor in 527 and in 528 appointed a commission to codify all valid imperial constitutions from Hadrian onwards; the first *Codex Justinianus* was issued in 529.

7. *Tribonian*: Tribonianus (d. AD 542/5) was a member of the commission for the first *Codex* and director of the work of the second, and of the *Digesta*, a collection of passages from classical jurists.

XIII 1. *Lisle*: Lille was captured by the Duke of Marlborough (see below, n. 1 to VI.XXI) in December 1708, but the subsequent reference is confused for the terrible winter that brought food shortages throughout Europe was that of 1708–9 not 1710.

XIV 1. *Tully's second Philippick*: The philippics were orations delivered by Cicero (see above, n. 2 to I.II) against Mark Antony, between 44 and 43 BC, after the death of Julius Caesar; the second is the longest.

2. *BAMBINO*: Child.

XVI 1. *granado*: Grenade.

XVIII 1. *pantoufles*: Slippers.

2. **Vid. Locke*: The substance of the passage derives from the *Essay Concerning Human Understanding*, II. xiv. 3.

3. *a clock in the kingdom*: An allusion to an anonymous one-shilling pamphlet, *The Clockmakers Outcry against the Author of The Life and Opinions of Tristram Shandy*, whose mock-serious attack on Sterne appeared in London in 1760.

4. *smoak-jack*: Smoke-jack; machine for turning roasting-spit by use of current of hot air in a chimney.

XIX   1. *Lucian*: Lucian (see n. 1 to I.xxIII) was best known for his works in dialogue form, influenced by Menippean humour, the Mime, and Attic comedy, of which Sterne is thinking here.

2. *Rabelais*: François Rabelais (?1483–1553), Franciscan priest, physician, and humanist, one of whose works was a (now lost) Latin translation of a dialogue of Lucian. He is best known for his *Gargantua and Pantagruel* (1532–64), from which Sterne frequently quotes, using the translation of Sir Thomas Urquhart, completed by Peter Motteux (and to which subsequent references are made).

3. *Cervantes*: Miguel de Cervantes Saavedra (1547–1616), author of *Don Quixote* (1605–15), one of the greatest literary influences on Sterne, who elsewhere refers to him as 'my beloved CERVANTES' (IX.xxIV 'THE INVOCATION'); see also n. 1 to I.x above.

4. *Ontologic treasury*: Ontology is the department of metaphysics relating to the being or essence of things.

XX   1. *Messina*: Messina was successfully besieged by the allies in 1719, during the War of the Quadruple Alliance (1718–20), which saw Britain, France, Austria, and the Dutch thwart Spanish ambitions in Italy.

2. *Agelastes*: 'One who is grave or gloomy'; Triptolemus was a judge in Greek mythology; Phutatorius derives from the Latin and means 'Copulator'.

3. *de fartandi et illustrandi fallaciis*: 'Of the deceptions of farting and of explaining', or possibly, though less correctly, 'Of farting and the explaining of deceptions'.

4. *thrice able critics*: Sterne's dedication of his preface parodies the opening of the 'Author's Preface' in *Gargantua and Pantagruel.*

5. *Monopolos*: Monopolos, 'Monopolist'; Kysarcius, 'Arsekisser', perhaps after Rabelais's Baise-cul (*Gargantua and Pantagruel*, II, x); Gastripheres is Sterne's coinage from the Greek, meaning 'One who carries a belly'; Somnolentius, 'One who is sleepy or drowsy'.

6. *Nova Zembla*: Nova Zemlya, two large islands in the Arctic Ocean off NE Russia.

7. *judgment*: The distinction between judgement and wit is discussed by Locke in his *Essay Concerning Human Understanding*, II. xi: 'Of Discerning, and other operations of the mind'.

8. *Angels and ministers of grace defend us!*: *Hamlet*, I. iv. 39.

9. *Swedeland*: Sweden.

10. *Angermania*: Angermanland, formerly a province of eastern Sweden, on the Gulf of Bothnia.

11. *Carelia*: Karelia, eastern region of Finland, ceded by Sweden to Russia in 1721.

12. *Petersbourg*: St. Petersburg, on the Karelian isthmus; founded in 1703, capital of Russia 1712–1917.

13. *Ingria*: Ingermanland, at the SE end of the Gulf of Finland; it includes St. Petersburg.

14. *Tartary*: Region of Central Asia, spreading eastwards from the Caspian Sea, inhabited by the Tatars.

15. *Suidas*: Hellenized form of the Suda, which Sterne uses for the author of the important encyclopedic lexicon compiled around AD 1000, but which more properly refers to the work itself.

16. *kennels*: Gutters.

17. *Esculapius*: Aesculapius, latinized form of Asclepius, the Greek god of healing.

18: *John o'Nokes ... Tom o'Stiles*: Fictitious names commonly used in law proceedings.

19. *centumvirate*: A hundred.

20. *'for what hinderance ... cane chair'*: Except for the last phrase, a quotation from *Gargantua and Pantagruel*, III. xvi.

XXII 1. *Marston-Moor*: Battle fought near York on 2 July 1644 during the English Civil War; it followed the siege of York by the parliamentary army and marked the first major defeat of the Royalist forces.

XXIII 1. *retrograde planet*: See above, n. 8 to I.xxi; one of the celestial movements to which astrology imputed particular significance.

XXIV 1. *Dunkirk*: See above, n. 1 to II.vii.

2. *opificers*: Makers.

3. *Aristotle*: Aristotle (see above, n. 10 to I.xix) is cited here as author of the *Poetics*, his major work of literary criticism.

4. *Pacuvius*: Marcus Pacuvius (220–c.130 BC), at one time considered the greatest Roman tragedian.

5. *Bossu*: See above, n. 2 to III.xii.

6. *Ricaboni*: Luigi Riccoboni (1675–1753), actor, dramatist and author of the *Histoire du théâtre italien* (1728–31), or perhaps his son Francesco Antonio (1707–72), author of *L'Art du Théâtre* (1750).

7. *Pompadour's vis a vis*: Jeanne Antoinette Poisson, marquise de Pompadour (1721–64), was mistress to Louis XV of France; a *vis à vis* was a light carriage for two, from the French 'face to face'.

8. *Mrs. Bridget*: It was still common in the eighteenth century for unmarried women to be called 'Mrs' or 'Mistress'.

9. *soss*: Heavily, with a dull thud.

10. *VINEA*: Shed for protecting besiegers.

11. *Tyre*: Tyre was besieged for seven months in 332 BC by Alexander the Great.

12. *BALLISTA*: Engine for hurling missiles.

13. *Marcellinus*: Ammianus Marcellinus (AD c.330–395), a Greek-educated Roman soldier and historian whose Latin work is a continuation of Tacitus, covering the years AD 96–378.

XXV 1. *Alberoni's*: Giulio Alberoni (1664–1752), Italian-born cleric and statesman who became *de facto* prime minister of Spain in 1716. He was not in fact personally responsible for the military expeditions to Sardinia (1717) and Sicily (1718) whose lack of success led to his banishment from Spain by Philip V in 1719 (see n. 1 to III.xx above).

2. *Spires*: Now Speyer, in SW Germany; destroyed by French troops in 1689.

3. *Brisac*: Now Breisach am Rhein, on the right bank of the Rhine.

4. *marquis d'Hôpital's*: The contributions of Guillaume François Antonine, marquis de l'Hôpital (1661–1704), and Jacques Bernoulli (1654–1705), a Swiss mathematician, to the *Acta Eruditorum* of Leipzig (Lipsia) are mentioned in the entry on bridges in Chambers's *Cyclopaedia*, from which Sterne's information derives.

XXVI 1. *Savoyard's box*: A peep-show, carried by itinerant Savoyard showmen.

XXIX 1. *hit the longitude*: The determination of longitude at sea was a vexed problem for most of the eighteenth century; see also below, n. 5 to VIII.xxxiii.

XXX 1. '*ALL* is not . . . purse.': A proverbial expression.

XXXI 1. *the fifty-second page of the second volume*: In the first edition; here on p. 82.

XXXII 1. *Pantagruel*: The gigantic son of the giant Gargantua.

2. *ENNASIN*: An island visited by Pantagruel whose inhabitants have noses shaped like the ace of clubs; *Gargantua and Pantagruel*, IV. ix.

XXXIII 1. *cawl*: Caul, the netted substructure of a wig.

XXXIV 1. *renitency*: Reluctance.

2. *ex confesso*: Beyond doubt.

3. *Tribonius*: An error for Tribonianus; see above, n. 7 to III.xii.

4. *Gregorius*: Supposed author of the *Codex Gregorianus* (AD c.291) of which only fragments remain; Hermogenes or Hermogenian was the supposed author of *Hermogenianus* (AD c.293–4), a supplementary code.

5. *Louis*: Louis XIV; Des Eaux is not an author but the abbreviated title of Louis XIV's ordinance of 1669, 'des eaux et forêts', 'of waters and forests'. Sterne's mistake arose from his misreading of the entry 'Code' in Chambers's *Cyclopaedia*, the source of all the preceding.

6. *exsudations*: Oozings, in the manner of sweat.

XXXV 1. *Bruscambille*: Theatrical name of the author and comic actor Jean Deslauriers (*fl.* 1610–34) who was active in Paris under Henri IV and Louis XIII; he was the author of *Prologues tant sérieux que facétieux* (1610), *Les Fantaisies* (1612), and *Les Nouvelles et plaisantes imaginations* (1613).

2. *Prignitz*: Imaginary authority, perhaps suggested by Prignitz, an area of Brandenburg in NE Germany; *Scroderus* is also imaginary.

3. *Andrea Paræus*: Ambroise Paré (*c.*1510–1590), distinguished French physician, often considered the father of modern surgery and, particularly, of military medicine.

4. *Bouchet's Evening Conferences*: *Les Sérées* (1584) by Guillaume Bouchet, sieur de Brocourt (1513–94), a series of evening conversations on a wide range of everyday topics, giving a vivid glimpse of sixteenth-century French provincial life.

5. *Hafen Slawkenbergius*: The name is Sterne's invention, from the German *hafen*, pot, and *schlackenberg*, mountain of clinker or excrement.

XXXVI 1. *Erasmus*: Desiderius Erasmus (?1466/9–1536), the Dutch humanist, is cited here as author of the *Colloquia Familiaria* (1518); *Pamphagus* and *Cocles* are the speakers in the colloquy 'De Captandis Sacerdotis'.

2. *Tickletoby's mare*: 'The filly of the convent—so they called a young mare that was never leaped yet' was ridden by Friar Stephen Tickletoby in *Gargantua and Pantagruel*, IV. xiii. Tickletoby is Urquhart's translation of Rabelais's *Tappecue*, implying a penis.

3. *ab urb. con.*: i.e. *ab urbe condita*, from the founding of the city, referring to the founding of Rome in 753 BC, the means of dating used by the Romans.

4. *the second Punic war*: The war began in 218 BC.

5. *Paraleipomenon*: Paralipomenon, a list of things omitted in the body of a work, and appended as a supplement.

6. *marbled page*: The reader could not 'penetrate the moral' of the marbled page since neither Sterne nor the printer could retain absolute control over the coloured marbling process, making copies impossible, and so ensuring that every marbled leaf would be unique; this feature of Sterne's book cannot be reproduced in modern editions, even those that print a coloured reproduction of a marbled leaf. See W. G. Day, 'Tristram Shandy: The Marbled Leaf', *The Library*, 27 (1972), 143–5, and Diana Patterson, 'Tristram's Marblings and Marblers', *The Shandean*, 3 (1991), 70–97.

XXXVII 1. '*Nihil me pœnitet hujus nasi,*': This nose does not displease me.

2. '*Nec est cur pœniteat,*': Nor is there any reason why it should displease you.

XXXVIII 1. *Disgrázias*: Misfortunes.

2. *Whitfield's*: George Whitefield (1714–70), noted preacher and leader of the Calvinistic wing of Methodism, controversially argued in his writings—e.g. *The Full Account of the Life and Dealings with God of the Reverend Mr George Whitefield* (1747)—that the soul could know intuitively whether it was motivated by the Devil or God. During his time in America, Harvard university had attacked such a view in *The Testimony of the President, Professors . . . of Harvard College in Cambridge against the Rev Mr. George*

Whitefield (1744), to which Whitefield replied in *A Letter to the Rev.
the President and Professors . . . of Harvard-college* (1745).

3. *dilucidating*: Elucidating.

4. *Crim Tartary*: The Crimea.

5. *Francis the ninth of France*: Paré (see above, n. 3 to III.xxxv) was
in fact surgeon to four French monarchs, Henri II, François II,
Charles IX, and Henri III, but not to Francis IX who never existed.

6. *Taliacotius's noses*: Gaspare Tagliacozzo or Taglicozzi (1545–99),
the Italian surgeon, reintroduced the method of reconstructing noses
from flaps of skin taken from the arm, anciently practised by Hindu
surgeons.

7. *puisne*: Puny.

8. *ad mensuram suam legitimam*: At its proper size.

9. *refocillated*: Revived.

10. *ratios*: Rations.

11. *Ponocrates and Grangousier*: Respectively, the Paris tutor and
father of Gargantua.

XXXIX 1. *damp tinder*: In the first edition, 'wet tinder'; the emendation was
probably Sterne's.

XL 1. *medius terminus*: In logic, the middle term of a syllogism; a ground
of proof or inference.

2. *Locke:* The observation occurs in the *Essay Concerning Human
Understanding*, IV. xvii. 18, though Locke has 'houses' for 'nine-pin-
alleys'.

XLI 1. *Grangousier's solution*: *Gargantua and Pantagruel,* I. xl.

VOLUME IV

frontispiece: The second illustration provided by William Hogarth and
engraved by Simon François Ravenet; the scene represents Tristram's
baptism by the curate and shows the maid Susannah and Walter
Shandy, who has arrived belatedly, having been unable to put on his
breeches in time to ensure that his son be christened Trismegistus, the
name that, according to his personal theory, 'shall bring all things to
rights' (see n. to I. frontispiece above, and IV.xi below).

Slawkenbergius's Tale   1. *Benedicity!*: Bless us!

2. *saint Radagunda*: St. Radegund (518–87), a prisoner and later the
wife of the Frankish king Clotaire I, who perhaps married her polyg-
amously; she subsequently left her husband and founded the Abbey
of the Holy Cross at Poitiers. She is one of the three contitulars of
Jesus College, Cambridge, where Sterne was a student.

3. *queen Mab*: The 'fairies' midwife', who reveals men's secret
hopes in the form of dreams, by driving 'athwart their noses' in her
chariot as they sleep; *Romeo and Juliet*, I. iv. 53 ff.

4. *abbess of Quedlingberg*: Sterne could have found mention of the 'Abbess, the Prioress, the Deaness, and the Canonesses' in the anonymous *The Present State of Germany* (1738) or Walter Harte's *The History of the Life of Gustavus Adolphus, King of Sweden* (1759).

5. *penitentiaries of the third order of saint Francis*: The Franciscans had a Third Order whose members, not necessarily under vows, engaged in charitable works.

6. *nuns of mount Calvary*: A community of Benedictines of Notre-Dame du Calvaire, founded by Antoinette d'Orléans-Longueville in 1617.

7. *Præmonstratenses*: Premonstratensians, also called Norbertines, were Canons Regular of Prémontré, founded by St. Norbert of Xanten (*c*.1080–1134) at Prémontré in 1120.

8. *Clunienses**: The important monastery at Cluny in Burgundy was established by William of Aquitaine in 910. Its first abbot (910–27) was St. Berno of Baume but its influence stemmed from the abbacy (927–42) of St. Odo (879–942); the first Cluniac convent, however, appears to date only from the mid-eleventh century.

9. *Carthusians*: The strict contemplative order, founded by St. Bruno in 1084, included nuns from the twelfth century onwards.

10. *saint Antony*: The intercession of St. Antony of Padua (1195–1231) was believed to bring relief from erysipelas, or St. Anthony's fire, a febrile disease accompanied by inflammation of the skin.

11. *nuns of saint Ursula*: The nuns who 'never attempted to go to bed at all' take their name from the legendary British saint, Ursula, traditionally associated with the eleven thousand virgins supposedly martyred by Huns near Cologne after returning from pilgrimage to Rome. They are not to be confused with the Ursulines founded in 1535 by St. Angela Merici (1474–1540) as a lay teaching order.

12. *capitulars*: Members of an ecclesiastical chapter.

13. *domiciliars*: Canons of a minor order having no voice in a chapter.

14. *butter'd buns*: Women enjoying sexual relations with several men in quick succession; the phrase appears in various works known to Sterne, including Rabelais and the *Works* (1707–11) of the miscellaneous writer Thomas Brown (1662/3–1704).

15. *Martin Luther*: Martin Luther (1483–1546), leader of the Reformation, whose doctrines turned Strasbourg into a predominantly Protestant city.

16. *Chrysippus*: See above, n. 3 to II.xix.

17. *Crantor*: Crantor (*c*.335-*c*.275 BC), a philosopher of the Old Academy.

18. *faculty*: Here, the medical faculty.

19. *in Utero*: In the womb.

20. *petitio principii*: The logical fallacy of taking for granted a

premiss which depends on the conclusion and which requires proof.

21. *civilians*: Professors or doctors of civil law.

22. *ex mero motu*: From mere impulse.

23. **Nonnulli ex . . . Vid. Idea*: Sterne's parodic note is nonsensical.

24. *Jacobus Sturmius*: Jakob Sturm (1489–1553), German reformer and statesman, associated with Strasbourg, where he founded the Protestant Gymnasium in 1538.

25. *Leopold, arch-duke of Austria*: Leopold V, Archduke of Austria (1586) became Bishop of Passau and Strasbourg in 1607. The substance of the passage is inaccurate for there were not two universities in Strasbourg but Sterne here closely follows *The Present State of Germany* (1738); see above, n. 4.

26. *in coition*: In conjunction.

27. **Haec mira . . . genituras examinatis*: The passage appears in the article on Luther in the *Dictionnaire historique et critique* (1695–7), trans. as *An Historical and Critical Dictionary* (1710; new edn. 1734–8), by the sceptical French Protestant philosopher Pierre Bayle (1647–1706), a source Sterne used elsewhere in *Tristram Shandy*. The cited passage is here corrected and translates: 'These are wonderful things and terrifying enough. The conjunction of the planets under the constellation Scorpio in the ninth house of heaven, which the Arabs assigned to religion, made Martin Luther a sacrilegious heretic, a most bitter and profane enemy of the Christian religion; from the direction of the horoscope to the conjunction of Mars, he perished and his most wicked soul sailed to hell—to be tortured perpetually with fiery scourges by Alecto, Tisiphone, and Megera.—Lucas Gauricus in his *Astrological treatise concerning the past mischances of many men, by means of an examination of their nativities*.' Luca Gaurico or Lucas Gauricus (1476–1558), Bishop of Civitate (San Severo), was a mathematician and astrologer, whose most celebrated work was the *Tractatus Astrologicus* (1552).

28. *Oct. 22, 1483*: It is now accepted that Luther was born on 10 November 1483, at Eisleben in Thuringian Saxony.

29. *Alexandrian library*: The most famous library of antiquity; probably founded by Ptolemy I in the fourth century BC, it survived until the third century AD; it was said to have held as many as 700,000 manuscripts.

30. *Thomas Aquinas*: St. Thomas Aquinas (c.1225–74), Dominican philosopher and the greatest theologian of the Western Church.

31. *Pantagruel and his companions*: The visit to the Oracle of the Holy Bottle Bacbuc occurs in *Gargantua and Pantagruel*, IV. i.

32. *Catastrophe*: The revolution producing the conclusion of a play.

33. *Peripeitia*: Peripeteia, a sudden change of fortune in tragedy.

34. *Protasis*: The first part of a play.

35. *Epitasis*: See n. 10 to II.v.

36. *Catastasis*: The part of a drama between the epitasis and the catastrophe.

37. *defluxion*: Discharge.

38. *Valadolid*: Valladolid, Spanish city NW of Madrid.

39. *Colbert*: Jean-Baptiste Colbert (1619–83), extremely influential minister of finance to Louis XIV.

40. *Suabia*: Swabia, medieval Duchy approximating to modern Baden-Württemberg, Hesse and West Bavaria.

III 1. *Makay's regiment*: Named for Lieutenant-General Hugh Mackay of Scourie (?1640–1692), who fought in Ireland under William III, and was commander of the British division of the grand army in Flanders; he was killed on 24 July 1692, at the Battle of Steinkirk, or Steenkerke (see p. 303 below).

VII 1. *Zooks!*: A minced oath, from gadzooks or God's hooks, the nails by which Christ was crucified.

2. *school of Athens*: The famous fresco of Raphael in the Stanza della Segnatura in the Vatican Palace, painted 1508–11, in which Socrates appears to the left of the central figures, Plato and Aristotle; R. F. Brissenden first noted that Sterne's source was apparently *An Account of some of the Statues, Bas-reliefs, Drawings and Pictures in Italy* (1722) by Jonathan Richardson the elder (1667–1745) and his son Jonathan Richardson the younger (1694–71).

VIII 1. *GEORGE or EDWARD*: George III, who had become king in 1760 at the age of twenty-two, and his younger brother.

IX 1. *balluster*: Bannister.

2. *anew*: Enough.

X 1. *a story of a roasted horse*: A story about nothing.

2. *Diana's temple*: Diana, a woodland goddess, later identified with the Greek virgin goddess Artemis, had an important temple in Rome on the Aventine.

3. *Longinus*: See above, n. 11 to I.xix.

4. *Avicenna*: Abū 'Alī al-Husayn ibn 'Abd Allāh ibn Sīnā (980–1037), a physician and philosopher, was master of the Muslim Aristotelians. He was an outstanding polymath whose *Book of Healing*, a philosophical and scientific encyclopaedia, is perhaps the largest work of its kind by a single author.

5. *Licetus*: Fortunio Liceti (1577–1657), physician and philosopher.

6. *de omni scribili*: 'Of all kinds of writing', or 'of all scribblings'.

7. **Ce Fœtus ... de l'Academie Françoise.*): Taken from Adrien Baillet's *Des Enfans devenus celebres* (1588), the passage translates: 'This foetus was no bigger than the palm of the hand; but its father having examined it in his capacity as a physician, and having found that it was something more than an embryo, had it carried alive to Rapallo, where he showed it to Jerôme Bardi and other physicians of

the place. They found that it lacked nothing essential to life, and its father, to make a trial of his experience, undertook to complete the work of Nature and to work for the formation of the child by the same means used to hatch chickens in Egypt. He instructed a wet-nurse in all she had to do, and having had his son placed in a properly appointed oven, he succeeded in raising him and making him grow normally, by the uniformity of an external heat measured exactly by degrees on a thermometer, or another equivalent instrument. (See Mich. Giustinian, in the Scritt. Liguri à Cart. 223.488.)

'One would still have been very satisfied with the industry of a father so skilled in the art of generation, had he been able to prolong his son's life for no more than a few months or a few years.

'But when one considers that the child lived nearly eighty years, and that he composed twenty-four different works, each the fruit of long reading, one must acknowledge that all that is incredible is not always false, and that appearance is not always on the side of truth.

'He was only nineteen when he composed *Gonopsychanthro-pologia de Origine Animæ humanæ.*

'(*Les enfans celebres*, revised and corrected by M. De la Mon-noye of the Académie Française.)'

The Greek and Latin titles of Licetus's work both translate: *Of the Origin of the Human Soul.*

XII   1. *Job's stock of asses*: Before his suffering Job possessed five hundred she-asses; later he received a double restitution (Job 1: 3; 42: 12).

XIII   1. *day-tall critick*: Day-tale, i.e. paid by the day; here a hack.

2. *as Horace advises*: In *Ars Poetica*, 1. 148, Horace suggests the epic writer should begin his work *in medias res*; see also n. 3 to I.iv above.

3. *the propagation of Geese*: Pens (i.e. Tristram's 'tools') were frequently made from goose quills.

XV   1. *'God's blessing, said Sancho Panca*: *Don Quixote*, II. iv. 68.

2. *what Montaigne advances upon it*: Sterne paraphrases, at times inaccurately, Montaigne's essay, III. xiii, 'Of Experience'.

3. *La Vraisemblance . . . du Cotè de la Verité*: 'Appearance is not always on the side of truth'; Baylet is here Baillet (see above, n. 7 to IV.x).

XVII   1. *riddles and mysteries . . . cannot penetrate into*: Sterne's fondness for the memorable phrase 'riddles and mysteries' or 'mysteries and riddles', which he also employs in IX.xxii (see p. 517 below) and in his sermon 'Felix's Behaviour towards Paul, examined' (*The Sermons of Mr. Yorick* (1766)), has been shown to derive from his near-verbatim quotation of *Practical Discourses* (1691) by John Norris (1657–1712); for a convincing demonstration of Norris's importance to Sterne, see M. New, 'The Odd Couple: Laurence Sterne and John Norris of Bemerton', *PQ* 75 (1996), 361–85.

2. *Pythagoras*: Pythagoras (*c*.580–*c*.500 BC), Greek philosopher, mathematician and founder of the Pythagorean brotherhood, whose followers' beliefs depended largely on their master's authority.

3. *Plato*: Plato (*c*.429–347 BC), the Greek philosopher whose extensive writings included the *Republic* and the *Laws*.

4. *Solon*: Solon (*c*.630-*c*.560 BC), statesman and poet who reformed the Athenian constitution, reputedly establishing a more humane code of justice in place of that of Draco.

5. *Licurgus*: Lycurgus (*fl.* ninth/seventh centuries BC?), the traditional but possibly apocryphal founder of the Spartan constitution.

6. *Mahomet*: Muhammad (*c*.570–632), the founder of Islam, who interpreted and expanded the Qur'ān (or Koran) for the first Muslim community, established in 622 at Medina.

XIX 1. *embryotic*: Embryonic.

2. *Goosecap*: Booby or simpleton.

XX 1. *a bishop*: An allusion to William Warburton (1698–1779), Bishop of Gloucester, and man of letters. In 1760 a rumour suggested that Sterne intended to caricature Warburton as Tristram's tutor. Sterne denied this in a letter to Garrick which the latter showed to Warburton, who in turn wrote a fulsome but perhaps not entirely convinced letter to Sterne. Subsequently, Warburton praised both *Tristram Shandy* and the volume of Sterne's sermons, but this reference brought about a permanent break in their relationship. See also below, n. 1 to IX.VIII.

2. *Mess. Le Moyne . . . the Sorbonne*: See above, n. 5 to I.xx.

XXI 1. *Francis the first of France*: François (1494–1547) was king of France from 1515 to 1547.

2. **Vide Menagiana, vol. 1*: *Menagiana* (1693) is a collection of *bons mots* and moral observations by the French scholar, Gilles Ménage (1613–92).

3. *Shadrach, Mesech, and Abed-nego*: The Jews who were bound and cast into the burning fiery furnace by Nebuchadnezzar and who emerged unharmed (Dan. 3: 8–30).

XXII 1. *christen-names*: Christian names.

2. *Francis the Ninth*: See above, n. 5 to III.xxxviii.

3. *the duke of Ormond*: Corporal Trim shares with the second Duke of Ormonde (1665–1745), soldier and statesman, the name James Butler (see above, p. 76 and n. 6 to II.v above). Ormonde fought in the Williamite wars and was appointed commander in chief of the army in the War of the Spanish Succession in 1711. An opponent of the Hanoverian Succession, he was impeached in 1715; he fled to France, joined the Old Pretender's abortive rebellion, and died in exile.

4. *succussations*: Violent shakings.

5. *inimicitious*: Inimical.

XXV 1. *ten pages*: In the first edition, only nine pages were in fact omitted, with the result that for the remainder of the fourth volume, the odd-numbered pages were on the verso of the leaf, the even numbers on the recto.

2. *visitations*: The official visit of a bishop to his diocese.

3. *Turpilius*: Turpilius (d. before AD 74), a Roman knight and painter, mentioned by Pliny both for the quality of his work and for painting with his left hand, which Pliny says was previously unheard of (*Natural History*, xxxv.xx).

4. *Hans Holbein*: Hans Holbein the Younger (1497/8–1543), German portraitist who began work in Basle in 1515 but who spent most of his working life in England.

5. *bend dexter*: A stripe in heraldry; the bend sinister signifies bastardy.

6. *the sound of the word siege*: Aside from its military signification, 'siege' also implies 'privy', 'evacuation', and 'anus'.

7. *Homenas*: The Bishop of Papimany in *Gargantua and Pantagruel*, IV. xlviii.

8. *Montaigne*: The passage alludes to and parodies 'Of the institution and education of children', *Essays*, I. xxv.

XXVII 1. *Phutatorius*: See above, n. 2 to III.xx.

2. *a twelve-penny oath*: The Profane Oaths Act 1745 (19 Geo. II, c. 21) attempted to discourage cursing and swearing by instituting a system of fines for offenders; a twelve-penny (1s.) fine was the lowest.

3. *the temple of Janus*: The god Janus was the *numen* of doorways and archways; the gates of his temple, the *Ianus geminus* in the forum at Rome, were closed when the state was at peace.

4. *Acrites*: 'One who is undecided or undiscriminating'; Mythogeras, 'Tale-bearer'.

5. *de Concubinis retinendis*: Of the Keeping of Concubines.

6. *compursions*: Pursing.

7. *Asker*: A dialect name for the newt in Yorkshire and some other parts of England.

8. *Euclid's*: Euclid (*fl. c.*300 BC), who taught at Alexandria, was author of the textbook on geometry, the *Elements*.

9. *Yorick . . . was a man of jest*: *Hamlet*, V. i; see also above, n. 4 to I.XII.

XXVIII 1. *de re concubinariâ*: Of a matter concerning concubinage.

XXIX 1 *in nomino patriæ & filia & spiritum sanctos*: A corrupt version of *in nomine patris et filii et spiritus sancti*, in the name of the Father and of the Son and of the Holy Ghost.

2. *Pope Leo the IIId*: Leo III (d. 816) did not make any significant statement concerning baptism, unlike Zachary (or Zacharias) III (d. 752) who, in correspondence with St. Boniface (d. 755), ruled that

baptism was valid even if the wrong formula was used as a result of ignorance on the part of the priest.

3. *Vid. Swinburn on Testaments, Part 7. §8:* Henry Swinburne (c.1551–1624), a York-born ecclesiastical lawyer, was author of *A Briefe Treatise of Testaments and Last Willes* (1591), Sterne's source for the Duke of Suffolk's case. Swinburne was also author of a posthumously published *Treatise of Spousals, or Matrimonial Contracts* (1686).

4. †*Vid. Brook Abridg. Tit. Administr. N.47:* Sir Robert Broke or Brooke (d. 1558), speaker of the House of Commons and chief justice of the common pleas. Sterne took the reference to *La Graunde Abridgement* from Swinburne.

5. *Lord Coke:* Sir Edward Coke (1552–1634), politician and important jurist, was author of the *Reports,* which details the Duke of Suffolk's case; Sterne's reference, though, derives from Swinburne.

6. *Edward the Sixth:* Edward VI (see above, n. 13 to II.xix) reigned from 1547 to 1553; the case dates from 5 Ed. 6.

7. *venter:* One or other of two or more wives who are sources of offspring to the same man.

8. *the juris-consulti—the juris-prudentes:* Synonyms for jurists, or men learned in the law.

9. *Mater non ... Verb. signific.:* Taken from Swinburne, Sterne's note alludes to a work of Baldo degli Ubaldi or Baldus de Ubaldis (1327–1400), a Perugia-born jurist.

10. *Liberi sunt ... de sanguine liberorum:* Children are of the blood of their father and mother, but the father and mother are not of the blood of their children.

11. *Selden:* John Selden (1584–1654), legal antiquarian, orientalist, and politician, whose occasional remarks were collected by his secretary, Richard Milward, and published as *Table Talk* (1689); the story is to be found under the heading 'King'.

12. *Argumentum commune:* Common argument.

XXXI   1. *Mississippi-scheme:* The scheme for colonizing Louisiana, the vast area drained by the Mississippi, the Ohio, and the Missouri rivers, was designed by the Scottish comptroller-general of France, John Law (1671–1729); after financing the settlement of New Orleans, Law's company went spectacularly bankrupt in 1720, destroying with it Law's entire banking system, and resulting in Law's expulsion from France.

2. *whinny:* Covered with whins or furze-bushes.

3. *tantum valet ... quantum sonat:* It is worth as much as it sounds.

XXXII   1. *since Adam:* Sharon Long Damoff suggests a play on the name of the Scottish architect Robert Adam (1728–92) who, along with John Carr (1723–1807) of York, was responsible for the building and decoration, between 1759 and 1771, of Harewood House in York-shire; see 'Laurence Sterne, Robert Adam, and the Lascelles Family', *N&Q* 45 (1998), 408.

2. *Sancho Pança*: Sancho speculates that if Don Quixote makes him governor of a land of negroes, he will ship them to Spain for ready money (*Don Quixote*, I. iv. 2).

VOLUME V

title pages 1. *Dixero ... dabis*—: The lines, adapted from Horace's *Satires*, IV. i, occur in the prefatory section, 'Democritus Junior to the Reader' of Burton's *Anatomy of Melancholy*. They translate: 'If perhaps I say anything too facetious, you will grant me this right indulgently.'

2. *Si quis ... Democritus dixit.*—: The motto is again taken from 'Democritus Junior to the Reader'; Burton's Latin is a loose para-phrase of some lines of Erasmus's 'Letter to Sir Thomas More' in the *Moriae Encomium* (*In Praise of Folly*). They translate: 'If any-one falsely charges that this is more light-hearted than becomes a theologian, or more biting than becomes a Christian—not I, but Democritus said it.'

3. *Si quis ... anathema esto*: The third motto first appeared in a Dublin edition of Volumes V and VI, published in 1762; it was then added, with minor variants, including an error, to the second London edition of 1767. It translates: 'If any priest or monk know jesting words exciting laughter, anathema upon him.' See also n. 11 to V.XLII below.

dedication 1. *Lord Viscount SPENCER*: Lord John Spencer (1734–83), a Whig politician, was a friend and patron of Sterne. There is no reason to doubt the sincerity of the dedication of Spencer though, in inscrib-ing the story of Le Fever in Volume VI—which would become one of the novel's most admired sentimental episodes—to Lady Spencer, Sterne certainly had commercial acumen, as well as gallantry, in mind. The first four volumes of *Tristram Shandy* had been not only hugely admired but also widely criticized as bawdy or even obscene; when Margaret Georgiana, Countess Spencer (1737–1814), accepted Sterne's dedication, however, no one could doubt that the novel was suitable even for women readers, and of the nicest sensibility. Sterne made a fair copy of the Le Fever episode to present to Lady Spencer (see note 1 to VI.x below), and in 1765 Lord Spencer would gift the writer a silver standish that he would greatly value.

1 1. *Stilton to Stamford*: A distance of some thirteen and a half miles on the Great North Road.

2. *Tell me ... so little to the stock?*: Sterne's cry humorously echoes

Burton's sentiments in 'Democritus Junior to the Reader' in which he describes modern authors as 'all theeves; they pilfer out of old Writers to stuff up their new Comments' while admitting that he had 'laboriously collected this Cento out of divers Writers'. Sterne's following paragraphs similarly recall *The Anatomy of Melancholy* I.I.I.I.

3. *Zoroaster*: Zoroaster, or Zarathustra (traditionally *c.*628–*c.*551 BC, but some scholars place him in the second millennium BC), the founder of Zoroastrianism, the principal pre-Islamic religion of Persia; the title of the book attributed to him is *Of Nature.* Having just thrown the key of his study door into the draw-well (see p. 275), Tristram (or Sterne) seems to rely on a fallible memory: beginning with an echo of Burton in *The Anatomy of Melancholy*, I.I.I.I, the passage subsequently draws on *A Discourse of the Light of Nature* (1652), esp. ch. xi, by the Cambridge Platonist Nathaniel Culverwell (d. 1651?), which mentions Zoroaster, Moses' description of man as the 'image of God', and the 'Divine Trismegist', within the space of three pages.

4. *SHEKINAH*: Hebrew term for the visible manifestation of God; the expression also appears, in Hebrew and Greek, in Culverwell's *Discourse*, 75.

5. *as abusive as Horace*: Horace apostrophized imitators as a 'slavish herd' (*Epistles*, I. xix. 19).

6. *mort main*: Literally, dead hand; Sterne uses the phrase figuratively to suggest the posthumous control of a testator over his legacy.

7. *Tartufs*: Tartuffe is the religious hypocrite in the comedy *Tartuffe; or, the Hypocrite* (1664) by Jean-Baptiste Poquelin (1622–73), known as Molière.

8. *the queen of Navarre*: Marguerite de Valois (1553–1615) was the first wife of Henry of Navarre, the future Henry IV of France; she was noted for her licentiousness. Several of the names in the Fragment appear, as members of her court, in Pierre Bayle's *Dictionary* (see n. 27 to IV, Slawkenbergius' Tale above).

9. *St. Francis*: There are several saints of the same name as all those in the following list, but the most likely ones Sterne had in mind are: St. Francis of Assisi (1181/2–1226), founder of the Franciscans; *St. Dominic* (*c.*1170–1221), founder of the Dominicans; *St. Benedict* (*c.*480–*c.*550), the Patriarch of Western monasticism; *St. Basil* (*c.*330–379), the Patriarch of Eastern monasticism; St. Brigitta or *Bridget* (*c.*1303–1373), founder of the Order of the Most Holy Saviour, or Brigittines.

10. *the curate of d'Estella*: Diego d'Estella, or Didacus Stella (1524–78), named from his birthplace in Navarre, a Franciscan and author of religious works, including *De la vanidad del mundo* (1562; rev. 1574), or *The contempt of the world, and the vanities thereof*, of which four editions appeared in English between 1584 and 1622.

11. *trouse*: Garment designed to cover the buttocks and thighs.

II 1. *Scotch horse*: An allusion to John Stuart, Earl of Bute (1713–92), adviser to George III (see above, n. 1 to IV.VIII) and, since March 1761, Secretary of State; he was greatly disliked for his personal influence over the young king and his mother, and for his supposed favouritism to his fellow-Scotsmen.

2. *PATRIOT*: 'Patriot' was the name given to those members of the opposition Country party avowedly working for the good of the nation as a whole, though Sterne may have had in mind William Pitt—who had been obliged to resign to make way for Bute (see n. 1 to V.II above)—to whom he would twice allude as a 'patriot' in his dedication to Pitt of Volume IX of *Tristram Shandy* (see pp. 483–4 below).

3. *Sanson's*: Nicolas Sanson (1600–67), geographer and founder of French cartography, who in 1644 published ten well-known maps of France.

4. *Agrippina*: Agrippina Major (*c.*14 BC–AD 33); the reference is a very confused one to Tacitus' *Annals*, 3, which Sterne took from Burton's *Anatomy*, 2.3.5. Agrippina's grief was in fact for the death of her husband Germanicus in AD 19.

III 1. *Plato*: See above, n. 3 to IV.XVII. The list of names which follows is taken from the *Anatomy*, 2.3.1.1.

2. *Plutarch*: Lucius Mestrus Plutarchus (before AD 50–after 120), philosopher and biographer, was author of the *Consolatio ad Uxorem*, a consolation written for his wife on the death of their infant daughter.

3. *Seneca*: Seneca (see above, n. 4 to III.IV) was author of the *Ad Marciam de consolatione*, written to console the daughter of Cremutius Cordus for the death of her sons.

4. *Xenophon*: Xenophon (*c.* 428–*c.* 354 BC), prolific author, admired as a philosopher and historian; his son Gryllus died at the Battle of Mantinea in 362 BC.

5. *Epictetus*: The Stoicism of Epictetus (see above, n. 1 to I, title page) touched on the question of the loss of close relations.

6. *Theophrastus*: Theophrastus (*c.*371–287 BC), philosopher and pupil and successor of Aristotle.

7. *Lucian*: see above, n. 1 to I.XXIII.

8. *Cardan*: Girolamo Cardano (1501–76), Italian physician, astrologer, and leading mathematician of his day; he refers to the execution of his son for the murder of his wife in an autobiography, *De propria vita liber.*

9. *Budæus*: Guillaume Budé (1467–1540), finest Greek scholar of his day and founder of the Collège de France in Paris.

10. *Petrarch*: Francesco Petrarca (1304–74), poet and humanist. One of his earliest surviving poems, *Epistolae metricae*, I. vii,

concerns the death of his mother, while the second part of his best-known work, *Rime in morte di Laura*, was written after Laura's death.

11. *Stella*: Didacus Stella, humanist name for Diego d'Estella (see above, n. 10 to V.1).

12. *Austin*: St. Augustine of Hippo (354–430) was greatly influenced by the life and death of his mother St. Monica (*c.*331–387).

13. *St. Cyprian*: St. Cyprian (*c.*200–58), Bishop of Carthage and the first African martyr.

14. *Barnard*: St. Bernard of Clairvaux (1090–1153) dated his full conversion from the death of his mother when he was seventeen.

15. *Seneca*: Lucius Annaeus Seneca, the Elder (*c.*50 BC–*c.* AD 40), the rhetorician; the reference is to the *Controversiae*, 5.30, which is noted by Burton in the *Anatomy*, 2.3.5.

16. *David ... Absalom*: 2 Sam. 18: 33.

17. *Adrian for his Antinous*: Antinous (*c.* AD 110/12–30), A FAVOURITE OF THE EMPEROR HADRIAN (AD 76–138), was drowned in the Nile; Hadrian's response included the foundation of a city in Middle Egypt called Antinoöpolis.

18. *Niobe*: Mythological figure whose children, traditionally six or seven of either sex, were killed by the two children of Leto; worn with grief, Niobe became a stone on Mt. Sipylon.

19. *Apollodorus and Crito*: Associates of the Athenian philosopher Socrates (469–399 BC), who carried out his own death sentence by drinking hemlock.

20. *Tully*: The death of Tullia in 45 BC was a bitter blow to Tully or Cicero, whose lost *Consolatio* was part of his response. The tone of Sterne's comment is an echo of Burton's in the *Anatomy*, 2.3.5.

21. '*Monarchs ... with us.*': Joseph Hall, *Epistles*, II. ix.

22. *Troy*: The most famous and elusive classical city, now identified by archaeologists with Layer VIIa (sometimes VI or VIIb) of the ancient stronghold Hisarlik in NW Asia Minor. The following list is largely taken from the *Anatomy*, 2.3.5.

23. *Mycenæ*: Mycenae, in the NE corner of the Argive plain, of great strategic importance, finally destroyed by the Dorians around 1120 BC.

24. *Thebes*: On the south edge of the Boeotian plain, whose influence as a great city did not survive its destruction for a revolt against Alexander the Great in 336 BC.

25. *Delos*: A small island in the Aegean, already famous in the *Odyssey*, which retained importance until the first century BC, after which it declined rapidly.

26. *Persepolis*: In Persia; residence of the Achaemenid kings, looted and burned by Alexander in 331 BC.

27. *Agrigentum*: Agrigento in Sicily, site of significant Greek (sixth to fifth century BC) and Roman (second century BC) ruins.

28. *Nineveh*: Capital of the Assyrian empire and leading city of the ancient world until it fell to Cyaxares and Nabopolassar in 612 BC.

29. *Babylon*: City of great commercial importance and influence under the Chaldean kings in the seventh and sixth centuries BC, it gradually declined thereafter and was found in ruins by Trajan in the second century AD.

30. *Cizicum*: Cyzicus, in modern NW Turkey, was traditionally founded in 756 BC and refounded in 675 BC; strategically situated, it rivalled Byzantium in commercial importance but was largely destroyed by the Arabs in AD 675.

31. *Mitylenæ*: Mytilene or Mitilini, port on Lesbos in the Aegean.

32. *Ægina towards Megara*: The passage is taken from the letter of Servius Sulpicius Rufus (d. 43 BC) to Cicero, consoling him on Tullia's death; it is paraphrased from the *Anatomy*, 2.3.5.

33. *Zant*: Zante (otherwise Zakinthos), capital of the southernmost of the principal Ionian islands.

34. *Vespasian*: Sterne's source for this and the following names was the essay 'Of Death' by Sir Francis Bacon (see below, n. 1 to V.XXXIV). According to Suetonius' life of Titus Flavius Vespasianus (AD 9–79), the emperor's last words were 'If I am not mistaken I am going to be a god.'

35. *Galba*: Servius Sulpicius Galba (3 BC–AD 69), whose last words before his assassination were, according to Plutarch, 'Strike, if this is better for the Roman people.'

36. *Septimius Severus*: Lucius Septimius Severus (AD 145–211), Roman emperor whose last words, says Dio Cassius, were 'Come, give it here, if anything is left for me to do.'

37. *Tiberius*: Tiberius Julius Caesar Augustus (42 BC–AD 37). In the *Annals*, Tacitus says of him on his death-bed: 'already his body and spirits failed him, but not his dissimulation', and he tells the story of how, when the emperor seemed to have died and Caligula had been proclaimed his successor, Tiberius suddenly sat up; Caligula promptly fled but Macro, commander of the Praetorian Guard, smothered Tiberius.

38. *Cæsar Augustus*: Suetonius reports that the dying words of Caesar Octavius Augustus (63 BC–AD 14) were 'Livia, remember our love while you live, and farewell.'

IV 1. *Cornelius Gallus*: It was Pliny, in the *Natural History*, 7.53, who reported that Gaius Cornelius Gallus (*c.*69–26 BC), soldier and author of widely read love poetry, died

*   *   *   *   *   *   *   *   *   *   *   *   *   *   *   *

V 1. *the listening slave*: Classical statue of a kneeling man, now better known as *l'Arrotino* or the Whetter, familiar to eighteenth-century tourists as it stood in the Tribuna in the Palazzo degli Uffizi in Florence.

2. *Goddess of Silence at his back*: The Roman Goddess of Silence was Angerona; of Etruscan origin, she was also associated with death, and was represented with a finger pressed to her bandaged mouth.

3. *Rapin*: Paul de Rapin de Thoyras (see above, n. 1 to II.I), various books of whose *The History of England, as well ecclesiastical as civil* conclude with a lengthy 'State of the Church of England'.

VII 1 *well might Locke*: Locke's chapter on the imperfection of words is chapter ix of book III of his *Essay Concerning Human Understanding* (see n. 5 to I.IV above).

2. *Barbati*: 'Bearded ones'; here venerable philosophers, and goats.

VIII 1. *green-gowns, and old hats*: 'Green-gowns' implies sexual sport, originally 'to tumble a woman on the grass'; 'old hat' is the female pudenda, 'because frequently felt'.

XI 1. *the river Nile*: The idea, anciently expressed by Diodorus Siculus (*fl.* first century BC), that spontaneous generation occurred in the warm mud of the Nile, was still maintained in the seventeenth century by Lucilio Vanini (1585–1619).

XII 1. *Josephus (de Bell. Judaic.)*: Sterne is drawing here on the *De Bello Judaico*, or *History of the Jewish War*, VII. vii, of Flavius Josephus (37/38–c.100), via John Donne's *Biathanatos* (1608–9; pub. 1647). Eleazar does not in fact attribute the sentiments to anyone, but Sterne is burlesquing serious accounts by antiquarians who attributed eastern origins to western learning.

2. *maroders*: Marauders.

3. *karrawans*: Caravans.

XV 1. *Caprichio*: Capriccio; short lively piece of music.

2. *Calliope*: The muse of heroic poetry.

3. *Cremona*: A violin, named for the Italian city famed for the making of stringed instruments in the seventeenth and eighteenth centuries.

4. *Jew's trump*: Jew's harp; small lyre-shaped instrument played with the mouth.

XVI 1. *Xenophon*: The works of Xenophon (see above, n. 4 to V.III) included the *Cyropaedia*, a historical fiction in eight books, having as hero Cyrus the Elder and containing an account of Cyrus's education and Xenophon's ideas on education and family life.

2. *hussive*: Pocket-case for needles and thread (from 'housewife').

3. *John de la Casse*: Giovanni della Casa (1503–56), author of the brief *Il galateo* (1558), one of the best-known treatises on manners of the Renaissance.

4. *Rider's Almanack*: *Rider's British Merlin* by Cardanus Rider ran to no more than 50 or 60 pages.

5 *to be fed—as to be famous*: In a self-justifying letter written in January 1760, after the initial success of the small York-printed

edition of *Tristram Shandy*, Sterne declared 'I wrote not [to] be *fed*, but to be *famous*' (*Letters*, 90); the phrase was a self-conscious reversal of the assertion by Colley Cibber (1671–1757), actor, theatre-manager, playwright, and Poet Laureate, who, in his *A Letter from Mr Cibber to Mr Pope* (1742), wrote that: 'I wrote more to be Fed, than to be Famous.' Sterne was fond of the remark, which he had also paraphrased in III.xx above (see p. 159).

XIX 1. *paderero*: Pedrero, a piece of ordnance for firing stones, broken iron, etc.

2. *demi-culverins*: Small cannon, about 4½ inch bore.

XX 1. *count Solmes*: Heinrich Maastricht, Count of Solms-Braunfels (1636–93), was commander of the allied forces when they were defeated by the French at the Battle of Steinkirk in 1692.

XXI 1. *Cutts's*: John Cutts, Baron Cutts of Gowran (1660/1–1707), fought as brigadier-general at Steinkirk where he was wounded; his regiment suffered heavy losses; for Mackay, see above, n. 1 to IV.III; James Douglas, Earl of Angus (1671–92), was killed at Steinkirk; Sir Charles Graham's was a Scots-Dutch regiment; Leven's was the regiment of David Melville, Earl of Leven (1660–1728).

XXVII 1. *de sede vel subjecto circumcisionis*: Of the foundation or subject of circumcision.

2. *Spencer . . . Ritualibus*: John Spencer (c. 1630–93), master of Corpus Christi College, Cambridge, from whose *De Legibus Hebraeorum, Ritualibus et earum Rationibus* (1685), I. iv, 2–6, Sterne took his material on circumcision.

3. *Maimonides*: Moses Maimonides (1135–1204), physician and the most important philosopher of medieval Judaism.

4. *COLCHI*: Colchians, inhabitants of region at eastern end of the Black Sea, south of the Caucasus.

XXVIII 1. *trine and sextil aspects*: The aspects of two heavenly bodies one third (120°) and one sixth (60°) part of the zodiac distant from each other.

2. *bo-peep*: The child's game; the whole passage is nonsense, though the use of astrological terms does owe something to the *Anatomy*, 1.2.1.4.

3. **Χαλεπῆζ . . . PHILO*: Philo Judaeus (c. 30 BC–AD 45) was a philosopher and head of the Jewish community at Alexandria. The quotation from his 'On Circumcision' translates: 'A release from a painful disease, difficult to cure, which they call carbuncle.'

4. *†Tὰ . . . εἶναι*: Again from Philo, Sterne's note translates: 'The circumcised races are the most prolific and the most populous.'

5. *‡Καθαφιότητος . . . BOCHART*: Sterne misattributes the source of the quotation, which is from the *History* of Herodotus; it translates: 'For the sake of cleanliness.'

6. *ʿΟ Ἴλος, ... *SANCHUNIATHO*: Sanchuniaton was the ancient Phoenician authority quoted by Philon of Byblos (AD 64–141). The quotation translates: 'Ilus circumcises his genitals, having compelled the allies with him to do the same.'

7. *Gymnast and captain Tripet*: The description of the battle in the following chapter occurs in *Gargantua and Pantagruel*, I. xxxv.

XXIX 1. *en croup*: En croupe, behind the saddle.

2. *demi-pommadas*: A pommada, or pomado, is an exercise of vaulting over a horse by putting one hand on the pommel of the saddle.

XXX 1. *scrutoir*: Escritoire, writing-desk.

XXXI 1. *Politian*: Angelo Poliziano or Ambrogini (1454–94), poet and humanist.

2. *Hesiod*: Hesiod (*fl. c.*700 BC), one of the earliest Greek epic poets, from whose *Works and Days* the following passage is taken; it translates: 'first of all a house, a woman, and an ox for ploughing'.

XXXII 1. *is big with jest—and has wit in it ... if we can but find it out*: Sterne paraphrases two lines from 'The Church-Porch', the opening poem of *The Temple* by George Herbert (1593–1633):

All Things are big with Jest: nothing that's plain
But may be witty, if thou has the Vein.

2. *bear-leaders*: Travelling tutors.

XXXIV 1. *Lord Verulam*: Francis Bacon, Lord Verulam (1561–1626), lawyer, statesman, philosopher, and essayist, from whose *Historia Vitae et Mortis* (1623) Sterne quotes at the beginning of Chapter xxxv, in each case (as the editors of the Florida edition point out) via James Mackenzie's *History of Health* (see n. 6 to II.1).

2. *Ars longa,—and Vita brevis*: 'Art is long, life is short'; the first of Hippocrates' *Aphorisms*.

XXXVI 1. *Van Helmont*: Jan Baptista van Helmont (1579–1644), Dutch chemist, philosopher, and physician, best known for his *Ortus Medicinae* (1648).

2. *'Quod omne ... triste.'*: After coition every animal is sad.

XXXVII 1. *the siege of Jerico*: Josh. 6.

2. *the siege of Limerick*: William III raised the siege of Limerick at the end of August 1690, after running out of ammunition and with rain threatening to turn the area into a morass.

3. *Œdipus*: In Greek myth, Oedipus solved the riddle of the Sphinx.

XXXIX 1. *phimosis*: A contraction of the orifice of the foreskin, so that it cannot be retracted.

XL 1. *consubstantials*: Consubstantials are things of the same substance or essence; *impriments* are things that impress or imprint; *occludents* are things that occlude, or stop up.

XLII 1. *Christ-cross-row to Malachi*: Christ-cross-row is the alphabet, so called from the figure of a cross prefixed to it in horn-books; Malachi is the last book of the Old Testament, which served as the reading-book for the highest class.

2. *more τυπτω-ing it* : τύπτω is to beat, or strike; the word was used as a paradigm of the Greek verb in eighteenth-century school grammars; *his probations and his negations*: i.e. the study of logic.

3. *Julius Scaliger*: Julius Caesar Scaliger (1484–1558) became known as a scholar only with an attack on Erasmus in 1531.

4. *Peter Damianus*: St. Peter Damian (1007–1072), Cardinal-Archbishop of Ostia and a Doctor of the Church, began his education late after being orphaned and neglected as a child.

5. *Baldus*: Baldus (see above, n. 9 to IV.xxix) was in fact remarkably precocious, taking his doctorate at seventeen.

6. *Eudamidas*: Eudamidas I, King of Sparta from 331 to 305 BC; the story appears in Plutarch's 'Sayings of Spartans'. Xenocrates was a disciple of Plato and head of the Academy from 339 to 314.

7. *Virgil's snake*: As the Florida editors note, Sterne has in mind Virgil's *Aeneid*, ii, ll. 510–14.

8. *Raymond Lullius*: Ramon Llull (c.1232–1316), Majorcan-born mystic and poet, who attempted to encompass all knowledge in a neoplatonic schema of Idealism intended to resolve all religious differences; viewing all reality as embodying some aspect of God, Llull endeavoured to teach theology, philosophy, and the natural sciences as analogues of one another.

9. *Pelegrini*: In his *Of Education. Especially of young gentlemen* (1673), I. xi, Obadiah Walker (1616–99) makes 'much use' of *Fonti dell'ingegno* (1650) by Matteo Pellegrini (1595?–1652), who reduced 'all *Predicates* that can be applied to a subject . . . to twelve *heads*'; Sterne in turn made much use of information from Walker in the preceding chapters, as he does in the following chapter also.

10. *Danes*: William III hired 6,000 troops from the King of Denmark to assist in his Irish campaign.

11. *And your honour . . . said the corporal:* These two sentences did not appear in the first edition of the novel but do appear in the Dublin edition of 1762 and were added to the second London edition of Volume V in 1767 (see above, n. 3 to V. title pages). Officers of equal quality who mount the same guards and do the same duty are said to roll.

XLIII 1. *The verbs auxiliary . . . Zodiac*: Sterne takes this material from Walker's *Of Education*, I. xi.

2. *a white bear?*: Mark Loveridge has linked Walter's white bear to

Thomas Sharp's Visitation Charge of 1756, later published in *Discourses on Preaching* [1787], where the 'white bears' are described as '*Emblems*, or *Similes*, as were too bold and striking as to be easily forgotten; and yet, from some strange Impropriety or Oddness in them, could not be remembered but with discredit to the brains that formed them' ('Walter Shandy's White Bear in *Tristram Shandy*', *N&Q* 244 (1999), 358–60), but this usage has a long history among preachers: see John Eachard, *A Vindication of the Clergy* (1672), 20.

VOLUME VI

II 1. *ten predicaments*: The ten categories of Aristotle, argued to be an enumeration of all things capable of being named: substance or being, quantity, quality, relation, place, time, posture, having or possession, action, passion.

2. *Vincent Quirino*: Vicenzo Quirino (1479–c.1514), while still a child, supposedly proposed and upheld 4,500 theses at Rome to the satisfaction of the philosophers who heard him.

3. *Cardinal Bembo*: Pietro Bembo (1470–1547), Venetian ecclesiastic and humanist, who refers to Quirino in *De Virgilii Culice*, though Sterne's source was Baillet's *Des Enfans devenus celebres*.

4. *Alphonsus Tostatus*: Alfonso Tostado (1400–55), Spanish theologian who received his doctorate at Salamanca at the age of twenty-two, by which time he had mastered languages, philosophy, civil and canon law, geography and history.

5. *Piereskius*: See above, n. 4 to II.xiv; as a child he showed a precocious curiosity and, according to Baillet, at the age of seven was acting as tutor to his five-year-old brother.

6. *Grotius*: Hugo Grotius or Huig de Groot (1583–1645), Dutch statesman, scholar, and important jurist, who began writing Latin poetry at the age of 8, entered the University of Leyden at 11, mastered its syllabus of philosophy, astronomy, mathematics, theology, and law in three years, and edited Martianus Capella (see below, n. 9 to VI.11) at 16; *Scioppius* (see above, n. 13 to I.xix) was a scholar from childhood and a respected author at 16; Daniel *Heinsius* (c.1580–1655), Flemish Latin poet, who began to write at 9 and published his first scholarly work before the age of 20; *Politian* (see above, n. 1 to V.xxxi) was a master of Latin and Greek verse at 12 and had made his poetical reputation at 14; Blaise *Pascal* (1623–62), mathematician and philosopher, mastered the *Elements* of Euclid at 12, and at 16 wrote a treatise on conic sections which astonished Descartes; Joseph Justus *Scaliger* (1540–1609) was fluent in Latin as a child, wrote a tragedy at 16, and taking up Greek at 19 had read Homer in three months; *Ferdinand* of Cordoba (*fl.* fifteenth century), Spanish scholar, who

could read, write, draw, and play the guitar at 5, and had mastered Latin and Rhetoric at 10, by which time he could memorize four or five pages of Cicero after a single reading.

7. *left off their substantial forms*: i.e. left off their studies in metaphysics; substantial forms are those independent of all matter or forms that are substances themselves.

8. *Servius*: Marius Servius Honoratus (late fourth/early fifth century AD), author of a commentary on Virgil, itself much commented upon.

9. *Martianus Capella*: Author of a didactic treatise, *De Nuptiis Mercurii et Philologiae*, composed between 410 and 439, and itself the subject of much medieval commentary.

10. *Lipsius*: Joest Lips (1547–1606), scholar and moral and political theorist, who published his first work at 22, was appointed to a chair at Jena at 25, and edited Tacitus at 27.

11. * *Nous aurions . . . ingenieux, &c. &c.*: Taken from *Des Enfans devenus celebres*, it translates: 'We should have some interest, says Baillet, in showing there is nothing ridiculous if it were true, at least in the enigmatic sense that Nicius Erythraeus has tried to give it. This author says that to understand how Lipsius could compose a work on the first day of his life, one must imagine that this first day is not that of his life in the flesh but that on which he began to use reason; he would have it that this would have been at the age of nine; and he wishes to persuade us that it was at this age that Lipsius composed a poem.—The attempt is ingenious, &c. &c.'

v 1. *Marcus Antoninus*: The Emperor Marcus Aurelius Antoninus (AD 121–80) was father of Lucius Aelius Aurelius Commodus (AD 161–92), joint emperor from 177 and sole emperor from 180; it was the latter's desire to appear in public as consul and gladiator that caused his outraged advisers to have him strangled; Sterne drew his account from Walker's *Of Education*, I. v (see n. 9 to V.XLII above).

2. *Gregory of Nazianzum*: St. Gregory of Nazianzus (329–89), who published two invectives against Flavius Claudius Julianus, Julian the Apostate (331–63), after the emperor had banned Christians from teaching the classics, though Julian had in fact avowed his apostasy upon becoming emperor.

3. *St. Ambrose*: St. Ambrose (*c*.339–397), Bishop of Milan and a Doctor of the Church.

4. *Democritus*: Democritus of Abdera (460/57–*c*.370/56 BC), known in later antiquity as the 'laughing philosopher'; in 'Democritus Junior to the Reader', Robert Burton says Democritus would 'laugh heartily' at the variety of ridiculous objects he saw.

5. *Protagoras*: Protagoras of Abdera (*c*.490–420 BC), the most celebrated of the Sophists.

6. **Vid. Pellegrina.*: See above, n. 9 to V.XLII.

7. *faceté*: Facetious.

VI 1. *Dendermond*: Dendermond in Flanders was taken by Marlborough in 1706.

2. *tennaile*: Tenaille, a small, low work, consisting of one or two reentering angles, placed before the curtain between two bastions.

VII 1. *death-watch*: Death-watch beetle.

2. *Breda*: Town in Brabant.

VIII 1. *a natural and a positive law*: Respectively, a law based on man's innate moral feeling and a formally enacted law.

X 1. *wishfully*: The fair copy of *The Story of* LE FEVER that Sterne presented to Lady Spencer (see n. 1 to V. Dedication) has 'wistfully'. As the principal Florida editor, Melvyn New, notes, the variant readings implicitly comment on editorial aspirations to produce a definitive edition of this, or any other, book (see 'A Manuscript of the Le Fever Episode', *N&Q* 23 (1991), 165–74). Here, the reading of the published text has been retained.

XI 1. *WATER-LANDISH*: Daniel Waterland (1683–1740), moralist, theologian, and author of *Advice to a Young Student* (1730), who in fact had some influence on Sterne's own sermons.

2. *tritical*: Trite.

3. *For this sermon . . . thief to catch a thief—*: In the 'Rabelaisian Fragment' (1759?)—unpublished during the author's lifetime, and sometimes considered a first draft of *Tristram Shandy*—Sterne touches on the subject of 'borrowings' by preachers from the sermons of their predecessors. Sterne, who himself borrowed heavily from the work of others, had reason to be concerned by this when he came to publish two volumes of his sermons in 1760, and still more so when he gathered together more existing sermons for a second collection in 1766. In a preface to the latter, he entered a nervous caveat to the reader, indicating that while he did not remember specific borrowings, such might be found by attentive readers. Paidagunes is a pedagogue.

4. *Moderato*: Moderate.

5. *Altieri's Italian dictionary*: Ferdinando Altieri's *Dizionario italiano ed inglese* (1726–7) appeared in a revised edition in 1749.

6. *lentamente*: Slowly; like *moderato* and the following, a musical term.

7. *tenutè*: Tenuto, sustained.

8. *grave*: Solemnly.

9. *adagio*: Slowly.

10. *a l'octava alta*: In the high octave.

11. *Con strepito*: Noisily; see also above n.3 to III.v.

12. *Scicilliana*: Siciliana, in the style of the *siciliano*, an old dance type in slowish time and swaying rhythm, particularly popular in the eighteenth century.

13. *Alla capella*: Literally, in the church style, though the term has three distinct musical meanings.

14. *Con l'arco*: With the bow.

15. *Senza l'arco*: Without the bow, *pizzicato*.

16. *a general review*: An aside by Sterne directed at the *Critical Review*, edited by the novelist and physician Tobias Smollett (1721–71), which had said of Volumes III and IV of *Tristram Shandy*, although in the course of a not altogether hostile review, that 'A spirit of petulance, an air of self-conceit, and an affectation of learning, are diffused through the whole performance, which is likewise blameable for some gross expressions, impure ideas, and a general want of decorum' (May 1761).

17. *ritratto*: Portrait.

18. *Mynheer Vander Blonederdondergewdenstronke*: This obvious nonsense word gestures towards the dullness generally imputed to the Dutch in eighteenth-century England; see also p. 506 below.

XII 1. *Eugene*: Prince Eugène of Savoy (1663–1736), French-born general of the Austrian imperial army, active in the War of the Spanish Succession, and considered the greatest strategist of his day.

XIII 1. *Belgrade*: Belgrade was the scene of Eugène's most famous victory, where in 1717 he successfully besieged the city despite being himself surrounded by a Turkish army four times the size of his own.

XVI 1. *beds of justice*: The literal translation of *lits de justice*, ceremonies in which pre-Revolutionary French kings, especially Louis XV (1710–74), made laws, while by-passing parliament; the name derives from the cushions on which the king reclined during the ceremony.

XVII 1. *Cluverius*: Philipp Clüver or Cluwer (1580–1622), founder of historical geography and author of, among others, *Philippi Cluveriæ Germanæ Antiquæ Libri Tres* (1616).

XVIII 1. *gig*: Whipping top.

XIX 1. *Albertus Rubenius*: Albert Rubens (1614–57), son of the painter, an archaeological scholar and author of *De Re Vestiaria Veterum, Praecipue de Lato Clavo* (1665), 'Of the clothing of the ancients, principally of the *latus clavus*'.

2. *The Chlamys*: A large upper garment of wool, worn especially by soldiers; *Ephod*, a Jewish priestly vestment without sleeves; *Synthesis*, a light upper garment or a dressing-gown; *Pænula*, a cloak for travelling; *Lacema*, an error for lacerna, a mantle worn over the toga on a journey; *Cucullus*, a hood; *Paludamentum*, a military cloak; *Prætexta*, the purple-edged toga worn by Roman magistrates, and by freeborn boys before they assumed the *toga virilis* on coming of age; *Trabea*, a white robe with scarlet stripes and a purple seam, variously worn by kings, knights, and augurs.

3. *Suetonius*: Gaius Suetonius Tranquillus (AD c.69–?130), Roman

biographer best known for his *Lives of the Caesars,* was also the author of a now lost work on the correct names for clothes.

4. *Juvenal*: Decimus Iunius Iuvenalis, or Juvenal (AD *c.*60–*c.*140), the Roman satirist, mentions the hobnailed military shoe in *Satires,* XVI. 13.

5. *calceus incisus*: Shoe cut with a net-like effect, so as to leave the foot partly bare; *calceus rostratus,* shoe with a hooked point.

6. *Latus Clavus*: A broad purple stripe on the tunic worn by senators.

7. *Egnatius*: Giambattista Cipelli (1478–1553), Venetian humanist; *Sigonius,* Carlo Sigonio (*c.*1520–84), Modenese historian; *Bossius Ticinensis,* Matteo Bosso (*c.*1427–1502), Veronese humanist; *Baifius,* Lazare de Baïf (*c.*1490–1547), the greatest French classical scholar of his day and author of *De re vestiaria* ('Of Clothing'); *Budæus,* see above, n. 9 to V.III; *Salmasius,* Claude de Saumaise (1588–1653), French classical scholar; *Lipsius,* see above, n. 10 to VI.II; *Lazius,* Wolfgang Lazius (1514–65), Viennese-born physician and antiquary; *Causabon,* Isaac Casaubon (1559–1614), French-born but English-naturalized classical scholar; *Scaliger,* see above, n. 6 to VI.II.

8. *tibula*: A mistranscription of *fibula,* a buckle, brooch, or clasp. Like the error of *lacema* for *lacerna,* this was more likely attributable to the printer than to Sterne himself, though the errors were left uncorrected in the second edition of 1767.

XX 1. *Poco-curante's*: Indifferent, uncaring persons.

XXI 1. *Duke of Marlborough*: John Churchill, Duke of Marlborough (1650–1722), one of England's greatest military leaders, fought in Flanders and Ireland between 1688 and 1691, and was commander of the British forces in the War of the Spanish Succession from 1701 to 1711, when he was dismissed by Queen Anne.

2. *first parallel*: The first trench (usually of three) parallel to the general face of the works attacked, serving as a means of communication for besiegers.

XXII 1. *the Gazette*: First published in 1665, the *London Gazette* contained lists of government and military appointments as well as accounts of military activity; the earliest English newspaper, it is still in existence.

2. *chamade*: A signal by drum or trumpet as an invitation to parley.

3. *Liege and Ruremond*: Both sieges took place in 1702.

4. *orgues*: Long, thick pieces of wood, armed with iron-plates and hung up separately by cord over a gate, to be let fall in case of surprise.

XXIII 1. *Amberg . . . Limbourg*: The victories all date from 1703.

2. *Proteus*: Minor sea-god having the power to take on any shape.

3. *Landen . . . Dendermond*: Various successful actions fought

between 1704 and 1706 (though, here, Landen is probably Sterne's, or the compositor's, error for Landau).

XXIV 1. *Montero-cap*: Spanish hunter's cap, with a spherical crown and a flap to cover the ears.

2. *ramallie wig*: A wig with a long plait behind with a bow at top and bottom, named for Ramillies, the scene of Marlborough's great victory of 1706.

XXV 1. *clod of the valley!*: 'The clods of the valley shall be sweet unto him, and every man shall draw after him, as there are innumerable before him' (Job 21: 33).

2. *rosemary*: For centuries, rosemary was used at funerals, often cast into the coffin or the grave, as an emblem of remembrance.

XXIX 1. *liver*: Referring to the ancient belief in the liver as the seat of love and of violent passion.

2. *had not served your purpose*. Sterne's characterization of the innocent, good-natured uncle Toby owes much throughout to the author's recollections of his father Roger Sterne (1683–1731), whom he had last seen when he was 9 or 10 years old. Here, Sterne echoes the account of his father he had written for his own daughter, Lydia: 'you might have cheated him ten times in a Day—if nine had not been sufficient' (*Sterne's Memoirs* (1985), 15).

XXX 1. *I wish . . . I had the key of my study out of my draw-well*: See p. 275 above.

2. *Aldrovandus*: Unable to recollect the names of real misogynists, Tristram provides a list whose connection with his theme is extremely doubtful, most being suggested by geographical locations. Only Charles XII of Sweden and Maria Aurora, Countess of Königsmark, can be definitely identified; the latter, famed for her beauty, was sent by Augustus II, Elector of Saxony and King of Poland, whose mistress she was, on an unsuccessful diplomatic mission to Charles XII.

3. *the peace of Utrecht*: A series of treaties enacted in 1713 and 1714 which put an end to the War of the Spanish Succession; it was violently debated in England.

XXXI 1. *Calais . . . Mary's heart*: In the *Chronicles*, Holinshed reports Queen Mary of England (1516–58), during whose reign Calais—England's last French possession—was lost, as saying: 'when I am dead and opened, you shall find Calis lieng in my hart'.

2. *Tertullus*: A 'certain orator' named Tertullus acted as prosecutor of the apostle Paul, before the governor of Caesarea; Acts 24: 1–8.

XXXII 1. *Guy, Earl of Warwick*: *Guy of Warwick* was a popular verse romance of the fourteenth century; Valentine and Orson were characters in an early French romance which appeared in English in 1550; for Parismus and Parismenus and the Seven Champions of England, see above, n. 2 and n. 3 to I.xx. All the stories were known in chap-book form by the eighteenth century.

2. *Helena*: Helen of Troy, wife of King Menelaus of Sparta, whose seduction by Paris, son of King Priam of Troy, led to the Trojan War.

3. *when King Priam . . . beg his body*: Priam's plea for the body of Hector, his eldest son, was in fact successful (*Iliad*, XXIV).

XXXIII 1. *Quanto . . . cavendum*: 'How much more carefully must we take heed in begetting children'; for Cardan, see above, n. 8 to V.III.

XXXIV 1. *the queen and the rest of the confederating powers*: i.e. between Queen Anne and the United Provinces of the Netherlands, Prussia, Savoy, and Portugal.

2. *Monsieur Tugghe*: Thomas-Ignace Tugghe who, on behalf of Dunkirk, petitioned Queen Anne not to demolish the town's port; his mission excited much hostile comment. Sterne here draws on Nicolas Tindal's *Continuation* of Rapin's *The History of England*.

XXXVI 1. *Plotinus*: Plotinus (AD c.205–269/70), Greek neoplatonist, perhaps the most important western thinker between Aristotle and Aquinas, cited here as author of the *Enneads*, though Sterne took his reference from Burton's *Anatomy*, 3.1.1.2.

2. *Ficinus*: Marsilio Ficino (1433–99), philosopher, theologian, and commentator on Plato and Plotinus; the reference is again from the *Anatomy*, 3.1.1.2.

3. *doctor Baynyard*: Edward Baynard (1641?–1717), physician and poet, whose letter 'containing an Account of many Eminent Cures done by the Cold Baths in England', to which Sterne alludes, was appended to Sir John Floyer's *The ancient Ψυχρολουσία revived: or, an Essay to prove Cold Bathing both safe and useful* (1702).

4. *Cantharidis.*: Cantharides, pharmacopoeial name for the Spanish fly, used for raising blisters on the skin, and as an aphrodisiac.

5. *Philagrius*: A correspondent of St. Gregory Nazianzen (see above, n. 2 to VI.v); the quotation from Gregory's *Epistola*, XXXII, translates: 'Well done! that you philosophize in your misfortunes', and is not there intended ironically.

6. *Rhasis*: Rhazes, or Abū Bakr Muhammad ibn Zakariya al-Rāzi (c.850–923/5), Persian alchemist, physician, and Muslim philosopher.

7. *Dioscorides*: Dioscorides Pedanius (first century AD), Greek physician and pharmacologist, author of *De Materia Medica*, or *Materials of Medicine*, the standard pharmacological work for sixteen centuries.

8. *Aætius*: Aetius of Amida (AD 502–75), Greek medical writer, and court physician at Byzantium.

9. *Hanea*: A herb mentioned by Burton (*Anatomy*, 3.2.6.1), from whom Sterne took many of the following details; Burton describes its use by Athenian women who found it 'asswaged those ardent flames of love, and freed them from the torments of that violent passion'.

10. *topaz-ring*: The topaz was anciently used in medicine, reduced to powder. Sterne would make jesting reference to his own topaz-ring in a letter of his daughter, 24 Aug. 1767 (*Letters*, 391).

11. *Gordonius*: Bernard Gordon (*fl.* 1285–1305 or 1318), celebrated French physician, mentioned by Burton who gives Latin and English versions of the remark Sterne quotes.

XXXVIII 1. *Thrice happy book! . . . cannot misrepresent*: Sterne here mischievously paraphrases comments by Henry Fielding (1707–54) on unacknowledged borrowings from other writers: '[T]here is no Conduct so fair and disinterested, but that it may be misunderstood by Ignorance, and misrepresented by Malice' (*The History of Tom Jones* (1749), XII. 1).

XL 1. *Inv. T.S*: Abbreviation for 'Invenit Tristram Shandy' or 'Tristram Shandy designed this'; 'Scul. T.S' is an abbreviated form of 'Sculpsit Tristram Shandy' or 'Tristram Shandy engraved this'.

2. *Archimedes*: The first assumption of the first book of Archimedes' *Of the sphere and the cylinder* is that 'Of all lines having the same extremities the straight line is the least.'

3. *birthday suits*: Dresses worn on birthdays, especially the King's, but here with a play on nakedness.

VOLUME VII

title page 1. *Non enim . . . Epistola sexta*: The motto is taken from the *Letters*, v. vi, of Pliny the Younger (see above, n. 1 to I.xx); it translates: 'For this is not a digression from it, but the work itself.'

I 1. *Eugenius . . . muscle*: For Eugenius, see n. 1 to I.XII above; muscle = mussel.

II 1. *the dock of Chatham*: The naval dockyard, established by Henry VIII, was one of the most important in eighteenth-century England.

2. *St. Thomas*: St. Thomas à Becket (*c.*1120–1170) has a shrine at Canterbury where he was murdered.

IV 1. *Addison*: In the preface to his *Remarks on Several Parts of Italy* (1705), Joseph Addison (1672–1719) relates how, before embarking on his travels, he collected passages from classical authors describing places he was to visit in order to compare them on the spot with contemporary reality.

2. *town-clerk of Ephesus*: Heracleitus (*c.*540–*c.*480 BC), pre-socratic philosopher; he became known as 'the weeping philosopher', hence a suitable contrast to Democritus (see above, n. 4 to VI.v), the 'laughing philosopher'.

V 1 *CALAIS, Calatium, Calusium, Calesium*: In an attempt to ward off the worst effects of the consumption, or pulmonary tuberculosis, from which he had suffered for many years, Sterne left England for France in the first week of January 1762 and remained abroad until late May 1764; the seventh volume of *Tristram Shandy* draws extensively on his own experience of travel in France. Among the books Sterne consulted was *Nouveau Voyage de France* (1724; rev. edn. 1755) by Jean-Aymar Piganiol de la Force (1673–1753), which he quotes, paraphrases, and parodies throughout this volume.

2. *town-house*: Hôtel de ville, or municipal building.

3. *La Tour de Guet*: Watch-tower.

4. *Tête de Gravelenes*: Part of the fortifications, facing east in the direction of Gravelines.

5. *Eustace de St. Pierre*: Eustache de Saint-Pierre (c.1287–1371), leader of the six burghers of Calais who, bareheaded and barefoot, with ropes around their necks, presented themselves to Edward III of England as hostages for the safety of Calais; they were pardoned at the instance of Queen Philippa.

6. *in Rapin's own words*: In fact, the account by Rapin (see n. 1 to II.1 above) extends only to about twenty-five lines.

VII 1. *size-ace!*: Usually, sice or syce-ace; a throw of a six and an ace at dice (here figurative).

2. *mine Irish host*: A number of inns frequented by English travellers in Channel ports were run by Irish or Scottish Jacobite exiles.

IX 1. *slut*: Impudent or bold girl.

2. *the abbey of Saint Austreberte*: St. Austreberta, or Eustreberta (d. 704), born near Thérouanne in Artois, was abbess of Port-sur-Somme, later Abbeville.

3. *devote*: Devotee.

4. *terce to a nine*: In piquet, a tierce is a sequence of three cards in a suit; here, an advantage.

5. *piqued ... capotted*: Had been beaten decisively; the terms are used in piquet.

XII 1. *glister*: Clyster, enema.

XIII 1. *'MAKE them like unto a wheel'*: Psalms 83: 13.

2. *grand tour*: In the eighteenth century, the Grand Tour took wealthy young men and their tutors on a circuit, lasting one or two years, of the principal cities and sights of France and Italy.

3. *an Ixion's wheel*: Ixion was attached to a revolving wheel as punishment for attempting the chastity of Hera.

4. *Pythagoreans*: Pythagoras (see above, n. 2 to IV.xvii) believed the soul to be a fallen divinity confined within the body as a tomb and condemned to a cycle of reincarnation (metempsychosis) from which it could gain release by the cultivation of an Apolline purity, though Sterne's source is again John Norris's *Practical Discourses* (see n. 1 to IV.xvii above).

XIV 1. *Lessius*: Leendert Leys (1554–1623), Flemish Jesuit theologian, from whose *De perfectionibus moribusque divinis* (1620) Sterne quotes, though via the *Anatomy*, 2.2.3.

 2. *Dutch mile*: Chambers's *Cyclopaedia* gives 24,000 feet, though other values are to be found.

 3. *Franciscus Ribbera's*: Francisco de Ribera (1537–91), Spanish Jesuit theologian, author of *In Sacram b. Johannis Apostoli et Evangelistae Apocalypsim commentarii* (1591) to which Sterne alludes, though again via Burton, 2.2.3.

 4. *Italian miles*: Chambers's *Cyclopaedia* gives 5,000 feet, though again other values occur.

 5. *tabid*: Consumptive, wasting.

 6. *Priapus*: God of fertility, whose symbol was a phallus.

XV 1. *thill-horse*: Horse attached to a thill, or shaft.

 2. *the chimes . . . through all France)*: During the Seven Years War, church bells were melted down to make cannons.

XVI 1. *avance-courier*: Outrider.

 2. *which will not pass*: There had been a change in the French coinage under Louis XV (1710–24).

 3. *liards*: A liard was worth a fourth of a sou.

 4. *shaveling*: Pejorative term for a tonsured friar, here a mendicant.

 5. *Chantilly*: The celebrated stables at Chantilly, constructed by Jean Aubert (*fl.* 1702–41) between 1719 and 1735.

 6. *Jaidas's lantern*: Joseph Hall (see above, n. 1 to I.XXII), in his *Quo Vadis? a just censure of travell as it is commonly undertaken by gentlemen of our nation* (1617), mentions the abbey's claim to possess the lantern of Judas Iscariot. The peculiar spelling of 'Jaidas', though almost certainly a compositorial error, is retained as it appears in all eighteenth-century editions.

XVII 1. *and no one gives the wall*: i.e., no one concedes the right or privilege of walking next to the wall, the cleaner and safer side of the pavement.

 2. *we shall all wear swords*: To wear a sword was the distinction of a gentleman.

XVIII 1. *seen it by day-light*: By the 1760s, London was perhaps the best-lit capital city in the world, Paris being very poorly lit by comparison.

 2. *Hôtel*: A large private house or mansion.

 3. *seen, felt, heard, and understood . . . Lilly*: The phrase occurs in 'An Introduction of the eight parts of Latin speech' in *A Short Introduction to Grammar* by William Lily (?1468–1522/3); in modified form, the grammar frequently reprinted in the eighteenth century.

 4. **Non Orbis . . . ulla parem*: Sterne's note translates: 'The earth has no other such a people, nor any people such a city.'

XIX 1. *Fontainbleau*: Fontainebleau, forty miles SE of Paris; a royal chateau, begun in 1527 and subsequently enlarged, with gardens by André Le Nôtre (1613–70), used especially for hunting.

xx 1. *consideratis, considerandis*: The things to be considered having been considered.

2. *Andoüillets*: An *andouillette* is a small sausage.

xxi 1. *sinovia*: Synovia, the lubricating fluid of the joints.

2. *man of Lystra*: St. Paul's healing of the man of Lystra is recounted in Acts 14: 8.

3. *hot baths of Bourbon*: The thermal baths of Bourbonne-les-Bains had been famous since Roman times.

4. *calesh*: Calash, a light low-wheeled carriage with a removable folding hood.

5. *a little tempting bush*: A bush indicated a tavern.

6. *to return the obligation downwards*: The mule, offspring of a he-ass and a mare, is generally sterile.

xxv 1. *bou, bou, bou*: 'Bouger' means to budge or move, though Sterne is suggesting a connection with 'bougre', a bugger, a word used previously with greater force than it now possesses (e.g. by Rabelais, *Gargantua and Pantagruel*, I. xx); 'fouter' or 'foutre', to fuck, *is* indecent.

xxvii 1. *coddling*: Stewing.

2. *monsieur Sequier*: Dominique Séguier (1593–1659), Bishop of Auxerre, had the tombs of sixty or so saints opened in 1636 and made a report on the condition of the bodies.

3. *St. Heribald*: St. Héribald (d. *c.*857), Abbot of St. Germanus, and Bishop of Auxerre.

4. *Charlemagne*: Charlemagne (*c.*742–814), his son Louis le Debonair, or the Pious (778–840), and Louis' son Charles the Bald (823–77), were successively rulers of large parts of France.

5. *Saint MAXIMA*: There were several saints Maxima and numerous saints Maximus, but Walter Shandy is playing on the Latin meaning of the names—the 'greatest'.

6. *Saint Optat*: St. Optatus (d. *c.*530) was briefly Bishop of Auxerre; his name signifies 'chosen' or 'elected'.

xxviii 1. **The same Don Pringello . . . small edit.*: Among the Demoniacs, a club he founded in imitation of the notorious 'Monks' of Medenham Abbey, John Hall-Stevenson (see above, n. 1 to I.xii) was known as Antony; he attributed to Pringello one of his *Crazy Tales* (1762).

xxix 1. *Hermitage and Coté roti*: Vineyards in the Rhône valley.

xxx 1. *Lippius of Basil*: Nicolas Lippius, maker of a clock (1598) in the Cathedral of St. Jean at Lyons, is mentioned in both the *Recherche des antiquités de curiosités de la ville de Lyon* (1683) of Jacob Spon (see below, n. 4 to VII.xxxi) and in Piganiol de la Force's *Nouveau Voyage*.

2. *squirrel cage*: A cylindrical cage in which squirrels were kept and which revolved as they moved.

3. *great library of the Jesuits*: One of the most important libraries in eighteenth- century France, containing over 40,000 volumes.

4. *valet de place*: Guide.

5. *church of St. Ireneus*: The church of St. Irenée supposedly held a part of the pillar to which Christ was bound while he was whipped.

6. *house where Pontius Pilate lived*: In *Recherches curieuses d'an-tiquité*, Spon writes of various buildings called 'Pilate's' and asserts they are named after an Italian, Pilati, secretary to the Dauphin Humbert.

7. *Tomb of the two lovers*: The celebrated tomb of the two lovers, in the faubourg de Vaise, was demolished, according to Piganiol de la Force, in June 1707.

XXXI 1. *fibrillous*: Composed of fibrils or parts of a fibre.

2. *Frusts:* Fragments.

3. *cullender*: Colander.

4. *Spon*: Jacob Spon (1647–85), French traveller and antiquarian.

5. *Santa Casa*: Literally, Holy House, the reputed home of the Blessed Virgin which, threatened with destruction at the hands of the Turks in 1291, was transported by angels to Europe, finally coming to rest at Loreto in the Italian Marches in 1295.

6. *Videnda*: Things to be seen.

7. *Basse Cour*: Stable-yard.

XXXIII 1. *CHAPTER XXXIII*: In the first edition, Chapter XXXIV, with subsequent chapters numbered accordingly through to the end of the volume; the numbering was corrected in the second edition, however, and seems to have been no more than a simple error.

XXXV 1. *PAR LE ROY*: By order of the king.

2. *fermiers*: Farmers of taxes.

3. *AND SO THE PEACE WAS MADE*: An allusion to the Treaty of Paris, signed on 10 February 1763, which concluded the Seven Years War, and whose conditions were widely debated in England.

XXXVI 1. *his ass's FURNITURE*: In fact, it is the loss of his ass that truly affects Sancho (*Don Quixote*, 1. iii, 9).

XXXVII 1. *Dodsley, or Becket*: Robert and James Dodsley published the first London edition of Volumes I and II of *Tristram Shandy*], and the first edition of Volumes III and IV; T. Beckett and P. A. Dehondt published Volumes V to IX.

XXXVIII 1. *papilliotes*: Papillotes, curl papers.

2. *a la folie:* To distraction.

XXXIX 1. *the JESUITS had got the cholic*: In 1764 the Society of Jesus had been declared illegal in France and her colonies.

XLI 1. *nothing to see*: Tristram deliberately ignores the principal sight of Avignon, the fourteenth-century palace built for the papacy, which had its seat in the city between 1309 and 1377.

2. *Ormond*: Ormonde (see above, n. 3 to IV.xxII) lived in exile in Avignon for some years, and died there in 1745.

3. *all Dukes, Marquisses, and Counts, there*: The profusion of titles among the French was a common cause of comment and ridicule among eighteenth-century British travellers.

XLIII 1. *Nismes*: Nîmes.

2. *Muscatto*: Sweet wine made from Muscat grapes.

3. *tabourin*: Taborin, a small drum beaten with one drumstick while a fife is played with the other hand.

4. *VIVA LA JOIA! FIDON LA TRISTESSA!*: Long live Joy! Then fie on Sadness!; 'Fidon' is Sterne's version of 'fi donc'.

5. *Perdrillo's pavillion*: Presumably an error for Pringello's; see above, n. 1 to VII.xxvIII.

VOLUME VIII

I 1. *Vid. Vol. VI. p. 152*: In this edition, p. 379.

II 1. *Vid. Pope's Portrait*: Probably an allusion to one of several engravings showing Alexander Pope receiving inspiration from the Muses, in William Warburton's well-known nine-volume edition of Pope's verse and letters, *The Works of Alexander Pope, Esq.* (1751).

III 1. *periclitating*: Imperilling.

V 1. *Longinus*: Longinus' version of the story to which Sterne alludes is in fact lost; John Rooke's translation (1729) of Arrian's *History of Alexander's Expedition* gives this version of the debate between Alexander the Great and Parmenio over Darius's proposed terms at the siege of Tyre: 'Parmenio is said to have told him, That if he was Alexander, he would accept the Terms; and, when the End of War was gain'd, no longer tempt the Hazard thereof. To which, the other is said to have reply'd, So would he, if he were Parmenio; but as he was Alexander, he must act worthy Alexander' (II. xxv, pp. 126–7).

VI 1. *thy fifth and sixth volumes still*: In his correspondence, Sterne refers several times to the slow sale of Volumes V and VI; see *Letters*, 166–7, 191–2, 199, 203–4, 211, 288.

2. *quirister*: Chorister.

VIII 1. *case-knife*: Knife kept in a case or sheath; also a large kitchen knife.

IX 1. *Flemish ells*: A Flemish ell was 27 inches.

XI 1. *Terra del Fuogo*: Tierra del Fuego, the southernmost tip of South America.

2. *gashly*: Literally, 'ghastly', but Sterne's choice of word is deliberate.

3. *staragen*: Tarragon.

xv 1. *meseraick*: The mesaraic or mesenteric veins are those of the mesentery, a fold of the peritoneum attaching some part of the intestinal canal to the posterior wall of the abdomen.

2. *Illion*: Ileum, third and last portion of the small intestine.

xvi 1. *from Dan to Beersheba*: A phrase used in the Old Testament (Judg. 20: 1; 1 Chron. 21: 2; 2 Sam. 24: 2) to denote the entire extent of Israel; here, from one end to the other.

xvii 1. *Bouchain*: Small, once fortified, town in northern France.

2. *St. Radagunda*: See above, n. 2 to IV, Slawkenbergius's Tale.

xix 1. *flatus*: An obvious expelling of air.

2. *Urbecondita's*: See above, n. 3 to III.xxxvi.

3. *Fagel*: François Nicolaas Fagel (1655–1718), Dutch Field-Marshal in the War of the Spanish Succession.

4. *Wencelaus*: Wenceslas IV (1361–1419), King of Bohemia, King of the Germans, and Holy Roman Emperor.

5. *Schwartz*: Berthold Schwarz, possibly apocryphal German Franciscan, once supposed to have invented gunpowder around 1313; Sterne's source for this, and subsequent, information was Chambers's *Cyclopaedia*, which gives the date 1380.

6. *Don Pedro the bishop of Leon*: Sterne in fact misread Chambers who gives Peter Mexia's *Various Readings* as his source for this information.

7. *King Alphonsus*: Alfonso XI (1311–50), King of Castile and Leon.

8. *Friar Bacon*: Roger Bacon (*c*.1220–92), English Franciscan, remarked on the explosive properties of a mixture of nitre, charcoal, and sulphur.

9. *the regiments of Wyndham, Lumley, and Galway*: Hugh Wyndham (d. 1708) was commissioned as a colonel in 1692; Richard Lumley (1650–1721), first Earl of Scarborough, fought in Flanders as a major-general (1692) and lieutenant-general (1694); Henri de Massue de Ruvigny (1648–1720), Earl of Galway, was commander of the English and Huguenot horse at Landen, where he displayed great bravery in covering William III's retreat.

10. *Luxembourg's brows*: François-Henri de Montmorency-Bouteville, duc de Luxembourg (1628–95), a leading French general in the War of the Grand Alliance.

11. *Conti*: François-Louis de Bourbon, prince de Conti (1664–1709), who fought in the War of the Grand Alliance.

12. *Talmash*: Thomas Talmash or Tollemache (*c*.1651–1694), lieutenant-general who commanded the centre at Landen, afterwards organizing the retreat of the infantry.

13. *cæteris paribus*: Other things being equal.

xxi 1. *with a sisserara*: With a siserary: i.e. with a vengeance.

XXIII 1. *Gotham*: According to legend, the villagers of Gotham, wanting to avoid the expense of a visit by King John, allowed royal emissaries to find them engaged in such tasks as trying to drown an eel, with the result that the king changed the route of his progress.

XXIV 1. **Rodope . . . I know not who*: Rhodopis (*fl. c.*600 BC) was a celebrated Greek courtesan. The note is taken from Heliodorus, as Sterne knew very well, for his immediate source was Burton's *Anatomy*, 3.2.3.3, where it is translated: 'Thracian Rodophe was so excellent at this dumb Rhetorick [of the eyes], that if she had but looked upon any one almost (saith Calisiris) she would have bewitched him, and he could not possibly escape it.'

2. *a spot in the sun*: Galileo's account of sunspots, published in support of Copernican theory, appeared in 1613, under the title *Istoria e dimostrazioni intorno alle macchie solari*.

XXVI 1. **This will be printed with my father's life of Socrates, &c. &c.*: The couplet appears in the *Anatomy*, 3.2.5.1, where it is attributed to R[obert] T[ofte].

2. *the dean and chapter were hewing down*: The dean and chapter of York Minster similarly sold off Langwith Wood near York in 1752.

3. *Wynnendale*: The Wyendael wood was of tactical importance in the battle fought there in 1708.

XXVII 1. *gap'd knife*: Gapped knife; a knife with a serrated edge.

XXVIII 1. *fresh into pipes*: Small articles made of pipe-clay, used to keep wigs in curl.

XXXI 1. *Hilarion*: St. Hilarion (*c.*291–371); the anecdote, which Sterne took from Burton's *Anatomy*, 3.2.6.1, derives from St. Jerome's life of Hilarion.

XXXIII 1. *gymnicks*: Gymnastics.

2. *nolens, volens*: Willingly or unwillingly; willy-nilly.

3. *Plato*: Walter's reference is to the *Symposium* 180D, but Sterne's source was the *Anatomy*, 3.1.1.2, where Pausanias' speech is translated: 'One Venus is ancient without a mother, and descended from heaven, whom we call coelestiall; The younger, begotten of Iupiter and Dione, whom commonly we call Venus.'

4. *Velasius*: Francisco Vallés (1524–92), Spanish physician; Ficino (see above, n. 2 to VI.xxxvi) could not have commented on him, but Sterne's mistake arises from a misreading of the *Anatomy*, 3.1.1.2, where both are referred to as commentators on Plato.

5. *finding out the longitude*: After numerous disasters at sea, the British government created a Board of Longitude which offered £20,000 to the inventor of the first accurate marine chronometer; John Harrison (1693–1776) submitted a series of chronometers from 1735 onwards, his fourth gaining him £5,000 in 1762 with the balance being tardily awarded in 1773.

XXXIV 1. *fourth general division*: Of his sermon.

2. *Scarron*: Paul Scarron (1610–60), French writer, celebrated here as author of the *Roman comique* (1651, 1657).

3. *didappers and water hens*—: Little grebes and moorhens.

4. *VERVAIN*: The medicinal herb *verbena*.

5. *Ælian*: Claudius Aelianus (AD c.170–235), teacher of rhetoric and author of *De Natura Animalium*; Sterne's source for this and much of the foregoing is Burton's *Anatomy*, 3.2.6.1.

VOLUME IX

title page 1. *Si quid . . . malè capias*: The motto is quoted from the *Anatomy of Melancholy*, 3.1.1.1, where Julius Caesar Scaliger is reported to have besought Cardan: 'If we have sported too facetiously with anything, by the Muses, the Graces, and the author of all the poets, I beg you not to take it too ill of me.'

dedication 1. *A DEDICATION TO A GREAT MAN*: Mr. *** is William Pit[t], to whom Sterne had also dedicated the first London edition of Volumes I and II, and who had been out of political office since 1761; *Lord* ******* is Lord Chatham, the title Pitt took when ennobled in 1766. This dedication also exists in two states, this being the second, with the emendation of the error *posteririori* for *posteriori*.

2. *Whose thoughts . . . him company*: As Morris Golden noticed, the lines, adapted from Alexander Pope's *An Essay on Man*, I. 101–12, satirize Pitt's erstwhile political ally and later opponent George Grenville (1712–70), whom Pitt publicly humiliated in a debate in the House of Commons in 1763 by bestowing on him the name 'Gentle shepherd' (after a popular air), by which he was subsequently known—though it did not prevent him succeeding Bute (see n. 1 to V.11) as prime minister between 1763 and 1765; see 'Periodical Context in the Imagined World of *Tristram Shandy*', *Age of Johnson*, 1 (1987), 237–60 (256–7).

III 1. *alout*: All out, entirely.

VIII 1. *Legation of Moses*: *The Divine Legation of Moses demonstrated* was the most celebrated and controversial work of William Warburton (see above, n. 1 to IV.xx); *A Tale of a Tub* (1704; 5th ed. 1710) by Jonathan Swift (1667–1745) is ironically dedicated to Prince Posterity.

XI 1. *fausse-brays*: Artificial mounds thrown up in front of the main rampart.

2. *a sacrament day*: The sacrament of Holy Communion would have been administered once a month, here on the first Sunday of the month; for Walter's embarrassment, compare p. 8.

XIII 1. *gummous*: Gum-like.

2. *take a plumb-lift*: Get directly out.

3. *topaz ring*: See above, n. 10 to VI.xxxvi.

4. *Ludovicus Sorbonensis*: Probably imaginary, suggested by the Sorbonne.

5. εξωτερίχη πραξίς: An external matter.

XIV 1. *thersitical*: Abusive, scurrilous.

2. *nasty Romance of the Galatea*: Sterne is not thinking of the *Galateo* (see above, n. 3 to V.xvi) but of one of della Casa's early licentious works: the *Capitolo del Forno, de'Bacci* or *Sopra il nome di Giovanni*.

XVII 1. *Rousseau*: Jean-Jacques Rousseau (1712–78) had described man's putative natural state, in which his needs were simple and no individual was subordinate to another, in his *Discours sur l'origine et les fondemens de l'inégalité parmi les hommes* (1755).

2. *Vestal*: The duty of the Vestal Virgins was to keep burning at all times the flame sacred to Vesta, the Roman hearth-goddess.

XXIII 1. *most concessible postulatums*: Most easily granted propositions.

2. *ten-ace*: In cards, the combination of the next highest and next lowest to the highest card in a suit held by the other side.

XXIV 1. *Pauls*: *Paolo*, obsolete Italian silver coin.

2. *a journey through France and Italy*: Sterne alludes to the *Travels through France and Italy* (1766) of Tobias Smollett (see above, n. 16 to VI.xi), in which the author is not backward in pointing out the possible annoyances awaiting the continental traveller; in *A Sentimental Journey* (1768), Sterne would memorably, if unfairly, caricature his fellow-novelist as 'the learned SMELFUNGUS'. Siena and Radicofani lay on the main western route from Florence to Rome, Capua on the main route from Rome to Naples.

3. *Lepanto*: Cervantes lost his left arm in the Battle of Lepanto, the great naval action fought on 7 October 1571 between the forces of the Holy Alliance and the Ottomans.

XXV 1. *Zeuxis*: Zeuxis (*fl. c.*413–399 BC), celebrated Greek painter; Sterne probably confused him with Nealces (*fl.* 245 BC) whom Pliny relates to have painted the foam at a horse's mouth by throwing his sponge at the picture (*Natural History*, xxxv. x).

2. *cake-bakers of Lernè*: Gargantua and Pantagruel, I. xxv.

3. *a Spanish proverb*: There is no obvious proverbial source in Spanish for these sentiments, but literary sources include Calderón de la Barca's 'En las venturas de amor/dice más el que más calla', *Ni amor se libra de amor*, III. iii.

4. REAL PRESENCE: The scholastic account of the Eucharist, adopted by the Roman Catholic but denied by the Anglican communion, asserts that the consecration of the elements transforms

them into the real body and blood of Christ whilst leaving the accidental, or empirically verifiable, forms unchanged.

5. *Common-Prayer Book*: In the Anglican Book of Common Prayer, the 'causes for which Matrimony was ordained' are 'the procreation of children', 'a remedy against sin, and to avoid fornication', and 'the mutual society, help, and comfort that the one ought to have of the other, both in prosperity and adversity'.

XXVI 1. *Drake's anatomy*: James Drake (bap. 1666–1707), physician and author of *Anthropologia Nova, or a New System of Anatomy* (1707).

2. *Wharton*: Thomas Wharton (1614–73), physician and author of *Adenographia; sive glandularum totius corporis descriptio* (1656).

3. *Graaf*: Reinier de Graaf (1641–73), Dutch physician, author of both the *Tractatus anatomico-medicus de succi panacreati natura & usu* (1671) and of *De virorum organis generationi inservientibus* (1668).

XXIX 1. *quart major to a terce*: In piquet, a quart major is the sequence of ace, king, queen, jack, while a tierce is a sequence of three cards, in any suit.

XXXIII 1. *Diogenes and Plato*: Sterne was probably thinking of Burton who refers to Diogenes and Plato on man's sexual passions in the *Anatomy*, 3.2.1.2 and 3.2.2.2.

2. *improprietor of the great tythes*: An impropriator was a layman to whom pre-Reformation ecclesiastical tithes were subsequently paid.

3. *pop-visit*: Short visit.

4. *Europa*: In Greek mythology, Europa was carried off to Crete by Zeus, who appeared in the form of a bull.

5. *Doctors Commons*: The College of Doctors of Civil Law in London, where divorce proceedings took place.

LIST OF EMENDATIONS

As described in the Note on the Text (p. xxxii), the text of this edition follows that of the first editions of the several volumes of *Tristram Shandy*. The following list records all emendations of copy-text and indicates (by the figure 2) where such emendations were made in the second editions of the several volumes.

VOL. I

p. 18 l. 17	nicety] 2; nicity	
l. 39	amount] 2; amout	
p. 19 l. 31	gentleman] 2; gentlemen	
p. 22 l. 41	likewise] 2; likwise	
p. 23 l. 5	or] 2; and	
p. 31 l. 16	circle] 2; cirle	
p. 32 ll. 3–4	contrary] 2; contray	
l. 32	reconcile:] 2; reconcile.	
p. 37 l. 18	weakness!”] weakness!⌃	
l. 20	him;] him;”	
p. 38 l. 7	herself] 2; hereself	
p. 42 l. 31	child.] 2; child,	
p. 44 l. 23	would] 2; w[ ]uld	
p. 49 l. 8	and the other] 2; and other	
l. 42	Vide Deventer . . .] v. n. XX, 6, p. 547	
p. 50 l. 38	à celui] 2; a'celui	
p. 51 l. 8	néantmoins] 2; néamoins	
p. 54 l. 34	knowledge] 2; knowldge	
p. 56 l. 19	comes] 2; come	
p. 58 l. 41	progressive] progessive	
ll. 41–2	movements] 2; movemets	
p. 60 l. 6	wrapt] 2; warpt	
l. 34	call'd] 2; calld	

VOL. II

p. [67] l. 11	Nicolas] 2; Nocolas	
p. 71 l. 20	it is] 2; is it	
p. 72 l. 20	diversions] 2; diversons	
p. 78 l. 24	sloped] 2; slopped	
l. 27	Honour] 2; Hnonour	
p. 80 l. 13	being] 2; been	
p. 81 l. 31	gives] give	
p. 84 l. 26	pressed——] pressed.——	
p. 85 l. 14	Pray] 2; Pay	
p. 90 ll. 21–2	tenaille——] 2; tenaille.——	
p. 92 l. 28	heartily] 2; heartly	
p. 93 l. 18	discourse] 2; discouse	
p. 94 l. 26	(especially] 2; ⌃especially	

p. 96 ll. 7–8	Corporal] 2; Coporal	
p. 97 l. 9	judge!] 2; judge?	
p. 110 l. 6	left.]] 2; left.⌃	
p. 111 l. 26	rate.]] 2; rate.⌃	
p. 114 l. 1	fit,] 2; fit.	
p. 115 l. 12	*fœtus*] 2; *fætus*	
p. 121 l. 14	*Trismegistus*] 2; *Tismegistus*	
l. 21	had read,] 2; had, read	
p. 122 ll. 4–5	the armour] 2; the the armour	
l. 27	*Alquife*] *Alquise*	

VOL. III

p. 127 l. 1	had he been] 2; had he had been	
p. 129 l. 25	father] 2; uncle	
p. 131 l. 3	children—the] 2; children.—The	
p. 136 l. 17	ut] et	
l. 23	resipuerit] respuerit	
p. 140 l. 9	harmis] harnis	
p. 144 l. 16	back?]; back.	
p. 148 l. 5	him] 2; hm	
l. 26	apple;] 2; apple,;	
p. 150 l. 7	things] 2; men	
p. 151 l. 19	are more like] 2; are like	
l. 25	regions] 2; r[ ]gions	
p. 153 l. 13	*Agelastes*] *Agalastes*	
l. 32	statesmen] 2; statesman	
p. 154 l. 11	the several] these veral	
p. 156 l. 4	you] 2; your	
p. 157 l. 33	driving a damn'd] 2; driving a a damn'd	
l. 34	main, the wrong] 2; main, the the wrong	
p. 158 l. 7	catching] 2; catechising	
l. 27	dissertations] 2; dessertations	
l. 32	about, you might] 2; about you, might	
p. 161 l. 6	eloquent] 2; elegant	

l. 21   he. ——] he.——
                |——

p. 429 l. 30   intention of buying] 2;
             intention of of
             buying

VOL. VIII

p. 436 l. 25   good-morrow!] good-
             morrow?
p. 437 ll. 21–2 *Nonsense*——]
             Nonsense——| ——
    l. 29   to] 2; so
p. 461 l. 25   two] 2; too
p. 466 l. 8   whenever] 2; wheneven
p. 467 l. 8   befell] 2; fefell
p. 469 l. 19   her *te Deum*] 2; her, *te
             Deum*
p. 471 l. 21   for the present] 2; for the the
             present

p. 473 l. 15   women] woman
p. 474 l. 16   own——] own—— | ——

VOL. IX

p. [483] l. 6   *posteriori*] *posteririori*
p. 497 l. 30   mother——] mother——
             | ——
p. 519 l. 5   *postulatums*] *postulatum*
p. 520 l. 5   to offer] to the offer
p. 522 l. 1   they had been] they been
p. 524 l. 20   Gargantua's] Garagantna's
p. 529 l. 2   et cætera,] et cætera.
p. 532 l. 4   shoulder——]
             shoulder—— |
             ——
p. 535 l. 6   over,] over [ ]

The Oxford World's Classics Website

www.worldsclassics.co.uk

- Browse the full range of Oxford World's Classics online

- Sign up for our monthly e-alert to receive information on new titles

- Read extracts from the Introductions

- Listen to our editors and translators talk about the world's greatest literature with our Oxford World's Classics audio guides

- Join the conversation, follow us on Twitter at OWC_Oxford

- Teachers and lecturers can order inspection copies quickly and simply via our website

www.worldsclassics.co.uk

American Literature

British and Irish Literature

Children's Literature

Classics and Ancient Literature

Colonial Literature

Eastern Literature

European Literature

Gothic Literature

History

Medieval Literature

Oxford English Drama

Poetry

Philosophy

Politics

Religion

The Oxford Shakespeare

A complete list of Oxford World's Classics, including Authors in Context, Oxford English Drama, and the Oxford Shakespeare, is available in the UK from the Marketing Services Department, Oxford University Press, Great Clarendon Street, Oxford OX2 6DP, or visit the website at www.oup.com/uk/worldsclassics.

In the USA, visit www.oup.com/us/owc for a complete title list.

Oxford World's Classics are available from all good bookshops. In case of difficulty, customers in the UK should contact Oxford University Press Bookshop, 116 High Street, Oxford OX1 4BR.